DUBLIN

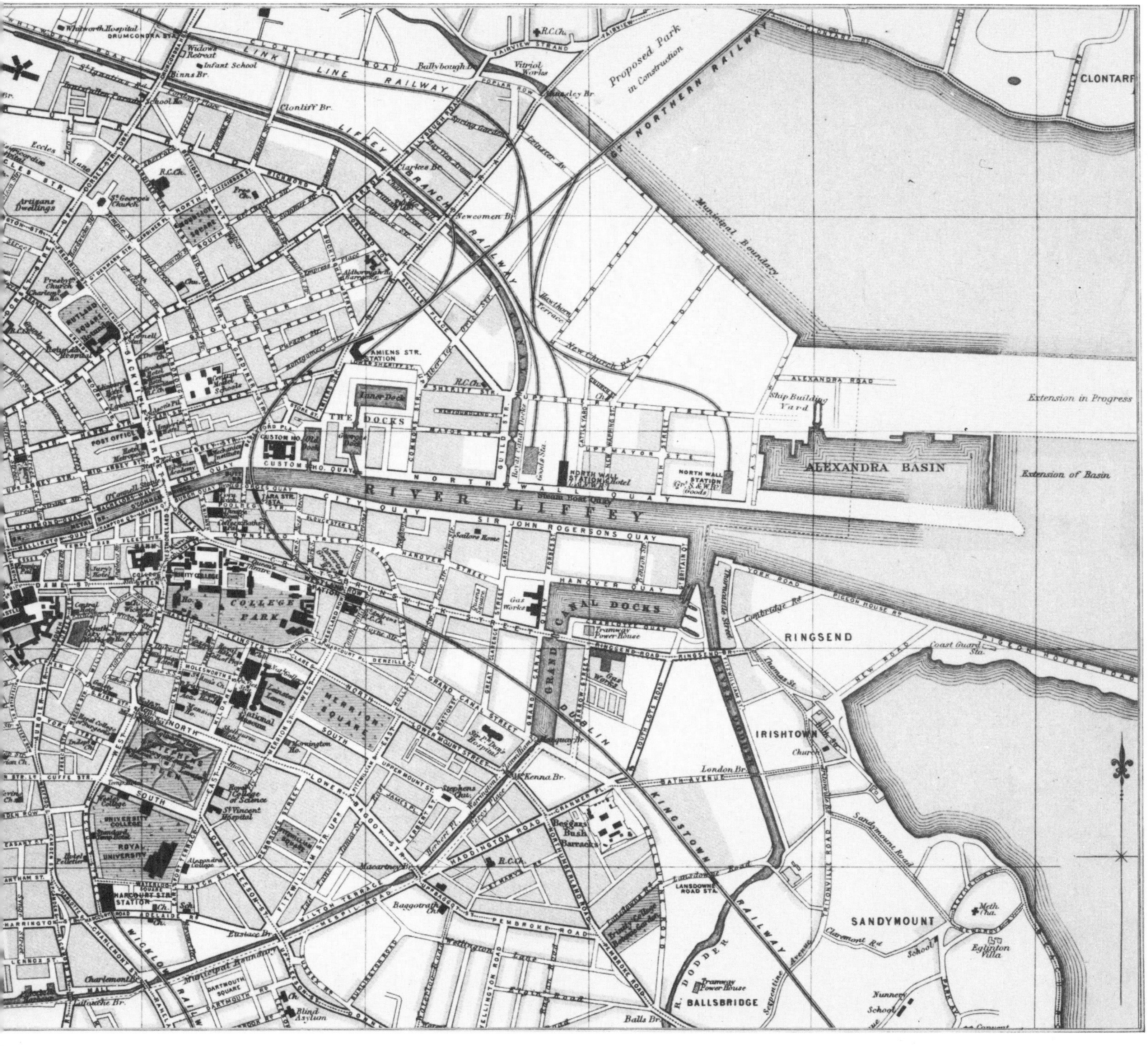

CLONTARF
Proposed Park in Construction
GT NORTHERN RAILWAY
Municipal Boundary
LINK LINE RAILWAY
LIFFEY BRANCH RAILWAY
ALEXANDRA ROAD
Ship Building Yard
Extension in Progress
ALEXANDRA BASIN
Extension of Basin
RIVER LIFFEY
NORTH WALL QUAY
SIR JOHN ROGERSONS QUAY
CITY QUAY
THE DOCKS
AMIENS STR. STATION
CUSTOM HO. QUAY
HANOVER QUAY
CANAL DOCKS
GRAND CANAL
RINGSEND
PIGEON HOUSE RD
IRISHTOWN
SANDYMOUNT
Sandymount Road
BALLSBRIDGE
R. DODDER
KINGSTOWN RAILWAY
DUBLIN
COLLEGE PARK
TRINITY COLLEGE
MERRION SQUARE
ROYAL UNIVERSITY
HARCOURT STR. STATION
WICKLOW RAILWAY
Municipal Boundary
Beggars Bush Barracks
RUTLAND SQUARE
Artisans Dwellings
Eglinton Villa

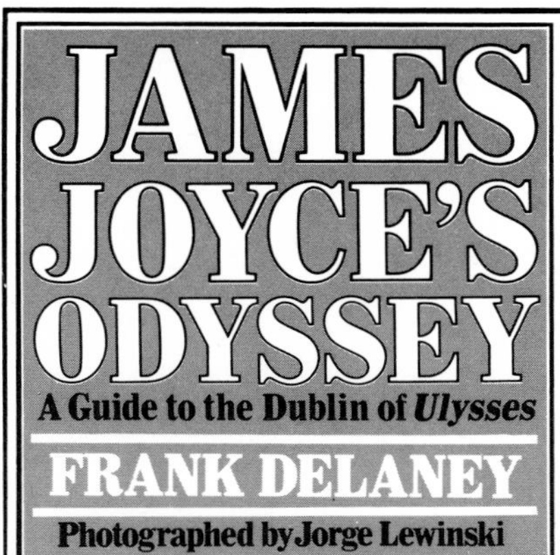
JAMES
JOYCE'S
ODYSSEY
A Guide to the Dublin of *Ulysses*
FRANK DELANEY
Photographed by Jorge Lewinski

JAMES JOYCE'S ODYSSEY

A Guide to the Dublin of *Ulysses*

FRANK DELANEY

Photographed by Jorge Lewinski

HODDER AND STOUGHTON
LONDON SYDNEY AUCKLAND TORONTO

Delaney, Frank
James Joyce's Odyssey.
1. Joyce, James, 1882-1941 – Ulysses
2. Joyce, James 1882-1941 – Homes and haunts –
Ireland – Dublin
823'.912 PRO 6019 09

ISBN 0 340 26885 9

 Typeset by King's English Typesetters, Ltd, Cambridge. Printed in Great Britain for Hodder and Stoughton Limited, Mill Road, Dunton Green, Sevenoaks, Kent by Morrison & Gibb Ltd, London and Edinburgh.

Book design: Sharyn Troughton

Hodder and Stoughton Editorial Office: 47 Bedford Square, London WC1B 3DP

This book is dedicated to my three sons,
Frank, Bryan and Owen Delaney,
who are already Dubliners and who
may yet become Joyceans.

EST LEATHER
ONLY USED
SINGER

CONTENTS

CHAPTER	PAGE
INTRODUCTION	NINE
TELEMACHUS	FOURTEEN
NESTOR	TWENTY SIX
PROTEUS	THIRTY FOUR
CALYPSO	FORTY ONE
LOTUS EATERS	FORTY EIGHT
HADES	FIFTY SIX
AEOLUS	SEVENTY ONE
LAESTRYGONIANS	SEVENTY EIGHT
SCYLLA AND CHARYBDIS	NINETY TWO
WANDERING ROCKS	NINETY EIGHT
SIRENS	ONE HUNDRED AND ELEVEN
CYCLOPS	ONE HUNDRED AND TWENTY
NAUSICAA	ONE HUNDRED AND THIRTY
OXEN OF THE SUN	ONE HUNDRED AND THIRTY NINE
CIRCE	ONE HUNDRED AND FORTY EIGHT
EUMAEUS	ONE HUNDRED AND FIFTY EIGHT
ITHACA	ONE HUNDRED AND SIXTY FIVE
PENELOPE	ONE HUNDRED AND SEVENTY FIVE
POSTSCRIPT	ONE HUNDRED AND EIGHTY ONE
BIBLIOGRAPHY	ONE HUNDRED AND EIGHTY FIVE
ACKNOWLEDGMENTS	ONE HUNDRED AND EIGHTY SEVEN
INDEX	ONE HUNDRED AND EIGHTY EIGHT

The distant Seychelles are not so remote
Nor Ctesiphon as ultimately dead
As this damp square round which tired echoes float
Of something brilliant that George Moore once said:
Where, still, in pitch-pine snugs pale poets quote
Verses rejected by the Bodley Head
For in this drained aquarium no breeze
Deposits pollen from more fertile shores
Or kills the smell of long unopened drawers
That clings forever to these dripping trees.
Where Bloom once wandered, gross and ill-at-ease,
Twice-pensioned heroes of forgotten wars
With misplaced confidence demand applause
Shouting stale slogans on the Liffey quays.

Osbert Lancaster, *Afternoons with Baedeker*

INTRODUCTION

Reading *Ulysses* is one of the pleasures of life. It is a vast, entertaining, funny, absorbing, exciting, complex, immensely *enjoyable* novel, a book to get lost in, a book to take to a desert island, a book to keep by your bedside and discover each day something new, a book to be quoted from, recalled, discussed, contemplated, bequeathed, bestowed, above all to be relished, savoured, a work of intelligence and delight. But ever since it was published on James Joyce's fortieth birthday, the 2nd of February, 1922, generations of readers have faltered. "I *will* finish it this time!" muttered the cinemagoers when Joseph Strick's film of *Ulysses* was shown: Joyce's novel is still, to many, a literary obstacle course and the reader whose stamina fails often feels guilty.

But is this surprising? The sheer length of the text (over three hundred thousand words), Joyce's genius with language (a rock-garden of classical references), the many interconnecting levels on which the author built his work (topographical, musical, theological, physiological, political, mythical) and the range of writing techniques (streams of consciousness, internal monologues, buried fact, synecdoche) all dumbfound the non-academic reader and exercise the scholar.

Ulysses has always controlled its readers, even the most learned, sending devoted students off to dig into every relevant archive (often inventing new ones in the process) and, alas, daunting those who just want to enjoy James Joyce. What other twentieth-century author has spawned such a huge body of academic and esoteric research? Universities, especially in America, dedicate entire areas of their English departments to him; translations, however unlikely given the particularity of the text, abound – Korean, Japanese, as well as European languages; Joyce's life and literature have consumed careers, imaginations, bibliographies. And though this body of academic attention would have delighted the author himself who desired to "keep the professors busy for years", has it not, by its size and daunting diligence, come between Joyce and the non-academic reader, the enthusiast?

Certainly even the most animated conversation about *Ulysses* will frequently include the comment: "I never managed it fully, tried several times, but somehow I couldn't get it finished". A pity – the perseverance is so well worth it, if only for the fun and the jokes, and the marvellous writing ability of the man, the superb use of language, the parody, the satire, the understanding of human nature.

A pity too, that *Ulysses* should somehow have been lodged outside the reach of the people about whom it was written. Joyce saw himself as essentially the chronicler of the common man. His companions were the "hundred-headed rabble of the cathedral close", waiters and tailors and fruit-sellers and porters: "nobody in any of my books is worth more than a hundred pounds". And he believed that the key to human nature lay in observing the commonest acts of man, ordering a drink, eating a meal, opening an umbrella, folding a newspaper. *Ulysses* and its behaviour exhibits Joyce's beliefs to the full. It was his third book of four – *Dubliners,* a collection of short stories; *A*

Portrait of the Artist as a Young Man, an autobiographical novel; and, after *Ulysses, Finnegans Wake,* "The Wake", as its affectionately called, which especially gave Joyce a reputation for obscurity, for recycling the English language.

"I want," said Joyce to a friend in Zurich, "to give a picture of Dublin so complete that if the city one day suddenly disappeared from the earth it could be reconstructed out of my book." He had been born and educated in Dublin, lived, loved, borrowed and begged in Dublin, was enhanced, betrayed and finally excluded by Dublin and up to the time he died, thirty-seven years after his self-imposed exile, chosen ascetically, exercised artistically, he taxed native Dubliners who visited him with his ability to remember the names and numbers of the shops and the houses in correct sequence.

Ulysses is James Joyce's incantation to, for and of Dublin. It was designed by him as a detailed account of ordinary life on an ordinary Dublin day, and he planned each movement of each character on each street as though he were playing chess. He placed them in houses he knew, drinking in pubs he had frequented, walking on cobblestones he retraced. He made the very air of Dublin, the atmosphere, the feeling, the place, almost indistinguishable, certainly inseparable, from his human characters – Dublin *is* a character in *Ulysses,* the "womancity" with her skirts lifted. Consequently, a feeling for Dublin as Joyce portrayed it, a knowledge of the city as it might have been in his time, and a modern catalogue of the geography of *Ulysses* may help to loosen the novel's bindings. A journey through its pages is a glistening, aromatic, atmospheric voyage in the company of believable, likeable, culpable human beings with ordinary vices, virtues and traits - recognisable people, comic, tragic, vulnerable, uncertain, carnal, aggressive, defensive, passionate, aloof, romantic, cynical.

At its simplest – dare I use the word! – *Ulysses* is a story of some random ramblings through a large part of Dublin on a single day, Thursday, 16th of June, 1904. Paths cross and criss-cross, characters pass by each other, knowingly and unknowingly. They greet, ignore, applaud and insult each other – their lives and the life of the city intermingle naturally and normally in the teeming streets. They are not remarkable people in any late-twentieth-century media-gilded way; few of these citizens would ever make the newspaper columns except by the announcement of a birth, marriage or death. But they are credible in their ordinariness, comic and tragic in their predicament and monumentally luminous, illuminating in their humanity. In the personalities of Leopold Bloom and his heaving wife Molly, Stephen Dedalus (Joyce himself at the age of twenty-two, the age he left Dublin) and various other assorted characters, Joyce drew, as he set out to, a map of human nature, a map whose symbols are everyday incidents, joys, tragedies, encounters, disappointments, boastings, betrayals, laughter and pain – a suitable case for the widest range of academic, philosophical and literary investigation.

> I who dishevelled ways forsook
> To hold the poets' grammar-book,
> Bringing to tavern and to brothel
> The mind of witty Aristotle,
> Lest bards in the attempt should err
> Must here be my interpreter:
> Wherefore receive now from my lip
> Peripatetic scholarship.

Taken out of context, the opening lines of Joyce's ballad *The Holy Office,* though intended differently (a vicious satire on old Dublin enemies) can be searched for a hint, no more, of the motivation for *Ulysses.* And then, as always, the danger with

Joyce is that just as you interpret him – or think you do – some other aspect, some digression, some pun, reference or vagary diverts you and once again he is the computer you cannot beat. He is, finally, his own interpreter. So why write a book of part-criticism, part-interpretation, part-illumination, a guide, any guide, to *Ulysses*? The answer is, simply, enthusiasm. (And, like Everest, it was *there* – the two efforts, scaling his heights, skirting precipice and crevasse, are not dissimilar!) I know I cannot possibly explicate, or even exhibit, every single reference on every single page – I only hope that the occasional delights I touch or trigger contribute to the overall score on the pinball machine. I know too, that a work of guidance to, or interpretation of, *Ulysses* which will be total and comprehensive in itself is perhaps impossible, certainly out of reach to someone not yet turned forty – and who has the ordinary necessities of life, such as eating and sleeping to attend to!

I am aware of, and am consumed with respect for, the huge body of academic work which Joyce has inspired. For example, who could possibly emulate, improve upon, the impeccable Richard Ellmann biography, the standard bible for all Joyce students? Agreed that there remains other work to be done; Anthony Burgess who, in his own novels, responds so warmly to Joyce, believes that the sequel to *Ulysses* must be written. But this book does not belong in any of those areas – this is a work of happy, gazetteering enthusiasm, sparked by a desire to share in the delights of an author whose city surrounded me for years, tinged me for ever. This is a plain man's guide to a novel, perhaps *the* novel, of the plain man. As befits such a project, the text of *Ulysses* from which I have quoted (trying wherever possible not to break the quotation internally – his prose is as music) is the 1969 edition published in the United Kingdom by Penguin, in paperback. In some cases where he did not, I have used capital letters in the interests of plainness, as I have decided, too, not to use the method of indicating speech – *Ulysses* employed the dash "–".

There is another notion underlying this book. *Ulysses* may, if you wish, become a guidebook, a literary Baedeker, by which a trip to Dublin becomes enlivened. Indeed, much of the more distinguished academic work, such as Clive Hart's, has examined that aspect. And after all, Joyce designed the novel from his own knowledge of the city, from details supplied by friends, relatives, books, newspapers – and from the information contained in *Thom's Directory of the United Kingdom of Great Britain and Ireland – Dublin Edition, 1904*. Each year this tome gazetted, alongside government and commerce, the city of Dublin, street by house, house by occupant and Joyce, for the purposes of *Ulysses*, interrogated Thom's. The characters and their bits and pieces were in his head already – he used *Thom's* to find them rooms to live in, places to go.

Dublin escaped the Second World War and the city of *Ulysses* is still there, forlorn, dishevelled and available. But only just available. Many of Joyce's streets have keeled over quietly, lanes have been suffocated, houses are lying, wounded and dying, on the kerbside. Only the big streets have survived and not always as Joyce utilised them. Even Mr. Bloom's house, Number Seven, Eccles Street, the most famous address in English literature, is on the verge of disappearing under the developer's pencil. Other areas have changed utterly. In fifty years from now it may well be that, public buildings and principal streets apart, the Dublin of *Ulysses* will be no more.

Yet Joyce's mist clings. It is to be found in the dingy lanes off the quays, in the web of streets leading to the river, through the railings at "Trinity's surly front", in Grafton Street still "gay with housed awnings", in the National Library, at the Martello Tower, preserved with dignity at Sandycove, behind the cypresses in the cemetery at

Glasnevin. Like old glass jars, parts of the city have bottled Joyce's smoky vapours.

Which is only as it should be. For long enough Joyce was reviled in his native city: Ireland in the 'Twenties was hardly sufficiently liberal to embrace an author who described woman as "an animal that micturates once a day, defecates once a week, menstruates once a month and parturates once a year": who satirised the principal ritual of the Roman Catholic Church (into which he was born) in his opening paragraph, and who described his native land as "the sow that eats her own farrow"! Nonetheless, as the years brought down benevolence, Joyce's genius was recognised and the city has come to regard its genius with that ironic affection it uses for compliments.

But if you have never read *Ulysses*, never visited Dublin, never known the work of James Joyce why do you need a guide to his odyssey? Well, he intended his work to be international, universal, the complete gazetteer of the human condition, a map of the body and the mind, as well as of the Dublin he knew. Leopold Bloom, Joyce's Common Man, leaves his home at eight o'clock on a Thursday morning in June, 1904, to buy his breakfast and returns finally, and sleeps at approximately two o'clock the following morning. In the hours between, he lands on the shores of many streets, endures misadventure and delight, tastes gall and honey before, as Homer's hero did, he regains the sanctuary of his terraced Ithaca where his wife spins at her loom of dreams. His voyage has taken him through the streets broad and narrow of Dublin on a parallel to one of the greatest adventure tales ever described – for the Isles of Greece read the streets of Dublin. If you accept, as a definition of the novel, the reflection of the human condition, Joyce's novel is the ultimate such exercise.

Who was this wayward genius, this odd, acerbic soul, who has been credited with changing the structure and course of the novel? He was a half-blind, irascible, impecunious spendthrift who quarrelled with his closest friends, made enemies of mere acquaintances, was a scathing critic, a devastating satirist, a man of immense imagination, learning and sheer brain-power. He lived most of his life in four cities, Dublin, Trieste, Zurich and Paris, and he was fifty-nine and famous when he died in 1941. Beckett took notes for him, Hemingway wrote letters to him, Proust asked him if he liked truffles.

Wrote one critic: "He wrote nothing that wasn't a masterpiece." Wrote another: "Mr. Joyce is a queasy undergraduate scratching his pimples." He opened Dublin's first cinema, the Volta in Mary Street, after he had persuaded some Italian businessmen to put up the money, and the rapt patrons sat for hours watching sepia waves washing a beach. Other failed ventures included the importation of Irish tweed into Italy, accounting for a bank in Rome, and litigation over real and/or imagined insults.

He was a delighted, devoted son, committed family man, remained in love with just one woman, whom he married after twenty-seven years of cohabitation. He was regarded by some literary critics and contemporaries – himself included – as the greatest writer since Shakespeare. Much of Joyce's work lay beneath its own surface. For example – at no point in *Ulysses* does he describe physically the streets of Dublin, yet you can recognise them. But in the National Library – by a pleasing coincidence the scene of an entire chapter in the novel – lies the famous Lawrence Collection, a wonderful, huge storehouse of photographs taken and preserved on glass plates by Robert French, a photographer, who worked for William Lawrence of O'Connell Street. The Lawrence Collection froze for ever Dublin as Joyce knew it and even though all the photographs reproduced in this book may not necessarily belong to the year 1904 (Lawrence's chronological cataloguing left something to be desired) they are of the Joycean period, that calm, pre-revolutionary period of Queen Victoria and her son, later King Edward VII. Robert French's photography all over Ireland embraced the period between 1880 and 1910 and the National Library acquired the forty thousand plates in 1942 for three hundred pounds.

When Jorge Lewinski, specially commissioned and committed, visited the scenes of *Ulysses,* he photographed them as much in a spirit of atmospheric enquiry as of geographical record. If on occasion you find it difficult to tell which pictures are Robert French's and which are Jorge Lewinski's – then, perhaps that, too, is a comment on Joyce.

So, with visual support, what of James Joyce's claim? Could Dublin, if required, be reconstructed out of the pages of *Ulysses*?

Well, should Joyce's comment be taken at face value? Always a dangerous thing to do with a man who after all, writing autobiographically, gave himself the name Dedalus, the mythological figure who devised the Labyrinth. To be regarded as an enigma was one of Joyce's better-known desires and therefore, whether Dublin could be rebuilt using *Ulysses* as a site-map is not, perhaps, the whole question, because did the architect mean physical or imaginative reconstruction? Or the means of finding out, the journey through Dublin and *Ulysses,* the hopeful travelling rather than the arrival, is that what Joyce intended? Maybe he wanted it to be a personal odyssey for each reader, an examination of self, enthusiasm? In which case. . .

FRANK DELANEY
London, 1981

TELEMACHUS

This Martello Tower, its original defensive menace muted, sits on a knuckle of Dublin coastline gnawed by the Irish Sea. Other such pocket-fortresses along the coast fell into decay, some were rescued as fashionably eccentric habitations and this one became a museum.

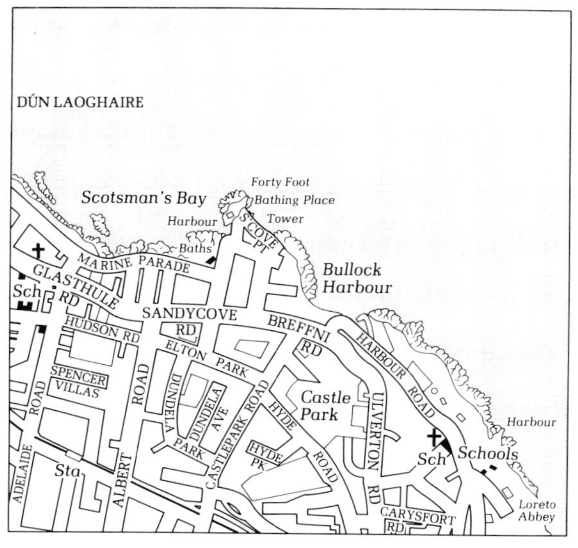

Leave Dublin, travel due south through Dun Laoire towards Dalkey and beyond the cluster of Glasthule village turn left into Sandycove Avenue West. Down the slope, adjacent to the Forty-Foot Bathing Place, you will find the Martello Tower and seasonally you may buy a ticket of admission, which reads:

> The Martello Tower at Sandycove, better known as James Joyce's Tower, was built in 1804 by the British in a series of defence measures to withstand a threatened Napoleonic invasion. The Tower, which is forty feet high with walls eight feet thick, was lived in by James Joyce in 1904 and provided the setting for part of the first chapter of *Ulysses*. It is now owned by the Eastern Regional Tourism Organisation who maintain it as a Joycean Museum.

On a Thursday night in 1904 three men lay asleep in the cold domed room of this tower. One, Samuel Chenevix Trench, had a nightmare about a black panther. He took his handgun, fired suddenly but harmlessly at the imaginary animal and went back to sleep. Not long afterwards he yelled again – same panther, different nightmare. Oliver St. John Gogarty, a wild medical student, grabbed the gun and fired gleefully at the pots and pans above the sleeping bed of the third man. This was James Joyce, who rose in fright, dressed in dudgeon and left to walk to Dublin in the rain.

The incident triggered Joyce's exile and planted the opening chapter of *Ulysses*. These three men are the characters whose conversation in and around the Martello Tower at Sandycove forms the opening episode. Samuel Chenevix Trench (who later blew his brains out, perhaps with the same revolver) appears as Haines the Englishman. Oliver St. John Gogarty, who fired at the pots and pans, is Buck Mulligan, mocker and roisterer. Most important is the author's depiction of himself, Stephen Dedalus as James Joyce.

Joyce had come to Sandycove by invitation, only six nights earlier, in September 1904, but had moodily outstayed the ebullient Gogarty's welcome. The coldness of Joyce's departure never thawed, even though Gogarty made several attempts at reconciliation, principally because he guessed, anxiously and correctly, that Joyce would lampoon him in literature. "He fears the lancet of my art as I fear that of his," is the cool observation which Joyce/Dedalus makes internally while being pilloried in the Tower by the irreverent medical student, Gogarty/Mulligan. And in time, indeed, Joyce exacted a humiliating literary revenge for Gogarty's nocturnal ballistics.

But why a Martello Tower? Apart from Joyce's interrupted repose there – Gogarty became a tenant in order to make it the Irish equivalent of the earth's navel-stone at Delphi, with himself as the Oracle – was it the imagery that appealed to Joyce, the round, smooth, impregnable, prominent fortification, a metaphor for his own personality? Or was it the fact that a Martello Tower seems a truncated version, a reducation, in phallic terms, of that other great Irish fortification, the Round Tower, used by monks to protect their sacred vessels and illuminated manuscripts from marauders?

In the days when Joyce stayed there Sandycove was already an orderly outpost of Dublin, a distant gardened suburb to which the middle classes had begun to gravitate. They bought good houses, or built well on private land, in order to enjoy the sea air, the lush, alluring countryside. Cottage families were still scattered throughout the hinterland. Some worked in the houses, some laboured on nearby farms and dairies, a few subsisted on local fishing or cockle-gathering.

The atmosphere was predominantly British and Protestant. Monarchists, professional classes, civil servants, officers – their occupations were dictated by their loyalties. The few middle-class Catholics among them were "Castle Catholics", those who by accidents of heritage or education were acceptable at Dublin Castle, the hub of rule. Home Rule and the late Charles Stewart Parnell were permissible conversation – even for ladies. Today all has changed in the natural order which folded Ireland into new shapes after the Anglo-Irish Treaty of 1922. But the change in Sandycove seems to have been slower. Many of the family names persist, the gardens exhibit the continuity, the perennation, of Anglo-Irish gentility in Dublin.

Dinner parties are comfortably hospitable, neighbours are friendly without intrusion, loyalties are more understood than emphasised and Sandycove, calm and neatly arranged, proceeds quietly with its life. Its citizens are solicitors, doctors, retired bankers and superannuated civil servants and there are no demarcation lines along religious grounds. Those Protestant families who flourish will always exercise their Irish franchise, but still take a keen interest in the affairs of the British Royal Family.

With all this gentility was Sandycove not an improbable location for the opening of *Ulysses*? When the novel appeared, on Joyce's fortieth birthday in 1922, there seemed to be only two schools of thought – and criticism. Ford Madox Ford wrote: "One feels admiration that is almost reverence for the incredible labours of this incredible genius." But Alfred Noyes suggested that it was "the foulest book that has ever found its way into print".

Ulysses is an account of ordinary life in a Dublin day on Thursday, June the 16th, 1904. It is a huge, wandering novel, intricate, comic, tragi-comic, explicit, carnal, cloacal. Within its punning idiom a celebrated Dublin punster described it as "more a public labyrinth than a Celtic toilet". Not for nothing did Joyce identify with Dedalus who created the labyrinth, and he scorned, denounced the soft lights of the more romantic Celtic literary twilight.

James Joyce's odyssey begins at the Tower at eight o'clock in the morning when "Stately, plump Buck Mulligan came from the stairhead, bearing a bowl of lather on which a mirror and a razor lay crossed". It ends eighteen jig-sawed hours later, on the far side of Dublin, when Stephen Dedalus has met Leopold Bloom; Telemachus has met his father Ulysses, the young, uncertain Joyce has met the assimilating maturity of the older Joyce – and Molly Bloom says "yes I will yes".

As in much day-to-day life the drama in *Ulysses* is small but incessant. There are disagreements, disappointments, betrayals, jokes, happinesses, hungers, thirsts, birth and death, wages, work and wonder. W. B. Yeats, the poet, called it "the vulgarity of a single Dublin day prolonged to seven hundred pages", an unnecessary and imperceptive disparagement; Joyce believed that the key to human character lay in observing the commonest acts of man. In *Ulysses* he exhibits the city's unremarkable inhabitants, and their commonplace activities are portrayed minutely.

The day Joyce chose was significant. On the 16th of June, 1904 he first walked out with Nora Barnacle, a dark-eyed full-blown woman from the West of Ireland with whom he fell endlessly in love. Was a woman ever so commemorated in literature? And she never even read *Ulysses*!

On the first page Buck Mulligan is shaving in the open air on top of the Tower, when Stephen Dedalus joins him. A conversation occurs in which Mulligan is unspeakably mocking about the death of Stephen's mother, a matter in which Stephen feels substantial guilt. "A light wind passed his brow, fanning softly his fair uncombed hair and stirring silver points of anxiety in his eyes."

Joyce's own mother had died a year before, after a long vomiting illness during which he rejected her wishes that he return to the practice and sacraments of Catholicism. Should Telemachus have listened to his mother, Penelope, and not gone in search of Ulysses, his father? Joyce's reasons for choosing Homer's *Odyssey* for creating his own epic have exercised scholars. It wasn't simply that the mythical wanderings of the Greek hero provided a convenient framework: Ulysses – as he preferred to call Odysseus – seemed to him the complete man in literature, a man who could

THE FORTY FOOT
GENTLEMEN'S
BATHING PLACE
WOMEN
WELCOME
NOT
DOGS

work his way through the misadventures of life, survive using wisdom and prudence as his only weapons and eventually return to the waiting Penelope.

Joyce divided his own odyssey into eighteen parts and gave them – in his mind and work, although not actually stated in the published book – titles corresponding to people or incidents in Homer's tale. Thus he cast Stephen Dedalus, aged twenty-two as Joyce then was, in the role of Telemachus.

The conversation in the Tower parapet grew even more acrimonius. Mulligan the medical student baited Stephen the poet. "And what is death, he asked, your mother's or yours or my own? You only saw your mother die. I see them pop off every day in the Mater and Richmond and cut up into tripes in the dissecting room." Downstairs Haines the Englishman is waiting and all three breakfast, while an old woman brings them new milk which she obtained "crouching by a patient cow at daybreak in the lush fields". Buck Mulligan wants to drink later; Stephen's wages from a nearby school are thus bespoken.

From the opening page when Buck Mulligan "held the bowl aloft and intoned: *Introibo ad altare Dei*" and mocked the Mass, to the last chapter where Molly Bloom lies languidly and explicitly in her erotic bed, Joyce's flouting of convention gave *Ulysses* a reputation for obscenity which caused litigation, censorship and attempted suppression.

"The most infamously obscene book in ancient or modern literature," *Sunday Express*.

"Our first impression is that of sheer disgust," *Daily Express*.

"Enough to make a Hottentot sick," *Sporting Times*.

Such reviews reflected the general opinion in which *Ulysses* has been held in Ireland. It was denounced and denied and the name James Joyce was a sulphurous cloud. So effective were the book's antagonists that there was no need to ban it – the stain stayed. Which is how I first came to hear the name of James Joyce. Some of my childhood holidays were spent near Dublin, and I first wandered around Sandycove and its Tower with the sons of my uncle. The leader of these cousins kicked the Tower dramatically one day and said it was in a dirty book by a man called Joyce.

Inside the Tower, long before my cousin kicked it, the trio finished their breakfast and Mulligan decided to swim in the Forty-Foot.

"And there's your Latin quarter hat, he said. Stephen picked it up and put it on. Haines called to them from the doorway: Are you coming, you fellows?" Stephen, Mulligan and Haines (who is no more than a scratching-post of a character) left the Tower, wearing, variously, second-hand breeks, stiff collars, rebellious ties, clean handkerchiefs, a primrose waistcoat even, and wandered down between "leader shoots of fern" to the Forty-Foot. The bathing-place is still a male bastion, a curious little place where myriad men sit about in aimless nakedness: a few years ago some heated Hibernian feminists tried to storm it. Mulligan immersed himself, Haines smoked on a rock, Stephen departed, vowing never to visit them again.

The Joycean mischiefs are beginning. Swimming with Mulligan is a young man who flickers much later. He is a student too, with a knowledge of the town of Mullingar and would have, if permitted, a knowledge of a young lady called Milly Bloom. But he merely flickers. With colons and commas, in brush-strokes and little daubs did Joyce portray Dublin – and therefore the world.

Today, James Joyce's Tower is much refined. The "dark, winding stairs" have been whitewashed, symbolically enough. The museum display cases contain Joyce's tie, waistcoat and guitar, some items presented by Samuel Beckett and other friends in literary endowment. Leaflets and pamphlets and booklets bear witness to the intellectual curiosity value of the man who swore that his work would "keep the professors busy for years".

In 1904 the place was shabbier, but today you can still feel Joyce's shade and shape. Tall, thin, aloof, a haughtiness that would grow into arrogance, the thick unwinking spectacles, the clothes shabby, or borrowed, or both, the manner compelling, the demeanour alternating between animation and broody silence. His conversation was always literary and intellectual but his personality was as grubby as his impecuniousness; his inability to get on with

people, and his general disenchantment with Ireland had become apparent early. Was it that Ireland, Dublin, had become too small for him? Yet, he wrote later: "If I can get to the heart of Dublin, I can get to the heart of every city in the world. In the particular is contained the universal". Perhaps he chose, instead, to be the surgeon who prefers not to look upon the face of the patient.

The Tower lingers on the land when you Sealink your way to England. It makes an appropriate point of departure: the incident with Gogarty/Mulligan and Trench/Haines finally convinced James Joyce to leave Ireland and seek silence, exile and cunning. Unhesitatingly he took with him that red-haired, dark-eyed woman of the 16th of June, Nora Barnacle: "I desire that you should share any happiness that may be mine and to assure you of my great respect for that love of yours which it is my wish to deserve and answer." Joyce never lived in Ireland again and he made few visits. His homes were to be in Trieste, Zurich and Paris. Nora bore him two children and immense love and they finally married in 1931.

"We'll see you again, Haines said, turning as Stephen walked up the path . . ." And the story has begun, the long bell of the day has commenced its ringing. Thursday, the 16th of June, 1904, was a normal, unremarkable Dublin day.

ULSTER

NESTOR

Dalkey, a hilly village, looks calmly and violetly down on Dublin Bay. In 1904, in these hushed and paved leafy avenues, James Joyce filled a temporary vacancy as "a gentleman usher" in an academy for boys.

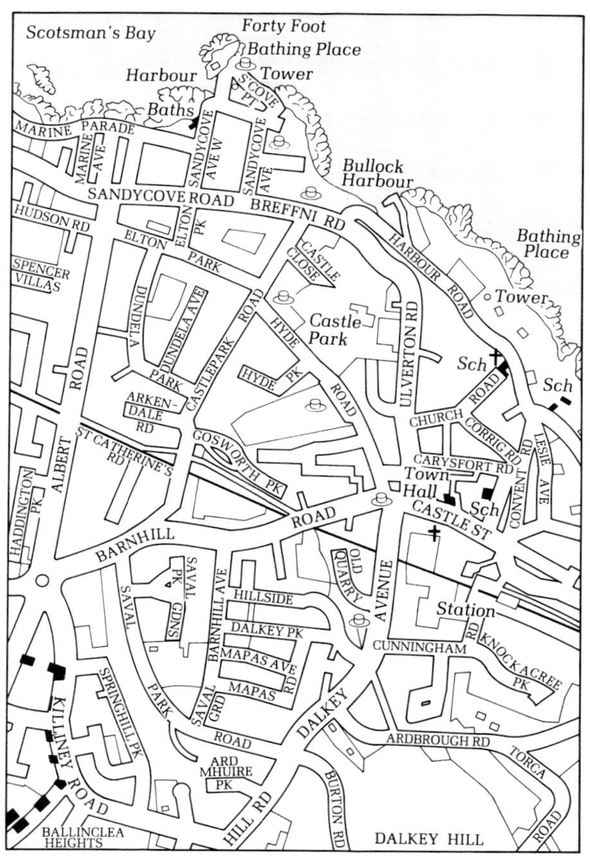

Summerfield Lodge is almost exactly one mile, as the crow flies, from the Martello Tower; and on foot, a distance of a mile and a tenth, a fit quarter of an hour. Stephen walked from Sandycove towards the glistening hill-housed countryside, then as now, bush-cushioned and buttressed, along Sandycove Avenue East and Breffni Road (a continuation of Sandycove Road), past creamy, louvred dwellings. Walk it now and you pass the gap of Bullock Harbour pretending to be a marina, into Ulverton Road where Our Lady's Manor genteels further a gentle home for the geriatric wealthy.

On a June morning in 1904 would an occasional carriage, a lady cyclist in, perhaps, her bloomers, a horseman, have passed Stephen? Now traffic lights stagger the journey. Some of the older houses along Ulverton Road have either been replaced by split-level enclaves, or their speculative demolition has simply left gaps in the gums. At the end of Ulverton Road there is a T-junction and Stephen turned right, ignoring the village of Dalkey, then sharp left up the hill of Dalkey Avenue. At his left hand, shadowed, shriven cottages blinked at him over their half-doors. Why are they empty now? So much of Joycean Dublin has disappeared. Did each character in *Ulysses* bear a wand? In Stephen's time the school was at the rear, and today a kindergarten occupies the same space. Through the branches of the willows the distant bay slides into view like a postcard.

By the time he was twenty-two, Stephen's age, Joyce's mind was a tapestry. He had been educated by the Jesuits, who had taught him "how to arrange things in such a way that they become easy to survey and to judge".

He met them first at six and a half years of age – "half-past-six", as he said – when he went to Clongowes Wood, in County Kildare, still the most eminent boys' school in Ireland. His biographer, Richard Ellmann, describes him as "already a well-behaved, slim little boy in adult company, with a pale face and eyes of the palest blue to lend, when he was not laughing, an impenetrable coolness, an odd self-sufficiency, to otherwise regular and predictable features. His nearsightedness was soon to make him wear

glasses . . ." But his father's eventual and continuous impecuniousness caused young James to be withdrawn from Clongowes after only three years; he spent two more years (which he always chose to forget) in a Christian Brothers school at North Richmond Street in Dublin and finally returned to the Jesuits in Belvedere College, where he remained until he went to University.

University College, Dublin, freed him from the compulsion to keep winning academic prizes and exhibitions at school in order to support the family, whose gentility grew shabbier and shabbier; the vagrant Joyces rented often and often used the banisters as firewood. James left the University in June 1902 with a lazy pass and decided to wade into the literary pool that was then Dublin, with William Butler Yeats, the flowing poet, John Millington Synge the playwright of the Western world, Lady Gregory, the self-appointed patron of the Celtic twilight, George Moore, the elegant bitch and George Russell ("A.E."), bearded, enthusiastic, enigmatic, who arranged the meeting between Joyce and Yeats which gave rise to the story:

"How old are you, Yeats?"

"I am forty."

"Then you are much too old for me to help you. Good day to you."

Apocryphal? Sadly, yes. But Yeats did comment on Joyce's appalling manners, even though he acknowledged the emerging talent.

Stephen was a sympathetic teacher, not a brilliant one. He always identified with the runt.

> "You, Armstrong. Do you know anything about Pyrrhus?"
>
> A bag of figrolls lay snugly in Armstrong's satchel. He curled them between his palms at whiles and swallowed them softly. Crumbs adhered to the tissues of his lips. A sweetened boy's breath. Welloff people, proud that their eldest son was in the navy. Vico Road, Dalkey,
>
> Pyrrhus, sir? Pyrrhus, a pier.
>
> All laughed. Mirthless high malicious laughter.

Dalkey village is not yet dragged into conurbated conformity. The streets, castled and churched, remain much as Stephen saw them along his left shoulder.

Joyce taught a boy who ate figrolls in the Clifton school on Dalkey Avenue in 1904. Stephen taught Roman history and English literature and then prepared himself for a discourse from Mr. Deasy. When Telemachus left the lovely lake of Ocean he stepped ashore to where Nestor, son of Neleus, glory of the Achaean race, sat with his sons and told stories of Trojan battles, voyages and sacrifices of bulls.

Mr. Deasy began to instruct Stephen in the cause of Irish nationalism and in the cure of foot-and-mouth disease in cattle, on which subject he had written a letter to the newspapers which he hoped Stephen might be able, with his literary connections, to have published. Most important, he paid Stephen's wages.

A sovereign fell, bright and new, on the soft pile of the tablecloth.

Three, Mr. Deasy said, turning his little savingsbox about in his hand. These are handy things to have. See. This is for sovereigns. This is for shillings, sixpences, halfcrowns. And here crowns. See.

He shot from it two crowns and two shillings.

Ireland then was at comparative peace. Victoria's calm had reigned. Home Rule was rising, a benign sun, over in the east, towards London. The ivy leaf of Parnell was still mourned. Nationalism meant earnest argument and logical discourse.

Mr. Deasy didn't mince his words:

Old England is dying.

He stepped swiftly off, his eyes coming to blue life as they passed a broad sunbeam. He faced about and back again.

Dying, he said, if not dead by now.

The harlot's cry from street to street
Shall weave old England's winding sheet.

Joyce had had immense difficulty with the Dublin publishers of his short stories, *Dubliners.* The publisher, George Roberts, demanded an amendment to what he considered an unflattering reference to the Queen. "Here's this chap come to the throne after his *old mother* keeping him out of it till the man was grey." Joyce amended it all right. It came back: ". . . his bloody old bitch of a mother . . ."

Quiet, residentially desirable, old-monied, Dalkey

Avenue leads on up into the heights of the hill. At night furtive eyes in the carpark gaze out over the lights of the strumpet city; by day dogs, children and walkers laugh through the groves on the hillside. Stephen Dedalus left that hillside to go to Dublin. "On his wise shoulders through the checkerwork of leaves the sun flung spangles, dancing coins." He is on his way to meet, ineluctably, his father Ulysses. No wonder Joyce was grateful to the Jesuits. "How to arrange things in such a way that they become easy to survey and to judge", indeed. So well did he learn from his teachers and priests that the characters who walk about inside his huge coiling novel even now still create the loudest whisper in the blessed mutter of Dublin's ghosts.

PROTEUS

Sandymount Strand is the palate of Dublin Bay, a horseshoe within a horseshoe, curving, lapping, long. Walkers and wild birds travel the ridged, cockled, herringbone sands.

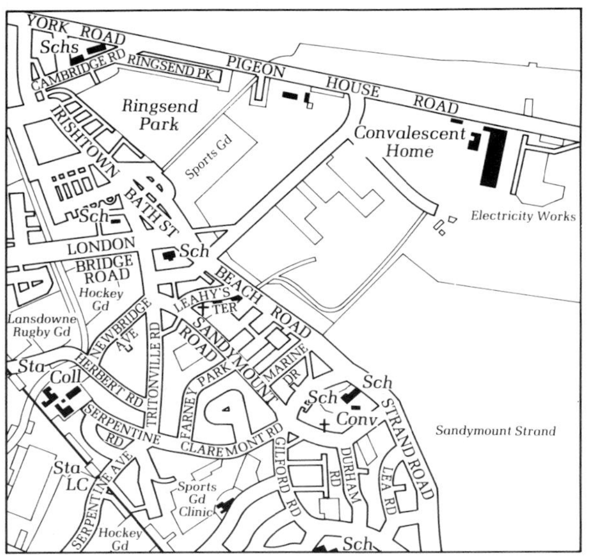

Two tall red-and-white chimneys mark the Pigeon House power station where the strand begins. Stephen must have taken the Dalkey tram to Haddington Road and there changed for the Sandymount tram to Tritonville Road, thence on foot by way of Leahy's Terrace to Sandymount Strand. In his footsteps today you will observe on one side of the street Massey's funeral parlour faced by (apt juxtaposition) a pub called Cheerio Ryan's, followed by Marie Basquille Confections, next to Brendella Skirts. Proceed, past the huge black hat of the Top Hat Roller Disco Fun For All The Family, which would have appealed to the young Joyce. By the wedding cake of Monkstown Church the Dedalus-bearing tram lurched, on through Blackrock village, through Booterstown, past the house of the tenor John McCormack – with whom Joyce once appeared in a concert – and on by Merrion. Did Stephen pass the brick Bank of Ireland in Ballsbridge where I ledger-clerked for a time and made fiscal history by granting a wayward customer an overdraft on his deposit account?

Certainly he passed by the grounds of the Royal Dublin Society and crossed Ball's Bridge over the Dodder River. Today the red roads of Ballsbridge, originally wide to let old regiments march through ceremonially, are interspersed with hotels never then intended, and the American Embassy, circular in design to commemorate the shape of the old Irish fort. The last lap of Stephen's journey to Sandymount is still a dribbling, nondescript passageway along streets of small houses to the sea.

I know a man who changed his name to protect this view of Dublin Bay. When Sandymount and its environs received notice of an impending oil refinery, he inserted the words "Dublin" and "Bay" between the words "Sean" and "Loftus", in order to get the issue named on the actual ballot paper when he was running for local office – a deed for the poll. He won both the election and the battle: there is no refinery.

At about eleven o'clock in the morning Stephen came to Sandymount – to think. "Proteus" is the first chapter in *Ulysses* in which Joyce makes extensive use of the device for which the novel became famous, the stream of consciousness, the *monologue interieur*. Many have parodied it since, none have accomplished it so brilliantly.

Are the opening words of "Proteus" James Joyce's keyboard? "Ineluctable modality of the visible, at least that, if no more, thought through my eyes", the towering phrase, the shining phrase of *Ulysses* sits grave and beautiful inside Stephen's head.

Ineluctable, *adj.*, that cannot be escaped from.

Modality, *n.*, the quality of being limited by a condition.

Sandymount Strand, ineluctable as sin, sweeps wide and grey and beige, stippled with gulls and aeroplanes and lighthouses and ships and lone Dedalus-walkers. "Signatures of all things I am here to read, seaspawn and seawrack, the nearing tide, that rusty boot." Most of the thoughts in Stephen's mind as he walked along Sandymount Strand were triggered by that ineluctable modality of the visible.

First he sees two worthy ladies from the Liberties of Dublin, "the two maries", out for the day, one of them carrying a midwife's bag. "What has she in the bag? A misbirth with a trailing navelcord, hushed in ruddy wool. The cord of all link back, strandentwining cable of all flesh", and Stephen fantasises that it might be possible, using this umbilical telephone line, to dial back to Adam and Eve. Then his mind wanders back and forth over his life so far, like a lazy sieve, recalling family incidents and persons. "In his broad bed nuncle Richie, pillowed and blanketed, extends over the hillock of his knees a sturdy forearm. Cleanchested. He has washed the upper moiety."

Stephen recalls incidents at school. "You told the Clongowes gentry you had an uncle a judge and an uncle a general in the army." Stephen reviews the religious and irreligious fits he used to have, all woman-inspired. "You were awfully holy, weren't you? You prayed to the Blessed Virgin that you might not have a red nose. You prayed to the devil in Serpentine Avenue that the fubsy widow in front might lift her clothes still more from the wet street."

"Ineluctable modality of the visible" was the phrase which ensured that *Ulysses* would first be published. The novel originally appeared, not in book form, but by instalment. *The Little Review,* an American publication, was run by two ladies who were interested in avant-garde prose. They deserve to be named – Margaret Anderson and Jane Heap; the intermediary between them and James Joyce was the poet Ezra Pound. When the two ladies read the ineluctable modality they immediately became daughters of a literary revolution and there and then declared their willingness to lay down their lives for *Ulysses* and its author.

Stephen Dedalus on Sandymount Strand was a troubled young man. The green mucous sea and Mulligan's sickening mockery had reminded him of his mother's illness and vomiting death. His failure to grant her dying wish and return to Catholicism has haunted him and, he knows, always will. So, there he was walking across the sands of Sandymount, a pale, blue-eyed, fair-haired young man, thin but too fine to be gaunt, with an aloofness that will yet be ascetic.

> The grainy sand had gone from under his feet. His boots trod again a damp, crackling mast, razorshells, squeaking pebbles, that on the unnumbered pebbles beats, wood sieved by the shipworm, lost Armada. Unwholesome sandflats waited to suck his treading soles, breathing upward sewage breath. He coasted them, walking warily. A porter-bottle stood up, stogged to its waist, in the cakey sand dough.

Nothing changes – except that they didn't have Coke tins and Polystyrene in 1904. Of the early parts of *Ulysses* the episode which pleased Joyce most was "Proteus". Even though Stephen wasn't an old man and didn't emerge from the waves, he still changed form. From being dull, sullen, listless and bitter he relaxed, became easy with himself, cheerful. And all around him the strand was changing with the tide, the landscape was changing with people wandering in and out of view, the sky was changing with clouds across it.

"His feet marched in sudden proud rhythm over the sand furrows, along by the boulders of the south wall. He stared at them proudly, piled stone mammoth skulls. Gold light on sea, on sand, on boulders. The sun is there, the slender trees, the lemon houses." Sandymount Strand still takes on a light you find further south in Europe, a cinnnamon-and-water light, I've seen it in towns near Rome, in villages near Marseilles, by shores where the Mediterranean stands still with thick, sickening pollution. In the Sandymount distance, to the south, three half-hearted hills; by the road, the railway line, Victorian terraces of houses, a shard of glassed architecture, sparse trees.

"He had come nearer the edge of the sea and wet sand slapped his boots. The new air greeted him, harping in wild nerves, wind of wild air of seeds of brightness." Each night six reliable lighthouses finger this shore with their gentle, yellow insistence.

Stephen saw a dead dog, then a live one, thought of panthers. Stephen mused on the man who was "drowned nine days ago off Maiden's Rock". Would his body float up, white-bloated? Stephen observed: "A woman and a man. I see her skirties. Pinned up, I bet." Stephen dreamed of a dead friend, a dynamitard in Paris, and of a girl he tried to pick up, he dreamed of corpses and ghosts, of longlashed eyes, of shells. He lay on the rocks at Sandymount Strand waiting for Proteus to come up from the sea and change all things. Over his shoulder "moving through the air high spars of a threemaster, her sails brailed up on the crosstrees, homing, upstream, silently moving, a silent ship".

CALYPSO

At eight o'clock on the morning of 16th of June, 1904, Mr. Leopold Bloom stepped out on the doorstep of Number Seven, Eccles Street, Dublin. As he stood beneath the lintel, drawing the door softly closed behind him, sunbeams glanced at the steeple of Saint George's Church.

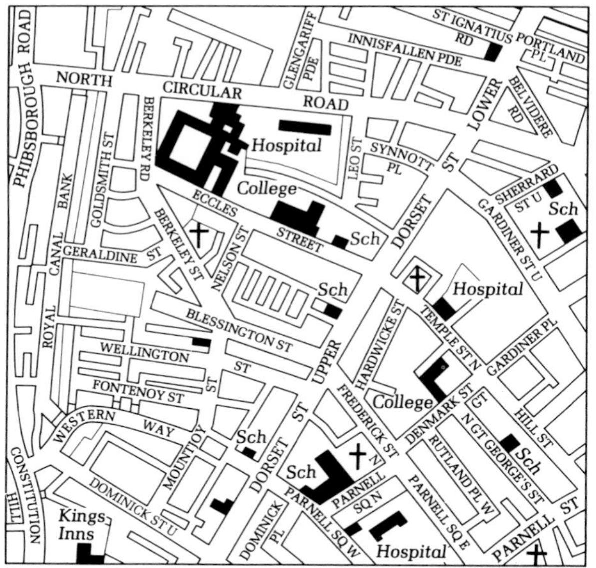

Mr. Bloom and his wife Molly lived quite near the Dorset Street corner of Eccles Street. At the other end Buck Mulligan in the Mater Misericordiae Hospital saw people every day "cut into tripes in the dissecting room". Eccles Street was part of the Georgian organisation of Dublin, and on the face of it now, a wrinkled, nondescript face, Eccles Street seems a curious choice for one of the most famous addresses in literature. But Joyce always had his reasons. Just as he chose the single day of *Ulysses* to commemorate Nora's arrival in his life, he gave Bloom an address which would also commemorate her.

According to Joyce's researches in *Thom's Directory* Number Seven, Eccles Street was vacant on the 16th of June, 1904: later it was to be the home of his great and good friend J. F. Byrne. On a brief return to Ireland in 1909, long before he began to write *Ulysses*, Joyce spent pleasant hours in conversation there but one afternoon, when he called to see Byrne, he was in a state of great misery.

Dublin is, always has been, a jealous city; metaphorically your throat may be cut while your back is turned. Joyce's genius, accompanying arrogance and cool, superior manner irritated his less talented "friends". One of these, an indolent called Cosgrave, told the holidaying Joyce that Nora had not, originally, been as faithful as she pretended. Cosgrave had once been an unsuccessful rival for Nora's attentions and now he informed Joyce that he had, in fact, been clandestinely successful, that when Joyce understood she was working late Cosgrave had been dallying with her. He may have hinted leeringly at sexual connexion too, "carnival knowledge" Dublin calls it.

Joyce was shattered. Even though his masochistic psyche had always needed moral martyrdom, this was terrible. A most tearful, pathetic letter was dashed off to Nora in Trieste:

> I have heard this only an hour ago from his lips. My eyes are full of tears, tears of sorrow and mortification. My heart is full of bitterness and

despair. I can see nothing but your face as it was then raised to meet another's. O, Nora, pity me for what I suffer now. I shall cry for days. My faith in that face I loved is broken. O, Nora, Nora, have pity for my poor wretched love. I cannot call you any dear name because tonight I have learned that the only being I believed in was not loyal to me.

The following morning at dawn, after a night of dark and anguish, he wrote again: "O Nora! Nora! Nora! I am speaking now to the girl I loved, who had red-brown hair and sauntered over to me and took me so easily into her arms and made me a man." Like a spirit possessed – which he was, by sorrow – he wandered, aimless and strained, around Dublin. Finally, two days after the awful information, he went to Number Seven, Eccles Street to confide in Byrne whom he trusted.

Byrne rallied and railed. Unlike Joyce, he hadn't left Dublin and had kept pace with the city's sense of jealousy and conspiracy. He soon smelt what had happened, that the story of Nora's infidelity was in fact a vengeful plan hatched by the envious Cosgrave and viciously encouraged by Gogarty. Subsequently Nora – who had behaved quietly and with dignity under such swingeing accusations – confided in Joyce's brother, Stanislaus, who was able to confirm Byrne's assessment. Cosgrave had previously admitted to Stanislaus his failure to oust Joyce from Nora's heart. It was never difficult to convince Joyce that people were conspiring against him and his relief was so complete that he commemorated Nora's fidelity by immortalising Number Seven, Eccles Street.

Dublin wakes slowly and mistily; the spires step forward from the mountains, the smoke carries the smell of fresh bread. "Mr. Leopold Bloom ate with relish the inner organs of beasts and fowls." When

Mr. Bloom appears in *Ulysses* for the first time, in the "Calypso" episode, he is preparing for a universally common experience, breakfast. "Kidneys were in his mind as he moved about the kitchen softly, righting her breakfast things on the humpy tray. Gelid light and air were in the kitchen but out of doors gentle summer morning everywhere. Made him feel a bit peckish."

Leopold Bloom is thirty-eight years old, and is descended from a Hungarian Jew. His father, Rudolph Virag, was fifty-nine when Leopold was born and had arrived in Ireland the previous year. Leopold's mother was Ellen Higgins, their only child was born in Clanbrassil Street, the Jewish area of Dublin, on the 6th of May, 1866. Joyce polished his verisimilitude until you could see his character's face in it.

"He heard then a warm heavy sigh, softer, as she turned over and the loose brass quoits of the bedstead jingled." (As they do in a recurring timpany throughout the novel.) Molly Bloom is lying in bed not yet fully awake. Dark-haired, wilful, plain-spoken, almost thirty-four years old, Mrs. Marion Bloom (neé Tweedy) is bountifully constructed. The daughter of a British soldier in Gibraltar and a girl of Spanish blood named Lunita Laredo – though there are doubts about both parentages – Molly Bloom's is the scent which stays in the nostrils of the entire novel, from the moment Mr. Bloom "pulled the halldoor to after him very quietly, more, till the footleaf dropped gently over the threshold, a limp lid".

Servants were about their employers' business as Mr Bloom walked to the corner of Eccles Street and Dorset Street, turned right past Larry O'Rourke's pub, to Dlugacz's meat shop. "His hand accepted the moist tender gland and slid it into a side-pocket." Threepence for the kidney for his breakfast and Mr. Bloom walks back along Dorset Street, reading from the piece of paper the meat-shop man used as wrapping paper. Larry O'Rourke's pub, under different ownership now, is still licensed to sell beer, wine and spirits but do not go looking for moist tender glands on Dorset Street, at least not in meat-shops: Dlugacz's is one of the few fictional addresses in *Ulysses*.

"A cloud began to cover the sun wholly slowly wholly", the same cloud that Stephen Dedalus, far away on the other side of the city, has seen "shadowing the bay in deeper green". Once, in this part of Dublin I trysted with a girl who, like me, had no timepiece, but we both lived in earshot, though in opposite directions, of the same church. So we left our separate residences when the bell began to ring. Thus, later, and through the entire day, the same bells ring in the ears of different characters in *Ulysses*, the same processions are saluted in different parts of the city, the same persons are observed in different streets.

Now, as Stephen Dedalus is massaging his chagrin at Buck Mulligan, Mr. Bloom is entering his hallway, and taking an anxious breath. On the floor, among the letters is one to his wife, addressing her as "Mrs. Marion Bloom"; she uses "Marion" when singing in popular concerts. The letter is from Blazes Boylan, the flash, straw-hatted, thuggish impresario who is cuckolding Bloom crudely and laughingly. Having already established him as the irreverent, insensitive Buck Mulligan, Joyce made it clear that Oliver St. John Gogarty was (spectrally at least) Blazes Boylan also – revenge to the full.

Letters in hand, "Entering the bedroom he half-closed his eyes and walked through the warm yellow twilight towards her tousled head." Molly, to whom Joyce's Bloom is as enslaved as Homer's Ulysses was to Queenly Calypso, lies there, on her island too: "She set the brasses jingling as she raised herself briskly, an elbow on the pillow."

He brings her "bread and butter, four, sugar, spoon, her cream" and explains that "metempsychosis", which she has just come across in her reading, means the transmigration of souls. "The warmth of her couched body rose on the air, mingling with the fragrance of the tea she poured." Suddenly, gently, you can feel the air around Mr Bloom grow heavy with sadness because of Blazes Boylan's letter. Down in the kitchen Mr Bloom finishes the cooking of the kidney and sits down to his own breakfast. Breakfast. What other meal could be so appropriate to begin the odyssey of Mr. Bloom? As dawn came with rosy fingers did not Calypso feed Ulysses before he sailed on the wine-dark seas away from her enchanted island?

Mr. Bloom reads a letter from his daughter, fifteen-year-old Milly in Mullingar, where she is working as a photographer's assistant and has taken a shine to a student called Bannon. Mr. Bloom ponders mildly the failures of his life: the death of their baby Rudy unsettled the sexual possibilities between him and Molly, and Blazes Boylan is going to call and see her later that day. But if Mr. Bloom cannot get his house in order he can at least get his body in order and after a "gentle loosening of his bowels" he leaves the house. The clock strikes a quarter to nine; Mr. Bloom is dressed darkly, because he is on his way to the funeral of poor Dignam. On the other side of the city Stephen has already heard a clock striking a quarter to nine; the long day's journey into night which will bring together Ulysses and Telemachus, Mr. Bloom and Stephen Dedalus, has begun. Mr. Leopold Bloom has had his breakfast and Mr. James Joyce has had his joke, a Jew breaking the fast from midnight before going forth to a multifarious communion.

Eccles Street is a quiet street now, the red brick is blackened, Mr. Bloom's house no more than an empty socket. You can still taste vicariously the genteel grandeur it once enjoyed: fanlights and

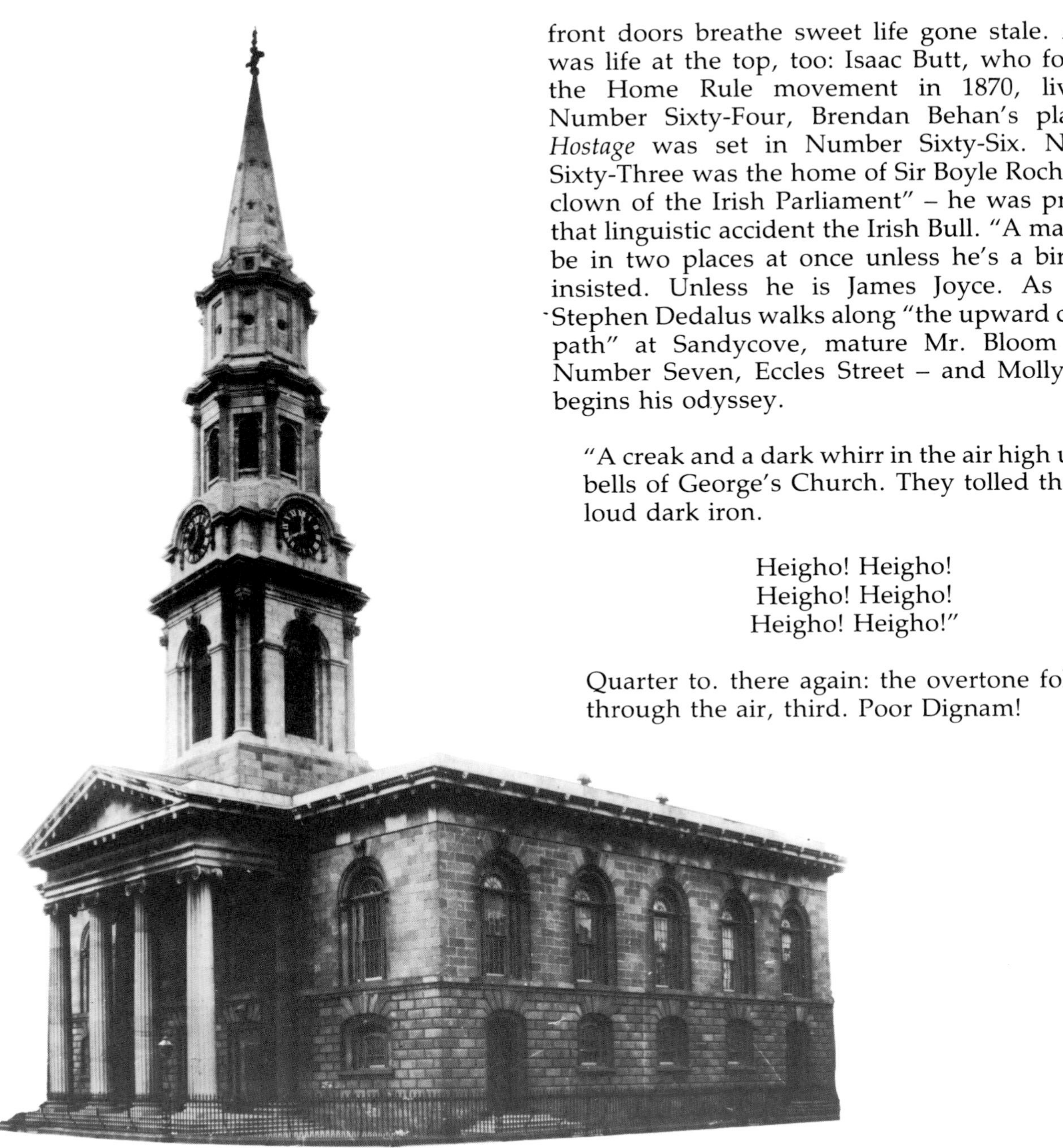

front doors breathe sweet life gone stale. And it was life at the top, too: Isaac Butt, who founded the Home Rule movement in 1870, lived at Number Sixty-Four, Brendan Behan's play *The Hostage* was set in Number Sixty-Six. Number Sixty-Three was the home of Sir Boyle Roche, "the clown of the Irish Parliament" – he was prone to that linguistic accident the Irish Bull. "A man can't be in two places at once unless he's a bird," he insisted. Unless he is James Joyce. As young Stephen Dedalus walks along "the upward curving path" at Sandycove, mature Mr. Bloom leaves Number Seven, Eccles Street – and Molly – and begins his odyssey.

> "A creak and a dark whirr in the air high up. The bells of George's Church. They tolled the hour: loud dark iron.
>
> Heigho! Heigho!
> Heigho! Heigho!
> Heigho! Heigho!"
>
> Quarter to. there again: the overtone following through the air, third. Poor Dignam!

LOTUS EATERS

Swans, sweepstakes, gunboats, Guinness, all have floated on the narrow green tide of the River Liffey, Anna Livia Plurabelle, Dublin's own stream of consciousness. Three hundred yards wide once, it formed a dark pool, the Dubh Linn of the Vikings.

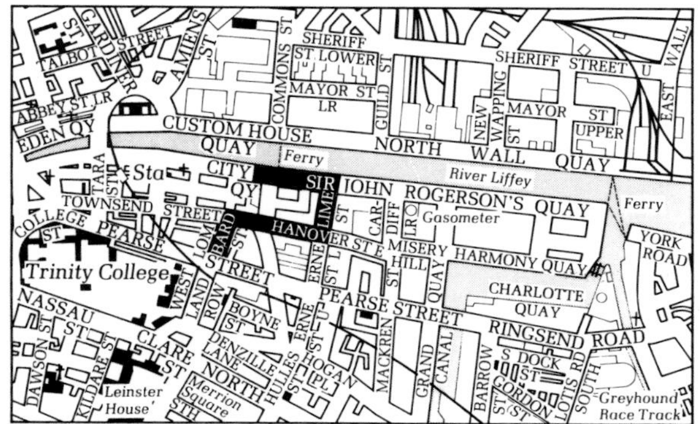

If you leave Number Seven, Eccles Street, cross Dorset Street and walk past St. George's Church, down the sloping streets towards the Liffey, you walk through a part of Dublin that has had a long day's dying. The houses are going, are gone, and the people with them. Corners boarded up, walls sloganed, skeletal tenements stalk you. On the street corners, erupting from behind the red traffic lights, thieves break car windows, snatch bags and disappear into the shadowed tenement tunnels.

Dublin is divided by the Liffey as a great house was divided by the staircase. Those "below stairs" were said to live on the North side, the grander folk on the south side. When Joyce's foe, Gogarty, escaped a Civil War execution by swimming across the Liffey he gave thanks later by bestowing on the river a gift of swans. Mindful of the sewage bobbing near his head, he subsequently described his escapade as "going through the motions". The Irish Hospital Sweepstakes launched exotic advertising campaigns on the Liffey. As one self-important Guinness skipper negotiated his barge the few hundred yards under the low bridges to the waiting ship a wag on a parapet yelled: "Hey, Mister – bring us back a parrot!"

Mr. Bloom's Thursday morning journey has an exotic intoxicating purpose too. Further to his enquiry – a discreet newspaper advertisement, actually – he has been engaged in a randy clandestine correspondence with a lady called Martha in the far south-western suburb of Dolphin's Barn. His post restante address is c/o Westland Row Post Office, his pen name is Henry Flower and he is expecting a letter. "By lorries along Sir John Rogerson's Quay Mr. Bloom walked soberly, past Windmill Lane, Leask's the linseed crushers, the postal telegraph office." He turned right and south into Lime Street, right again along Hanover Street to turn left into Lombard Street. Then he walked along Lombard Street, crossed Great Brunswick Street (now Pearse Street) and into Westland Row.

He could have approached Westland Row by a much more direct route; he didn't need to go down the quays as far as Lime Street and then turn back. But his conscience interrogated him about this naughty letter – and he did not want to bump into any friends or acquaintances who might accompany him and discover his purpose, thus he took a devious route. And if you trace Mr. Bloom's steps from the quayside to the post office, you will find that it describes a huge question mark – which must have been deliberate on Joyce's part, since he measured his characters' movements with a ruler, compass and stop-watch.

As Mr. Bloom crossed the Liffey and walked parallel to the river the Custom House sat on the river, watching him, busier then; the ships dock further down now. The architect, James Gandon, wore his sword to the Custom House building site to protect himself from the hostilities of the merchants – who feared it would reduce upriver trading – of the neighbours, who worried that the building would attract "a low and vulgar crowd with the manners of Billingsgate". Ten years build-

LENWOOD
CASH & CARRY
MOTOR ACCESSORIES ETC.
TRADE ONLY
THE GROSVENOR
HOTEL - LOUNGE - GRILL - BAR
GROSVENOR
THE BLADS
STARDUST
MON 8th
WAH! HEAT

ing, 1781 to 1791, half a million pounds and Gandon was a Palladian hero. The Custom House is the grace of Dublin, and the riverine gods, whose corniced faces adorn the façade, brought art and commerce together when they were chosen to appear on the Irish banknotes.

Dublin in 1904 was hardly the land of the lotus eaters but, nonetheless, Mr Bloom is lotus eating, prompted principally by the prospect of a letter from Martha, prompted too by the yellow light of the morning, by the sounds of the shining, sluggish river, by the sensation of a digesting breakfast. Mr. Bloom takes off his hat and inhales his own hairoil. Joyce piles on the lotus-eating images. In a shop window, tea from Ceylon evokes the Far East. "Lovely spot it must be: the garden of the world, big lazy leaves to float about on, cactuses, flowery meads, snaky lianas they call them" and on to waterlilies, tired petals, roseleaves until finally contemplating the bath he is about to take, Mr. Bloom recalls "the chap I saw in that picture somewhere? Ah, in the dead sea, floating on his bank, reading a book with a parasol open."

At the post office "he handed the card through the brass grill. Are there any letters for me? he asked." And Henry Flower receives a letter full of promise. (The Hungarian "Virag", Bloom's father's name before he changed it by deed poll, means "flower".)

As well as having a Homeric counterpart, Joyce intended each chapter in *Ulysses* to represent an organ of the body; thus the kidney, for Mr. Bloom's breakfast. In "Lotus Eaters" Joyce displays the genitals. He used symbols; a newspaper rolled "lengthwise in a baton"; suggestions: "you darling manflower"; comment: "an army half-rotten with venereal disease". Now, in early heat, before he can read his letter, an acquaintance accosts him. "Hello, Bloom. Where are you off to? Hello, M'Coy. Nowhere in particular", and Mr. Bloom manages to prevent M'Coy from borrowing a leather valise, "capped corners, riveted edges, double action lever lock". Mr Bloom is too polite to show his impatience but he feels from fingering the letter in his pocket that Martha has sent him something, "A photo it isn't. A badge maybe."

Across the road, a horse-drawn vehicle, an "outsider" by the Grosvenor Hotel, a sleek woman waits to climb aboard. "Stylish kind of coat with that roll collar, warm for a day like this, looks like blanketcloth. Careless stand of her with her hands in those patch pockets. Like that haughty creature at the polo match." A passing tram foils Mr. Bloom's view of the climbing "silk flash rich stockings white". Mr. Bloom feels excluded. Today the Grosvenor Hotel is locked, barred and boarded, a reduced direlict, rattled by high heedless trains crossing the bridge at first-floor level. Mr. Bloom and M'Coy part with talk of poor Dignam who is about to be buried and for whom Mr. Bloom has dressed in black.

From the corner of Great Brunswick Street Mr. Bloom turns right and immediately right again. Mr. Bloom stands on the dingy cobbles soaking in the scent of the illicit flower – containing letter. The lotus blooms below the barren peak – and by every winding creek – but it is all in the mind of Mr. Bloom, dreams of domination, hazy, lazy, dreaming dreams of exotic Martha who has sent him a, and who will open to him like a, flower.

James Joyce based Leopold Bloom on Alfred Hunter, a good Samaritan. Joyce's affair with Nora, six days young, had not as yet gelled, and on the 22nd of June, 1904, the bold James, never backward in coming forward, approached a girl who was merely taking the air. She was already vigorously escorted, so Joyce's nose was out of joint – and bloodied. Alfred Hunter, a Dublin Jew with a straying wife, chanced by, comforted Joyce and bound his wounds. But there is more to Bloom than just Hunter's kindness. Joyce admired the Jews because they chose isolation and because they maintained the closest family ties, qualities evident and abundant in the man himself.

Under the archway Mr. Bloom tears up the envelope, scattering the petals of Henry Flower. Mr. Bloom, a Jew by race, a Christian by conversion, goes to "the backdoor of All Hallows", the Catholic Church on Westland Row, where the "cold smell of sacred stone called him". Why a Jew? Joyce believed that a Jew was king and priest in his own house.

The lotus eating Mr. Bloom kneels to eucharist and incense and contemplates wine. "Makes it more aristocratic than for example if he drank what they are used to Guinness's porter or some temperance beverage Wheatley's Dublin hop bitters or Cantrell and Cochrane's ginger ale (aromatic)."

Mr. Bloom stands a moment "unseeing by the cold black marble bowl while before him and behind two worshippers dipped furtive hands in the low tide of holy water". Intoned a television commentator once as the camera panned across bowed heads and yellow flickering candles: "Whenever I hear of an Irishman losing the faith I hear the cock crow thrice."

Westland Row was the birthplace of two distinguished and elegant institutions. Twenty years apart, both occasioned remarkable comment, initiated new styles of things, and eventually suffered decrepitude to varying degrees. One was the Dublin to Kingstown railway line, born at Westland Row Station in 1834, the other was Oscar Fingal

O'Flahertie Wills Wilde, born at Number Twenty-One, Westland Row, in 1854.

Mr. Bloom turns left from the Church door and walks along Westland Row to Sweny the chemist, to purchase for Molly a facial lotion of "sweet almond oil and tincture of benzoin", and orangeflower water and then a cake of soap for himself of a sweet lemony wax. Outside he meets Bantam Lyons who is lurking for a tip for the Gold Cup to be run that afternoon. Mr. Bloom says that he is just about to throw away his newspaper. "Throwaway" is the name of a horse in the race and Bantam Lyons mistakes Mr. Bloom's generosity for a nod and a wink. But not so – Mr. Bloom is too prudent to gamble and anyway he has other things on his mind. He walks cheerfully towards the baths. "Remind you of a mosque, redbaked bricks, the minarets."

Lotus eating, this is my body eucharist taking, and in the stream the long-leaved flowers weep and from the craggy ledge the poppy hangs in sleep. He lies quiet, dazed and dreamy. He observes his navel, "bud of flesh", and watches the dark "tangled curls of his bush floating, floating hair of the stream around the limp father of thousands, a languid floating flower". All the aromas, the scents, the spiced vapours of early-morning Dublin have been released. He lies in the bath, "naked, in a womb of warmth, oiled by scented melting soap, softly laved". Homer, Christ, Tennyson, Joyce, meet on the page, in the mind.

It is cricket weather. It is the day of the Sports in Trinity College Park (where "Captain Buller broke a window in the Kildare Street Club with a slog to square leg" – so much for W. G. Grace). It is Bloom's day.

HADES

Like the ribboned silver spoor of a snail the funeral path of poor Dignam curled and trailed in the passages of the city. While his soul flew upwards plumed hearse-horses drew his body downwards to Joyce's Hades – the alabaster groves of Glasnevin cemetery.

Even the carriages had a tombstone smell. Buttoned, cracked leather, blinds, top-hatted coachmen – and at the end of it all acres of stilled marbles, heavy-lidded unseeing memorials.

Martin Cunningham, first, poked his silkhatted head into the carriage and, entering deftly, seated himself. Mr. Power stepped in after him, curving his height with care.
Come on, Simon.
After you, Mr. Bloom said.
Mr. Dedalus covered himself quickly and got in.

Poor Dignam, who died from drink-induced apoplexy, lived at Number Nine, Newbridge Avenue, Sandymount, near where Stephen Dedalus is crackling his boots across the seawrack and shells. The grave in Glasnevin is at the very far side of the city. "What way is he taking us? Mr. Power asked through both windows. Irishtown, Martin Cunningham said. Ringsend, Brunswick Street." The journey to Hades begins, a clipping pace in clopping, swaying, creaking carriages.
"All watched awhile through their windows caps and hats lifted by passers. Respect. The carriage swerved from the tramtrack to the smoother road past Watery Lane. Mr. Bloom at gaze saw a lithe young man, clad in mourning, a wide hat": the first epiphany of Stephen and Mr. Bloom. And during a funeral procession? O, Joyce! From January to April, 1903, James Joyce lounged around Paris, cadging subsistence by visiting friends at mealtimes, borrowing money from everybody he could touch. He inhabited libraries, brothels, and cafés: he drank absinthe, met literati and stayed in a small room at the Hotel Corneille in the Latin Quarter (where he bought a hat). On Saturday, the 11th of April, he received a telegram: "Mother dying. Come home. Father." Mr. Joyce left Paris.

May Murray Joyce spent a long time dying, that kindly, concerned, gentle woman. She lay in bed vomiting cancer. She begged her Jim to turn back to the sacraments of the Church. Otherwise tender and yielding, he sang Yeats to her:

Who will go drive with Fergus now,
And pierce the deep wood's woven shade,
And dance upon the level shore?
Young man, lift up your russet brow,
And lift your tender eyelids, maid
And brood on hopes and fear no more.

His hair was long, his bow tie floppy, a small beard straggled across his uneasy face. He wrote little, drank to ease his mother's pain, refused to kneel in prayer by her dying coma. She died in August, he dressed all in Hamlet-black and sat on the staircase, his arm around his alarmed nine-year-old sister, Mabel, advising her not to cry. His mother's forty-four-year-old body was buried in Glasnevin.

"They went past the bleak pulpit of Saint Mark's, under the railway bridge, past the Queen's Theatre: in silence. Hoardings." How to see the great and small streets of Dublin? Follow poor Dignam to Hades. Great Brunswick Street, where Mr. Bloom has earlier stood, now Pearse Street, is still derelict of character. On opposite corners a bank and anonymous shops, then a cinema once the Antient Concert Rooms (sic) incongruously beside St. Mark's Parish Church, whose bleak pulpit was made from the poop of a ship wrecked in the bay: wherein Oscar etc. Wilde was baptised: over which the railway bridge uglily services Westland Row Station.

The street promises to improve, but nothing comes of it – extensions of Trinity College, drab commercial offices, a lone pub, engineering companies and a plaque at Number Twenty-Seven to commemorate the Pearse Brothers, Patrick and Willie, who died in the Poets' Rising of 1916. Junctions now begin to take life away from the street; the Fire Station at Tara Street with its Florentine spire is younger than Mr. Bloom, on the left a block of offices supplanted the Queen's

Theatre of Variety where the Abbey Theatre lodged from 1951 to 1966, until its phoenix rose again across the river.

"Mr. Dedalus bent across to salute. From the door of the Red Bank a white disc of a straw hat flashed reply: passed." It is impossible now for a funeral to go straight from Pearse Street into D'Olier Street. It is just as impossible for a Blazes Boylan to tip his hat outside the Red Bank Restaurant. D'Olier Street is one-way in the other direction: so is the Red Bank – it is a church.

In Paris, James Joyce told Arthur Power, a young Dublin renaissance man, that *Ulysses* was the book of his maturity, which he preferred to his violent and painful youth.

Power replied with a motto he had seen on the dial of an Italian clock: "Every one hurts and the last one kills." Joyce liked it – time as a further ineluctable modality, another key. "We are going the pace, I think, Martin Cunningham said. God grant he doesn't upset us on the road, Mr. Power said." When *Ulysses* first became available in Dublin one asked another: "Am I in it?" Peter-like, a former associate denied all knowledge, ever, of Joyce. "But you're in *Ulysses,*" said the journalist. "I am not a character in fiction. I am a living human being." Martin Cunningham was based on a friend of Joyce's father, the bearded Matthew Kane. Mr. Power was Tom Devan, who espied the farewelling Jim and Nora come clandestinely together after they boarded ship and told John Joyce his son hadn't gone alone. Simon Dedalus is John Joyce, a Corkman whose tidal fortunes receded permanently, who sang, sported, drank and married above himself. His firstborn, like Mr. Bloom's, didn't survive, nine of the ten children felt hostile to him, James, his living oldest, adored him, emulated him in music, passion for gossipy detail and penury, tried to commemorate him in stone, set-

HOTEL METROPOLE. SACKVILLE ST. DUBLIN. 4818.

tled for prose. In *A Portrait of the Artist as a Young Man*

> Stephen began to enumerate glibly his father's attributes. A medical student, an oarsman, a tenor, an amateur actor, a shouting politician, a small landlord, a small investor, a drinker, a good fellow, a story-teller, somebody's secretary, something in a distillery, a tax-gatherer, a bankrupt, and at present a raiser of his own past.

Undoubtedly John Joyce was the inspiration for many of his son's expressions. Old argot, half-forgotten soldier's words, cliches from penny ballads, sudden truths glinted in his conversation – his ear for music listened to him speaking.

"Oot: a dullgarbed old man from the curbstone tendered his wares, his mouth opening: oot. Four bootlaces for a penny." From D'Olier Street, named for a Huguenot called Jeremiah of the family of Olier; Mr. Cunningham, Mr. Power, Mr. Dedalus and Mr. Bloom corteged over O'Connell Bridge, named for a talking, hunting, arguing, laughing, womanising advocate from Kerry.

Daniel O'Connell, fighting the Act of Union which in 1800 manacled Ireland to England, said that Pitt the Prime Minister had a smile "like the brass plate on a coffin".

"They passed the hugecloaked Liberator's form." Daniel O'Connell, the Liberator, died on his sad, broken way to Rome. In keeping with his beliefs, activities and instincts his heart went to Rome, his body to Glasnevin, his genitals to his native Kerry.

Mr. Cunningham, Mr. Power, Mr. Dedalus and Mr. Bloom sat in the carriage and peeped out at the world moving slowly by. Sackville Street, now O'Connell Street, furlonged ahead.

Tritonville Road, Ringsend Road, Pearse Street, D'Olier Street, O'Connell Street, Parnell Square, Blessington Street, Berkeley Road, North Circular Road, Phibsborough Road, Prospect Road, Finglas Road – a postman's chorus.

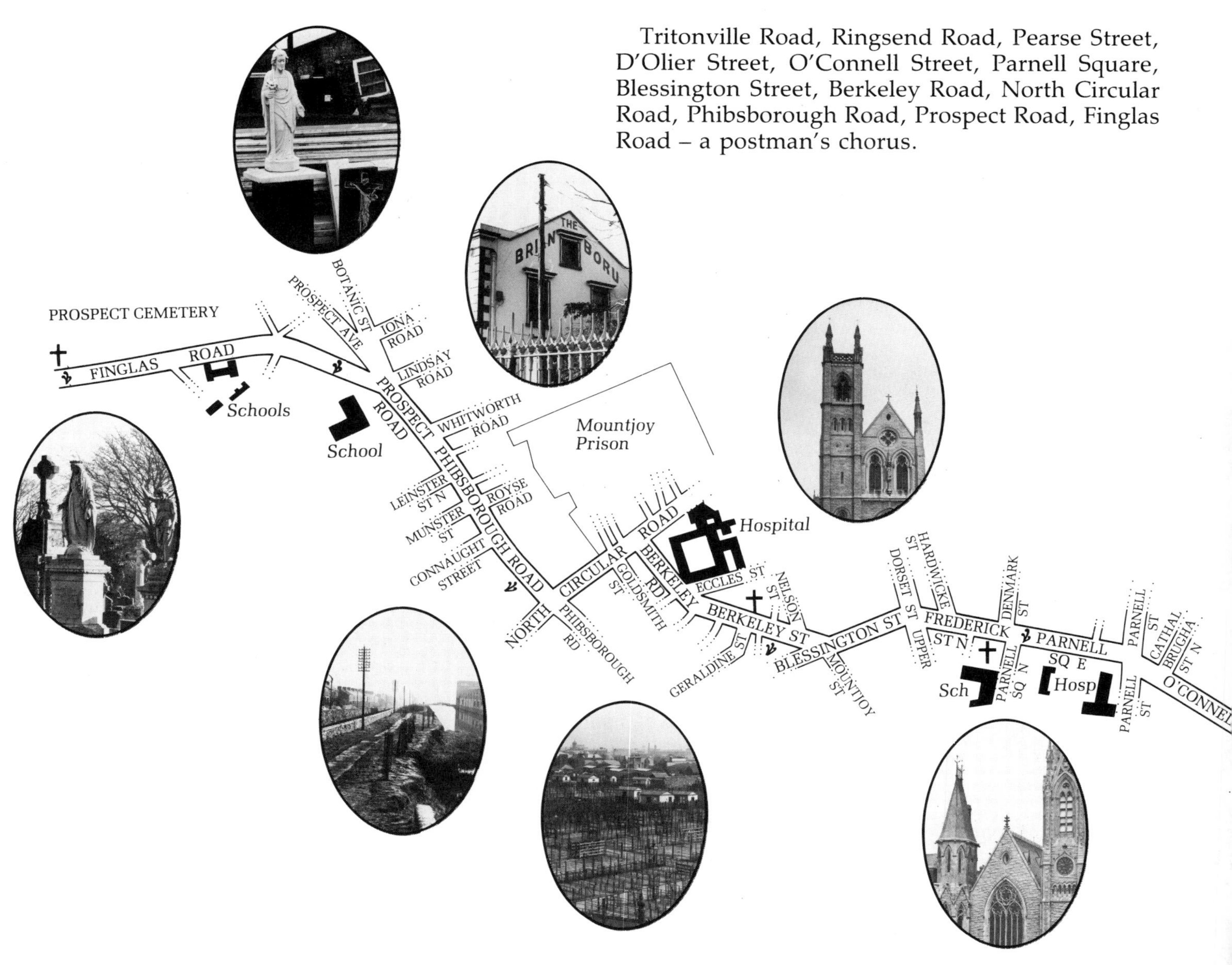

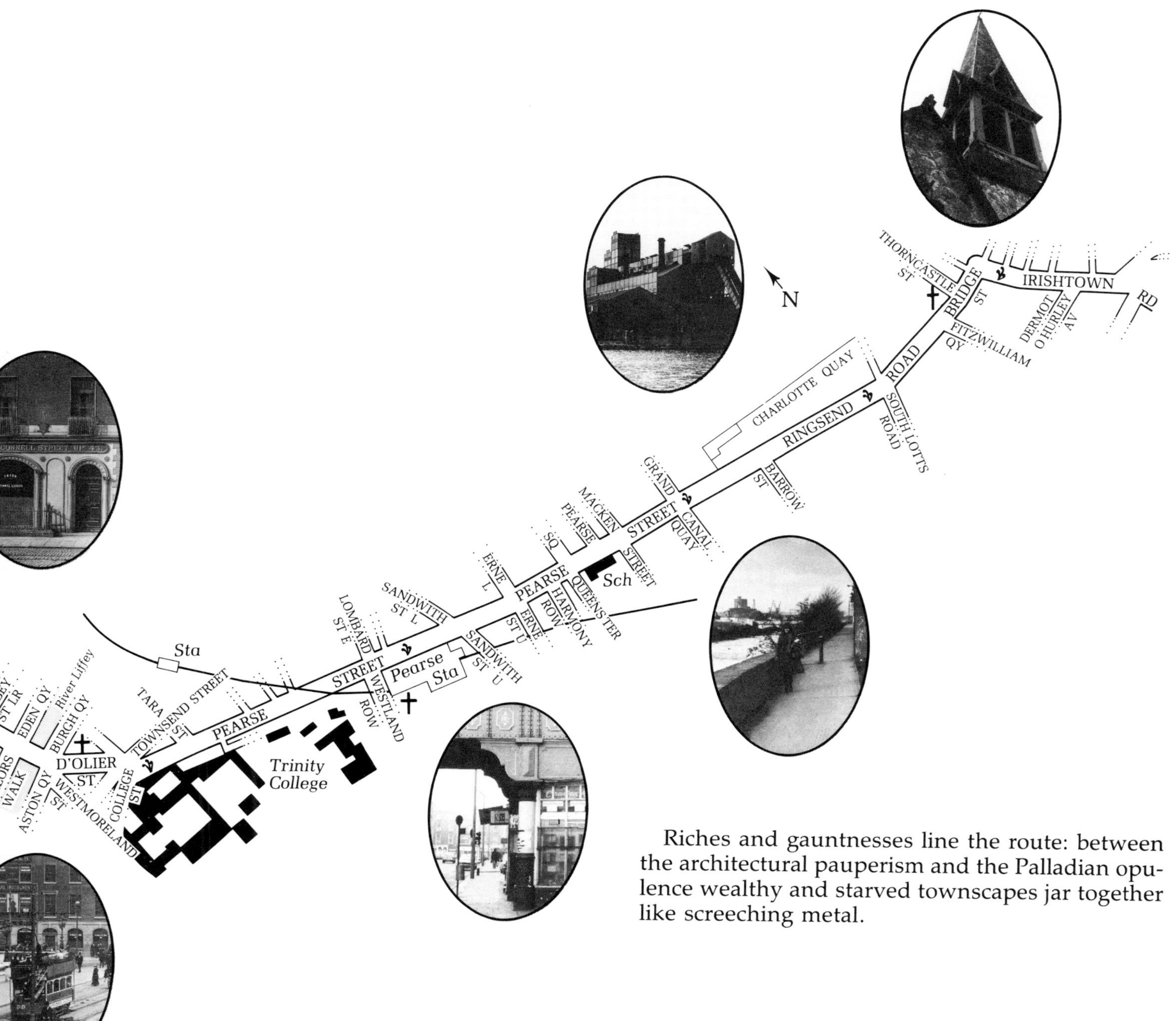

Riches and gauntnesses line the route: between the architectural pauperism and the Palladian opulence wealthy and starved townscapes jar together like screeching metal.

Stately, sombre, stepping slow
The white-plumed funeral horses go
With coaches crawling in their wake
A long and slow black glittering snake.
Inside of every crawling yoke
Silent cronies sit and smoke . . .

(This poet, Seumas O'Sullivan, had an eve-of-departure letter from Joyce: "1 toothbrush and powder. 1 nail brush. 1 pair of black boots and any coat and vest you have to spare.")

The General Post Office porticoed by, where a nation without a placenta was born in 1916 and to whose fame generations of patriots laid subsequent claim – the building simply isn't big enough to house everybody who pint-insists he was there on Easter Monday. Atop, Hibernia, Mercury, Fidelity: inside, the mythical warrior Cuchulainn, the Hound of Ulster, undead to his enemies until a raven pranced on his shoulder. Trollope was an official of the Post Office; up the street, Percy Bysshe Shelley threw pamphlets from his window encouraging the Irish to cast off the yoke. In 1966 they blew up the last vestiges of imperial Sackville Street by toppling Nelson and his pillar in the small furtive hours – plastic explosives marked fifty years of freedom, independence and maturity.

"Dead side of the street this. Dull business by day, land agents, temperance hotel, Falconer's railway guide, civil service college, Gill's, catholic club, the industrious blind." Hasn't changed much since Mr. Bloom's mental procession, fast food, an airline, a cinema sit suitable side by side, "under the patronage of Father Mathew", the apostle who laid temperance with a capital T on the Irish nation of drinkers in the mid-nineteenth century. "Ah, Father Mathew. A decent man – but a bit narrow-minded," declared a thirsty Abbey play, and every year in front of his Tipperary home the daffodils grow "T.M.", Theobald Mathew.

"White horses with white frontlet plumes came round the Rotunda corner, galloping. A tiny coffin flashed by. In a hurry to bury. A mourning coach. Unmarried. Black for the married. Piebald for bachelors. Dun for a nun."

There were thatched cottages once where the Rotunda is now, the first maternity hospital. The Assembly Rooms, by the lying-in hospital, became by Joycean juxtaposition the Gate Theatre. Up Rutland Square, indexed by the high frosted cornices of Findlater's Church, all one-way now. Is it a Joycean joke, or an affirmation of life, that one-way Dublin runs from, not *to*, Glasnevin cemetery? "The carriage climbed more slowly the hill of Rutland Square. Rattle his bones. Over the stones. Only a pauper. Nobody owns." Round the corner from Rutland Square Joyce was a pupil at Belvedere College. His academic skills brought the family spasms of prosperity, improvident trips to Jammet's Restaurant. His father asked once what gift Jim wanted if he won a forthcoming prize. "Two chops."

Up the hill, Blessington Street, Berkeley Street, Berkeley Road.

The carriage galloped round a corner: stopped.
What's wrong now?
A divided drove of branded cattle passed the windows, lowing, slouching by on padded hoofs, whisking their tails slowly on their clotted bony croups. Outside them and through them ran raddled sheep bleating their fear.
Emigrants, Mr. Power said.

For the boat certainly, down from the iron-clad acres of the cattle market, of the squared, hutted, fenced cobbleyards, came the browned, heaving, glinting, streaming kine, lurching to death.

Past the other end of Eccles Street. "My house down there." Molly, gleaming by now in the

TYLERS BOOTS
ROTUNDA. DUBLIN. 6427. W.L.

morning. Left into North Circular Road, up the slope. "Dunphy's Corner. Mourning coaches drawn up drowning their grief. A pause by the wayside. Tiptop position for a pub. Expect we'll pull up here on the way back to drink his health. Pass round the consolation. Elixir of life." Turned right again down Phibsborough Road over Cross Guns Bridge, past the Brian Boru pub, left into Prospect Road. On the right, at the bridge, the towers of Mountjoy Jail: on the left the Royal Canal sidles sluggishly into the bright fields of Kildare.

The carriage steered left for Finglas Road.

The stonecutter's yard on the right. Last lap. Crowded on the spit of land silent shapes appeared, white, sorrowful, holding out calm hands, knelt in grief, pointing. Fragments of shapes, hewn. In white silence: appealing. The best obtainable. Thos. H. Dennany, monumental builder and sculptor.

Glasnevin at last, poplar trees, groves of graves, little avenues of silence, O'Connell, Parnell, the towering dead.

Joyce believed that the word *Odysseus* came from *Outis* and *Zeus* – "nobody" and "god". Outis-zeus-Ulysses-Bloom went down to the place of graves. The gods had warned Ulysses that in order to enter Hades safely he had to cut a trench in the ground a cubit long and a cubit broad. On the walls around Glasnevin are nineteenth century watch-towers erected to spotlight body-snatchers, often led by that knave of spades, the Sexton.

"White shapes thronged amid the trees, white forms and fragments streaming by mutely sustaining vain gestures on the air." In Hades Ulysses met the shades of the great and grateful dead. In Glasnevin Mr. Bloom eyed his way past the O'Connell circle, outward by Parnell's harped grave, thinking of rot and worm and shroud and

corpse. When John Joyce died Jim sent a friend out into the street to give money in commemoration to any indigent old man. And he wrote a poem: "O Father forsaken Forgive your son." In a letter to T. S. Eliot: "He had an intense love for me and it adds anew to my grief and remorse that I did not go to Dublin to see him for so many years." "Hades" is the chapter of the heart; "a man's inmost heart": "through the heart"; "hearts of grace", as many as twenty hearts in the chapter.

Poor Dignam is in the ground, noon approaches. "Mr. Bloom walked unheeded along his grove by saddened angels, crosses, broken pillars, family vaults, stone hopes praying with upcast eyes, old Ireland's hearts and hands."

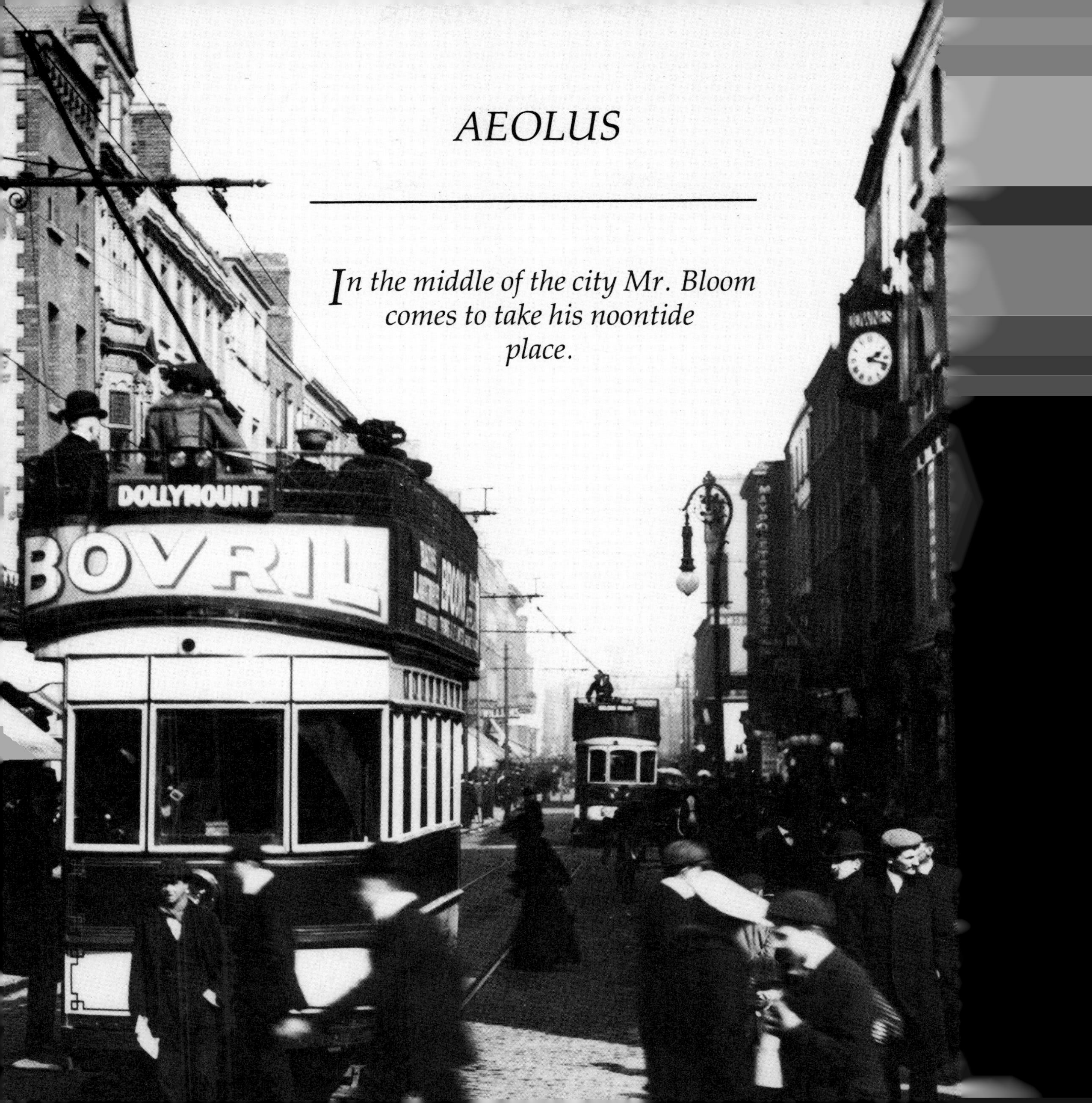

AEOLUS

In the middle of the city Mr. Bloom comes to take his noontide place.

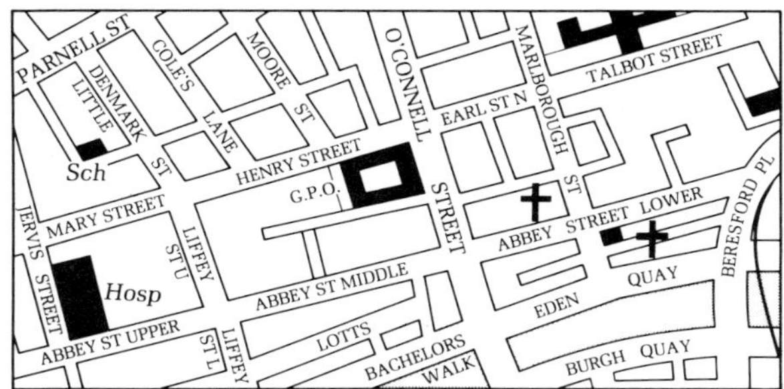

Mr. Leopold Bloom is a canvasser for newspaper advertisements, paid by results, a purchaser of time and space. When Ulysses arrived at the cave of Aeolus, the guardian of the breezes, that inventor of sail gave him a wine-skin full of propitious winds to speed him home. Mr. Bloom has arrived at the offices of the *Freeman's Journal* where he intends to transact business. In "Aeolus" Mr. Joyce gives the first hint that perhaps not everybody is endeared to Mr. Bloom.

The *Freeman's Journal* eventually, after a burning and a breaking of its presses by I.R.A. Civil Warriors, merged with Parnell's newspaper, the *Irish Independent,* whose main entrance is on Middle Abbey Street. Princes Street and O'Connell Street complete a wedge of buildings from which flow several newspapers. Joyce used the lungs as the symbol, the organic motto of the "Aeolus" chapter; news is inhaled, dwelt upon, and exhaled gustily, gaseously.

James Joyce's career as a writer began in University debates on his new passion, Ibsen. "I have read, or rather, spelt out", wrote Ibsen to an intermediary "a review by Mr. James Joyce in the *Fortnightly Review* which is very benevolent and for which I should greatly like to thank the author if only I had sufficient knowledge of the language." Joyce replied that he was a mere eighteen-year-old Irishman, that he would keep the words of Ibsen in his heart all his life, – and spent the twelve-guinea fee in glee and haste. Richard Ellman in his biography comments that Joyce had entered the world of literature "under the best auspices". With such Parnassian encouragement, he read voraciously, learned, enquired, rampaged through the minds of authors,novelists, playwrights, poets and essayists. Even language was no barrier: his headlong propulsion into literature culminated in a fulsome, flowing letter to Ibsen where despite "highest excellence" and "lofty impersonal power", he decreed that he, Joyce, was no hero-worshipper: but he had nonetheless deliberately acquired Dano-Norwegian, in order to write to Ibsen.

EVENING
PRESS
for small ads

GENTLEMEN OF THE PRESS

Grossbooted draymen rolled barrels dullthudding out of Prince's stores and bumped them up on the brewery float. On the brewery float bumped dullthudding barrels rolled by grossbooted draymen out of Prince's stores.

There it is, Red Murray said. Alexander Keyes.

Just cut it out, will you? Mr Bloom said, and I'll take it round to the *Telegraph* office.

Mr. Bloom is in the offices of the *Freeman's Journal* where he is reviving an advertisement for a purveyor of tea, wine and spirits. His client, Alexander Keyes, wants something special, two keys crossed at the top of his advertisement, already used successfully in a Kilkenny newspaper. Mr. Keyes' enterprise will be puffed editorially, provided the merchant takes three months of advertising in the newspaper. Mr. Bloom agrees to solicit time in return for space.

A DAYFATHER

He walked on through the caseroom, passing an old man, bowed, spectacled, aproned. Old Monks, the dayfather. Queer lot of stuff he must have put through his hands in his time: obituary notices, pubs' ads, speeches, divorce suits, found drowned.

Joyce wrote the "Aeolus" chapter in a parody of the newspaperman's style, headlines blowing forth from the Cave of the Winds.

AND IT WAS THE FEAST OF THE PASSOVER

He stayed in his walk to watch a typesetter neatly distributing type. Reads it backwards

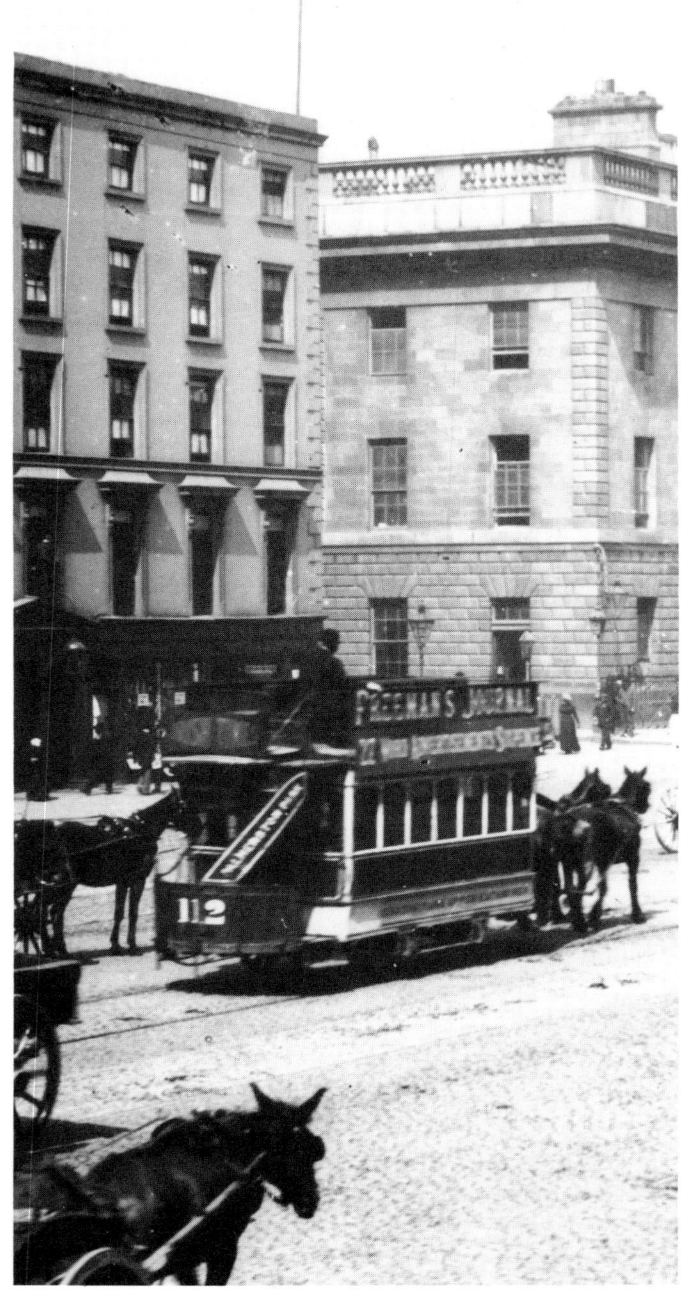

first. Quickly he does it. Must require some practice that. mangiD. kcirtaP. Poor Papa with his hagadah book, reading backwards with his finger to me.

James Joyce's father, redundant from his official position, took an occasional job as an advertisement canvasser for the *Freeman's Journal*. James Joyce himself wrote several reports and reviews. His career with one newspaper ended so acrimoniously that the editor finally threatened to kick him down the stairs.

SPOT THE WINNER

Lenehan came out of the inner office with *Sports* tissues.

Who wants a dead cert for the Gold Cup? he asked. Sceptre with O. Madden up.

He tossed the tissues on to the table.

Screams of newsboys barefoot in the hall rushed near and the door was flung open.

Hush, Lenehan said. I hear footsteps.

Professor MacHugh strode across the room and seized the cringing urchin by the collar as the others scampered out of the hall and down the steps.

Mr. Bloom is hurrying back and forth, buffeted by the winds of advertising and editorial: he leaves the newspaper offices to find his client in a nearby auction room. There follows mocking his mazurka walk, "a file of capering newsboys in Mr. Bloom's wake, the last zigzagging white on the breeze a mocking kite, a tail of white bowknots".

Bachelor's Walk, where Bloom is headed, runs at right angles to O'Connell Street. Mr. Bloom's view, had he cared to stop, was of ships and seafarers, of bonneted ladies and bucks, of trams and tramp steamers: and for the second time that day he has missed Stephen Dedalus, who has arrived to deliver Mr. Deasy's letter.

Today, on Bachelor's Walk, the same small auction rooms (frequented by Alexander Keyes, purveyor of tea, wine and spirits, where he is discovered by Mr. Bloom): brass, the wood of ages, carpets, gathered in, and exhaled with the auctioneer's ten per cent added. Outside Mr. Bloom accosts the pubward editor, Myles Crawford.

House of keys, don't you see? His name is Keyes. It's a play on the name. But he practically promised he'd give the renewal. But he wants just a little puff. What will I tell him, Mr. Crawford?

K.M.A.

Will you tell him he can kiss by arse? Myles Crawford said, throwing out his arm for emphasis. Tell him that straight from the stable.

And Mr. Bloom, excluded, stands diplomatically on the street, watches the receding back of young Dedalus, "the moving spirit. Has a good pair of boots on him today. Last time I saw him he had his heels on view. Been walking in muck somewhere. Careless chap. What was he doing in Irishtown?" The tram which went from Glasnevin to Rialto bore a brown lozenge badge to indicate its route. From Nelson's pillar to Sandymount was indicated by a green crescent. A green shamrocked tram bore you to Dalkey, a green Maltese Cross from Rathfarnham to Drumcondra. Two blue diamonds decorated the tram which linked Donnybrook to the Phoenix Park and a white circle tram reached the quiet pools of Palmerston Park. It didn't, therefore, matter whether you could read. All that mattered was whether you walked. The tram conductor's

16
RATHFARNHAM
810

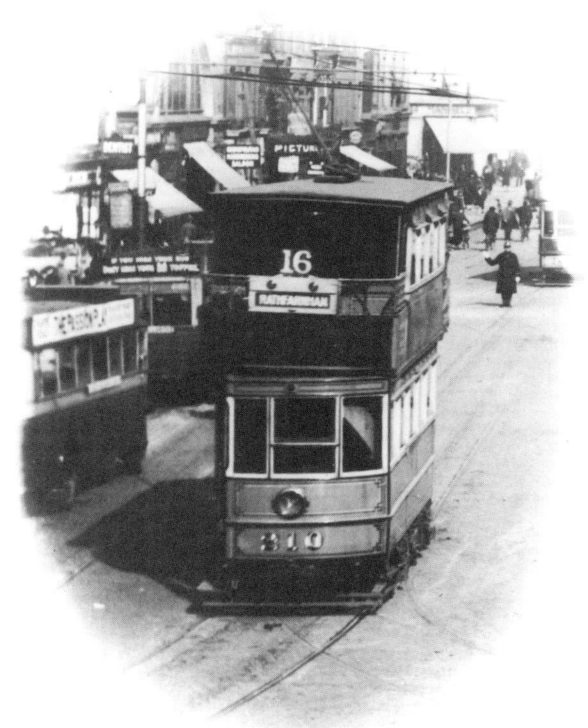

manual urged: "Keep a sharp lookout for passengers and by signalling, induce persons to travel who would otherwise walk."

A little phenomenon touched the tramways on Bloomsday – a little electrical phenomenon.

HELLO THERE, CENTRAL!

At various points along the eight lines tramcars with motionless trolleys stood in their tracks, bound for or from Rathmines, Rathfarnham, Blackrock, Kingstown and Dalkey, Sandymount Green, Ringsend and Sandymount Tower, Donnybrook, Palmerston Park and Upper Rathmines, all still, becalmed in short circuit.

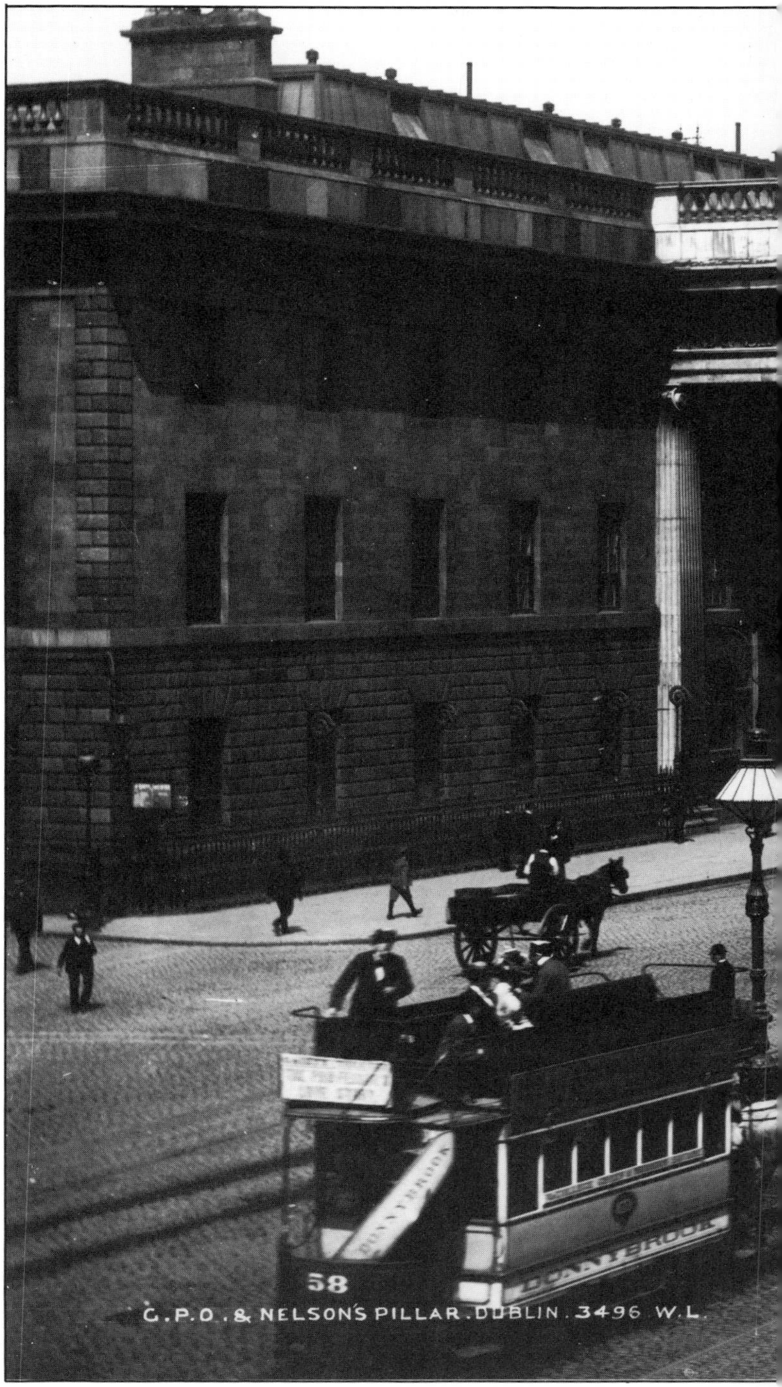
58
DONNYBROOK
G.P.O. & NELSON'S PILLAR. DUBLIN. 3496 W.L.

CADBURY'S
COCOA
KEHOE, DONNELLY & PAKENHAM
LAWN MOWERS
139
LAWN MOWERS
XXI

LAESTRYGONIANS

From the square splay of O'Connell Bridge wide streets feel their way southward into an easier and richer city. The generous horizons forsake the common brick: elegant buildings ennoble Dublin with their cut stone.

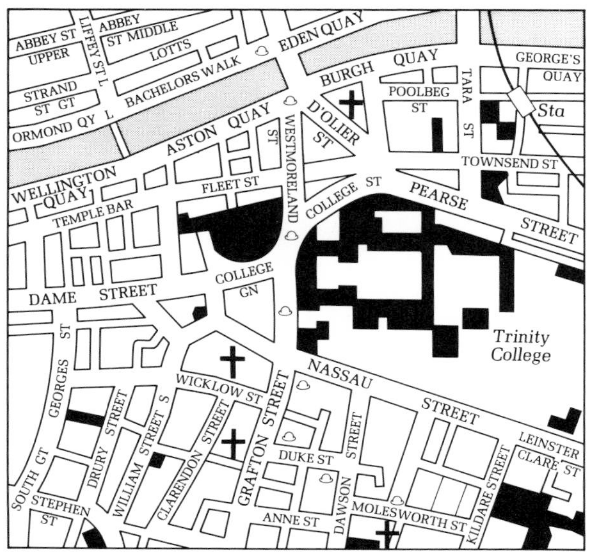

Think of O'Connell Street as the arm, O'Connell Bridge the hand: from the palm four fingers – Burgh Quay, D'Olier Street, Westmoreland Street, Aston Quay. The long finger is Westmoreland Street along which Mr. Bloom walked his pursed thoughtful way via College Green and Grafton Street; Duke Street means lunch: then over Dawson Street, to Molesworth Street, eventually faltering to a halt in Kildare Street. His journey begins at one o'clock, there is fitful sunshine, gently blown cloud.

"Pineapple rock, lemon platt, butter scotch. A sugar-sticky girl shovelling scoopfuls of cream for a christian brother." Mr. Bloom is thinking of food, of lunch, of Molly, of love. His destination is the National Library of Ireland in Kildare Street where he needs to make reference to that Kilkenny newspaper which has carried Mr. Keyes' advertisement with the keys crossed. "A sombre Y.M.C.A. young man, watchful among the warm sweet fumes of Graham Lemon's, placed a throwaway in a hand of Mr. Bloom." You will recall that Mr. Bloom has unwittingly tipped a horse called "Throwaway" (of whose existence he is unaware) for the Gold Cup. Now he is handed a throwaway piece of paper by a young evangelist: it suggests that Mr. Bloom be "washed in the blood of the lamb".

O'Connell Bridge was once Carlisle Bridge. "POPULACE APPLAUDS AS QUEEN VICTORIA PASSES OVER CARLISLE BRIDGE": but the *Irish Times* mischief-makers changed the "A" in "PASSES" to "I". Legend? How many bridges – and newspapers – claim the same tale? It took ten years to build Carlisle Bridge and its scaffolding was used as a gallows to hang renegade soldiers, with their coats turned inside out. "As he set foot on O'Connell Bridge a puffball of smoke plumed up from the parapet. Brewery barge with export stout." Dubliners, priorities in order, jest biblically about "the Book of Guinnesses". When Lord Moyne, brewery proprietor, was elevated to the House of Lords in London, one ancient blue-blooded peer, outraged at this ingress of trade, this mere brewer, queried querulously: "Who is this fellow Moyne, anyway?" The new noble Lord was jubil-

O'CONNELL BRIDGE, DUBLIN

ant: "Moyne's a Guinness." An Ulster poet Louis MacNeice coopered into shape the view from O'Connell Bridge:

. . . And the brewery tugs and the swans
On the balustraded stream
And the bare bones of a fanlight
Over a hungry door
And the air soft on the cheek
And porter running from the taps
With a head of yellow cream . . .

Flowers and lanterns light this broad bridge and political protestors pollute it with bearded shouts. "He threw down among them a crumpled paper ball." But Mr. Bloom's kind heart gets the better of him and he offers the kee-haaring gulls two crumbed Banbury cakes which he buys for a penny. Bread after the "blood of the lamb"? "Aware of their greed and cunning he shook the powdery crumb from his hands. They never expected that. Manna." Watch – Joyce is at it again. Mannanaan MacLir is the god of the waters and Mannanaan MacLir possesses magic pigs which though killed and eaten are re-generated every day. And, sure enough, a few lines later: "eat pig like pig". Manna, Mannanaan MacLir. Pig like pig. O, Joyce!

"Timeball on the ballast office is down." It is one o'clock, Mr. Bloom is thinking of food and Molly's sharp wit. "She used to say Ben Dollard had a base barreltone voice. He had legs like barrels and you'd think he was singing into a barrel." The ballast office is no more, and this corner of Westmoreland Street and Aston Quay is housed anew. Mr. Bloom stood and watched a procession of whitesmocked sandwich boards. "He read the scarlet letters on their five tall white hats: H.E.L.Y.S. Wisdom Hely's. Y lagging behind drew a chunk of bread from under his foreboard, crammed into his mouth and munched as he walked.

Mr. Bloom crosses Westmoreland Street "when apostrophe S had plodded by." Thinking still about Molly and food and Molly and rabbit pie, "he walked along the curbstone. Stream of life." Mr. Bloom loves his wife.

O, Mr. Bloom, how do you do?

O, how do you do, Mrs. Breen?

No use complaining. How is Molly those times? Haven't seen her for ages.

In the pink, Mr. Bloom said gaily, Milly has a position down in Mullingar, you know.

A typical Dublin greeting, it even has a tune.

How is your oul' wan? Game Ball.
Who was she out with? Meehawl.
What did she give him? Damn-all.

Mr. Bloom tells of the death of poor Dignam. "Sad to lose the old friends, Mrs. Breen's womaneyes said melancholily." Mrs. Breen's daft husband is a great one for the litigation. "He's a caution to rattlesnakes." Mr. Bloom's tastebuds begin to blossom, to bloom even, in his nostrils "hot mockturtle vapour and steam of newbaked jampuffs rolypoly". Mrs. Breen's husband is difficult – the new moon.

Mr. Bloom said:

Mind! Let this man pass.

A bony form strode along the curbstone from the river, staring with a rapt gaze into the sunlight through a heavy stringed glass. Tight as a skullpiece a tiny hat gripped his head. From his arm a folded dustcoat, a stick and an umbrella dangled to his stride.

OINTMENT

Watch him, Mr. Bloom said. He always walks outside the lampposts. Watch!

Cashel Boyle O'Connor Fitzmaurice Tisdall Farrell always walked at great speed *outside* the lampposts.

Bang-bang from Inchicore brandished, gun-like, a large key, yelling, "Bang. Bang. You're dead". Zozimus, the blind ballad-maker, wandered in the walled shadows of the Old City making songs for the children. The Bird Flanagan bought and paid for a Christmas turkey hanging outdoors in Nassau Street. Telling the shopkeeper he would collect it later, he hung about until he saw two patrolling policemen. Then he charged along the pavement, grabbed the bird from its hook and ran, luring the policemen into a full hue and cry. Endymion Farrell was the son of a brewer. He fell into a vat and never recovered his equilibrium: he carried a sword and a fishing rod and his little bowler hat had large holes in it for ventilation.

Cashel Boyle O'Connor Fitzmaurice Tisdall Farrell recurs in *Ulysses*, a rushing breeze along the pavements.

Mr. Bloom moves on, Mrs. Breen moves off.

Same blue dress she had two years ago, the nap bleaching. Seen its best days. Wispish hair over her ears. And that dowdy toque, three old grapes to take the harm out of it. Shabby genteel. She used to be a tasty dresser. Lines round her mouth. Only a year or so older than Molly.

Mr. Bloom passed the *Irish Times*, since moved round the corner. In it he had placed the advertisement which found Martha: "Wanted lady typist to aid gentleman in literary work." Mr. Bloom reflects on the *Irish Times'* small ads, its news of earls and clergy, thoughts of ladies astride horses, the woman climbing on the sidecar outside the Gros-

DUFF

venor Hotel that morning, Lady Mountcashel with the Ward Union Staghounds "riding astride", daring. A Tipperary huntress, Mrs. Delaney, galloped to hounds blowing a hunting horn and smoking a cigarette simultaneously. And when challenged with the cruel knowledge that her poor horse was sweating distressedly, said between hunting horn and cigarette: "Little man, if you'd been between my legs for the past five hours you'd be sweating too."

When James Joyce met Nora Barnacle for the first time (on the 10th of June 1904) she thought he was a sailor. He wore a yachting cap, had deep blue eyes. Swedish? She was a chambermaid in Finn's Hotel on South Leinster Street, tall, strong and striking and he addressed her, serendipitily, on Nassau Street. She came from Galway and when Joyce's father heard her name, "Barnacle", he is said to have exclaimed: "Jaysus, I suppose she'll stick to him anyway." They made an appointment to meet, on the 14th, outside the Wildes of Merrion Square. Nora jilted, but a letter later she agreed to meet again, and on the 16th of June they went walking. She was a straightforward, simple country girl who satisfied Joyce's need for the ordinary – but could be tart and brusque when stirred. Joyce loved her as Mr. Bloom loves Molly, thought of her constantly, laughed at her wit, addressed his letters: "Dear Little Brown Head". She had elementary education, at thirteen was a menial employee, rarely read, never her husband's work, but defended him vigorously, even when a priest asked her during Confession to try and stop her husband writing "those terrible books". In later life Nora observed: "I *don't* know whether he's a genius, but I *do* know there's nobody like him." Joyce's Ulysses also thinks endlessly about his Molly, a sensuous debt on his soul, a watermark.

"He crossed under Tommy Moore's roguish finger." Moore was a social climber with courtly ambitions and despite his sweet, sweet, song-making Dublin turned against him. "They did right to put him up over a urinal: meeting of the waters." Old Dublin joke. Moore's melody went: "There is not in this wide world a valley so sweet/ As that vale in whose bosom the bright waters meet." The lavatory attendant under Moore's statue, questioned on the unsavoury raw materials, the commodities he dealt with every day, protested: "Sure, isn't it my bread and butter."

"His smile faded as he walked, a heavy cloud hiding the sun slowly, shadowing Trinity's surly front." This is College Green: before the light of learning filtered through its railings and pillars it was an archery green, and Mystery Plays were performed. Trinity College was created in 1592, blessed from afar by Queen Elizabeth I: founded on the site of a priory whose tower was a navigation aid to sailors in the bay: developed as a "breeding-ground for Protestants and patriots". Once it was an excommunicable act for a Catholic to attend Trinity – now the majority rules. On the lawn, rented from the Dublin Corporation in exchange for a chicken towards the Lord Mayor's pot, stand statues of Edmund Burke and Oliver Goldsmith, politician and poet. They shared a sculptor, their legs are identical. Impoverished Goldsmith attended Trinity as a sizar, a position obtainable elsewhere only in Cambridge – the College paid his fees, he paid in pride. He served the Fellows, cleaned the Squares, wore a humiliatingly obvious red cap. In London later, in the company of Dr. Johnson and Sir Joshua Reynolds, he gained subtle, social revenge by assuring Society that whereas they chewed with the lower jaw he alone chewed with the upper!

Across College Green the twenty-two pillars of the Bank of Ireland support statues of, left to right, Commerce, Hibernia, Fidelity. A bank since 1789,

Reckitts Blue
ZEBRA
GRATE POLISH

it once Housed the Parliament – and official Irish Bulls: "Why should we do anything for posterity," debated Boyle Roche, "what has posterity ever done for us?" Banking halls of high ceilings and old triumphal tapestries, brass and mahogany, long, whispering stone corridors, green lampshades and deep vaults, counting-houses, correspondence rooms, cobbled courtyards and a court of directors.

In the early 1960s I worked in this building, a slave to commercial splendour. Lunch was by ticket, promotion by age, survival by servility. Paternalism was pervasive, the right parlance and preoccupations – golf, hockey, tennis, rugby football, choir membership – important. Young men from mild commercial and professional families in country towns came to Dublin in new suits and stiff gaits to earn respect and a pension. Young women wore blue bodycoats and an air of passive distinction.

Much of the work was subterranean – in silvered neon Hadean vaults we counted coins from sacks into bags. The tedium was relieved by the wild Joycean language of the bucks whose recounted weekend exploits, no less entertaining for their apocryphy, whitewashed the ache until Wednesday when it was possible to look forward again.

The irreverence was endless. An elderly, haughty bank auditor was accustomed to wearing two pairs of trousers, the old protecting the striped. As he fumbled through his outside flies for his change inside, the bus conductor interpreted his action incorrectly and ejected him with angry prudery. Downstairs we laughed for a month.

J. R. R. Tolkien, a Visiting Examiner at Trinity, needed to cash a cheque, hadn't made the necessary advices, was refused upstairs in the banking hall. As he insisted on a confirmation by telephone to Trinity the reluctant clerk took down his name. "Tolkien," said the discomfited professor: "T-O-L-K-I-E-N. J.R.R.," wrote the clerk immediately and smiled up: "And how much money does the Lord of the Rings want today?" J. R. R. Tolkien always said Dublin was the most civilised city in Europe.

"Provost's House. The reverend Dr. Salmon: tinned salmon." Food again as Mr. Bloom treads past the most perfect house in Ireland, designed by Palladio himself. When Sir John Pentland Mahaffy, Oscar Wilde's tutor, was Provost of Trinity a cocktailed lady tweeted: "Dr. Mahaffy, you are a man, I a woman. In your learned opinion what, pray, is the essential difference between us?" "Madame, I can't conceive." Town and gown have merged since then.

Mr. Bloom sees the "haunting face" of John Howard Parnell, brother of Charles Stewart Parnell, the lost leader. Mr. Bloom is overtaken by two cyclists, George Russell of the famous pseudonym "A.E.", and Miss Lizzie Twigg, the literatus and his emanuensis. "His eyes followed the high figure in homespun, beard and bicycle, a listening woman at his side." Is this the same Lizzie Twigg who has replied to his advertisement in the *Irish Times*? "He crossed at Nassau Street corner and stood before the window of Yeates and Son, pricing the field glasses." Is it true that each side of Nassau Street is the sunny side?

"Grafton Street gay with housed awnings lured his senses. Muslin prints, silk, dames and dowagers, jingle of harnesses, hoofthuds lowringing in the baking causeway." The shopping area for the cream of Dublin – rich and thick. Very old Dublin joke. Coffee grinding in Bewleys' window, svelte mincing young women in fashion, Dublin on high heels. "He passed, dallying, the windows of Brown Thomas, silk mercers. Cascades of ribbons. Flimsy China silks. A tilted urn poured from its mouth a flood of bloodhued poplin: lustrous blood." The sun has come out again and Mr. Bloom's hunger drives him to seek a collation, but the diners in the Burton Restaurant on Duke Street are repellent. "Perched on high stools by the bar, hats shoved back, at the tables calling for more bread no charge, swilling, wolfing gobfuls of sloppy food, their eyes bulging, wiping wetted moustaches. A pallid suetfaced young man polished his tumbler knife fork and spoon with his napkin." Poor Mr. Bloom. "A man with an infant's saucestained napkin tucked around him shovelled gurgling soup down his gullet. A man spitting back on his plate: halfmasticated gristle: no teeth to chewchewchew it." Mr. Bloom made an excuse and left, went along the street to Davy Byrne's. In Duke Street now, the Bailey Restuarant enlightenedly houses the door of Number Seven Eccles Street. Across in Davy Byrne's Mr Bloom takes a glass of Burgundy and a sandwich. Watch! Again! "Sandwich? Ham and his descendants mustered and bred there." Bloom the Jew. Ham. Mustard. Bread. Grrr! Joyce!

It was not unusual for James Joyce to be hungry.

LUAN-AOINE
16.00 18.30
MON-FRI
Telefon

Richard Ellmann recounts a meeting between Joyce and Gogarty.

> Gogarty asked: "Where have you been for two days, Were you ill?" "Yes." "What were you suffering from?" "Inanition," Joyce answered without hesitation. His hunger fed his pride.

In Paris he cadged meals, in Trieste the Joyces frequently went without. On his visit home to Dublin in 1909 relatives remarked on how thin he had become. And in London in the Thirties he cooled for ever to a friend who took him to an indifferent restaurant.

Joyce wrote the "Laestrygonians" episode of *Ulysses* as a peristaltic parallel to the human digestive system: food is the dominant commodity, streetside sweetstalls, cakes cast upon the waters, Dr. Salmon, John Howard Parnell has "poached eyes on ghost" in his haunting face, Mrs. Breen was a "tasty dresser". When Ulysses finally left Aeolus and the Cave of the Winds he and his crew sailed for six days and six nights and on the seventh day reached Laestrygonia. There, his scouts were devoured and his ships attacked by the giant Laestrygonian cannibals who speared men like fish and ate them raw. Ulysses Bloom escaped too, from the ogred foulness of the Burton Restaurant to the calm of Davy Byrnes.

"Mr. Bloom ate his strips of sandwich, fresh clean bread, with relish of disgust, pungent mustard, the feety savour of green cheese." Not ham, of course, gorgonzola. "Glowing wine on his palate lingered swallowed." A memory is touched, of Molly lying on Howth Head, in fern beneath him, kissing, yielding, wild. As Mr. Bloom goes out to the yard Nosey Flynn and Davy Byrne discuss him. Paddy Leonard, Bantam Lyons and Tom Rochford enter and discuss the Gold Cup. "Mr. Bloom on his way out raised three fingers in greeting." Nobody yet believes Bantam Lyons that he received a tip for "Throwaway" from the prudent Jew.

"Mr. Bloom walked towards Dawson Street, his tongue brushing his teeth smooth." It is almost two o'clock and he helps a blind youth across Dawson Street into Molesworth Street. Up ahead, Leinster House is a broad forehead, to the left the Masonic Headquarters. Molesworth Street has fared better than some: the new architecture is not entirely without character. Mr. Bloom sees yet again "straw hat in sunlight. Tan shoes. Turnedup trousers. It is. It is." Blazes Boylan, the organiser of Molly Bloom. Agitated, wrinkled with cuckoldry, Mr. Bloom flees with the wine on his face. As if he were referring to papers in his pocket he flutters off-course to the Museum instead of the nearby Library. "Yes. Gate. Safe!."

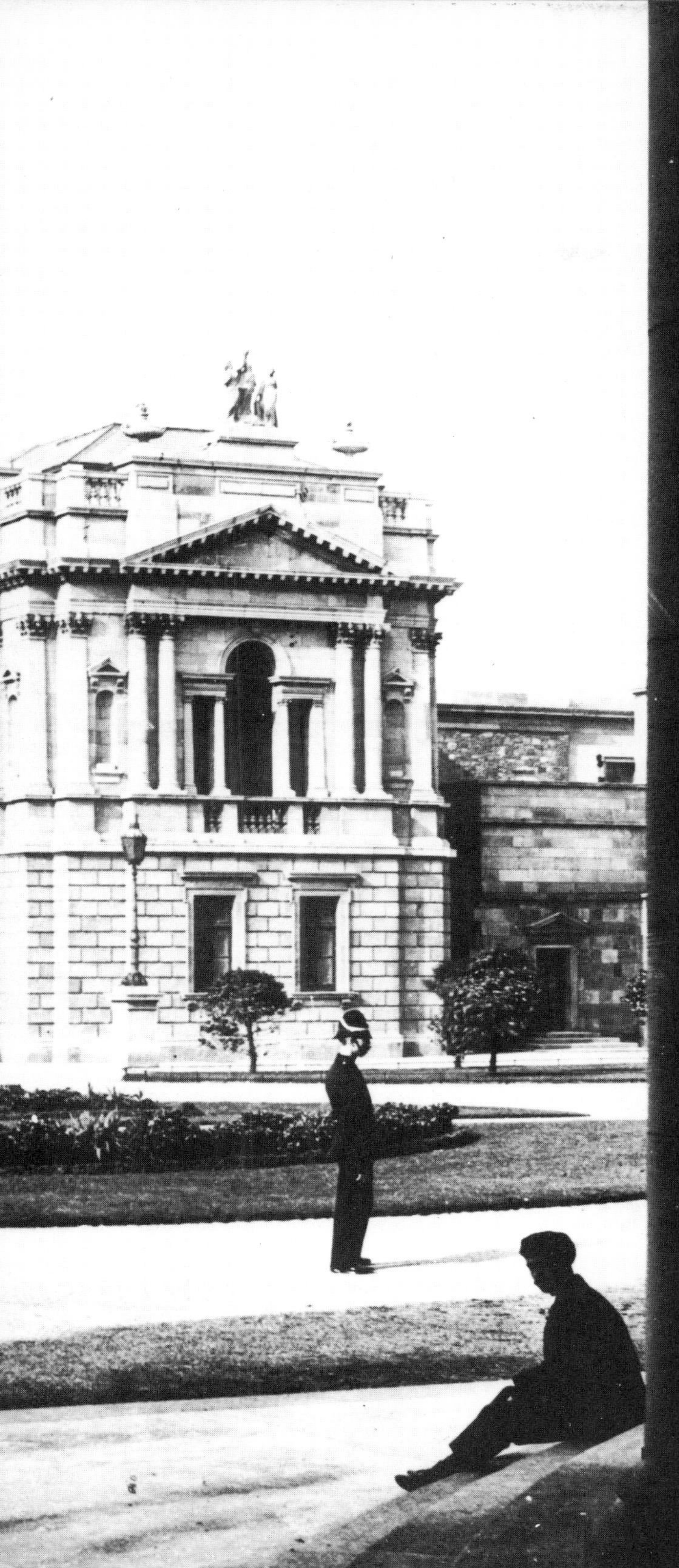

SCYLLA AND CHARYBDIS

The National Library of Ireland is a rounded fort, a columned temple. Like twin stone urns, the Library and the Museum stand in the yard of Government, storing the essence of the nation.

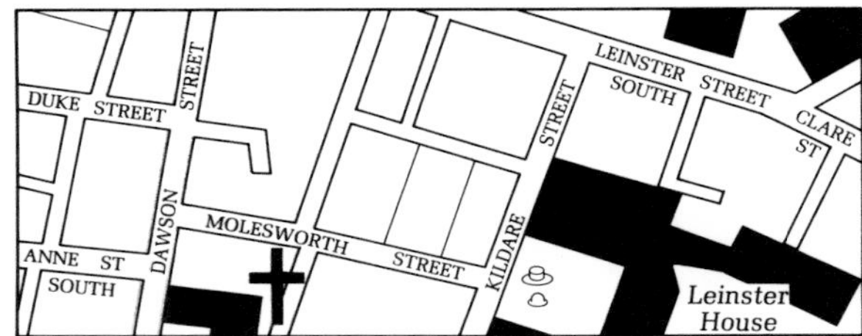

Uncurved Kildare Street is quiet and wide from St. Stephen's Green in the south to College Park wall on Nassau Street to the north. Trees dress each end. Nubian princesses and their slaves light the entrance to the Shelbourne Hotel on the Green corner, monkeys and birds are chased into the wall of the old Kildare Street Club on the Nassau Street corner. This is an official street, dominated by Dail Eireann, the Irish Lower House and Senate. Government offices stand civilly by, a few happy little shops wink from behind the official skirts.

When Joyce left the Martello Tower in Sandycove in a frightened huff, he walked the nine miles to the National Library to expand a theory. Stephen Dedalus, since quaffing with newspapermen, makes his way to the National Library to discourse upon acquaintances. The first is "Bald, most zealous" Lyster, the Quaker librarian. Then, "Mr. Best entered, tall, young, mild, light" and destined to be Lyster's successor, refuser of small loans to J. Joyce, Esq.

W. K. Magee, also on the Library staff, used the nom-de-plume "John Eglinton", was nicknamed "Stiff-breeches" by Joyce; a careful man, elegant essayist, he eschewed drink, women, wild imaginings and was, therefore, in Joyce's ink, a butt:

There once was a Celtic librarian
Whose essays were voted Spencerian
His name is Magee
But it seems that to me
He's a flavour that's more Presbyterian.

The fourth of Stephen's energetic listeners is George Russell, Mr. Bloom's high, tweedy cyclist. As "A.E.", Russell was Dublin's principal literary host. Joyce, at twenty, ambitiously anticipatory, wanted his name scribbled in Russell's address book and called on him unannounced one chiming midnight, and used two hours to damn all Russell's literary ilk by comparison with the Artist as a young man. Kind, mystic and bearded, Russell thought Joyce the wildest young man he had ever known:

"Proud as Lucifer and writes verses perfect in their technique and sometimes beautiful in quality." It worked. Russell spoke in his circle, a new cup-and-saucer was put on the tray for tea. But he told the youth to acquire more chaos.

> "What is a ghost? Stephen said with tingling energy. One who has faded into impalpability through death, through absence, through change of manners. Elizabethan London lay as far from Stratford as corrupt Paris lies from virgin Dublin. Who is the ghost from *limbo patrum,* returning to the world that has forgotten him? Who is King Hamlet?

Even as Joyce dwelt in the Tower at Sandycove he had begun to work out his theory that Shakespeare was Hamlet's father, the dead King whom Will loved to play. That Hamlet was the young Hamnet Shakespeare, Will's only son who died at the age of twelve. That while Shakespeare was in London Ann Hathaway enjoyed Will's brothers, a betraying Queen. Leopold Bloom is a cuckold with a dead son.

The Reading Room of the National Library of Ireland, Kildare Street, Dublin, 2, is a fertile, peaceful acre. Curvilinear, styled like the Parliament in Oslo, built in 1890 by Sir Thomas Deane and Sir Thomas Deane – Deane and Son – it houses the photographs in the Lawrence Collection, the stiffened ghosts of ribboned ladies, hatted gentlemen and harnessed animals recorded on glass, preserved on microfilm. Of the thousand copies printed in the Shakespeare and Co. first edition of *Ulysses*, published by Sylvia Beach in Paris in 1922, the National Library contains volume number 999 and volume number one. Rich wood, green shades, old files of newspapers with the names of mythical citizens: *The Kerryman, The Clare Champion, The Dundalk Argus, The Cork Examiner, The Anglo-Celt, The Munster Tribune, The Nationalist*, printed provincial demigods awaiting consultation.

Joyce believed that the brain was busiest and best in the afternoon. The episode in the National Library represents the brain. Scylla and Charybdis, to complicate matters, are the twin cliffs of Platonic and Aristotleian thought between which Stephen is trying to steer, without being sucked into the eddy of confusion. "Ineffable", "Supreme", "deepest", "heavenly", "beautiful" are globes which glow in Stephen's illumination of the Bard.

Shakespeare was one of Joyce's few gods. Stephen is about to insist that Shakespeare's well-known inferiority complex was due to Ann Hathaway's seducing him, stealing the sexual initiative, when: "Amen! responded from the doorway." And "with a ribald face, sullen as a dean's, Buck Mulligan came forwards then blithe in motley, towards the greeting of their smiles". The mocker is back, double-dactyl Malachi Mulligan.

Stephen hadn't kept their tavern appointment, ("The Ship, Buck Mulligan cried. Half twelve" – remember?) and telegraphed his absence to the exaggeratedly aggrieved Buck. "And we to be there, mavrone, and you to be unbeknownst sending us your conglomerations the way we to have our tongues out a yard long like the drouthy clerics do be fainting for a pussful." It was a Golden Age in Dublin. Synge, Gogarty, Shaw, Russell, Moore, Colum, O'Sullivan, O'Casey – foothills on whom the lava flowed from the high fiery cones of Yeats and Joyce. "Mr. Lyster, an attendant said from the door ajar." Enter Mr. Bloom. "There's a gentleman here, sir, the attendant said, coming forward and offering a card. From the *Freeman*. He wants to see the files of the *Kilkenny People* for last year." Mulligan has just seen Mr. Bloom by the statues in the museum, and Bloom knows Stephen's father, Simon. Shakespeare is resumed – much more lightly with mocking Mulligan. Stephen even tells the Shakespearean joke. Burbage, playing the Hunchback, arrived at the door of a lady fan. The Bard had intercepted the curtain call, and cried from the boudoir: "William the Conqueror came before Richard the Third." And Stephen is still brooding over his dead mother "hurrying to her squalid deathlain from gay Paris". Mother dying. Come home. Father.

"Every life is many days, day after day. We walk through ourselves, meeting robbers, ghosts, giants, old men, young men, wives, widows, brothers-in-love. But always meeting ourselves." Shakespeare ended, Stephen and the Buck Mulligan stand in the doorway "a man passed out between them, bowing, greeting". The Third Time. "The wandering Jew, Buck Mulligan whispered with clown's awe", mocking as the newsboys did, Mr. Bloom's departing back. Stephen still resents the Buck who chants airily of whores and mariners. Joyce softens. "Kind air defined the coigns of houses in Kildare Street. No birds. Frail from the housetops two plumes of smoke ascended, pluming, and in a flaw of softness softly were blown."

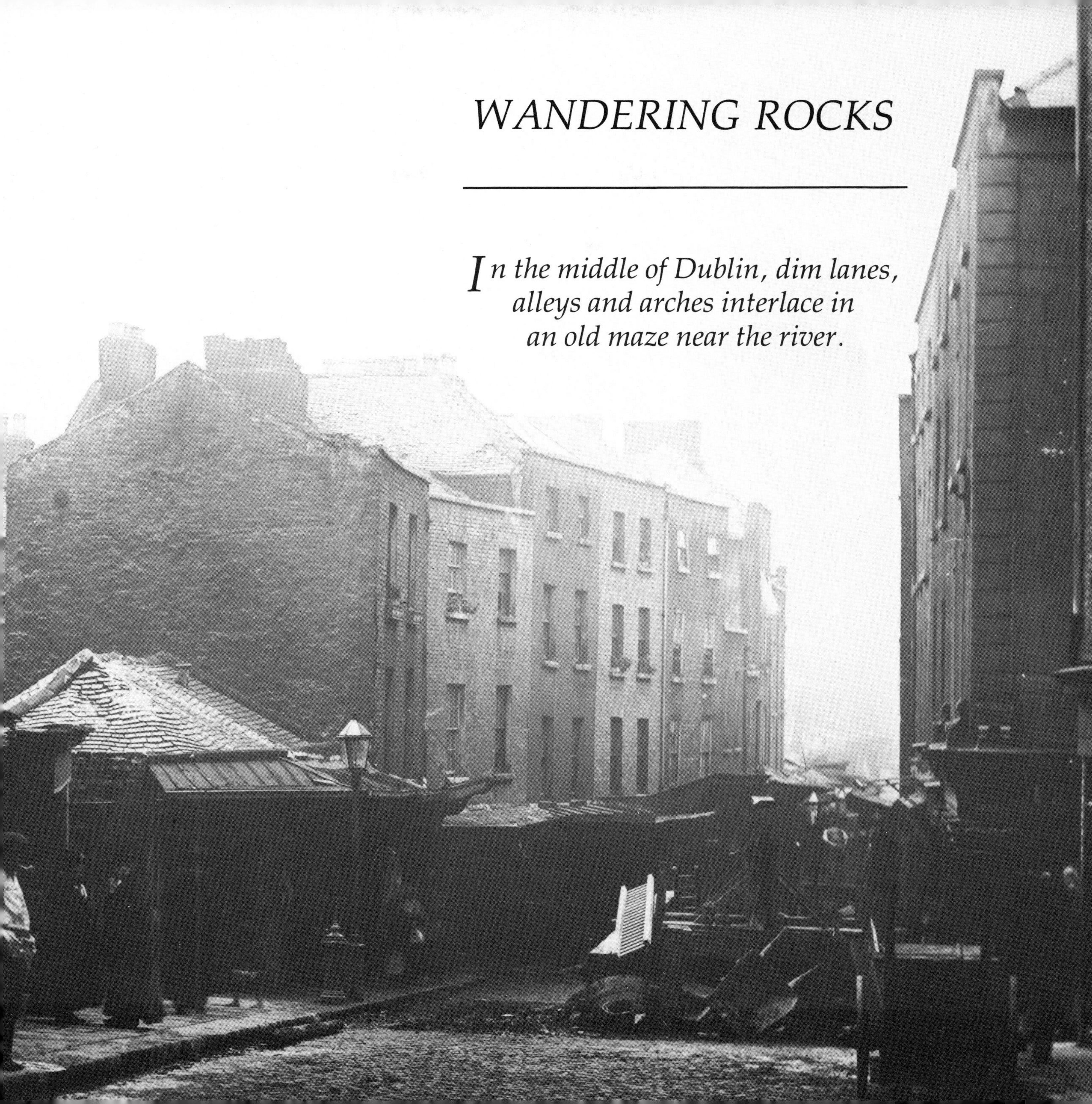

WANDERING ROCKS

In the middle of Dublin, dim lanes, alleys and arches interlace in an old maze near the river.

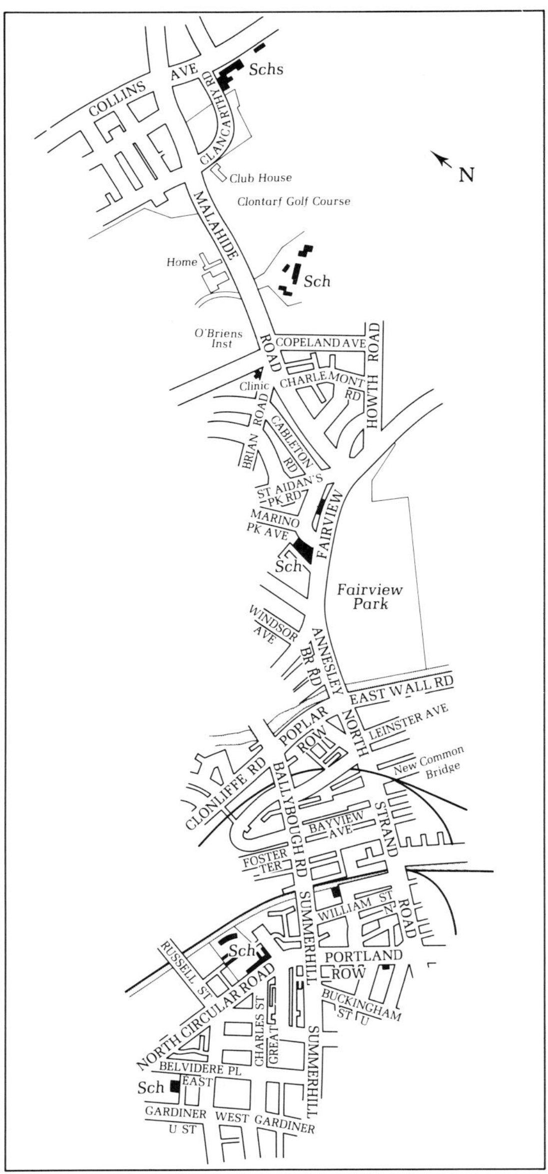

A broker of Space and Time, Joyce, while devising "Wandering Rocks", used compass, set-square, ruler and map – and a timepiece to arrange the movements of the characters in the episode; as a further aid he played every night a board game called "Labyrinth" with his daughter Lucia. In "Wandering Rocks", which comes halfway in the novel, neither Stephen Dedalus nor Leopold Bloom dominates. Here is the nub and core of Joycean Dublin; the "woman-city" is the central character, hostess to her own people; her shores are mapped by her citizens on their un-epic voyages.

In his planning Joyce traced the two principal voyages in red ink – the first journey, made by a priest, the final one by the King's Governor-General. And between those parameters of Church and State a procession of the people of Dublin wander, walk, talk and wind their way about the business of the hour between three and four o'clock in the afternoon. Think of it as a busy Dutch painting, sixteenth or seventeenth century, Pieter Brueghel or Hendrik Avercamp – all those little figures dancing, skating, hunting, harvesting. In Dublin on the 16th of June, 1904, they are walking, talking, standing still.

Homer's heroes were advised to steer clear of the rocks which his blessed gods called the wanderers, past which it was fatal to sail, over which it was dangerous to fly. Joyce's people navigate their streams of consciousness with a similar weather eye to fortune and comedy, tragedy and mischance.

> The superior, the very Reverend John Conmee S.J., reset his smooth watch in his interior pocket as he came down the presbytery steps. Five to three. Just nice time to walk to Artane. What was that boy's name again? Dignam, yes. *Vere dignum et justum est.*

Father Conmee is on his way to the orphanage to see whether the son of the deceased Patrick Dignam may be admitted. A one-legged sailor held out a cap, and Father Conmee blessed him and crossed to Mountjoy Square, thinking of God and soldiers and sailors and cannonballs.

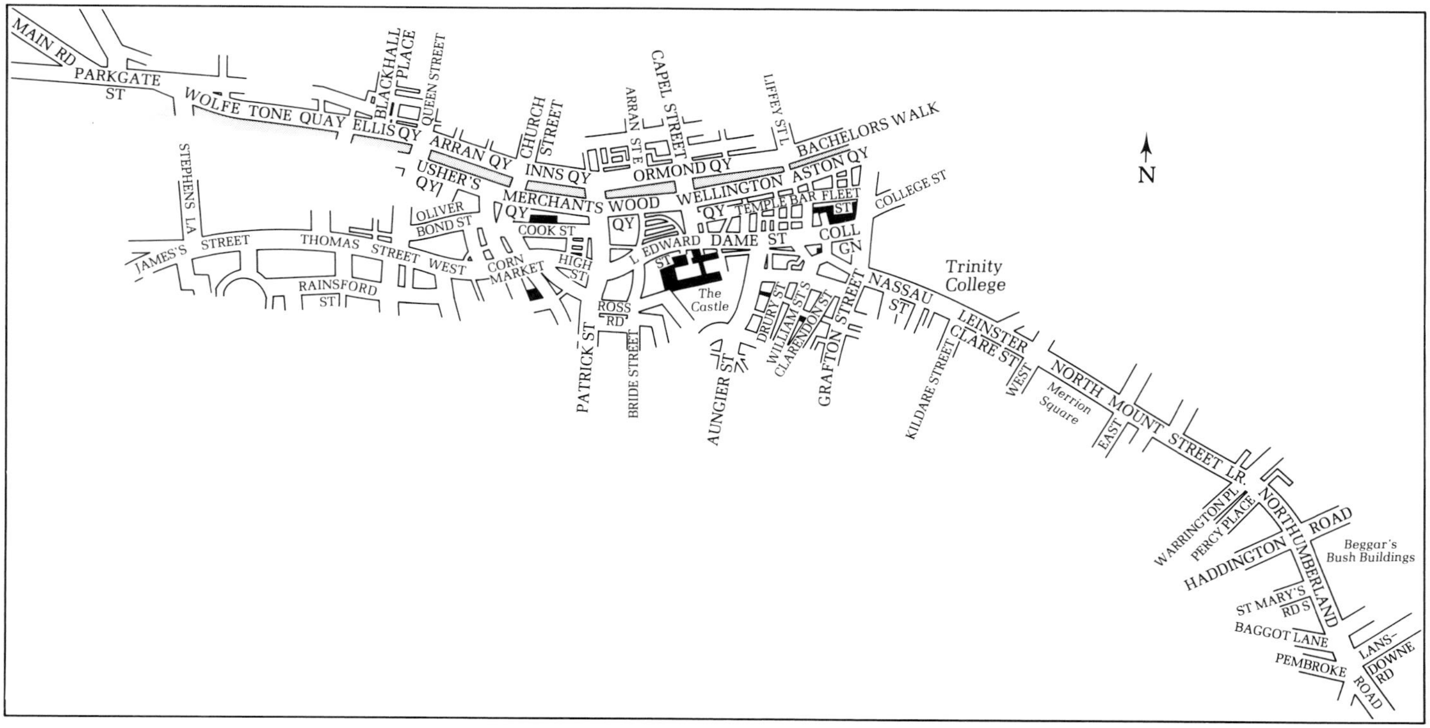

MAIN RD
PARKGATE ST
WOLFE TONE QUAY
BLACKHALL PLACE
QUEEN STREET
ELLIS QY
ARRAN QY
CHURCH STREET
USHER'S QY
INNS QY
ARRAN ST E
CAPEL STREET
ORMOND QY
LIFFEY ST
BACHELORS WALK
WELLINGTON QY
ASTON QY
MERCHANTS QY
WOOD QY
TEMPLE BAR
FLEET ST
COLLEGE ST
STEPHENS LA
JAMES'S STREET
THOMAS STREET WEST
OLIVER BOND ST
COOK ST
L. EDWARD ST
DAME ST
COLL GN
Trinity College
CORN MARKET
HIGH ST
RAINSFORD ST
The Castle
ROSS RD
NASSAU ST
PATRICK ST
BRIDE STREET
AUNGIER ST
DRURY ST
WILLIAM ST S
CLARENDON ST
GRAFTON STREET
KILDARE STREET
LEINSTER
CLARE ST
WEST
Merrion Square
EAST
NORTH MOUNT STREET LR.
N
WARRINGTON PL.
PERCY PLACE
NORTHUMBERLAND ROAD
HADDINGTON ROAD
Beggar's Bush Buildings
ST MARY'S RD S
BAGGOT LANE
PEMBROKE ROAD
LANSDOWNE RD

Father Conmee was the Rector of Clongowes Wood, Joyce's first school. He was the Jesuit whom Joyce's dilapidated father met in Mountjoy Square one day and who immediately offered James a place in Belvedere College, nearby, where he had just become Prefect of Studies. To Joyce he was ever after "a bland and courtly humanist".

"Father Conmee walked down Great Charles Street and glanced at the shutup free church on his left", to the North Circular Road where there is "strangely no tramline", past the schools of Saint Joseph and by Aldborough House with its own theatre; it was the last genuine Palladian mansion to be built in Ireland. Father Conmee walked along the North Strand Road, smelling incense and baconflitches and butter, past Corny Kelleher, poor Dignam's undertaker, who "totted figures in the daybook while he chewed a blade of hay". Past

policemen and porkbutchers and bargemen and their horses on Newcomen Bridge, he "stepped on to an outward bound tram".

Bombs fell here in Hitler's war, neutral Eire's only wound. A limping German aircraft either jettisoned for speed, or got it all wrong, and the night came apart. This is no-man's-land, not city, not suburb, suitable only for travelling through and halting, as did Father Conmee's tram. By Annesley Bridge he descended and read his Latin breviary, hic-haec-hocking his way to Artane: into his path "a flushed young man came from a gap of the hedge and after him a young woman with wild nodding daisies in her hand". Father Conmee blessed them both "gravely and turned a thin page of his breviary". In "Wandering Rocks" only the representatives of Church and State move away from the city's heart.

"Mr. Dennis J. Maginni, professor of dancing, etc., in silk hat, slate frockcoat with silk facings, white kerchief tie, tight lavender trousers, canary gloves and pointed patent boots, walking with grave deportment . . ." Another of Dublin's characters on his way from his home in North Great Georges Street to the city centre. Is the dancing-master included to observe the element of time? With metronomic precision, the characters in "Wandering Rocks" walk only minutes away from each other. One-two, one-two-three-four. Tempo? Well, strict enough.

"Corny Kelleher sped a silent jet of hayjuice arching from his mouth while a generous white arm from a window in Eccles Street flung forth a coin", two glittering arcs simultaneously, miles apart. A one-legged sailor who earlier importuned Father John Conmee for alms, received instead a blessing, has pegged his way around the corner from Upper Gardiner Street into Dorset Street. As he turned into Eccles Street Molly Bloom flung the sailor a coin. "A plump bare generous arm shone, was seen, held forth from a white petticoatbodice and taut shiftstraps." All through "Wandering Rocks" Joyce, who founded Dublin's first cinema, keeps more than one projector running.

"Katey and Boody Dedalus shoved in the door of the close steaming kitchen." They are the sisters of Stephen, and the daughters of feckless Simon. They live at Number Seven, St. Peter's Terrace, Cabra, where they boil shirts and lament their lack of money, even though they have just pawned Stephen's books. Another sister, Dilly, has gone to meet their "father who are not in heaven" to get money. The artist on home ground – in June 1904 the Joyce family lived in tumult and penury at Number Seven, St. Peter's Terrace, Cabra.

Blazes Boylan, Bloom's cuckoldiser has gone into Thornton's the fruit shop at Sixty-Three, Grafton Street, to order some fruit to be sent ahead – to "somebody". While he ogles the "young pullet" bosom of a blond girl, "H.E.L.Y.'S. filed before him, tallwhitehatted". He asks to use the telephone.

Stephen has walked from the library down Kildare Street, turned left into Nassau Street and then to College Green and the statues in front of Trinity. Carrying his ashplant walking stick, he meets Almidano Artifoni, his singing-master, under "Goldsmith's knobby poll". Another pun? "Here lies Oliver Goldsmith More often called Noll Who wrote like an angel But talked like poor Poll", was the poet's own epitaph. Poll? Parrot? Head? In name, Almidano Artifoni was the principal at the Trieste Berlitz Institute, who gave Joyce a teaching job. In character, he was the Jesuit Father, Charles Ghezzi, who taught Joyce Dante.

The phone rings in Boylan's house of business at Number Fifteen, D'Olier Street, just around the corner from where Stephen is. The message passes on the wires somewhere in the air above and near Stephen; he is between Boylan in Grafton Street and Boylan's secretary in D'Olier Street. Miss Dunne's conversation with Mr. Boylan closes with the words that he is to meet Mr. Lenehan at the Ormond Hotel at four. The citizens of *Ulysses* are on the move.

J. J. O'Molloy is a Dublin gurrier – in low common parlance he only leaves his street corner or bar stool to cadge. Now he comes to Ned Lambert in the chapterhouse of Mary's Abbey, finds Ned at work showing a clergyman, the Reverend Hugh C. Love, the vaulted arches of the old chapterhouse: "We are standing in the historic council chamber of

Saint Mary's Abbey where silken Thomas proclaimed himself a rebel in 1534."

Had you been standing on O'Connell Bridge between the hours of three and four o'clock on that faraway Thursday afternoon nothing would have appeared different. But nothing was different: all these citizens were only doing what they did every day. They came, stayed, went, and the commonest acts of man became the brush-strokes on Joyce's canvas, the detail in his portrait of everyman.

Tom Rochford is displaying a machine he has invented to tell theatre latecomers which variety act is on. Richie Goulding, Stephen's cousin, is on his professional way to the courts across the river. Lenehan and M'Coy walk out of Crampton Court and into the labyrinth between Dame Street and the river, on their way to the Ormond Hotel to meet Boylan at four o'clock. A stop at the bookmakers, praise for Tom Rochford who saved a man from a sewer, what about the Gold Cup?

> They went up the steps and under Merchants' Arch. A darkbacked figure scanned books on the hawker's cart.
>
> There he is, Lenehan said.
>
> Wonder what he is buying. M'Coy said, glancing behind.
>
> Leopoldo or the Bloom is on the Rye, Lenehan said.

The wandering Jew – whom they discuss. Bloom's hobby is astronomy: "he's a cultured allroundman Bloom is". The two worthies walk from Crampton Court to Dame Street, Sycamore Street, Essex Street and Temple Bar.

At breakfast Molly asked Mr. Bloom to get her a book. "Get another of Paul de Kock's. Nice name he has." There is still a book barrow at Merchants' Arch. "*Sweets of Sin*, he said, tapping on it. That's a good one." And on O'Connell Bridge "many persons observed the grave deportment and gay apparel of Mr. Denis J. Maginni, professor of dancing".

On Bachelor's Walk, directly across the river, Dilly Dedalus stands in wait for her father Simon. Deflecting, Mr. Dedalus urges her not to slouch and abusively tries to straighten her shoulders. After his wife died and was buried in Glasnevin, John Joyce treated his family appallingly, too. "I'll break your bloody heart," he used to yell, "I'll break your stomach first, ye buggers." Now, Dilly insists that Simon Dedalus has more money than the shilling he hands over. Eventually, because she grins at his joke, he surrenders two pennies more. And at this moment "the viceregal cavalcade passed, greeted by obsequious policemen, out of Parkgate".

The St. James's Gate brewery of Arthur Guinness and Company was, in Joyce's time, the biggest in the world. Mr. Kernan walks towards it: on the way he preens himself in the sloping mirror of Peter Kennedy, hairdresser, at Forty-Eight, James's Street. He thinks he sees Ned Lambert's brother Sam "over the way". But the sun flashes in the windscreen of a motor-car and he is not sure. Who is Mr. Kernan? You may as well ask who is Ned Lambert? And his brother Sam? Who is J. J. O'Molloy, Tom Rochford, Mrs. Breen, M'Coy, Lenehan, the one-legged sailor? People, citizens of Dublin, Joycean corpuscles. And as Mr. Kernan turned down Watling Street "by the corner of Guinness' visitors' waitingroom", Mrs. Breen, who lately had a conversation with Mr. Bloom, goes over O'Connell Bridge, half a mile away, with her husband who is not the full shilling. "A cavalcade in easy trot along Pembroke quay passed, outriders leaping, leaping in their, in their saddles. Frockcoats. Cream sunshades."

In Bedford Row "Stephen Dedalus watched through the webbed window the lapidary's fingers prove a timedulled chain". In Clohissey's window "a faded 1860 print of Heenan boxing Sayers held his eye". Mr. Bloom is a few minutes away, in Merchants' Arch, book-buying.

Stephen, too – in Bedford Row, still – "turned and halted by the slanted bookcart". Perhaps he will see and re-purchase some of the "schoolprizes" his hungry sisters pawned. Could they still be there, on today's bookcarts? Oh – the temptation to look for a flyleaved "S. Dedalus, 1904". Dilly comes forward to Stephen bearing shyly a coverless *Chardeual's French Primer*. She blushes when he wrings from her that she spent one of her pennies on it to learn French.

The picture hangs. Stephen – at a book-barrow in one of the little streets, his scrawny sister standing before him: Bloom – bent "darkbacked" over another barrow around the corner: Lenehan and M'Coy walking past, clouds scudding slow across the sky, the viceregal cavalcade clip-clopping along the quays.

Simon Dedalus meets "Father" Cowley outside the premises of Reddy and Daughters on Ormond Quay where they "clasped hands loudly". Cowley complains that Reuben J. Dodd, the moneylender, has two bailiffs pursuing him. But who can approach the subsheriff and have the bailiffs hauled off? Aha! "Ben Dollard's loose blue cutaway and square hat above large slops crossed the quay in full gait from the metal bridge."

"The youngster will be all right, Martin Cunningham said, as they passed out of the Castleyard Gate", the youngster being poor Dignam's son. The mourners have convened to care for the bereaved. "Yes, Martin Cunningham said, fingering his beard. I wrote to Father Conmee and laid the whole case before him." From the gate of Dublin Castle to Kavanagh's winerooms at Twenty-Seven, Parliament Street is but a short journey, around the corner and down the hill. Martin Cunningham is making the trip – to see the subsheriff, Long John Fanning, about the case of the Dignams. "Horses pass Parliament Street, harness and glossy posterns in sunlight glimmering."

"As they trod across the thick carpet Buck Mulligan whispered behind his panama to Haines. 'Parnell's brother. There in the corner'." The Buck has parted company with Stephen and is about to take tea at the Dublin Bakery Company's tearooms, Thirty-Five, Dame Street. Haines and Mulligan order *mélanges* and scones and butter and cakes. The Buck chuckles: "We call it D.B.C. because they have damn bad cakes." Cashel Boyle O'Connor Fitzmaurice Tisdall Farrell is outside the lampposts of Merrion Square a mile away, behind him the blind stripling whom Bloom guided earlier, before him, Almidano Artifoni, homegoing. The characters walk in each other's footsteps, in a long-stretched straight line, by the walls of College Park, along Nassau Street, South Leinster Street and Clare Street into Merrion Square and ahead as far as Mount Street.

"Opposite Ruggy O'Donohoe's Master Patrick Aloysius Dignam, pawing the pound and half of Mangan's, late Fehrenbach's, porksteaks he had been sent for, went along warm Wicklow Street dawdling."

Bored with the mourners sitting in the parlour, he

goes to get the bidden meat. Master Dignam sees a poster in a window advertising a boxing match. "Myler Keogh, Dublin's pet lamb, will meet sergeantmajor Bennett, the Portobello bruiser, for a purse of fifty sovereigns" and Master Dignam contemplates on how much he would like to see that match. But he notices with chagrin that the date on the poster is May the twentysecond. "Sure, the blooming thing is all over." "In Grafton Street Master Dignam saw a red flower in a toff's mouth and a swell pair of kicks on him." Blazes Boylan, none other. Master Dignam continues his slow schoolboy's journey into Nassau Street.

Four o'clock approaches and there is sunlight and warm air and soft clouds. Pause. Let us not be boggled by this dazzling chess-player, Joyce, let us survey the board.

An hour ago play commenced when Father John Conmee set off on a journey to get a boy into a school, a mercy inspired by Martin Cunningham who shared a funeral carriage with Mr. Bloom and Mr. Dedalus and Mr. Power.

Professor Maginni is dancing, the five whitehatted H.E.L.Y.'S. sandwichmen are eeling, through the city. Corny Kelleher, the undertaker, spits. A one-legged sailor, blessed by Father Conmee, fetches the coin thrown by Molly Bloom. The Dedalus sisters are burning books to boil shirts. Blazes Boylan buys fruit for "someone", telephones his secretary. Stephen Dedalus meets his kind singing teacher, Almidano Artifoni. Lenehan tells M'Coy stories about Molly Bloom. J. J. O'Molloy tries to borrow money from Ned Lambert who is showing a historic building to the Reverend Hugh C. Love. Bob Cowley is off fending the Reverend Hugh C. Love's bailiffs, Simon Dedalus is fending off his equally distraining daughter. Under Merchants' Arch, near Lenehan and M'Coy, Mr. Bloom obtains *Sweets of Sin,* a book for his

wife. Mr. Kernan gleams at his reflection in a barber's looking-glass. Father Conmee blesses gravely a young couple who come flushed through the hedge. Martin Cunningham talks to the sub-sheriff, Long John Fanning, about the relatives of the late poor Dignam. Buck Mulligan and Haines see Parnell's brother in a teashop. Cashel Boyle what's-his-name bumps into a blind youth. Master Dignam, unknowing of Jews and Blooms, buys porksteaks.

Through the glittering green valleys of the Phoenix Park "William Humble, Earl of Dudley, and Lady Dudley, accompanied by lieutenantcolonel Hesseltine, drove out after luncheon from the viceregal lodge. In the following carriage were the honourable Mrs. Paget, Miss de Courcy and the honourable Gerald Ward, A.D.C., in attendance", along the long Liffey quays, by bridges to Parliament Street, Dame Street, College Green and Nassau Street – to Sandymount, to open the Mirus Bazaar in aid of funds for Mercer's Hospital. Dublin salutes the Viceroy – one way and another. On Ormond Quay Simon Dedalus gestures rudely. The Reverend Hugh C. Love's greeting goes unperceived, because he is out of sight. Lenehan and M'Coy look from Grattan/Essex Bridge.

Tom Rochford doffs his cap. Buck Mulligan and Haines, eating Damn Bad Cakes in Dame Street, look gaily and gravely down. Dilly Dedalus sees "sunshades spanned and wheelspokes spinning in the glare" of Fownes's Street. In Dame Street poor Mr. Breen is hauled from under the cavalcade wheels by his wife. The H.E.L.Y.'S., tallwhitehatted, come to a halt in Grafton Street. Mr. Denis J. Maginni pays absolutely no attention in Westmoreland Street. Blazes Boylan acknowledges, at the wall of the Provost's house, in "a skyblue tie, a widebrimmed straw hat at a rakish angle and a suit of indigo serge". Cashel Boyle and-so-forth turns back along Clare Street defiant in the opposite direction. Master Dignam "raised his new black cap". The blind stripling listens to the cavalcade on Mount Street. And Signor Artifoni goes through the door of his home, Number Fourteen Lansdowne Road.

SIRENS

Jingling, cleartinkling music and strong song rises on the sighing afternoon. Over the bridges and down the cobbled quays you may meet singers and golden liquids in a sunbeamed, dim, woodgrained bar.

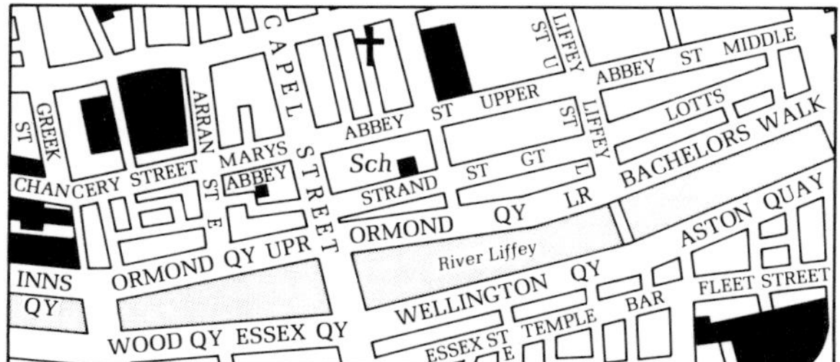

"Bronze by gold, Miss Douce's head by Miss Kennedy's head, over the crossblind of the Ormond Bar heard the viceregal hoofs go by." The two barmaids in the Ormond Hotel had been watching the progress of the viceregal cavalcade as it sped by the Liffey. Miss Douce's head was the colour of bronze, Miss Kennedy's head was the colour of gold and they were lively, vulgar young things. They were excited by the passing silk and grey of the cavalcade and when they left the window to resume duty on their island behind the bar the insolent Boots served them tea. "They cowered under their reef of counter, waiting on footstools, crates upturned, waiting for their teas to draw. They pawed their blouses, both of black satin, two and nine a yard, waiting for their teas to draw, and two and seven."

The barmaids lured the men of the city to their reefs at the bar of the Ormond Hotel. The Sirens were beautiful to the waist but in the lower regions had the bodies of birds, from the neck down, or the tails of fish from the waist down. Miss Kennedy and Miss Douce looked pristine and angelic when seen at the height of a bar counter, but their skirts and footwear were much shabbier than their black satin blouses and bronzegold features.

The Ormond Hotel still stands on a Liffey Quay. It has undergone considerable renovations since 1904 but parts of the old hotel are still to be seen. The panelling in the dining-room is of the colour and fabric which Joyce knew; at the back, some as yet unrenovated, used for meetings now, are the very rooms in which the singing of the Sirens took place. Outside, the river view has not changed. Downstream, stared at by the half-lidded eyes of many bridges, the considered skyline is gently jagged, scalloped, by the domes of churches, the squares of warehouses, the minaret of a malting tower and the narrowing tallness of an occasional residence. Lowering windows, warping sashes, upstairs musty apartments, old offices: below, the old shops still serve country customers. The Liffey is untroubled here, the line of its containing rampart is even, unbroken – save for the arched bridges and hanging tongues of piped water. Churches face each

other: and in a final agreement between Church and State the Franciscans and the Four Courts, green-domed and austere, sentry the stream.

The parallel quays palpitate the city. Inwards, with the river's tide, the veins: from Kingsbridge, past Usher's Island and Merchants' Arch come the new citizens, to O'Connell Bridge. On the opposite side, against the tide, the artery of Bachelor's Walk, the Four Courts, the Ormond Hotel, the way home to the west, past Kingsbridge, past Islandbridge, Phoenix Park, Chapelizod, the road for drovers, dealers and their goods and cattle, the way to *Finnegans Wake*.

When Joyce had finished writing the "Sirens" he lost all interest in music for a time. He had put so much into the chapter, in the notes, chords and contrapuntals of the prose, that he felt had it all been drained out of his system. As a boy he sang sweetly, as a man, publicly. He appeared on the same concert platform as the celebrated tenor John McCormack, he came second in Dublin's premier singing competition – and threw the medal away, disgusted both at losing, and at not being able to pawn it. But his singing performances were reviewed by the newspapers. After he appeared on the 27th of August, 1904 in a Grand Irish Concert at the Antient (sic) Concert Rooms, now the Academy Cinema on Pearse Street, the *Freeman's Journal* wrote:

"Mr. James A. Joyce, the possessor of a sweet tenor voice, sang charmingly 'The Sally Gardens' and gave a pathetic rendering of 'The Croppy Boy'." Another critic wrote: "Mr. Joyce possesses a light tenor voice, which he is inclined to force on the high notes but he sings with artistic emotionalism." Nora often said he should have stuck to the singing.

Ulysses had been warned that the sweet song of the Sirens would lure, had lured, all mortal men to

their deaths on the ferocious island of the Sirens. He sealed the ears of his companions with wax and lashed himself to the mast in order to resist the temptation. Behind the counter of the Ormond Hotel Miss Douce and Miss Kennedy greet a variety of men who wander in. As the afternoon shines on, one man departs, lured by another Siren, others stay: soon, sweet sounds, long notes, come from the concert-room.

The first strolling player is Simon Dedalus, father of the bard. He hoped Miss Douce had nice holiday weather in Rostrevor.

> Gorgeous, she said. Look at the holy show I am. Lying out on the strand all day.
>
> Bronze whiteness.
>
> That was exceedingly naughty of you, Mr. Dedalus told her and pressed her hand indulgently. Tempting poor simple males.
>
> Miss Douce of satin douced her arm away.
>
> O go away, she said. You're very simple, I don't think.

The next arrival is Lenehan, looking for Blazes Boylan. He informs Mr. Dedalus that Stephen has earlier had the elite of Erin hanging on his lips while he drank with the newspapermen in Mooneys.

And Mr. Bloom is still wandering. He has crossed the river at Essex Bridge, bought "two sheets cream vellum paper one reserve two envelopes" to reply to Martha's letter. As he emerges from the shop, eye falling on a poster with a mermaid advertising cigarettes, Mr. Bloom's heart stops again. "He eyed and saw afar on Essex Bridge a gay hat riding on a jauntingcar. It is. Third time. Coincidence." Blazes Boylan is on his way to the Ormond Hotel to meet Lenehan. Then he has an appointment at Number Seven, Eccles Street, with

Mrs. Marion Bloom, as per the letter she received from him that morning.

Dublin in 1904 heard many songs. The music-hall soldiery loved Victorian drawing-room ballads. All classes and creeds – who could afford it – went to the opera. The ceaseless flow of international operatic stars through Dublin was always assured of an attentive audience. Once, a visiting tenor in *La Traviata* was unable to resume, by dint of beverage, in the second act. "Ladies and gentlemen," apologised the manager, "I regret to announce that our tenor will not be appearing in Act Two. He is, I'm afraid, suffering an attack of malaria." A raucous voice from the pit yelled: "Malaria! Jaysus! I'd love a bottle of that meself."

In the Ormond Hotel, "from the saloon a call came, long in dying. That was a tuning-fork the tuner had that he forgot that he now struck. A call again. That he now poised that it throbbed. You hear? It throbbed, pure, purer, softly and softlier, its buzzing prongs. Longer in dying call." Lured to the Ormond Hotel, "Blazes Boylan's smart tan shoes creaked on the barfloor where he strode", greeted by barmaids and Lenehan. The poor nervous Mr. Bloom, aware that Boylan is about to visit Molly, slips unseen into the dining-room while in the concert-room "a voiceless song sang from within".

Three levels of awareness – Mr. Bloom on the outside, not wanting to see Boylan, able to hear the unseen song. At the bar "Boylan bespoke potions"; Mr. Bloom ordered liver and bacon; deep inside the inner ear the Ormond rang with song.

Richard Ellman quotes James Joyce's conversation with a friend on the 18th of June, 1919.

> I finished the "Sirens" chapter during the last few days. A big job. I wrote this chapter with the technical resources of music. It is a fugue with all

> musical notations: piano, forte, rallentando, and so on. A quintet occurs in it too, as in *Die Meistersinger*, my favourite Wagnerian opera . . . Since exploring the resources and artifices of music and employing them in this chapter, I haven't cared for music any more. I, the great friend of music, can no longer listen to it. I see through all the tricks and can't enjoy it any more.

Ellmann tells too, the story of Joyce reading "Sirens" to a friend just before they left for *Die Walküre*. At the interval Joyce asked the friend, an enthusiastic Wagnerian, whether he didn't think that the musical efforts of "Sirens" were better than Wagner's? When the friend disagreed Joyce departed in a huff.

A different kind of music is organised from Miss Douce. "Smack. She let free sudden in rebound her nipped elastic garter smackwarm against her smackable woman's warmhosed thigh" to the vast amusement of Blazes and acolyte Lenehan. "Boylan eyed, eyed. Tossed to fat lips his chalice, drankoff his tiny chalice, sucking the last fat violet syrupy drops." Blazes Boylan departed for his appointment. Poor Mr. Bloom. "Bloom heard a jing, a little sound. He's off. Light sob of breath." The tension, the lust rises. "By Bachelor's Walk jogjaunty jingled Blazes Boylan, bachelor, in sun, in heat, mare's glossy rump atrot, with a flick of whip, on bounding tyres: sprawled, warmseated, Boylan impatience, ardentbold." And back at the Ormond Hotel, like a sound-track, barreltoned Ben Dollard's voice booms: "When love absorbs my ardent soul . . ." Blazes Boylan the impressario, and Mrs. Marion Bloom are about to rehearse "Love's Old Sweet Song". Joyce was attracted/repelled by the notion that Nora was attractive to other men – despite her fidelity to him. But when a journalist in Trieste called Prezioso, whose friendship Joyce encouraged, wanted Nora to become his mistress, Joyce tonguelashed him to tears.

"In liver gravy Bloom mashed mashed potatoes." It is just past four o'clock. Mr. Bloom sits at the table "married in silence" to Richie Goulding who has ordered steak and kidney pie, all brought by Pat the bald, deaf waiter. Within, watched by Miss Douce and Miss Kennedy, there is to be a splendid singing. The piano is now in tune, thanks to a certain blind stripling who came this morning but left his tuning fork behind him. Came Simon Dedalus' voice:

> It soared like a bird, it held its flight, a swift pure cry, soar silver orb it leaped serene, speeding, sustained, to come, don't spin it out too long long breath he breath long life, soaring high, high resplendent, aflame, crowned, high in the effulgence symbolistic, high, of the ethereal bosom, high of the vast irradiation everywhere all soaring all around about the all, the endlessnessnessness . . .

"Sirens" has often been described as the most beautiful episode in *Ulysses*. It represents the ear, and all through the chapter, songs and sounds resound like various sections of an orchestra. Even the opening passages are shaped like an overture, tiny quotes and phrases dotted and pitched across the page, notes for the fuller chords to come.

Then the sounds of the afternoon – the recurring jingle of Boylan's jauntingcar matching the jingling brass quoits on Molly's bed of brass, the tap-tap-tapping of the blind stripling coming back for his tuning-fork, the clap-clap-clapping which greeted each song sung, the "cockcarracarra" rat-tat-tat-tat of Boylan with the doorknocker of Number Seven, Eccles Street.

Ben Dollard stands up to sing "The Croppy Boy", a song of betrayal. Mr. Bloom writes to

"Martha Clifford c/o P.O. Dolphin's Barn Lane Dublin". Miss Lydia Douce displays the shell she brought back from holiday. Bob Cowley plays the piano in F sharp major. Blazes Boylan knocks on Molly's door and she titivates lingeringly in the hall mirror before opening up. The blind stripling piano-tuner tap-taps his way down the quays. Lonely, Mr. Bloom leaves the music of the Ormond Hotel.

While Joyce was writing the *Sirens* he went with a friend to Locarno. He had heard of an old baroness who made dolls on an island in Lake Maggiore. She was known locally as the Siren because she lived a curious life on her little isle and was reputed to have buried seven husbands. Clearly she embraced her nickname; she had the walls of her rooms decorated with Homeric themes. Joyce wrote to her à propos his own *Ulysses*, requesting a viewing of her pictures. She invited him to the island where she gave him access to a chest full of obscene letters and erotic books.

"A frowsy whore with a black sailor hat askew came glazily in the day along the quay towards Mr. Bloom." He is so lonely, so lonely, trying to keep the pictures of Blazes and Molly out of his mind, but on a previous assignation the whore mentioned Molly," stout lady does be with you in the brown costume". So lonely Mr. Bloom turns instead to a shop window, and introverts himself into the lanes, burrows and furrows behind the Ormond Hotel.

CYCLOPS

Surrounded by echoes of previous patriots, the policemen at Green Street Court protect the city and the world from rebellious sentiment. The ruined corner by Barney Kiernan's pub is cordoned by slogans taken down and used in evidence.

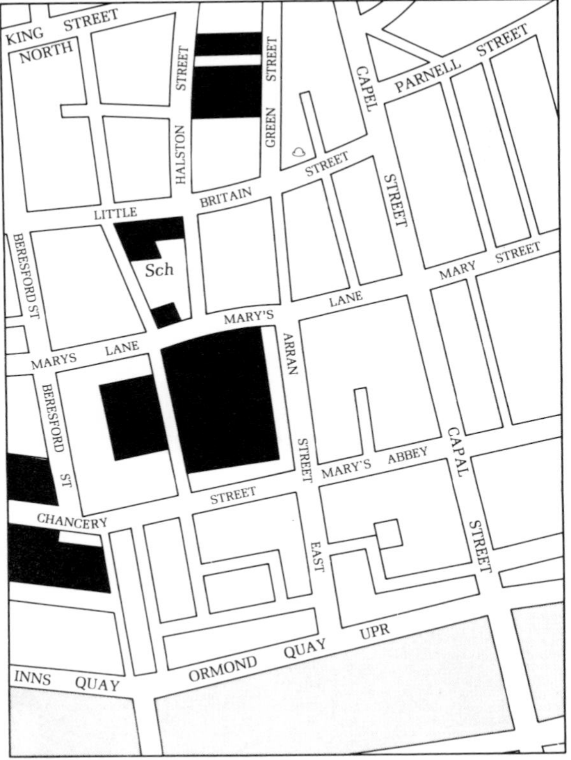

A nameless narrator, after a brief conversation with Constable Troy of the Dublin Metropolitan Police, an altercation with the bristles of a chimneysweep, an encounter with a friend, is on his way to Barney Kiernan's pub in Little Britain Street for the most savagely satirical chapter in *Ulysses*. The time is five o'clock in the afternoon: Barney Kiernan's pub is now vanished, a dying parish by Green Street Courthouse, in the heart of the markets.

I was just passing the time of day with old Troy of the D.M.P. at the corner of Arbour Hill there and be damned but a boody old sweep came along and he near drove his gear into my eye. I turned around to let him have the weight of my tongue when who should I see dodging along Stony Batter only Joe Hynes.

Lo, Joe, says I. How are you blowing? Did you see that bloody chimneysweep near shove my eye out with his brush?

Mr. Bloom is wandering somewhere in the dingy labyrinth between Ormond Quay and Little Britain Street. He has agreed to meet Martin Cunningham at the Courthouse in order to establish a charitable fund for the relatives of poor Dignam. He has purchased a postal order gift for Martha, and a stamp: needing solitude he walks sadly into the warren of streets on his way to five o'clock. In these streets the pubs have always had special licensing laws to open in the early morning hours of the markets, a special tipple is poured. Old Dublin still clings, small houses, broken terraces, sparse now. Citizens here are unto the second and third generation, do not want to leave. But an old person living alone falls ill, is moved to hospital, never returns and the dead house is boarded up. Eventually it is incorporated into town planning.

The style of "Cyclops" is garrulous and malicious: the narrator adopts a pretence of friendship and familiarity sufficiently ingratiating to encourage free drink. An old Irish pastime: at funerals unfamiliar wellwishers were a familiar sight, offering condolence in exchange for drink at

the wake. Sometimes they were disappointed. Once, near my home, a regular was chagrined at the dryness of the house. Days later when queried as to "What did poor Mr. Hogan die of?" this "mourner" snorted: "Drought." In the bar of Barney Kiernan's sits "the citizen up in the corner having a great confab with himself and that bloody mangy mongrel, Garryowen, and he waiting for what the sky would drop in the way of drink". Enter the citizen, the central character in "Cyclops".

By the time Joyce left Dublin in 1904 he was convinced that his fellow citizens were the most malicious, priest-ridden, treacherous, calumnious, politically dubious, devious breed. He was the deer, the antlered intellect, the nervous, elegant animal – his countrymen were the hounds, ready, anxious to tear him down. It was his favourite image of his young self – but was he aware of his own emotional and social malice, his multifarious, unrestituted borrowings, his tidal contempt for every living Irish writer?

"So begob the citizen claps his paw on his knee and he says: Foreign wars is the cause of it." Ulysses fought the one-eyed giant, Cyclops. The citizen can only see the Irish Question from one nationalistic point of view. He is entirely blind to the view of somebody who doesn't believe that "The Cause" is all, he is blind to all other points of view, to reason, to logic. It is a literary irony that Barney Kiernan's pub stood on a corner across from Green Street Courthouse, which for a decade and more has been the venue for those on trial for politically-claimed crimes. And Joyce calls up the old, old images, the legends, the stuff of slogans: ". . . Cuchulin, Conn of hundred battles, Niall of nine hostages, Brian of Kincora, the Ardri Malachi. Art MacMurragh, Shane O'Neill, Father John Murphy, Owen Roe, Patrick Sarsfield, Red Hugh O'Donnell. Red Jim McDermott . . ." and on, and on, and on until the ludicrous emerges . . . ". . . the Mother of the Maccabees, the Last of the Mohicans, the Rose of Castille, the Man for Galway, the Man that Broke the Bank at Monte Carlo, the Man in the Gap, the Woman who Didn't . . ."

It is only five o'clock but this is Dublin and there are plenty of conversationalists in the pub. "What's that bloody freemason doing, says the citizen, prawling up and down outside?" Mr. Bloom is waiting for his appointment. A minor civil servant produces a batch of letters, applications for the post of hangman. One is signed "H. Rumbold". In Zurich in 1918 Joyce had a violent disagreement with the British diplomatic authorities whose Minister to Switzerland was Sir Horace Rumbold. Joyce later referred to him as "Sir Whorearse Rumhole"; two of his staff, Gann and Smith, appear as hanged murderers in the hangman's application.

> There he is again, says the citizen, staring out.
> Who? says I.
> Bloom, says he. He's on point duty up and down there for the last ten minutes.
> And, begob, I saw his physog do a peep in and then slidder off again.

There was endless conversation in the Joyce household, as often as not politics, Parnell's fall from grace – and because of a woman! – was a sore point with Joyce's father whose every drink mourned the ivy leaf, Parnell's symbol. At University, books, literature, theology and the destiny of man prevailed. In Trieste and Zurich and Paris there were long, long hours of café conversation: the slim figure with the thick, disconcerting spectacles drank coffee when his wife was there, absinthe and anything when she was not. Since alcohol affected, aggravated, his appalling eye

JAMESON
GOLD LABEL

AN CHUIRT

troubles – over a dozen operations – she looked unkindly on any visitor who might tempt him. And testimony exists to the rowdiness of her welcome if he came home intoxicated. Mr. Bloom is offered a drink: "he wouldn't and couldn't and excuse him no offence and all to that and then he said well he'd just take a cigar. Gob, he's a prudent member and no mistake."

Arthur Griffith, founder of Sinn Fein, editor of the *United Irishman,* signatory of the 1921 Anglo-Irish Treaty was born on Little Britain Street.

In Green Street Courthouse they tried Young Irelanders, Fenians, I.R.A., Invincibles, Robert Emmet, "the darling of Erin", the Sheares Brothers; patriotism in the dock. Joyce modelled the Citizen on Michael Cusack, the patriot who founded the Gaelic Athletic Association, Ireland's largest sporting body; Joyce had met the ineluctably patriotic Cusack, found him narrow-minded, was delighted to dislike him intensely.

> And the citizen and Bloom having an argument about the point, the brothers Sheares and Wolfe Tone beyond on Arbour Hill and Robert Emmet and die for your country, the Tommy Moore touch about Sara Curran and she's far from the land. And Bloom, of course, with his knockmedown cigar putting on swank with his lardy face.

The Cyclops was blinded when a stake was stabbed in his one eye.

"So anyhow in came John Wyse Nolan and Lenehan with him with a face on him as long as a late breakfast. Well, says the citizen, what's the latest from the scene of the action?" "Throwaway", twenty to one, won the Gold Cup, much recrimination, regret.

Mr. Bloom's friends still haven't arrived, he goes in search.

A Dublin saying: if you value your repute, never leave a group of three or more. And sure enough:

> Isn't that a fact, says John Wyse, what I was telling the citizen about Bloom and the Sinn Fein?
> That's so, says Martin. Or so they allege.
> Who made those allegations? says Alf.
> I, says Joe. I'm the alligator.
> And after all, says John Wyse, why can't a jew love his country like the next fellow?

Mr. Bloom has offered Arthur Griffith some neutral political advice – but much more serious is the idea that he may have made money on "Throwaway" and gone to collect it. They believe it may even be five pounds, that Bloom won't tell them lest he has to buy a drink. "Do you know what I'm telling you? It'd be an act of God to take hold of a fellow the like of that and throw him in the bloody sea. Justifiable homicide, so it would. Then sloping off with his five quid without putting up a pint of stuff like a man."

The citizen represents all that Joyce hated about his fellow man. He is a characterless scrounger, good for nothing except drink and calumny, without a good word to say for anybody alive, capable only of looking for and seeing the worst in everybody, suspicious, narrow-minded and dogmatic,

thriving on the mishaps of others and all too willing to recount them – a loud-mouthed, opinionated, unfair, unsporting, bigoted, cant-carrying, know-all. When Joyce's own enemies drew their own portrait of the artist, he seemed not unlike the citizen.

Martin Cunningham smells trouble. The citizen has the courage of drink and rage on him. Mr. Bloom is eased out to the jauntingcar that will take them to Dignam's widow in Sandymount. The citizen rushes out. There is a ferocious verbal altercation, with the citizen hurling abuse at Mr. Bloom, mainly aimed at his Jewishness. Mr. Bloom as usual tries to reason the point: "Your God was a jew. Christ was a jew like me. Gob, the citizen

made a plunge back into the shop. By Jesus, says he, I'll brain that bloody jewman for using the holy name. By Jesus, I'll crucify him, so I will", and he hurls a biscuit tin after the departing jauntingcar, while the citizen's dog, Garryowen, pursues ineffectually.

> The catastrophe was terrific and instantaneous in its effect. The observatory of Dunsink registered in all eleven shocks, all of the fifth grade of Mercalli's scale, and there is no record extant of a similar seismic disturbance in our island since the earthquake of 1534, the year of the rebellion of Silken Thomas.

In "Cyclops", Ireland is a land where shining palaces rise with crystal glittering roofs: "The figure seated on a large boulder at the foot of a round tower was that of a broadshouldered deepchested stronglimbed frankeyed redhaired freely freckled shaggybearded widemouthed largenosed longheaded deepvoiced barekneed brawnyhanded hairylegged ruddyfaced sinewyarmed hero." At a mythical hanging, to lampoon friend Rumbold further, "a word of praise is due to the Little Sisters of the Poor for their excellent idea of affording the good fatherless and motherless children a genuinely instructive treat". The Catholic Church – against whom Joyce railed for ever – doesn't escape: ". . . S. Denis and S. Cornelius and S. Leopold and S. Bernard and S. Terence and S. Edward and S. Owen Caniculus and S. Anonymous and S. Eponymous and S. Pseudonymous and S. Homonymous and S. Paronymous and S. Synonymous . . ."

Joyce said once, not without sadness, to Nora: "The pity is the public will demand and find a moral in my book, or worse, they may take it in some serious way, and on the honour of a gentleman, there is not one serious single line in it."

NAUSICAA

The sun set on Bloomsday at twenty-seven minutes past eight and its undertaking shadows wrapped the rocks of Sandymount Strand in deep purple thought.

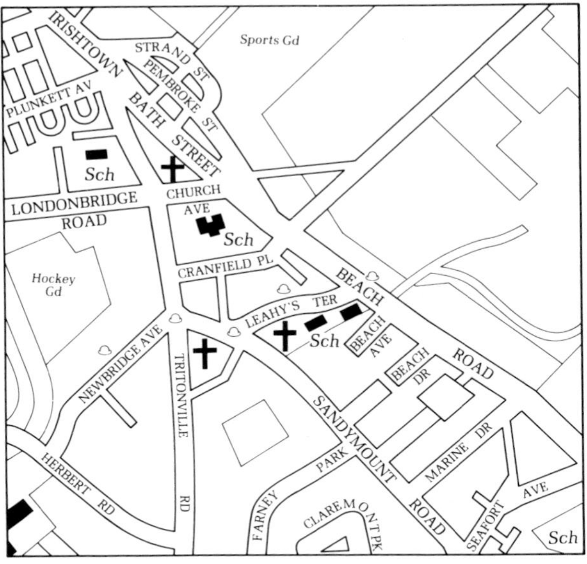

Sandymount was a resort then, where men bathed naked and old women sold crabs and cockles from hand-held, homeweave baskets to the strollers. It was broad and bright and within sufficiently easy reach of Dublin for the men of heart and quality to maintain mistresses there. In the distance Howth Head lay, snout to the waves like a farrowing sow. Carriages and horsemen clopped by; at that hour of the evening the last businessmen were coming home to Blackrock and Kingstown. Nearby the noise of a train perhaps, sparks lighting the fireman's face?

Mr. Bloom saw, at that gathering hour, three girls sitting on the rocks, caring the while for curlyheaded four-year-old twin boys and a baby in a pushchair. Mr. Bloom has just completed his errand of mercy to Mrs. Dignam at Newbridge Avenue nearby; poor Dignam's policy is to be straightened out and paid over. Then, as Stephen did at noon, he walked on to Sandymount Strand via Leahy's Terrace.

On Sandymount Strand now, the twin red-and-white towers of the Pigeon House are studded with red flashing lights to warn aircraft. Cars bound by, both ways; the lights of the bay form a horseshoe to Howth. The summer evening is calm upon the lovers walking the sands, the last sunlight shafts the terraces and churches along the shore to Seapoint, to the smoke-plumed mailboat at Dun Laoire and inevitably to the round shadow of the Martello Tower in Sandycove.

Leopold Bloom comes to Sandymount to gather himself, to take away the pain of the day. His watch, he finds, stopped at half past four – the moment of conjunction between Molly and Boylan? "Was that just when he, she?"

In the holy time breathless with adoration litanies are said in a nearby church. Cissy Caffrey and Edy Boardman are looking after Tommy and Jacky Caffrey and Baby Boardman and Gerty MacDowell is looking on, gently aloof.

> Her figure was slight and graceful, inclining even to fragility but those iron jelloids she had been taking of

late had done her a world of good much better than the Widow Welch's female pills and she was much better of those discharges she used to get and that tired feeling. The waxen pallor of her face was almost spiritual in its ivorylike purity though her rosebud mouth was a genuine Cupid's bow, Greekly perfect. Her hands were of finely veined alabaster with tapering fingers and as white as lemon juice and queen of ointments could make them thought it was not true that she used to wear kid gloves in bed or take a milk footbath either. Bertha Supple told that once to Edy Boardman, a deliberate lie, when she was black out at daggers drawn with Gerty . . .

The slight action of "Nausicaa" is overwhelming on several levels. In the nearby church, the organ pealed during the men's temperance retreat while "still the voices rang in supplication to the Virgin most powerful, Virgin most merciful".

Gerty MacDowell dreams of love and a boy she knows. Leaning back upon the rocks, half-consciously she allows Mr. Bloom see her underwear:

> four dinky sets, with awfully pretty stitchery, three garments and nighties extra, and each set slotted with different coloured ribbons, rosepink, pale blue, mauve and peagreen and she aired them herself and blued them when they came home from the wash and ironed them and she had a brickbat to keep the iron on because she wouldn't trust those washerwomen as far as she'd see them scorching the things.

As Mr. Bloom sees her thighs, the fireworks display at the bazaar, opened earlier by the viceroy, burst a Roman candle in the sky "and it was like a sigh of O! and everyone cried O! O! in raptures and it gushed out of it a stream of rain gold hair threads and they shed and ah!" Mr. Bloom, excited, has become his own Roman candle; and now he "stands silent, with bowed head before those young guileless eyes. What a brute he had been! At it again?" Gerty MacDowell, by some sweet telepathy, suspects what it is Mr. Bloom has been at and never having spoken, or moved closer than some yards, she walks sadly away giving him "a sweet forgiving smile, a smile that verged on tears, and then they parted". Mr. Bloom notices that she is lame, thinks she is pre-menstrual and wonders about women in general and, it has to be said, in particular too. In the church the devotions have ended.

One day, late in 1918 – he lived in Zurich then and was almost thirty-seven-years-old – James Joyce walked home to his flat behind a dark-haired, dark-eyed young woman who had a slight limp. He was electrified. He watched her go into her house and discovered she lived around the corner from him. Her name was Martha Fleischmann, she was Swiss, conceited, and kept by an engineer. Joyce prevailed upon her, wrote to her, watched her from his own windows, was moved passionately by her and in his mind at least – for she was not so forthcoming – had a sizzling affair with her.

On his thirty-seventh birthday, the 2nd of February, 1919, she agreed to allow him call on her, which he did bearing a borrowed ceremonial candlestick, for it was Candlemas Day. What transpired in the glow? Neither said – but they did not meet again for some time. Their correspondence ended, too; Martha's jealous lover (who was, after all, paying the bills) found out.

Gerty MacDowell must have been based on Martha Fleischmann. Joyce began the "Nausicaa" episode a few months later – and wrote it in the flowery, simpering style common to the romantic magazines and novels which Martha read all day. Nora Barnacle never knew about the candlelight relationship and if in fact Joyce succeeded with Martha it is one of the very few, perhaps two, occasions in his life when he was unfaithful to Nora.

Curiously – bearing the mood of "Nausicaa" in mind – the organ of the body it represents is the eye. The nose is included too, but the eye dominates.

> And while she gazed her heart went pitapat. Yes, it was her he was looking at and there was meaning in his look. His eyes burned into her as though they would search her through and through, read her very soul. Wonderful eyes they were, superbly expressive, but could you trust them? She could see at once by his dark eyes and his pale intellectual face that he was a foreigner, the image of the photo she had of Martin Harvey, the matinée idol . . .

In all, the presence of Gerty MacDowell in "Nausicaa", up to the time she leaves the area of Mr. Bloom, generates over a hundred references to eyes, pictures, looking, glancing, seeing, viewing, eyeing.

Sandymount Strand is greatly changed since Bloomsday. The footpaths by the sands have been trimmed and gardened; an enormous rubbish dump has been levelled and grassed. Why did Mr. Bloom and Gerty MacDowell meet in the twilight of Sandymount Strand? Was it because of Joyce's concern with his ailing eyes? Or was he simply tempted by Homer's story of Nausicaa, who finds Ulysses lying exhausted, naked shipwrecked? Nausicaa, as sumptuously attractive as any of the immortal goddesses, is preparing for her wedding and goes to the beach with some handmaidens to wash her clothes and when she finds Ulysses lying there gives him a tunic, a cloak, some sweet oil in a golden flask and a new stature.

Certainly Mr. Bloom leaves Sandymount Strand in a different condition from the one in which he arrived there. His physical excesses brought on by watching Gerty have left him exhausted and drained, but her clear though unspoken romantic interest in him has restored him psychologically. He dozes.

Joyce described "Nausicaa" as written "in a namby-pamby jammy marmalady drawersy style with effects of incense, mariolatry, masturbations, stewed cockles, painter's palette, chit-chat, circumlocution, etc., etc."

He wrote back to Dublin, asking his aunt to send him novelettes. He asked too whether there were trees behind the Church in Sandymount, whether they would be visible from the shore, whether there were steps down from Leahy's Terrace and whether she could send him a penny hymnbook.

"Nausicaa" had *Ulysses* banned in the United States. When it was published in the *Little Review*, a civil servant responsible for protecting New York from Vice brought the publishers to court. Intellectual and artistic defences, the thoughts of Freud and Cubists, were produced to confound the allegations of obscenity. But finally it was Gerty MacDowell showing Mr. Bloom her drawers that lost the publishers' case. The two ladies were fined fifty dollars each, were disappointed not to have been jailed as martyrs to freedom. But the fact that the *Little Review* could no longer publish the emerging chapters of *Ulysses* encouraged Sylvia Beach, a young American in Paris, to offer to publish a book. Thus did Gerty MacDowell's drawers get *Ulysses* published in book form.

In Sandymount now the Strand has been foreshortened: you could never hear the hymns in the Star of the Sea church, nor, easily see fireworks over Ballsbridge. "A bat flew. Here. There. Here. Far in the grey a bell chimed. Mr. Bloom with open mouth, his left boot sanded sidways, leaned, breathed."

A clock chimes, a cuckoo clock, cuckoo
for Bloom, cuckoo for Boylan,
cuckoo for Molly, cuckoo, cuckoo . . .

OXEN OF THE SUN

Squared in regular bricks, the National Maternity Hospital stands at the bottom corner of Merrion Square, lit by the evening sun. Behind it, vaguely symbolic, stands a huge gasometer.

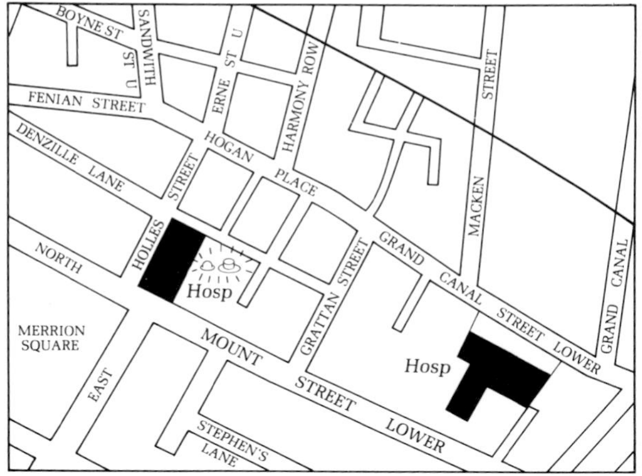

Holles Street Hospital lies along Merion Square, bridging into Lower Mount Street cornering into Holles Street. Merrion Square, on the 16th of June, 1904, was a place of quiet grandeur. It was once a beach, washed by a tide from Ringsend. As a square it was laid out in 1762, elegant and controlled by the Wide Streets Commission. Merrion Square's development spanned the turn of the eighteenth century: it became a place of residence for the gentry and members of the professions.

Their houses were substantial: several, if not all, had mews at the end of the garden for the servants, and these quarters were connected to the main residence by a tunnel or enclosed corridor, mustn't let them blot the landscape. It was a closed, extremely snobbish enclave. People of class and society lived in this encrusted enclave. Dublin was enjoying the beginnings of its great era of medicine, and the physicians who lived in Merrion Square were redoubtable figures, their ladies venturing forth only to visit by carriage or to take the air in the railed enclosure which formed the middle of the square, a locked sward opened only by residents' keys.

The Wildes, Sir William and Speranza, lived at Number One on the same side as the Maternity Hospital. Sheridan Le Fanu drank green tea and wrote his eerie tales at Number Sixty, Merrion Square. In 1904 it was still posh, only slightly bruised by the poverty in the adjacent tenements. It had managed to remain aloft from the squalid city, stayed and secured by its affluence. Once when rebels erupted in a southern county, old men in Merrion Square formed a militia and patrolled their properties in sedan chairs, muskets angled through the curtained windows.

Today the doctors prefer nearby Fitzwilliam Square. The houses and mews of Merrion Square are divided over and over again. Offshoot government departments, dairy produce bodies, solicitors, barristers, controllers of the betting laws, consultant engineers, have purchased corners of corners in these old high houses. Sometimes the subdivision is so obvious: in an office the exquisite frieze will be abruptly bisected by a wooden partition. Ceilings never

complete their expanse. Hallways have suffered most: if you stand in a beautiful small antechamber to a huge hallway and as the shining mahogany and brassed door swings back – you are greeted by plywood and glass. A few brave people of taste have taken high apartments and have restored ceilings, panels, plasterwork. For their efforts – a residential bonus.

For generations, the centre of the square had been designated as a site for a Catholic cathedral. Successive Archbishops of Dublin had retained exclusive access – the square was closed, no constitutional walks could be taken without ecclesiastical permission. Now – *nihil obstat*: a new Archbishop elevated the square into a park, squared by embassies, by the National Gallery of Ireland, rich from Shaw, bequeathed by *My Fair Lady*, and by Government Buildings.

> Now let us speak of that fellowship that was there to the intent to be drunken an they might. There was a sort of scholars along either side the board, that is to wit, Dixon yclept junior of saint Mary Merciable's with other his fellows Lynch and Madden, scholars of medicine, and the franklin that hight Lenehan and one from Alba Longa, one Crotthers, and young Stephen that had mien of a frere that was at head of the board and Costello that men clepen Punch Costello all long of a mastery of him erstwhile gested (and all of them, reserved young Stephen, he was the most drunken that demanded still of more mead) and beside the meek Sir Leopold. But on young Malachi they waited for that he promised to have come and such as intended to no goodness said how he had broke his avow. And Sir Leopold sat with them for he bore fast friendship to Sir Simon and to this his son young Stephen and for that his langour becalmed him there after longest wanderings . . .

NATIONAL GALLERY OF IRELAND

"Oxen of the Sun" is the episode in which Mr. Bloom and Stephen meet. A bunch of medical students, Dixon, Lynch, Madden, the hanger-on Lenehan, a Scot called Crotthers, Stephen Dedalus and Punch Costello have been sitting in an anteroom of the maternity hospital waiting for Buck Mulligan to appear, when Mr. Bloom slips in and sits next to drunken Stephen. It is ten o'clock at night and Mr. Bloom enquires into the health of Mrs. Purefoy who is in labour and having a bad time.

Joyce took her name from that of the leading obstetrician of the day in Dublin, Dr. R. Damon Purefoy, and the Christian postnatal ritual of "churching" a woman is intended to purify after birth. The proprietor of the maternity hospital is Sir Andrew Horne: a bull forms a substantial topic of conversation but Joyce's joke is sexual rather than agricultural.

"Oxen of the Sun" is the most complex chapter in *Ulysses*. It took Joyce, by his own reckoning, a thousand hours to write. He designed it in nine segments – to correspond with pregnancy – and while he was working on it he kept before him an onion-shaped diagram to which he crayoned monthly the growth of the embryo. The episode is a literary parody of most of the major writers, Shakespeare excepted, from Mandeville, Swift, Sterne and Dickens, with a loud blast of slang, jargon and pidgin English at the end.

The students and their associates are sitting around discussing birth, sex and women in an extremely coarse fashion. They range over contraception, bestial sexual activity, congress and conquests, and the old dilemma of whom do you save, mother or child, in a difficult birth? Reasoned, quiet Mr. Bloom attempts to defuse: "laying hand to jaw, he said dissembling, as his wont was, that as it was informed him, who had ever loved the art of physic as might a layman, and agreeing also with his experience of so seldom seen an accident". The argument rises until: "Nurse Quigley from the door angerly bid them hist ye should shame you"; as the students are ordered to lower their voices a thunderstorm broke out and electrified Stephen: "and he that had erst challenged to be so doughty waxed pale". Joyce was terrified of lightning.

Lenehan refers to Mr. Deasy's letter about foot-and-mouth disease and cattle. Stephen has arranged publication in the evening paper.

The bull is proffered as a symbol of all that is dominant, male and mythological. "Our worthy acquaintance, Mr. Malachi Mulligan", now appeared in the doorway, accompanied with a friend, Alec Bannon, who has been attempting his luck with Mr. Bloom's daughter Milly in Mullingar. Mulligan amuses everyone vastly and bawdily.

Miss Callan, a nursing sister, arrives to tell Dixon he is required in the ward; Mina Purefoy, to great relief, has given birth to a bouncing boy, her ninth. After more bawdry, melancholy from Mr. Bloom, a sudden appearance by Haines the Englishman, more pouring from bottles, they all leave to drink in a nearby pub called Burke's. J. Burke, publican, licensed his premises at 17, Holles Street. No more, no more, the medicals to-day drink at more suitably-named Ulyssean places.

Even though George Bernard Shaw never finished reading Ulysses he was particularly struck by "Oxen of the Sun". He believed it conveyed such an accurate picture of the foul-mouthed young Dublin rakes, the notorious "medicals", that he wanted to form clubs of them for the sole purpose of making them read *Ulysses*, dare they continue to live, he opined, without reforming profoundly and extensively.

Joyce found the episode the most difficult part of the novel. Ulysses' appeal to his fellow travellers not to destroy the legendary cattle of the sun was a parallel along which Joyce could, he felt, outline the medical students' disrespect for fertility for the women labouring upstairs. Ulysses alone took no part in the slaughter of the oxen, Bloom never contributed to the coarse student exchanges. Ulysses groaned aloud when he came upon the wanton slaughter: Bloom wished inwardly that the young men didn't drink quite so heavily and showed more respect for their patients.

While he was constructing it, Joyce told a friend that he wanted the chapter to convey a crime against fecundity; the students discuss the valuable fruitlessness of contraception. The organ he wished to represent is the womb, medicine the chosen art, white the colour and embryonic

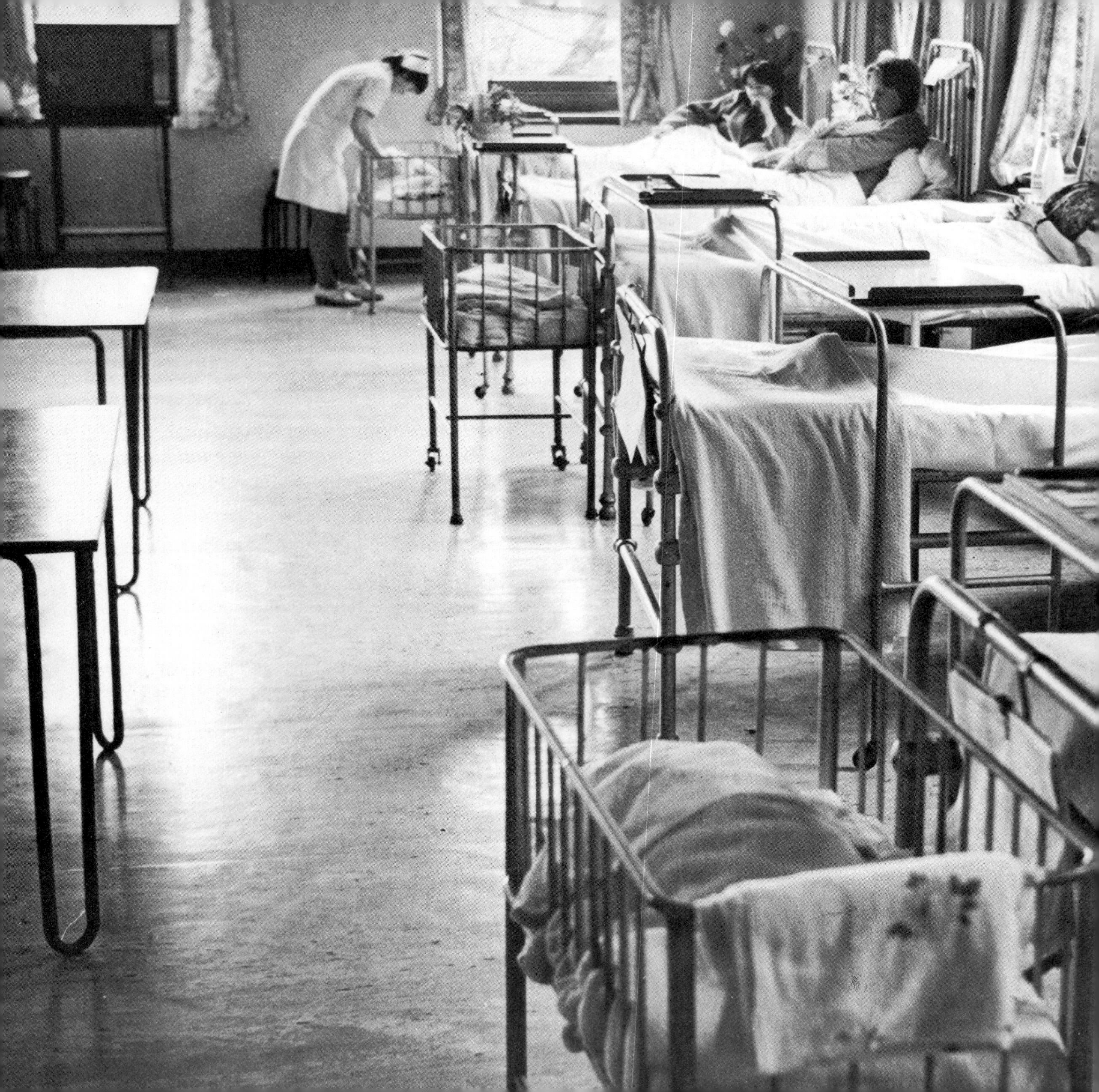

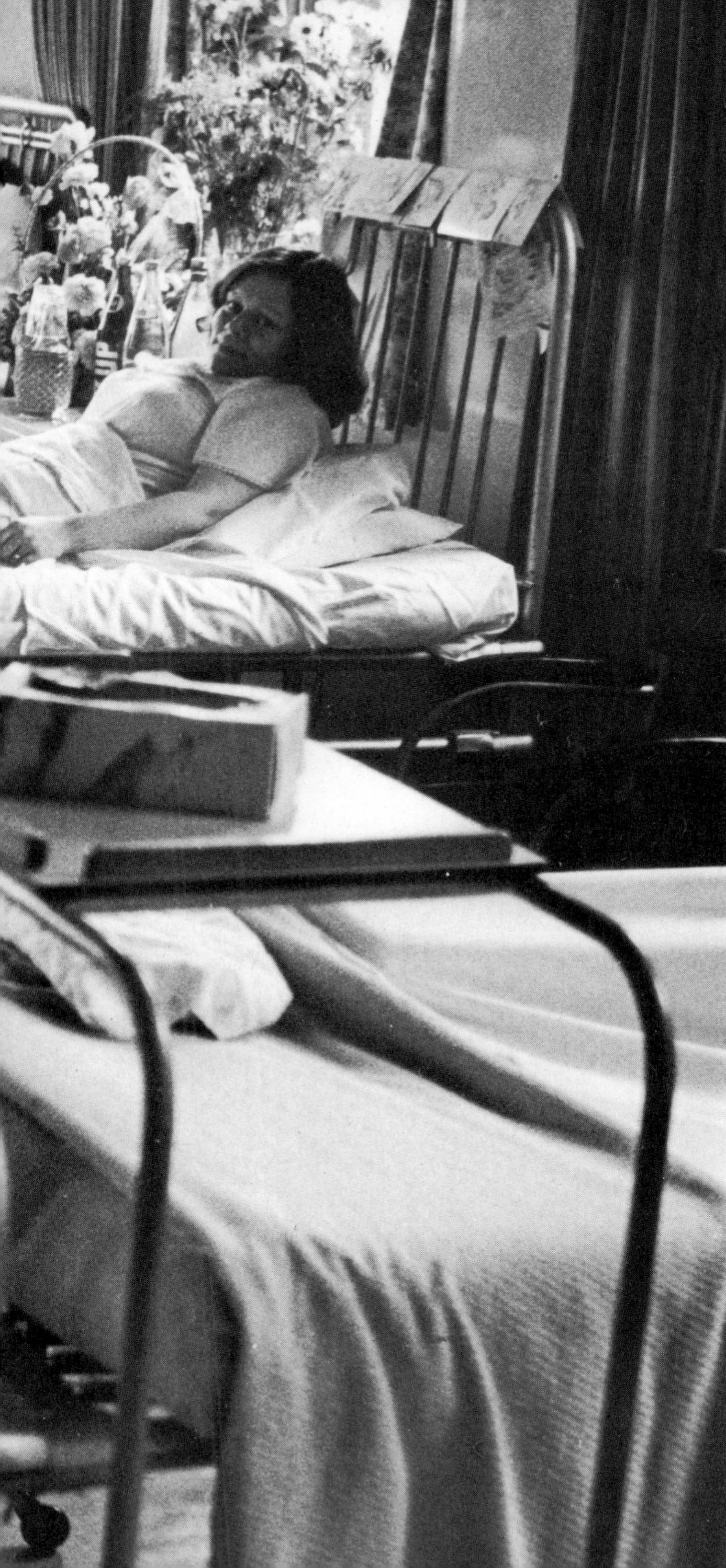

development the technique. He became so involved with the Homeric theme that he felt he himself had eaten oxen, and for months he couldn't sit down to a meal without feeling nauseous.

First he tickled her, then he patted her
Then he passed the female catheter

Dr. Oliver St. John Gogarty, the Buck Mulligan, epitomised the rakish medical student about Dublin. When a colleague who had made a fortune through his renowned surgery lost it all in the divorce that followed a sexual indiscretion, Gogarty described him as "the only man I ever knew who made a fortune with his knife and lost it with his fork". The National Maternity Hospital is no longer the noisome unhygienic building of Bloomsday. And it is involved in an activity which would have appealed to Joyce's symbolic mind. Umbilical cords are gathered, adjusted and converted into bypass transplants for varicose veins.

"The Oxen of the Sun" episode is the most difficult to read in *Ulysses* All Joyce's linguistic interests are on exhibition and he gives a foretaste of what was to come in *Finnegans Wake*. That it exhausted him is certain: in several communications with friends he referred to "the Oxen of the bloody, bleeding Sun" and he admitted freely that the control of all the ideas, the mathematical nine-part divisions, the embryonic developments and the endless parodies were almost as much as he could master. He managed brilliantly.

Pubwards, Mr. Bloom leaves the hospital where Mina Purefoy is relaxing in the hands of "Doctor Diet and Doctor Quiet". After closing time Mr. Bloom and Stephen Dedalus "will seek the kips where shady Mari is. Righto, any old time".

CIRCE

Nighttown that crawling, hag-haunted, gaseous sump, is now derelict. This was the red-light district of gaslit, foggy streets where sin, wild laughter and nightmares were private property.

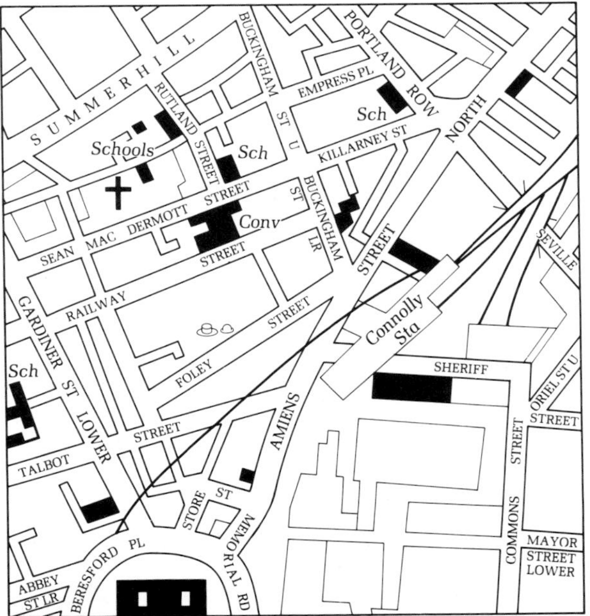

Montgomery Street, "Monto", was Nighttown. So was Corporation Street, Railway Street and Foley Street, all radiating off Talbot Street. Officers, gentlemen and soldiers spent many thirds of their lives there in circumstances as unhygienic as they were bawdy. Montgomery Street, it was agreed, was then the worst slum in Western Europe. In the area between Monto and O'Connell Street two thousand prostitutes urged trade.

The heyday of Nighttown began in the middle of the nineteenth century when a fashionable group of streets gave way to two regiments and their retinue. Nighttown gained Dublin a reputation for unlimited bawdry.

The women flocked to do business in the creaking streets, "those crowds of young girls who take possession of the city when darkness comes and whose demeanour by no means suggests the modesty and decorum we are wont to regard as inseparable from the Irish maiden", was how an eminent Jesuit of the day worried about them.

Some of the women passed into immediate legend. There was Becky Cooper who loved her work so much that she plied enjoyable young men with gifts – and with economic gestures:

Italy's maids are fair to see
And France's maids are willing
But less expensive 'tis to me:
Becky's for a shilling.

Julia Hooligan, engrossed in conversation with a friend in Grafton Street one day, was unwittingly barring the path of a well-known lawyer. "Out of my way, woman," he throated. "And who do you think you are?" Julia nipped back. "Madam – I am the most famous Crown solicitor from here to Balbriggan." "That's nuthin'," chuckled the undaunted Julia. "I'm the most famous *half*-crown solicitor from here to Belfast." Another, Mrs Mack, is alleged to have been visited by the Prince of Wales.

The Prince of Wales lost more than virtue in Dublin. As King Edward the Seventh he later came to the city for an investiture, but the insignia of the Knights of the Order of

JOEY
RF

Saint Patrick were mysteriously stolen from Dublin Castle days before and consequently no investiture even occurred.

O, there goes Mrs. Mack;
She keeps a house of imprudence,
She keeps an old back parlour
For us poxy medical students.

Mrs. Mack's bedroom had a large washstand containing two jugs in bright yellow basins, a large bed hammocked with age, a sewing-machine, spools of silk, slippers, cigarettes, greasy curl-papers, empty cigarette tins, and on the mantelpiece mottled with cigarette burns were several rancid tumblers and a photograph of a smart trapful of girls. Mrs. Mack's face – Gogarty's description – was brick red "on which avarice was written like a hieroglyphic, and a laugh like a guffaw in hell". Mrs. Mack's parlour was inhabited by a pianist who sat with his face turned to the wall in front of a cottage piano on which stood a half-empty measure of stout.

Florry Talbot's father was asked by the priests why he wouldn't do something about his daughter's disgraceful way of life. "Well," he said thoughtfully and agreeably, "the girl appears to be enjoying herself and besides, well – she's a source of income to me."

Piano Mary dwelt:

Where Hell's gates leave the street,
And all the tunes she used to play
Along your spine beneath the sheet?
She was a morsel passing sweet
And warmer than the gates of Hell.

There was May Oblong and fresh Nellie and Lady Betty and Mrs. Lawless. Some had their own houses full of religious pictures behind which they hid coshes of lead piping in case of trouble. Some worked the Hay Hotel; the windowsills and lower windows were packed with hay to comfort the waiting horses of the visiting gentlemen.

Some became immortal through literature, like the lady at Number Eighty-Two, Railway Street, then Mecklenburgh Street. Here lived Bella Cohen the Circe who lured Mr. Bloom. Her chandelier was covered with mauve tissue paper, an oilcloth on the floor had patterns and colours in mosaics of jade and azure and cinnabar rhomboids. The walls were hung with paper of yew fronds and clear glades and a screen of peacock feathers filled the grate while Bella Cohen sang endlessly.

(The Mabbot Street entrance of Nighttown, before which stretches an uncobbled tramsiding set with skeleton tracks, red and green will-o'-the-wisps and danger signals. Rows of flimsy houses with gaping doors. Rare lamps with faint rainbow fans. Round Rabaiotti's halted ice gondola stunted men and women squabble. They grab wafers between which are wedged lumps of coal and copper snow. Sucking, they scatter slowly. Children. The swancomb of the gondola, highreared, forges on through the murk, white and blue under a lighthouse. Whistles call and answer.)

THE CALLS : Wait, my love, and I'll be with you.

THE ANSWERS : Round behind the stable.

Mr. Bloom leaves the pub loses his way, jumps into a first class carriage by mistake, goes a station too far. He is concerned about the very drunken Stephen, realises that the students are bound for the brothels.

"Circe" is fantasy merging slowly and cruelly into fact. The longest chapter in the entire novel, it is a psychedelic hallucination, fantastic nightmare, written as dramatic performance with actions,

characterisations and descriptions embodied in the "stage directions" – reactions, imaginations and subconscious fears in the verbal exchanges. All sorts of echoes ring out – for Macbeth's three witches Joyce has Kitty, Zoe and Florry; Gerty MacDowell, Cissy Caffrey and Edy Boardman appear bawdily transmuted from the sweet-smelling moments on Sandymount Strand; Paddy Dignam returns from the grave: "Half of one ear, all the nose and thumbs are ghouleaten." Mrs. Breen, J. J. O'Molloy. Tom Rochford, Bob Doran, Myles Crawford, several of the minor characters from previous chapters reappear – and a few others, Edward VII, Shakespeare and Alfred Lord Tennyson; Philip Drunk and Philip Sober, two Oxford dons – they are Siamese twins with lawnmowers.

Mr. Bloom undergoes a mock trial for interfering with Mary Driscoll, a housemaid: his ancestors offer advice, his wife abuse, and finally he succumbs to the longed-for violence of Bella Cohen.

> (*The door opens. Bella Cohen, a massive whoremistress enters. She is dressed in a three-quarter ivory gown, fringed round the hem with tasselled selvedge, and cools herself, flirting a black horn fan like Minni Hauck in* Carmen. *On her left hand are wedding and keeper rings. Her eyes are deeply carboned. She has a sprouting moustache. Her olive face is heavy, slightly sweated and fullnosed, with orange-tainted nostrils. She has large pendant beryl eardrops*).
> BELLA : My word! I'm all of a mucksweat.
> (*She glances around her at the couples. Then her eyes rest on Bloom with hard insistence. Her large fan winnows wind towards her heated face, neck and embonpoint. Her falcon eyes glitter.*)
> THE FAN : (*flirting quickly, then slowly*) Married, I see.

And from then on Mr. Bloom gets who-began-it, vile abuse, to his great delight, even being obliged to lace Bella's boot.

The fan is not the only inanimate object with a speaking part. Yew trees, Sleepy Hollow, Halcyon Days, an Echo, a Dummy, a Waterfall, a Pianola, a Gasjet, a Horse, a Retriever, Brass Quoits, and assorted nymphs, hobgoblins and bracelets clamour and clang in a long, mad, luminous, swirling saraband of images that fog and fill your mind and drag you along in a crazy punk rag-doll, dervish, dance.

> *(Gazelles are leaping, feeding on the mountains. Near are lakes. Round their shores file shadows black of cedargroves. Aroma rises, a strong hairgrowth of resin. It burns, the orient, a sky of sapphire, cleft by the bronze flight of eagles. Under it lies the womancity, nude, white, still, cool, in luxury. A fountain murmurs among damask roses. Mammoth roses murmur of scarlet winegrapes. A wine of shame, lust, blood exudes, strangely murmuring.)*

> There is a young fellow named Joyce
> Who possesses a sweet tenor voice.
> He goes down to the kips,
> With a psalm on his lips,
> And biddeth the harlots rejoice.
> Oliver St. J. Gogarty

Joyce's first sexual experience was with a prostitute on a canal bank when he was fourteen. Subsequently in Nighttown and in Paris he paid them frequent visits and got, as well as such sexual gratification as he sought, the Irish thrill of religious guilt. At the time of that first vivid canalbank moment he was an active member of the sodality of the Blessed Virgin Mary in School: thereafter all

carnal knowledge was tinged with guilt and shame in some way. When his relationship with Nora filled out, his wanderings largely ceased. He did record to friends his encounter with Martha Fleischmann, the lame girl who was the prototype for Gerty MacDowell. After his "sojourn" with Martha on the night of his thirty-seventh birthday, Candlemas Day, the 2nd of February, 1919, he told a friend that he had "explored the hottest and coldest parts of a woman's body".

The bulk of the action in "Circe" takes place, appropriately, around midnight. Stephen shows up, is knocked down brutally in a confrontation between two foul-mouthed soldiers to whom Joyce gave the names of two British civil servants he had argued with in Zurich. The widening circles which Mr. Bloom and Stephen have described about each other all day, around the book-barrows, around the National Library, along Sandymount Strand, close inwards when Mr. Bloom takes charge of Stephen who is too bruised, too shocked and too drunk to take care of himself. Endless references in "Circe" to the Mass, Stephen a sacrificial victim, a Christ figure, blood and wine, all set Ireland's teeth on edge against Joyce.

The motor parts of the body, the endless need to move, were the physiological parallels. Magic glitters, religious, literary, scientific, artistic, linguistic, topographical, social, political magic. When he had written "Circe" and re-written it up to nine times, Joyce allowed himself a rare compliment by asserting his belief that it was perhaps "the best thing he had ever done".

May Oblong's gone and Mrs. Mack,
Fresh Nellie's gone and Number Five
Where you could get so good a back
And drinks were so superlative.
Of all their nights, oh man alive!
There is not left an oyster shell
Where greens are gone the grays will thrive;
There's only left the Hay Hotel.

The Gogarty lament became redundant in 1925 when a preaching priest dared suggest that such

ERRUM TRADING

an unsavoury place existed in Dublin. And on the 12th of March, in the middle of Lent, Catholic vigilantes, supported by the police, went in like an army. That well-known Irish disease, "Scuffles", broke out; whores were arrested, so were citizens and visitors, including a member of the Irish Parliament who protested until he was red in the face (which he was anyway) that he was only in there for a drink. The Legion of Mary, a white army which still marches under the banner of the Mother of God, was the conqueror: when the back-up force of Legion ladies rosaried through the area within days the saddened, remaining, redundant whores knelt in the streets, and watched the silent, compassionate, benign conquerors pin holy pictures on the brothel doors.

No such area as Nighttown exists in Dublin now. Prostitution is no longer a "problem". When Gogarty became a senator the trees on the canal bank, under which the descendants of fresh Nellie, Mrs. Mack, and Piano Mary entertained their clients, were threatened by zealous politicians. Gogarty pleaded for the trees, argued that they were "more sinned against than sinning". As Mr. Bloom leaves Nighttown, he has a vision.

> *(Against the dark wall a figure appears slowly, a fairy boy of eleven, a changeling, kidnapped, dressed in an Eton suit with glass shoes and a little bronze helmet, holding a book in his hand. He reads from right to left inaudibly, smiling, kissing the page.)*
>
> BLOOM: *(Wonderstruck, calls inaudibly)* Rudy!

If his baby son Rudy had lived he would be eleven. Bloom, in fact, with Stephen, and in fantasy with Rudy, has found his son. His odyssey is coming to a long, slow, thoughtful, curling conclusion.

EUMAEUS

The sadness, the dark, in Dublin late at night is swingeing. People who do not want to go home, who will not go home, who have not got a home, lurch and stagger in the gloom, moths without a candle.

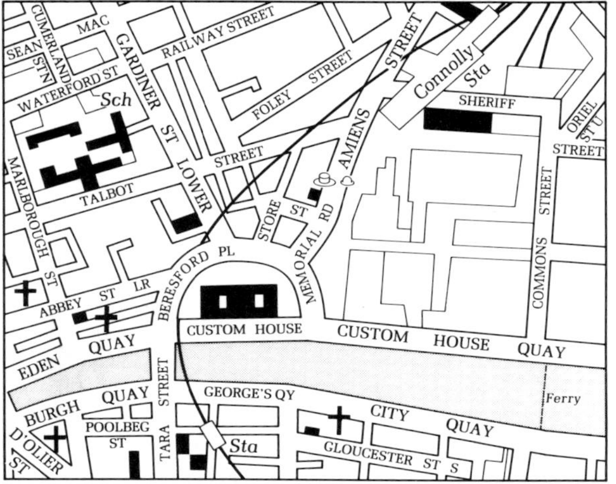

When Mr. Bloom left Nighttown, Stephen Dedalus in tow, he turned into Amiens Street, sought a cab – in vain – and steered a course for Butt Bridge. Ahead, the Custom House; to the left of Mr. Bloom, then as now, the Italianate pile of Amiens Street railway station from which you may bear north through Balbriggan and Drogheda and Dundalk to Belfast, an old, historic journey. Here, in easier times, the Thursday shopping excursions departed for Belfast: here returned the Contraceptive Express, a train of women testing the laws which forbade the sale of, the use of. A canvassed government whig, stoutly, Catholicly, insisted against contraceptives. "But I wouldn't mind using a French letter."

"Preparatory to anything else Mr. Bloom brushed off the greater bulk of the shavings and handed Stephen the hat and ashplant and bucked him up generally in orthodox Samaritan fashion, which he very badly needed." Stephen has had an altercation with a couple of private soldiers at the entrance to Nighttown and is none the better for it. He is dusted down by Mr. Bloom, as James Joyce was once dusted down by that Jewish good Samaritan, Alfred Hunter.

Stephen has a drink in mind and Mr. Bloom imagined the possibilities of perhaps a glass of milk or a mineral or even some pure water from the River Vartry, reservoired into Dublin. The cabman's shelter at Butt Bridge will provide the necessary facilities. Getting there – Stephen is intoxicated and Mr. Bloom is tired – makes walking a weary hazard.

It is after midnight.

> They passed the main entrance of the Great Northern Railway Station, the starting point for Belfast, where of course all traffic was suspended at that late hour, and, passing the back door of the morgue (a not very enticing locality, not to say gruesome to a degree, more especially at night), ultimately gained the Dock Tavern and in due course turned into Store Street, famous for its C division police station.

Today, Store Street is still a busy police station. A building has been added, Bus Áras, the house of the omnibus: from here towns are connected to Dublin like a childrens' puzzle which joins the numbered dots. This clanging building was unwrapped in 1953, the first postwar attempt at modern Irish architecture, a gallant try. Slowly, with tired certainty, "they made a beeline across the back of the Customhouse and passed under the Loop Line bridge when a brazier of coke burning in front of a sentrybox, or something like one, attracted their rather lagging footsteps".

Somniferously, James Joyce is winding down his long odyssey. Stephen and Mr. Bloom have met. Telemachus has met his father Ulysses, the young man has met the older Everyman, youth and maturity are in each other's arms.

Mr. Bloom is concerned about Stephen, even advises him that going down to the kips, to be Gogartian about it, was not a good idea,

> spoke a word of caution *re* the dangers of Nighttown, women of ill fame and swell mobsmen, which, barely permissible once in a while, though not as a habitual practice, was of the nature of a regular deathtrap for young fellows of his age particularly if they had acquired drinking habits under the influence of liquor unless you knew a little jujitsu for every contingency as even a fellow on the broad of his back could administer a nasty kick if you didn't look out.

Mr. Bloom, tired man, is beginning to drone a little; young Dedalus, on home-made wings, is flying above, a little ahead, far enough away for earshot to be unimportant. Joyce controlled most of his male relationships in such a fashion. He was the acceptor, rarely the initiator. Only where there was blood relationship did he show his colours.

The three significant male relatives were his father John, his brother Stanislaus, his son Giorgio. His father died in Dublin in 1931 at the age of eighty-two, Stanislaus died in Trieste on the 16th of June, 1955, at the age of seventy-one, Giorgio was born in July 1905. Joyce and Nora had one other child, Lucia. Since 1945 she has lived in England, cared for in a hospice in Northampton, the survivor.

The relationship between John Joyce and his son was loving, lifelong, despite their separation. As a child Joyce was delighted in, encouraged, admired by his father, who took him on business trips – usually to patch a hole in some sinking argosy. He was shrewd enough to know that his son's mind had possibilities, vain enough to boast about him. When *Ulysses* was published in Dublin and the city was reeling under its scatology and its fingerprinting of Dubliners John Joyce, who did not pretend to read or understand it, accepted mystification, smiled at the effects his genius son was having on Dublin: Jim was "a nice sort of blackguard".

The relationship with Stanislaus was a different matter altogether. He was two years and ten months younger than James, he was the third child in the family. His earlier literary ambitions were doomed to shadow. Stanislaus was the more responsible, had a quieter air, a more serious visage. He followed to Trieste, where his role lay halfway between butler and lord chamberlain. He came to the domestic rescue on several occasions, dealt with debt collectors, consoled Nora when times were hard, was often a protesting provider.

He took it upon himself to be his brother's literary critic, unwelcomed by James. He greatly admired *Ulysses*, condemned one or two chapters. For *Finnegans Wake* he employed words like "drivelling rigmarole" and "witless wandering" – James' brain was finally softening. His diary's earlier perceptions of his older brother are revealing.

> He has extraordinary moral courage – courage so great that I have hoped he will one day become the Rousseau of Ireland . . . His manner is generally very engaging and courteous with strangers, but, though he greatly dislikes to be rude, I think there is little courtesy in his nature . . . As he sits on the hearthrug, his arms embracing his knees, his head thrown a little back, his hair brushed up straight off his forehead, his long face red as an Indian's in the reflexion of the fire, there is a look of cruelty on his face . . . Jim is a genius of character . . . But few people will love him in spite of his graces and his genius and whosoever exchanges kindnesses with him is likely to get the worst of the bargain . . .

Stanislaus was always jealous of James' attentiveness to surrounding friends and acquaintances. From University days this jealousy persisted: he loathed Gogarty, for example, whom he described as like Punch, hooked nose and chin to match. Gogarty, ineffably true to form, had written a cruel poem about Stanislaus (Gogarty's nickname for Joyce was Kinch – the word "felt like a blade"):

Poet Kinch has a brother called Thug
His imitator, and jackal, and mug.
His stride like a lord's is
His pretension absurd is
In fact he's an *awful* thick-lug.

Stanislaus Joyce was a good, kind man who was never wanded with his brother's magic. But oh! How he wished to be!

Giorgio Joyce sang like an angel and swam like an athlete. He was tall and handsome like his father, brushed with some of his mother's good looks. He was agreeably fiery, wasn't easily pushed about by his father. Giorgio received the exaggerated affectionate courtesy which Joyce bestowed quietly upon his children.

"Stephen of his own accord stopped for no special reason to look at the heap of barren cobblestones and by the light emanating from the brazier he could just make out the darker figure of the corporation watchman inside the gloom of the sentrybox." Eumaeus, the swineherd, sits in a little hut and discourses in the direction of Ulysses, who is reunited with Telemachus in front of the hut. "Mr. Bloom in the meanwhile kept dodging about in the vicinity of the cobblestones near the brazier of coke in front of the corporation watchman's sentrybox, who, evidently a glutton for work, it struck him, was having a quiet forty winks for all intents and purposes on his own private account while Dublin slept." The "Eumaeus" episode of *Ulysses* represents the nervous system: Stephen is under the influence of drink, Mr. Bloom is under the influence of Stephen and wishes to see to him, feed and rest him. Excised from Mulligan and Haines where will Stephen stay? "I don't mean to presume to dictate to you in the slightest degree but why did you leave your father's house? To seek misfortune, was Stephen's answer". Both men lurch easily to the cabmen's shelter at Butt Bridge.

Night in Dublin makes the city dark and old and Victorian and Edwardian. Gaslight would not be too surprising: Dublin is a nightcity. Isolated forgotten tramps phantom the pavements, police patrol in cars or pairs. A few open cafés gather in the drifters, the jilted, the jetsam, as a pound rounds up strays.

"Mr. Bloom and Stephen entered the cabman's shelter, an unpretentious wooden structure, where, prior to then, he had rarely, if ever, been before"; and to where they have now come in

search of a night's collation. It has disappeared now, this anteroom to Purgatory, flotsammed with a "decidedly miscellaneous collection of waifs and strays and other nondescript specimens of the genus *homo*". Mr. Bloom and his new-found friend – who, by dint of his writing and musical abilities may yet assist Mr. Bloom's suddenly budding impresario ambitions – attempt sustenance. An able seaman, one W. B. Murphy, addresses them, tells tall stories. This sailor came up the river at eleven o'clock in the morning. He was on board that high ship Stephen saw, from Sandymount Strand "the threemaster *Rosevean* from Bridgwater with bricks". There is much conversation between the able seaman and the assembled company, which includes the notorious proprietor Skin-the-Goat, a man who has been involved in dark deeds. The sailor displays his chest tattoo, a face named Antonio, who may be made to smile by the manipulation of the flesh.

Mr. Bloom, however, displays a photograph of his wife:

> a large sized lady, with her fleshy charms on evidence in an open fashion, as she was in the full bloom of womanhood, in evening dress cut ostentatiously low for the occasion to give a liberal display of bosom, with more than vision of breasts, her full lips parted, and some perfect teeth, standing near, ostensibly with gravity, a piano . . .

O, it is late and Mr. Bloom is tired, his mind wanders. He picks up a newspaper which contains the report of poor Dignam's death, of the Throwaway victory in the Gold Cup. Coffee bad, conversation not much better: Joyce's style is deliberately tabloid. He draws Stephen away from the cabmen's shelter where the talk is of Parnell, the lost leader.

What has come together now? In the newspaper poor Dignam's funeral, the Gold Cup, the foot-and-mouth letter from Mr. Deasy, the threemaster *Rosevean* from Bridgwater. Mr. Joyce is drawing all the strings together, plucks the last notes from them. There is yet a reprise to come, Mr. Joyce will not let the orchestra go home without a last long note. At a friend's house in Switzerland late one night Joyce and Giorgio sang sweet sad songs for their host. He begged them to stay. Joyce, smiling, spoke a gracious "No". Mr. Bloom, too, must go home.

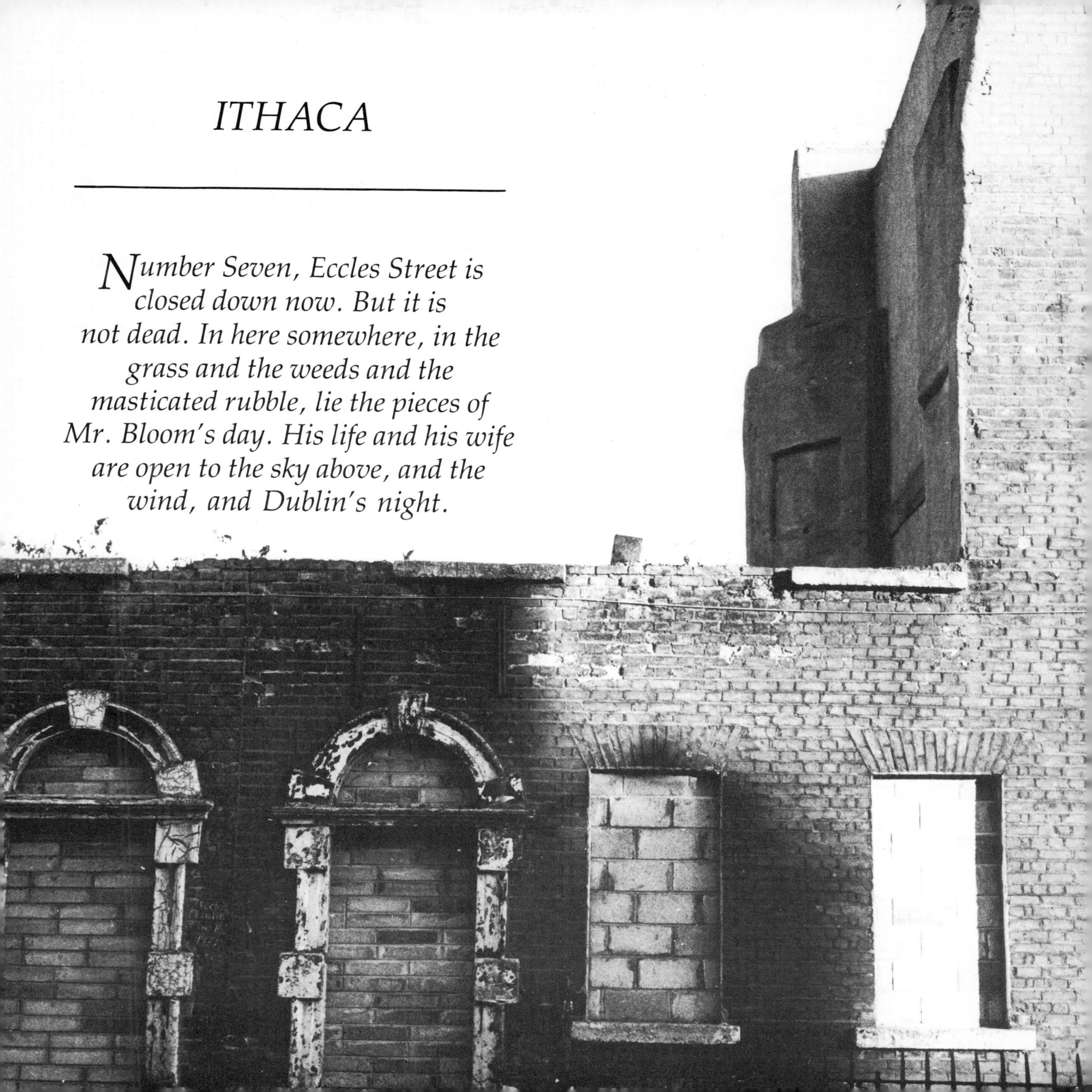

ITHACA

Number Seven, Eccles Street is closed down now. But it is not dead. In here somewhere, in the grass and the weeds and the masticated rubble, lie the pieces of Mr. Bloom's day. His life and his wife are open to the sky above, and the wind, and Dublin's night.

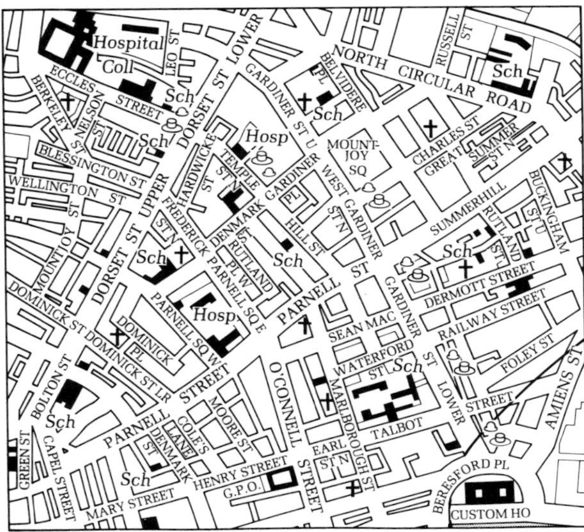

What parallel courses did Bloom and Stephen follow returning?

Starting united both at normal walking pace from Beresford Place they followed in the order named Lower and Middle Gardiner streets and Mountjoy square, west: then, at reduced pace, each bearing left, Gardiner's place by an inadvertence as far as the farther corner of Temple street, north: then at reduced pace with interruptions of halt, bearing right, Temple street, north, as far as Hardwicke place. Approaching, disparate, at relaxed walking pace they crossed both the circus before George's church diametrically, the chord in any circle being less than the arc which it subtends.

Mr. Bloom is home, the Wanderer has returned, Ulysses has come back to Ithaca bringing Telemachus, his son, with him. Murmuring, singing snatches of song, Mr. Bloom and Stephen Dedalus have wound a slow, friendly way home, meshed simply, loosely, inconsequentially in tiredness, inebriation, feeble thought. Music, medicine, the world at large, women – topics which come out at night. It is one o'clock in the morning of the 17th of June, 1904, it is still Bloomsday in lonely Dublin. Mr. Bloom has taken Stephen fully under his wing; kindness and respect for learning.

What action did Bloom make on their arrival at their destination?

At the housesteps of the 4th of the equidifferent uneven numbers, number 7 Eccles Street, he inserted his hand mechanically into the back pocket of his trousers to obtain his latchkey.

Joyce described the style of "Ithaca". the penultimate chapter in *Ulysses*, as the form of a mathematical catechism. Every passage either begins with a question or a statement.

"Was it there? It was in the corresponding pocket of the trousers which he had worn on the day but one preceding."

Mr. Bloom lowers himself into the basement area and drops gently into the space beside the door.

Did he fall?

By his body's known weight of eleven stone and four pounds in avoirdupois measure, as certified by the graduated machine for periodical selfweighing in the premises of Francis Froedman, pharmaceutical chemist of Nineteen, Frederick Street, North, on the last feast of the Ascension, to wit, the twelfth day of May of the bissextile year one thousand nine hundred and four of the christian era (jewish era five thousand six hundred and sixtyfour, mohammedan era one thousand three hundred and twentytwo), golden number five, epact thirteen, solar cycle nine, dominical letters C.B. Roman indication two, Julian period 6617, MXMIV.

Whew! And the entire chapter displays the same knowledge. Everything is grist to the Joycean mill. Mr. Bloom turns on a tap – there is a detailed account of the flowing water in the Roundwood reservoir to Number Seven, Eccles Street. Mr. Bloom's budget for the day occasions a detailed, furnished account of the kind of property an affluent Mr. Bloom would purchase.

"Ithaca" is James Joyce in the highest of high spirits. ". . . Wonderworker, the world's greatest remedy for rectal complaints direct from Wonderworker." Wonderworker is the suppository which apparently "assists nature in the most formidable way" both in men and in ladies who "find Wonderworker especially useful, a pleasant surprise when they note delightful result like a cool drink of fresh spring water on a sultry summer's day". Wonderworker has numerous testimonials, too

from clergyman, British naval officer, well-known author, city man, hospital nurse, lady, mother of five, absentminded beggar.

How did absentminded beggar's concluding testimonial conclude?

What a pity the government did not supply our men with wonderworkers during the South African campaign! What a relief it would have been!

Who, or what, or which manner of man was James A. Joyce? He was born on the 2nd of February, 1882 at Number Forty-One, Brighton Square West in Rathgar. Already his epiphenomena had begun: Brighton Square is not a square, but a triangle! He died in Zurich on the 13th of January, 1941 and is buried there. He was devoted, in his fashion, to his woman Nora Barnacle and his two children, Giorgio and Lucia. He was a remote man who had difficulty trusting anyone. His chief emotional appetite was a psychological one too: happily for him his birth and membership of the Irish race fed his paranoia. He worked harder than most writers in the world have ever done, noting down, making important the ordinary events of life, making what seems small important, what seems commonplace extraordinary.

He was a thin man, in personality and physique: once when his family were tired from want of food he lay back in desultory exultation and announced that he had retired from public life, such as it was. He borrowed clothes, money and food, for himself, his family and his lifestyle. When money was available he dressed like a dandy, lived like a lord in the best restaurants. He was patronised by wealthy women on whom he unfailingly turned. He never smiled without thinking about it first.

He quarrelled with people outside his domain – outside, that is, his inner world, and that included his family and his writings. His greeting to a fellow writer might as easily have been abusive – as when

he told James Stephens at their first meeting that he (Stephens) didn't know the difference between a colon and a semi-colon; a true Joycean will dart immediately to the cloacal pun which Joyce may or may not have intended and it is that "may or may not" which perennates his fascination. He had little patience with intellectual scroungers and scant respect, in the same vein, for those who built sheds instead of castles – even the effort was not worthy of his consideration. From the earliest adulthood he believed himself to be a genius and he worked hard at proving to himself and to the world that he was. He eschewed vociferously and cholerically the Catholic faith of his upbringing – yet his books are full of religious references, some not at all irreverent or blasphemous, his chief crime in Ireland. He was immensely cutting to people who frightened him – even more so to those who did not. He was impatient of commerce, failed at it several times; his essays into enterprise included an attempt to found the first cinema in Dublin (it folded), to import Irish Tweed into Trieste (it faded). He was a teacher, a tenant, a trial. "A man of small virtue, inclined to alcoholism," he told his doctor.

As an author, his biographer Richard Ellmann summarised him:

> Joyce is the porcupine of authors. His heroes are grudged heroes – the impossible young man, the passive adult, the whisky-drinking greybeard. It is hard to like them, harder to admire them. Joyce prefers it so. Unequivocal sympathy would be romancing. He denudes man of what we are accustomed to respect, then summons us to sympathise. For Joyce, as for Socrates, understanding is a struggle, best when humiliating. We can move closer to him by climbing over the obstacles of our pretensions, but as we do so he tasks our prowess again by his difficult language. He requires that we adapt ourselves in form as well as in content to his new point of view. His heroes are not easy liking, his books are not easy reading. He does not wish to conquer us, but to have us conquer him. There are, in other words, no invitations, but the door is ajar.

Mr. Bloom negotiated safely the drop into the area, opened the door by its latch. Joyce had written home to his aunt to enquire whether a man might safely descend from the railings on the street into the open basement of the house and drop the remaining few feet, as he had once seen his friend Byrne do. Stephen waited on the pavement outside until Mr. Bloom, candlelit, let him through the silent darkened hall door.

The island of Ithaca, south-west of the heel of Italy, north-east of the head of the Peloponnese, below Corfu, was the home of Ulysses. While he was away presumed dead, his faithful wife Penelope wove and waited, beset with suitors. To each one, she made the same answer, that she would choose when she finished her loomful. But every night, to ward off decision, she unravelled all she had woven that day and always had work in progress. And when Ulysses came home, the walls of Ithaca ran red with the blood of the suitors.

Mr. Bloom is aware that there have been suitors to his Penelope during the afternoon – rehearsing "Love's Old Sweet Song", no less. He bids Stephen a good night as the clock on Saint George's Church steeple rings half past one.

Heigho, heigho,
Heigho, heigho.

Where were the several members of the company which with Bloom that day at the bidding of that peal had travelled from Sandymount in the south to Glasnevin in the north?

Martin Cunningham (in bed), Jack Power (in bed), Simon Dedalus (in bed), Tom Kernan (in bed), Ned Lambert (in bed), Joe Hynes (in bed), John Henry Menton (in bed), Bernard Corrigan (in bed), Patsy Dignam (in bed), Paddy Dignam (in the grave).

All Mr Bloom's side of Eccles Street is hollow now. From the Mater Hospital to Dorset Street is a sad facade. Even the Dominican Convent with its little baroque basilica will go the way of all developers flesh. Behind the facade of Mr Bloom's house there are weeds in the rubble. Some of the houses have yet to fall – nearby, by poking into the creaking hallway it is still possible to follow Mr Bloom's footsteps as he returns to his little Ithaca and surrounds himself with his possessions which invaders have touched in his absence. In these rooms dwelt the first of Dublin's twentieth-century petit-bourgeoisie: here among their old calendars and almanacs and milk-bottles they became, in time, a risen people.

Mr. Bloom, thoughts whirling in his mind like planets, enters his front room to find furniture rearranged, presumably by the visiting Boylan. Joyce catalogues the room's contents, furniture, books. It is an ordinary sort of room, easy chairs, rectangular rug, "a sofa upholstered in prune plush", a blue and white majolica-topped table, a piano, "its musicrest supporting the music in the key of G natural for voice and piano of *Love's Old Sweet Song* (words by G. Clifton Bingham, composed by J. L. Molloy, sung by Madam Antoinette Sterling) open at the last page with the final indications *ad libitum, forte,* pedal, *animato,* sustained, pedal, *ritirando,* close".

Mr. Bloom's house was laid out as follows: through the hallway the front room, parlour, living-room, is on the left, behind it the bow-windowed bedroom where Molly sleeps in her brassquoitjingling bed. After a short flight of stairs down to a small landing, a door leads to the back garden and the privy. Continue down the stairs to the kitchen, opening on to the area into which keyforgetting Mr. Bloom has dropped gently and safely.

How did Bloom prepare a collation for a gentile?

He poured into two teacups two level spoonfuls, four in all, of Epp's soluble cocoa and proceeded according to the directions for use printed on the label, to each adding after sufficient time for infusion the prescribed ingredients for diffusion in the manner and quantity prescribed.

Being a kindly and courteous gentleman, Mr. Bloom decides to use, not his own favourite moustache cup of imitation Crown Derby "but a cup identical with that of his guest". He and Stephen sit and drink cocoa, Mr. Bloom drinking somewhat quicker than his young guest. Stephen's jacket is torn, Stephen has refused to wash his stained face and hands, "distrusting aquacities". Such firm eccentricity in one so learned makes Mr. Bloom think of poetry and literature.

An ambition to squint
At my verses in print
Makes me hope that for these you'll find room.
If you so condescend
Then please place at the end
The name of yours truly, L. Bloom.

There were a few families of Bloom in Dublin in Joyce's time. One was a dentist whose son was a dentist. Another Mr. Bloom murdered a girl in some sort of rural death pact. He failed, however, to kill himself and, Manson-like, scrawled the word "LOVE" on the wall, but could not get the spelling right – it emerged as a scarlet, dripping "LIOVE".

The last notes of Blazes Boylan fade away – yesterday's hit parade . . .

Joyce intended "Ithaca" to represent the skeleton. The bones of the day are recorded in Mr. Bloom's budget, from the first kidney in Dlugacz's meat shop, to the coffee and bun in the cabman's shelter. Such financial considerations excite Mr. Bloom's ambitions and he dreams of being a sleek landed gentleman, a man attractive to courtesans, a businessman, a financier, a man apart. Mr. Bloom in his own home at nearly two o'clock in the morning, looking through the drawers of his life and his household, emerges finally as a lovable, harmless, slightly gormless man: mildly crafty, often lonely, gently enquiring, a loner who pays his own ticket, a dreamer of dreams which he is afraid to make come true, a hurt, slightly odd, generous, undriving, wandering thirty-eight-year-old Dublin Jew.

£5 reward lost, stolen or strayed from his residence Seven Eccles Street, missing gent about forty, answering to the name of Bloom, Leopold (Poldy), height 5ft. 9½ inches, full build, olive complexion, may have since grown a beard, when last seen was wearing a black suit. Above sum will be paid for information leading to his discovery.

What universal binomial denominations would be his as entity and nonentity?

Assumed by any or known to none. Everyman or Noman.

Mr. Bloom is alive and well and is going to bed. Mr. Bloom puts on a white nightshirt and climbs into bed beside his wife. "He kissed the plump mellow yellow smellow melons of her rump . . ." and lay with his feet beside her head, his head at the foot of the bed. Not since five weeks before their son Rudy was born have Mr. Bloom and Molly made love. That was ten years, five months and eighteen days before Bloomsday.

Wakened Molly mutters. They lie there in the dim. They are "at rest relatively to themselves and to each other. In motion being each and both carried westward, forward and rereward respectively, by the proper perpetual motion of the earth through everchanging tracks of neverchanging space." The globe spins on and Mr. and Mrs. Bloom, upside down in bed, spin with it.

PENELOPE

Molly Bloom is life itself. When kissed and yielding in Howth, when deep asleep upstairs, she is the end, and the beginning, and the continuation of Bloom's day.

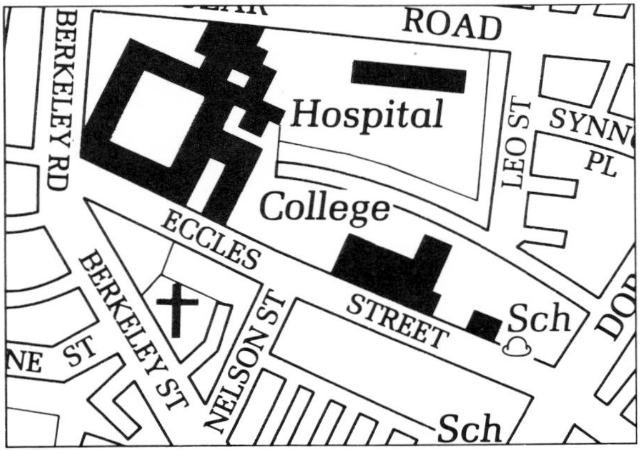

"I can't write," came a letter from Joyce to his brother. "Nora is trying on a pair of drawers by the wardrobe. Excuse me."

"He knows at all nothing about women," said his wife once. He signed ceremonially the first copy of *Ulysses* for Nora and she immediately offered to sell it to a young friend who was there at the time. Later, when they were invited to the ballet to celebrate the 16th of June, she didn't know why the date was significant.

In May 1921 Joyce said that he was completing "Ithaca", a "mathematico-astronomico-physico-mechanico-geometrico-chemico sublimation of Bloom and Stephen (devil take 'em both) to prepare for the final amplitudinously curvilinear episode, 'Penelope'." The first sentence was to contain two and half thousand words, the entire chapter no more than eight sentences, to begin and end with "the most positive word in the English language, the word *yes*". It takes place in Molly's bed-mind, a stream of life flowing through her. ("Yes because he never did a thing like that before as ask to get his breakfast in bed with a couple of eggs . . .") Molly Bloom's soliloquy was regarded as the most obscene chapter in the novel. The monologue interieur, is brought to its highest point in Molly's ramblings across her life, her world in Number Seven, Eccles Street, her husband, her lovers, her prospects.

Joyce was better with women than with men. When he fell in love with Nora, and she with him, he decided to be as true as he could to her. They had a difficult life: he was generally uncaring and hereditarily accustomed to living on his wits, tomorrow would take care of the debt collector. The greater burden of their world fell on Nora. She had come from candid Catholic West of Ireland stock and bravely dashed into exile with a complex man she hardly knew. She adored Joyce without being overawed by him: no matter what pinnacle the world built for him she stayed within reach of herself.

He relished her tartness, her rigid propriety, moral disciplines, her friendliness and hospitality. More than one friend has borne witness that Nora was the one who

kept the house under control, to such a degree that even intimates of the family never felt that they could bring just any casual, occasional, one-night partner to the Joyce's apartment, it had to be a relationship of a more permanent nature.

She watched over his health, with good reason. He suffered acutely from iritis, a painful and distressing inflammation of the eye. Several operations did not cure the problem. Drinking inflamed the condition: Nora consequently behaved with considerable aggression towards tempters.

It was an ordinary house, the Blooms', convenient to shops, churches, schools and public transport. The occupants had some pretensions, sufficient prudence. Molly is thirty-four, the daughter of a soldier, a disappointed wife. Is Molly Bloom's soliloquy no more than Joyce's idea of how a woman's mind works? Or, to be more accurate, how he would like to *believe* a woman's mind works? Lying in the dark she ranges over the full scope of her sexual imagination, recalling her lurid afternoon activities with Boylan. Every man she has known is mentioned either directly or obliquely: her husband's sexual predilections draw comment: ". . . drawers drawers the whole blessed time till I promised to give him the pair off my doll to carry about in his waistcoat pocket . . ."

Once, in Dublin, Joyce and Gogarty played a practical joke on the celibate National Librarian. They stretched a pair of drawers across a chair, strategically accosted them with a propped-up broom handle, placarded it "John Eglinton". Friends at a restaurant table recall Joyce taking out a tiny pair of drawers and fingerwalking it across the table. Jung reading *Ulysses,* told Joyce that "the forty pages of non stop run in the end is a string of veritable psychological peaches". Joyce referred to Jung as "the Swiss Tweedledum, not to

be confused with the Austrian Tweedledee, Freud".

Joyce's Ulysses has won too. He has returned to his palace, defeated his suitors. Molly may have been unfaithful, but she lies in his bed beside him now, albeit upside down: peace, reason and consideration have carried the day.

When Joyce was buried in the cemetery at Zurich in the Friedhofkpalle, it was cold and snowing. Only a few people stood there. The cemetery adjoins the zoological gardens, which pleased Nora. She said he was "awfully fond of the lions" and it pleased her to imagine him lying there and hearing them roar. She lived on in Zurich, lonely, unheeding of what went on in the world of literature which had beaten a path to her husband's door. She paid no attention to any other writers: when you have been married "to the greatest writer in the world, how could you be thinking of the little ones". She died in 1951 and the priest who spoke at her funeral described her as "a great sinner".

Molly hears the clock chime. She thinks of the day they spent out in Howth gazing down on the island of Ireland's Eye, she thinks of the time Poldy called her a flower of the mountain, ". . . and first I put my arms around him yes and drew him down to me so he could feel my breasts all perfume yes and his heart was going like mad and yes I said yes I will Yes". The clock has struck at a quarter past two in the morning at the end of Bloomsday.

A friend was arranging a birthday party for Joyce and even though he was depressed he didn't object. "Birth, departure, sickness, death, life is so tragic we are permitted to distract ourselves and forget a little . . ."

Exiled in Trieste, in Zurich, in Paris, whenever, James Joyce closed his eyes every day and took a walk around Dublin . . .

POSTSCRIPT

He wore a white coat, dentist-like: it enhanced the light by which to write. Those who met him commented on the high forehead and how disconcerting the thickness of the spectacles was. He wrote to his daughter when her mind was troubled to the point of illness: "Why do you always sit at the window? No doubt it makes a pretty picture but a girl walking in the fields also makes a pretty picture."

Facts, facts, facts: as he immured himself within them, behind them, so they pursue him, in town and gown. At dinner in Dublin people argue over his frailties as though he had just left the room. In academe his epiphanies provide agonised, ambitious conversation. A mark of distinction, like a physical characteristic, is claimed by those whose relatives or ancestors were mentioned in his books.

Now that the embarrassment surrounding him is dying – it was the result of a conflict between distaste and liberalism – Ireland will take pride in James Joyce who wrote, they say, "the most difficult of entertaining novels and the most entertaining of difficult ones". Remember that he was spreadeagled by abusers. He loved to quote, in a paranoid wallow, the tale of the man who asked for *Ulysses* in a Dublin bookshop. The bookseller did not stock it, much to the customer's delight. "The man who wrote it," he trumpeted, "had better not come back to Ireland – ever." Hot on the heels of this delicious terror came Joyce's defence to a relative: "If *Ulysses* isn't fit to read, life isn't fit to live –" pause – "of *course* life is fit to live – and *Ulysses* to read."

When it emerged from the embroidery of proofs – he corrected up to six sets of galleys – *Ulysses* stimulated, broadly, three responses. First came an undoubted, if intellectually fashionable, appreciation – albeit from those who had been pre-conditioned by the *Little Review* serialisation, or by respectful word-of-mouth, or by regard for the author's earlier works. Elsewhere, distaste, running up the scale to disgust. To this opinion clung several critics (including Virginia Woolf and Alfred Noyes), the American legal system, the British customs authorities and the Irish nation who, presciently, did not need to read *Ulysses* in order to establish the fact that it ought to be burned. A third school was bewildered – by the language, by the exhilarated tapestries woven by the author, by his mixture of erudition and cunning; readers either fell away completely, or came eventually to enjoy, to be consumed.

The publication was, still is, one of the great dates in literary history. When the first two copies arrived in Paris Joyce was happily talismanned. It was his fortieth birthday: the first two copies of the thousand in the limited edition were numbers 901 and 902, and the next two he received from the printer's steaming, erratic press were 251 and 252: buyers kept calling at Sylvia Beach's shop on the day – the word had wildfired – only to be disappointed for lack of copies: the copy numbered "1" was presented by post – he did much of his own packaging and dispatching – to his great patron, Harriet Shaw Weaver (whose very surname he found engagingly satisfying) and the first review, a month after publication, in the London *Observer* brought requests by the next post for 136 copies. A second edition, published eight months later, in

October 1922, at two guineas per copy, sold its entire two thousand copies in four days.

A new planet had, therefore, appeared in Joyce's skies. His letters to his friends were dominated by the orbit of *Ulysses*: the comments of the critics, the attitudes of the public, the reactions of the booksellers, were rehearsed again and again. To one friend he advised that he ought not "throw *Ulysses* out of the window. Pyrrhus was killed in Argos like that. Also Socrates might be passing in the street." To a relative who had given or lent her copy – which though unsigned was immediately worth forty pounds in London: "There is a difference between a present of a pound of chops and a present of a book like *Ulysses*. You can acknowledge receipt of a present of a pound of chops by simply nodding gratefully, supposing, that is, you have your mouth full of as much of the chops as it will conveniently hold, but you cannot do so with a large book on account of the difficulty of fitting it into the mouth."

For whatever reasons, and despite the book's alleged obscurity, *Ulysses* and Joyce eventually became fixed in the popular mind – even in Ireland. Whether for notoriety, or for the fact that he was iconoclastic, he clamped a hold, even on the minds of those who were never expected to read him. I have heard bank clerks revelling in his language: Molly Bloom was taken, unwittingly, to Confession; an artist in Dublin, Jewish, sensitive and shrewd, dresses now as Leopold Bloom, walks the city bowler-hatted and wistful.

Joyce once wrote to Nora: "Dublin is a detestable city and the people in it are most repulsive to me", but he was nonetheless quintessentially Irish. There is a myth, accepted by the world, not denied by the natives, that the Irish are a warm, friendly people. Not wholly true: that open, hospitable spirit is as the rind on cheese. Caution is the decree of experience – historically, friendship and easy confidence often led to betrayal, to the militia, to the landlord. Abroad, James Joyce was able to build upon this aloofness, a stranger among strangers. He may have been surrounded by friends, acquaintances, fellow-writers (many of whom made a reputation by having known Joyce while they and he were in the same place at the same time), he may have entertained at his favourite restaurants when he was in funds and in Paris – but he chose distance.

There are other manifestations of Joyce's Irishry – contradictions in speech, in language, as with the small boy's jibe: "Eh, mister, your fly is open, mister," whereas in English such form of address indicates politeness. There is the need too – chronically Hibernian – to identify with somebody of historical or spiritual significance. When the poet Yeats made a rich and honeyed filibuster in the Irish Senate, a scarcely-lettered colleague, who had difficulty with articulation and pronunciation, sprang to his feet and cawed: "Jaysus, Mr. Yates – you took the very words outa me mouth." And Joyce, delighted, discovered that he had a physical parallel too with his Classical mentor, blind Homer, "blind from glaucoma according to one of my doctors, Dr. Berman, as iridectomy [Joyce's own complaint] had not been thought of."

Joyce signifies frustration. The endlessness of his enlightenment breeds feeble mortality. One scholar of my acquaintance claims that he can point out over seven hundred liminal and subliminal references, connections, jokes, puns, on the first page of *Finnegans Wake*. Joyce tantalises too: there is trickery in every paragraph, every sentence, a new meaning with each sighting. Further frustration then – the desire of the writer to keep secrets seems to transfer itself to the reader: does one shout the discovery or not? (Which may be the reason why "Penelope" is the shortest chapter in this book.) Does it explain too, why Joyce as an author and a subject of study arouses such feelings of possessiveness? The interest which students of Joyce exhibit in each other's work-in-progress amounts to a form of industrial espionage and every new thesis, unless its scholarship is incontrovertible (well-nigh impossible, even for an Ellmann, a Burgess, a Groden or a Gilbert) is challenged to a frazzle.

What, finally (taking one's words in one's hands), attracts so many people to this pied piper? That his claim is true, that he has contained the universal in his particular? Or humanity? Real and imagined, it belied his acerbity. Once, Nora threatened to leave him and commenced an explanatory letter to her mother with a small "i". Joyce wondered humorously over her shoulder whether such an event did not merit at least a capital letter. "Counterparts", a story in *Dubliners*, ends: "The boy uttered a squeal of pain as the stick cut his thigh. He clasped his hands together in the air and his voice shook with fright. 'Oh, pa!' he cried. 'Don't beat me, pa! And I'll . . . I'll say a Hail Mary for you . . . I'll say a Hail Mary for you, pa, if you don't beat me . . . I'll say a Hail Mary . . .'" To his daughter, Lucia, Joyce wrote: "The trees you love change their leaves with the passing of the months" and promised to send her cuttings from newspaper articles about him or the family where her name was mentioned. Mr. Bloom bought buns for the seagulls because he first fooled them with a throwaway piece of paper.

Where *Ulysses* is concerned his appeal must also be the way in which he omnipotently contained Dublin and its inhabitants. One visiting Joycean student expressed the wish that all the Dublin of *Ulysses* would collapse and disappear (the City Fathers and town planners are doing their damnable best) in order to have the sheer comfort of imagination only. And the marvel of the Joycean achievement often becomes too much to encompass – *Ulysses* was created before he was forty years old.

And is it in that dimension, in his web of Dublin, that all the strands of James Joyce are drawn together? Human beings and their habitations are the subject of literature, since we have little else to write about. Joyce drew together the city and the world and all the inhabitants therein residing – a dolls' house, a shelf of specimens.

With customary monumental arrogance he had stated early in life that he wished to "forge the uncreated conscience" of his race, that he would do so grandiosely by going forth to greet experience. Contradictorily, he chose a simple vehicle for his journey forth, the day on which he came to love. Some lovers have written symphonies, some have built temples. Infinitely and multitudinously, James Joyce wrote *Ulysses*.

Entrance
to The National Library and
The National College of Art

BIBLIOGRAPHY

A note on the bibliography: The books listed here are those which have proved particularly useful in the preparation of *James Joyce's Odyssey*. If a full bibliography were to be included there would neither be space enough nor time enough: many references come from memory and have been gathered through the years from books on Joyce, Dublin and Ireland.

Allen, Walter, *The Short Story in English*, Clarendon Press, Oxford, England, 1981.

Anderson, Chester G., *James Joyce and His World*, Thames and Hudson, London, 1967.

Blamires, Harry, *The Bloomsday Book*, Methuen and Co., London, 1966.

Budgen, Frank, *James Joyce and the Making of Ulysses*, Indiana University Press, Bloomington, 1960.

Burgess, Anthony, *Joysprick – An Introduction to the Language of James Joyce*, André Deutsch, London, 1973.

Craig, Maurice, *Dublin, 1660-1860*, 1952.

Ellman, Richard, *James Joyce*, Oxford University Press, 1959.
(Ed.) *Letters of James Joyce*, Vols. II and III, Faber and Faber, 1966.
James Joyce's Tower, Eastern Regional Tourism Organisation, Dun Laoire, Dublin, 1969.
Ulysses on the Liffey, Faber and Faber, London, 1972.
Yeats – The Man and the Masks, Macmillan, London, 1949.

Gilbert, Stuart, *James Joyce's "Ulysses" – A Study:* New York, 1930.
(Ed.) *Letters of James Joyce*, Vol. I: Faber and Faber, London, 1957.

Groden, Michael, *Ulysses in Progress*, Princeton University Press, 1977.

Hart, Clive and Knuth, Leo, *A Topographical Guide to James Joyce's "Ulysses"*: Pub. by "A Wake Newslitter", Department of Literature, Essex University, England, 1975.

Hickey, D. J. and J. E., *A Dictionary of Irish History since 1800*, Gill and Macmillan, Dublin, 1980.

Hutchins, Patricia, *James Joyce's Dublin*, London, 1950.

Jeffares, A. Norman, *W. B. Yeats, Man and Poet*, Routledge and Kegan Paul, London, 1949.

Joyce, James, *Ulysses*, first published, Shakespeare and Co., Paris, 1922; Bodley Head, London, 1936; Penguin Books, Harmondsworth, Middlesex, England 1969. In the U.S. first published, Random House, 1934.
Dubliners, Grant Richards, London, 1914; B.W. Huebsch

(later of Viking Press), New York, 1916; Jonathan Cape, London, 1967; Granada Publishing, London (in Panther Books), 1977.
A Portrait of the Artist as a Young Man, B.W. Huebsch (later of Viking Press), New York, 1916; Jonathan Cape, London, 1924; Penguin Books, 1960.
Finnegans Wake, Faber and Faber, London, 1939; Viking Press, New York, 1939.

Kenner, Hugh, *Joyce's Voices,* Faber and Faber, London, 1978.

Lyon, F. S. L., *James Joyce's Dublin,* Twentieth-Century Studies, IV, November 1970.

Lyons, J. B., *Oliver St. John Gogarty* – a Biography, Blackwater Press, Dublin, 1980.

McHugh, Roland, *Annotations to "Finnegans Wake",* Routledge and Kegan Paul, London, 1980.

McLoughlin, Adrian, *Guide to Historic Dublin,* Gill and Macmillan, Dublin, 1979.

O'Connor, Ulick, *Oliver St. John Gogarty,* Jonathan Cape, London, 1964, Granada Publishing, London, 1981.

Peake, C. H., *James Joyce – the Citizen and the Artist,* Edward Arnold, London, 1977

Power, Arthur, *Conversations with James Joyce,* Millington Books, London, 1974.

Raleigh, John Henry, *The Chronicle of Leopold and Molly Bloom,* University of California Press, Berkeley, 1977.

Ryan, John, (Ed.) *A Bash in the Tunnel: James Joyce by the Irish,* Clifton Books, London, 1970.
Remembering How We Stood, Gill and Macmillan, Dublin, 1975.

Schleifer, Ronald, *The Genres of the Irish Literary Revival,* Pilgrim Books, Norman, Oklahoma and Wolfhound Press, Dublin, 1980.

Shewring, Walter, (Trans) *The Odyssey* by Homer, Oxford University Press, England, 1980.

Somerville-Large, Peter, *Dublin,* Hamish Hamilton, London, 1979.

Thom's Official Directory of the United Kingdom of Great Britain and Ireland, 1904, London, 1905.

ACKNOWLEDGMENTS

The author wishes to make acknowledgment, with gratitude, to the following:

The Bodley Head in London, and Random House, Inc. in New York for permission to quote extensively from *Ulysses*; Faber & Faber in London and Viking Press in New York for permission to quote from *My Brother's Keeper* by Stanislaus Joyce; from *The Letters of James Joyce* edited by Stuart Gilbert (Vol. I) and Richard Ellmann, (Vols. II & III); Jonathan Cape in London and Viking Press in New York for permission to quote from *A Portrait of the Artist as a Young Man* and *Dubliners*; to the Society of Authors protecting the Literary Estate of James Joyce for permission to quote from *The Holy Office*; Faber & Faber in London for permission to quote from *Dublin* by Louis MacNeice; Sir Osbert Lancaster and John Murray Ltd. for permission to quote from *Afternoons with Baedeker* in *Facades and Faces*; to the Representatives of the late Seumas O'Sullivan for permission to quote from his works; Mr. Oliver D. Gogarty for permission to quote from the works of the late Dr. Oliver St. John Gogarty; Mr. Michael Yeats for permission to quote from *Who Goes with Fergus* by the late W. B. Yeats; The Ordnance Survey of Ireland, Phoenix Park, Dublin for permission to reproduce and quote from maps of Dublin – Permit No. 3631; Dr. Alf MacLochlainn, Director of the National Library of Ireland, Kildare Street, Dublin, for permission to reproduce pictures from the Lawrence Collection and his Staff for their unflagging courtesy and assistance; to the Trustees of the British Museum in London for permission to reproduce the Plan of Dublin as of 1904, and to the staff of the Map Room in the British Museum for such diligent effort on the author's behalf; to Mr. Patrick Long, Director of the Eastern Regional Tourism Board, Dun Laoghaire, Co. Dublin and to Mr. Robert Nicholson, Curator of the James Joyce Museum in Sandycove for their kind permission to quote from the ticket of admission to the Museum and to photograph the Museum and its exhibits; to the Master and Staff of the National Maternity Hospital in Dublin for permission to photograph within the hospital; to the Directors of Arthur Guinness, Son & Company Ltd. for permission to photograph from their rooftops; to Mike O'Malley and Ray Hollidge of Chartwell Illustrations, Ltd., Croydon, Surrey, for the chapter maps.

Gratitude born of admiration is due to Professor Richard Ellman; it is impossible to progress with any research into the world of James Joyce without relying heavily on Professor Ellmann's unrivalled scholarship in the field; likewise Dr. Anthony Burgess, who supplied words of kind encouragement; Roland McHugh's example and enthusiasm are daunting and exhilarating, Vivien Igoe uncovered some extra and enthralling sources and Ulick O'Connor offered assistance unselfishly.

Acknowledgments of a particular kind are due to Sharyn Troughton of Hodder & Stoughton who designed this book with affection and zeal; to Ion Trewin who as Senior Non-Fiction Editor edited it and nursed it into life; to Clare Bristow who transfused it, Amanda Batten who guarded it, Tracy Loveman who typed it impeccably; to Jorge Lewinski for taking an interpretative as well as a photographic role – and to Brigid Roden who helped so competently in all sorts of ways.

INDEX

Abbey Theatre, 2
Aldborough House, 102
All Hallows Church, Westland Row, 54
American Embassy, 36
Amiens Street, 160
Anderson, Margaret, 40
Annesley Bridge, 103
Ancient Concert Rooms (now Academy Cinema), 60, 114
Arbour Hill, 103
Artane, 103
Artifoni, Almidano, 105
Assembly Rooms, *see* Gate Theatre
Aston Quay, 80, 82
Avercamp, Hendrik, 100

Bachelor's Walk, 75, 107, 114, 118
Bailey Restaurant/Pub, 89
Ballsbridge, 36
Bank of Ireland, 36, 86
Barnacle, Nora (Mrs James Joyce), 18, 24, 86, 114, 135, 168, 176, 178, 179, 182, 183
Beach, Sylvia, 97, 138, 181
Beckett, Samuel, 12
Bedford Row, 108
Behan, Brendan, 47
Belvedere College, 30, 66, 102
Beresford Place, 166
Berkeley Road, 64, 66
Berkeley Street, 66
Berlitz Institute, 105
Berman, Dr., 182
Best, Richard, 94
Bewley's, 88
Blackrock, 36, 132
Blessington Street, 64, 66
Bodley Head, The, 8
Booterstown, 36

Breffni Road, 28
Brueghel, Pieter, 100
Brian Boru Pub, 68
Brown Thomas, 88
Brunswick Street, Great, *see* Pearse Street
Bullock Harbour, 28
Burbage, Richard, 97
Burgess, Anthony, 11, 183
Burgh Quay, 80
Burke, Edmund, 86
Burke's Pub, 144
Burton Restaurant, 88, 90
Bus Aras, 161
Butt Bridge, 160, 162
Butt, Isaac, 47
Byrne's Davy, 89, 90
Byrne, J. F., 42, 44

Cabra, 104
Carlisle Bridge, *see* O'Connell Bridge
Cattle Market, 66
Chapelizod, 114
Clanbrassil Street, 45
Clare Street, 108, 110
Clongowes Wood School, 28, 30, 37, 102
Cohen, Bella, 152
College Green, 80, 86, 105, 110
Colum, Padraic, 97
Conmee, Father John, 100, 102, 103, 104, 110
Cooper, Becky, 150
Corporation Street, 150
Cosgrave, Vincent, 42, 44
Crampton Court, 107
Cross Guns Bridge, 68
Cusack, Michael, 127
Custom House, 51, 53, 160, 161

Dail Eireann, *see* Leinster House
Daily Express, 21
Dalkey, 16, 27, 30, 36, 75
Dalkey Avenue, 28
Dame Street, 107, 108, 110
Dawson Street, 80, 91
Deane & Son, Sir Thomas & Sir Thomas, 97
Delaney, Mrs., 86
Devan, Tom, 62
Dickens, Charles, 144
Dock Tavern, 160
Dodder River, 36
D'Olier Street, 62, 63, 64, 80, 105
Dolphin's Barn, 50, 119
Dominican Convent, 172
Donnybrook, 75
Drumcondra, 75
Dublin Bakery Company, 108
Dublin Castle, 108, 152
Duke Street, 80, 88
Dun Laoghaire (formerly Kingstown), 16, 132
Dunphy's Corner, 68
Dunsink Observatory, 129

Eccles Street, 11, 41, 42, 46, 50, 66, 89, 104, 115, 118, 165, 166, 168, 172, 174, 176
Edward the Seventh, King, 13, 150, 154
"Eglinton, John", *see* Magee, W. K.
Eliot, T. S., 70
Elizabeth I, Queen, 86
Ellmann, Richard, 11, 72, 91, 115, 118, 170, 183
Emmett, Robert, 127
Essex Bridge, 115
Essex Street, 107

Farrell, Endymion, 84
Findlater's Church, 68
Finglas Road, 64, 68
Finn's Hotel, 86
Fitzwilliam Square, 140
Flanagan, Bird, 84
Fleischmann, Martha, 135, 155
Foley Street, 150
Ford, Ford Madox, 18
Fortnightly Review, 72
Forty-Foot Bathing Place, 16, 21
Four Courts, 114
Fownes Street, 110
Fanciscan Church, Merchants Quay, 114
Freeman's Journal, 72, 74, 75, 114
French, Robert, 12, 13
Fresh Nellie, 152, 155

G.A.A. (Gaelic Athletic Association), 127
Gandon, James, 51, 53
Gardiner's Place, 166
Gate Theatre, 68
General Post Office, 66
Ghezzi, Father Charles, 105
Gilbert, Stuart, 183
Glasnevin, 57, 58, 60, 63, 68, 75, 107, 172
Glasthule, 16
Gogarty, Oliver St. John, 16, 44, 46, 50, 91, 97, 147, 152, 154, 157, 162, 178
Goldsmith, Oliver, 86
Grace, W. G., 55
Grafton Street, 11, 80, 88, 105, 109, 110
Grattan Bridge, 110
Great Charles Street, 102
Great Georges Street, North, 104
Green Street, 121, 122, 123, 124, 127
Gregory, Lady Augusta, 30
Griffith, Arthur, 127, 128
Groden, Michael, 183
Grosvenor Hotel, 53, 86
Guinness, Arthur, Son & Company Ltd., 49, 50, 80, 107

Haddington Road, 36
Hanover Street, 50
Hardwicke Place, 166
Hart, Clive, 11
Hathaway, Anne, 95, 97

Heap, Jane, 40
Hemingway, Ernest, 12
Holles Street, 140, 144
Homer, 55, 182
Hooligan, Julia, 150
Horne, Sir Andrew, 144
Howth, 91, 132, 179
Hunter, Alfred, 53, 54, 160

Ibsen, Henrik, 72
Irish Hospitals Sweepstakes, 50
Irish Independent, 72
Irish Times, 80, 84, 88
Irishtown, 58, 75
Islandbridge, 114

James's Street, 107
Jammet's Restaurant, 66
Jesus Christ, 55
Johnson, Dr. Samuel, 86
Joyce, Giorgio, 161, 162, 164, 168
Joyce, John, 58, 62, 63, 70, 75, 161
Joyce, Lucia, 100, 161, 168, 183
Joyce, Mabel, 60
Joyce, May Murray, 58
Joyce, Nora, *see* Barnacle, Nora
Joyce, Stanislaus, 44, 161, 162

Kane, Matthew, 62
Kiernan's, Barney, 121, 124
Kildare, 68
Kildare Street, 80, 94, 97
Kildare Street Club, 94
Kingsbridge, 114
Kingstown, *see* Dun Laoghaire

Lady Betty, 152
Lake Maggiore, 119
Lancaster, Osbert, 8
Lansdowne Road, 110
Lawless, Mrs., 152
Lawrence Collection, 12, 97
Lawrence, Mrs., 12
Leahy's Terrace, 36, 132, 138
Leasks, the linseed crushers, 50
Le Fanu, Sheridan, 140
Legion of Mary, 157
Lewinski, Jorge, 13
Leinster House, 91, 94
Liberty Hall, 50
Liffey Quay, 112
Liffey, River, 18, 49, 50, 51, 112
Lime Street, 50
Little Britain Street, 122
Little Review, The, 40, 138
Locarno, 119
Loftus, Sean, Dublin Bay, 36
Lombard Street, 50
Lower Gardiner Street, 166
Lyster, T. W., 94, 97

McCormack, John, 114
McNeice, Louis, 82
Mack, Mrs., 150, 152, 155, 157
Magee, W. K. 94, 178
Mahaffy, John Pentland, 88
Mandeville, 144
Martello Tower, Sandycove, 11, 15, 17, 132
Mary St., 12
Masonic Headquarters, 91
Mater Misericordiae Hospital, 42, 172
Mathew, Fr. Theobald, 66
Mercer's Hospital, 110
Merchants Arch, 107, 108, 109, 114
Merrion, 36
Merrion Square, 86, 108, 139, 140
Middle Abbey Street, 72
Middle Gardiner Street, 166
Molesworth Street, 80, 91
Monkstown, 36
Montgomery Street, 150
Moore, George, 8, 30, 97
Moore, Thomas, 86
Mount Street, 108, 110, 140
Mountjoy Jail, 68
Mountjoy Square, 100, 102, 166

Moyne, Lord, 80
Museum, James Joyce, 22
Museum, National, 91, 93

Nassau Street, 86, 88, 94, 105, 108, 109, 110
National Gallery, 142
National Library, 11, 12, 13, 80, 93, 94, 97, 155
National Maternity Hospital, 139, 147
Nelson, Admiral Lord Horatio, 66, 75
Newbridge Avenue, 58, 132
Newcomer Bridge, 103
North Circular Road, 64, 68, 102
North Frederick Street, 168
North Strand, 102
Noyes, Alfred, 18, 181

Oblong, May, 152, 155
Observer, 181
O'Casey, Sean, 97
O'Connell Bridge (formerly Carlisle Bridge), 79, 80, 107
O'Connell, Daniel, 63, 68
O'Connell Street (formerly Sackville Street), 12, 63, 64, 66, 72, 75, 80, 150
Ormond Hotel, 105, 107, 112, 115, 117, 118, 119
Ormond Quay, 108, 110, 122
O'Rourke, Larry, 45, 46
O'Sullivan, Seumas, 66, 97

Palmerston Park, 75
Paris, 12, 24, 91, 124, 179
Parkgate, 107
Parliament Street, 108, 110
Parnell, Charles Stewart, 68, 88, 124, 164
Parnell, John Howard, 88, 91, 110
Parnell Square, 64, 66
Pearse Brothers, 60
Pearse Street (formerly Great Brunswick Street), 50, 53, 58, 64
Pembroke Quay, 108
Phibsborough Road, 64, 68
Phoenix Park, 75, 114
Piano, Mary, 152, 157
Pigeon House, 36, 132
Pitt, William, 63
Post Office, *see* General Post Office
Pound, Ezra, 40
Power, Arthur, 62
Prezioso, Roberto, 118
Prince's Street, 72
Prospect Road, 64, 68
Proust, Marcel, 12
Purefoy, Dr. R. Damon, 144

Queens Theatre of Variety, 60, 62

Railway Street, 150, 152
Rathfarnham, 75
Rathgar, 168
Rathmines, 76
Red Bank Restaurant, 62
Reynolds, Sir Joshua, 86
Rialto, 75
Richmond Street (North), 30
Ringsend, 58, 64, 140
Roberts, George, 32
Roche, Sir Boyle, 47, 88
Rotunda Hospital, 66
Royal Canal, 68
Royal Dublin Society, 36
Rumbold, Sir Horace, 124
Russell, George ("AE"), 30, 88, 94, 95, 97
Rutland Square, *see* Parnell Square

Sackville Street, *see* O'Connell Street
Saint George's Church, 41, 47, 50, 166, 172
Saint James's Gate, 107
Saint Joseph's School, 102
Saint Mark's Church, 60

Saint Mary's Abbey, 105
Saint Peter's Terrace, 104
Saint Stephen's Green, 94
Sandycove, 11, 16, 17, 18, 28, 47, 94, 132
Sandymount, 34, 36, 37, 40, 58, 75, 110, 129, 131, 132, 136, 138, 154, 155, 164, 172
Serpentine Avenue, 37
Shakespeare & Co., 97
Shakespeare, Hamnet, 95
Shakespeare, William, 95, 97, 144, 154
Shaw, George Bernard, 97, 142, 144
Sheares Brothers, 127
Shelbourne Hotel, 12
Shelley, Percy Bysshe, 66
Silken, Thomas, 107, 129
Sinn Fein, 127
Sir John Rogerson's Quay, 50
Skin-the-Goat, 164
South Leinster Street, 86, 108
Sporting Times, 21
Stephens, James, 169
Sterne, L., 144
Store Street, 160
Strick, Joseph, 9
Summerfield Lodge, 28
Sunday Express, 21
Sweny's Chemists, 54
Swift, Dr. Jonathan, 144
Sycamore Street, 107
Synge, John Millington, 30, 97

Talbot, Florry, 152
Talbot Street, 150
Tara Street, 60
Temple Bar, 107
Temple Street, 166
Tennyson, Lord Alfred, 55, 154
Thom's Directory, 11, 42
Tolkien, J. R. R., 88
Trench, Samuel Chevenix, 16
Trieste, 12, 24, 42, 91, 105, 118, 124, 161, 170, 179
Trinity College, 11, 55, 60, 86
Tritonville Road, 36, 64
Trollope, Anthony, 66

Ulverton Road, 28
University College, Dublin, 30
Upper Gardiner Street, 104
Ushers Island, 114

Vartry River, 160
Victoria, Queen, 13, 80

Wagner, R., 118
Ward Union, 86
Watery Lane, 58
Watling Street, 107
Weaver, Harriet Shaw, 181
West Brighton Square, 168
Westland Row, 50, 54, 55, 60
Westmoreland Street, 80, 82, 110
Wicklow Street, 108
Wide Streets Commission, 140
Wilde, Oscar, 55, 60, 140
Windmill Lane, 50
Woolf, Virginia, 181

Yeates & Son, 88
Yeats, William B., 18, 30, 58, 182

Zurich, 9, 11, 12, 24, 124, 135, 168, 179
Zozimus, 84, 155

D-Day: Dawn to midnight J

To Dad
From Calum
Christmas 1977.

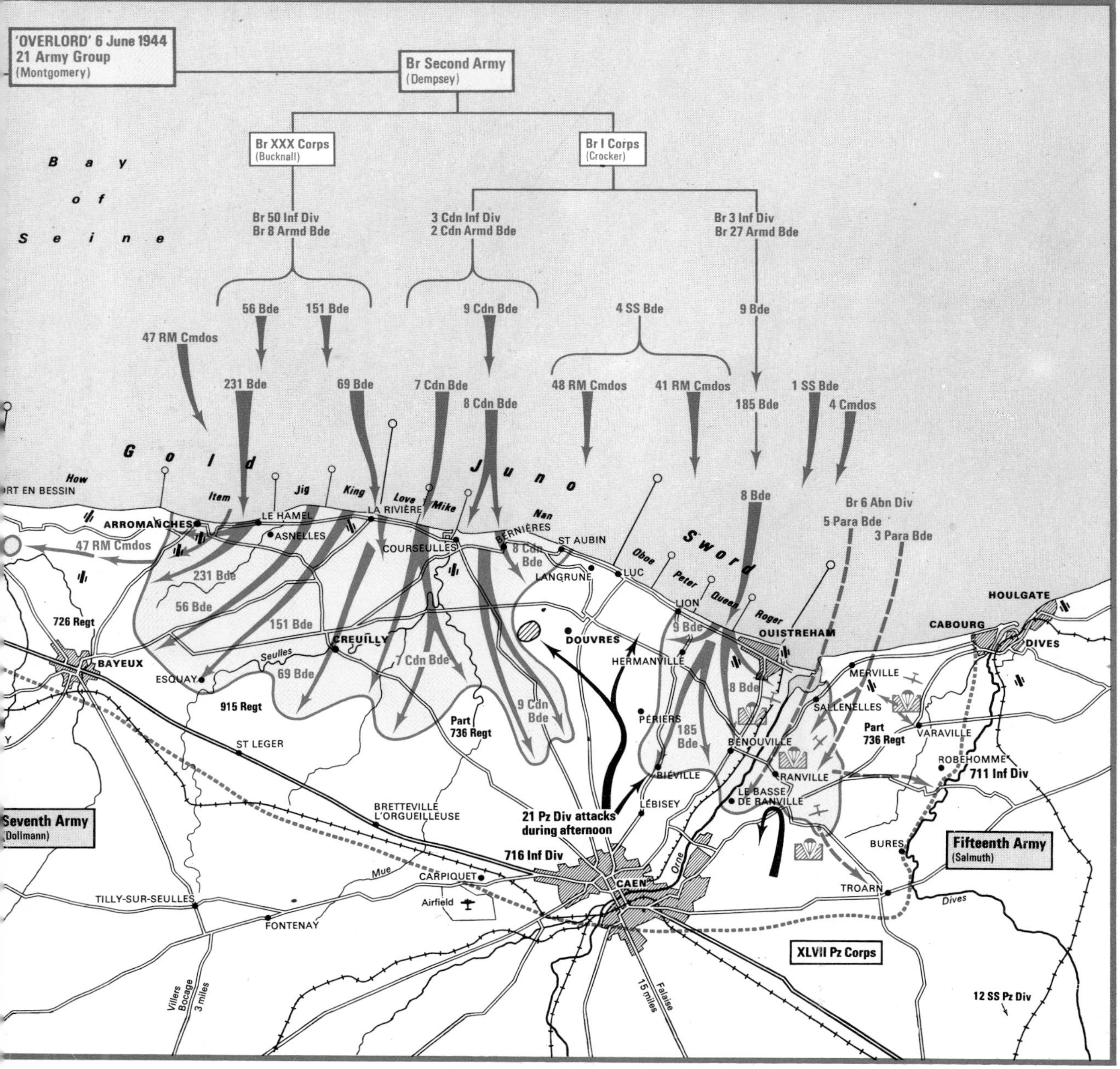

'OVERLORD' 6 June 1944
21 Army Group
(Montgomery)

Br Second Army
(Dempsey)

Br XXX Corps
(Bucknall)

Br I Corps
(Crocker)

Bay of Seine

Br 50 Inf Div
Br 8 Armd Bde

3 Cdn Inf Div
2 Cdn Armd Bde

Br 3 Inf Div
Br 27 Armd Bde

56 Bde
151 Bde
9 Cdn Bde
4 SS Bde
9 Bde
47 RM Cmdos
231 Bde
69 Bde
7 Cdn Bde
8 Cdn Bde
48 RM Cmdos
41 RM Cmdos
185 Bde
1 SS Bde
4 Cmdos

Gold
Juno
Sword
How
Item
Jig
King
Love
Mike
Nan
Oboe
Peter
Queen
Roger

8 Bde
Br 6 Abn Div
5 Para Bde
3 Para Bde

PORT EN BESSIN
ARROMANCHES
LE HAMEL
ASNELLES
LA RIVIÈRE
COURSEULLES
BERNIÈRES
ST AUBIN
LANGRUNE
LUC
LION
OUISTREHAM
HOULGATE
CABOURG
DIVES
MERVILLE
SALLENELLES
VARAVILLE
ROBEHOMME
RANVILLE
LE BASSE DE RANVILLE
BÉNOUVILLE
BIÉVILLE
PÉRIERS
HERMANVILLE
DOUVRES
LÉBISEY
CREULLY
BAYEUX
ESQUAY
ST LEGER
BRETTEVILLE L'ORGUEILLEUSE
CARPIQUET
Airfield
CAEN
TILLY-SUR-SEULLES
FONTENAY
BURES
TROARN

Seulles
Mue
Orne
Dives

47 RM Cmdos
231 Bde
56 Bde
151 Bde
69 Bde
7 Cdn Bde
8 Cdn Bde
9 Cdn Bde
9 Bde
8 Bde
185 Bde

726 Regt
915 Regt
Part 736 Regt
Part 736 Regt
716 Inf Div
711 Inf Div
21 Pz Div attacks during afternoon

Seventh Army
(Dollmann)

Fifteenth Army
(Salmuth)

XLVII Pz Corps

12 SS Pz Div

Villers Bocage 3 miles
Falaise 15 miles

SUPREME HEADQUARTERS

ALLIED EXPEDITIONARY FORCE

Soldiers, Sailors and Airmen of the Allied Expeditionary Force!

You are about to embark upon the Great Crusade, toward which we have striven these many months. The eyes of the world are upon you. The hopes and prayers of liberty-loving people everywhere march with you. In company with our brave Allies and brothers-in-arms on other Fronts, you will bring about the destruction of the German war machine, the elimination of Nazi tyranny over the oppressed peoples of Europe, and security for ourselves in a free world.

Your task will not be an easy one. Your enemy is well trained, well equipped and battle-hardened. He will fight savagely.

But this is the year 1944! Much has happened since the Nazi triumphs of 1940-41. The United Nations have inflicted upon the Germans great defeats, in open battle, man-to-man. Our air offensive has seriously reduced their strength in the air and their capacity to wage war on the ground. Our Home Fronts have given us an overwhelming superiority in weapons and munitions of war, and placed at our disposal great reserves of trained fighting men. The tide has turned! The free men of the world are marching together to Victory!

I have full confidence in your courage, devotion to duty and skill in battle. We will accept nothing less than full Victory!

Good Luck! And let us all beseech the blessing of Almighty God upon this great and noble undertaking.

Dwight D. Eisenhower

Designed by Paul Watkins
Picture Research by
Jonathan Moore and Judy Harkison
Maps by Richard Natkiel

Contents

	Foreword by Admiral of the Fleet The Earl Mountbatten of Burma	4
1	**'We Shall Go Back'**	6
2	**Forging the Alliance, 1942**	20
3	**The Torch is Lit**	28
4	**COSSAC**	34
5	**Festung Europa**	42
6	**SHAEF**	56
7	**The Enemy Observed**	60
8	**Engineering an Invasion**	70
9	**'Tougher than D-Day'**	78
10	**Master Plan**	90
11	**'O.K., Let's Go'**	108
	The Second Front: a record in colour	113
12	**H-Hour Approaches**	150
13	**Dawn Assault**	162
	Utah	176
	Omaha	184
	Gold	196
	Juno	203
	Sword	210
14	**Day of Destiny**	218
15	**Race Against Time**	226
16	**Break-out to Victory**	236
	Authors' Note	250
	Acknowledgements	251
	Selected Bibliography	251
	List of Regiments	252
	List of Contributors	253
	Index	255

Warren Tute/John Costello & Terry Hughes

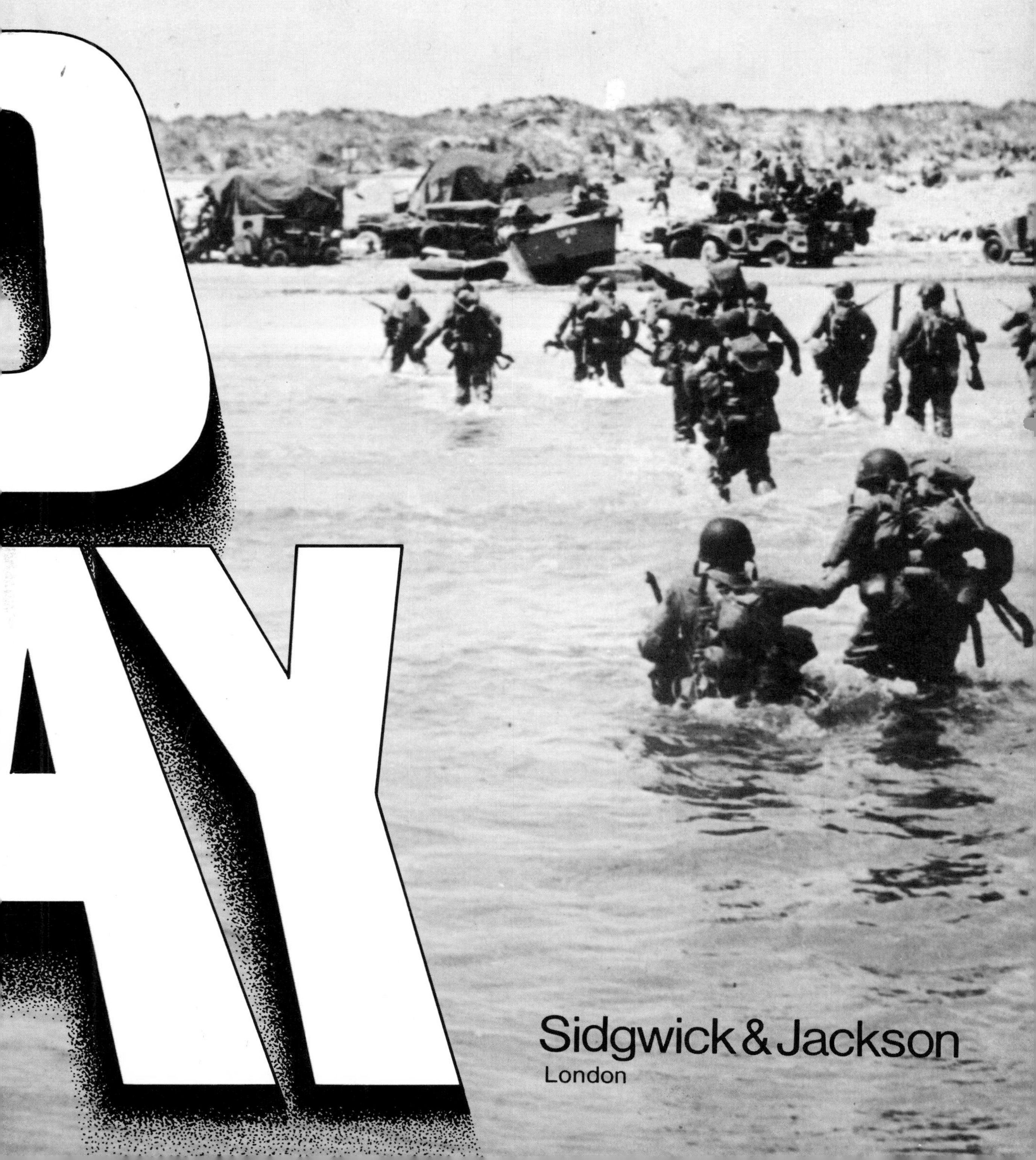

Sidgwick & Jackson
London

Foreword by **Admiral of the Fleet The Earl Mountbatten of Burma**

KG, PC, GCB, OM, GCSI, GCIE, GCVO, DSO, FRS

On 10 October 1941, when I had taken over command of the Aircraft Carrier *Illustrious* after having been sunk in the Battle of Crete in my destroyer Flotilla Leader *Kelly*, I received a signal from the Prime Minister: 'We want you home here at once for something which you will find of the highest interest'. When I got back Winston Churchill told me he wanted me to succeed Admiral of the Fleet Lord Keyes in charge of 'Combined Operations'.

I felt far from pleased at leaving the fleet; Churchill must have spotted this for he stuck out his jaw and said, 'Well, what have you got to say to that?' I replied I'd rather be back at sea. That really made him snort!

'Have you no sense of glory? Here I give you a chance to take part in the highest direction of the war and all you want to do is to go back to sea! What could you hope to achieve, except to be sunk in a bigger and more expensive ship?' I gave in. Winston then gave me his directive in more or less these words: 'You will continue with the Commando raids in order to keep up the offensive spirit and gain essential experience of landing on enemy occupied coasts, and to harass the enemy. But, above all, I now want you to start the preparations for our great counter-invasion of Europe. Unless we can land overwhelming forces and beat the Nazis in battle in France, Hitler will never be defeated. So this must be your prime task.

'I want you to work out the philosophy of invasion, to land and advance against the enemy. You must collect the most brilliant planners in the three services to help you. You must devise and design new landing craft, appurtenances and appliances and train the three services to act together as a single force in combined operation.

'All other Headquarters in England are engaged on defensive measures; your Headquarters must think only of offence. The south coast of England is a bastion of defence against Hitler's invasion; you must turn it into a springboard to launch an attack.'

You can imagine how inspiring this talk was in October 1941 when most people thought we had our backs to the wall.

I went to Combined Operations Headquarters and

First published in Great Britain in 1974

ISBN 0 283 98144 X

Printed in Great Britain by
W. S. Cowell Limited, Ipswich
for Sidgwick and Jackson Limited
1 Tavistock Chambers, Bloomsbury Way
London WC1A 2SG

found there were only twenty-six persons all told and not a single regular active-service officer or man among them. Before I left, this number had increased twenty-fold, all working at full pressure. The actual sailors, soldiers and airmen in the Combined Operations Command increased to 50,000 trained experts. We really put our backs into it. I could not find any guidelines so I enunciated my own philosophy of invasion briefly as follows:

(1) To be certain of obtaining a firm lodgement at the desired place on the enemy-held coast against all known defences.

(2) To break quickly out of the beachheads while reinforcements of men, vehicles, munitions, and stores continued ceaselessly to follow up the spearhead no matter what the weather conditions during the following weeks.

(3) At the same time to keep the main enemy forces far from the landing area by deception and prevent them, when they discovered the deception, from moving reinforcements to the landing area faster than the 'build up' of the invasion force, by bombing all road and rail communications over a wide area for several months beforehand.

In November 1941 I was ordered, in conjunction with General Paget, Commander-in-Chief of Home Forces, to prepare for a large-scale raid, and two months later we were told to work or plan for Allied permanent re-entry into the Continent of Europe. Other senior officers, British, American and Canadian, became associated with us and we came to be known as the 'Combined Commanders'.

From the start, all the Allied Generals and Air Marshals decided that they wished the invasion to take place from the Dover area across the straits to land in the Pas de Calais area. I alone resolutely and ceaselessly opposed them. I pointed out that the German Generals had come to the same conclusion as them and were rapidly building up reinforcements in the Calais area which reached a force of no less than twenty-five divisions before we landed in France.

Our intelligence showed the Germans had developed a really powerful coast defence system, which could dominate our ships, and had established strong defence in depth behind Calais. The Luftwaffe would easily be able to attack the small assembly ports in our south-eastern area and destroy or damage the thousands of landing craft we would have to assemble. Continental Channel ports from Le Havre to the eastward were all shallow ports with narrow entrances and capable of complete protection by minefields. Even if enough of our landing craft survived to force a lodgement by our forces we had not the remotest hope of building these forces up quickly enough to match the enemy concentration.

So I insisted we should land in the Baie de la Seine area just to the eastward of Cherbourg. I put my case to Churchill and our Chiefs of Staff direct, for I was a member of their Committee. Space does not permit me to enlarge on the dispute that raged over the target area. Thank God, I won through and we landed successfully in Normandy, where we were able to put up a really credible deception plan that we meant to land in the Calais area, which kept all the enemy forces and strong defences concentrated in the wrong place.

And then in the autumn of 1943 I was sent out to set up the Supreme Allied Command in south-east Asia and so was many thousands of miles away on D-Day. It is most kind of the authors to have recognized the part I played in planning and preparing for Overlord before D-Day by inviting me to write this Foreword.

Warren Tute was a naval officer actively involved in all Combined Operations from February 1942 and ended with my successor in Combined Operations Headquarters; thus he is one of the few people to realize the part 'Combined Operations' played in the success of Overlord. I wasn't there so I have read this manuscript with particular interest and am sure the book will prove a real success.

Mountbatten of Burma

A.F.

For author's note on Lord Mountbatten, see p.250

1 'We Shall Go Back'

**'Britain will fight on . . .
if necessary for years . . .
if necessary alone . . .
We shall go back.'**

Winston Churchill 1940

Previous pages: The battle for France is lost. June 1940, and a last look at the Continent for some of the 330,000 British troops evacuated from the beaches of Dunkirk. It will be four years before they return to France
Left: 'Bands of Brothers'. The commandos were established in 1940, shortly after Dunkirk, as Britain's amphibious raiding force. Their first cross-Channel attack was on 23 June 1940
Below: 'We shall fight on the beaches' – the British defiance of Nazi Germany was characterized in this Churchill cartoon published by the *Daily Express* on 8 June 1940

On the night of 23 June 1940, hours after France had signed her humiliating surrender to Hitler's Reich in the forest of Compiègne, a group of R.A.F. high-speed launches nosed silently out of the English south-coast harbours of Folkestone, Dover and Newhaven. They glided past the battered naval craft, pleasure steamers, yachts and fishing boats which had – miraculously – brought home the 330,000 British and French soldiers from the beaches of Dunkirk only three weeks before.

This tiny fleet turned into the Channel and headed towards France. On board were the first British fighting men – just over a hundred of them – to attack Nazi-occupied Europe even before the world could assess what the French armistice really meant. In mid-Channel the assault force of men, soon to be called Commandos, blackened their faces with grease paint hurriedly purchased from a Soho theatrical costumier. Armed with twenty tommy-guns (all the army could spare from its total surviving reserve of only forty) they reached the French coast.

One party landed on the dunes near Boulogne, after running down a seaplane in the harbour, and surprised some Wehrmacht sentries. Others went ashore near Le Touquet and attacked a large building which looked like a garrison H.Q., killing two Germans. No one could claim such results as a spectacular contribution to the grand strategy of the war, yet when they returned home they were cheered by every vessel they passed on the way into harbour. This was the first gesture of defiance, the first tiny presage of things to come.

By the summer of 1940 the 'blitzkrieg' had conquered Europe. War had been revolutionized by the brilliant German combination of armour, air-power and speed. Hitler had changed the balance of European power as dramatically as Napoleon. By the summer of 1940, Czechoslovakia, Poland, Denmark, Norway, the Netherlands, Belgium and France had all been overrun. This hitherto unthinkable situation generated in the British their ancient fear of a continent united against them controlled by a determined enemy. For millions of people the world they had known had gone, and Hitler's New Order now dominated their lives.

The British and French High Commands suffered the greatest shock. Their military preparations for a 'second round' to the Great War of 1914–18 had been based on a defensive strategy. That bloody struggle had seen millions of men confronting each other from trenches in the Flanders mud. Movement was slight and thousands of lives could be lost for the temporary gain of a few yards. In the twenties and thirties it seemed logical to the French to construct round themselves a sort of Great Wall of China which could never be breached. This was the Maginot Line – but it stopped at the Belgian frontier, 200 miles from the sea.

The huge guns and the concrete fortifications of the Maginot Line were indeed a formidable deterrent to any frontal attack. Whether or not it would have held will never be known since, when Hitler attacked on 10 May 1940, he simply drove his Panzers through the 'impossible, impenetrable' Ardennes forests and outflanked the Maginot Line.

Three weeks later, the French army had collapsed and the British Expeditionary Force had

Master of Europe

Left: Adolf Hitler surveys Paris after the fall of France
Top right: Britain's front line. A squadron of Hurricane fighters at the time of the Battle of Britain, August–September 1940
Bottom right: Preparations for Sea Lion

been thrown off the continent of Europe, its precious equipment littering the seafront of Dunkirk. France called back as her leader the aged Marshal Pétain, who had saved the country in the First World War, and sued for peace. Great Britain was expected to follow suit in a matter of weeks.

Britain alone

In June 1940, as the victorious Wehrmacht polished its boots for a victory parade down the Champs Elysées, Britain found herself forced back on an island strategy. She stood alone against a Nazi-dominated Europe. Only one obstacle blocked the way to Hitler's total mastery and that was the English Channel. 'I must admit you have a very good anti-tank obstacle,' General Weygand, the French Commander-in-Chief, had said to Churchill at their last tragic meeting before the collapse, and in that remark lay his sober assessment of Britain's chances of survival. When France signed her armistice, the rest of the world virtually wrote Britain off.

But the 'anti-tank obstacle' of the English Channel proved to be crucial. Although it began as England's moat against Hitler, four years later it was the Nazi aggressors' best defence. But first it was Hitler's opportunity for an invasion.

Like it or not, from June 1940 onwards, if Hitler and his Oberkommando der Wehrmacht (O.K.W.) staff wanted to strike finally and decisively at Britain, they had to face the problem of moving a large military force across a defended sea barrier. It was not a task they relished. The British Army might well have lost what inadequate equipment it had, but the powerful Royal Navy remained supreme and the R.A.F. still commanded British skies. Time, initially on Hitler's side, would not stay that way for long and the Führer's hesitation to invade was, in the event, to prove fatal. His caution was based on a deep-rooted instinct that when Great Britain totted up the odds against her, after the fall of France, she would be bound to sue for peace. He had told his Generals in 1939 that 'if Holland and Belgium are successfully occupied and if France is also defeated, the fundamental conditions for a successful war against England will have been secured. England can then be blockaded from

The German Operation Sea Lion plan ordered under Directive No. 16 laid down overall requirements for the invasion of Britain. It started with the daunting command that 'preparations for the entire operation must be completed by the middle of August'. The landing, which was to be a surprise crossing between the Isle of Wight and Ramsgate, would be carried out by one army group. There were three main prerequisites for its success. First: 'The English Air Force must be so reduced morally and physically that it is unable to deliver any significant attack against the German crossing.' Then, in order to compensate for German naval weakness in the face of what would obviously be bitter resistance by the Royal Navy: 'The Straits of Dover must be closely sealed off with minefields on both flanks; also the western entrance to the Channel approximately on the line Alderney–Portland.'

The whole operation was dominated by the interests of the army which was to 'draw up the operational and crossing plans for all formations of the first wave of the invasion'. The German Navy was reduced to the role of a mere carrier, to 'procure the means for the invasion and will take them in accordance with the wishes of the Army . . . to the various embarkation points'.

Against this German force, which originally started as a forty-division army group but was whittled down to thirty-two divisions, none of which were Panzers (armour was included with the infantry formations), Britain could bring into action on the south coast sixteen divisions, of which three were armoured, as well as coastal forces and local defence formations. German control of the sea could also only be transitory.

Air supremacy was the one vital factor which could turn the scales.

MIGHTIER YET!
In ships, tonnage
the British Empire
million tons
force in the world
of British
ALDWYCH

Top left: Threat from the skies. German propaganda cartoon of August 1940. Left: 'London can take it' – sheltering from Luftwaffe bombs in tube stations during the Blitz
Right: 'France is not alone' – Charles de Gaulle broadcasts his historic call to French patriots from London, 18 June 1940

western France at close quarters by the air force, while the navy with its U-boats can extend the range of the blockade. When that is done, England will not be able to fight on the continent and daily attacks by the air force and navy will cut her lines. The moment England's supply routes are severed, she will be forced to capitulate.'

The reluctant invader

In 1940, the British military leaders took the invasion threat very seriously indeed. Churchill feared a rapid strike by small groups of armour and airborne troops which could evade the naval defences. This was urged by some of Hitler's Generals even before the campaign in France was over but was fortunately not taken seriously. Nobody knows what might have happened if Hitler had risked his hand at that time. The British land defences were virtually non-existent and what became known as the Home Guard, though as brave and ferocious as a terrier, would have been just about as effective.

The paramount reason for Hitler's reluctance to launch an invasion of Britain, however, remained political. Odd as it seems, he had no wish to destroy the British Empire. Hitler had long admired the two great stabilizing powers in the world – the British Empire and the Roman Catholic Church. He intended to keep both in being but under strong German control. Why wreck the British Empire for the ultimate benefit of America, Russia and Japan? He hoped to negotiate Britain out of the war.

In June 1940, General Halder of the O.K.W. recorded in his diary: 'There was talk of negotiations being conducted through Sweden; then through the Duke of Alba, but nothing definitive came in the way of confrontation.'

On 19 July, Hitler made a conciliatory speech in the Reichstag claiming that he did not want war with the British Empire but warning that 'a great Empire will be destroyed . . . an Empire it was never my intention to destroy or even harm'.

Then, in language hardly likely to appease Churchill, he went on, 'I consider myself in a position to make this appeal since I am not the vanquished begging favours but the victor speaking in the name of reason.'

In London the offer was treated with icy contempt. It was formally brushed aside on 22 July.

If Britain would not surrender she had to be eliminated, even if, in the Führer's view, 'this is not just a river crossing but the crossing of a sea which is dominated by the enemy'. In spite of all his fears and O.K.W. scepticism about a successful military operation, Hitler had to accept Britain's challenge. Almost every free government of the nations overrun by German armies was now sheltered in London. Hotels, boarding houses and private homes housed ministers and political leaders of the occupied powers. They had formed legal governments-in-exile serving as a constant reminder to Hitler of his own illegitimate rule. Governments and cabinets met and worked in London. The monarchs of Norway and the Netherlands, and the President of Poland all symbolized their countries' will to resist. Allegiance to the Third Reich or any of its puppet regimes would automatically be an act of treason.

The most difficult case was the most important of all – that of France. On 18 June, de Gaulle had spoken in defiant terms to the French people: 'I ask you to believe me when I say that the cause of France is not lost. The very factors that brought about our defeat may one day lead us to victory. For remember France does not stand alone. She is not isolated. . . . This war is not limited to our unfortunate country. The outcome of the struggle has not been decided by the Battle of France. This is a world war. . . . The flames of French resistance must not and shall not die.'

In early July, Hitler decided that an invasion of Britain was possible, 'provided that air superiority can be attained and certain other necessary conditions fulfilled.' On 16 July Hitler decreed in Directive No. 16: 'Since England, in spite of her hopeless military position, shows no sign of coming to terms, I have decided to prepare a landing operation against England and, if necessary, to carry it out.'

Churchill saw Hitler's problem quite clearly. These 'certain other necessary conditions' were just as formidable for the German Führer as the winning of air supremacy. They were to provide the British Prime Minister with invaluable experience

Attacking the Life-line

when it came to launching the great Allied seaborne expeditions later in the war.

In Churchill's view, 'the invasion of England in the summer and autumn of 1940 required from Germany local naval superiority and immense special fleets and landing craft'. In the summer of 1940 none of these conditions obtained. In comparison with the plans evolved by the Allies four years later, the *ad hoc* efforts of Hitler's commanders in contemplating the first cross-Channel plan of the war were highly risky and woefully inadequate.

The broken eagle

Air supremacy was the one vital factor which could turn the scales. Ships had shown their vulnerability to air attack at Narvik and Dunkirk where 218 vessels out of 765 had been sunk, including six destroyers. Once the R.A.F. had been destroyed by raids on airfields and aircraft production, the Luftwaffe would concentrate on coastal fortifications and would 'aim to break the first resistance of the enemy land forces, dispersing reserves on their way to the front'. Thus, in addition to the British fleet, road and rail communications would also be top targets.

Churchill was indeed right when he wrote: 'Our fate now depended upon victory in the air.'

Everything now turned on air-power. On 2 August Goering issued the first orders listing as objectives the destruction of the R.A.F., command of the air over southern England and attacks on the British fleet.

The first air assaults started on 13 August with Air Fleets 1 and 2 launching attacks with 485 bombers and 1,000 fighters. Nine airfields were attacked. As August wore on the battle reached its peak. Hitler had ruled that all services were to be ready to launch Operation Sea Lion on 15 September but the air battle was far from won. Luftwaffe losses mounted. On 3 September the invasion was postponed until 21 September.

R.A.F. victories provided Hitler with an excuse to abandon all thoughts of a landing in Britain in the immediate future. On 17 September, Sea Lion was indefinitely postponed.

The double threat. Far left: The U-boat offensive was stepped up and the Battle of the Atlantic raged for three years. Left: Luftwaffe bomber crews rained down high explosive on British cities and industry in the winter of 1941

Below right: Hitler's eastern strategy, 1941. The Führer, Goering and Field-Marshal Keitel plan Operation Barbarossa – the invasion of Russia

The invasion fleet of 168 transports, 1,910 barges, 419 tugs and trawlers as well as 1,600 motor-boats dispersed. The German armies would be released for land-warfare; this was the kind they understood. In the meantime Britain was to be attacked by air and sea. A U-boat offensive would be waged against Britain's lifelines and the Luftwaffe was ordered to blitz London and other cities, with the aim of destroying the British economy and terrorizing the population. A drive was also mounted against British imperial shipping lanes in the Mediterranean and her sources of oil in the Middle East.

Hitler had now to take his most crucial decision of the war. In order to have the power and the freedom to deal with Britain, he would have to remove the Russian menace once and for all. Hitler had always regarded it as his mission to protect western civilization from Bolshevism. Now, with his superb fighting machine, he would destroy it, at the same time removing all hope for Britain.

According to General Warlimont, then Deputy Chief of Operations at O.K.W., Hitler underlined the record of a planning conference which had noted that, 'Russia is the factor by which England sets the greatest store . . . if Russia is beaten England's last hope is gone. Germany is then master of Europe and the Balkans . . . As a result of this argument, Russia must be dealt with in spring 1941'.

For Britain without allies – or only token allies so far as military strength was concerned – 1940 and early 1941 were grim years indeed. Britain now had to defend the Middle East not only against the Italian army, but also against Rommel's Afrika Korps. Moreover, German troops had helped the luckless Duce to conquer Greece in May 1941 and British forces had then been hurled out of Crete by a daring German airborne assault. Luftwaffe Stukas then painfully demonstrated for a second time the vulnerability of ships to air attack, inflicting high naval losses on the British at Crete. This showed the British Chiefs of Staff, still anxious about a possible invasion of the United Kingdom, how a sea barrier could be successfully passed, given air supremacy.

A further strain on British sea-power was the growing militancy of Japan in the Far East. Some of the richer possessions of the British Empire could be threatened by a Pacific aggressor. But Churchill's main anxiety in this dark period of the war continued to be the rising losses of vital shipping from U-boat attacks. Britain seemed to be in a long dark tunnel with only the smallest pinprick of light to be seen. Hopes which had risen after the Battle of Britain sank now to their lowest ebb. Britain simply did not have the strength to defend both herself and her world-wide commitments. She was building an army of fifty divisions and 7,000 front-line aircraft to be ready by 1942, but on 8 December 1940 – a year before Pearl Harbor – Churchill was writing to Roosevelt: 'The form which this war has taken and seems likely to hold does not enable us to match the immense armies of Germany in any theatre where their main power can be brought to bear. We can, however, by the use of sea-power and air-power meet the German armies in regions where only comparatively small forces can be brought to action.'

Then in June 1941 Britain suddenly acquired a new, unexpected but welcome ally which was to

change the whole course of the war. On 22 June 1941 the Wehrmacht smashed across the Russian frontier. Advancing in swift Panzer drives, 120 divisions, nineteen of them armoured, went into action on a 500-mile front. Three army groups in the north, centre and south drove in the Russian forces. Soviet losses were staggering.

Churchill's reaction was immediate and characteristic. A lifelong opponent of communism, he had said, 'If Hitler invaded Hell, I would at least make a favourable reference to the Devil in the House of Commons'. The course was clear. On B.B.C. radio at nine o'clock on the day of the Russian invasion, Churchill urged the nation in unforgettable tones to stand alongside the Russians in a common cause: 'We have but one aim and one single irrevocable purpose. We are resolved to destroy Hitler and every vestige of the Nazi régime. From this nothing will turn us, nothing! We will never parley, we will never negotiate with Hitler or with any of his gang.'

Churchill left the people of Britain in no doubt as to the immense issues at stake in Russia. 'He [Hitler] wishes to destroy the Russian power because he hopes that if he succeeds in this he will be able to bring back the main strength of his army and air force from the east and hurl it upon this island, which he knows he must conquer or suffer the penalty for his crimes. His invasion of Russia is no more than a prelude to an invasion of the British Isles.'

'Second Front Now!'

Churchill's stirring call to arms was greeted by twenty-six days of silence from the Kremlin.

Barbarossa, as Hitler called his blitzkrieg on Russia, was biting deeply before Stalin saw fit to reply. The Soviet leader wanted anything that would relieve the pressure on his reeling armies, and his response struck a note which was to reverberate, waspishly at times, until D-Day itself. In his first message to Churchill on 18 July 1941, Stalin called for a second front to help relieve the hard-pressed Red Armies. This was the beginning of unrelenting Soviet pressure for a cross-Channel invasion and was to colour all relations between the Kremlin and the British and, later, the Americans for the remainder of the war. Stalin had even less understanding of sea-power than Hitler. He saw the matter in simple terms and expressed it forcefully: 'It seems to me, therefore, that the military situation of the Soviet Union as well as of Great Britain would be considerably improved if there could be established a front against Hitler in the west – northern France – and in the north – the Arctic. A front in northern France could not only divert Hitler's forces from the east but at the same time would make it impossible for Hitler to invade Great Britain. The establishment of the front just mentioned would be popular with the British Army as well as with the whole population of southern England.'

For Britain, however, such an operation in 1941, or even 1942, was unthinkable, in spite of Stalin's last 'helpful' remark. The risks far outweighed the chance of success. British military leaders such as Admiral Ramsay, who had managed to change the disaster of Dunkirk into something of a triumph, Generals Alexander, Alan Brooke and Montgomery, who had been overwhelmed in battle by the German preponderance in armour and air support, and Air Marshal Leigh Mallory, who had known how close defeat had loomed in the Battle of Britain – all these experienced commanders had

Barbarossa unleashed. Hitler launched his eastern offensive on 22 June 1941. The Panzers plunged swiftly into Russian territory; on the first day, 10,000 prisoners were captured

a healthy respect for the toughness of the German military machine. Their sober assessment of what was and what was not possible had the full backing of the British War Cabinet. It would be a long time before British forces could cross the Channel. As Churchill wrote: 'The Russians never understood in the smallest degree the nature of the amphibious operation necessary to disembark and maintain a great invasion army upon a well defended, hostile coast. Even the Americans were at this time largely unaware of the difficulties. Not only sea but air superiority was indispensable. Moreover, there was a third vital factor. A vast armada of specially constructed landing craft, above all tank-landing craft in numerous varieties, was the foundation of any successful heavily opposed landing.'

At the time of Stalin's appeal, the British Army could barely muster a front-line strength equal to that of the British Expeditionary Force which had been evacuated from Dunkirk. Landing craft were almost non-existent.

It is not surprising that Churchill replied to Stalin on 20 July 1941, 'The Chiefs of Staff do not see any way of doing anything on a scale likely to be of the slightest use to you'. Churchill went on, 'To attempt a landing in force would be to encounter a bloody repulse, and petty raids would only lead to fiascos doing far more harm than good to both of us.'

The 'butcher's bill'

The awareness of 'a bloody repulse' and what it could mean became a deep preoccupation of the British government and their Chiefs of Staff. It tended to dominate their thinking almost until D-Day itself to the exasperation not only of the Russians but also of the Americans once they had entered the fray. Despite the immense pressure brought to bear on them not only by their Allies but also by a vociferous section of public opinion in Britain, the War Cabinet never liked the idea of a landing in France. The fear lay deep of what Lieutenant-General Frederick Morgan, later to be Eisenhower's chief planner, called the 'butcher's bill', and the shades of 1914–18. The British were not keen on 'sticking their necks out further than they had ever stuck them before'.

A hasty cross-Channel thrust, followed by a slaughter on the dunes of Calais or Boulogne, would rule out any successful invasion for years. To Stalin this was incomprehensible. He saw his own armies locked in a desperate struggle with seventy-five per cent of the Wehrmacht. What, then, was this British reluctance to attack the Germans who were only a few miles across the Channel? Stalin even went so far as to suggest sending a Red Army corps to assist Churchill, if the British were frightened of taking on the much-vaunted Germans by themselves.

Yet while there was a real danger of Soviet collapse – or, worse, the kind of disenchantment which would drive Stalin to do another deal with Hitler and so allow the Germans to turn all their forces on Britain – Churchill had to keep open the option of a landing in France which would effectively draw German forces away from the eastern front. At the same time it was hoped that the Russian armies, reeling back though they were, would be able to hold out until the United States could throw in her immense strength on the Allied side. One fact was clear, and entered all British calculations: without massive American help, the British could never invade Hitler's '*Festung Europa*', ['Fortress Europe'].

Under an obscure act of 1892 the United States Secretary of Defence could lease war equipment to anyone he chose, 'when, in his discretion, it will be for the public good'. There was no doubt about what was good for the American public in Roosevelt's mind and he defended his actions at a press conference on 16 December 1940. Already, since Dunkirk, Britain had traded the use of British bases in Newfoundland and the West Indies for fifty old but invaluable U.S. destroyers and had continued to buy arms from American factories. Now, under Lease-Lend, she could press on with her rearmament programme, undeterred by the knowledge that her dollars were getting scarcer. They would never run out whilst Britain remained in the war.

The friendship and underlying identity of interests – at any rate as far as the war was concerned – between the two great English-speaking nations was symbolized by the warm understanding which existed between Roosevelt and Churchill. One of the first practical gestures made by Roosevelt after his re-election as President in November 1940 was to sanction what Churchill called 'the most unsordid act in the history of nations'. This went by the name of Lease-Lend. It dismayed the Axis and delighted the Allies.

Atlantic Charter

The first Allied summit meeting took place at Placentia Bay in Newfoundland in August 1941. Churchill crossed the Atlantic in the new battleship H.M.S. *Prince of Wales*. Roosevelt travelled north in the U.S.S. *Augusta*, a heavy cruiser of the United States Navy.

When the news of this meeting broke, the world saw it as symbolic and sensational; from it came the historic Atlantic Charter on which the future conduct of the war was based. The Joint Declaration of 19 August 1941 spelt out principles common to both the United States and Great Britain. They declared their resounding opposition to any 'territorial changes that do not accord with the freely expressed wishes of the peoples concerned'. All peoples had the right to 'choose the form of government under which they will live and rights would be restored to those who had lost them'.

It was an extraordinary statement of intent by a neutral country in support of a belligerent. It meant that the war was now both global and ideological.

Those cynics who had expected America's declaration of war to be made at that time – a virtual impossibility in the United States' political scene of the day – and had then described the outcome of the meeting as nothing but a nebulous profession of good intentions, were confounded by Roosevelt's subsequent and forthright broadcast in which he referred bluntly to 'the final destruction of Nazi tyranny'.

The British Chiefs of Staff then outlined their limited strategy for the continuation of the war against Germany. The possibility of the British Army landing in north-west Europe and taking on the Wehrmacht on its own territory now seemed distinctly remote. British hopes lay in blockading and carrying out an increasing air offensive against the German heartland. It was hoped this would produce a deterioration in morale as the Nazi war machine and economy ran short of materials.

Pressure from within

At the same time, the oppressed nations of Europe were to be encouraged to develop underground resistance campaigns against their German rulers. These factors, it was hoped, would crack the fortress from within and then the British Army could safely be landed in the ports of northern and western Europe to finish off Hitler's war machine. Any contribution by the Russians, who were then falling back rapidly before the German blitzkrieg, was discounted. Many in Britain expected a decisive German victory by the turn of 1941.

The accent was still on defence and no end to the struggle was in sight. However, the idea of an eventual return to France lived on, and it was during this dark, uncertain period that the nucleus of what would become the British component of the D-Day team was unobtrusively assembled. The design, manufacture and testing of specialized equipment such as landing craft were begun and the problems of where to go, how to do it – and when – started to be intensively studied. Although the British were certainly not strong enough to invade Europe alone, the essential groundwork was being undertaken in the full expectation that one day the Allies would indeed be going back.

The seeds of D-Day

Early attempts to marshal Anglo-American talent, however, revealed the difficulties which the two nations would soon have to solve in the forthcoming combined role. On board the *Augusta* at the Newfoundland meeting, the British Chiefs of Staff had initiated discussion of an operation to put ashore an Allied force in Europe. Sadly, the American Chiefs of Staff replied that with the United States still at peace they had no authority to deal with

Opposite: 'The Union Strong and Great'. The first meeting between Roosevelt and Churchill on board a British battleship at Placentia Bay, Newfoundland, 10 August 1941. From it came the declaration of the Atlantic Charter

Day of infamy – 7 December 1941. Japanese carrier aircraft strike Pearl Harbor, bringing the United States into the war. The U.S.S. *Maryland* survived the attack (left) but the U.S.S. *Oklahoma* capsized (right)

major strategic problems.

As early as July 1941 a plan had been drawn up by the Inter Services Training and Development Centre (I.S.T.D.C.) in England. This was then the expert department on amphibious warfare. It examined the 'scope of the future operation which will be necessary to secure the ultimate defeat of Germany *on the assumption that the U.S.A. is a belligerent*'. This was one of the first seeds of D-Day.

The plan estimated that fifteen armoured and twenty infantry divisions would be needed for the invasion of north-west Europe, plus the support of local patriot forces. On the vital question of supply, the report concluded that: 'Forces will have to be maintained from England, the Channel being regarded as a river rather than the sea.'

This plan was valuable for drawing attention to the most critical problem of all – shipping. The broadest calculation assumed that 'one division including non-divisional troops and their components could total 45,000 men and 6,000 vehicles, all of which was to be shipped from the United States'. This would require half a million tons of shipping. Even the United States would need four months to build this tonnage without any allowance being made for the heavy losses mounting up in the Battle of the Atlantic. In the six months to July 1941 nearly $1\frac{1}{2}$ million tons of shipping had been sunk.

Pearl Harbor

On 7 December 1941 waves of Japanese carrier-borne aircraft attacked the American Pacific Fleet at Pearl Harbor. U.S. naval power in the Pacific was crippled in one stunning blow. The imperial armies of Japan then went on to attack Malaya, Singapore, the Dutch East Indies, the Philippines and other islands of the Pacific – in every case with alarming success. However, the shock of Pearl Harbor brought the United States, with all her resources, into the war.

Pearl Harbor was a strategic misfortune for the Führer. Hitler had done everything in his power to induce the Japanese to attack Russia at Vladivostok rather than America. He warned that this would inevitably bring the combined strength of the two Anglo-Saxon powers to bear on his western front, whilst no decision had yet been reached in the east.

Strategic concepts on the Allied side were totally transformed by the Japanese attack. As Churchill said, 'Hitler's fate was sealed. Mussolini's fate was sealed. As for the Japanese they would be ground to powder. All the rest was merely the proper application of overwhelming force.'

2 Forging the Alliance
1942

Grand Alliance. Two weeks after Pearl Harbor, Churchill travelled to Washington to meet Roosevelt and to agree a grand strategy of 'Europe first'. The British Prime Minister addressed a joint session of Congress on 26 December (opposite right) and told them, 'We shall never cease to persevere against the enemy until we have taught them a lesson which the world will never forget'. Opposite left: President Roosevelt marshalled the American nation behind the 'Europe first' strategy, in spite of strong pressure to avenge Pearl Harbor

The entry of the United States into the war, although providing the industrial and economic power for a final victory, raised awkward questions. How were American resources best to be deployed? The jubilation of Churchill and the British War Cabinet at having the Americans by their side was tempered by the fact that powerful voices in Washington placed a higher priority on defeating Japan rather than Germany.

The chief protagonist of the 'Pacific first' strategy was the U.S. Navy, led by Admiral Ernest J. King, the Chief of Staff, who is alleged to have said, 'I fought under the goddam British in the First World War, and if I can help it no ship of mine will fight under them again.' He saw the fundamental responsibility of the U.S. Navy as the defence of the Pacific; this was a task that only the American fleet could undertake. As the Japanese advanced from island to island, King took the initiative in calling for containment. In the Atlantic and in European waters the U.S. Navy's role would be much less dramatic and would in all likelihood entail being subordinate to or under the operational control of the Royal Navy. The British found it difficult to sympathize with the U.S. Navy's position.

A major conference was held in Washington over the Christmas period of 1941 at which Churchill, Roosevelt and their staffs planned the basic Allied strategy. The British point of view was put bluntly enough: 'The war cannot be ended by driving Japan back to her own bounds and defeating her overseas forces. The war can only be ended through the defeat in Europe of the German armies, or through the internal convulsions in Germany produced by the unfavourable course of the war.'

The immediate aim should therefore be to close the ring around Germany, by dominating the Mediterranean and liberating north Africa, whilst Japan was contained in the Far East. The next step, hopefully slated for 1943, was 'to prepare for the liberation of the captive countries of western and southern Europe by the landing at suitable points successively or simultaneously of British and American armies strong enough to enable the conquered populations to revolt'.

Although this did not suit Admiral King, in the Washington discussions the British received the welcome support of the American Army Chief of Staff, General George C. Marshall, as well as that of the President himself.

Memorandum WW.1 of the Washington Conference set out the final conclusions of the Chiefs of Staff: 'The two powers would maintain only such positions in the Eastern Theatre as will safeguard vital interests and deny to Japan access to raw materials vital to her continuous war effort while we are concentrating on the defeat of Germany.'

Churchill had won his point. To achieve the objectives American forces would be built up in Britain under a plan code-named Operation Bolero. In addition, there would be an operation to clear north Africa in 1942. The Washington Conference was an impressive display of Anglo-American unity, and one of its most important aspects was the setting up of a basic Allied command structure. Although Britain had her own Chiefs of Staff, and the U.S. its Joint Chiefs, senior officers were posted to each country's capital to maintain liaison.

Pressure on the Alliance

The clear-cut agreements reached at Washington in December 1941 did not remain clear for long. Although they had adopted the British strategy of attrition, the Americans began to grow uneasy about what appeared to be the slow and rather dilatory way of bringing the Germans to decisive battle. The British appeared to prefer to blockade and throttle the enemy rather than confront him. The first months of 1942 threw all plans into doubt. The war was going very badly indeed for the Allies. By March, Churchill was writing to Roosevelt: 'I find it difficult to realize how gravely British affairs have deteriorated by what has happened since December 7th.'

In the Far East, the Japanese had inflicted a humiliating military disaster on the British by capturing Singapore. The Bay of Bengal and the Indian Ocean were now directly threatened by the Japanese Navy. In the Middle East, Rommel had been sent to support the ailing Italians and was already driving the British out of Cyrenaica and opening

Far right: A plan called Sledgehammer was considered for a small landing on the mainland of Europe in 1944 to relieve German pressure on the Red Army. It was quickly abandoned as being too risky
Right: Stalin in Moscow, 1941. Throughout the winter the Soviet capital defied the German attacks. In spring 1942, the Soviet leader put diplomatic pressure on his allies to open a second front

the road to Egypt. Malta was under siege, and at sea the U-boats were sinking an alarming amount of tonnage; in the first three months of 1942 over a million tons had been sunk.

Finally, on the biggest and most important front of all, the Red Army had suffered immense losses since the beginning of Operation Barbarossa. Hitler claimed that Russia had lost over 2½ million men, 1,400 aircraft and 18,000 tanks. The Moscow offensive late in 1941 yielded another 600,000 Russian prisoners. The British and Americans began to wonder how long the Soviet Union could survive such punishment. As Churchill confessed: 'The whole of the Levant and Caspian Front now depends entirely upon the success of the Russian armies . . . the attack which the Germans will deliver upon Russia in the spring will, I fear, be most formidable.' It began to look as if Hitler's strategy would actually work, that his gigantic gamble would pay off.

There is little wonder that the British and Americans scarcely knew where to turn. The Chiefs of Staff began to realize they might be forced to attack across the English Channel, whether they were ready or not.

Soon Roosevelt was adding his weight to the pressure on Churchill to provide Russia with some relief apart from all other commitments. In March 1942, Roosevelt wrote to Churchill that 'he was becoming more and more interested in the establishment of a new front this summer on the European continent'.

The British Chiefs of Staff were not prepared to be so easily swayed by this outburst of American energy. Some American military opinion began to express itself that the British, with their distaste for the cross-Channel offensive and their preference for operations in the Mediterranean, were in reality only preserving their Empire. The plan to clear north Africa was declared by some U.S. military planners to be 'motivated more largely by political than by sound strategical purposes'.

An acid expression of this American frustration came from General Albert C. Wedemeyer of the Operations and Planning Staff: 'The British were masters in negotiation; particularly were they adept in the use of phrases or words which were capable of more than one interpretation . . . when matters of state were involved our British opposite numbers had elastic scruples. To skirt the facts for King and Country was justified in the conscience of these British gentlemen . . . what I witnessed was the British power of finesse in its finest hour – a power that had been developed over centuries of successful international intrigue, cajolery and tacit compulsions.'

The British, of course, did not quite see it that way.

U.S. calls for action

In the spring of 1942 the U.S. Army produced *its* plan for winning the war. This was pressed forward by Marshall to try to stem the cries of King's Pacific lobby which was calling for a maximum effort against Japan. Eisenhower's team in the Operations and Planning Department had worked on certain essential facts for a cross-Channel invasion with Britain as the base for the attack.

On 8 April 1942, the President's two emissaries, Harry Hopkins and General Marshall, arrived in London. They carried in their briefcases Eisenhower's plan, earnestly recommended by the President. In the first sentence it clearly set out American intentions:

'Western Europe is favoured as the theatre in which to stage the first major offensive by the United States and Great Britain. Only there could their combined land and air resources be fully developed and the maximum support given to Russia.'

Preparations should be made at once, therefore, the plan went on, for a forty-eight-division invasion of France. Eighteen of these divisions would be British. Supporting air forces would number 5,800 combat aircraft of which Britain would supply 2,550. Since the plan stated 'Speed is the essence of the problem', everything should be ready by 1 April 1943. Seven thousand landing craft would need to be assembled. The landing should take place somewhere between Boulogne and Le Havre on a six-division front. Reinforcements would need to be at the rate of 100,000 men a week.

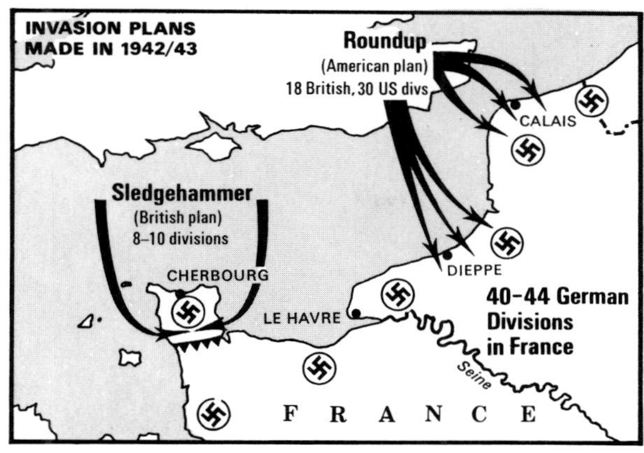

General Eisenhower, then Chief of the U.S. Army Operations and Planning Staff, believed: 'We've got to go to Europe and fight – and we've got to quit wasting resources all over the world and, still worse, wasting time. If we're going to keep Russia in, save the Middle East, India and Burma, we've got to begin slugging with air at West Europe, to be followed by a land attack as soon as possible.'

Marshall had added an important rider which took care of the ever-present anxiety for them that by 1943 it might all be too late. The Red Army might collapse at any time: 'A plan must be prepared and kept up to date for immediate action by such forces as may be available from time to time. This may have to be put into effect as an emergency measure either (a) to take advantage of a sudden German disintegration or (b) as a sacrifice to avert an imminent collapse of Russian resistance.'

The chief burden of this action would fall on the British, since the American industrial machine was only just gearing itself up for total war production.

Churchill had no hesitation in cordially accepting the overall plan, subject to the defence of India and the Middle East. This was supported by the British Chief of the Imperial General Staff (C.I.G.S.), Sir Alan Brooke. However, the British war leaders were strongly against Marshall's proposal for a short, sharp cross-Channel operation before the main landing. They saw this as a suicide attempt to take the pressure off the Red Army.

It was left to the politician, Harry Hopkins, who was Roosevelt's right-hand man, to remind the military of other important facts of life. 'If public opinion had its way,' he said, 'the weight of American effort would be directed against Japan.' But the British war leaders could read between the lines; the pressure for American diversion to the Pacific might not be resisted for much longer.

Molotov's demands

The main invasion plan was now given the code name of 'Round-up', the smaller cross-Channel operation being entitled 'Sledgehammer'. In essence, this plan was similar to various other plans which had been drawn up by the British since 1940 for the occupation of either the Cherbourg Peninsula or Brittany.

After the meeting Churchill cabled Roosevelt his agreement that all preparations for Round-up should be made for a successful landing in 1943. There was no suggestion from any quarter that the previously agreed plan to clear the north African coast would be in any way affected.

Although the British accepted the American proposal for Round-up and Eisenhower was transferred to command the build-up of American forces in Britain (under the daunting title of European Theatre of Operations United States Army – ETOUSA), nothing could induce the British Chiefs of Staff to like Sledgehammer which they regarded as a totally unacceptable risk.

Accordingly, a small team of experienced British commanders was assembled in London to examine and analyse the conflicting views of Sledgehammer and Round-up. This group consisted of General Sir Bernard Paget, Air Chief Marshal Sir Sholto Douglas and Admiral Sir Bertram Ramsay – each being appointed as Commander-in-Chief of his respective service for the Expeditionary Force as it was then called. Ramsay, a quiet Scot who had added to his already high reputation by successfully organizing the evacuation from Dunkirk, wrote scathingly in the summer of 1942: 'Things have been in a proper mess in higher direction circles owing to the American desire to do something quickly without knowing what it is possible to do. Consequently their perspective is all wrong and they have shown it. However I think that after much argument they do see things a little more clearly.'

Pressure for action soon came from another source which could not be ignored. On 20 May 1942 the Soviet Foreign Minister, Molotov, passed through London on his way to see Roosevelt. He was blunt and desperate. Stalin required the immediate opening of a second front in France to divert a minimum of forty Wehrmacht divisions from the east. This demand was particularly awkward for Churchill. Russia had to be kept in the war at all costs. Churchill tried to make the Soviet leaders understand the serious risks of an inadequately prepared cross-Channel invasion. Substantial air cover was essential and he stressed that Britain's small resources could be squandered in a week.

Molotov's obduracy, however, secured him Roosevelt's support and on his return via London, the British Prime Minister found it expedient to issue a communiqué on 11 June which stated: 'Full understanding was reached with regard to the

The commandos developed their expertise by embarking on a lively programme of raids on the Lofotens, Spitzbergen and Vaagso. An ambitious scheme was worked out by Keyes for the capture of the Italian island of Pantelleria in the Mediterranean off the African coast. But this was never tried since, in October 1941, Churchill decided that a younger and more dynamic man was needed for these new techniques. Keyes was replaced by forty-one-year-old Lord Louis Mountbatten, a naval officer whose personality and training gave him unique qualifications for the job. Under 'new management' Combined Operations rapidly became a power-house providing major experience for amphibious operations and assault techniques.

urgent tasks of creating a Second Front in Europe in 1942.'

However, Churchill also took the precaution of preparing an *aide-mémoire* which he handed to Molotov before his dangerous flight back to Moscow. This said unequivocally: 'It is impossible to say in advance whether the situation will be such as to make this operation feasible when the time comes. We can therefore give no promise in the matter.' This was an escape clause for the British War Cabinet, which they were determined to use.

It was not only at diplomatic level that the Russians pursued their campaign for a second front. They knew that the British people as a whole were keen for some sort of decisive action to be taken against Hitler whilst his hands were full in Russia. Soon the walls of British cities were blazoned with the slogan 'Second Front Now'. The Soviet Ambassador Maisky, persistent and tetchy as ever, complained: 'There is no time to wait until the last button is sown to the last uniform of the last soldier.' The *Daily Mail* praised his 'sound sense'.

As the British call for a second front became a moral issue, the Chiefs of Staff remained unmoved in their view that a cross-Channel invasion in 1942, unless as a last desperate act to stave off a Russian collapse, would be madness.

Churchill remained adamant. In a memorandum to Roosevelt on 8 July, he claimed that 'no responsible British General, Admiral or Air Marshal is prepared to recommend Sledgehammer as a practical operation in 1942'.

Instead, he urged a north African landing as the best chance of effecting relief to the Russian front. Roosevelt himself was known to favour this policy. It had the added advantage of creating a major political crisis for Vichy France. The French government of Algeria, which had remained loyal to Pétain, would then have to choose sides – whether to support the British and Americans or to shoot back, so identifying France with the German cause.

But just as the British had disliked Sledgehammer, so the American Chiefs of Staff distrusted the idea of directing large forces into the Mediterranean. The Pacific lobby grew in strength and demanded that U.S. effort be diverted to the war against Japan. In Washington, Field-Marshal Sir John Dill, Britain's representative on the Joint Chiefs of Staff, warned that 'there are highly placed Americans who do not believe that anything better than a stalemate with Germany is possible'.

It was clear to both Roosevelt and Churchill that matters could not go on in this fashion for very much longer. Accordingly, Marshall, King and Harry Hopkins were despatched to London with instructions to reach agreement within a week on some suitable military operation for 1942. Dill foresaw the danger and told Churchill, 'unless you can convince them of your unswerving devotion to

Left: Commando raids. Combined Operations was established under Admiral Keyes (far left) in 1940 to harass the enemy coastline with raiding parties. After Lord Louis Mountbatten (centre) became Chief of Combined Operations in 1941, plans for amphibious assaults received a new impetus
Bottom left: 'He promised you shall go'. By abandoning invasion plans for 1942, the British public were left wondering when a second front would be opened. This was summed up in a *Daily Mail* cartoon of 29 July 1942
Bottom right: The Bulldog has Wings'. This *Punch* cartoon of 26 August coincided with Churchill's hazardous flight to Moscow to explain why it was impossible to invade in 1942

"Bolero", everything points to a complete reversal of our present strategy and the withdrawal of America to a war of her own in the Pacific'. The crisis point had been reached. Britain would have to declare herself for the invasion of north-west Europe.

The British held a trump card in that a large proportion of their forces would necessarily have to be committed in any early operation – with the obvious risks this entailed. So, after days of tense negotiation in London, agreement was suddenly reached to invade French North Africa. But Britain had also committed herself to the final objective of a major cross-Channel invasion. On 25 July, Roosevelt ratified these proposals and Operation Torch began, the date for its execution being set as not later than 30 October 1942. The planners had a bare three months in which to prepare the first great Allied landing of the war. This was to be the second front. All that remained was to sell the idea to Stalin.

On 10 August 1942, Churchill flew to Moscow, via Persia, dodging the peaks of Kurdistan, and the first extraordinary meeting between the British and Russian leaders took place. The Prime Minister's plane skirted the Stalingrad battle area. Over the Soviet capital the Moscow anti-aircraft batteries had been warned to expect a British plane and soon Churchill was safely installed in State Villa No. 7 in Moscow. He was dourly received. 'Stalin, whose glumness had by now much increased, said that, as he understood it, we were unable to create a second front with any large force and unwilling even to land six divisions.'

He was hard to convince and was patently unable, or unwilling, to see the difficulties involved. Only when Churchill drew a picture of a crocodile and pointed to its soft underbelly did Marshal Stalin begin to understand the point of attacking the Axis in north Africa. But he could not resist a taunt. He asked Churchill if the British were afraid of the Germans?

Stalin did not like the Anglo-American decision but he had no alternative other than to accept it. Nevertheless, the British War Cabinet decided to mount some form of cross-Channel expedition.

The lessons of Dieppe

The British services were developing the all-important techniques of amphibious warfare which could determine the success or failure of invasion.

In 1940 Churchill recalled to active service the first war expert in amphibious operations who had commanded the Zeebrugge raid, Admiral of the Fleet Sir Roger Keyes, and set up the Directorate of Combined Operations.

The role of this department was to train troops and provide equipment for 'pinprick raids' against the 3,000-mile enemy coastline. Apart from the tac-

Dieppe, 1942

On 19 August, the assault groups drawn from the Canadian regiments in Britain set out on the sixty-mile voyage to the French coast. Fighters provided air cover, and no less than seventy-four Allied air squadrons were on call in anticipation of a major air battle with the Luftwaffe. Although commandos successfully scaled the high cliffs flanking the town to disable the German batteries, assaults on the inner flanks of the beachhead failed to prevent the defences opening a deadly fire on the main landing on the beaches. Casualties were exceptionally heavy and the infantry had great difficulty in surmounting the sea wall. Only a handful managed to penetrate the streets of the Norman town. The tanks also fell victim to the Wall and proved unable to climb on to the promenade. One by one they were destroyed. Out of the 6,100 Canadian and British troops that took part, over 3,500 were killed, missing or taken prisoner. Even the air battle was not a success. One hundred and six Allied planes were shot down to a loss of only forty-eight by the Luftwaffe.

It gave Dr Goebbels an immense propaganda bonus which he immediately exploited. Headlines in the Nazi press proclaimed the Allied disaster, 'CATASTROPHIC DEFEAT A SETBACK TO INVASION . . . WHAT DOES STALIN SAY ABOUT THIS DISASTER TO CHURCHILL'S INVASION?' To serve his purpose, Goebbels had promoted the raid into a full-scale invasion. German confidence in their ability to throw an Allied assault back into the sea received an immense fillip.

tical and morale value of such raids, they were designed to lead, through experience, to bigger operations. The nub of this idea was to develop the design and operation of landing craft and to coordinate the three fighting services in their use.

The target chosen for the cross-Channel expedition was Dieppe and ministers hoped that their action would convince British public opinion of their enthusiasm for cross-Channel operations. The raid was also planned as the biggest test of Combined Operations techniques to date. No fewer than 6,000 men and thirty of the new Churchill tanks were to be used in a plan to seize the harbour and fortifications of Dieppe. The operation, however, was dogged by ill-fortune. In the attack of 19 August 1942 casualties were heavy. The tanks failed to enter the town. Out of the Canadian and British troops taking part, over 3,500 were killed, missing, or taken prisoner.

Dieppe contained hard lessons for the Allies, but they were not wasted. The costly 'reconnaissance in force' proved to the Combined Chiefs of Staff that no fortified Channel port could be taken by direct assault with the resources available in 1942.

A second lesson was that the Atlantic Wall could not be stormed at bearable cost unless the first waves of assault troops were supported by the fire-power of tanks. Work speeded up after Dieppe on the development of specialized armoured assault vehicles.

Yet the Dieppe raid had a profound effect on Hitler's overall strategy. He reacted to the threat to his western front by transferring seven divisions, four of them Panzers, from the Russian front. In the case of the Luftwaffe, the relief for the Soviet forces was greater. Less than half the available aircraft were thrown into the battle on the eastern front. Churchill could justifiably show that the cross-Channel attack, though it had been immensely costly in lives and material, had given some small relief to the Russians at a critical time. But the spectre of the appalling casualties involved in storming the Channel coast never really left the British Prime Minister. He was still haunted by the memory of Gallipoli. Dieppe did nothing to allay that fear.

Aftermath of Dieppe. Wehrmacht troops inspect the new British Churchill tank used for the first time on the raid. Although Dieppe provided an invaluable lesson on cross-Channel attack, it was extremely costly in men and equipment

3 The Torch is Lit

Operation Torch, which took place in November 1942, shortly after Montgomery's desert victory at El Alamein, was an important test for the Allies. The command structure was new and set an important precedent for D-Day. An American, General Eisenhower, was given supreme responsibility for the landing. The 'supremo's' commanders were all British. Admiral Sir Andrew Browne Cunningham for the navy, General Sir Kenneth Anderson for the army and Air Marshal Tedder for the Allied air forces. The operation was successful and comparatively bloodless but good fortune played a major part.

Torch was the greatest invasion the Allies had undertaken, the risks being enormous since the huge convoys had to run the gauntlet of the U-boat infested waters in the north Atlantic and Bay of Biscay. Yet the Germans were taken by surprise.

The aims of Torch were as much political as military. The intention was to bring the French Army in north Africa over to the Allied side and to give the Vichy régime which governed the 'unoccupied' zone of France the chance of joining the Allies. The latter were not deterred by de Gaulle's

On 8 November 1942, over 200 warships, 350 merchant ships carrying 70,000 troops, and 1,000 aircraft converged on three north African targets – two, Algiers and Oran, in the Mediterranean, and one on the Atlantic coast at Casablanca. Twenty thousand British and U.S. assault troops were landed at Algiers, followed by the First British Army under the command of General Anderson. At Oran, 19,000 Americans were put ashore to be followed by more Americans. The forces for these two landings set out from Britain. The third force of 31,000 American G.I.s which was to land at Casablanca sailed directly from the United States. This landing, which encountered only token opposition from the Vichy French, took place through heavy surf. The three assaults were launched simultaneously, air support being provided by carriers and a continuous covering operation from Gibraltar.

Nevertheless, the liberating forces were not welcomed by every Frenchman. General Giraud, whom the Americans backed as head of the French north African forces, received little support. A deal had to be struck with Admiral Darlan, Pétain's deputy, who, by coincidence, happened to be in Algiers at the time of the invasion. This certainly saved any unnecessary bloodshed but aroused great unpopularity in Britain and a raging fury among de Gaulle's Free French. On Christmas Eve 1942, the complicated situation worsened when Darlan was assassinated in Algiers. De Gaulle and Giraud were brought together almost forcibly by Eisenhower and his political advisers. De Gaulle, who strongly disliked the British, now turned against the Americans for what he believed to be their high-handed and callous attitude.

interests as leader of the Free French from lobbying Admiral Darlan, Pétain's deputy, and other high Vichy officers. Eisenhower was ordered 'under no circumstances to communicate any information about the proposed expedition to General de Gaulle'.

Surprise and speed were essential if the French were not to resist the Allied landings. In Oran, anti-British feeling stemmed from the Royal Navy's destruction of the French Atlantic fleet there in July 1940. The Allied stratagem, adopted for French benefit, was to pretend that the whole operation was American. Vehicles and equipment bore the stars and stripes. British troops were kept in the background; at one stage Churchill even considered dressing them in American uniforms.

Hitler's immediate reaction to the landings was to rush in reinforcements by sea and air. Swiftly the Germans occupied the rest of France and General Jodl defined the north African problem from the O.K.W. viewpoint: 'North Africa is the glacis of Europe and must therefore be held in all circumstances. If it is lost we must expect an Anglo-Saxon attack against south-eastern Europe via the

'At last we're on our way'. The American landings at Sourcouf, north Africa, on 9 November 1942

The rapid transit of German forces mainly by air (a minimum of 750 troops a day were lifted into Tunisia for the first months of 1943) slowed down the north African campaign to a tough slogging match. The heavy fighting tested the resources of Allied teamwork. The battles soon drew in Montgomery's Eighth Army advancing on the Tripoli front, having pursued Rommel for 1,500 miles across the desert from Alamein.

The Allies had realized they were in for a hard battle ever since General Anderson's First Army had been halted in front of Bizerta after a frantic drive east from Algiers. Hitler stubbornly refused to let Rommel withdraw from north Africa. His army fought on with its head in a noose. By the end of the campaign nearly a quarter of a million Axis troops had been knocked out of the war. This came on top of the great Red Army victory at Stalingrad in February, when 108,000 Germans, including twenty-four Generals, were captured. Another 72,000 had been killed or wounded. Kesselring, the German Commander-in-Chief responsible for the theatre, wrote: 'The final battles left the enemy with a sense of superiority which gave an extraordinary boost to his morale.'

The tide turns. Opposite above: Stalingrad, 19 November 1942. Soviet armies trap the Germans at the city they had besieged for a year.

Below: Alamein. Montgomery's offensive began on 23 October 1942; two weeks later, Rommel's Afrika Corps were in headlong retreat across the western desert, pursued by British tanks

Left: Reconciliation at Casablanca, January 1943. The Free French leaders, General Giraud (far left) and Charles de Gaulle, were brought together for an uneasy meeting by Roosevelt and Churchill in the garden of the President's villa

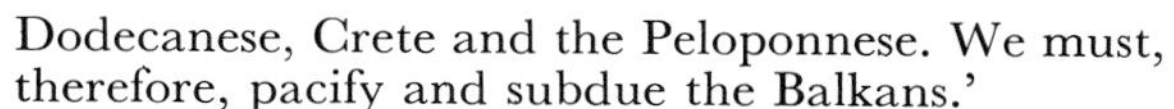

Dodecanese, Crete and the Peloponnese. We must, therefore, pacify and subdue the Balkans.'

Although it had not yet received American approval, the Germans were correctly reading the British 'soft underbelly strategy'.

Churchill and the British Chiefs of Staff were only too well aware of the possibilities of attacking southern Europe. This had always been a favourite idea.

Throughout 1943 the British continued to press this strategy on the American Chiefs of Staff. General Marshall, backed by the President, was still determined on a frontal attack on Germany in what he considered to be the supreme and decisive theatre – north-west Europe.

Decisions at Casablanca

At the Casablanca Conference in January 1943, attended by Churchill, Roosevelt and the Combined Chiefs of Staff, an agreement was won by Churchill, supported by Eisenhower, for the invasion of Sicily (Operation Husky). But the British found themselves constantly being forced to reassure the Americans, especially Marshall and Eisenhower, that they were determined to go through with Round-up, for a full-scale cross-Channel invasion. 'General, I have heard here,' Churchill said to Eisenhower at Casablanca, 'that we British are planning to scuttle Round-up. This is not so. I have given my word and I shall keep it. But now we have a glorious opportunity before us; we must not fail to seize it.'

The Americans, however, continued in their deep distrust of this point of view. Although they had agreed to an attack on Sicily once the north African campaign had been cleared up, they were very uneasy about extending the Mediterranean front. Indeed Eisenhower was directed to prepare for a landing in either Sicily or Sardinia, since the latter would bring him closer to the European mainland, rather than furthering a British drive to the east into the Balkans.

The Washington Conference of May 1943 failed to produce agreement on yet a further landing in Italy if Sicily were taken. The Americans still strongly believed that the British would divert far

The assault on Sicily differed from that on north Africa not only in its precision but also because the Germans expected a landing to be made and were dug in to resist it. With no accurate plan of German defensive positions on the island, a rapid build-up from the beachhead was clearly an essential part of the assault.
Training was a priority and an Operations Training Centre was set up in the Middle East. Seasoned troops of the Eighth Army could be intensively trained in the techniques of beach landings. Instructors were sent out from Combined Operations in Britain and a pier on the Great Bitter Lakes in the Suez Canal was rigged up to resemble an assembly area and the side of a ship. Altogether over 65,000 men were put through the course and dryshod training was also arranged with dummy landing craft in Palestine, Syria, Iraq and Persia. Then came intensive wetshod training so that assault troops could learn how to keep their equipment safe and dry when they hit the sea or had to come ashore through surf.

The landings were successful and the assault techniques more polished than they had been for Torch. Each assault group had a headquarters ship and was protected by a quota of AA ships, escorts and minesweepers as well as bombarding forces for tackling shore batteries. The big landing ships, some of which arrived only days before the assault direct from the United States, dispersed to their positions some seven miles off-shore and then lowered their assault craft. As the day wore on, guns, tanks, vehicles and supplies were landed directly on to the beaches. Opposition was slight. The Italians gave in almost at once and there turned out to be only two German divisions in Sicily. Altogether, 160,000 men were landed together with 14,000 vehicles, 600 tanks and 1,800 guns, 3,000 aircraft and 3,200 ships and craft taking part. The forces were assembled from the United States, Britain, north Africa and Egypt. By the end of August, Sicily was in Allied hands. The Italian mainland awaited the next Allied thrust.

Tunis, the end of the Axis in north Africa. On 7 May 1943, a quarter of a million troops surrendered to the Allies. The Germans dubbed the catastrophe 'Tunisgrad'

Operation Husky. The British Army lands in Sicily on 10 July 1943 near Syracuse

too many resources to this campaign, their motives were suspect and, as Henry Stimson reported, having visited London in the summer of 1943: 'We cannot now rationally hope to cross the Channel and come to grips with our German enemy under a British commander. The Prime Minister and the Chief of the Imperial General Staff are frankly at variance with such a proposal. The shadows of Passchendaele and Dunkerque still hang too heavily over the imagination of these leaders of the government.'

Churchill sought to reassure the Americans and often he repeated his acceptance of Round-up as being the main objective of the Allies. In fact, the Mediterranean operations were having a major effect on the preparations for Round-up. In any event the build-up of American forces in Britain was very slow; only 238,000 U.S. troops were in Britain by mid-1943. Less than a year later there were to be 1½ million.

The Joint Chiefs of Staff, however, only agreed to allow the possibility of operations against Italy provided the primacy of Round-up was settled and seven divisions withdrawn for the purpose. At the same time, Marshall asked that the date of the cross-Channel attack be fixed, proposing 1 May 1944. The operation now had a new code name, 'Overlord'.

The British had little choice but to accept and General Eisenhower was given the decision whether or not to allow precious landing craft and highly trained divisions to be used in further Mediterranean operations. He was authorized 'to mount such operations in exploitation of Husky as are best calculated to eliminate Italy from the war and to contain the maximum number of German forces'.

In July 1943, the invasion of Sicily was mounted. Eisenhower was in supreme command with Tedder, Cunningham and Montgomery as the subordinate Service Commanders. Admiral Ramsay was made the chief naval planner and by now expertise in the techniques of invasion was being raised to a much higher pitch. Husky, in fact, provided invaluable experience for D-Day.

4 COSSAC

COSSAC: Lieutenant-General F. E. Morgan (top), chosen at the Casablanca Conference to draw up plans for the invasion of Europe
Below: Allied Chiefs of Staff at the Casablanca Conference. Left to right, front: Admiral Ernest J. King (U.S.), Churchill, Roosevelt, General Sir Alan Brooke (G.B.), Admiral Sir Dudley Pound (G.B.), General Marshall (U.S.); Second row: General Arnold (U.S.), Maj-Gen. Ismay (G.B.), Admiral Mountbatten (G.B.), Field-Marshal Sir John Dill (G.B.), Air Chief Marshal Sir Charles Portal (G.B.)

COSSAC became a remarkable international success. Divisions of opinion were along specialist and professional lines rather than according to nationality. There were, however, one or two points of friction in day-to-day working. Although the British and Americans spoke the English language they could use it in different ways. Morgan confessed to reading and re-reading an American document, 'until it dawned on me that I did not understand a single word of it'.
For their part, the American officers disliked the British committee system which they regarded as 'one of the safest ways that positive action is postponed indefinitely'. Of the twenty-nine committees meeting regularly at Norfolk House, Morgan scrapped twenty-five. The Americans became happier.

At the Casablanca Conference in January 1943, Churchill and Roosevelt with the Combined Chiefs of Staff had decided that Round-up planning should start. Concentrated staff work started in London. Lieutenant-General Sir Frederick Morgan was appointed to the post of Chief of Staff to the Supreme Allied Commander (Designate) in March. This title was soon shortened to COSSAC.

Morgan was given a mixed Anglo-American staff. Brigadier-General Ray Barker of the U.S. Army acted as his deputy and the multi-national team was allocated the elegant St James's Square office-block called Norfolk House as its headquarters. Ironically, as the Americans never ceased to point out, the house of the same name on that site had been the birthplace of George III, whose military exploits had not been very successful.

COSSAC's brief was threefold. First he was to prepare plans for a diversion against the Pas de Calais to encourage the Germans to concentrate their defences in the wrong place. Second, he was to plan for a sudden cross-Channel attack to be known as Operation Rankin, to relieve Russia or exploit a sudden collapse in German morale. Finally, the most important role of COSSAC was to 'prepare plans for: . . . a full-scale assault against the Continent in 1944 as early as possible.' This was Operation Overlord.

The strains being felt in the British and American High Command quickly became apparent inside the COSSAC headquarters. There was a markedly different style in working between the British and Americans. As Morgan wrote, the Americans, 'having decided to go to war, determined to fight a bigger and better war than was ever fought before and, to enable them to do so, had endowed themselves with more armaments on sea, on land and in the air.'

The British were not so enthusiastic. COSSAC had the distinct impression after the Casablanca meeting that the Chiefs of Staff were 'not pleased at having to commit themselves to the cross-Channel adventure more than a year ahead of time . . . sticking their necks out further than they had ever stuck them before'.

The Americans believed that at heart the British still preferred a Mediterranean strategy. The great debate which continued in the higher councils of war was felt throughout COSSAC. Morgan knew that 'in certain American quarters there was the gravest possible doubt about the honesty of intention on the part of British strategists. They had the most disquieting suspicions with regard to the Mediterranean campaign' and 'the British kept nattering about Rome and about all kinds of wild-cat adventures in the Balkans to be based on Italy'.

Whatever the controversies that existed both before and after D-Day, for everyone who took part there is virtual unanimity on one major aspect: that every detail of the slightest importance had been taken care of – from the intense pre-invasion reconnaissance of the beaches themselves to seemingly minor details like the provision of sacramental wine in the landing craft and the provision of condoms for the rifle-carrying infantry. The rubber sheaths were not for the purpose that their manufacturers intended – but to put over the muzzles of the rifles to keep out the seawater without impeding the need for instant fire.

The credit for this exceptional 'success in depth' must first be given to General Morgan and his staff whose work was later taken over, expanded and developed by the Overlord commanders. It was no easy assignment. The calculation of logistics, which now would be computerized, depended in 1943 and 1944 on the tireless brainwork, at abacus level, of specialists in every field with, as it appeared at times, all oppositon, including their Allies'.

The first operation that came from COSSAC's planning, dubbed Starkey, was a pantomime. On instructions to prepare a feint across the Pas de Calais, a mock invasion force of string and plywood was assembled ostentatiously in the Thames estuary and Channel ports. At zero hour, battle-ready troops were marched down to the few real landing craft which would go to sea. Like the Duke of York's army, they were promptly marched back again. The landing craft sailed without them, bristling with anti-aircraft guns. The Allied Air Force took to the skies in great strength, hoping to lure the Luftwaffe into a set battle. The Germans, however, failed to oblige. For Rundstedt, German

C.-in-C. West, it was all too obvious, and the only reaction picked up on British radio was of a Wehrmacht officer asking what all the fuss was about.

The Overlord plan drew on the immense wealth of material which had already been produced by previous study groups including the Combined Operations Directorate and Admiral Ramsay's Sledgehammer team. Getting maximum co-operation from all services was no easy task. The British and American Air Forces were particularly difficult. They did not always see eye to eye, not only with each other but with the aims of COSSAC as a whole. The 'bomber barons' led by Air Marshal Sir Arthur Harris still believed they could beat Germany unaided. According to Morgan, 'in the case of the Air, even more difficulty was encountered than in the case of the Navy on the score of clashes of personality and inter-service rivalries'.

The resources for COSSAC were slender considering its task. There was even a suggestion that a cross-Channel attack would be impossible before 1945.

Limited resources

Allied shipping losses rose alarmingly in the first months of 1943 until April, when there was a dramatic improvement. This spelt the defeat of the U-boats and the Battle of the Atlantic was being won. But an immense demand existed at the shipyards to make up the backlog of vessels lost, particularly for warship construction.

The shortage of ocean-going ships was serious enough but the lack of landing craft completely hamstrung COSSAC. Britain had already pressed engineering companies, bridge builders, furniture factories and small boatyards into turning out as many landing craft as possible, but far more were needed. The position was aggravated by the attitude of Admiral Ernest J. King, U.S. Navy Chief of Staff, who controlled the construction and supply of naval vessels in the United States. King was supported by General Marshall who believed that if additional landing craft were sent to Europe Britain would only be encouraged to indulge in peripheral Mediterranean adventures of which he disapproved. The supply of landing craft became an important means of bringing American pressure to bear on the British Prime Minister and his Chiefs of Staff.

The great debate

The key problem was to select a suitable beach to land an expeditionary force on once it was ready. The choice was limited by the short range of British fighters which ruled out the Bay of Biscay and Norway. The most obvious landing zone was the Pas de Calais, strongly favoured by some of the British planners. It was the shortest shipping route, making naval operations easier and allowing a quick turnaround in landing craft. On the other hand, a port the size of Dover would be needed to supply the armies once they were ashore; none could compare with Normandy's Cherbourg or Le Havre.

A final choice would be influenced by the German defences. There was no comparison between the heavy fortifications of the Pas de Calais and the comparatively thin defences of the Normandy coast. Antwerp was too far away and like all the Channel ports, heavily defended. At Norfolk House arguments became heated about where to land and, to make matters worse, the British contingent began to get cold feet about the risks of undertaking any invasion at all. Morgan wondered whether 'It was wrong to listen to such die-hardism as was contended by the Americans in particular. After all, these Americans knew at first hand of the immense power and resources that the United States could throw into the battle. We British had as yet no personal knowledge of this and it was hard entirely to overcome the effects of a lifetime of niggling, cheeseparing, parsimony and making do . . .'

The great debate which now threatened the confidence of COSSAC and the British Chiefs of Staff

Assault warfare. Amphibious landing techniques were developed and tested by Combined Operations' specialists led by Vice-Admiral Lord Louis Mountbatten (opposite) with his Vice-Chief, Maj.-Gen. J. C. Heidon, and his deputy chief, Air Vice-Marshal J. M. Robb

in the whole invasion was solved by the dramatic intervention of the head of Combined Operations, Lord Louis Mountbatten. Since early 1942, Mountbatten had been intensively studying the problems of landing in France. As a member of the British Chiefs of Staff Committee, Mountbatten wielded great authority and had learnt how to break down inter-service rivalry. Combined Operations H.Q. felt confident that a landing could be successfully mounted and that new ideas like artificial harbours (Mulberries) and pipelines under the ocean (Pluto) could supply the army ashore.

Mountbatten suggested that the invasion planners should leave London for the clear air of Largs in Scotland where there was a Combined Operations training school. A conference, code-named Rattle, began on 28 June 1943, chaired by Lord Mountbatten himself. It examined every aspect of the invasion plan. No fewer than twenty Generals, eleven Air Marshals and Commodores, as well as eight Admirals, were among the officers who gathered at the Hollywood Hotel, then part of H.M.S. *Warren*. Security was very tight. Commandos and military police guarded the compound.

All aspects of the invasion were covered, and twenty-three detailed papers discussed. The problems seemed daunting, but Mountbatten and Morgan were determined to find solutions. After the first day, pacing the lawn with Mountbatten, Morgan confessed that the prospect of a united front seemed remote. But Mountbatten was more confident and agreed to give it one more day. 'And during that day,' recalls Morgan, 'what we hoped for began to happen. A member of the opposition was seen to smile . . . By the end of the course, there was not only unanimity but enthusiasm that a cross-Channel invasion could work.'

The many practical ideas and proposals which had been aired at the Rattle Conference, including Captain John Hughes-Hallett's report of artificial harbours, now led to a flurry of activity. The Conference had also clarified the decision on where the landings should take place. They concluded that this should be in the Bay of the Seine between the Cotentin and Dieppe where 'suitable assault and landing beaches and an appropriate lodgement area can and must be found'.

Now, as far as COSSAC and his staff were concerned, Overlord was definitely on. One senior officer commented, 'For the first time I really believe in this operation.' Morgan himself recorded that the Rattle Conference marked the beginning of Operation Overlord.

Normandy was selected as the place for the landing. The staff worked day and night sifting and assembling evidence. Pre-war tide-tables were studied, and a vast amount of intelligence started pouring in on the Channel beaches. It came from sources as diverse as Michelin Guides, picture postcards, midget submarines and reconnaissance aircraft.

The biggest single logistic problem of all was the shortage of landing craft because this would limit the number of men landed and the rate of build-up.

Destination Normandy

Mountbatten, reporting to the Chiefs of Staff, underlined the key problems still facing the planners. There were three of major concern:

'Firstly, that the strength of the enemy defences and the limitations imposed on the degree of supporting fire which can be brought to bear during the landing are such that it will obviously be essential to subject the area of the assault to the most intense bombardment.'

Secondly, there was no solution to the problem of 'the most critical period' between 'the lifting of the naval and air bombardment and the time when the army can get its own guns into action'. Special rocket-firing barges and close-support naval vessels would be needed.

Thirdly, the army were keen to land in darkness although the navy hated the idea. Mountbatten now called for practical trials to solve all the problems of the assault.

Agreement at Quebec

In August 1943 Churchill and the British Chiefs of Staff sailed for the Quadrant Conference at Quebec. They travelled aboard the *Queen Mary* in company with 5,000 German P.O.W.s. The former Wehrmacht troops going to north America could hardly have known that the ship carried the top-secret plans for the eventual downfall of the Fatherland. En route, lying in his bunk, with a cigar in his mouth, the Prime Minister listened to the whole co-ordinated plan for Overlord.

Morgan had done his best with the 'pitiful resources' allocated to him. His plan visualized an assault on Normandy with three seaborne and two airborne divisions, plus two more divisions already aboard landing craft for immediate follow-up. After securing the beachheads on a 35-mile front between Caen and Carentan, the Anglo-American forces were to concentrate on the capture of Cherbourg. To cope with the problems of supplying the army across open beaches, two artificial harbours called Mulberries were to be prefabricated in England and towed in sections across the Channel.

The plan called for the landing of eighteen divisions in the first two weeks. By that time the bridgehead had to be extended to include the Cherbourg peninsula and most of western Normandy bounded by the line Mont St Michel-Alençon-Trouville. COSSAC was careful to elaborate the conditions that he saw as essential for the success of his plan. The first of what Morgan called the 'set of circumstances' was 'an overall reduction of the German fighter force between now and the time of surface assault'.

Second, because of the severe restrictions of men and material that COSSAC had been allocated, German opposition must be at a minimum. Morgan spelt this out, 'the German reserves in France and the Low Countries as a whole, excluding the divisions holding the coast . . . should not exceed on the day of the assault twelve full-strength, first-quality divisions'.

Finally, there was the question of keeping the army supplied in the face of heavily defended Channel ports and the uncertain weather. Morgan stressed the need for 'sheltered waters' and underlined the great deal of work going into the artificial harbours. Sir Harold Wernher, the scientist behind the Mulberry project, was part of the COSSAC team and he explained how the harbours might be built.

Morgan was at pains to underline that his plan rested on a knife-edge balance – it would only just be feasible, he warned, 'If not more than twelve reserve, mobile field divisions should be available to the Germans in France – and that in the Caen area they should have not more than three of these divisions on D-Day, five by D plus 2 and nine by D plus 8.'

When Stalin was first told of the plan, he was convinced that a twelve-division attack was too puny – the Russians were committing hundreds against the Germans on the eastern front. 'What happens if there are thirteen German divisions?' he is reported to have asked sardonically later. 'Will the invasion be cancelled?'

Churchill approved Morgan's plan but also had several reservations: 'The objections I had to the cross-Channel operation were . . . now removed. I thought that every effort should be made to add at least 25 per cent to the first assault. This would mean finding more landing craft.' The Prime Minister had spotted one weakness in the scheme: the fact that no landing would take place on the Cotentin peninsula itself. This could lead to a very

The Quebec Conference set the invasion for spring 1944. On the citadel terrace overlooking the Château Frontenac, Roosevelt, Churchill, and the Canadian Prime Minister, Mackenzie King (front left), assemble for photographs with the British and American Chiefs of Staff. Left to right: General Arnold (U.S.), Air Chief Marshal Sir Charles Portal (G.B.), General Sir Alan Brooke (G.B.), Admiral King (U.S.), Field-Marshal Sir John Dill (G.B.), General George C. Marshall (U.S.), Admiral Sir Dudley Pound (G.B.), Admiral Leahy (U.S.)

hard fight through the difficult marshy estuary of the Vire and the bocage to capture Cherbourg. The C.I.G.S., Sir Alan Brooke, shared these misgivings, noting that it was 'a good plan, but too optimistic as to rate of advance to be expected'.

The Quebec Conference consisted mainly of staff meetings and there were two plenary sessions, in which Churchill and Roosevelt took part. The disagreements between the British and American Chiefs of Staff now became very acrimonious. So determined were the Americans to concentrate British efforts on a cross-Channel attack and away from the Mediterranean campaign of attrition, that a staff paper told how they had 'analysed at length the technique of previous conferences, the debating techniques of the British and even the precise number of planners required to cope on equal terms with the British staffs'.

They went to Quebec determined to make their ideas prevail. Already Stimson, the U.S. Secretary of War, had been pressing Roosevelt for a strong line, saying: 'The time has come for you to decide that your government must assume the responsibility of leadership . . . We cannot afford to confer again and close with a lip-tribute to Bolero which we have tried twice and failed to carry out.'

Yet the differences at Quebec were patched up. The British got most of what they wanted by a combination of skilful committee tactics and stubbornness. They were helped by the fact that halfway through the Conference news came in of Badoglio's offer to surrender. It now seemed ridiculous not to land an Allied army in Italy. Marshall conceded that Rome should be taken, although he did not share Churchill's view of pushing up towards the line of the Po, or fanning out into the Balkans. The C.I.G.S. won his argument that any efforts in the Mediterranean could only serve to draw off German divisions from Normandy. Although this logic was conceded, the Americans suggested that any diversionary activity should embrace an attack on the south of France, code-named Anvil. For this operation there was to be no increase in forces already allocated for the Mediterranean. Most of the landing craft were still to go to the Pacific.

On the face of it, Anvil was a sound idea. Churchill, however, accepted it only with reluctance. It was a good 500 miles from the south of France to the Normandy area and Churchill felt that the threat of invasion, rather than an invasion itself, would pin down the necessary German divisions.

Foothold in Europe

The Mediterranean did not cease to be a bone of contention after Quebec. Italy was invaded on 3 September by Montgomery's Eighth Army, which landed in Calabria, and the Anglo-American Fifth, which went in at Salerno, south of Naples, on 8 September. Now British Chiefs of Staff wanted to push forcefully towards Rome. The Anglo-American disagreements and Marshall's refusal to allow any more than diversionary activity in Italy had even affected the choice of an Allied landing place. German Headquarters at O.K.W. was amazed when the Allies landed south of Naples, when they had expected a landing further up the coast in the region of Rome. 'Why should we crawl up the leg like a harvest bug from the ankle upwards? Let us rather strike at the knee . . .' Churchill had said, but Eisenhower had played safe, not wishing to move outside Allied air cover.

The Italian invasion had an effect on Hitler that would profoundly affect the attitude of the Ger-

Salerno, 'a close-run thing'. Five days after the British Eighth Army crossed the Straits of Messina and Italy had surrendered, General Mark Clark's Fifth Army landed on the beaches of the Bay of Salerno (below). The new tank landing ships played a key role in the assault (right); the armour they landed was vital in holding the beachhead against the fierce German counter-attacks that for ten days threatened the whole invasion

Far right: Dinner at Tehran. In November 1943, Roosevelt, Churchill and Stalin met together for the first time to decide on a final strategy

mans towards the later invasion. The Führer decided to reinforce Italy. He abandoned his plan of sacrificing Kesselring's divisions in the south and formed a new defence line under Rommel which stretched from Pisa to Rimini. In the face of concerted Panzer and air counter-attacks, for the first time an Allied landing was very nearly thrown back into the sea.

Counter-punch

At Salerno, Mark Clark's Fifth Army landing on a three-division front had been suddenly and vigorously struck by Kesselring's Panzer divisions. Only round-the-clock bombing by the Allied Air Force and heavy naval bombardment had saved the landings from disaster.

The British charged the Americans with the responsibility for this narrow escape, claiming that they would not devote enough resources to Italy. That autumn General Brooke wrote in his diary: 'Our build-up in Italy is much slower than that of the Germans, and far slower than I expected. We shall have an almighty row with the Americans who put us in this position with their insistence to abandon the Mediterranean operations for the very problematical cross-Channel operations.'

The last British stand for a Mediterranean strategy came at the Tehran Conference in November 1943. Roosevelt, Churchill and Stalin assembled for the first time; all attended with their Foreign Ministers and Chiefs of Staff. It was a remarkable gathering of war leadership. The security was exceptionally tight, and some American commanders had difficulty passing the solid phalanx of Soviet security men guarding the Embassy gates in the capital.

It was this conference that set the seal on the strategy which was to take the Allies to victory.

The Prime Minister used all his immense eloquence to persuade the other two war leaders to agree to a British thrust to prize Yugoslavia and Greece away from Germany and to drag Turkey into the war.

The Americans' worst fears were confirmed about British military adventures and the Russians were deeply sceptical. Stalin sensed a British attempt to restore their position in the eastern Medi-

terranean. The Soviet Union already regarded this territory as her preserve. Churchill wrote: 'Overlord remained top of the bill but this operation should not be such a tyrant as to rule out every other activity in the Mediterranean.' He saw that there was an opportunity open to 'take Rome in January, and Rhodes in February, to renew our supplies to the Yugoslavs, settle the Command arrangements and open the Aegean, subject to the outcome of an approach to Turkey; all preparations for Overlord to go full-steam ahead within the framework of the foregoing policy for the Mediterranean'.

Stalin sided strongly with the Americans in maintaining that the only advantage of Mediterranean activities was to support Overlord. This meant the Allies would be committed 2:1 to Anvil. All through the conference the Soviet leader had needled Churchill, suggesting that the British did not want to fight the Germans. Once Churchill stormed out of the conference, only to be restrained by Eden. Finally Stalin asked Churchill point-blank, 'Do the Prime Minister and the British Staff really believe in Overlord?' To which Churchill replied that he did, provided the proper conditions of drawing off German forces had been carried out.

5 Festung Europa

Previous pages: The Channel watch. A coastal gun emplacement on the Atlantic Wall

In December 1941, just after the United States had committed herself to the war, and on the eve of his first winter campaign in Russia, Hitler had laid down in descending order of importance the places he thought the Allies would invade. These were:

1. Norway
2. The Atlantic ports between Bordeaux and Brest
3. The Channel ports between the Seine and Antwerp
4. The Channel Isles
5. The beaches of Brittany and Normandy.

'Little minds,' said Frederick the Great, 'want to defend everything; sensible men concentrate on the essentials.' For the German C.-in-C. West, Field-Marshal von Rundstedt, the problem was where he should concentrate his forces to resist the expected Allied attack. The Prussian General who lived like a Roman proconsul in a magnificent château, St Germain-en-Laye, overlooking the Seine, had never lost a campaign.

He was a soldier of the old school, an aristocrat with a private contempt for Hitler, which he took great pains to disguise. It was ironic that the man mainly responsible for the brilliant 1940 blitzkreig which had defeated France enjoyed the French lifestyle. He had then gone on to Russia but his criticisms of the Führer's strategy in the east, bluntly expressed and true though they proved to be, caused him to be replaced. He had been sent back to the west and to what was, at first sight, an impossible task.

To comprehend the extent of von Rundstedt's responsibilities, it is necessary to survey Europe's coastal frontiers. 'I had over 3,000 miles of coastline to cover from the Italian frontier in the south to the German frontier in the north,' he said after the war, 'and only sixty divisions with which to defend it. Most of them were low-grade divisions and some of them were skeletons.'

Even after the Dieppe raid in August 1942 German strategic thinking did not basically change. Normandy was not high on the list. Von Rundstedt and the more experienced of the High Command took Dieppe for what it was – an experimental attack to probe the coastal defences.

Goebbels, certainly, treated Dieppe as the glorious repulse of an Allied invasion. His propaganda harped on this theme. 'We have fortified the coast of Europe,' he said, 'from North Cape to the Mediterranean, and installed the most deadly weapons that the twentieth century can produce. This is why an enemy attack, even the most powerful and furious possible to imagine, is bound to fail . . . At Dieppe they held on for nine hours and there was no Wall. If they hold on for nine hours next time they'll do well.' He also voiced the profound preoccupation of the Nazi hierarchy when he said, 'The final decision will be won on the Western Front.'

In this he was right. Another Dunkirk would shatter British morale and give the Germans time to reorganize themselves with their new V-weapons and jet fighters. But where would the invasion come?

Unfortunately for von Rundstedt, Hitler's military commanders were divided and kept that way by the Führer. He decreed that the defence of a naval port should be the responsibility of the navy. Other possible landing zones were to be a Wehrmacht charge. However, coastal artillery, whether naval or military, was put under naval command. The material was different, the training was different and liaison between the two services kept purposely weak. Eventually, this state of affairs and the fact that any decision of any importance had to be taken by the Führer himself drove von Rundstedt to comment caustically, 'As C.-in-C. West, my sole prerogative was to change the guard in front of my gate.'

The anxious Führer

During 1943, Hitler became increasingly anxious about a possible landing in the south of France. In fact, as General von Blumentritt remarked, 'That year he was constantly on the jump – at one moment he expected an invasion in Norway, at another moment in Holland, then near the Somme, or Normandy or Brittany, in Portugal, in Spain, in the Adriatic.' His eyes raced round the map.

Professional soldiers under von Rundstedt discounted most of their Führer's frenzied thinking for valid military reasons (such as the lack of Allied air cover at vital points). However, they had to put up with Hitler's interference and also with the fact that the divisions in the west were, up to 1943, continually being replaced by badly mauled units pulled out from the Russian front. In many cases a full divisional strength hardly existed, except on paper.

During 1943, therefore, coast defence divisions were formed with a specialized organization adapted to their particular sectors. The inevitable handicap was that both officers and men were

Field-Marshal von Rundstedt, the man with the impossible task of defending 3,000 miles of coastline. 'As C.-in-C. West, my sole prerogative was to change the guard in front of my gate'

mostly of the older classes, their armament on a lower scale than that of the active divisions.

Rundstedt's defences were however backed up by what Hitler called his Atlantic Wall, the westward bastion of *Festung Europa*. As early as December 1941, the Führer had given orders to O.K.W. Operations staff to draw up plans 'for the construction of a new West Wall to assure protection of the Arctic, North Sea and Atlantic coasts'. Its object was 'to assure protection against any landing operation of very considerable strength with the employment of the smallest number of static forces'. On 23 March 1942, although Hitler was at the height of his success, he showed his anxiety about the west in Directive No. 40 which set out in great detail the responsibilities of coastal commanders. They were told bluntly that 'enemy forces which have landed must be destroyed or thrown back into the sea by immediate counter-attack'. All personnel, irrespective of service, would be involved.

The Atlantic Wall was started in earnest in 1942 and extended along the Channel coast from the Pas de Calais to the Bay of Biscay. It was however very uneven with massive preparations in some places where the Germans expected an Allied landing such as Cap Gris Nez, the mouth of the Seine, Brest and Lorient. The long line of the coast however, from the Netherlands to the Atlantic coast of France, meant that the building of a line of pillboxes and fortifications was beyond even the German construction industry with its Todt Organization of press-ganged foreign workers. The massive defences were therefore concentrated around ports such as Cherbourg where every step was taken to make them impregnable. Hitler and O.K.W. knew that the Allies would have to capture a port very early in any campaign if they were to build up an army capable of tackling von Rundstedt's forces. All the same, the Todt Organization managed to build a network of strong and comprehensive defence works which worried the Allied Command. Moreover, the tempo of construction was quickening with 17·3 million cubic yards of concrete, and 1·2 million tons of steel absorbed in two frantic years.

A British intelligence report of early 1944 set out

The Atlantic Wall

The Maginot mentality. Above left: Troops exercising in part of the underground fortifications
Above centre: The Todt Construction Organization poured nearly 18 million tons of concrete into the vast Maginot-like strongpoints
Above right: A massive railway gun in the Calais sector
Right: The strongest fortifications and guns were concentrated around the Channel ports
Below: Drawings of a Type-C gun emplacement from a British intelligence brief of 1944

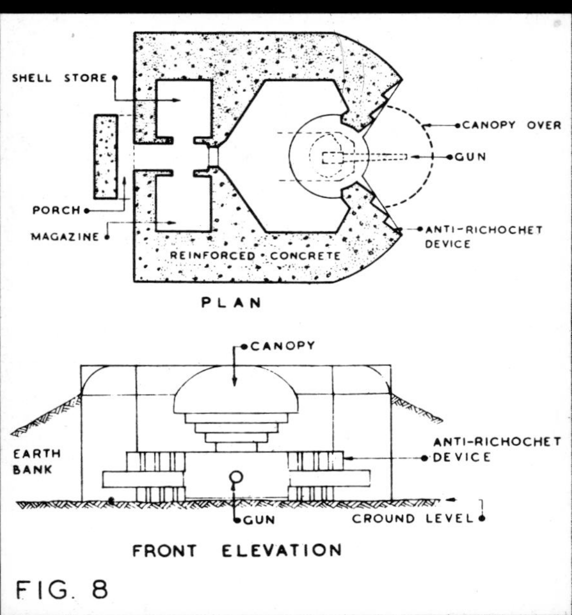

RIE TODT

Fortifying the beaches. Right: Barbed wire on the promenade. Far right: 'Dragon's Teeth' anti-tank obstacles. Below and below right: Seafront machine-gun nest and waterline obstacles from a British intelligence brief

the detailed elevations and drawings of the bunkers and gun emplacements like some fiendish builder's catalogue. According to Albert Speer, who was responsible as Minister of Armaments, most of the architecture was designed by Hitler himself. 'Hitler planned these defensive installations down to the smallest details. He even designed the various types of bunkers and pillboxes, usually in the small hours of the night. Never sparing in self-praise, he often remarked that his designs ideally met all the requirements of a frontline soldier.' The Führer's sketches were adopted almost without revision, though few of the men who manned them fully appreciated their leader's concern was not for their comfort. Their job was to fight.

The Atlantic Wall included various fortifications. There were *Wiederstandsnest* which could hold a platoon armed with machine-guns or anti-tank weapons. There were *Stutzpunkt* or strongpoints which were mutually self-supporting. They could be garrisoned by a company or battalion supported by artillery. There was then a still larger fortified position known as a *Verteidigungsbereich* supported by a mobile reserve. As Allied bombing tests revealed, some of these were impenetrable to the heaviest air attack, which says something for Hitler's misplaced architectural talent.

The top secret report succinctly summarized the principles on which the fortifications were laid out. 'All defence positions, including artillery positions, except for howitzers, will be sited well forward, wherever possible on the back line of the beaches.' They all had to 'cover with fire the beaches and the sea off the beaches'. They were grouped round ports and made maximum use of automatic weapons. Seafront towns and villages had been turned into miniature fortresses.

The makeshift Maginot

Ingenious obstacles were then sited to be concealed under water for as long as possible. They were normally set out in several rows between 12 and 17 feet above the low-tide mark. They were particularly vicious and designed to rip through the bottoms of landing craft or the bellies of tanks. Materials had been plundered from the fortifica-

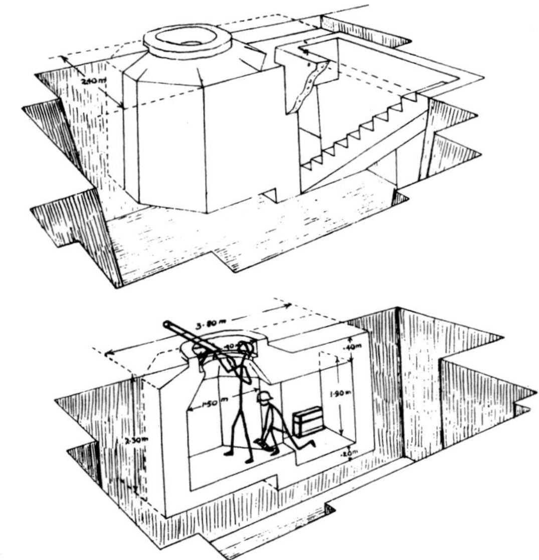

GERMAN ANTI-TANK OBSTACLES USED AS UNDERWATER OBSTACLES

TETRAHEDRA. I.

TETRAHEDRA. II

GERMAN STEEL OBSTACLES–HEDGEHOG

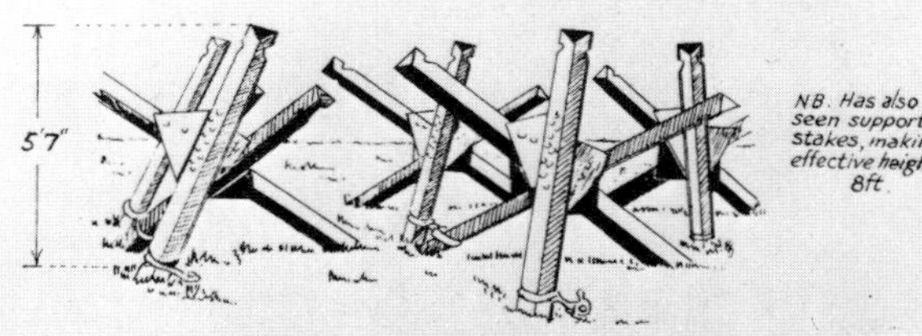

tions of occupied countries to build rows of tetrahydra and curved rail obstructions. The Czech defences, built originally to stop Wehrmacht Panzers invading Bohemia, were now transplanted to the Channel beaches. Steel girders were transported across Europe to make Czech hedgehogs, which were jagged steel stakes. Even movable steel doors from the ill-starred Maginot Line found their way into the Atlantic Wall.

If any invasion force managed to fight its way past these formidable obstacles, there were many more unpleasant surprises in store. It would run up against minefields up to 300 yards in depth. Thick concrete walls were concealed in hedgerows and sand dunes to block the advance of men and tanks, with artillery carefully sited to bring down a murderous fire. In the open Norman countryside, behind the beach exits, fields and meadows had been flooded to stop glider landings and trap parachutists.

Fortunately for the Allies, the Atlantic Wall, the first defence of Hitler's Fortress Europe, was not complete. It was far stronger at Cap Gris Nez and Boulogne than further down the French coast. Over two and a half times as many troops were

Manning the Atlantic Wall. Right: Artillery range-finder positions
Far right: An isolated clifftop machine-gun position
Below: A contingent of Wehrmacht infantry march up to man the front-line batteries
Below right: A unit of Cossack 'volunteers', part of the motley collection of non-German forces who were stationed on the Channel coast

stationed in the north than in Normandy, and there was a great disparity in gun emplacements. In the invasion year some 132 heavy guns were deployed between Calais and Boulogne, ninety-three of which were protected. In Normandy, there were forty-seven, of which only twenty-seven were in concrete emplacements. Many of these weapons were also captured from earlier Wehrmacht campaigns, but it added to the difficulties of the German defenders since there were over twenty-eight different calibres, often without standard range-finding equipment. Many were put hastily in position, mounted in concrete casements which, although providing protection, did not allow the guns to cover a wide field of fire. They were particularly unsuitable against moving sea targets, as the veterans and boys manning them were to find out.

Transport for the army was in extremely short supply, and the Wehrmacht scoured France for anything on wheels. Whether it had an engine or not was hardly relevant since the Allied air bombardment was affecting fuel supplies and many commanders were resorting to horse-drawn transport and bicycles. All the same, elite formations were still highly mobile, although the crack 6th Parachute Regiment had to use fifty different types of lorry, even though there were only seventy trucks in their total motor pool.

Many of the defending troops in Normandy could hardly match the world's image of the resolute and highly trained Wehrmacht. In fact many of them were not German at all but prisoners of war captured on the eastern front who had agreed to serve in the German Army rather than live in the misery of a concentration camp.

'A mere showpiece'

Von Rundstedt did not believe in the invincibility of the Atlantic Wall. It ran against all his military principles of flexibility and mobile attack. 'The Wall was a myth,' he said, 'nothing in front of it, nothing behind – a mere showpiece. The best that could be hoped for was that it might hold up an attack for twenty-four hours, but any resolute assault was bound to make a breakthrough anywhere

along it in a day at most. And, once through, all the rest could be taken from the rear, for it all faced out to sea and became quite useless.'

Then in November 1943 a further complication was added to the scene. Hitler appointed Rommel to inspect and improve the coast defences from Denmark to the Spanish frontier. After dealing with those in Denmark, he moved to France just before Christmas and thus came into the sphere of von Rundstedt. Rommel held a special brief from the Führer to whom he reported but his relationship to von Rundstedt had been left undefined, no doubt on purpose. As with any visiting Inquisitor, disagreement naturally developed, the more so since their ideas of what should be done were different. Soon the armies in France began to question whether they were under the command of von

An extraordinary document captured by the advancing Canadians reveals the composition of the 276th Division:

Infantry Regiment 987 — Regimental H.Q.
Personnel Branch — 9 August 1944
Subject: Paybooks for volunteers in German units.

In order to issue paybooks to volunteers in German units a nominal roll of such volunteers, separated according to their nationality, will be handed in to Regimental Headquarters by 11 August 1944.
The paybooks will be issued in eight different forms, i.e.:

(i) For Russians, Ukrainians and White Ruthenians – Russian paybook.
(ii) For Cossacks – Cossack paybook.
(iii) For Armenians – Armenian paybook.
(iv) For Aserbaijans – Aserbaijan paybook.
(v) For Georgians (including Adschars, South Ossetans and Abschars) – Georgian paybook.
(vi) For Adigis, Karbadins, Karatjers, Balkars, Kherkasians, North Ossetans, Ingus, Takjenen, Dagastares, (Calmuckes, Awares, Lakes, Dargines etc.) – North Caucasian paybook.
(vii) For Turkemen, Usbeks, Kazaks, Khirgiz, Karakalpaks, Tadschiks – Turkestan paybook.
(viii) For Volga Tartars (Kazan Tartars), Bashkires, Tartar-speaking Tschuwashi, Maris, Merdwiners, Udmuns – Volga Tartar paybook.

By order

(Signature illegible)
Lt and Regtl. Adjutant

Rundstedt or Rommel since the latter immediately set about putting his principles of coast defence into practice.

Von Rundstedt solved the problem by setting the most important sector from the Dutch–German border to the Loire under Rommel, as Commander-in-Chief Army Group B, whilst the southern sector, from the Loire to the Alps, was entrusted to General Blaskowitz, Army Group G. This helped, but the basic difference in views between Rundstedt and Rommel continued.

'We Germans,' von Rundstedt said to a correspondent early in 1944, 'do not indulge in the tired Maginot spirit.' Behind this statement (natural, perhaps, in the man who had brilliantly exposed the Maginot Line as an overvalued white elephant) lay the C.-in-C.'s belief that actual landings by the Allies could not be prevented. Hitler had made many propaganda statements – especially for home consumption – about the invulnerability of the Atlantic Wall, most of it filmed by Goebbel's propaganda units around the heavily fortified Cap Gris Nez. Both von Rundstedt and Rommel knew this 'Atlantic Wall' was largely an illusion, and totally inadequate to counter the great strategic flexibility which the Allies possessed in their command of the sea and, latterly, of the air.

Von Rundstedt, therefore, planned to concentrate his forces at only the most vulnerable sections of the coast – the Pas de Calais, the mouths of the Somme and the Seine, Cherbourg and Brest – and

Far left: Rommel and his staff inspecting the Normandy defences early in 1944; he wanted the Panzer divisions moved up to the coast. Below: Guderian, Hitler's Inspector of Panzers, refused to give Rommel full control of the armoured reserves. Left: Panzer divisions. The key to any defeat of the invasion was the concentration of the German armoured forces against the beachhead

to make the major ports impregnable against direct attack.

Rommel, on the other hand, whom von Rundstedt considered to be 'a brave man and a very capable commander in small operations, but not really qualified for high command', believed in hitting the invader as hard as possible the moment he got ashore and, if practicable, before. It was more important, he believed, to have one Panzer division in the assaulted sector on the day of the invasion, than to have three there three days later.

Rommel's dilemma

Rommel, the dashing Panzer leader who had broken through the French lines in 1940, advancing a hundred miles in a day, and who had brilliantly exploited armoured warfare in the desert, had fundamentally changed his military thinking as a result of fighting the British and Americans. He knew of the immense power of the Allied air forces which had broken the nerve of even his veteran Afrika Korps. He had been trapped on Montgomery's defensive minefields at Alam Halfa, the turning point before the British Alamein offensive. Finally, the 'Desert Fox' had seen how Kesselring's forces in Italy had almost hurled the Allied Fifth Army back into the sea at Salerno, with a rapid Panzer counter-attack. He had come to the conclusion that it would be vital to try and stop the enemy landing and consolidating his foothold. The Panzer reserves, whose Tigers and Panthers were far superior to anything used by the British and Americans, would have to be deployed behind the beaches, on call and not exposing themselves to long journeys over heavily strafed roads and railways.

The success of Rommel's strategy depended almost entirely upon the location of the only formidable reserves the Wehrmacht possessed in the west, the ten Panzer divisions. Of the fifty-eight divisions in the west in the spring of 1944, more than half were in coast defence and training divisions, strung along the Atlantic Wall with a massive concentration in the Pas de Calais. Of the twenty-four field divisions only ten were armoured, and of these three were allocated to Blaskowitz's Army Group G defending the south of France. A further armoured division was held near Antwerp, leaving the remainder to form a mobile reserve under Geyr von Schweppenburg. Yet Rommel did not control any of these divisions. If they were not close to the beaches he could only plead with both von Rundstedt and Geyr von Schweppenburg to move them there.

Rommel's impotence and the wrong location of the Panzers triggered a first-class row inside the German Command. Rundstedt did not want to tie the Panzers down and still believed the Allies might strike anywhere, in particular across the Straits of Dover, because this would open the way to north-west Germany and cut off the German forces in France. There was another serious reason why the Allies should be interested in the shortest route to France. In 1944, Hitler's new V-weapons were prepared for an attack on Britain. In Directive No. 51 of November 1943, Hitler had spelt out: 'I can no longer take responsibility for further weakening the west in favour of other theatres of war. I have therefore decided to reinforce its defences, particularly those places from which a long-range bombardment of England will begin.'

The Atlantic Wall was now to serve a dual purpose, protecting the V.1 flying bomb sites against what seemed an almost certain Allied attack.

Rundstedt's ally in maintaining a central mobile reserve was the bustling General in Command of Armoured Forces in the West, Geyr von Schwep-

Fortress of Oppression

Below: Nazi anti-liberation propaganda leaflet, distributed in Paris during the winter of 1943/44, pours scorn on a reference, taken out of context, from Churchill's speech on 30 June 1943. He was construed as saying the Allies would land *'before the falling of the leaves'* (autumn 1943). Right: A Gestapo raid. All over Europe the civilian population lived in fear of lightning arrests and deportation to concentration camps by the Gestapo. Together with the S.S., they saw to it that *Festung Europa* imprisoned a continent

penburg. He was not answerable to Rommel and intended to keep his forces 'under cover from air attack in the forests north-west and south of Paris, from which they could mount their assault when the enemy is deeply committed in the country'. The reserve would also be prepared to meet any airborne assault far behind the coast. Rommel sarcastically noted that 'contrary to myself, General von Schweppenburg who may well know the British in peacetime has never yet met them in battle'; he wished to be in a position to mount a quick counter-attack. Since the Luftwaffe had virtually disappeared from the skies of France, there was no chance of Panzers moving in open country by daylight without courting disaster. Rommel warned the High Command: 'Failing a tight command under one single hand of all available forces for defence, failing the early engagement of our mobile forces in the battle for the coast, victory will be in grave doubt.'

In March 1944, the row between the Generals could no longer be ignored. Hitler sent the Inspector General of Panzers, General Guderian, to try and sort out the argument. Meeting at Rommel's headquarters at the elegant mansion of La Roche Guyon in Normandy, the Generals thrashed it out. Guderian was not convinced by Rommel's case. If the Field-Marshal placed his Panzer reserves close to the beaches, Guderian remarked that 'his reserves would be in the wrong place if his opinion of the presumed landing sector of the Allies should be wrong'.

Eventually, after a visit by the exasperated Geyr to Berchtesgaden to plead with Hitler, who instinctively favoured Rommel's approach, the Führer arranged a compromise which pleased nobody. Four of the Panzer divisions in the west would be taken under the Führer's own control and they would not be moved without O.K.W. sanction. Even Rundstedt did not like this, and proposed that the whole of southern France should be evacuated by the Wehrmacht to a line of the Loire thus building up a stronger reserve from forces formed from Army Group G. This did not please Hitler at all. The man who had sacrificed at least two armies holding lost ground would not give up half of France.

Such, then, were the outer defence and the attitudes of the German High Command. Behind this dangerously patchy plan to be carried out by Generals at loggerheads with each other and with the Führer himself, the deprived, underfed millions of occupied Europe waited patiently for liberation. Theirs were the realities of the Gestapo-enforced Nazi domination with its whole apparatus of forced labour and concentration camps to be dealt with by the as yet unknown Anglo-American liberators. *Festung Europa* was as much an inner fortress of the human mind and spirit as a wall of concrete and steel fortifications.

Pol

6 SHAEF

Top: General Dwight D. Eisenhower (Supreme Allied Commander-in-Chief Allied Forces of Liberation)
Middle row, left to right: Major-General W. Bedell Smith (Chief of Staff), Air Chief Marshal Sir Arthur Tedder (Deputy Supreme C.-in-C.)
Bottom row, left to right: Admiral Sir Bertram Ramsay (Allied Naval C.-in-C.), General Sir Bernard Montgomery (C.-in-C. British Armies of Liberation), Lt-General Omar Bradley (Commander U.S. Army in the Field), Air Chief Marshal Sir Trafford Leigh Mallory (Allied Air C.-in-C.)

On 7 December, President Roosevelt broke his journey at Tunis on his way home from the Cairo Conference. General Eisenhower met the Commander-in-Chief of the American Republic at the airport. In the back of the car, before the General made his report, Roosevelt turned to him and said, 'Well, Ike, you are going to command Overlord.'

Eisenhower, who sensed how politically difficult the decision must have been, replied, 'Mr President, I hope you will not be disappointed'.

The choice of Supreme Commander had been a complicated minefield of domestic and Allied politics. The British knew that he would be American. The overwhelming weight of U.S. forces in the invasion made this inevitable; but they were alarmed at a suggestion of the American Joint Chiefs of Staff that the Supreme Commander should be responsible for *all* Allied forces engaged against Germany. Roosevelt was expected to propose General Marshall for the job. He would take command of the cross-Channel invasion and would remain a central figure of the Combined Chiefs of Staff, becoming the most powerful Allied military leader.

The British would have none of this. They were already feeling bruised at what seemed to be an American take-over of the British war effort. When the proposal was formally advanced by Roosevelt at Tehran, Churchill rejected the American case, in a reasoned memorandum, saying that, 'the proposal has immense political implications', and that since 'he will only be able to make a decision without reference to high authority on comparatively minor and strictly military questions . . . He will thus be an extra and unnecessary link in the chain of command.' Britain did not want this 'novel experiment' which 'will surely lead to disillusionment and disappointment'. Marshall's chances of becoming the Supremo were effectively stopped.

The choice fell upon Eisenhower, who was at least a known quantity and extremely popular with the British. After endless haggling between the British and American Chiefs of Staff on precise terms of reference, Eisenhower was finally instructed: 'You will enter the continent of Europe and in conjunction with other United Nations undertake operations aimed at the heart of Germany.'

The British were keen that there should be no mention of invasion, as it would plainly upset the French. The Allied Expeditionary Force was technically not an army but a United Nations' force whose mission was liberation.

The Supremo's team

There was a ruthless search for the ablest commanders to support Eisenhower, and the highly successful Allied Mediterranean Command was the obvious place for candidates. Air Chief Marshal Tedder, C.-in-C. of Allied Air Forces in the Mediterranean, was nominated Eisenhower's deputy, to the immense delight of the Supreme Commander since he had always believed in the close coordination of air and ground forces. Their combination of personalities would do much to forge a genuinely united leadership at the top of the command chain.

It did not please the Germans. A Luftwaffe appraisal said, 'Tedder is on good terms with Eisenhower to whom he is superior in both intelligence and energy. The coming operations will be conducted by him to a very large extent . . . Obviously we are dealing here with one of the most eminent personalities amongst the invasion leaders.'

As Naval Commander, Eisenhower was assigned Admiral Ramsay, who had planned the north African invasion and evacuated the British from Dunkirk. In the air, Air Marshal Leigh Mallory was given responsibility for the Allied Tactical Air Force. This was to consist of the R.A.F.'s Second Tactical Air Force and the U.S. Ninth. Leigh Mallory was a tough, uncompromising airman who would fight the 'bomber barons' almost as hard as the Germans in deploying Allied air-power against the Wehrmacht.

The most vital choice of all, however, was that of Ground Commander of the Allied Armies. He would be responsible for establishing the beachhead and withstanding the fierce and inevitable Wehrmacht counter-attack.

Eisenhower badly wanted General Alexander for this key job, but the British government decided

The Friendly Invasion

Right: The English 'cuppa' welded many Anglo-American friendships. Far right: Fougasse cartoon from *Punch*, 1944

that he was indispensable if the gruelling Italian campaign was to be pushed forward to success. The choice naturally fell upon the brusque and highly successful General Sir Bernard Montgomery. The American First Army was put under General Omar Bradley.

Eisenhower arrived in London in January 1944. He did not want Supreme Allied H.Q. (SHAEF) to be located in the heart of the metropolis, and soon a canvas township, code-named Widewing, had sprouted in Bushey Park on the western outskirts of the city. The headquarters, as the nerve-centre of the vast operation, grew into a huge and complex machine, with no fewer than six functional divisions: G1 – Personnel; G2 – Intelligence; G3 – Operations and Planning (the heart of SHAEF); G4 – Supply; G5 – Civil Affairs (for setting up political control in liberated countries); and G6 – Psychological Warfare and Public Relations (later separated). There were dozens of highly trained specialists, in everything ranging from medicine to heavy engineering, and by March 1944 SHAEF could claim some 750 officers and 6,000 men working at Widewing. At the heart of the whole organization, in contact with the subordinate H.Q.s all over Britain, was the SHAEF Chief of Staff, General Bedell Smith. He was in many ways the complement to Eisenhower, for whom he had worked as Chief of Staff in the Mediterranean. A determined man, he protected Eisenhower from endless interruption and involvement in detail, acting as the Supreme Commander's filter. But he could also be diplomatic and was soon known as Eisenhower's hatchet man. 'Bedell, tell them to go to hell,' Eisenhower once said in referring to a mission to SHAEF, 'but put it so they won't be offended'.

The friendly invasion

The Allied invasion force was now rapidly building up in Britain. By early 1944 the British began to wonder whether they were not subject to a 'friendly invasion'. This caused some anxiety for American commanders, not knowing how the reserved British would react to the arrival of millions of tough young troops in their towns and villages. Since the first American troops had arrived in January 1942, the U.S. Army had risen to over 950,000 by January 1944. They formed the major part of Eisenhower's Expeditionary Force, and were concentrated in the beautiful counties of south and west England. The Devon and Dorset villages shook with the rumble of their Sherman tanks; the pubs of Cornwall and Somerset were suddenly filled with men who spoke in every variety of American accent, from the Boston twang to the lazy drawl of Louisiana. On the downs near Newbury, west of London, American paratroopers of the 101st Airborne Division rehearsed their battle drills, and there were far more jeeps than British cars in the country lanes.

The Americans were not the only army in Britain. The home-grown Second Army was of comparable size. The whole island seemed in danger of sinking under the weight of the huge masses of soldiers and military material. Every spare yard of flat ground had been turned into an airfield! Air-crews joked that there was no need to worry about coming to the end of the runway because it did not end until John O'Groats. Every creek and harbour on the south coast held a naval vessel, and the woods and heathland were crowded with military vehicles.

The British forces were concentrated in the south and south-east of England where the famous regiments of the 50th Infantry Division were ready to march down the long road to Southampton in the footsteps of the B.E.F. which had marched on its way to France thirty years before. In Kent and Sussex the woods and forests concealed the armour

of the Canadian First Army and the seaside towns were packed with troops. In London the drab wartime atmosphere was lifted by the cosmopolitan characters and accents of Poles, Czechs, Frenchmen, Norwegians, Dutch, Canadians, Australians, New Zealanders, and, of course, Americans. For many a young woman 'bliss was it then to be alive'.

The G.I.s gave the British cartoonists and comedians a field-day. There were many music-hall jokes about their behaviour. There was only one thing wrong with G.I.s, said the comedians, they were 'over-paid, over-fed, over-sexed and *over-here*!' They seemed endlessly supplied with all the luxuries the British had been missing since 1939. To the British, oranges and bananas were like manna from heaven, but eaten abundantly by the Yanks. Candy like Hershey Bars and Lifesavers astonished British children who hung around hopefully at American bases. Cigarettes, extremely scarce for the natives, were supplied in vast cartons of Lucky Strike and Chesterfields. Apart from anything else, the average G.I. had far more money than his British counterpart and knew how to spend it, often monopolizing taxis, bars and restaurants.

The impact on British women of this tough and lusty young army was immense. A vogue with many girls out for a good time became peroxided hair, because the G.I.s liked blondes. They whistled at them whenever they had a chance.

The G.I.s' friendly invasion made a great impact on national life and culture which remains even today. British speech and vocabulary were affected. The impact on British music was also impossible to exaggerate with the American forces' jazz bands playing at parties and socials in towns and villages all over Britain. If the Expeditionary Force had a music of its own it was not any brassy, nationalist tune, but the soft music of Glenn Miller, which the British loved as much as the Americans.

Much of the credit for the American build-up passing without friction devolves once more on Eisenhower's shrewdness and imagination when dealing with people. He insisted that the press should be free to report American forces' behaviour in Britain, even though sometimes this could hurt the American image. British newspapers reacted strongly to friction between negro and white soldiers which came into the open at public dances. All was reported freely in the press.

There was considerable co-operation from the Ministry of Information, where Brendan Bracken, Minister and confidant of Churchill, saw the dangers of not smoothing the path for the American forces in Britain. G.I.s were issued with special booklets to help them understand the British. Although the two countries spoke the same language, the words could have very different meanings – the word 'bum' in American parlance meant something very different in English! The Americans were warned about using terms like rubbers for the Ebflus contraceptive, which led to misunderstanding and embarrassment when the British discovered they did not mean erasers or wellington boots! On the whole, the Americans were accepted, and, although some lived in England for only a few weeks before D-Day, there was remarkably little tension and indeed a great deal of harmony with the British.

7 The Enemy Observed

Aerial reconnaissance of beach obstacles (left). As the aircraft swoops in for a close shot (right) the Wehrmacht troops abandon their work and dive for cover

Below: A U.S. bomber prepares for a photographic mission, its delicate camera heavily protected against the cold at altitude
Right: 'Dicing for the I.S.T.D.' Spitfire pilots flew dangerous low-altitude missions along the coast at zero height dodging German flak (shell splashes can be seen clearly on the left – this pilot was lucky, others were less fortunate). The photographs together made a continuous panorama and were used to compile detailed maps of the defences (opposite below); they proved invaluable for briefing troops and the naval bombardment. This section shows Ouistreham beach; the estuary of the River Orne on the left of the picture is shown at the centre of the map

Throughout 1942 and 1943 the whole coast of northern France was photographed from the Belgian frontier to Brest by high-flying reconnaissance aircraft. The pictures were so clear and accurate that when they were blown up, all kinds of detail of the beaches, including rock formations, currents and tidal movements, could be deduced. Low-flying R.A.F. Spitfires flew at zero height along the French coast to snatch continuous panoramic photographs of the beaches. Midget submarines and motor launches with sounding parties visited beaches all along the coast of northern France collecting valuable hydrographic information. French beaches were visited with an astonishing frequency and regularity by groups of British frogmen and swimmers. They did not know where the landing would be, but they covered every location from the Belgian frontier to the Bay of Biscay. If the invasion were to take place with the minimum of risk then two things had to be discovered and weighed by the planners: first, the topography of the beaches and their immediate hinterland, and, secondly, the strength and nature of the German defences.

First COSSAC and then SHAEF received invaluable reports from the French Resistance. Although the beaches were sealed off, hundreds of pairs of eyes kept watch for any small detail that could be transmitted to London to create a fuller picture of the German occupation.

In the Caen and Cherbourg areas a steady stream of information filtered through a dozen sources. Patriotic artists and Resistance photographers with box cameras surreptitiously sketched and snapped details of fortifications behind the Germans' backs. Information on troops and new dispositions found its way through underground channels to London. Café proprietors and restaurateurs collected morsels of gossip from French and German customers passing on any details of information that would give Allied intelligence a clearer picture of what Rommel and his troops were doing behind the beaches.

The main cog of the whole D-Day intelligence operation was in the unlikely location of the medieval University of Oxford. Here a quiet don, Frederick Wells, worked assiduously with Royal Marine Colonel Sam Bassett in the Inter-Services Topographical Unit which had been set up by Churchill after the relative ignorance of British officers in the Norwegian campaign. Then, they only had 1912 Baedekers to try to find the Wehrmacht. By 1944 the unit gleaned information from professors of geology, geography, economics and every kind of subject to build up an accurate picture of the French coastal zone. An army of draughtsmen and photographers worked in a rapidly expanding library at the Ashmolean. In 1942 Lord Mountbatten called for comprehensive

information about possible landing beaches. Bassett persuaded the B.B.C. to broadcast an appeal for pictures from any part of the world. Since the British were great travellers and had hiked and cycled all over Europe, he believed that many valuable points could be established from these snapshots, such as the height of tides, and beach exits. Bassett's idea paid off, 'I had a frantic phone call from the B.B.C. to say that Broadcasting House had been snowed under with letters. Thirty thousand had arrived by the morning post.'

Eventually, after a press and radio campaign, over ten million pictures were collected. Fifty American girls were flown over specially to help organize the material. The Oxford Unit began building models of the beaches and coastal strongpoints to familiarize the assault troops. In 1944, Ramsay had a complete picture of the coast. It was so accurate that grids could be drawn and superimposed on the pictures for Allied gunners. Eisenhower was enthusiastic about the panoramic photos, and ordered forty sets. When forty were delivered he had to spell out that he meant 40,000! Britain did not have the photographic paper for

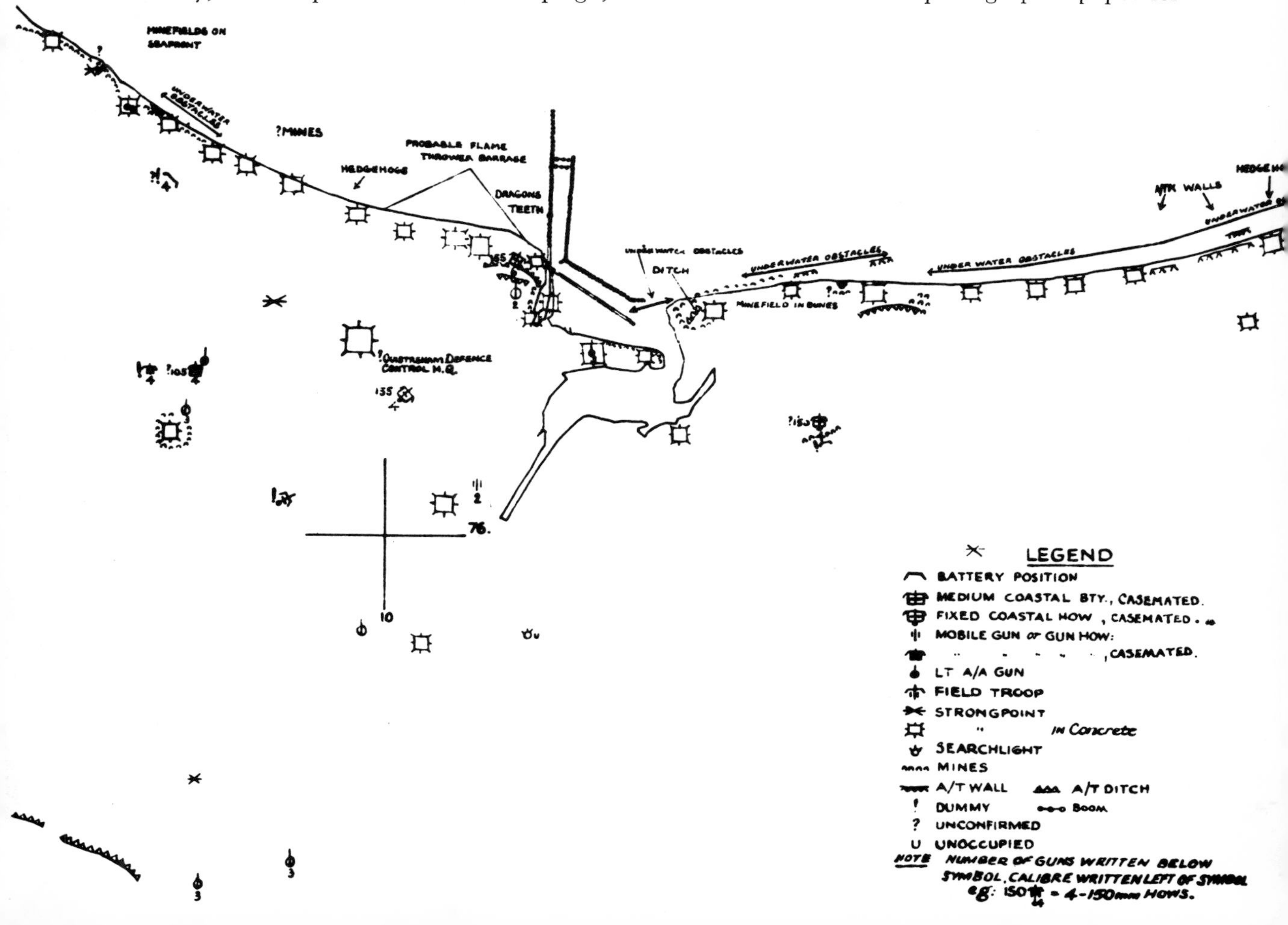

Undercover Survey

MISSION.

1. Carry out a personal recce of the area enclosed by R. Orne - Caen, Bayeux - Arromanches.
2. Confirm position and strength of all known obstacles and defences.
3. Identify and pin-point any new ones
4. Supervise laying of buoys & Nav. a marking channels to assault beache
5. Position marker vessels on night of assault.
6. Establish and develop Headquarters in neighborhood of Courseulles.
7. Assume S.O.(M) duties, and supervise landing of personnel & vehicles, and their rapid movement to front.

MOST SECRET

such an undertaking and American bombers flew in the 730 miles of paper and ten tons of chemicals needed every other day until the maps were finished.

Tides, currents, topography, even weather, could be studied from known information dug out of old guidebooks, yachting manuals and the dusty libraries of universities, but there was one vital factor still to be discovered – the composition of the beaches. Could they withstand the huge weight of armour and transport which would be poured over the sand on D-Day? The only way to find this out was to send men on to the French beaches under the German guns.

Throughout 1943 and 1944 reconnaissance parties were sent across the Channel. In Operation KJH on 31 December 1943, a launch dropped two swimmers, Major Scott Bowden and Sergeant B. Ogden-Smith, in six and a half feet of water off La Rivière to examine beach exit no. 5. The craft waited 400 yards off shore whilst, unperturbed by enemy lights, the two swimmers dug into the shore with augurs and scooped up samples of the beach to take home for analysis. By careful probing they found that there was rock beneath most of the sand with a few soft spots here and there.

A staggering total of 170 million maps was printed by the War Office for Overlord, all under cover of total security. As part of the elaborate deception plan, British agents in the early months of 1944 bought all the stocks of Michelin maps of the Pas de Calais in neutral European towns like Madrid.

Panic over peat

Suddenly there was panic. On 12 January 1944, 21st Army Group H.Q. reported that there was a danger of soft spots which could bog down vehicles and tanks, resulting from patches of peat and clay which were all unfortunately near to the beach exits. 'It is clear that out of several main exits which we intended to use for all vehicles which can be put ashore on the first tide, at least five on the existing assessment must be expected to present serious difficulties to the speedy landing of vehicles. A large part of the area between Asnelles and La Rivière will be impassable even to lightly equipped infantry without vehicles.'

This alarming discovery had been made by Professor J. D. Bernal, 21st Army Group Scientific Adviser, after glancing through a Guide Bleu of Normandy which told of peat-digging in the sands. Free French geologists were smuggled into Paris to secure four volumes of geological maps, which they brought successfully out of Occupied France to the Topographical Unit at Oxford. Combined Operations Pilotage Parties (COPPs) like KJH were sent to look for peat on the Normandy beaches. Reconnaissance was stepped up. Between 17 and 21 January 1944, Lt-Commander Willmott took midget submarine X-20 to the Normandy coast. It was a hard trip. Once again Major Scott Bowden and Sergeant Ogden-Smith were dropped in the sea whilst the submarine with its crew of four settled on the bottom only 380 yards offshore with Willmott studying German movements through X-20's periscope. Suddenly it was disturbed by 'that familiar Boer war sound, the whip crack of mauser bullets'. Willmott felt vulnerable, but no German forces appeared. A short time later the swimmers were taken aboard, Willmott noting in his report, 'it was a very creditable effort for them to swim out so far'. For another day the submarine lay on the bottom. With a crew of four and the two swimmers, it became very uncomfortable and some men felt very ill. It was a relief when night fell and the submarine could surface for fresh air.

X-20 brought back a mass of information on

The Resistance was also inadvertently involved in the operation. Monsieur Philippe de Bourgoing, now a Senator and Mayor of Tracy-sur-Mer near Arromanches, had had his château requisitioned by the Germans as an officers' mess. Apart from listening to the B.B.C. on one of the batmen's radios (the batman was a Pole), he kept quietly and generally in touch with everything going on in that sector of the Atlantic Wall. One day, he was brought a strange instrument which had been found by a local farmer on his land. M. de Bourgoing recognized it as a geologist's boring tool. A visiting British expert had left it behind and it was obvious to M. de Bourgoing that someone had landed from a submarine to survey supplies of water. An army descending on a strange area needs water in quantity. Monsieur de Bourgoing realized the implications of this and hid away the tool. A single incident of this kind, had it been known to the Germans, might well have given the game away.

Left: Page from a secret notebook of a reconnaissance mission conducted by Lieutenant G. Honour in 1943

Below: German gun position overlooking Arromanches

surf, tides, substrata, rocks, runnels and the composition of the beach. In particular the swimmers reported that 'there were no obstacles and the sand was firm'.

Even this evidence was still not enough to calm Ramsay's fears about the invasion becoming disastrously bogged down. He was not happy until he had sent the expert himself. Colonel Sam Bassett, the head of the Oxford I.S.T.D. operation and a middle-aged executive officer, was ordered to Normandy himself in the middle of the winter. There was a big risk involved; if Bassett were caught he actually knew the secret of where the Allies planned to land. He was put ashore with an infrared torch and a trowel. 'I stepped ashore from a dinghy on to Hitler's Europe . . . Although I had never stepped on these beaches in my life they had already become more familiar to me than the beaches of England.' He dipped his arms into the beaches more than 200 times, and then returned home. The sand appeared to be firm. The naval planners breathed a sigh of relief but no chances were taken; the 79th Armoured Division began to design a Bobbin tank which would lay a mat across the beaches to prevent transport floundering.

The resistance forces kept up a stream of information for the Allies, particularly about German reinforcements but it was a very risky business. The German sentries patrolled day and night and military police made constant snap checks, but considerable information filtered out of Normandy. Dominic Ponchardier, acting as an estate agent, managed to tour the coastal towns looking for property that nobody now wanted with an invasion expected. A fisherman, Cardron, cast his nets close to German positions, but hid an old Kodak camera in them to take pictures. Information was gathered in a myriad of small ways. Although German units were ordered to remove their shoulder flashes and identification marks, spies in laundries knew what was going on by removing name tags from underwear. Information constantly came back that the Wall was not all that it was meant to be. In the Cherbourg area the Centurie group had over 120 agents organized. Others worked from Caen.

The ubiquitous Field-Marshal

The Germans fought back. They tried to fool the French agents into believing that the coast was securely held, with false railway movement orders and orders to farmers about massive practice shoots. Their scheme of deception did not work. Early in 1944, tougher tactics were adopted and the Gestapo moved in with their black Citroëns. Security was tightened but they could never stop the flow of material to the London headquarters. During May 1944 over 700 wireless reports and 3,000 written despatches were sent to London on German military positions. Colonel Remy of the Free French and a team of 120 people in Palace Street, London, processed the information ready for assessment by SHAEF intelligence. From here it began to be issued to the assault formations now being actively trained in England. Like a stream of weather forecasts, and with the same regularity, updated information about minefields, troop movements and obstacles came daily out of France. The Germans knew about it, but were unable to stop it. Some of the coastal regiments could only make target practice on the carrier pigeons they saw heading out to sea.

Early in 1944, the French Resistance group

Tackling the beaches. Below: In January 1944, Rommel ordered a massive mining and obstacle plan for the Normandy beaches. The streets of seafront towns (right) were blocked by concrete obstructions

'Never in history was there a defence of such an extent with such an obstacle as the sea. The enemy must be annihilated before he reaches our main battlefield . . . From day to day, week to week, the Atlantic Wall will be stronger and the equipment of our troops will be better . . . It will and must lead to the destruction of the attackers and that will be our contribution to the revenge we owe the English and Americans for the inhuman warfare they are raging against our homeland.'
Rommel

Soises, led by Dominic Ponchardier, had a stroke of luck. Tired of receiving sceptical messages from London about their reports on the weakness of the Atlantic Wall, the group had raided German headquarters at St Malo. At the bottom of a sackful of maps and documents they found nothing less than Field-Marshal Erwin Rommel's latest report on his inspection of the Atlantic Wall, and his instructions to the army on the jobs still to be done. The report showed Rommel's typically buoyant spirit, but any shrewd intelligence officer could detect a large number of weaknesses, by reading between the lines. The Field-Marshal admitted '. . . almost without exception unusual progress has been made in all sectors of the defence groups in accordance with the seriousness of the situation', but here and there he had noticed 'units that do not seem to have recognized the graveness of the hour and who do not even follow instructions'. In one sector, several hundred kilometres wide, only a handful of mines had been installed, although orders had been issued that this should be carried out.

Rommel's report then catalogued the new beach obstacles which had to be installed, such as Tetrahedra, strengthened by concrete, to impale heavy landing craft. Ram logs were also to carry Teller mines so that they could blow a hole in large vessels. One test had shown that a 500-ton landing craft had been sunk in three minutes with this device. If mines were not suitable, then ram logs could be provided with saw-teeth and iron spikes 'to cut open the bottom of the ship and prevent it from slipping off to the side'. Rommel also showed deep anxiety about the need to improve the defences against airborne troops. He told his Generals, 'The time seems to be near when the coast cannot be penetrated any more on account of the strength of the K obstacles and the fortress-like defences by sea forces alone, but the enemy has to employ the very numerous airborne troops to solve the problem from the land'. Rommel urged minefields to be placed in the probable landing places and the installation of dummy fortifications, emphasizing particularly the region of the Somme.

Rommel's impact on the Reich's western de-

fences was becoming far more obvious to SHAEF planners in other ways. In May aerial reconnaissance from Spitfires flying at zero height showed the Normandy beaches bristling with obstacles. Even worse, Rommel's efforts were moving towards the very beaches chosen for the invasion. The Field-Marshal was not alone in his appreciation of the landing zone. The Führer also had become increasingly aware that the invasion could take place in Normandy. At a March 20th Conference Hitler had stated: 'At no place along our front is a landing impossible except perhaps where the coast is broken by cliffs. The most suitable, and hence the most threatened, areas are the two west-coast peninsulas, Cherbourg and Brest, which are very tempting and offer the best possibilities for the formation of a bridgehead, which would be systematically enlarged.'

The O.K.W. Deputy Chief of Operations, General Warlimont, saw Hitler more and more absorbed with the possibility of Normandy. 'Hitler was the first who came to the conclusion that Normandy was the most probable spot . . . Besides his deductions from troop movements Hitler based his conclusions on the consideration that the Allies from the outset would need a big port which had to be situated in such a way as to be quickly protected by a rather short front line. The conditions would be essentially met by the port of Cherbourg and the Cotentin Peninsula.'

Hitler ordered the Normandy coast to be reinforced, but although the 91st Airborne Division was moved into position near Carentan, there were few reserves left to strengthen the west.

For the Germans to have any chance of repulsing the D-Day landing, everything now depended on Rommel. In the last three months before the invasion he threw himself into the work of building up the fortifications with demonic energy, driving hundreds of miles over Army Group B area from the Scheldt to the Loire.

Rommel had firmly decided on the tactics in resisting the landing. In his initial report to the Führer, early in 1944, he had stressed that the Allied invasion would come in such strength that: 'With the coastline held as thinly as it is at present the enemy will probably succeed in creating bridgeheads at several different points and in achieving a major penetration of our coastal defences. Once this has happened it will only be by the rapid intervention of our operation reserves that he will be thrown back into the sea.'

Hamstrung in Normandy

Rommel had decided that a great deal would depend on mines because, 'We have learnt from our engagements with the British that large minefields with isolated strongpoints dispersed within them (field positions) are extremely difficult to take.'

These mined zones would also make the best use of the inferior fortress troops with which Rommel had to resist the well-equipped Anglo-American divisions. Work on the minefields started immediately with a breathtaking plan for an impregnable thousand-yard strip along the French coast and a similar zone inland to defend the coastal defences from the rear. Some ten mines to the yard were to be laid, making a total of 20 million mines for the whole of the French coast. Even this was only the beginning. A second, deeper, zone of 8,000 yards was planned, packed with mines. According to the Engineer Commander of Army Group B this would take 200 million mines. Rommel was already beginning to establish this formidable barrier. By 20 May, over four million mines were in place on the Channel coast, and half had been laid on Rommel's initiative. It was small wonder that he wrote confidently: 'If the enemy should ever set foot on land, an attack through the minefields against the defence works sited within them will present him with a task of immense difficulty. He will have to fight his way through the zone of death in the defensive fire of the whole of our artillery. And not only on the coast . . . any airborne troops who attempt to penetrate to the coast from the rear will make the acquaintance of this mined zone.'

The Germans tried continuously to discover the vital details of the invasion plan. They knew it would come in the summer months, but little else. For all the speculation about Normandy, many in the High Command, including von Rundstedt,

The army working parties steadily increased the number of beach obstacles, often under attack from marauding R.A.F. and U.S.A.A.F. aircraft. By the end of May, 517,000 obstacles were in place. Rommel was a great improviser who paid close attention to making the best use of any material available. One of his ideas was to put a Teller mine on the end of a pole where it would be touched off by a landing glider. The Wehrmacht dubbed it *Rommel-spagel*. This strange crop began to appear in some of the landing zones which the Allies had already marked on their maps for airborne attack

Opposite: Type-C obstacles, and a detail of an Allied invasion map

still believed other locations were more likely, particularly the Pas de Calais. Both the Führer and Rommel believed that two attacks were possible, on Normandy and the Pas de Calais. Indications were coming in that the invasion would take place in May. Indeed, on 10 May, the Kriegsmarine flashed a warning to expect a Normandy landing on the night of 18 May, with an attack on Brittany as a diversion. Large-scale parachute drops were expected and the troops were turned out all along the Atlantic Wall.

SHAEF intelligence watched these movements with great apprehension. They began to wonder at what point Rommel's defences would become so strong that they would seriously threaten the success of D-Day.

But Rommel had to fight shortages and compete for man-power and armaments. He did not control the Todt Organization and he had to contend with a totally divided command structure, with many of his forces answerable to other commanders: the airborne troops to the Luftwaffe; the S.S. to Himmler, and the fortresses to the navy. Even within the army there was von Schweppenburg to advise Rundstedt on Panzers, and, over all, the final unpredictable control of O.K.W. and the Führer.

Request for armour

There was little O.K.W. or von Rundstedt could do to help Rommel. The Todt Organization was now being drawn back to Germany to help clear bomb-damaged cities, and Rundstedt's attempt to build a second line of defence behind the coast was cancelled for lack of concrete and labour. There was also a desperate shortage of first-class fighting units. Rommel asked O.K.W. for an anti-aircraft corps of twenty-four batteries to be placed between the Orne and the Vire, as well as a brigade of *Nebelwerfer* (heavy mortar) to be positioned south of Carentan, but O.K.W. did nothing. Hitler's promises to strengthen the Luftwaffe with a thousand Me 262s also failed to materialize. Finally, in perhaps his most significant request, Rommel asked for two O.K.W. Panzer divisions, writing on 4 May: 'The Commander-in-Chief of Army Group B has reported that in his view, the best way to strengthen the defence potential of Normandy and Brittany is to move up and bring under command the High Command Reserves Corps Headquarters 1st S.S. Panzer Corps, Panzer Lehr Division and 12th S.S. Panzer.' This would place them all within an hour of the Normandy beaches. But O.K.W., on the advice of von Rundstedt, refused to authorize the move.

The Allies, conscious of a race against time, did all they could to hamper the improvements in the German defences. The Allied Tactical Air Force was used in strength to strafe the Todt Organization and German soldiers were shot up as they worked on the sandy French beaches.

Meanwhile, the Resistance inside France was growing in strength and began to enter the battle. Over 100,000 men were believed to be in the Maquis by early 1944. According to COSSAC, a plan had been worked out for the Resistance forces to be used on a phased basis throughout France, with co-ordinated risings and actions by the Maquis taking place region by region.

In March, General de Gaulle ordered from Algiers the formation of the Forces Françaises de l'Intérieur, under the command of General Koenig. 'Resistance,' said de Gaulle, 'had to become consistent enough to play a part in Allied strategy', to 'lead the army of the shadows to fuse with the rest into a single French Army.'

Attacks on railways were stepped up and there were small but effective gestures such as throwing lumps of sugar into concrete mixers to prevent the concrete setting, labourers digging holes for the Rommel Asparagus making them shallow and beach obstacles not being securely anchored down.

The Germans however cracked down hard on the Resistance in the Pas de Calais where the coastal areas were evacuated and rigid screening took place. In Normandy, too, it was becoming far tougher for the groups to operate and send out messages about the latest belts of obstacles. The Gestapo had started a crackdown from Antwerp to the Loire.

Studying Rommel's vigorous actions, SHAEF began to have serious anxieties about the invasion.

STAKES
STRONGPOINTS
PILLBOX
MACHINE-GUN PIT
A/T GUN EMPLACEMENT
TRENCH
ANTI-TANK DITCH
xxxxx WIRE BARRIER
WIRE FENCE
LAND MINES
CABLE
SHELTER
BEACH OBSTACLES
ELEMENT "C"
CURVED RAIL OR RAMP
HEDGEHOGS AND TETRAHEDRA OBSTACLES
STAKES OR FENCES
RESERVOIR
RUQUET
HIGH HIGH WATER MARK
BEACH EXIT
HEDGEHOGS, 3 TO 4 DEEP
RANDOM PATTERN
RAMPS
STAKES
RANDOM STAKES OCCUR THROUGHOUT
LOW LOW WATER MARK

8 Engineering an Invasion

A typical allied landing fleet in 1944, a contemporary illustration by C. E. Turner for *Illustrated London News*. Left background: Troop-carrying assault ships (converted liners) lowering assault craft from their lifeboat davits. Centre: An L.C.S. (Landing Craft Support), a miniature gunboat for giving fire support close inshore. Right: A large ocean-going L.S.T. (Landing Ship Tank) with bow doors and carrying 60 or more tanks and vehicles which could be driven off after beaching. Middle left: An L.C.F. (Landing Craft Flak), a converted L.S.T. with anti-aircraft guns. Centre: A type of smaller U.S. L.S.T., and (right) an L.C.T. (Landing Craft Tank), a flat-bottomed craft designed to land tanks and vehicles by running up on shore and lowering the bow door. In the foreground (left) a typical L.C.I. (Landing Craft Infantry), a craft like a motor yacht with bow ramps for discharging the 240 troops carried after beaching on shore; (centre) an L.C.A. (Landing Craft Assault), 'a floating . . . box pretending to be a motor-boat', a 10-ton shell for carrying 36 troops ashore. Right: A D.U.K.W. ('Duck') amphibious truck

Right: Commodore John Hughes-Hallett. When 'horns were inextricably locked', he argued the case for the Mulberry harbour. Over 200 concrete caissons (far right) would be needed for the sea wall. The 6,000-ton monsters were built all over Britain in just seven months (below)

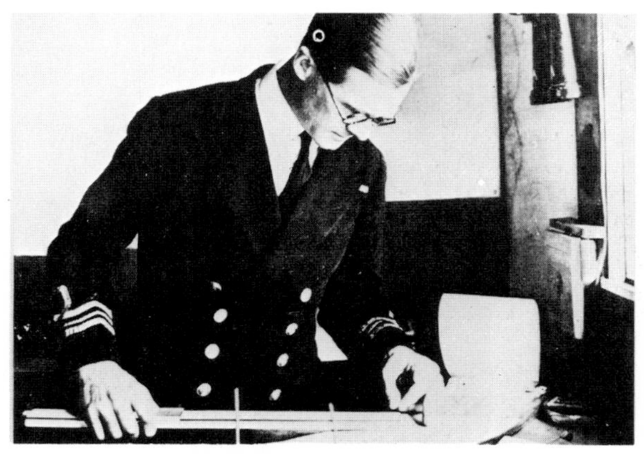

The brilliance of the D-Day plan was its use of technology to overcome the disadvantages of landing on a defended shore at the mercy of the weather. The choice facing the Allies was stark: either to attempt a frontal assault on one of the ports which Hitler had turned into a fortress, or, according to the Admiralty report on the Mulberry harbour, 'to attack the less heavily defended beaches between the port areas and to submit the consequent build-up and maintenance of the force to the vagaries of the Channel weather until a major port could be taken from the rear'.

The invasion would require the facilities of a port the size of Dover. COSSAC had stressed the need for 'sheltered water', envisaging an assault on the lightly held beaches, 'bringing a couple of artificial harbours with us'. Churchill had always been in favour of devising some method of providing sheltered water; his memo of 1942 had called for piers which, 'must float up and down with the tide; the anchoring problem must be mastered. Let me have the best solution worked out. Don't argue the matter. The difficulties will argue for themselves'.

When the proposal for an artificial harbour was presented at the Quebec Conference in September 1943, the British naturally pressed the idea. The Combined Chiefs of Staff agreed to the construction of two such harbours, one for each Ally. The specifications were formidable. By D plus 21 they were to be capable of shifting 12,000 tons of cargo and 2,500 vehicles a day. They would have to cope with the full 26-foot draught of Liberty ships and provide a shelter for landing craft in bad weather. Furthermore, each harbour had to have a minimum life of ninety days. They were to be ready by 1 May 1944 – a mere seven months to build two full-scale harbours the size of Dover.

In many ways the decision to build artificial harbours emerged from the sad experience of Dieppe where planners had realized that any heavy bombardment to soften up the defences could also destroy any existing port facilities, making reinforcement impossible. The only way to supply the army ashore was by means of a prefabricated harbour. As early as December 1941, the staff at Combined Operations Headquarters had been studying a scheme for creating sheltered water. Acceptance of the idea was, however, far from easy and first became accepted only at the Combined Operations Conference (Rattle), held at Largs in 1943, where two naval captains, Hughes-Hallett and Hussey, 'provided a ray of hope' by outlining their scheme for the Mulberries.

Many bright ideas were examined in wrestling with the problems of beating both the English Channel and the Germans at the same time. One of the most original was to try to create an artificial breakwater from a wall of bubbles released from the sea bed, but this was abandoned as far too risky. The final plan called for a breakwater created by sunken blockships, and the construction of an outer sea wall made up of huge boxes of concrete, some the size of three-storey buildings, known as Phoenixes. There would also be floating roadways, called Whales, made of articulated steel sections capable of moving with the 23-foot Nor-

A fortunate accident to one of the Mulberry units prevented what could have been a major disaster for the Allies. One of the concrete Phoenix had gone aground at the Brambles near Southampton. The engineers started to pump it out but discovered that they could not raise the unit because the pumps were not strong enough. According to Admiral Tennant, 'a salvage expert was necessary to take charge of the work . . . and the salvage resources of the country must be employed if the job was to be done on time'. The salvage expert was found and so were the additional heavy-duty pumps. Finding enough tugs which were sufficiently powerful to pull these concrete giants against Channel currents created a major headache for the navy. But 150 tugs were selected as suitable for the Channel crossing and were 'marked with an M for Mulberry on their funnels; all took great pride in their M'

mandy tide. At the end of each roadway would be a pier known as a Spud. In addition to these two Mulberry harbours, even more blockships were to be used to create five Gooseberries, which were sheltered anchorages for landing craft, one off each of the assault beaches.

Building the Mulberries strained the administrative abilities of the senior officer, Major-General Sir Harold Wernher. As the report claimed, 'Perhaps the greatest difficulty in getting the project underway after the plan was approved was the vast number of interested parties who had to be consulted or thought they ought to be consulted.'

A team was assembled of 'three of the best brains from the consultant engineers in Britain, and alongside them were placed leading contractors in naval installation together with British and American officers'. At first, the whole team were in almost continuous session trying to solve the crucial problem of the design of the outer breakwater. As the report recorded: 'The main harbours were to accommodate deep draught ships of the Liberty type. These ships, when loaded, drew approximately 26 feet and it was therefore necessary to include in the sheltered water an area with a depth of some 5 fathoms [30 feet] at low tide. The maximum rise and fall of the tide on the Normandy coast is 23 feet; over and above that, it was necessary for the walls to have adequate freeboard at high water; thus a structure with overall height of some 60 feet was required.'

The largest type of Phoenix which the constructors eventually designed was 200 feet long, 60 feet high and weighed more than 6,000 tons. Over 213 of all types were made, which took over one million tons of reinforced concrete and 70,000 tons of steel reinforcement. The piers, code-named Lobnitz, were attached to massive steel pylons that rested on the sea bed. Following Churchill's directive, the piers did indeed 'float up and down with the tide' – with the assistance of an ingenious system of hydraulic jacks. Linking the piers to the land was a floating roadway made up of steel pontoon bridges, called Whales. Although the navy was unenthusiastic about releasing any usable merchant ships, sixty blockships were assembled in Scotland and loaded with explosive charges. They were to be sunk off the D-Day beaches.

Dozens of construction companies and 20,000 workers sweated to complete the Mulberry harbours in time for D-Day. The work was carried out all over Britain with huge excavations being made in the banks of the Thames and Medway to allow the mammoth Phoenix units to be built. Two hundred tugs were used to tow the parts of the harbour to their moorings. Various pieces of the Mulberry meccano were stored in creeks and inlets around the British coast before their D-Day assembly, some even within the range of German guns at Calais. This was deliberately to confuse the enemy about the intended invasion route. The Mulberry project was so secret that many who built the components did not know what they would be used for, nor did the Germans, although they were certain that they must be floating moorings or fuel storage-tanks for use in the invasion. Lord Haw Haw confidently told Britain in May 1944: 'We

The D.U.K.W. Eisenhower regarded this $2\frac{1}{2}$-ton amphibious truck as one of the crucial weapons of the war

know what you're doing with those caissons [Mulberry units]. You intend to sink them off the coast when the attack takes place. Well, chaps, we've decided to help you. We'll save you trouble and sink the caissons before you arrive.'

A week before the day of the invasion the blockships were to sail from Scotland to rendezvous with the rest of the Mulberries. The invasion would be vitally dependent on the successful functioning of the Mulberry harbours, but until there was the chance to test one in action, no one knew just what their capabilities would be – this test would not happen until they were actually in place in Normandy.

D-Day meccano

The Allied army was perhaps the most mobile army that had ever existed. The plan was to land 14,000 vehicles on D-Day and 95,000 by D plus 12. Millions of gallons of fuel would be needed to move it into action. Normally this would be transported by tankers but, as General Morgan knew, 'few better targets can be imagined than that to be presented by a tanker at anchor off an open beach engaged in the lengthy process of pumping its cargo ashore'.

The COSSAC planners thought that the obvious way to overcome this problem was to lay a pipeline from Britain to France, but it was not quite so simple. Experiments in early 1943 with a pipeline between Swansea and Ilfracombe revealed difficulties of operation. An alternative idea was developed: this was to tow concrete barges across the Channel to serve as floating reservoirs. Nevertheless, SHAEF decided to persevere with Pluto, as the scheme for a submarine pipeline from the Isle of Wight to Cherbourg was called. Pluto would not fare very satisfactorily in the first weeks of the invasion but it was later perfected in 1944 to pump fuel from Liverpool across the Straits of Dover to the Rhine.

D-Day was impossible without the specialized landing ships and craft. There were various breeds.

The key landing craft of all the Allied operations was the Landing Ship Tank (L.S.T.). On 7 July 1940, Churchill had minuted: 'Let there be built great ships which can cast up on a beach in any weather large numbers of the heaviest tanks.'

The L.S.T. was to be capable not only of carrying anything up to sixty tanks, but of crossing the oceans so that it could be used in any theatre of war. It presented difficult design problems, needing a shallow draught for cruising on to a gently sloping beach so that the tanks could roll off safely, as well as rugged sea-keeping qualities.

There was the Landing Craft Tank (L.C.T.), which was a self-propelled barge, with bow door and ramp, able to carry three to five tanks. The British versions could land tanks in three feet of water.

The infantry troops were carried ashore on either L.C.I.s or L.C.A.s. The Landing Craft Infantry were largish vessels, each able to carry troops who disembarked down ramps on either side of the bows. Their smaller versions, the Landing Craft Assault, L.C.A., could be carried aboard large merchant ships and troop carriers, being released from davits.

By far the most awe-inspiring landing craft was the L.C.T. (R), adapted for shore bombardment. The lessons of Dieppe had shown the need for maximum fire support when infantry and armour hit the beach. To solve the problem, Colonel F. H. C. Langley of Combined Operations designed a rocket-firing L.C.T. A demonstration of this craft was arranged at Portsmouth; it carried banks of 5-inch rockets and was provided with H2S radar to scan the shore. The first test was hardly auspicious when 360 rockets were accidentally fired at one go. Langley said, 'It was enough to remove my eyelashes and eyebrows as well as much of my hair.' But the potential of the L.C.T.(R) was immense, and in service it became capable of firing 1,080 rockets in half a minute, in rapid salvos. This devastating fire-power equalled that of eighty cruisers shooting simultaneously. Thirty-six L.C.T.s were built for the Mediterranean and Normandy.

Despite these spectacular weapons, the SHAEF commanders had also learnt to respect the war-winning potential of less glamorous but equally important equipment in amphibious operations.

Eisenhower wrote, 'Four other pieces of equipment that most senior officers came to regard as

among the most vital to our success in Africa and Europe were the bulldozer, the jeep, the 2½-ton truck and the C-47 airplane. Curiously enough, none of these items is designed for combat.'

Of these, the one craft specifically valuable in the assault phase of the invasion, and almost indispensable as the war dragged on, was the D.U.K.W. This amphibious truck could be driven into the sea to float like a boat or roll on to dry land just like a truck. It fulfilled the vital role of bridging the gap between the landing craft and the dry shore. Designed by Hartley Rowe, Chief Engineer of the United Fruit Company, who had experience of moving cargoes over difficult shores in South America, it was based on the standard 2½-ton U.S. Army truck. In 1942, after thirty-eight days, General Motors had the first prototype ready for testing. In the view of many Generals, its versatility made it a war-winning weapon.

Hobart's 'Funnies'

Far and away the most important technical development for D-Day for the army was the specialized armour designed by Major-General Percy Hobart's 79th Armoured Division, known as 'Hobart's Funnies'. The 79th Armoured Division had been set up in March 1943 on the orders of Sir Alan Brooke, C.I.G.S. Hobart worked out many different ways of tackling the problem of giving amphibious assault troops immediate armoured support and of using new techniques to breach the concrete and minefields of the Atlantic Wall. Most remarkable was the D.D., or swimming tank. Using a Sherman M4, Hobart's engineers worked out a way in which the tanks could swim ashore under their own power.

The tank, known as a Duplex Drive (D.D.), was fitted with twin propellers working off its main engine. A larger waterproof canvas screen was erected all round the hull, giving it the appearance of a baby carriage, with caterpillar tracks. The tanks could be launched into the sea several miles off the enemy beach and be driven ashore. Once they hit the beach, the canvas skirts were lowered and the Sherman operated in its normal fighting capacity.

The beach obstacles of the Atlantic Wall were also taken very seriously and Hobart developed special armour to protect the engineers as they blasted or by-passed any fortifications. Churchill tanks were converted to carry a 40-foot box-girder bridge for crossing tank ditches and walls. The flail tank, or Crab, was specially developed to scythe through Rommel's minefields. A rotating drum in front thrashed the ground with steel chains, detonating any mines in its path. It was uncomfortable for the crew who had to endure the deafening explosions, but the flails could beat a path 10 feet wide for other vehicles to follow up. Hobart produced even more specialized fighting vehicles such as the A.V.R.E. Mk III which carried a powerful mortar capable of hurling 'dustbin'-sized explosive charges to blast block-houses. Most terrible was the Mark VII Crocodile which towed a 400-gallon trailer of fuel, which it shot as a high-pressure jet of flame over ranges of 100 yards.

1

2

3

4

5

6

7

Hobart's Funnies

The 'Funnies' were the brainchildren of Major-General Percy Hobart (right) of the 79th Armoured Division. (1) The D.D. or 'swimming tank' was a conversion of a standard Sherman that turned it into an amphibious tank to give vital fire support; its canvas skirts (2) turned the 33-ton Sherman into a clumsy boat. (3) The Churchill Mk VIII A.V.R.E. fired a 25-lb. 'flying dustbin' of high explosive pointblank at Hitler's pillboxes. (4) The Bobbin tank – its canvas roadway unrolled across soft and treacherous sand. (5) A Sherman 'Crab' tank, its whirling chain flails scything a path through a minefield. (6) A tank equipped with a special bridge approaching a ditch; (7) the bridge is hydraulically extended to close the gap. Below: A D.D. tank takes to the water Bottom: Propelled by two propellers attached to the tracks, the clumsy 'boat' heads for shore in choppy seas. With a freeboard of less than a foot or two, it could be swamped and sunk in seconds

9 'Tougher than D-Day'

Training for invasion. On Devon beaches, American troops and landing craft practise assault landings under the fire of bullets and explosives. Inset: The Supreme Commander, Churchill and General Bradley get on to the firing line during one of their many tours of inspection. Ike scored hits on target but Churchill's target was tactfully removed before his score could be counted

The Allied commanders needed to train their men not only in the specialist role for each fighting arm, but also to co-ordinate all operations in one smooth overall plan. The British and American officers who were to carry out the D-Day plans had gained experience of seaborne landings in the Mediterranean. Eisenhower had been responsible for the successful landings in north Africa, Sicily and Italy; Montgomery, Bradley and Patton had all been adept in securing a lodgement on an enemy-held shore. Admiral Ramsay had also always understood the close relationship between the naval, land and air direction necessary for amphibious assault, together with the importance of maintaining a smooth supply build-up for the army ashore. Air Marshals Tedder and Coningham had developed the techniques of tactical air support with ground troops in the desert and Italy.

If D-Day was to be a success, the fighting units had to co-operate with each other. The army assault regiments would have to practise closely with the navy and air force; the navy would have to rely on air spotting to carry out its bombardment, and the army would, in turn, be totally dependent on the navy for supplies.

The D-Day planners knew that the men who were to go on the D-Day operation differed greatly in fighting experience.

The Americans in particular were very raw. They had only a few battle-trained infantry divisions: the 'Big Red One', the 1st and 4th Infantry Divisions, which had taken part in the earlier north African and Italian campaigns. Most of the U.S. divisions allocated to France would be sent direct from the United States. Others would have the chance of a few weeks' training in Britain.

The airborne forces were rigorous in their training. Those with special objectives like Lt-Colonel Otway's Regiment of 6th Airborne, which had to capture the dominating battery at Hermanville, practised for months on accurately constructed replicas of German guns made out of scaffolding at a secret area in Berkshire. Their mission was by parachute and glider, to land on the top of the battery itself; lack of precision could mean total disaster.

Welding the team. American infantrymen training on Slapton Sands in Devon; this beach would be the scene of the nearly disastrous practice assault in April 1944. Left: Preparing Sherman tanks, part of the vast assault of armour transported from America. Far left: General Montgomery addressing Allied troops. His morale-boosting trips took him to every major unit, British, Canadian and American. Above: The Supreme Commander and his deputy, Air Chief Marshal Tedder, with a Sherman crew during invasion manoeuvres in February 1944

Armoured vehicles ready for invasion
Below: Specially constructed model of landing beach

Specialist troops included the crews of the D.D. tanks. They had to practise erecting the canvas walls around their tanks floating off L.C.T.s and swimming these '30-ton yachts with lead keels'.

In the autumn of 1943, COSSAC carried out syndicate discussions to try to work out training doctrine for D-Day. They concluded that 'in short, the cart has been put in front of the horse – and the horse is pulling it backwards'. Nobody knew what was required of them, few soldiers had any idea of the effectiveness of D.D. tanks, or even if they would work, and some units were training for the wrong kind of landings. The syndicate thought that all the tasks would be far too much for one body of assault troops. They would have to overcome the local enemy and clear routes inland. Fresh troops should be employed to pass through the assault and man the covering position. Commando-style training should be given to the assault groups.

Compensation

Suitable places had to be found that resembled the terrain of the French beaches. Five were finally selected and added to Studland Bay and Ringstead Bay. These were Slapton Sands, the Gower peninsula, the Tarbat peninsula, Culbin Sands and Burghead Bay. Southwold in East Suffolk was also required for divisional training. This meant the inhabitants of small villages and farms would have to be evacuated from their homes. 2,750 people were involved at Slapton and several hundred at the other sites. At a meeting of Ministers chaired by Deputy Prime Minister Clement Attlee, the army's requirements were examined. The problem was delicate since 'It would be difficult to compensate people for loss of livelihood under existing statute, which provided for compensation for loss of rent but not for loss of profit'. The judgement would hit small tradesmen and farmers very hard, but the meeting pointed out that any compensation for damage would fall upon the services themselves. This later caused the august Board of Admiralty to enter into a lively argument with Mr F. A. Pickett, of Harberton, Devon, who claimed that compensation was inadequate, following the use of his property for training for the D-Day assault. Loftily, their Lordships stated that 'compensation has been paid on as full a scale as possible . . . My Lords fully appreciate the concern that must be felt by those whose homes these properties are, but they feel that perhaps those affected may derive some measure of consolation from the brilliant successes which the use of the area has enabled the troops to achieve.'

Mr Pickett was unimpressed. He replied, 'We do appreciate the brilliant success which the use of

"Pity you couldn't have seen the garden a fortnight earlier."

the area has enabled the troops to achieve, and so, presumably, do others outside the area, but we do not appreciate why all the burden should fall on this area, and it is no consolation to us. The whole country has benefited by our misfortunes and the whole country should be called upon to provide.'

Chaotic rehearsals

In April and May there was a major rehearsal for Operation Neptune to practise marshalling, the embarkation and sailing of the assault forces; the approach and assault landings; the quick setting-up of beach organization. The operation, code-named Fabius, took place in five separate stages, testing all aspects of the inter-service operation.

Fabius 1 was a full-scale exercise for Naval Assault Force O, landing the 1st U.S. Infantry Division on Slapton Sands from Portland.

Fabius 2 carried Assault Force G, 50th Northumbrian Division, landing at Hayling Island from Portsmouth and Southampton.

Fabius 3: Naval Assault Force J landed the 3rd Canadian Infantry Division at Bracklesham Bay from Portsmouth and Southampton.

Fabius 4: Naval Assault Forces landed the 3rd British Infantry Division at Littlehampton from Portsmouth and Southampton.

Fabius 5 familiarized staff in the Thames estuary and east-coast ports in the embarkation of the build-up forces.

The air forces also rehearsed their role during Fabius. They practised methods of protecting marshalling areas and the passage of the many convoys, right up to the moment of assault. As Allied Tactical Air Force put it, 'It is important that the pilots of all aircraft should see a large concentration of assault forces at sea . . . Conversely, it is of importance that personnel in assault forces should obtain an idea of the degree of air cover and support which they might expect, and have an opportunity of seeing the different types of Allied aircraft in the air over the forces.'

The 21st Army Group exercises were carried out successfully. The troops were issued with chewing gum to ward off sea-sickness, and maximum security was imposed on the D.D. tanks which had to be kept covered up until the last moments before use.

If a bad rehearsal means a good show, then General Omar Bradley had reason to feel relieved. The American exercise at Slapton Sands was a disaster. Bradley and Brereton, Commander of the Ninth U.S. Air Force, which had been charged with tactical support, watched the assault on the mock Utah. The visibility was bad and the American fighters did not turn up. Bradley became anxious in case they arrived late, bombing his assault wave. Rocket barges opened fire and the troops went in. Everything was in a mess: 'The beach-engineer organization had broken down and air support failed to show.' In Bradley's view, 'These were two very serious breakdowns because the beach-engineers were longshoreman, trucker, traffic cop and warehouseman.' What Bradley did not know until later was that the chaos had been caused by an E-boat attack. The German Navy, making a bold appearance, had sunk two L.S.T.s with the loss of over 700 men.

Careless talk costs lives

In the spring of 1944 the British people found themselves in the odd position of witnessing the assembly of a huge armada in their island without knowing exactly where it was going. The great public enthusiasm and interest in the expedition frightened SHAEF in case top-secret details concerning Overlord should leak out. Lt-Gen. Morgan bluntly stated their fears, 'If the enemy obtains as much as forty-eight hours warning of the location of the assault area, the chances of success are small, and any longer warning spells certain defeat.'

Although few people knew the complete D-Day plans, Sir Alan Brooke, C.I.G.S., knew that a skilled intelligence service could piece together the minutiae of apparently unrelated facts to gain a convincing overall picture of enemy intentions. The Germans knew that because of their relative weakness they could throw the Allies into the sea if only they knew where the landings were going to take place. Careless talk really could cost lives – that of D-Day literally thousands. For example, there were over 20,000 men working flat out on Mulberry

Bigot

BIGOT
TOP SECRET

SUPREME HEADQUARTERS
ALLIED EXPEDITIONARY FORCE
Office of the Assistant Chief of Staff, G-2

TOP SECRET

Copy No. 18

SHAEF/2DX/1/INT

5th May, 1944.

G-2 ESTIMATE OF THE ENEMY BUILD UP AGAINST OPERATION 'OVERLORD'

(Based on information available up to 2 May)

OBJECT

1. The object of this paper is to estimate the rate of build up of enemy formations against Operation OVERLORD, between D day and D + 25.

ASSUMPTION

2. That enemy dispositions in FRANCE and the LOW COUNTRIES are as shown on the attached map (Appendix A).

harbours. If any of them talked about the strange concrete caissons, or the articulated roadways, the Germans could soon start to gather the secrets of the giant meccano puzzle. If its true purpose were discovered, then von Rundstedt and Rommel could work out the invasion beaches by a process of elimination.

The number of officers who knew all the Overlord secrets was kept very small, to reduce any possibility of leakage. The Bigot system was used to keep a strict security check on all those who had access to the complete plan. Many knew about details, but only the select band of Bigot officers knew how the jigsaw pieced together. Documents and plans that were stamped BIGOT were treated with a confidentiality even more secure than TOP SECRET.

The nearer D-Day approached, the greater the number of officers and men who had to be briefed in detail on their assignments. Airborne troops had to be briefed about the kind of terrain they would be landing on, commandos given the details of the beaches they would assault. The pilotage and demolition parties, as well as the engineers in the naval beach parties, had to know every detail of their sector and practise on obstacles and beaches in the south of England. SHAEF and the army commanders were so anxious about minimizing the risks of a leak that rigid steps were taken to corral assault troops behind the barbed wire of what appeared to be concentration camps. In a note to the War Cabinet the Chiefs of Staff said that, 'After briefing, perimeter and interior guards will be established by S.O.S. and tactical units, in order to prevent communication between briefed troops and persons not entitled to operational knowledge.'

Just in case somebody wished to say farewell to his wife or sweetheart, steps were also taken 'to ensure that troops will not have access to civilian letterboxes or to civilian telephones'.

Despite barbed wire fencing as strict security, some men did get out. The last-minute urge to see a wife or girlfriend proved too great for any physical barrier. One sapper from a Royal Engineers battalion made his way from near Portsmouth to Newcastle in the week before D-Day. Evading the

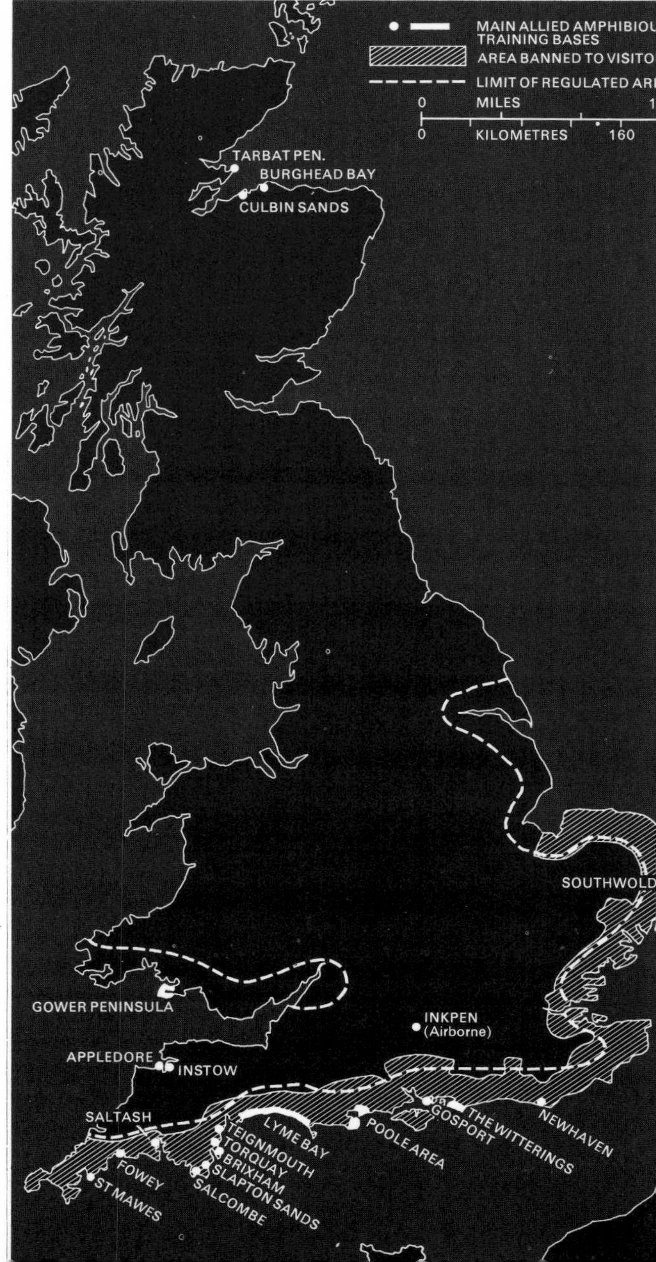

Where and when would the invasion come? This was Hitler's nightmare as visualized by a British cartoonist. But German agents failed to break the extremely tight security with which the invasion plan was surrounded (left)

Overleaf: The secrets of D-Day lay scattered over the whole of the south of England. Military convoys were parked in quiet backstreets, and training camps for the troops abounded in parkland and country villages near the embarkation ports

military police who combed England for him, he finally returned to his unit, under his own steam, the night before the unit embarked. It was a huge joke to his mates that 'he went to invade France under close arrest'.

Alarums and excursions

One of the greatest threats to Overlord security arose from an incident involving the loss of Bigot officers. During the E-boat attack on the U.S. 4th Division's Fabius rehearsal at Slapton Sands in May, two L.S.T.s sank and 700 men were drowned. Ten Bigot officers were discovered to be among the missing. SHAEF security was extremely alarmed. It was quite possible for the Germans to capture one of these men, or discover documents on his body. A gruesome operation began of scouring Lyme Bay to recover the bodies of the Bigot officers. Not until the last Bigot corpse, still stiff in his life-jacket, was fished out of the water, did SHAEF know that the secrets were secure.

This incident apart, military security for Overlord remained incredibly tight. Many soberly remembered the two disastrous earlier landings at Dakar and Dieppe when the enemy appeared to have been tipped off in advance.

But in spite of all the officers who knew the secret, there was no major break of security, and only the occasional slip. A U.S. Major-General, having drinks at Claridges, was overheard saying that he could not get any supplies through until after the invasion, and that would not, of course, be until after 15 June. He was sent packing to the United States within twenty-four hours.

The British, too, had the occasional problem. One young British officer told his parents about the invasion when he was on leave. Unfortunately for their son, their sense of duty obliged them to tell the military authorities.

There were other scares, mainly from press sources whose speculation about the date and place of the landings became the issue of the year.

On 2 May, SHAEF intelligence pounced on the innocent compiler of the *Daily Telegraph* crossword puzzle that morning. Answers to two of the clues were Utah and Omaha.

NO CURE FOR INSOMNIA

One journalist who ran foul of British intelligence was from the *Chicago Herald Tribune*. He had come to Britain just before the invasion, determined to scoop the most sensational story of the war, the invasion plan. When he tried to return to America, three days before the invasion was launched, he found that security would not let him leave the country. He spent the next three weeks creating 'one helluva scene' and his case was even discussed by the British War Cabinet. But the story of the century did not break.

In the final weeks before D-Day, there was a whole series of heart-stopping incidents, each one of which could have leaked the secret. In Exeter, a railway employee found a briefcase abandoned in a train compartment. In it was a complete set of Overlord plans. In Whitehall, on a morning in late May, a gust of wind blew a dozen copies of an Overlord resumé into the street. Security officers raced out on to the pavement and chased paper amongst the traffic. They only recovered eleven. After two hours, the twelfth copy was handed in by an unknown civilian.

The Chicago post office, repacking a parcel from England that had broken apart, found a set of Bigot documents, with details of Operation Overlord. Subsequent investigation revealed that they had been sent by accident to the sister of an American officer working at SHAEF headquarters. But,

incredibly, in spite of these accidents the secret did not leak out, and German intelligence failed to gain any information of real significance about D-Day. Such evidence that did come in from scattered sources around the world and through neutral European capitals was wasted. At the time when the German Generals vitally needed accurate intelligence, the S.S. and Hitler finally succeeded in ousting Admiral Canaris. He was the master spy whose intelligence network was acknowledged to be the finest in the world. An eccentric, whose personal filing cabinet held secrets about the Nazi High Command as well as his pet dachshund, he ran a private war against the Nazi bosses. But by 1944 he had fallen under the Führer's suspicion and the S.S., under Schellenberg, took over Canaris's outfit. Many of his 16,000 agents, who owed the master spy an almost personal loyalty, showed their disapproval of their new S.S. masters by a lack of co-operation in getting information.

The S.S. takeover also put paid to the last-ditch scheme devised by Canaris to get information about the invasion. He had created an English-speaking commando unit whose mission would be to make a lightning raid on the English coast to seize officers and information. This unit had the unlikely title of the Brandenberger Division, but it was never used because neither the S.S. nor the Führer trusted it.

One important clue, however, had been unearthed by the activity of Cicero in the British Embassy in Ankara. By 1944 German intelligence knew the invasion was called 'Overlock', later corrected to 'Overlord'. An analysis by the Chief of O.K.H., section Fremde Heere West, stated: 'For 1944 an operation is planned outside the Mediterranean that will seek to force a decision and therefore will be carried out with all available forces. This operation is probably being prepared under the code name of Overlord . . . On 18 January 1944, therefore, the Anglo-Saxon command was committed to a large-scale operation which would seek a final decision (second front).'

The desperate need to cover all trace of Overlord encouraged the Allied intelligence services to indulge their wilder imaginative and theatrical

talents. One clever British idea was to exploit General Montgomery's strong personality and flair for publicity. The Germans knew well the familiar features of the black-bereted figure who gained so much attention from the press and news-reels. British intelligence searched for Monty's double, a man who, when dressed in the commander's uniform, would be exactly like him. When he was found, Monty's double was sent far away from the invasion area to distract German attention.

The Americans had their own cloak-and-dagger methods. Shortly before D-Day, Eisenhower ordered Miles Copeland of the Office of Strategic Services (O.S.S.) and another of his security staff to give in their own identity papers, and to be issued with the false documents of German spies. They were to find out the date and place of the invasion. They did not succeed, though they had some valuable pointers.

Censorship and security blackout

Britain did possess one great advantage in tackling its security problems. It was an island and there could be firm control of movement in and out of the country. Eisenhower urged Churchill to 'draw a cordon round the British Isles, regulate all traffic from abroad, censor all communications, including diplomatic, by whatever means, and stop all air and sea traffic from the British Isles not under our direct control.'

The War Cabinet set up a security sub-committee to examine the security risks. Top of the list was Ireland, which Churchill regarded as 'a most useful base for enemy agents'. A hundred-per-cent censorship on all mail to both Eire and Northern Ireland was imposed and telephone calls were continuously monitored. Aer Lingus services were stopped and Irish ships continued to be searched by the navy.

As the result of one particular source of intelligence leaks, as from 17 April, foreign diplomats were forbidden to enter or leave the country and their communications were censored. This led to a first-class row with de Gaulle, especially as the U.S.A. and U.S.S.R. were exempt from censorship.

De Gaulle's headquarters was now in Algiers where the French Committee of National Libera-

'The U.S. First Army is known to be concerned about the numbers of women of the worst type from large cities, the type that has supplied so many instruments of espionage, and their visits to U.S. forces give cause for concern'.

General Eisenhower

'The fixing of Montgomery's headquarters south of London confirms that the main strength of the enemy's forces is centred on south and south-east England.'

Rommel, 21 May

tion was preparing to assume power. The British and Americans, although recognizing the value of de Gaulle's control over the 'army of the shadows' which could rise behind the Germans on D-Day, did not trust de Gaulle's security arrangements. Important information could easily be passed on by disaffected factions inside the French Committee of National Liberation.

De Gaulle expected his government to be treated on an equal footing with Britain, the U.S. and Russia. He regarded the censorship of his ciphers as insupportable.

No notes passed between London and Algiers so that no discussions would be possible on the establishment of a post-liberation government in France. Eventually, however, Koenig sorted out the censorship problem. The Allies allowed him to encode messages in French cipher after they had been first checked by Allied censors. Koenig gave his word not to make any changes. Churchill also invited de Gaulle to London to tell him the place and date of D-Day.

The British and the Americans also considered it inadvisable to let the Russians know the full details of the plan in advance. Although they were allies, mutual suspicion and the increased chance of leakage from Moscow made them hold out in spite of Stalin's demand for a marked map and full details of the plan.

Whilst a rigid ban was brought down on travel and communications with the world outside Britain, SHAEF became concerned about the behaviour of people inside Britain. Eisenhower was particularly worried about visitors to coastal areas and D-Day bases, who could go back to their homes and talk about what they had seen. A visitors' ban on a huge section of the British coast would, in Eisenhower's view, reduce the risks of disclosure. The War Cabinet was unhappy about these restrictions, but the Supreme Commander continued to press for action. He illustrated his case by pointing out that there was an alarming jump in day-return rail tickets from London to the seaside resort of Brighton, which was right in the middle of the build-up area of the British and Canadian assault formations. Brighton gained a great deal of attention from the Americans because, apart from anything else, the town had a certain reputation as being the rendezvous of ladies of disrepute, who were naturally attracted by the large number of young men based there.

Churchill was sceptical, but, in the face of Eisenhower's insistent demands, the War Cabinet agreed to bring down heavy controls on movement in Britain in 'a belt on the east and south coasts extending from the Wash to Land's End, and also to a small area in the Firth of Forth'. It came into force on 2 April.

German agents were already operational in both London and the south-coast areas. They were regularly feeding back reports by radio to Berlin. The Germans knew that they were not enemy hands that tapped out the morse messages about troop concentrations and possible dates because they compared the 'signature' of the senders' keying with taped records made before the agents had been infiltrated into England. One of their most reliable informants, Hans Schmidt, had been parachuted into Britain in 1942 and was living happily with a wife and young children right in the heart of the south-coast assembly area. Another agent, a Frenchwoman, was working in a British Ministry and regularly chatted to British and American officers at select cocktail parties. Afterwards she was driven to a house in Hampstead where she transmitted her reports to Berlin. Her messages always underlined the fact that her information, supposedly gathered from contact with the French General Koenig, was that the invasion was coming at Calais in July.

These were the agents who survived. Hundreds didn't. They were arrested remarkably rapidly by British authorities and they had no chance of doing harm. In fact, what the Germans reported as their most reliable and trustworthy sources were feeding false information. They had been 'turned round' by British counter-intelligence and the 'messages' were specially prepared to mislead their erstwhile masters.

Captured German records showed that on the vital question of the real date they were totally confused. The Germans had intercepted reports claim-

Security was a major worry for the Allied leaders – and a national joke for the cartoonists, as Fougasse illustrated for *Punch*

ing that the mission would take place on a variety of dates from May to September and in a dozen locations from Norway to Bordeaux. Only one, from a French Colonel in Algiers, had given the correct date and place – 6 June, Normandy. This source had been 'turned round' too; in fact the Germans had been used to seeing so many misleading reports from the Colonel on the Sicily and Italy invasions that they had discounted his information.

Keeping Hitler guessing

The Germans had one source of intelligence that could not be turned round. By sending out air reconnaissance missions over Britain, they could still try to piece together the Allied intentions from troop and transport concentrations, but the number of photographic missions possible in 1944 was drastically reduced owing to the supremacy of the Allied Air Force. Soon aircraft were deliberately allowed to get through in the south-east and saw massive ground concentrations with ships and landing craft filling almost every English harbour and creek. In fact this was exactly what SHAEF wanted them to see – an Allied build-up in south-east England. Dummy landing craft known as Bigbobs had been grouped in the Thames estuary and the Channel ports. Squadrons of wooden tanks had been gathered in the Kent and Sussex meadows.

Movements of landing craft took place ostentatiously down the east of England. The Pluto terminal at Dover and the Mulberry units near Folkestone added to the impression that something big would be landing across the Straits of Dover. In order to complete the deception, all the 21st Army Group signals' traffic went from the genuine headquarters in Portsmouth via land-line before being broadcast from Kent. So successfully did this ruse work, that it was instrumental in persuading Rommel that von Rundstedt was perhaps right after all when he said the invasion was coming across the Straits of Dover.

The deception plan was so elaborate that it was a shadow operation all of its own, called Operation Fortitude. Air-power was skilfully used in deceiving Rundstedt and O.K.W. Repeated fighter-bomber attacks were made against the Pas de Calais. At the same time, under Operation Crossbow, heavy bombers flew hundreds of sorties to attack the V-weapon sites behind Boulogne and Calais. The overall effect on German H.Q. was to indicate a big softening-up campaign prior to a seaborne assault.

Fortitude kept the Fifteenth Army in place, and Hitler and von Rundstedt were made to wonder about diversionary support for Normandy. The Fifteenth Army stayed in this position, ready to repulse the invaders north of the Seine, leaving the Seventh Army to fight the Allied armada on its own.

It was vital, according to Eisenhower, that the Germans did not bring all their available units into battle before 15 July when enough Allied divisions could meet them. To confirm his view of how the German Command was interpreting the Allied invasion plans, the Supreme Commander had set up his own 'Nazi command' structure in London. Commanders who conformed to the known characteristics of von Rundstedt, Rommel, Hitler, Goering, Jodl, or the other Germans in High Command, were regularly assembled for a fantastic war game. They would go through specially briefed intelligence reports prepared by SHAEF which accurately assessed how much the Germans could have found out. They would then test these against the Allied invasion operations. The results of this intensive war gaming convinced Eisenhower that if the Germans could be kept guessing about the invasion, even after it had been landed, his 15 July deadline for the arrival of German reserves would be possible.

Intelligence reports and Resistance information reaching London from Normandy at the end of May worried Allied planners. It seemed as though the German Command in Normandy was concentrating its forces behind the beaches. In the first week of May, Panzer Lehr moved to Le Mans and the 21st Panzer Division moved up to Caen. The 91st Division was first of all moved to Brittany and the 17th Machine-gun Battalion moved up into the area of the Cotentin peninsula. Pessimists at SHAEF suspected that the Germans had cracked the secret.

10 Master Plan

Anglo-American anxiety. Before D-Day, Anglo-American relations were severely strained. Churchill was convinced that the U.S. plan to land in the south of France (Anvil) in support of Overlord was futile. He argued instead for continuing the push in Italy and the Balkans. Churchill and his Chiefs of Staff were also uneasy about Eisenhower's demands, as Supreme Commander, for control of a major part of R.A.F. Bomber Command, Britain's strategic weapon. Shortly after his appointment, Eisenhower found himself confronting Churchill and the British Chiefs of Staff

On 6 June 1944, two landings were planned to take place in France. The Combined Chiefs of Staff intended that the invasion of Normandy, although the main effort, should share its glory with a second landing in the south of France. A small army of two divisions was to be found from the Mediterranean forces and put ashore among the luxury villas and hotels of the Côte d'Azur. The operation was appropriately called Anvil, but although it was meant to assist D-Day by diverting the Germans away from Normandy, the plan almost ruined chances of success in Normandy and placed an intense strain on Anglo-American relations. The row over Anvil was sparked off early in 1944 by the decision of Eisenhower and Montgomery to increase the strength of the D-Day assault from three divisions to five, with two follow-up divisions landing on the second tide. On Montgomery's advice, SHAEF also agreed to widen the beachhead to include the Cotentin peninsula so that Cherbourg could be immediately threatened, and German reserves stretched over a longer perimeter. The Chiefs of Staff in Washington were told unequivocally, 'Nothing less will give us an adequate margin for success!'

The naval implications of these decisions were enormous. The original COSSAC plan had called for 3,323 landing craft of all shapes and sizes, 467 warships and 150 minesweepers; this now needed to be increased by doubling the number of minesweepers, and adding at least another 1,000 landing craft. Yet landing craft, particularly the big L.S.T.s, were in desperately short supply. The British had no spare capacity to produce them, but the U.S. Navy held most of the spare reserves. Admiral King, however, had now gone on to the offensive in the Pacific war, regardless of the 'Europe-first' decisions of the 1941 Washington Conference.

General Marshall, the chief advocate of the Europe-first policy, and Eisenhower's Chief, took up a strangely equivocal stance on the question of landing craft. He had always advocated a cross-Channel attack and, like Eisenhower, firmly believed Anvil would support the invasion, but he strongly suspected that the British would use any U.S. craft allocated by King to the European theatre for their own Mediterranean ventures. Churchill and the British Chiefs of Staff still held to the view that there were wonderful opportunities in attacking the 'soft underbelly of Europe'. They also thought Anvil rather pointless as it would absorb men and material not only from Overlord but also from the Italian front, where fighting had bogged down into a hard slog against Kesselring's army. Marshall merely saw these British objections as an attempt to dodge the issue of a cross-Channel assault. In January, Italian developments placed the possibility of an Anvil landing in the gravest doubt. A belated attempt to land an army behind Kesselring's lines at Anzio to ease the path to Rome met fierce German resistance and the army narrowly escaped being driven into the sea. The Anzio divisions were pinned down and a large part of the Mediterranean landing-craft fleet was needed to supply them over the beaches.

Eisenhower still wanted the Anvil landings; they would relieve pressure on Normandy and also bring the French North African army back to France to fight the Germans. But the difficulties mounted and Montgomery's insistence that Overlord should be as strong as possible persuaded Eisenhower to abandon the Mediterranean scheme. General Marshall took a decidedly different view. In February he rapped Eisenhower over the knuckles for succumbing to 'localities', as a result of British pressure, which he hoped 'has not warped your judgement'. The British were certainly unrepentant about their dislike for Anvil. They wanted to keep up the pressure in Italy and capture Rome. If a second front was to be opened in the Mediterranean after a maximum effort in Italy, why not make a landing somewhere more profitable than the south of France, which the Germans could easily defend? On 9 February Churchill wrote to Roosevelt: 'I am concerned at the divergence of thought which is growing up between our staffs as we approach the momentous period. It is not simply a question of whether the lift of one division in L.S.T.s should be transferred from Anvil to Overlord, though that would seem desirable.' The Prime Minister went on to say that he had asked, 'the British Staffs to examine the logistics of moving two or three . . .

divisions in the next few months unostentatiously by land into Morocco . . . This army would be very near the main battle and could be brought in by the Commanders at any time and at any point on the French Channel or Atlantic coasts which they might consider desirable.'

The Americans held fast to Anvil and the row continued. By March Eisenhower confessed, 'Uncertainty is having a marked effect on everyone responsible for planning and executing Operation Overlord.'

On 28 April, with only five weeks to D-Day, an unexpected piece of bad luck settled the Anvil debate. Five precious L.S.T.s were torpedoed by an E-boat attack during a rehearsal of the Utah landings at Slapton Sands, and two were sunk.

This was a major setback. There was no choice other than to postpone Anvil, drawing all available craft from the Mediterranean to help D-Day although even this would not be enough. Admiral King was persuaded to relent and supply additional lift to the Mediterranean, rather than despatching everything he held in American reserve for the forthcoming Pacific offensive. But he insisted that these landing craft could only be used for Anvil. This shocked the British. Sir Alan Brooke commented, 'History will never forgive them for bargaining equipment against strategy and for trying to blackmail us into agreeing with them by holding the pistol of withdrawing craft at our heads.'

The disagreement was finally settled by a compromise on 15 April. Eisenhower's Normandy landing would be supported by Anvil, but not until 10 July. All decisions in the Mediterranean would not be confirmed until after the Anzio army had broken out and Rome had been taken. Churchill was to have his own British victory. Alexander's armies took the ancient capital on 5 June, the eve of D-Day. Anvil, which did not take place until August, was a sad anticlimax. Much to the satisfaction of the British Prime Minister, the downgraded landings were re-named 'Dragoon', because he felt that the British had been 'dragooned' into accepting it all.

The bomber row

Although the row over Anvil produced great frustration for Eisenhower and the SHAEF planners, an even bigger dispute raged at the same time. This centred on the effective use of the supreme Anglo-American weapon – the strategic bomber force – and could have had disastrous political and military consequences. Eisenhower was a strong advocate of air-power as a decisive support for ground war. With the help of Air Chief Marshal

Far left: The invasion that almost failed. Allied troops go ashore at Anzio, 40 miles south of Rome, in late January 1944. Kesselring's aggressive counter-attacks and Allied caution in exploiting their initial gains could have led to Anglo-American disaster. The Allies were pinned down until May, all-important landing craft were diverted from the D-Day build-up, and the Anvil landing in the south of France had to be postponed until August

Left: General Koenig, de Gaulle's man in London. The Free French victor of the battle of Bir Hakeim in 1942 was created Commander of the French Forces of the Interior before D-Day. This 'army of the shadows' was 100,000 strong and poised to take the offensive against the Wehrmacht

Tedder and General Carl Spaatz of the American Eighth Air Force, he had applied these ideas in the Mediterranean. The Allied Tactical Air Forces had ruthlessly battered enemy troop concentrations and airfields, as well as strafing communications so that reinforcements could not reach the battlefield. Air operations were planned in close liaison with the army, and Eisenhower as Supreme Commander also controlled the air forces. The Americans were certain to press for a similar command structure for Overlord. On 6 November 1943 Sir Charles Portal, British Chief of Air Staff, wrote to Churchill: 'I would like to warn you that we may be confronted with a demand that the Overlord Supreme Commander shall command the whole of the strategic bomber forces, British and American, probably from an early date after his appointment and certainly from about D minus 14. I think you will agree that this would be just as unacceptable as, for instance, a claim to command the Home Fleet.'

The situation in Britain was quite different from that of the Mediterranean. Coastal Command was waging a vital and decisive battle against the U-boats and R.A.F. Bomber Command, commanded by the redoubtable Sir Arthur Harris, had been waging a massive air offensive against Germany since 1943. Along with the U.S. Eighth Air Force, the R.A.F. had been executing the Casablanca directive and was engaged in 'the progressive destruction and dislocation of the German military, industrial and economic systems and the undermining of the morale of the German people to a point where their capacity for armed resistance is fatally weakened'.

'Bomber' Harris believed that the war could be won by this elite force alone, and General Carl Spaatz shared his views. These 'bomber barons' had once claimed that a mere thirty clear operational days would see the end of the Third Reich. One thing was certain, it would not be easy persuading Harris to relinquish control over his bombers. As Tedder knew, he 'was by way of being something of a dictator, who had very much the reputation for not taking kindly to directions from outside his own command'.

The Prime Minister shared the misgivings of Portal and Harris, but he replied to Portal's note: 'I am not sure that we could resist a claim from General Marshall, if he were Commander-in-Chief, to control all the strategic bomber forces during the actual period of Overlord as they are an integral and vital part of his operation and are connected with it in a way in which the Home Fleet certainly is not. We should however allow the demand to be developed and only concede it when we are generally satisfied on the whole policy.'

When the SHAEF command structure was set up in January 1944, the row exploded.

The British Air Staff regarded Overlord as just another theatre of operations. In his letter to Churchill of 6 November 1943, Portal had envisaged only a short period during which the bomber force would be diverted from its other duties. He wrote: 'Since the British and American heavy bomber forces have an essential part to play in creating the conditions which will make Overlord possible, it is (in theory at any rate) unlikely that they will be diverted substantially from the attack on Germany until shortly before Overlord begins, probably about fourteen days.'

Yet Eisenhower, Tedder and Leigh Mallory knew that this was not enough. Even though the British Second Tactical Air Force and the U.S. Ninth were allocated to the Supreme Commander

with the latest fighter-bombers, the task of ensuring a successful landing demanded the use of far more air-power. In Eisenhower's view, 'The greatest contribution that he could imagine the Air Forces making to this [Overlord] aim was that they should hinder enemy movement.'

Eisenhower badly needed full operational control of the strategic bombers. He dug his heels in. Tedder began to express grave doubts. In February 1944 he wrote to Portal:

'I very much fear that if the British Chiefs of Staff and the P.M. are going to take up a position regarding Bomber Command which prevents . . . unified control, very serious issues will arise affecting Anglo-American cooperation in "Overlord" . . . A split on the question of air forces might well, since the issues are very clear, precipitate a quite irremediable cleavage.'

The Transportation Plan

Behind the argument about command of the air forces was a serious division on strategy. Although the bomber offensive against Germany, known as Pointblank, was certainly of indirect assistance to Overlord by weakening German strength, particularly her fighter forces, the real dispute was over the three-month run-up period to D-Day itself. Harris and Spaatz knew that their squadrons would be ordered to pound the Germans immediately before the landing, but they could not agree that the best use of Lancasters and Fortresses and their highly trained crews lay in what Harris contemptuously called 'army support' for as much as three months preceding the invasion. Yet this is exactly what Tedder and Leigh Mallory wanted. They had drawn up a Transportation Plan, which aimed at the total destruction of the rail network in northern France. It was based on the scientific analysis of Professor Zuckerman, an anatomist who had studied the effects of the bombing attacks of the Allied Tactical Air Force in Sicily and southern Italy. His work had convinced Tedder that the destruction of the rail network and repair facilities had been decisive in stopping German reinforcement. But in Harris's view, bombing railway yards was a criminal waste of his bombers and would 'commit the irremediable error of diverting our best weapon from the military function for which it has been equipped and trained to tasks it cannot effectively carry out. Though this might give the specious appearance of supporting the army, in reality it would be the greatest disservice we could do them. It would lead directly to disaster'.

Churchill was still unconvinced about the virtues of the Transportation Plan. A mistaken decision could mean disaster, allowing the Luftwaffe to recover and the Germans to strengthen the air defences of the Reich. Already there were disturbing statistics that showed signs of a rise in German fighter strength in spite of Pointblank. Yet Eisenhower believed Overlord was equally crucial. He bluntly told the Prime Minister that if he did not receive what he wanted, he would 'simply have to go home'.

Now Portal acted with great diplomatic skill by trying to get the warring airmen to co-operate with each other. He set up a bombing policy committee to clear targets with Eisenhower and Tedder, thus by-passing Leigh Mallory. He also ordered a test raid on the rail centre of Trappes in northern France to see how effective Bomber Command's Lancasters could be against such a target. The raid carried out on 6 March brought excellent results, destroying sixty engines and immobilizing the marshalling yard for weeks. He also gained agreement from everybody concerned that once the target list was agreed, 'command should pass through the Supreme Commander'. This unfortunately was not good enough for Eisenhower or Washington. On 22 March he wrote in his diary: 'If a satisfactory answer is not reached I am going to take drastic action and inform the Combined Chiefs of Staff that unless the matter is settled at once I will request relief from this Command.'

By the time Eisenhower had won his point it was little over two months before D-Day. Now began the attempt to secure an agreed bombing policy.

Portal worked skilfully to bridge the gap between the airmen and SHAEF. On 25 March Eisenhower brought together all the commanders at his H.Q. It was a bristling confrontation. Harris wanted to go on bombing German industrial

Left to right: Air Chief Marshal Sir Arthur Harris, C.-in-C. of R.A.F. Bomber Command. He had created a powerful strategic weapon and would resist any interference. Air Chief Marshal Sir Charles Portal, British Chief of Air Staff. Great diplomacy was needed on his part to bring the bomber barons to accept Eisenhower's request for overall command of their forces Lieutenant-General Carl Spaatz, Commander U.S. Strategic Air Forces. He wanted to knock out the Reich's oil installations and reserves. Below: American Flying Fortresses were flown in daylight raids over Germany to carry out Operation Pointblank against Hitler's war potential

'If the country in which an army is operating is not kept alive, it will itself become a heavy commitment on that army. Neptune area [Normandy] is not self-supporting and I am certain the Hun cannot afford to turn off the tap.'

Air Chief Marshal Tedder

'Murderers always return to the scene of their crime.' Vichy propaganda and emotive posters in the spring of 1944 attempted to stir up French feelings against the Allied bombing campaign aimed at the destruction of vital rail junctions and bridges in France. But the French people accepted their casualties stoically. In London, General Koenig spoke for them all: 'This is war and it must be expected that people will be killed. We would take the anticipated loss to be rid of the Germans'

centres, but now the American bomber chief, General Carl Spaatz, put forward his objections – in his view, the Eighth Air Force could best help Overlord by striking at Germany's fuel supplies according to an overall Oil Plan. There were only two dozen synthetic oil plants in Germany and Spaatz believed they could be knocked out one by one until the Panzers had no fuel to fight on. Leigh Mallory and Tedder dismissed this argument as being far too slow in bringing results.

Eisenhower backed the Transportation Plan. Now, however, the British War Cabinet entered the fray and blocked the scheme. For Churchill there was a new issue – how many of Britain's French allies would be killed in the raids? He believed the arguments for the Transportation Plan 'very nicely balanced on military grounds', and that use of the heavy bombers would kill thousands of French citizens, and would 'smear the name of the Royal Air Force across the world'.

R.A.F. Operations Research had come up with figures showing that anything from 80,000 to 160,000 casualties could be expected. This appalled Churchill, whilst Eden, the Foreign Secretary, believed it would present Goebbels with a marvellous chance to vilify the Allies. At first the War Cabinet asked that only targets where casualties not exceeding 100 to 150 could be expected should be attacked. Surprisingly, General Koenig, de Gaulle's man commanding the Free French in London, raised no objections.

Before making a final decision, the Prime Minister consulted Roosevelt and the President's view was unequivocal: 'However regrettable the attendant loss of civilian lives is, I am not prepared to impose from this distance any restriction on military action by the responsible commanders that in their opinion might militate against the success of "Overlord" or cause additional loss of life to our Allied forces of invasion.'

In April the bombing campaign to seal off Normandy began in earnest. Over 70,000 tons of bombs were dropped on the rail network of northern France.

The Allied air offensive took its toll of German communications. By D-Day most Normandy bridges had been destroyed and engines and rolling-stock knocked out.

Strategic bombers methodically struck rail centres and marshalling yards, moving remorselessly through the eighty transportation targets on Tedder's list. They also began to turn their attention to the heavy coastal defences. Medium bombers and fighters struck radar stations – only eighteen out of a normal ninety-two were working on the eve of D-Day, and all the time raids had to be continued on German V-weapon sites now being built near Calais.

Tank busting became almost a sport for the Allied Air Force fighter pilots. Waves of Spitfires, Thunderbolts, Mustangs and Typhoons swept across northern France, shooting up anything that moved. Locomotives were smashed by 5-inch rockets, bridges were blasted by precision bombing.

Ammunition dumps, camps, depots and headquarters were all sought out and furiously attacked. In April and May the Allied Air Forces flew over 200,000 sorties, and dropped 195,400 tons of bombs. But losses were heavy too. German flak was improving even though the Luftwaffe had become a less familiar sight in the western skies. Between 28 April and 6 June, 1,953 Allied aircraft were shot down and 12,000 airmen lost their lives.

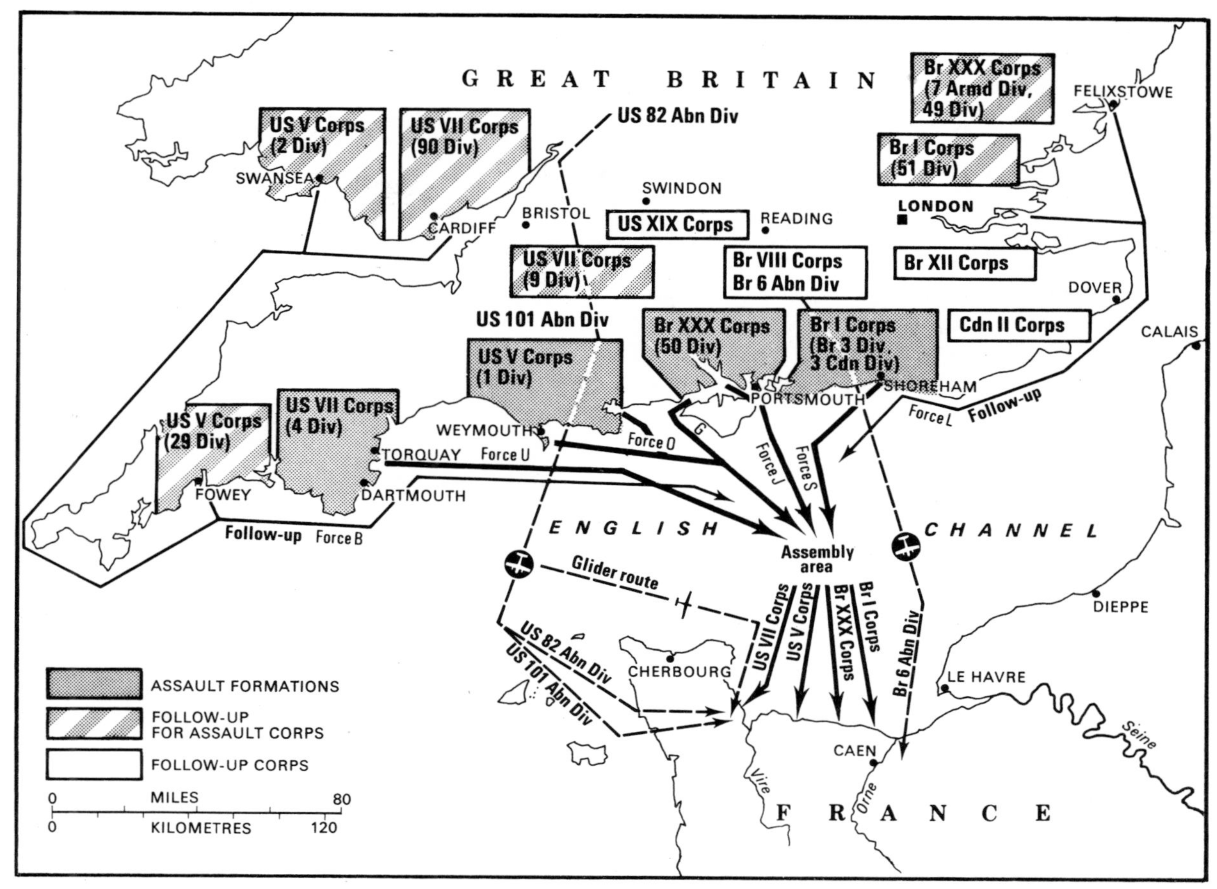

The overall invasion plan showing the disposition of the Allied divisions and their routes to Normandy

Briefing at St Paul's

On 15 May 1944, three weeks before the great armada was due to sail, an act of almost medieval theatricality took place at St Paul's School, in west London. There, in the bowl-like model room, the Supreme Commander had gathered the men who had planned D-Day and who would be responsible for its success or failure. Using a map as wide as a city street, their duty was to explain the plan for the liberation of Europe to the King and Churchill.

King George VI sat on a hard narrow bench in the front row, with Churchill on his right, and the Supreme Commander on his left. Eisenhower's deputies sat in order on his left – Air Chief Marshal Tedder, his deputy, Admiral Ramsay, the Commander of the Naval Forces, General Montgomery, Ground Force Commander, Air Chief Marshal Leigh Mallory, and Admiral Creasey, who would lead the British naval assault forces. The rest of the room was filled with naval force commanders, divisional Generals, staff officers and Air Marshals.

Admiral Deyo, U.S.N., who was to command the bombardment group for Force U attacking Utah beach, described the scene: 'As we took those uncompromisingly hard and narrow seats, the room was hushed and the tension palpable. It seemed to most of us that the proper meshing of so many gears would need nothing less than divine guidance. A failure at one point could throw the momentum out of balance and result in chaos. All in that room were aware of the gravity of the elements to be dealt with . . .

'The first to rise and break the silence was the Supreme Commander himself. It had been said that his smile was worth twenty divisions. That day it was worth more. He spoke for ten minutes. Before the warmth of his quiet confidence the mists of doubt dissolved. When he had finished the tension was gone. Not often has one man been called upon to accept so great a burden of responsibility. But here was one at peace with his soul.'

Montgomery, however, speaking after Ike, provided a bromide. He relished the distinguished audience. As General Bradley recalled, 'With rare skill Monty traced his 21st Group plan of manoeuvre as he tramped like a giant through Lilliputian France.' He described the basic objectives of the ground forces. The American First Army was to make an assault on two beaches with the aim of cutting off Cherbourg and establishing the western flank of the bridgehead. The British effort was to be on the stretch of coast between the Orne and Port-en-Bessin. Their objectives were the communications centre of Caen and Bayeux.

Bradley recalled that, 'As Monty discussed this plan for Caen there in St Paul's School, he became increasingly optimistic. Pointing toward Falaise he talked of breaking his tanks free on D-Day "to knock about a bit down there".'

Slowly and impressively the complete D-Day plan emerged. Once the British and American armies had been landed ashore, there was to be a massive build-up of Allied forces capable of matching the Wehrmacht in a pitched battle for control of the west. The eight divisions landed on D-Day would rise to thirteen on D-Day plus 1, seventeen on D-Day plus 3, and twenty-one by D-Day plus 12, and eventually to an army of some thirty-nine divisions by D-Day plus 90.

The U.S. forces were to go in first north and east of the Vire to seize the base of the Cotentin which the Germans could otherwise turn into a strong defensive area behind the natural defence line of the Vire.

The most westward American beach, Utah, was on the Cotentin itself, between La Madeleine and Varreville. The assault was to be led by Major-General Lawton Collins' VII U.S. Corps. The 4th Infantry Division would be followed by the 90th, 9th and 79th Divisions. The Utah force would strike north towards Cherbourg and south to cut off the Cotentin. Bradley hoped to capture Cherbourg within a month.

Omaha beach was a little over four miles long, with towering cliffs at each end. It was bounded by Colleville-sur-Mer and Vierville-sur-Mer. The first troops ashore under the command of Major-General Gerow's V U.S. Corps would be the 1st U.S. Infantry Division, the 'Big Red One'. It would be joined by the 16th Regimental Combat Team, a part of the 29th which had been the first to arrive in Britain under Operation Bolero in 1942. The rest of the 29th and the 2nd Divisions were to reinforce the assault. These units would link up with the British in the east at Port-en-Bessin and move south to establish a bridgehead on the Aure east of Trévières. In the west, the ground towards Isigny would be occupied; U.S. Rangers were to capture the commanding Pointe-du-Hoc, and in the east the Pointe-de-la-Percée.

To assist the U.S. divisions ashore, a bold airborne attack was planned which would isolate the Cherbourg peninsula. The 82nd Airborne, commanded by General Matthew Ridgway, would be dropped to capture both banks of the Merderet south and west of Ste Mère-Église. The 101st, led by General Maxwell Taylor, would seize the beach exits, and the bridges over the Douve, north of Carentan.

Operation Caen

The British troops of the Second Army, commanded by General Dempsey, were to land in three coastal sectors code-named Sword, Juno and Gold. The total British front ran for twenty-four miles along the shore and since only a small section was to be taken in the first assault, there were dangerous gaps between the attacking formations. These could

The Commanders

Left to Right: Rear-Admiral Sir Philip Vian, R.N., Eastern Naval Task Force; Rear-Admiral A. G. Kirk, U.S.N., Western Naval Task Force; Lieutenant-General Lewis H. Brereton, U.S. Ninth Air Force; Air Marshal Sir Arthur Coningham, R.A.F., Second Tactical Air Force; Major-General Matthew Ridgway, 82nd U.S. Airborne Division; Major-General Maxwell D. Taylor, 101st U.S. Airborne Division; Major-General R. N. Gale, 6th British Airborne Division; Lieutenant-General J. T. Crocker, I British Corps; Lieutenant-General Sir Miles Dempsey, Second British Army; Lieutenant-General G. C. Bucknall, XXX Corps; Lieutenant-General H. D. G. Crerar, First Canadian Army; Major-General J. Lawton Collins, U.S. VII Corps; Major-General Leonard T. Gerow, V U.S. Corps

only be plugged by using Royal Marine Commandos to seize decisive points.

The main British thrust on Caen was to be mounted from Sword beach between Lion-sur-Mer and Ouistreham. Both had been fortified and the coastline was exposed to the heavy German batteries east and west of the Orne estuary. The assault was to be carried out by the 3rd Division of General Crocker's I Corps. They would be preceded by men of the 6th Airborne Division dropped on to landing zones on the east bank of the Orne in the early hours of D-Day. Their task would be to seize the bridges over the river, in particular the defended bridge at Bénouville. In this way they would secure the flank of Sword beach and prevent incursions from German forces which could be concentrated behind the river. The parachutists would also assist the seaborne attack by neutralizing the powerful German battery at Merville, a task demanding the highest military skill and precision.

A gap of three miles stretched between the western flank of Sword beach at Lion-sur-Mer and Juno. This was to be assaulted over five miles between St Aubin and La Rivière by the 3rd Canadian Infantry Division, attacking in two brigades with a third to follow up. The D.D. tanks would go ashore with the 6th and 10th Canadian Armoured Regiments, followed by sappers and beach specialists. The troops were from the North Shore Regiment, the Queen's Own of Canada Regiment, the Regina Rifles and Royal Winnipeg Rifles.

The Canadian division was also under the command of Crocker and would move rapidly to seize the Caen–Bayeux road and the airfield at Carpiquet, as well as occupying high ground. Juno beach presented some difficult navigational problems with its outcrop of rocks and dangerous currents swirling round them, but once ashore, the Canadians would be reinforced by the 51st Highlanders and the 4th Armoured Brigade. The 41st and 48th R.M. Commandos would land at Lion-sur-Mer and St Aubin, to protect the flanks of Juno.

The remaining British beach, code-named Gold, stretched between La Rivière and Le Hamel. It had been strongly fortified by the Germans. XXX British Corps, under the command of General Bucknall, was responsible for the landing. This was to be led by the 50th Northumbrian Division, the formation Montgomery had used in many earlier campaigns. They had been in Tobruk, Alamein, Sicily and Italy. Now they were to take on the most important landing of all. The Northumbrian division was supported by the 8th Armoured Brigade.

The 69th Brigade of the Northumbrian division was to march south to cut the Caen–Bayeux road near St Léger, whilst the 231st drove west to link up with the American forces. The 56th and 151st Brigades would then drive forward in the centre to capture Bayeux, and occupy positions south of the town. The 7th Armoured and 49th Infantry Divisions were to follow up on Gold, and the 47th R.M. Commando were to attack Port-en-Bessin on the western flank of Gold to link up with the Americans.

Assault technique. Diagram illustrating a landing on a typical beach sector. After the naval and air bombardment the formation of landing craft approach the shore. The inshore destroyers (left) provided close fire cover, backed up by gunfire from the leading support landing craft, and the powerful batteries of the L.C.T.R., S.P. artillery, and flak landing craft which were to deal with any enemy aircraft. The first wave is led ashore by D.D. tanks backed up by L.C.T.s carrying the 'Funnies' (A.V.R.E.s). Behind them are the assault landing craft carrying the assault troops. The infantry are carried ashore in the L.C.A.s which shuttle back and forth from the Landing Ship Infantry (right)

Right: In a typical troopship, H.M.S. *Empire Mace*, the L.C.A.s, like the one alongside, are carried on the lifeboat davits

To land this formidable force taxed the skill of the navy to the limit. The problem was described well by a supply officer interviewed by *Picture Post* on 6 May 1944.

'We've got a fairly big job on. Something comparable to the city of Birmingham hasn't merely got to be shifted: it's got to be kept moving when it's on the other side . . . We must take everything with us – and take it in the teeth of the fiercest opposition. We are, in fact, undertaking the greatest amphibious operation in history, so vast in scale and so complex in detail that the supreme consideration must be the orderly carrying out of a Plan.'

Admiral Ramsay was a punctilious man who left nothing to chance. This drew criticism from some of the American admirals about the detail of the Neptune orders, but at least he knew the immense risks of failing to carry out some essential operation.

Ramsay could now dispose of 4,126 ships and landing craft which would be used in the assault and follow-up phases. These were brought to an extraordinary peak of efficiency by the British and American Navies, with over ninety per cent of all craft ready and available for D-Day. This fleet would be protected and supported by a force of 1,213 naval combatant ships, serviced by 736 ancillary craft and supplied by 864 merchant ships. It made a fleet of nearly 7,000 vessels, seventy-nine per cent of which were British.

Ramsay's immense naval forces were concentrated all around Britain's coast. Large warships allocated to the bombardment groups were ready to sail from bases in Scotland and northern England. The Mulberry blockships were being prepared in the Clyde and Firth of Forth.

The D-Day armada was divided into two: an Eastern Task Force commanded by Admiral Vian for the British beaches and an American Western Task Force directed by Rear-Admiral Kirk, U.S.N. The Task Forces themselves broke down into five smaller forces, each of which would tackle one of the D-Day beaches. There were also two follow-up groups ready to reinforce the beach.

Each force was organized as a small armada. There were the landing ships carrying infantry and tanks, the backbone of the amphibious assault, and

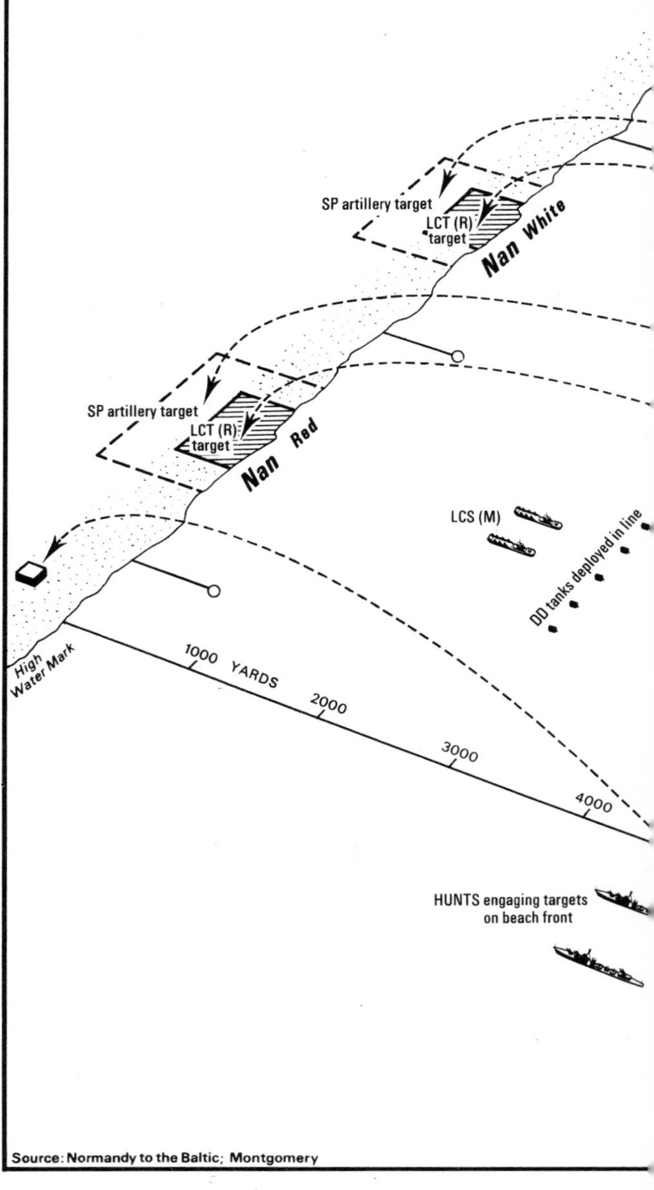

Source: Normandy to the Baltic; Montgomery

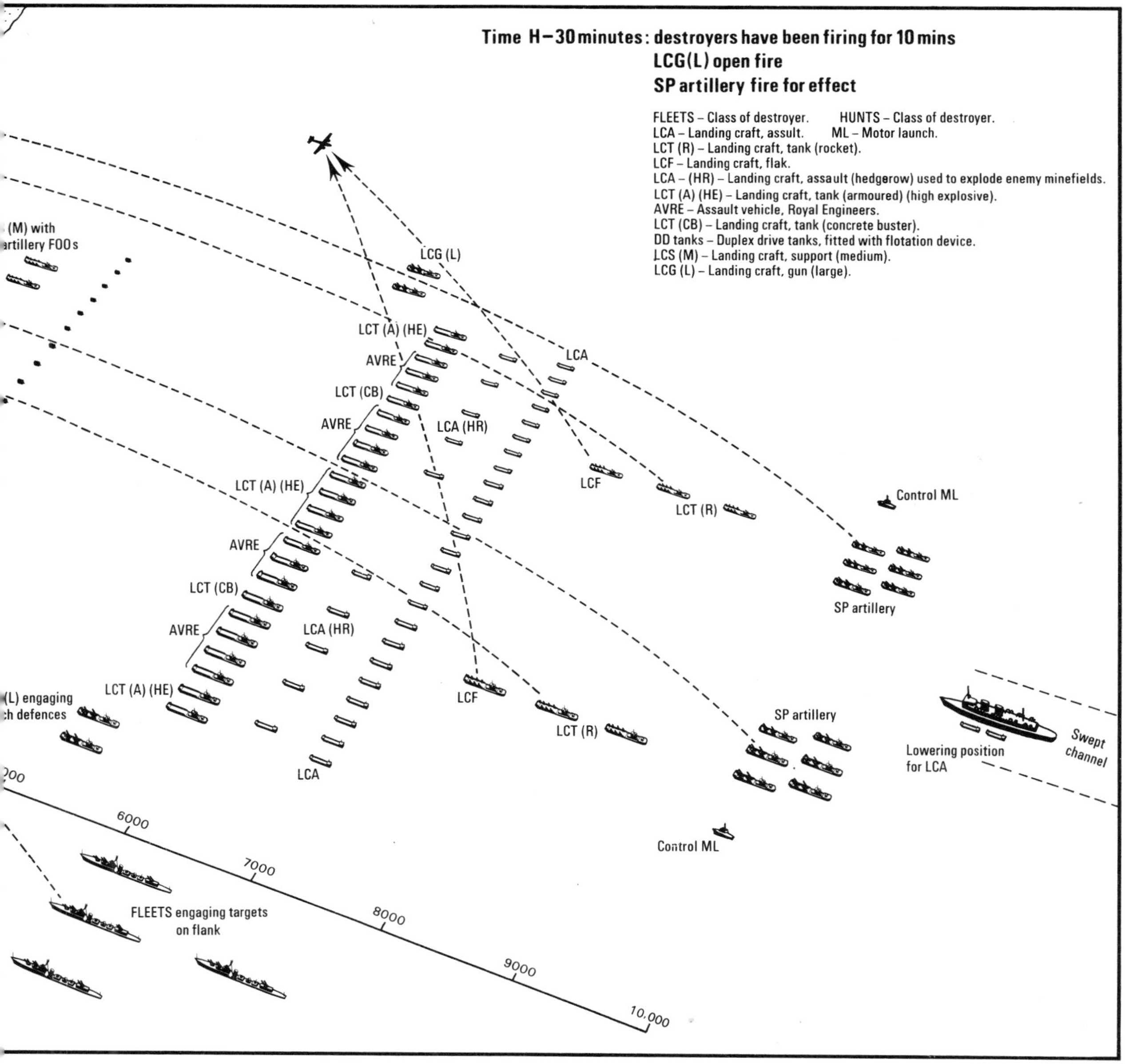

Time H–30 minutes: destroyers have been firing for 10 mins
LCG(L) open fire
SP artillery fire for effect

FLEETS – Class of destroyer. HUNTS – Class of destroyer.
LCA – Landing craft, assult. ML – Motor launch.
LCT (R) – Landing craft, tank (rocket).
LCF – Landing craft, flak.
LCA – (HR) – Landing craft, assault (hedgerow) used to explode enemy minefields.
LCT (A) (HE) – Landing craft, tank (armoured) (high explosive).
AVRE – Assault vehicle, Royal Engineers.
LCT (CB) – Landing craft, tank (concrete buster).
DD tanks – Duplex drive tanks, fitted with flotation device.
LCS (M) – Landing craft, support (medium).
LCG (L) – Landing craft, gun (large).

(M) with
artillery FOOs
LCG (L)
LCT (A) (HE)
AVRE
LCA
LCT (CB)
AVRE
LCA (HR)
LCT (A) (HE)
LCF
LCT (R)
Control ML
AVRE
LCT (CB)
SP artillery
AVRE
LCA (HR)
LCT (A) (HE)
LCF
(L) engaging
ch defences
SP artillery
LCT (R)
Swept channel
Lowering position for LCA
LCA
200
6000
7000
Control ML
8000
FLEETS engaging targets on flank
9000
10,000

hundreds of smaller landing craft, sailing in line ahead. Most of these could run directly on to the enemy shore. They included L.C.T.s and L.C.I.s as well as vehicle and personnel carriers. Finally there was a wide variety of support craft, ranging from boats carrying guns and rockets to landing craft especially adapted for cooking and repair. The task forces were escorted by strong covering groups of destroyers, sloops and anti-submarine trawlers. Beyond that the Home Fleet would be on the alert at Scapa Flow to watch for any moves by the remnants of the German battle fleet which might dare to venture out.

Covering forces of destroyers, anti-submarine trawlers and escorts were deployed by Ramsay to hold the flanks of the convoys. Apart from protecting the army during the Channel crossing, their fire-power was going to be used in the assault. The Allied planners knew that the strength of the German gun emplacements was such that they could not be certain of the effectiveness of air bombardment. Also there was deep anxiety about the need for close fire support to compensate for the lack of land artillery in the first waves.

An essential element of each force was its bombarding group. One hundred and thirty-seven warships had been mustered for a drenching bombardment of the German defenders. The group contained seven battleships. The Royal Navy provided H.M.S. *Nelson*, *Warspite* and *Ramillies*, with *Rodney* in reserve, whilst the U.S.S. *Texas*, *Nevada* and *Arkansas* were supplied by the U.S.N. Two moni-

Loaded up and ready. L.C.T.s lined up at Southampton docks where luxury ocean liners berthed before the war. Every sizeable harbour on the south coast of England was packed with invasion craft by May 1944

tors with 15-inch guns, H.M.S. *Roberts* and *Erebus*, added to this massive punch. The battleships were supported by twenty-three cruisers including the American ships, U.S.S. *Augusta*, *Quincy* and *Tuscaloosa*, and the British cruisers, H.M.S. *Belfast*, *Glasgow*, *Hawkins*, *Enterprise*, *Black Prince*, *Scylla*, *Orion*, *Argonaut*, *Emerald*, *Diadem*, *Mauritius*, *Arethusa*, *Frobisher*, *Danae* and *Ajax*.

Two Free French cruisers were also to be in the fray, the F.F.S. *Montcalm* and *Georges Leygues* (known as 'George's Legs' by the irreverent Anglo-Saxons). Fifty-eight Fleet destroyers and nineteen Hunt destroyers were also on call for inshore shooting. They had proved their value in the Italian campaign by taking on German tanks at close quarters, saving the Anzio beachhead.

Each force was controlled by a headquarters ship rigged with all the complex communications needed to direct an amphibious operation. In addition to these vessels, there were specialist repair ships and flak barges, as well as the fighter control tenders.

When the force approached the far shore each ship had to take up its position and perform its task with immense precision. First, the minesweepers would precede the main force as far as the beach itself. The troop carriers and landing craft would heave to several miles off the enemy shore. Assault craft would be lowered on command from the bigger ships and the troops would scramble over the side nets to take up their positions ready for the attack. Meanwhile the bombardment ships would take up their positions, seeking pre-arranged targets. The battleships would fire from 10,000 yards off shore, whilst the destroyers would close to 5,000 yards.

Even closer to the shore, and ready to accompany the first landing craft, would be fire-support vessels, usually L.C.T.s armed with 4-inch guns or racks of rocket batteries.

As H-Hour approached, the first assault craft would leave the assembly area and forge towards the beach. In the van would be the L.C.T.s carrying D.D. tanks to be released a few thousand yards from the beach. A launch would go forward for each sector and, aided by two Landing Craft (Control) equipped with radar, would guide the assault waves ashore.

Other assault craft would also pour out infantry. Hard on their heels would come naval and marine demolition teams, allowed only half an hour to clear the worst obstacles before the next assault wave arrived. Engineers would be sent ashore to tackle other defence works on the eastern beaches; they would be backed up by 79th Armoured Division's 'Funnies'.

Throughout the day wave after wave would arrive. They would deliver, according to a precise order, engineering specialists to blow a hole in the Atlantic Wall, tanks to give fire support to the infantry, and, inevitably, more and more infantry, to press ahead for the first objectives.

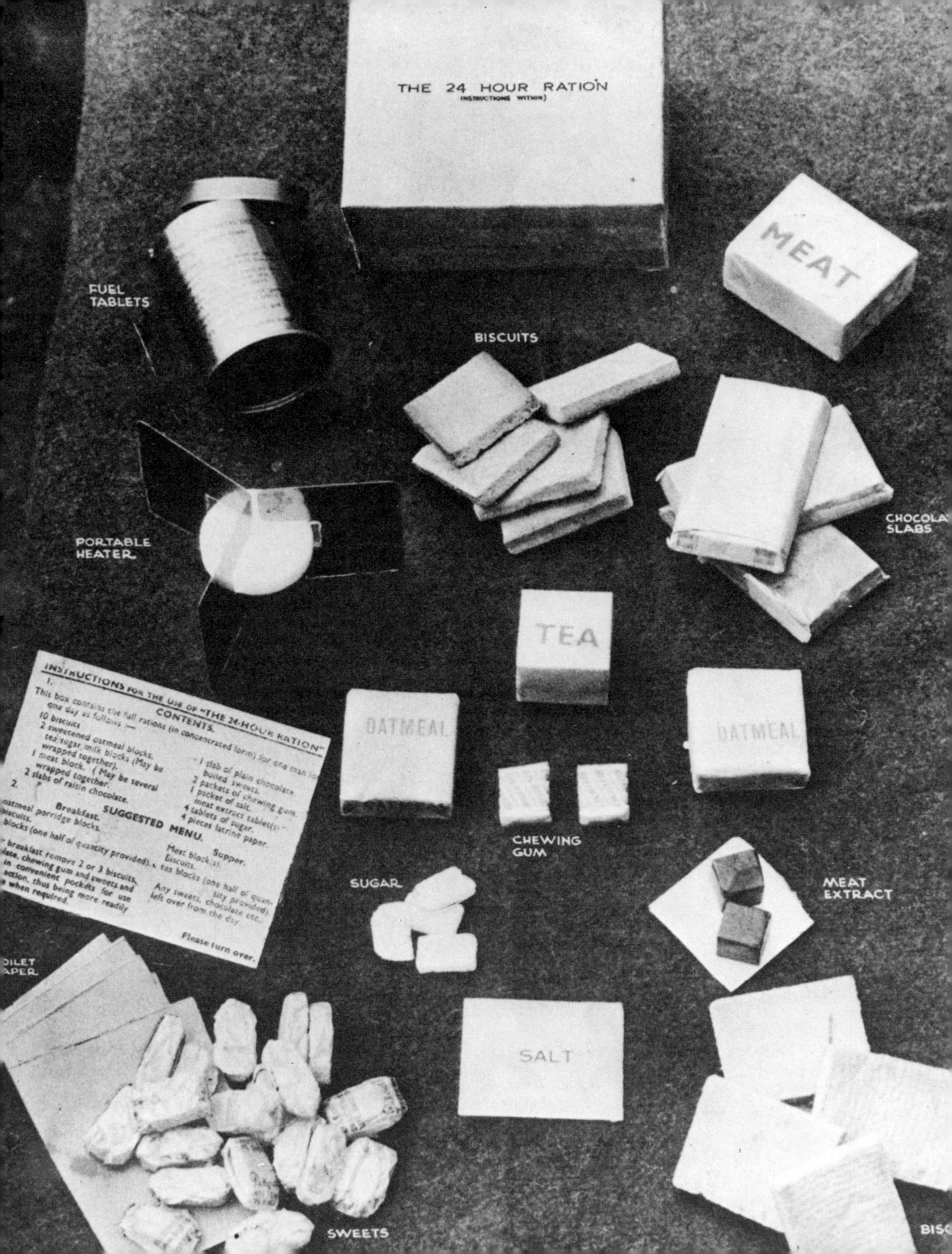

THE 24 HOUR RATION
(INSTRUCTIONS WITHIN)
MEAT
FUEL TABLETS
BISCUITS
PORTABLE HEATER
TEA
OATMEAL
OATMEAL
CHEWING GUM
INSTRUCTIONS FOR THE USE OF "THE 24-HOUR RATION"
1.
CONTENTS.
This box contains the full rations (in concentrated form) for one man for one day as follows :—
10 biscuits
2 sweetened oatmeal blocks.
tea/sugar/milk blocks (May be wrapped together).
1 meat block. (May be several wrapped together.
2 slabs of raisin chocolate.
1 slab of plain chocolate.
boiled sweets.
2 packets of chewing gum.
1 packet of salt.
meat extract tablet(s).
4 tablets of sugar.
4 pieces latrine paper.
2.
SUGGESTED MENU.
Breakfast.
oatmeal porridge blocks.
blocks (one half of quantity provided).
Supper.
Meat block(s).
Biscuits.
tea blocks (one half of quantity provided).
Any sweets, chocolate etc., left over from the day
Please turn over.
SUGAR
MEAT EXTRACT
SALT
SWEETS

The Quartermaster's Plan for the U.S. Armies specified the equipment to be carried by each soldier in his attack on the Atlantic Wall. In addition to his rifle or carbine, he was to wear and carry the following articles of clothing and equipment in the assault and follow-up:

Individual clothing	
Belt, web, waist	1 ea.
Drawers, wool	1 pr.
Gloves, cotton, protective	1 pr.
Helmet, steel w/liner	1 ea.
Handkerchiefs	2 ea.
Hood, wool, protective	1 ea.
Jacket, field or Jacket, combat, winter	1 ea.
Leggings, canvas, protective	1 pr.
Socks, protective	1 pr.
Shoes, service	1 pr.
Shirt, flannel, protective	1 ea.
Trousers, wool, protective	1 pr.
Undershirt, wool	1 ea.

Individual equipment	
Belt, cartridge, belt pistol, or belt, B-A-R	1 ea.
Bag, canvas, field w/strap carrying and suspenders	1 ea.
Canteen	1 ea.
Cover, canteen	1 ea.
Cup, canteen	1 ea.
Haversack	1 ea.
Carrier, pack	1 ea.
Pouch, first aid	1 ea.
Pocket, magazine D.W. or Pocket, carbine	1 ea.
Tags, identification w/n	1 ea.

Each landing craft was to carry a supply of food carefully calculated on the basis of '1 Man for 7 Days'. Quartermasters were quick to point out that the 3½ lbs. of bread, 7 lbs. of potatoes, 15 oz. of tinned vegetables, haricot beans, rice, marrowfat peas, ½ lb. of jam, ¼ lb. of tea, ½ tin of sausages, 1 tin of salmon, plus other goodies like margarine and baked beans, were 'NOT the same as "7 men for 1 day" as the above scale of rations is designed to provide a reasonably varied menu for a week.'

Finally, there were detailed and bureaucratic instructions on how to deal with Allied and enemy dead, including the selection and operation of cemeteries in strict order – U.S., Allied and enemy.

Assault from the sky

The Allied Air Force would be above the beachhead in great strength to stifle any German action. Air Chief Marshal Leigh Mallory could dispose of no less than 11,500 aircraft. His air fleet was the strongest ever assembled. There were 1,470 heavy Lancasters and Halifaxes of R.A.F. Bomber Command, as well as 1,970 Fortresses and Liberators of the Eighth U.S.A.A.F. They supplied the heavy bomber forces for raids on German communications and coast defences. Their attacks would be supported by another 930 medium bombers, mostly American Mitchells, Marauders and Bostons for tactical support. Allied air supremacy would be maintained by no less than 1,530 R.A.F. and 2,300 American fighters. Spitfires, Typhoons, Mustangs and Thunderbolts would place a continuous umbrella over the Channel crossing at the beachhead, and strafe German forces. A massive airlift would also be mounted to carry the three parachute divisions into action. Four hundred and sixty British transport aircraft were available to join the fleet of 900 U.S. carriers, mostly Dakotas, which would fly slowly over the French coast to drop their parachutists and equipment in the precise zone. Heavy equipment would be taken in 3,500 gliders. All the time, 500 reconnaissance planes would act as the eyes of the Expeditionary Force, spotting the critical movement of Rommel's reserves, and, far removed from the Normandy battle-zone, 1,000 aircraft of Coastal Command would make sure that no U-boats approached the vulnerable invasion fleet. The 'chops of the Channel' from Devon to Brittany would be under constant surveillance.

Gallic sensitivities

U.S. Army intelligence had taken great pains to forecast the likely reaction to the landings. In a special appendix to the Neptune Plan they discounted any hopes that the Wehrmacht would present the Allies with a quick and painless victory.

The report sifted all known political, military and economic intelligence about Nazi-occupied France and stated that, 'The survival of the Nazi regime dictates the prevention of invasion of Germany. This means, in turn, determined resistance to our landings in France. Politically, the German hope for victory has dwindled into a desire for stalemate. With a deadlock, the Nazis believe they can maintain their regime. To achieve stalemate in France, there is one course they can take: to try to meet the British–American invasion with such force that it is entirely repelled, or, so costly in the initial stages that political pressure in Great Britain and the United States will force a compromise with the Germans.'

The intelligence staff believed that the Allied Expeditionary Force would be welcomed by the French. 'The Normans have a political record of antagonism to strong authority. At present, their dislike is directed against the Germans and their Vichy puppets.'

They summed up the Norman character in the following way: 'In France, the Norman is considered to be a difficult person. The fact that he is anti-German and anti-Vichy does not mean he will remain enthusiastically pro-British or American after the Liberation comes. His attitude will be influenced by the losses he has suffered from Allied air raids and by the attitude of the liberating troops.'

SHAEF commanders hoped that the delicate task of justifying the invasion of France to its war-weary citizens could be mitigated by General de Gaulle. The General was in Algiers, busily organizing the political takeover of his country by the

The British menu for D-Day. Blocks of oatmeal, slabs of chocolate and the inevitable supply of tea

The Uncomfortable Alliance

In February 1944 a U.S. Army intelligence report predicted the German Army plot, which actually took place six weeks after the landings: 'If the first weeks of invasion indicate that the United Nations cannot be stopped, high-ranking officers of the German Army, recognizing the war weariness of the German people, may act quickly against Hitler'

French National Committee of Liberation, but relations with the British and Americans were far from happy.

President Eisenhower, the Supreme Commander, counted on de Gaulle's assistance in two ways. First, he wanted to avoid the occupation of France with precious Anglo-American troops which would be needed for the onslaught against Germany. This would be accomplished if de Gaulle could take over responsibility for civil administration as the Vichyites were removed from office. Secondly, Eisenhower appreciated the military support which could be brought to the Allied cause by the mobilization of French forces. They took orders from General Koenig, de Gaulle's Commander of the French Forces of the Interior.

Roosevelt was stubborn in not allowing de Gaulle to assume power without the sanction of the French people. There was animosity between the two men which did not help negotiations, and the American President suspected that de Gaulle would turn France into an anti-American force on the liberated continent. The President claimed that he was 'perfectly willing to have de Gaulle made President, Emperor, or King, or anything else so long as action comes in an untrammeled forceful way from the French people themselves.'

De Gaulle and the Anglo-Saxons

De Gaulle regarded Roosevelt's attitude as impossibly presumptuous. He demanded the exercise of French sovereignty in the liberated territories. When the British and Americans planned to introduce invasion currency, he protested vigorously, maintaining that the Allies had stepped beyond their powers; only the French Committee of National Liberation could issue money. Churchill was embarrassed and sought some accommodation with de Gaulle, but Roosevelt stood firm and refused. If de Gaulle wanted to issue his own currency there was no reason why he should not do this in parallel with the new francs backed by the dollar. If the General chose to go his own way, the President said that the General could sign the currency 'in any capacity he desires, even that of King of Siam. Prima donnas do not change their spots.'

The British Prime Minister, who had worked with de Gaulle since the dark days of 1940, wanted to bridge the gap between Roosevelt and the General. He therefore suggested that the General should be invited to London to be told the secrets of D-Day in order to enlist his co-operation in the difficult days ahead.

Churchill started the interview by saying, 'that he had wished to see de Gaulle in order to tell him, as he had been unable to do by telegraph, of the forthcoming operation. He felt that it would have been a very bad thing in the history of our two countries if an operation designed to liberate France had been undertaken by British and American forces without the French being informed.' De Gaulle thanked the Prime Minister. 'He said that the operation was clearly an affair of momentous importance,' adding rather pompously that 'he had himself thought that now was the moment to carry it out'. The General also promised, at the Prime Minister's request, to broadcast to the French people. This could be of great value to the Allies. The difficult question of the recognition of the French Committee of National Liberation inevitably surfaced. The General said that 'He was quite content about the battle, which he felt showed that the United States, Great Britain and France were all together. But on the practical question of the administration of territories he had difficulties.' He made no attempt to hide his bitterness about the American President's attitude, and a row between the two very strong personalities of Churchill and de Gaulle developed. Churchill is reported as saying, 'Each time we must choose between Europe and the open sea, we shall always choose the open sea. Each time I must choose between you and Roosevelt, I shall always choose Roosevelt.'

The official record tactfully stated that, 'if after every effort had been exhausted, the President was on one side and the French Committee of National Liberation on the other, he, Mr Churchill, would almost certainly side with the President, and that anyhow no quarrel would ever arise between Britain and the United States on account of France.'

The prickly General at least seemed willing to broadcast to the French nation as the only credible

General Charles de Gaulle, the defender of French liberty since 1940, resented Roosevelt's plans to train 'a group of politico-military specialists who will ensure the administration of France until democracy has been re-established.' To the General, Roosevelt's intentions were 'of the same order as Alice's Adventures in Wonderland.' The Free French leader was kept in the dark over the precise date of D-Day until only two days before the landing

alternative to Vichy, but the row was not over. Eisenhower was scheduled to speak first on D-Day, and de Gaulle wanted to know what he would say – would he take the Roosevelt line? At Southwick House, the Supreme Commander showed his address to de Gaulle, who was mortified. Eisenhower had made no mention whatsoever of the French Committee of National Liberation, and had gone so far as to say that 'the French themselves would choose their own representatives and their government'. Only after intense diplomatic pressure did the General consent to speak at a different time to Eisenhower. He skilfully nullified Eisenhower's previous message by saying that 'The orders given by the French government [his own committee] and by the leaders which it has recognized must be followed precisely.'

Certainly the General made Eisenhower's job far more difficult on the eve of D-Day. Butcher, Eisenhower's aide, reported, 'Ike looks worn and tired'. To add to his problems, Air Marshal Leigh Mallory still expressed anxiety about the landings of airborne forces on the Cotentin. He was convinced that the slow-moving transports flying over the peninsula would be a sitting target for German flak, and the paratroops would be scattered and easily mopped up on the ground. According to Bradley, Leigh Mallory claimed, 'I cannot approve your plan. It is much too hazardous an undertaking. Your losses will be excessive – certainly far more than the gains are worth.'

Bradley disagreed. He conceded the dangers and the possibility of disaster, but those risks 'must be subordinated to the importance of Utah beach and to the prompt capture of Cherbourg. Certainly I would not willingly risk the lives of 17,000 airborne troops if we could accomplish our mission without them. But I would willingly risk them to insure against failure of the invasion. This in a nutshell was the issue.'

Eisenhower agreed with Bradley, but even then the First Army Commander was forced to change his airborne plans at the last minute by the movement of three German divisions into the planned landing zone. This merely made Leigh Mallory a greater prophet of doom.

11 'OK, Let's Go'

Previous pages: Waiting for the off – 1 June. A U.S. armoured unit: men, equipment, and pet member of the crew, 'Oscar', packed aboard an L.C.T. in Portland harbour, Dorset

Opposite: On the way. American troops march through Torquay on 3 June to board their assault craft. All over the south coast the scene was repeated

'Some of them shout farewells, some of them sing. Some are silent. Some of them laugh, some smile, some look thoughtful, some look grim. One thing is common to all of them – an unmistakable air of purpose and resolve. You will now hear some of them calling out: . . . "Hallo, Betty darling – how're you getting on? Back soon when it's all over – don't get worried. George." "Cheerio, mother – keep smiling. Up John Smith." "Hello, some public house. Save us a pint!" "We're off on a little trip. Love to you all. Frank." "Hallo, Mum and Dad. This is Derek speaking. All the best. We're going to give Jerry all he gave us at Dunkirk, and, boy, we're going to give it to him strong." '

B.B.C. reporter, Colin Wills, watching the embarkation

On 8 May General Eisenhower set D-Day for Y plus 4 – 5 June (Y-Day was 1 June when all preparation were complete). The plans were laid, the troops trained and the bombing offensive well under way. Now it was only a matter of embarking the men and giving the order to go. In the last days of May and the first few days in June, the vastly complicated process began of ferrying the assault troops from their sealed compounds to their appointed ships and landing craft. The people of Britain sensed the greatness of the event about to unfold as all over the south coast of England convoys of lorries rumbled through narrow streets carrying men and their equipment down to the crowded harbours and quays. From Fowey to Poole, Portsmouth to Shoreham, people lined the streets to cheer them on. Few were unmoved by the occasion.

The tension mounted as the men, packed in their landing craft and assault ships, waited for the signal to go. At the nerve centre for the whole operation in Southwick House, the elegant regency mansion behind the hills overlooking Portsmouth harbour, Admiral Ramsay, the Allied Naval Commander, organized a cricket match for his staff.

Under the hot sun of early June troops thumbed through their copies of the specially issued French Guide. Admiral Ramsay, whose responsibility was to get them safely to France, reflected, 'It is a tragic situation that this is the scene of a stage set for terrible human sacrifice. But if out of it comes peace and happiness, who would have it otherwise.'

Gambling on the weather

The final decision to go depended on one vital factor beyond SHAEF's control – the weather. Only the Supreme Commander could give the order, and Eisenhower knew from the north African and Sicily landings just how difficult this decision would be. The Channel weather could ruin the assault before it ever reached France.

From 1 June the Commanders-in-Chief met daily to consider the weather reports – the deadline for a final decision was 3 June if D-Day on 5 June was to be kept.

The diary kept by General Eisenhower's aide, Captain Harry Butcher, U.S.N., recorded the Supreme Commander's preoccupation with the uncertain Channel weather: 'It is the same old story of gambling on the weather and knowing there is nothing that can be done about it, yet myriads of units will be ready to move or be actually on the high seas when announcement of postponement for twenty-four hours or more might have to be made. This has always been the most anguishing period for Ike and now is no exception.'

Churchill, too, was anxious. He wrote a personal minute to the First Sea Lord on 30 May: 'Pray let me have the weather forecast. How does this hot spell fit in with our dates? Does it tend to bring about a violent reaction or is it all clear ahead? Let me have the best your meteorologists can do, but do not fill it up with technical terms. I would like a daily return.'

The fine weather broke on 1 June, but already the first convoys had started sailing from distant ports and the colossal machinery of invasion was turning. That night the B.B.C. broadcast twenty-eight messages to the French Resistance after the nine o'clock news. German intelligence intercepted them and realized that this was the first stage of the alert.

By 3 June the Germans were sure something was imminent. That day Rommel signed his report: 'Concentrated air attacks on the coastal defences between Dunkirk and Dieppe and on the ports strengthen the supposition that the main invasion effort will be made in that area . . . Since 1 June an increasing number of warning messages has been broadcast to the French Resistance . . . Air reconnaissance has not observed a great increase in the number of invasion craft in the Dover sector. No flights have been made over the other ports along the south coast of England. It is essential to send recce planes over all the harbours of the south coast.'

The weather was continuing to deteriorate, and German forecasts confirmed that it would settle in for at least a week. Unlike the Allies, the Germans did not have a continuous line of watching weather-ships strung out across the Atlantic providing continuous advance reports. For Rommel the threat

'I remember D-Day, 6 June. I was working in Plessey's underground tunnel at Redbridge, Wanstead, making Spitfire vacuum pumps. I was walking to the top of the road towards East Ham High Street to get my 101 bus from Woolwich when I heard such a noise and thundering. I reached the High Street and thousands of lorries and tanks loaded with soldiers were making their way to Woolwich. They were laughing and waving their hands and Mrs Larkin from Larkins sweetshop was throwing them packets of cigarettes and chocolates and peanuts. They were catching them and saying, "Thank you, darling". The older people were standing by the kerb crying and saying, "Good Luck, boys", "God Bless You" . . . When I walked across the road to get my bus, they all gave me the wolf whistle. I smiled and waved my hand . . . needless to say, I was crying too.'

Mrs Nellie Nowlan of Basildon, Essex

'Getting light now and a few people coming out of doorways, on their way to work I suppose, so are we in a different sort of way . . . turn down a narrow road, must be near docks – wonder which. A few more people about now – suppose it's around half six . . . not the kind of send off we would have liked . . . their faces half awake – wonder – a few waves and one silver-haired old lady coming to our side of the truck and saying, "Have a fag, boy, and Good Luck!" . . . we're through the dock gates and there are the L.C.T.s which are to be our life on the ocean wave . . . I wonder what my wife and daughter are doing . . . I had a sinking feeling at that moment . . . my father already dead, my brother shot down in S. France, my father-in-law blinded at Hill 60 in the '14–'18 war . . . was it going to be my turn next?'

H. L. Barclay, 33rd Armoured Brigade Company, R.A.S.C.

'The time has come to deal the enemy a terrific blow in western Europe. The blow will be struck by the combined sea, land and air forces of the Allies, together constituting one great Allied team, under the Supreme command of General Eisenhower. On the eve of this great adventure I send my best wishes to every soldier in the Allied team . . . With stout heart and with enthusiasm for the contest, let us go forward to victory and, as we enter the battle, let us recall the words of a famous soldier spoken so many years ago. These are the words he said . . . HE EITHER FEARS HIS FATE TOO MUCH OR HIS DESSERTS ARE SMALL WHO DARE NOT PUT IT TO THE TOUCH TO WIN OR LOSE IT ALL . . . Good luck to each one of you and good hunting on the mainland of Europe.'

General Montgomery's message to the troops

seemed to be diminishing. Experts from Admiral Krancke's naval staff had assured him that the enemy would need at least five clear days to launch their attack. Rommel decided to ask permission to visit Hitler, to make a last personal plea for the release of the Panzer divisions before the attack came.

D-Day postponed

Saturday, 3 June, was a day of mounting anxiety at SHAEF Headquarters. The advance forecasts were increasingly bad, but that evening, hoping for some improvement, Eisenhower ordered advance units to sail for a D-Day on 5 June.

If the invasion was to take place on the appointed date, a final decision had to be taken at 0400 hours on Sunday. It was a night fraught with worry, made worse when an Associated Press teletype operator unwittingly sent out: URGENT A.P. NYK FLASH EISENHOWERS H.Q. ANNOUNCE ALLIED LANDINGS IN FRANCE. Twenty-three minutes later it had been corrected, but not before it had been put out in America, Berlin and Moscow.

At 0415 hours on Sunday morning, the Allied Commanders-in-Chief assembled to hear the gaunt and uncompromising figure of Group-Captain Stagg confirm a dismal forecast of mounting seas, poor visibility and low cloud over the Normandy beaches for Monday, 5 June. Eisenhower was left with no choice. The invasion was postponed for twenty-four hours. The huge machine was halted. Men, already keyed up for action, had to wait and bite their lips in frustration.

The bombarding warships on their way from Scotland received the signal to return and reduced speed. But parts of Kirk's Force U convoy were already out at sea heading for Utah beach when they were recalled. The man responsible for sending the signals from Southwick House Operations Room was Captain Richard Courage, R.N.

'In the early hours of 4 June I got a signal to send out in cipher giving a twenty-four hour postponement of the Operation. I sent that off, but we didn't know whether it had got through to everyone. They couldn't answer back because of radio silence and we could not guarantee that they had received the signal. So we had to send out Walrus amphibian

The Second Front
a record in colour

H-Hour – painted by official war artist, Norman Wilkinson, from sketches he made on D-Day

rman propaganda view of the Atlantic Wall. Right: onster railway-gun firing across the Pas de Calais t: The might of the Pa[illegible]ers a 'Hummel' howitzer

The Way to Liberation

Right: The decision at Quebec, 18 August 1943. After finally agreeing on Operation Overlord, Churchill and Roosevelt were photographed with their host, Mackenzie King, the Canadian Prime Minister, and the Earl of Athlone, Governor-General of Canada

Far right: General Charles de Gaulle at Free French headquarters in London 1943. 'Le Général' embodied the spirit of French resistance and the determination for liberation, but he proved a prickly ally

Below left: Lord Louis Mountbatten, the dynamic Chief of Combined Operations, who established the amphibious assault techniques which made the invasion possible

Below right: 'Second Front Now' rallies supporting the Soviet Union, like this one in 1943 at the Albert Hall, put pressure on the British government for a cross-Channel invasion

Festung Europa

Postcards and pictures of the impenetrable fortress were distributed by the Nazi propaganda machine. In reality, these guns and fortifications were concentrated in very few places: Pas de Calais, Cherbourg, Le Havre

Below: Wehrmacht artillery covered potential landing beaches

Right: Heavy guns were sheltered in massive concrete emplacements

Far right: Menacing guns, protected by impenetrable concrete and camouflage, were much photographed by Dr Goebbels' Ministry of Propaganda and Enlightenment

Below right: Flak batteries were deployed to cover the Wall against Allied air-power. But by 1944, most had been withdrawn to protect the Reich's industrial plant

Aux frontières de l'Europe
Cliché du Lieutenant [illegible] (PK)

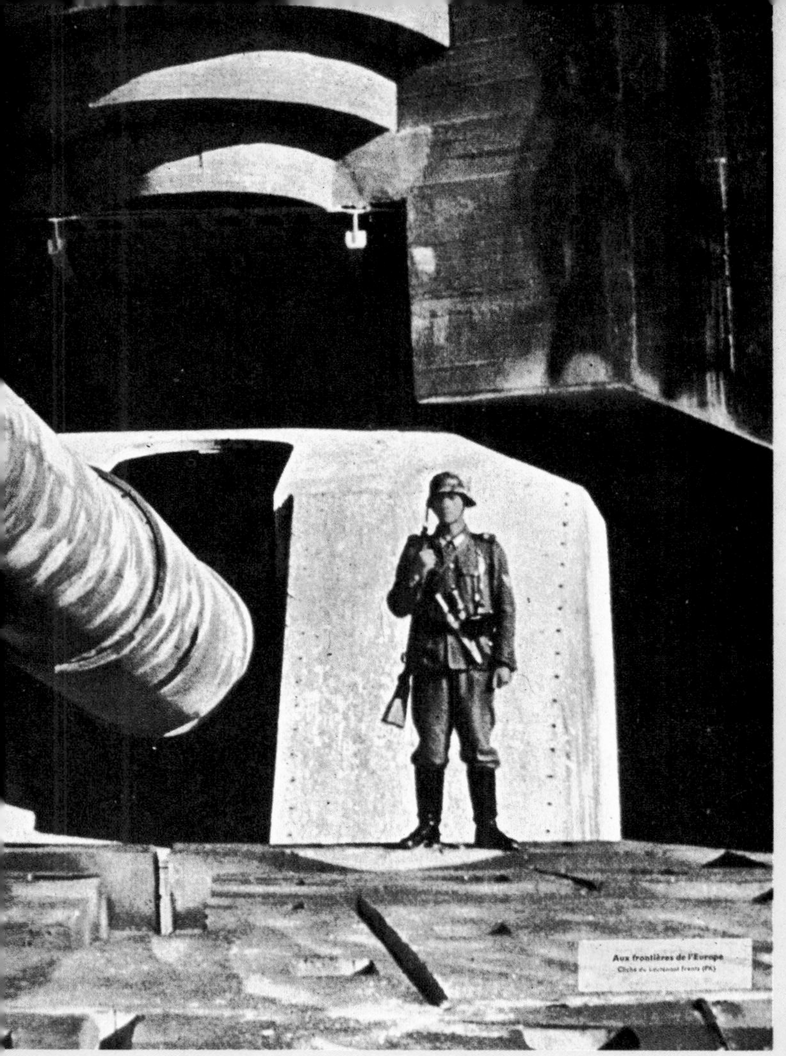

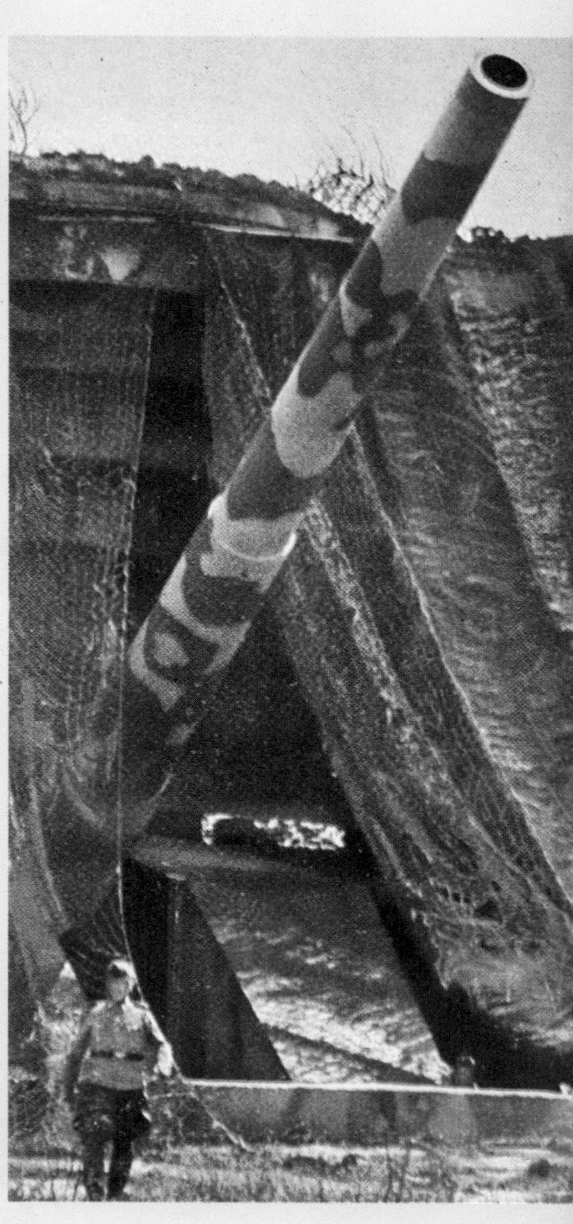

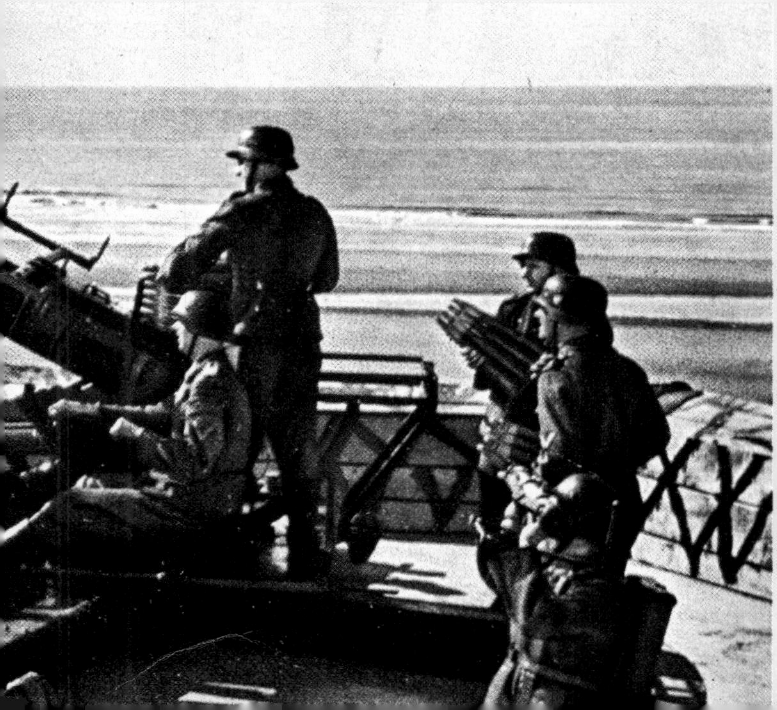

Arsenal for Invasion

In June 1944 more than 2,000,000 men, 6,600 ships and 11,500 aircraft were ready to take part in Overlord

Below: Convoys had ferried ammunition, food and equipment from America at the rate of 750,000 tons a month during 1944. This Atlantic convoy in February 1944 was photographed from the American battleship U.S.S. *Arkansas*

Right: In Britain's factories women had been mobilized to meet the demands of war production

Far right: A production line for Mosquito fighter-bombers – its largely wooden airframe allowed it to be produced by the thousand in British factories

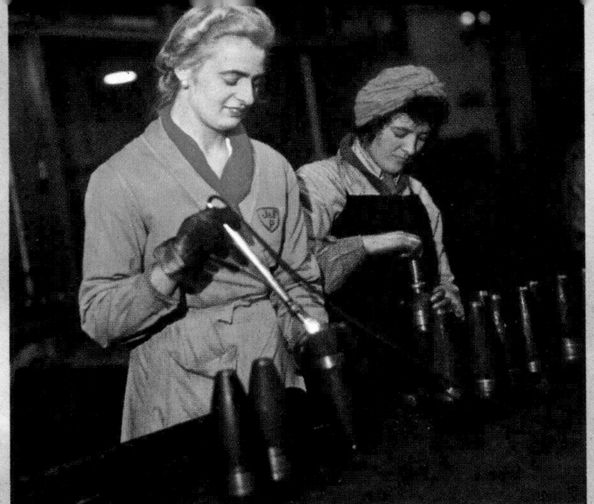

LR264

Assault from the Sky

The assault on Hitler's fortress would begin with the largest airborne operation in history. Pre-invasion training was intensive

Below left: Many of the paratroops were to be landed by glider. Here a British unit of the Red Berets prepares for a training exercise

Right: Mass parachute drops were rehearsed over Salisbury Plain in daylight. Later, the 'real thing' would take place at night

Below right: Airborne forces 20,000 strong would be ferried to France in 1,400 transport aircraft and 3,500 gliders. Loaded up with heavy equipment, paratroops make the best of the confined space

L
V

L
S

L
P
GB

The B17 Flying Fortress of the U.S. Eighth Air Force, with a bomb-load of some 12,000 lbs, played a major role in the Transportation Plan. Hundreds of B17s (inset) were ferried across the Atlantic to take part in the air offensive against Germany. Very accurate bombsights, and the daylight fighter cover from the accompanying American Mustang fighter seen at top right, allowed Flying Fortresses to knock out rail and bridge targets. By D-Day, three-quarters of the railway system of northern France had been incapacitated

Air Power: the Key to Overlord

The Allied bomber force struck heavily against the German war machine, supply and communication lines. The Transportation Plan smashed vital road, rail and bridge links. The bombers paved the way for the invasion, dislocating the rail system and knocking out German gun emplacements and fortifications in the landing areas. Over 70,000 tons of bombs were dropped on enemy communications from February to June 1944

Lancaster Bombers, the mainstay of the R.A.F. Bomber Command, carried a maximum bomb-load of some 18,000 lbs

Previous pages: The Allied Commanders in February 1944 at their headquarters in Norfolk House, St James's Square

Left to right:
Lieutenant-General Omar N. Bradley
Commander U.S. First Army

Admiral Sir Bertram Ramsay
Commander Allied Naval Expeditionary Force

Air Chief Marshal Sir Arthur Tedder
Deputy Supreme Commander

General Dwight D. Eisenhower
Supreme Commander Allied Expeditionary Force

General Sir Bernard Montgomery
Commander 21st Army Group

Air Chief Marshal Sir Trafford Leigh Mallory
Commander Allied Expeditionary Air Force

Lieutenant-General Walter Bedell Smith
Chief of Staff

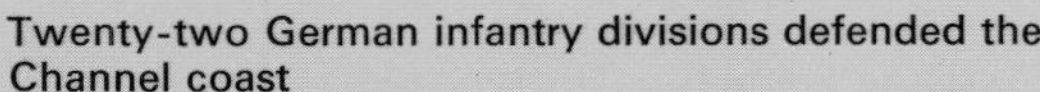

Twenty-two German infantry divisions defended the Channel coast

Left: Wehrmacht gunners man an artillery position on the French coast

Below left: The man whom Hitler had charged with stopping the invasion on the beaches – Field-Marshal Erwin Rommel

Centre: The elite of the Wehrmacht infantry – a Panzer grenadier with an MG 43 machine-gun

Right: An artillery officer sighting one of the heavy guns

The Hammer behind the Wall

Five powerful Panzer divisions were ranged inland in north France

Left: German infantry were highly trained in exploiting tank advances

Below left: A battle-group of Panthers moving up to an attack. These were the fast hard-hitting backbone of the Panzers

Below right: The formidable Tiger, most powerful and heavily armoured of all the German tanks

British and Canadian Forces

Left: A 'Tommy' in an aggressive spirit during training

Right: General Montgomery addressing officers and N.C.O.s of the British 50th Division in France, after they had spearheaded the landings

Shoulder flashes of the British and Canadian forces that landed on D-Day

Top:
21st Army Group

Middle:
British I Corps
British Second Army
British XXX Corps

Bottom:
3rd Infantry Division (Sword)
50th Infantry Division (Gold)
6th Airborne Division
3rd Canadian Division (Juno)

American Forces

Left: The Supreme Commander, General Eisenhower, visiting an American unit training in Britain. Accompanying him are his Deputy, Air Chief Marshal Tedder (*left*), and General Montgomery (*centre*)

Shoulder flashes of the U.S. forces that landed on D-Day

Top:
U.S. First Army

Middle:
V Corps
VII Corps
1st Infantry Division, 'The Big Red One' (Omaha)
4th Infantry Division, 'Ivy' (Utah)
29th Infantry Division, 'Blue and Grey' (Omaha)

Bottom:
82nd Airborne Division, 'All American'
101st Airborne Division, 'Screaming Eagles'

US 134
BERTH
E

Opposite: Trucks and equipment being loaded through the bow doors of an American L.S.T.

Below: American troops board L.C.I.s at a west-country harbour, prior to D-Day. Barrage balloons are ready for protecting the ships against enemy aircraft

Following pages: Top left. A British Churchill tank tackling rough hedgerow country

Bottom left: First-rate medical back-up was insisted on by SHAEF. A battle casualty receives prompt blood transfusion in a British field hospital

Right: The infantry soldier was the backbone of the Allied invasion forces. A U.S. mortar squad is fighting its way through a wrecked French town

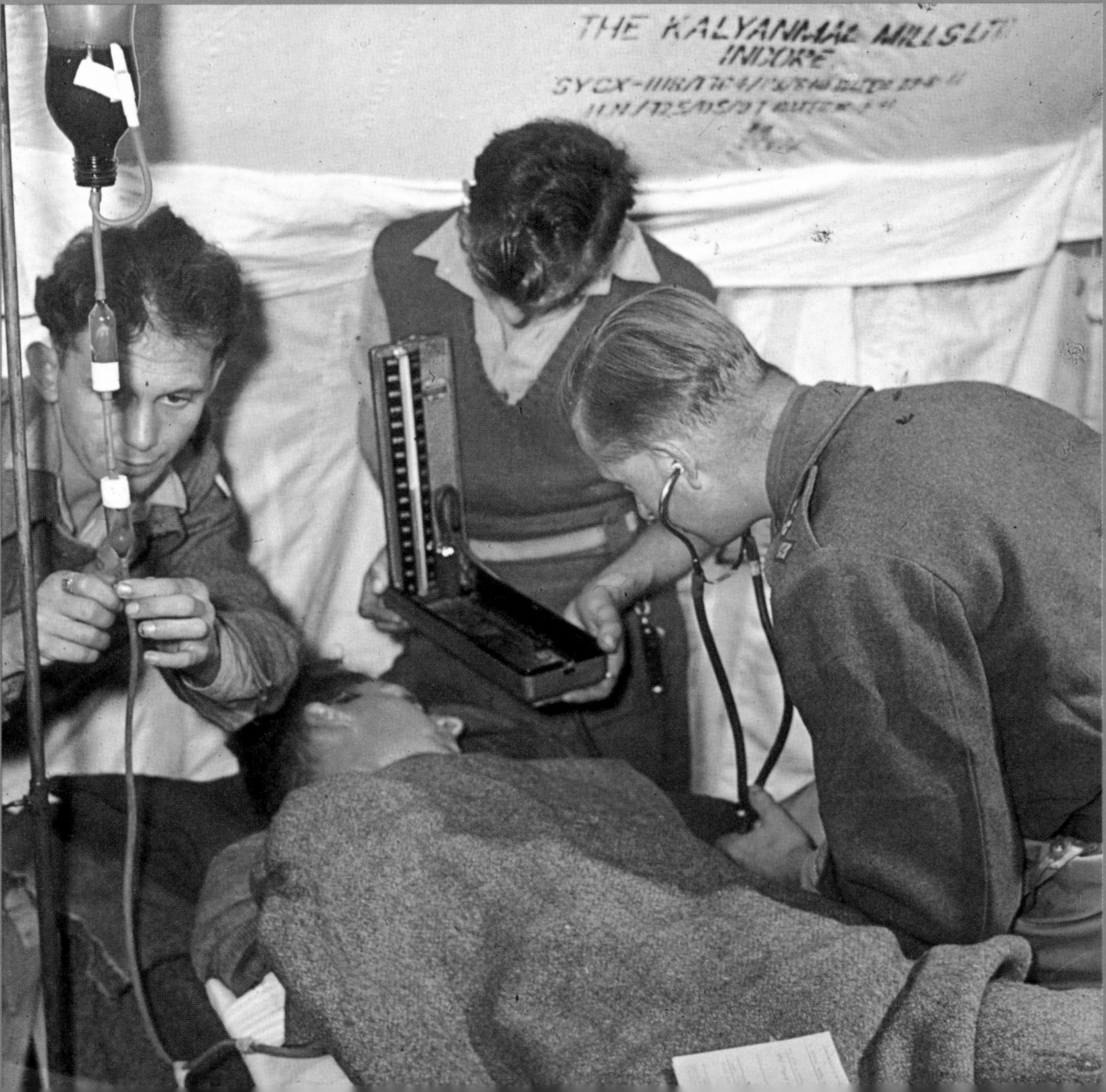

Relics of Invasion

Above: The remains at Asnelles of Phoenix breakwaters of the Mulberry harbour from Gold beach

Below: Arromanches, seen from the German gun emplacement, was the site of Port Winston, the British Mulberry harbour. Scattered concrete sections are still stranded on the beach

Above right: Wreckage uncovered at low tide on Utah beach at La Madeleine

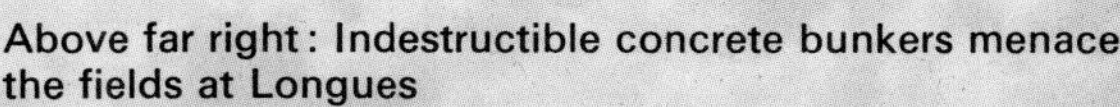

Above far right: Indestructible concrete bunkers menace the fields at Longues

Far centre: A Sherman tank in the dunes at Utah beach freezes a moment in history

Far right: A Krupp gun-barrel in the Longues battery still juts out from its concrete emplacement towards the Channel

Above: 14 July 1944 – the Allies join the local French population at Courseulles to commemorate Bastille Day at the Memorial to the First War

Below: Thirty years on – a rusting German gun mounts silent vigil over a now deserted beach

Opposite: Final briefing for the airborne assault. The message from their commander read, 'Keep cool, maintain that offensive eagerness and see to it that the Red Berets of the Air-Landing Brigade become a symbol of terror to the Germans.' Below: The gliders and aircraft that were to carry them to France were lined up on the runway, freshly painted with the white invasion identification stripes

Right: Nerve centre of the invasion, Southwick House, near Portsmouth. In the library behind the colonnade, Eisenhower took the decision to go

aircraft flying low over the sea to make sure that they had come back.'

Eventually all the units were rounded up, and headed back through a mounting gale to the nearest port.

It was not until 0900 hours on Sunday that an anxious Admiral Ramsay knew that all units were safely on their way to shelter as the Admiralty issued a gale warning.

On board the crowded troopships briefings took place for the troops. Up-to-date maps and aerial photographs of the sectors of the beaches were distributed with code names. Even at this stage security was so tight that many people did not know the exact name of the beach they would be landing on. Some were code-named after famous poets, others after Walt Disney characters, or else they read more like a lesson in world geography. A group of Royal Engineers heard that they would be landing on a piece of the French coast called 'Cape Town'. Practice boarding drills were held on the small assault landing craft that the troopships carried on the lifeboat davits. On board *Clan Lamont*, Sergeant Smith of the Royal Engineers acquired an unwilling addition to their company. 'We practised jumping into the canvas chutes and sliding down into the landing craft. Unfortunately, one of the soldiers ripped up the chute with the foresight of his rifle. They had to send ashore for a naval sailmaker. And having got this chap on board to sew it up they then discovered that he was a security risk. So this poor chap, who was about sixty-five, had to come with us. He's the only man I ever saw panic in the whole operation.'

'I would say – go'

It was a dismal day for the Allied Commanders. Late in the afternoon they drove back in the pouring rain for a series of fateful meetings, knowing that each postponement would increase the hazard of the invasion. Only eight days in June provided a favourable combination of tide and dawn light. Any lengthy postponement would wreck the morale of the assault troops and jeopardize the security of the whole operation. Eisenhower snatched a quick supper and dashed over to the meeting at 2130 hours in the oak-panelled room that had been the library in Southwick House. The wind and rain beat against the blacked-out bow windows as Stagg, to everyone's surprise, stood up and announced that a break in the weather was on its way. The rain-front over the assault area was expected to clear for forty-eight hours. Cloud conditions would permit heavy bombing on Monday night, 5 June, and the cloud base at H-Hour would be just high enough to permit spotting for the navy's guns. The wind would moderate, but the seas still remain choppy and rough. There was just half an hour for a decision. They knew that if Admiral Kirk's forces sailed for a D-Day on 6 June and were again recalled, they would not have enough fuel left to make a Wednesday invasion. 6 June was the last day for two weeks in which dawn and the tide were suitable for the assault. The Supreme Commander went round the group, who were sitting in easy chairs, and asked for advice. Air Chief Marshal Leigh Mallory was pessimistic. He believed, with Air Chief Marshal Tedder, that it would be 'chancy'. Admiral Ramsay thought that the assault should go ahead. Eisenhower turned to General Montgomery and asked, 'Do you see any reason for not going Tuesday?'

'I would say – go,' Montgomery replied.

Eisenhower summed up the issue facing them all: 'Just how long can you hang this operation on the end of a limb and let it hang there?'

The discussion continued for a few more minutes but only one man could decide. General Bedell Smith was struck by 'the loneliness and isolation of a Commander at a time when such a momentous decision was to be taken by him, with the full knowledge that failure or success rested on his individual decision.'

After reflecting for a few moments, Eisenhower calmly announced, 'I am quite positive we must give the order . . . I don't like it, but there it is . . . I don't see how we can possibly do anything else.'

A final meeting was arranged at 0400 hours on 5 June. When they heard that the decision was to go, at least one Admiral leaving Southwick House looked up to the sky as the rain poured down and said, 'Bloody nonsense, I call it.'

'All afternoon, Monday, 5 June, the *Augusta* scudded past the Utah-bound convoys, heading for her rendezvous with the Omaha force. High above the cruiser's bridge a radar antenna rotated monotonously under the woolly sky. In the plotting room below, an officer bent before the radar screen searching for the tell-tale pips that would signify enemy air. But day passed and evening came without a bogey report. "Seems hard to believe," I said to Kirk, "maybe we're going to have a Sicily all over again." There, too, we had held our breaths in anticipation of air attack against the convoys. Yet in Sicily the enemy had slumbered on until we piled up on his beaches. But in the narrow English Channel we could scarcely count on slipping through the enemy's alert without sounding an alarm.'

General Bradley

5 June 1944 'Tonight I have seen the assault force move out from Spithead from the bridge of H.M.S. *Southern Prince* in order to break open the defences of the northern coast of France. Nothing as great, nothing as world changing and gigantic has been undertaken in these waters since 1066. This night we invade the continent of Europe from the west, the awaited hour has poured itself through the hour-glass, and tomorrow morning we strike.

'The sky's grey overhead but the wind is veering northwards and the glass shows signs of rising. The moment is one of great suspense and tomorrow will bring us news of the battle as we await our orders to go forth.'

Lieutenant Michael Chodzko, R.N.V.R.

The Supreme Commander retired to his caravan, with the Sunday newspapers and his favourite Westerns, to rest before the dawn conference. At 0330 hours on Monday, 5 June, Eisenhower set out on his mile-long trip through the park to Southwick House. 'Our little camp,' he wrote, 'was shaking and shuddering under a wind of hurricane proportions, and the accompanying rain seemed to be travelling in horizontal streaks. It seemed impossible in such conditions there was any reason for discussing the situation.' This was the third time that Eisenhower had had to gamble on the weather. As he jangled the lucky coins that he had put in his pocket at north Africa and Sicily he went into the meeting. The Met. report was still favourable for the morning of 6 June. It was agreed that Air Operations would be practical. Ramsay and Montgomery were in no doubt that they should go ahead. The Supreme Commander, almost nonchalantly, set the seal on Overlord with the words, 'O.K. Let's go.'

As the meeting broke up, Montgomery asked Ramsay, upon whose 4,000 ships the success of D-Day now depended, what he was going to do. His reply was characteristically calm and urbane: 'The operation has begun and it is too late to stop it now . . . There is wireless silence and we can expect no signals. I am going to bed.'

Neptune under way

By morning, the weather had started to improve and the naval commanders flashed out their signals: CARRY OUT OPERATION NEPTUNE. Michael Standing of the B.B.C., on board H.M.S. *Hilary*, described the scene as D-Day got under way:

'This morning the anchorage has suddenly come to life, not as in the last few days with sporadic movement here and there, but this is a large-scale business with columns of smaller ships and craft threading their way down the Channel between the larger ships that still lie moored. These are the preliminary moves that, weather, and weather alone, permitting, will develop into the greatest assault on the European shore. We've watched in the last hour or so a flotilla of fleet sweepers moving down in line ahead down to – down to the west. And among the many hundreds of the larger vessels that still crowd the anchorage as far as the eye can see – the smoke is beginning to pour from their funnels.

'So the long months of preparation – the weeks of waiting – are within hours of perhaps being over. The first move has been made, and under the providence of God the mammoth fleet is now ready to sail.'

Spirits were high throughout the great concentrations of ships leaving Plymouth, Portland, Portsmouth and Southampton for Point Z, the rendezvous off the southernmost tip of the Isle of Wight, the starting-point for the trip to France, unofficially called Piccadilly Circus. One commander reported: 'Anyone might have thought we were taking a batch of troops home on leave, such were the high spirits prevailing.'

'The dice are on the table'

At the headquarters of Army Group West at the Château of St Germain near Paris that morning, Field-Marshal von Rundstedt received the Luftwaffe report for the day: 'The enemy command is still trying by all means to prevent us from observing his activities. The continued air attack on Dunkirk and the coast as far as Dieppe leads us to suppose that the enemy will attack in that sector.' Von Rundstedt noted with some satisfaction that the report concluded: 'However, it is unlikely that the invasion is imminent.' It confirmed his own opinion and he signed his personal situation brief for O.K.W. before leaving for a long lunch at his regular restaurant, the Côq Hardi. His lunch would have been less enjoyable had he known that over 4,000 ships were heading for Normandy, and that in every airfield in southern England ground crews were busily applying tons of white paint as identification stripes on thousands of Allied aircraft.

By the afternoon of 5 June the English Channel was an extraordinary sight with ships converging on the Isle of Wight from every direction. The convoys stretched for miles.

By late afternoon the anchorage at Spithead was becoming strangely empty after the immense crowding of the previous weeks.

Neptune's Trident'. As the great armada gets under way, Admiral Ramsay (right), Allied Naval Commander, watches units head out into the Channel Below: Passing a troopship with the L.C.A.s on davits, a column of L.C.T.s fly barrage balloons to ward off enemy fighters

Ike's farewell. Left: The Supreme Commander with the 101st U.S. Airborne Division, 'Hundreds of paratroopers, with blackened and grotesque faces, packing up for the big hop and jump. Ike wandered around them, stepping over packs, guns and a variety of equipment such as only paratroop people can devise, chinning with this one and that one. All were put at ease. He was promised a job after the war by a Texan who said he roped, not dallied, his cows, and at least there was enough to eat in the work.' Captain Harry Butcher

Below: In gathering dusk, the paratroops board waiting Dakotas near Newbury, Berkshire – a scene that was taking place at dozens of airfields on the evening of 5 June 1944

As the last of the assault ships left harbour late that afternoon the airborne forces were preparing for their assault.

The Supreme Commander felt an almost personal responsibility for the fate of these men. Their mission was to take part in the biggest airborne assault ever mounted. He drove to see the 101st Airborne Division leave from its base at Greenham Common near Newbury. There were 'hundreds of paratroopers, with blackened and grotesque faces, packing up for the big hop and jump.'

As General Eisenhower sped back through the sleeping countryside to his headquarters, the German listening posts picked up another transmission that could have profoundly affected Overlord. The B.B.C. nine o'clock news announcing the fall of Rome was followed by a string of messages to the Resistance. At least one section of German intelligence, forewarned by Gestapo agents, knew what the strange sounding phrases meant. 'I am looking for four-leafed clovers.' 'The tomatoes should be picked.' 'The dice are on the table.' 'It is hot in Suez.' 'The children are bored on Sundays.' These were the Code B messages which triggered the carefully laid Resistance Scheme. The Fifteenth Army headquarters near the Belgian frontier heard the most important signal of all, which they, like the Resistance, had been awaiting for days. It warned of an imminent Allied invasion: it was the second line of Verlaine's poem 'Ode to Autumn', 'Pierce my heart with a dull languor.'

Fifteenth Army headquarters signalled to all German units in the west that invasion was about to start, and Fifteenth Army troops were put on full alert. But at Rundstedt's headquarters at St Germain, the Field-Marshal dismissed it as a false alarm. He was in the middle of his dinner when the signal arrived. As one officer commented, 'Does any one really think the enemy is stupid enough to announce its arrival over the radio.' Rundstedt had already been told by his naval advisers that the Channel was far too rough for an invasion.

At Cherbourg, German Naval Headquarters entered the Fifteenth Army signal on its record with a comment, 'Of course, nothing *will* happen.'

'We took off from Lyneham aerodrome on the night of 5 June. Somebody – I think it was the Padre – had the bright idea of getting a piano to keep the lads amused while we were waiting. A driver, called Jack Young, found one from somewhere and brought it in his truck to the airfield. As I could play a bit, I was detailed to play a few tunes and we had a sing-song alongside the waiting planes. When the time came, we climbed into the aircraft and flew off to France to play our part in the invasion, leaving the piano in the middle of the airfield . . . it seems that next morning Jack Young went back to the airfield to collect it, but the piano had completely disappeared. He searched everywhere but could not find it. He said I must have taken it to France and flogged it . . .'

Sergeant A. G. Reading, M.M., 8th Parachute Regiment

'The first aircraft that is going to lead the very front in the early hours of tomorrow morning is turning on the end of the tarmac to make its take-off – a graceful machine, and its wing-tip lights shining red and green over the heads of the dark, small figures of people on the aerodrome watching it taking off. Taking off from here loaded with parachutists – taking with it perhaps the hopes and the fears and the prayers of millions of people of this country who sleep tonight not knowing that this operation is taking place. There she goes now, the first aircraft leading the attack on Europe . . .'

Richard Dimbleby, B.B.C.

12 H-Hour Approaches

Previous pages: The Channel watch. At sunset on the evening of 5 June, unsuspecting German sentries from Calais to Bordeaux resigned themselves to another night of inactivity, unaware that thousands of ships and aircraft were heading for Normandy

Right: Destination Normandy. The invasion convoys round the Isle of Wight and head out into a choppy Channel

Dusk was closing over the grimy government buildings in Whitehall. For Londoners, 5 June 1944 was just another night of dreary black-out and possible blitz. But deep under one of the administrative blocks near St James's Park, the Cabinet War Rooms were a hive of activity. In the subterranean headquarters of the British government, Churchill and his staff prepared to share the tensions of the night with the thousands of Allied soldiers, sailors and airmen who were already heading for their encounter in Normandy.

All appeared to be going well, the gigantic plan was unfolding smoothly and the Germans were still ignorant that the operation had started. But the lack of real information did little to dispel the steadily mounting tension. Churchill did not enjoy the waiting period. He knew, better than anyone, how much was at stake on the waters of the Channel and in the skies above the armada. His personal assistant, Commander Thompson, noted, 'He was much on edge. Once again, he could hear the tramping of Housman's ghostly legions.

Far and near, low and louder
On the roads of earth go by
Dear to friends and food for powder
Soldiers marching, all to die.

When Mrs Churchill joined him for a few moments before retiring he said to her, 'Do you realize that by the time you wake up in the morning 20,000 men may have been killed?'

The 'Former Naval Person' would have much preferred to be out on the Channel with the soldiers that night, leading the invasion in his own warship. He had, in fact, arranged to board H.M.S. *Belfast*, but at the eleventh hour the King had firmly instructed him not to go.

'Nelson in the van'

The whole armada was converging on the Normandy coast along ten channels which were being buoyed and swept of mines by flotillas of small minesweepers taking their sweeps far ahead.

The minesweeper, H.M.S. *Pelorus*, played a leading part in clearing the Channel. She left the Solent early on Monday after their Captain had told the crew: 'We have the honour and the privilege to lead the Invasion Fleet across the Channel to the beaches of Cherbourg.' A. F. Wilby recalls, 'A senior Petty Officer alongside me muttered, "what did 'e say? The Honour or the 'orrer?"

'We steamed out with the halliards streaming the flags – "Nelson in the Van". It seemed no different from all our previous trips to sea as a flotilla, except that as far as one could see on each side, stretching back away from us, were minesweepers. *Pelorus* was the point of a very large arrow. We were now at action stations of course, and at about midnight the Captain spliced the mainbrace.'

The cumbersome landing craft were struggling through the rough Channel crossing. An official British report noted that: 'Craft such as the L.C.T. (A) who were routed at 5 knots (their best cruising speed) and the L.C.T. "D.D.", who were tied to proceeding at $4\frac{3}{4}$ knots for a large part of the passage, found navigation in the existing conditions extremely difficult.'

One American L.C.T. in particular was having problems. 'We were located in one of the inside columns and spent our entire time trying to keep station', runs the official report of U.S. Navy Lieutenant, Stanley C. Bodell. 'We had the misfortune to have a British "lettered craft" behind us which had the ability to go ahead twice as fast as the Americans, but lacked the backing power that we had. We would pound along, the whole boat

'On the decks, in the holds . . . the soldiers were waiting. For the most part standing about looking out to sea, talking now and then and thinking. In the wardroom, dinner. From the menu, soup, roast beef and green peas and apples and cream. It might have been a crossing to Cherbourg in peacetime. And then you realized that your hand was moving just a little sluggishly to your mouth. Your tummy wasn't just where it usually was. The men around you were rather silent, and when they spoke they were self-conscious. It was a roomful of men on the way. Wondering, waiting and listening. On deck, signals were flashing between ships. *Enterprise* had run up a flag signal. Boat crews were making their final preparations. There was a tenseness and a sense of good humour and good fellowship that were impossible of translation into words.'

Robin Duff, B.B.C.

'On the whole, everyone is glad. We have known for the past three weeks now that once more *Orion* would have a place in the front line and knowing this, the feeling has been – it's got to come, the sooner the better. Many people will be killed, it certainly will be many, many times worse than Anzio. He's ready for us, knows it must be soon – let's hope that no one has told him where. This afternoon will be one of tension and nervousness – I feel it now, it's only natural. But when the dirt begins to fly tomorrow, I don't think we'll have time to worry about things. If it's our turn, it'll come too quick for us to think about it.'

Ian A. Michie, Leading Radio Mechanic

bending and buckling; then the one ahead would slow down. We would go into full reverse to keep from riding up its stern, then the Britisher would start to climb ours. To avoid collision, we would go full speed ahead with full right rudder, and sheer off towards the other column. The vessels of different columns would close to about five feet or less, usually crashing together then separating with one going full speed at right angles to the course of the convoy. All day there was always someone heading off by himself having a wonderful time. Sleep was almost impossible, as you couldn't stay in your sack.'

Some of the British commanders on convoy S-7 shepherding the L.S.I.s enjoyed easier navigation. Lieutenant-Commander A. J. R. White, R.N., reported: 'It was like driving to a race meeting with the A.A. controlling the traffic.'

'We didn't feel much like sleeping that night,' remembered Major Smith who was on the deck of his troopship. 'In any case, even if anyone had wanted any sleep on my boat they could not have got it. It was full of French Canadians, the Chauderie and the Winnipeg Rifles. All they did all night was sharpen up their knives!

'In one respect, I don't think anyone wanted to miss anything. After months and months of training we were suddenly aware that everything was fitting into place. Naturally, there was tension. Everybody was really frightened of letting the other bloke know that underneath it all you were really afraid. The sum total of this was that nobody appeared to be afraid. Yet, if we were honest, we were all terribly afraid.

'It was easier on deck because it was all so impressive to us to see these hundreds of ships with destroyers and minesweepers on either side. The whole thing going across in one steady pattern – just steaming across to France. Then, late at night, there were the waves and waves of planes going across overhead. It really was impressive, very impressive.'

Waiting to jump

High overhead, the airborne troops were already on their way to land on French soil. Only hours away from the dropping zone, General Matthew B. Ridgway was in command of the U.S. 82nd Airborne Division.

'Eastward, over the Channel, the skies were darkening. Two hours later night had fallen, and below us we could see the glints of yellow flame from the German anti-aircraft guns on the Channel Islands. We watched them curiously, and without fear, as high flying duck may watch a hunter, knowing that we were too high and far away for their fire to reach us. In the plane, the men sat quietly, deep in their own thoughts. They joked a little and broke, now and then, into ribald laughter. Nervousness and tension, and the cold that blasted

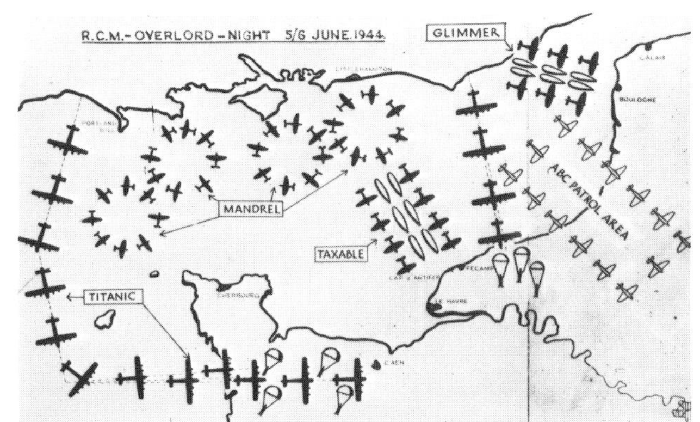

'The enemy did mistake the Glimmer convoy simulation for a genuine threat and . . . believed that the A.B.C. Patrol [flown backwards and forwards with radar-jamming equipment to confuse German fighter defences] was cover for operations in the Somme area. As well as sending a number of E-boats to investigate the Glimmer operations the enemy opened up with searchlights and guns on the imaginary "convoy" . . . The night-fighter force . . . was sent into the A.B.C. area . . . [supposedly], into the main bomber stream of a major attack. On their arrival in the area, the fighters found that they were being subjected to serious jamming on the R/T communications channel. They returned toward their control points, but appeared to have received instructions to go on hunting in the "bomber stream" as there was sporadic fighter activity in that area between 0105 and 0355 hours.'
Official Report

Opposite: The fake invasion. Above: A contemporary map showing the feint attacks on the night of 5/6 June that confused the German defences. Glimmer and Taxable were the 'invasion convoys' which, together with Mandrel, threw German radar into disarray. Titanic was the dummy paratroop drop, and A.B.C. the false fighter-cover simulation

Below: The real invaders. U.S. paratroops, their faces revealing mixed emotions at the prospect of being 'on their way at last'. In a few hours they would jump out into the darkness to become the 'first liberators'

through the open door, had its effect upon us all. Now and then a paratrooper would rise, lumber heavily to the little bathroom in the tail of the plane, find he could not get through the narrow doorway in his bulky gear, and come back, mumbling his profane opinion of the designers of the C47 airplane. Soon the crew chief passed the bucket around, but this did not entirely solve our problem. A man strapped and buckled into full combat gear finds it extremely difficult to reach certain essential portions of his anatomy, and his efforts are not made easier by the fact that his comrades are watching him, jeering derisively and offering gratuitous advice.'

Everyone held their breath

Brief signals indicating 'Enemy Intelligence unchanged' were the only news that Supreme Headquarters had of the early progress of the invasion. The assault fleet observed radio silence. As Captain Courage, who was in charge of Fleet Signals at Southwick House that night, recalled: 'I remember the tension was greatest when we felt that the time was approaching when any German E-boat patrols from Cherbourg might have met the invasion fleet in mid-Channel. But, contrary to expectations, they didn't appear.'

'Everyone held their breath at that time when we were watching the plot to see if the E-boats came out from Cherbourg,' remembered Mrs Fanny Hughill, who was a Wren plotter in the Operational Headquarters that night. 'General Eisenhower, Admiral Ramsay, and, of course, the top brass generally, used to come and pop in for a few minutes, have a look round, look at the plot. They didn't really discuss things in front of us. They tended to come in here for a look and then return and obviously had their conferences back in their own headquarters.'

At 2310 the teleprinter clattered through a signal in cipher from the Naval Officer commanding Newhaven: 'Operation Glimmersailed Harbour Defence M.L.s 1390, 1060, 1279, 1410, 1413, 1379, 1071, 1310, 1414, 1420, 1049, 1058 and Pinnace 1249.'

In the Operations Room, the Wren plotters moved out counters to mark the launching of a second 'invasion'. In contrast to the thousands of ships and aircraft heading for Normandy, this armada consisted of a couple of dozen motor-launches and aircraft. Their job would be to fool the German defences and radar into believing that there was a massive assault heading for Boulogne and the Cap d'Antifer near Dieppe, code-named Glimmer and Taxable. They consisted of motor-launches equipped with radar devices and bombers of the R.A.F. 617 Squadron flying in carefully worked out circles, dropping aluminium foil called Window. The impression on the enemy radar screens would be of a vast invasion fleet heading for the French coast.

German Intelligence had still not reported the real invasion by the time Eisenhower returned to his caravan. For him, more than anyone else, that day and night must have seemed the longest in his life. For Butcher, his close friend and aide, the waiting soon became too much. 'We returned about 0115, sat around in the nickel-plated office caravan in courteous silence, each with his own thoughts and trying to borrow by psychological osmosis those of the Supreme Commander, until I became the first to say to hell with it, and excused myself – to bed.'

Alarm at midnight

Meanwhile, the streams of bombers, paratroop transports and glider-towing Dakotas were roaring over the still peaceful beaches of Normandy.

One man who was waiting to jump was Guy Byam of the B.B.C. 'In the crowded fuselage all you see in the pale light of an orange bulb is the man next to you.

'And you fly out over the Channel and the minutes go by and the stock commander says that the pilot has told him we are over a great armada of naval ships. And then it is something else he says – something that gives you a dry feeling in your mouth – flak – and the word is passed from man to man. The machine starts to rock and jump with it. Ahead of us – a comforting thought – Lancasters are going for the flak, and a coastal battery is one of the objectives.'

As the coastal flak batteries opened up on the approaching airborne armada, one of the strangest components of Overlord went into operation. Titanic 1, 3 and 4 was a diversionary operation in which three groups of aircraft broke away from the mainstream and headed for points far inland of the main invasion areas. At the same time, the bomber crews discharged large quantities of Window and then, simulating a parachute drop, pushed out straw dummies over dropping zones near Rouen, Caen and Avranches. As the dummy parachutists floated into the fields, isolated German units rushed into the alert, creating confusion miles away from where the real airborne landings were taking place.

The bad weather had lulled the Germans into a false sense of security. Admiral Krancke, Naval Commander at Cherbourg, had cancelled the night's reconnaissance patrol by the E-boat flotilla.

The storm had brought relief from a constant alert to the defenders all round the coast. Monday had been a day off for the troops in the centre of the invasion front. In any case they were confident that nobody would be foolhardy enough to try to land amongst the shoals and rocks of Calvados. That evening the German local command held a party at their headquarters near Tracy-sur-Mer, the comfortable seventeenth-century château of Philippe de Bourgoing, requisitioned by the Germans.

'The day before D-Day they had a concert for the officers and troops in the garden behind the house,' recalled M. de Bourgoing, whose family had been allocated a single floor. 'In the evening they had a big dinner and the party was finishing after midnight, when suddenly the alarm came. All the officers then rushed out down the garden to their bunkers which were in the woods. About one hour after the alarm, very heavy bombing began. It seemed to be all over the country. The first waves of planes were very, very high in the sky but as the night went on they came lower and lower and the bombing around us became more intense.'

All over Normandy, German headquarters were empty of senior officers. They were taking advantage of the weather for a break in the constant alerts that they had been on since that spring. The practice alert for the night of the 5th/6th had been cancelled. A number of senior officers were on the road to Rennes where there was to be a *kriegspiel* the following morning. Prophetically, the theme for the 'staff war game' was 'enemy landings in Normandy, preceded by parachute drops'. At Caen, earlier that evening, a weekly staff conference ended with General Richter jokingly informing his officers of the 716th Division that the wires were buzzing with a rumour that an invasion was imminent. They had, he said, suffered so many false alarms that they could certainly expect it to happen that night! But General Dollman, Commander of the Seventh Army, had an afterthought that evening; worried about the exodus of officers for Rennes, he ordered them not to leave Normandy before dawn. It was too late. Many had taken the opportunity to snatch an evening off duty.

In St Lô a midnight birthday party in honour of General Erich Marcks was under way. One of his staff officers was present: 'He disliked all forms of celebration, so he looked surprised; his gaunt strong-willed, deeply lined face might have been that of a scientist or scholar. He had lost a leg in Russia and the joint of his artificial limb creaked as he stood up; he raised his hand in a friendly, but nevertheless cool gesture.

'We each drank a glass of Chablis standing and the little ceremony was over in a few minutes.'

'Out with a yell!'

The party at St Lô would soon be over. A few miles to the north, the first of the American paratroops were approaching their dropping zones in the Cherbourg peninsula. *Time Magazine* captured the moment: 'The paratroops dozed, or pretended to. They were the Army's elite, the tough boys – lean wiry men clad in green camouflaged battledress, faces stained with cocoa and linseed oil ("We'll have something to eat if our rations run out!")'

General Ridgway's 82nd Paratroop Division was part of that drop:

'A bell rang loudly, a green light glowed. The jump-master, crouched in the door, went out with a yell – "Let's go!" With a paratrooper still laugh-

'Each time an explosion took place we bounced a couple of hundred feet or so and it was on one of these occasions that the leader of our paratroop stick – still waiting for the order to jump with the red preparation light on – was jerked through the hole head downwards, *and completely blocked it.*

'I could hear through the intercom the verbal and physical efforts of my wireless operator and gunner to pull him out but he was solidly stuck. We reached home some three hours after take-off with the unfortunate paratroop leader still blocking the hole.

'The problem remained as to how I could land, there being a very real danger that the landing itself might throw him out of the aircraft. After three orbits of the airfield, a triumphant shout from my crew indicated that they had managed to pull him back inside the aircraft.'

D. S. C. Brierly, 570 Squadron, R.A.F.

Opposite: Softening up. A squadron of B24 Liberators bomb French coastal defences. All through the night before D-Day, the Allied bombers plastered bridges, road and rail communications, and German positions

ing, breathing hard on my neck, I leapt out after him.'

All over the narrow neck of the Cotentin, the U.S. airborne troops were floating down from the summer sky. Many were far from their planned dropping zones. General Taylor's 101st Division landed nearest Utah beach – and right on to the meadows flooded by the Germans. Their allotted task was to assemble and secure the exits to the beachhead. They had planned to regroup in the dark by signalling to each other with the clicking of toy crickets. Unfortunately, a German patrol had captured a number of the early arrivals, and, hearing the mechanical chirruping, realized its significance and, like bird-catchers on a hunting expedition, lured other paratroopers into their gunfire. For many it became a nightmare of confusion, unable to tell friend from foe.

The largest airborne operation ever attempted very nearly became the disastrous failure that Air Chief Marshal Leigh Mallory had predicted. On an individual level too, it had its moments of horror.

Time reported: 'One paratroop lieutenant survived to return and tell how the Germans "were machine-gunning us all the way down". Another officer told of seeing German tracers ripping through other men's parachutes as they descended. In one plane, a soldier laden with his 90 pounds of equipment got momentarily stuck in the door. A 20-mm. shell hit him in the belly. Fuse-caps in his pockets began to go off. Part of the wounded man's load was T.N.T. Before this human bomb could explode, his mates behind him pushed him out. The last they saw of him, his parachute had opened and he was drifting to earth in a shroud of bursting flame.'

General Ridgway's 82nd Division suffered an even worse scattering than the 101st. Some paratroopers landed as much as twenty-five miles from the dropping zone west of Ste Mère-Église which was their primary target. More than sixty per cent of their equipment was lost. They only pulled something together out of potential disaster through a dogged determination. Their very wide dispersion helped to confuse the Germans, as did the sudden unexpected nature of the first drop.

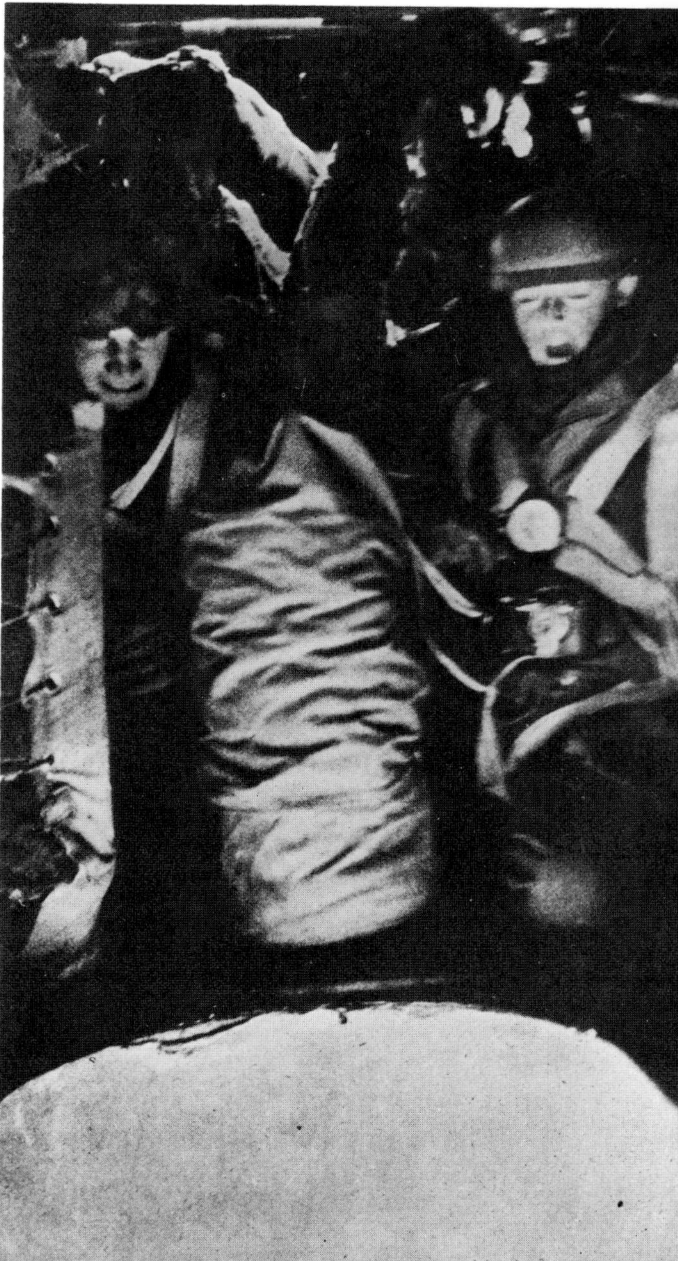

Below: 'Jump!' The moment of truth for the paratroops came shortly before 0100 hours

Below: General Erich Marcks, commander of the LXXXIV Corps. His birthday celebration was interrupted by news of the airborne assault

Opposite: Empty British gliders after making a successful landing at Ranville in spite of Rommel's Asparagus (right of picture)

'The run has started – one minute and thirty seconds. Red light – green and out – get on, out, out fast into the cool night air, out, out, out over France – and we know that the dropping zone is obstructed. We're jumping into fields covered with poles! And / hit my parachute and lower my kitbag which is suspended on the end of a forty foot rope from my harness. And then the ground comes up to hit me. And I find myself in the middle of a cornfield. I look around, and even with a compass I can't be sure where I am – and overhead hundreds of parachutes and containers are coming down.

'The whole sky is a fantastic chimera of lights and flak and one plane gets hit and disintegrates wholesale in the sky, sprinkling a myriad of burning pieces all over the sky.'

Guy Byam

The first news of the landings when it reached General Marck's headquarters at St Lô was electrifying:

'At 0111 hours – unforgettable moment – the field telephone rang. Something important was coming through; whilst listening to it, the General stood up stiffly, his hand gripping the edge of the table. With a nod, he beckoned his chief of staff to listen in. "Enemy parachute troops dropped east of the Orne estuary. Main area Bréville-Ranville and the north edge of the Bavent Forest. Counter measures are in progress". This message from 716 intelligence service struck like lightning.

'Was this, at last, the invasion, the storming of *Festung Europa*? Someone said haltingly "Perhaps they are only supply troops for the French Resistance?" '

Although the landings had nothing to do with the Resistance, French saboteurs were helping the scattered American troops by cutting telephone lines all over Normandy. This added to the Germans' confusion over the extent and disposition of the landings. Incoherent reports were coming in from all directions that parachutists were coming down. Some were the dummies. These, too, helped General Ridgway who, with eleven officers and men, had set up an H.Q. in an apple orchard.

'The Germans were all around us, of course, sometimes within 500 yards of my command post, but in the fierce and confused fighting that was going on all about they did not launch the strong attack that could have wiped out our eggshell perimeter defence.'

The American paratroops had created chaos in the Cotentin. They cut all the telephone lines leaving the Germans completely bewildered about what was really happening. The Commander of the 91st German Airborne Division who went to find things out for himself was caught by an American patrol and killed. Ridgway ruefully commented to his men, 'Well, in our present situation, killing Division Commanders does not strike me as being particularly hilarious.'

'This is it'

Sixty-three miles away, on the eastern bank of the Orne river, between Caen and the sea, the British 6th Airborne Division's near-total success contrasted with American difficulties. A paratroop brigade was coming in by glider to capture the bridges over the Orne including the swing-bridge over the shipping canal to Caen. These would be vital in preventing the German armoured divisions racing for the eastern flank of the invasion beaches.

The official report, in its clipped prose, indicates the success of this daring mission. The small brigade achieved its significant victory with six flimsy plywood gliders.

(a) 'Gliders came in exactly on time. Very little flak was encountered when crossing the coast or in landing.

(b) The three gliders for the CANAL bridge landed exactly on the pre-arranged spot. The troops from those gliders were completely successful in their assault and very little resistance was encountered from the strong defences on the EAST bank, the enemy withdrawing hastily across the bridge, and NORTH between the river and canal.

The party detailed to cross the bridge met some opposition from machine guns in entrenchments on the WEST bank, and suffered casualties, including the platoon commander killed, in crossing the open bridge. The Germans on the WEST bank withdrew in the face of a determined assault, which was carried out at the double, with the greatest dash and without pause.

A close bridgehead was then consolidated on the WEST bank by the *Coup de main* party.

(c) The glider detachment on the EAST bridge did not land with quite such accuracy as was the case at the CANAL bridge, but there was an appreciable opposition on the bridge, and the bridgehead on the EASTERN bank was secured.'

The signals HAM and JAM were sent out, indicating that the bridges were both safe and secure.

Other gliders were circling around in the skies above Ranville. On one of them was Sergeant-Major Scriven, of the 195th Field Ambulance Division.

'Soon we were flying over the Channel, and what a sight that was! It seemed that everyone in England was on an excursion to the shores of Normandy. The noise from the engines of the towing planes made conversation difficult but people did not seem to have much to say except, "This is it", and that summed up the total conversation.

'Soon we were crossing over France, then the towing planes released their tow ropes and the gliders were on their way down; the silence after the planes left us made the soldiers feel as if they were in a new world. The next thing I recall was the glider landing. The tail of the glider fell off and I was struggling in a bed of poppies. I wondered whether I was in this world or the next, then there were things to do and I was off.'

One of the most vital objectives for the paratroopers that night was to seize the guns of the Merville battery. If they were not put out of action by dawn, they could wreak havoc with the landings on Sword beach.

An army from the sky

Lt-Colonel T. B. N. Otway, Royal Ulster Rifles, led a contingent of paratroops. One stick of Otway's paratroops dropped thirty miles away from the battery; he himself had been flung out of the Dakota in advance of the main drop. He had marked the target area for the bombers, but the Lancasters had dropped their 4,000-lb bombs on a herd of cows and not the concrete casemates. Two gliders only had landed in the area of the batteries, but immediately Otway led his band, whose average age was twenty-one and who had never been in battle before, into the fortifications. It was hand-to-hand combat, until the Germans recognized the parachutists' battle-smocks, and, yelling '*Fallschirmjager*', they rapidly lost heart and surrendered. The demolition party then destroyed the guns – one by firing two shells up the barrel. It was only left for the battalion signals officer to pull a battered carrier-pigeon from his smock and throw it into the air. Some hours later it arrived in England with the news.

By 0200 hours on D-Day, the skies over the British dropping zones were filled with parachutists and gliders. As one pilot reported, 'There was a terrific congestion in the DZ and several crews nearly collided with other Dakotas. Altogether, there were approximately 250 aircraft dropping troops in the area at the same time.'

One who jumped was W. G. Lloyd of Ipswich, then part of the 12th Parachute Brigade. 'In the very early hours of D-Day we were dropped at about 600 feet a few miles inland behind the Normandy beaches. As I left the aircraft, I could see some light flak coming up slowly, it seemed like long strings of flaming sausages, and fires were burning inland, probably part of the work of Allied bombing.

Mission accomplished. Right: Success for the contingent of the British 6th Airborne Division which captured the 'Pegasus' swing-bridge over the Orne canal, just visible at the extreme top of the picture. The pinpoint accuracy of the attack is revealed by the almost incredible proximity of the gliders to the target

Below: Broken birds. At first light, aerial reconnaissance revealed the fields near Ranville covered with British gliders. The detached tail sections show that the troops they carried are already successfully dug in with their weapons

'After landing safely in open country, my first impression was not what I'd expected. It was very quiet, considering. After releasing myself from my 'chute and retrieving my kitbag which contained a small radio set, I commenced my steady walk towards what I thought should be our rendezvous. But to my dismay my feet became entangled in what I took to be broken telephone wires. What a horrible twanging noise they made and I felt sure that being so loud, must be heard by the enemy, but of course this was all exaggerated due to my being keyed up. I found a crossroads and a few of my comrades.'

The invasion could not have come at a worse time. 'The Corps Command post resembled a disturbed beehive,' was the impression of one of Marcks' Staff Officers. 'Priority messages were sent in all directions.' For some it was a relief, 'At last the suspense was over, the constant round of "stand to" and partial "full" state of readiness. Since the middle of April this had kept the troops in suspense and they had in the end got used to it and it wasn't taken seriously any more.'

But in spite of the urgent signals flashed from Marcks' headquarters, Army Command West and O.K.W. decided to play it cool; they were not prepared to take all the evidence as warning of an immediate invasion. Von Rundstedt believed it was a diversion. The main attack would come later at Calais.

The German Command lost vital hours wondering whether to move the Panzer divisions to Normandy to counter the invasion threat. In following days this would become increasingly impossible because of continual bombing attacks. Already, the two days of heavy bombing had knocked out rail links, and the Seine bridges were being relentlessly destroyed. Too late the German Generals would see Allied bombers rapidly isolating Normandy from the rest of France.

A *Times* correspondent watched the bombing of the coastal batteries. They were to receive 5,000 tons of bombs in twenty-four hours.

'E for Easy eased its way gently through the not very frightening flak and took its place in the queue of Lancasters moving steadily over the target. After the usual directions of 'Right, Right, Steady, Steady,' from the bomb-aimer lying prone in the nose of the fuselage, the bomber gave a slight jump as it was relieved of its burden of 1,000-lb. bombs. After what seemed like a long interval, the bombs exploded among earlier ones which had already ignited ammunition dumps near the guns.'

'Bonjour'

On the ground with the paratroops, B.B.C. man Guy Byam watched the prelude to the assault: 'On the dropping zone, shock paratroop engineers are finishing blowing the poles that obstruct the dropping zone, and soon the gliders come in scores, coming out of the sky like a sign.

'And the night wears on, and soon it is light and to the northwest the cannonade begins on the beaches. While our paratroop unit fights a terrific battle over the bridges, actually repelling an attack by a Panzer formation – paratroops able to deal with the Panzers. I think that one surprised the German High Command. These airborne units

fight magnificently with terrific morale and vigour.

'The people are pleased to see us. We apologize for the bringing of war to their homes. But in little ways they show they are glad to see us. A dead paratroop is laid out on a bed in the best bedroom covered from head to foot with local flowers.'

Mr E. Purchase was in 225 Parachute Field Ambulance, and dropped with the 6th Airborne Division close to Ranville:

'We made our way to a prearranged rendezvous, thence to Ranville where villagers in the dark (approx. 0350 hours) whispered "Bonjour" from bedroom windows.

'Arrived at a chateau (picked previously from aerial photographs). Our second-in-command knocked and asked if there were any Germans inside. There were, and four or five surrendered and were made prisoners. We then entered and set up our various departments. I was in a surgical team, and we started operating about the time of the main seaborne landing, which was announced to us by a thunderous barrage from the Navy.'

13 Dawn Assault

Previous pages: A German's view of the invasion. The British bombardment at Ouistreham and Sword beachhead, seen from across the Orne estuary near the Houlgate battery

Right: A midget submarine of the type which marked the invasion route on to the British beaches

Below: U.S. destroyers off the American beaches steaming close inshore at high speed. These 'mobile batteries' were highly effective in dealing with those on the shore

Far right: On the receiving end. Inside the German dugouts and pillboxes, the coastal defence troops had to face a massive bombardment from sea and air

Dawn was breaking as midget submarine X-23, captained by Lt G. Honour, surfaced off the French coast. It was joined fifty minutes later and a few miles to the east by X-20, captained by Lt K. Hudspeth, D.S.C., R.A.N.V.R. They had been patiently waiting on the bottom for forty-eight hours, a few hundred yards from the invasion beaches. Their mission was to mark the critical lowering point for D.D. tanks on two of the British invasion beaches and they carefully checked their bearings and radar beacons on the slippery decks. No mean achievement as, they reported, 'the craft was rolling and pitching considerably . . . The sea and swirl made exit and entry difficult and considerable water was shipped, necessitating continual pumping.'

The long vigil in the tin-can atmosphere of a thirty-foot long midget submarine must surely be one of the feats of D-Day. 'Diet consisted mainly of nutty, bread and jam, chocolate biscuits, orange juice, hyocine and oxygen, and this proved adequate. Only two hot meals were prepared; smell and oxygen used when heating made more undesirable.'

The postponement of D-Day increased the danger and the risks that the premature discovery of the X-craft would reveal the whole of the invasion plan. The submarine crews were as least rewarded with a grandstand view of the biggest invasion ever known in history. As Lieutenant Honour later recalled, 'I suppose we saw D-Day as the Germans must have seen it. It was really a tremendous sight as the hundreds of invasion craft came in with the bombarding warships' shells whistling over our heads, and waves of bombers blasting the beaches.'

'The Führer sleeps'

The naval bombardment was an important weapon in creating tactical surprise against the coastal batteries. The psychological effect of this colossal bombardment at dawn is illustrated by the prisoner-of-war interrogation report. 'Many said after the event that when they saw what was being massed against them, fleets and aircraft and fire-power, they knew "the game was up" and complained they had been misled by their High Command and propaganda.' Even making allowances for what the report called 'the well-known instability of German attitudes', which made it difficult to know how confident the men manning the coast defence units and beach defences were, there were certainly too few and too low-grade troops manning the defences. They were 'pretty soft' and 'fed up with military service'. Predictably, as the P.O.W.s were being grilled by Allied intelligence, German commanders were busily filing reports stating 'our own troops were in a state of constant readiness'. Suggesting measures to be taken as a result of the experience, one German

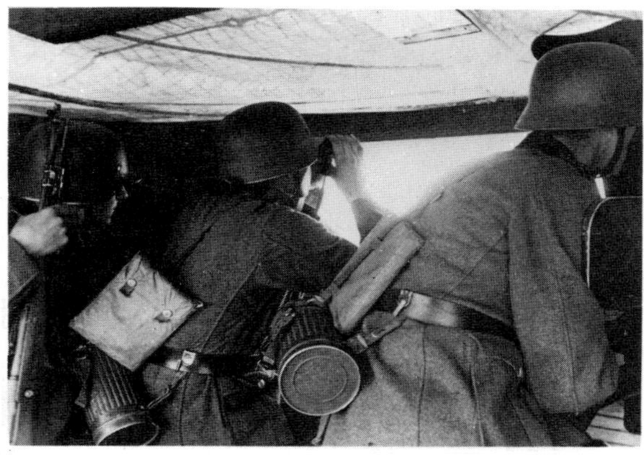

'The enemy invasion was preceded from 0200 hours onwards by successive waves of air raids and on the first signs of dawn by extremely intensive naval shelling directed against the landing points and terrain immediately behind. No reports are available of the effects on defence posts and strongpoints, *as no member of their crews has so far returned and the lines of communication with them were very soon cut.*'
German Army report

report acidly advised that 'when installing advance beach obstacles or in mining operations carried out by the Navy, particular attention should be paid to those parts of the coastline which are alleged to be only conditionally suitable for landing owing to the existence of natural obstacles'.

The German official reports do not explain the incredible fact that, although they knew of the landings by paratroops from soon after 0100 hours, they were unable to put the coastal defences, the vital first line, on full alert.

As early as 0150 the Chief of Operations of Naval Group West at his headquarters in the Bois de Boulogne in Paris called an urgent conference in the situation room. Reports had been pouring in from naval radar stations indicating large numbers of blips on the screens. At first the German radar operators had dismissed this as interference. They did not believe that there could be so many ships approaching, but soon there was no doubt. Admiral Hoffman, the Chief of Staff, arrived in the situation room in his dressing-gown. After studying the reports and discussing them, Hoffman came to the inescapable conclusion that 'this can only be the invasion fleet. Signal to the Führer's headquarters the invasion is on'.

General Marcks, commander of the LXXXIV Corps at St Lô, was also in no doubt. 'Alarm coast' – the signal for the invasion – was passing out through field telephones to battalions, artillery batteries and troops before dawn. Field police were sent out to comb the cafés and restaurants of Caen to round up everybody. But at German High Command, no firm action was taken. Field-Marshal Keitel refused to wake the Führer. It could be another false alarm. Like all the Field-Marshals in the west, he believed that the invasion would come at Calais. The landings in Normandy could only be a diversion.

On the outskirts of Caen at St Pierre-sur-Dives, fifteen miles from the coast, 170 armoured vehicles and tanks of the 21st Panzer division prepared for action. This was the one Panzer division close enough to intervene in the early stages of the assault. Lt-Gen. Feuchtinger, its commander, prepared to act on his own initiative. 'I waited impatiently all night for some instructions. But not a single order from a higher formation was received by me. Realizing that my armoured division was closest to the scene of operations, I finally decided at 6.30 in the morning that I had to take some action. I ordered my tanks to attack the 6th Airborne Division which had entrenched itself in a bridgehead over the Orne. To me this constituted the most immediate threat to the German position.

'Hardly had I made this decision when at 7 o'clock I received my first intimation that a higher command did still exist. I was told by Army

'At dawn I went to the little village of Tracy, where happily, nobody had been killed during the night, and I went along to the top of the cliff. The cliff itself was mined so I couldn't go right up to the edge but I climbed on to the top of a wall – there I saw a sight on the sea that has remained part of my life.'
Philippe de Bourgoing

Right: The biggest naval bombardment in history. The map shows the disposition of the Allied battleships and their principal targets

Group B that I was now under command of the Seventh Army. But I received no further orders as to my role.' Higher command, in the shape of Field-Marshal von Rundstedt, had come to the conclusion that the military situation demanded action. 'At four o'clock in the morning, three hours after I received the first reports of the invasion, I decided that these landings in Normandy had to be dealt with. I asked the Supreme Command in Berlin for authority to commit these two divisions into the battle.

'Although Panzer Lehr and the 12th S.S. Panzer Divisions were under my command, I could not move them until I had received permission from Berlin. Berlin replied that it was still uncertain as to whether or not these first assaults were the main Allied efforts or merely a diversion.'

At LXXXIV Corps H.Q. at St Lô, the development of the invasion was being plotted.

'The location of the landing north of the Carentan estuary could be fixed exactly. This was in the sector of the 919th Infantry Regiment . . . Strongpoint 5 was the first to be in immediate contact with the enemy . . . the garrison of which got buried and had to be dug out by the Americans . . . The minutes dragged by. Nerves were tense. One individual report followed another; they confirmed or contradicted each other. Army or Army Group H.Q. were constantly telephoning. But all the Corps staff could do was to wait, wait, wait until the confused overall picture had been clarified, until the main centres of the dropping and landing zones had become apparent, until we had heard from strongpoints either encircled by the enemy or by-passed by him, or until reconnaissance thrusts had brought in important statements by prisoners. What complicated matters was that all reports came from the Army exclusively. Support from our own air force was non-existent from the very first minute. That was why the facts as they became apparent did not add up to a fixed overall picture.'

'I was at Quinéville when the invasion started,' a German corporal later recalled for the benefit of B.B.C. listeners. 'The number of ships, aircraft, and tanks thrown in against us defies any description. The guns of the Allied warships pulverized one position after another. Planes overhead reported on the accuracy of the guns, quite undisturbed, and with uncanny precision. Every moment we expected our own fighters to appear. The whole sky was darkened by planes, but they were Marauders, Typhoons, Liberators, Flying Fortresses and Mustangs, attacking our posts, our machine-gun nests and artillery positions with their bombs and guns. As far as I could see, there was no anti-aircraft fire with the exception of a few two-centimetre rifles.'

The Allies were achieving an astonishing feat of tactical surprise. 'I was the wireless operator on night duty from 1900, 5 June, to 0700, 6 June,' recalled the then corporal T. W. Hausdorfer of the Luftwaffe Signal Corps. 'Our radar installation was some miles south-west of Rennes (Brittany) and I had to listen in to the whole company wavelength all over Brittany. At times this could be very boring through non-action, so sometimes I used the spare communication set to listen in on the wavelength of our sister company in Normandy. In the early morning hours I seemed to get some weird Q groups (signals which, translated, gave us certain events in certain sectors). Amongst many others about hundreds of planes, came "Battleships, cruisers, etc. off the coast", "shelling" and the one which opened my eyes to events, "tank battle in Bayeux". All of a sudden, I realized that the invasion must have started.

'But in our sector everything was quiet and peaceful. The question was – what to do, as it was against regulations to listen to any other wavelength than your own? So at 0630 our Company Commander came in to ask for the latest report which I gave him "Nothing to report but . . ." and he said, "But?" So I had to tell him the truth, that I had listened in to the wavelength and believed, according to my Q groups, the invasion had started. After a severe ticking off by him, he got interested in what I had taken down on scrap paper about the events.

'After he studied it he went to the phone to contact regimental headquarters in Rennes and enquired after the position. For a while he listened quietly, and then all of a sudden he blew his top at

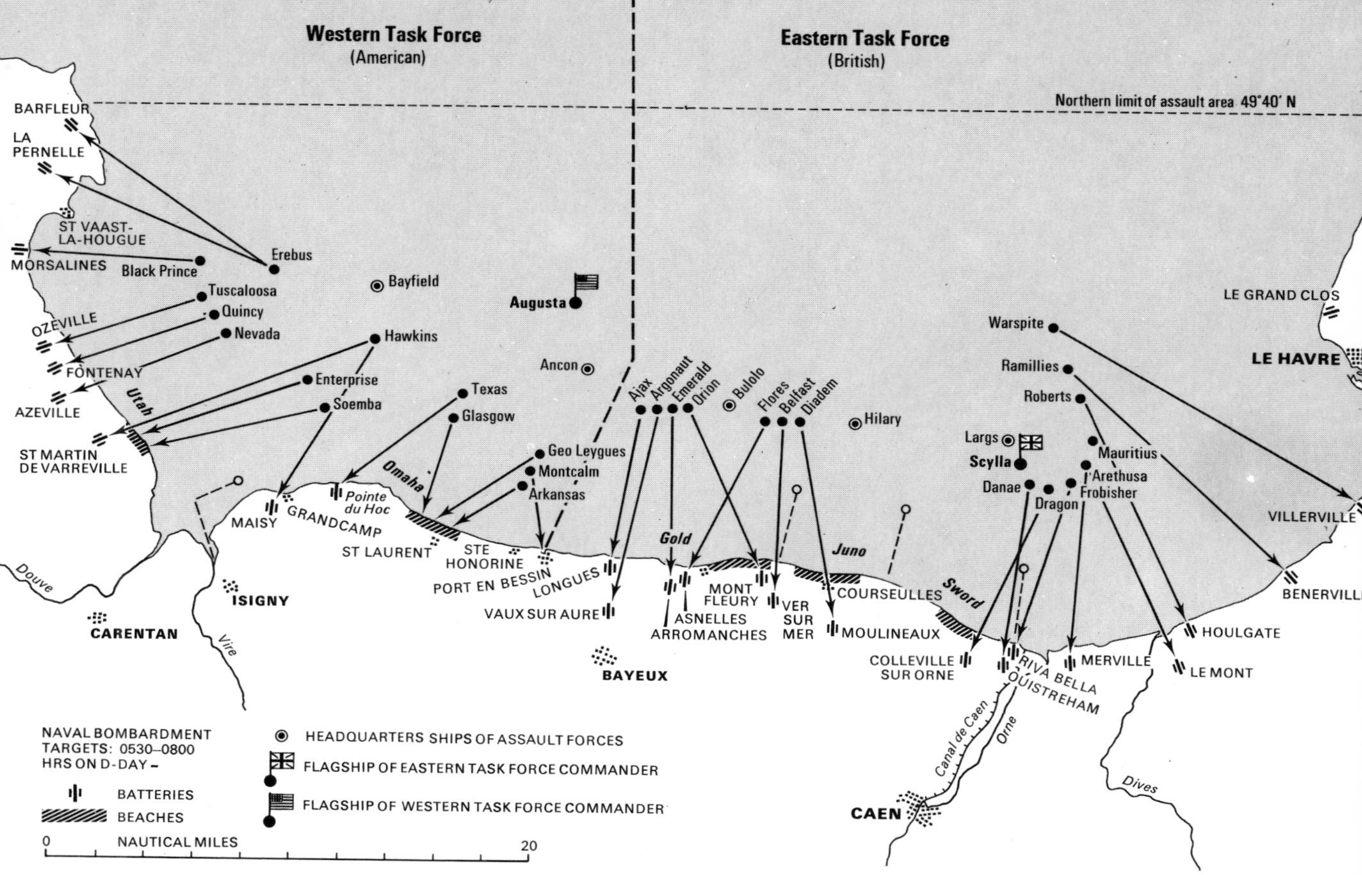

the person on the other end of the telephone and said in no uncertain tone: "I suppose if my wireless operator had not listened in, you would have waited till the Yankees nabbed us, still in slippers and pyjamas, and then told us about the invasion." '

The bombardment squadrons were forming up at sea. Captain Parham stood on the bridge of H.M.S. *Belfast*. 'H.M.S. *Belfast* led the bombarding squadron into the pre-arranged position. I remember very well it had been a difficult passage down, where we were almost continually under helm dodging the small craft carrying the soldiers in. At about 0530 we were one of the first warships to fire on our target battery.'

It was the same story across the long front. 'At four o'clock this morning we had gone to surface action stations,' recorded Ian Michie in H.M.S. *Orion*. 'Those on the flag deck reported that targets inland were getting a very heavy battering from the R.A.F. We were then moving slowly down the swept channel towards our bombardment position. The Commander reported that the sweepers had made a much wider channel than was expected and we'd have room to manoeuvre (audible sighs of relief!).

'At 0510 *Orion* was the first cruiser to open fire. Good old *Orion* – always first there! Our shooting was very good and direct hits were soon being recorded. We scored thirteen direct hits on the battery before shifting target. The other cruisers were all ripping away – *Belfast* was firing tracer.'

On the eastern flank of Omaha beach the American battleships were preparing to open up. 'During the final approach radar was used and all prominent landmarks could be readily identified and the ship's position accurately fixed. The shoreline stood out on the screen exactly as presented on the charts. At no time during the approach was the Q H or radar jammed. By 0300 all ships of the bombardment group were in position to commence the pre H-Hour bombardment, H-Hour being at 0630. At 0530 the *Texas* opened fire on the Pointe-du-Hoc according to schedule. It is believed that not one of the six guns in this battery returned the fire.'

Across the bay in front of Utah beach, 'enemy fire began somewhat early, though not as early as expected, the first flashes being seen at 0530'. The official report continues, 'Upon coming under fire, several ships requested permission to return fire. Permission was withheld, however, as ships were not seriously endangered and it was desired to wait until the plan could be placed in effect as a whole with all ships having plane spotters. *Black Prince* was narrowly missed many times by the larger batteries, the closest fire apparently coming from battery no. 8, which had not been fired upon in the belief that it would be unable to bear on ships in the assault area. *Tuscaloosa* and *Quincy* were also taken under fire and received close misses from time to time.'

Below: One of the flotilla of German torpedo boats which set out at dawn from Le Havre with orders to stop the invasion. After sinking one Allied destroyer, they were driven off by H.M.S. *Warspite*, so ending the only serious German attempt at interfering with the seaborne landings

Right: Air cover above Utah beach. Waves of Allied bombers fly over landing craft heading for the shore

Far right: The big guns speak. Inside a British battleship's 15-in. turret. Orders ring out above the din from the commander, his head protected by anti-flash gear

Opposite below: H.M.S. *Warspite* sends ashore a salvo of 15-in. 'bricks'

One ship at least was having trouble raising any response from her targets. The official report from H.M.S. *Frobisher*, a British cruiser off Sword beach, reads, 'No communication could be established with the spotting aircraft. A most regrettable thing in which the bombarding force were not alone. However, we had the great advantage of being able to see our target and fire was opened upon it at 0547.

'Up to this hour there had been no sign of life from Ouistreham One Battery nor, as far as I am aware, did it ever open fire. Whether there was any life left in it after its aerial bombardment or whether it was playing possum and waiting for H-Hour and whether the ship's fire thwarted that purpose we shall never know.' It was later established that her target was a dummy battery!

David Divine, a naval war correspondent, who was in an L.C.T. carrying A.V.R.E.s, saw this Norwegian destroyer 'fished' – 'We went through and under the battleship fire and passed the *Svenner* which had been struck amidships and went down like a V . . . we actually passed her when the men were still jumping off. We had no loss going in – a number of ships were damaged, but on the whole minor damage, the sea was roughly half-tide when we went in but we had a gap and we went through that gap so that our first tank was the first ashore. She went up shortly after that on a mine, the next tank managed to wriggle round her and went up right across the beach and got over the sea wall. I think we then landed two Bangalore torpedo tanks and two armoured bulldozers . . . and that was our load.'

Overture to H-Hour

The British battleship *Warspite* was already engaging the Villerville battery when it tackled the only serious German naval attempt to interfere with the landings. At 0600 hours three enemy warships, which were assumed to be destroyers, were seen approaching from Le Havre. They were rapidly engaged by the *Warspite* sinking one before they were driven off. The Villerville battery was neutralized with three direct hits which were accurately spotted by the aircraft. The accuracy and effectiveness of the naval gunfire was largely due to the efficient spotting by the R.A.F. planes flying up and down observing the beachhead. Wing Commander L. C. Glover, a fighter reconnaissance pilot with No. 26 Squadron R.A.F., directed the ship's gunfire on to the targets.

'I arrived over the beachhead at H-Hour for the first of five sorties on D-Day. We were flying Spitfires Mk 5 in pairs and speaking by R.T. directly with the gunnery officers aboard the ships. The fireworks display which ensued as every craft opened up, viewed from 10,000 feet in the dawn

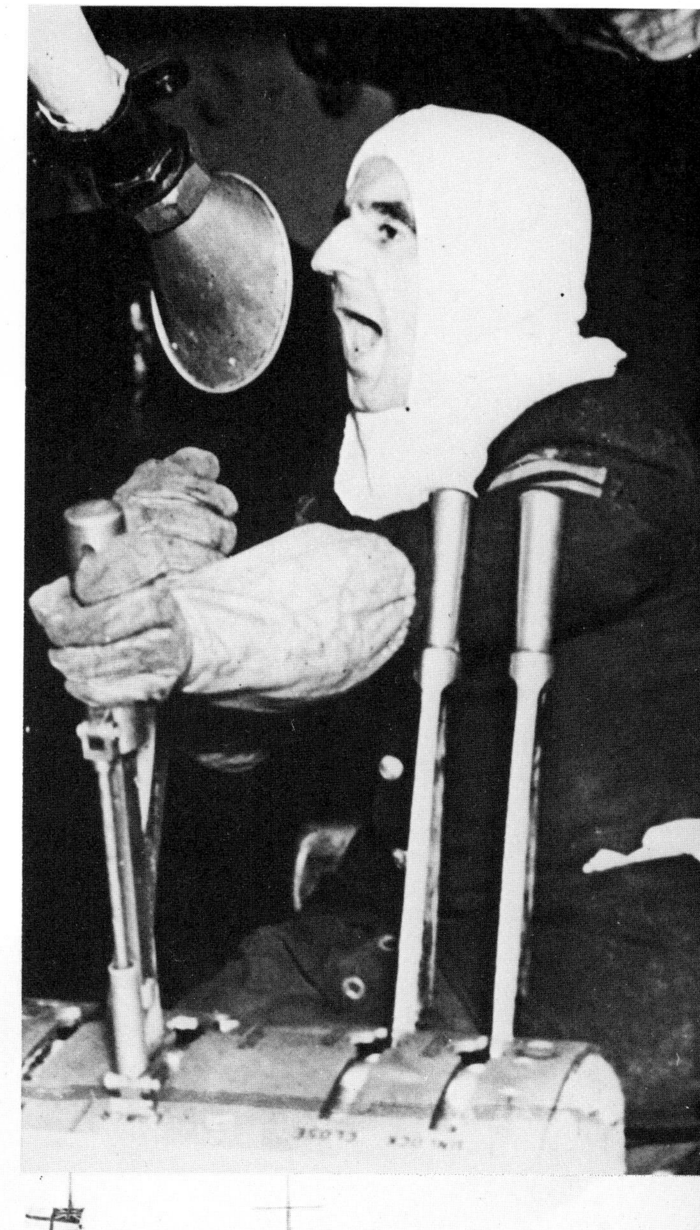

light, is something I shall never forget.

'The battleships, with armaments ranging from 14- to 16-inch guns, were lying about twenty miles off-shore so the shells had quite a high trajectory and a 15- to 20-second time of flight. On one occasion when firing with H.M.S. *Warspite* (15-inch guns) and flying midway between the ship and the beachhead at between 9,000 and 10,000 feet, I gave the order "fire" and turned slowly broadside on to the shore to wait for the fall of shot. Suddenly, in the clear sky my aircraft experienced a most violent bump which practically shook me out of my wits. At the same moment, I saw two enormous objects moving rapidly away from me towards the shore and immediately realized that I had flown at right angles through the slipstream of *Warspite*'s two ranging 15-inch "bricks". Awestruck, I followed the shells down quite easily with my eyes during the rest of their curved flight and saw one of them actually hit the gun emplacement we were engaging! Not only that, the German gun was blasted out of the rear of the emplacement.

'I think my report of the fall of shot to *Warspite* was a little incoherent but I did manage to assure them that no further "fire for effect" was needed and after congratulations all round, we switched to another target . . . we had one or two inexplicable losses during those weeks which we finally had to attribute to pilots being hit by their "own" shells.'

The crescendo of the bombardment was moving to its terrible climax on the beaches, whilst back at the Operations Room at Southwick Park the long night of waiting was nearly over. As the seconds ticked away to H-Hour, the actual moment of the first landing, the plot showed a cluster of markers lined up against the outline of the Normandy coast.

'There was certainly some talk. It was not hushed like a church or anything like that,' remembered Mrs Fanny Hughill. 'People were behaving completely naturally. After all, we had been exercising in this room for months and so we were quite at home with the situation. The atmosphere was tense, certainly, but everyone was very confident and very friendly. I don't think any one of us dreamed that things could go badly wrong now.'

In the grounds of Southwick House, Eisenhower's aide stirred himself from sleep, 'At H-Hour, by coincidence, I was awake, that being 6.40, and was contemplating the underside of the drab tent roof, wondering how come such a quiet night in contrast with other D-nights when this was supposed to be the biggest and most super-duper of all . . . I tiptoed down the cinder path to Ike's circus wagon to see if he was asleep and saw him silhouetted in bed behind a Western. Ike grinned as he lit a cigarette. I was almost the first with good news, but Admiral Ramsay was just on the phone, telling him things seemed to be going by plan and he had no bad news at all.'

The long run in

Across the choppy waters of the Channel the thousands of men who had to be 'up front' were in the last stages of making ready for their ordeal. Those fortunate enough to be in the larger troopships had the chance of a hearty breakfast. Most preferred seasick pills. One who didn't was Sergeant Reg Cole, 'I remember that breakfast on the *Clan Lamont* was really first class. We had pork chops and a choice of stewed prunes, apricots or fresh fruit. A lot of the men couldn't face it but one had

Left: Operations Room at Southwick House on D-Day, recorded by official war artist, Barnett Friedmann. The deciphered signals bringing news of the landings arrived along the scaffolding-like transport apparatus on the left wall; they were distributed from the tables at the left, and the information transferred to the plotting tables on the right and the large map on the end wall. This historic map was preserved after the invasion at Admiral Ramsay's express wish. Today it is still in place (below), in what has now become the officers' mess of H.M.S. *Dryad* at Southwick House. It is set out exactly as it was at H-Hour, the moment the first troops came ashore

Overleaf: Going in. Allied troops in the last quiet moments before they face enemy fire on the beaches

to be sensible about this – you didn't know when you were going to eat again.'

They all had the same feeling in the pit of their stomachs. Those on the larger troopships had to pay for their comfortable crossing with a hazardous drop down chutes and scramble nets into the landing craft that would take them on the final stage of what was for many the most significant journey of their lives. 'We were lucky,' remembers Reg Cole, 'We were able to get into our landing craft on the davits. The little assault craft were on davits and were lowered like lifeboats. But it was a big bump when they hit the water.'

'We were supposed to be going down a Jacob's Ladder, but it was so rough that one moment the craft was 10 feet above you and the next right down below so we went down a scramble net.

'It was dangerous, you had to watch it. You had to catch the craft as it was going down and drop into it. One of our chaps didn't and the boat caught him and the force broke both his ankles. There was nothing we could do about it. We had to take him in to the beach even though he was wounded.'

'No one remembers the date of the Battle of Shiloh. But the day we took Fox Green Beach was 6 June, and the wind was blowing hard out of the north-west. As we moved in toward land in the grey early light, the thirty-six-foot coffin-shaped steel boat took solid green sheets of water that fell on the helmeted heads of the troops packed shoulder to shoulder in the stiff, awkward, uncomfortable, lonely companionship of men going to battle.'

Ernest Hemingway

' "What are you waiting for?"

' "There are still five minutes to go before H plus 90," the Captain, a young R.N.V.R. officer, replies.

' "I don't think anyone will mind if we're five minutes early on D-Day."

' "Then in we go."

'Another shellburst almost overhead. This time a splinter hits the front of my jacket. Someone ducks and his helmet clangs on the deck. Another flash from in front of Ouistreham. This time the next craft is the target – a near miss, or a hit, maybe. The craft shies like a horse. Our craft is to port of the rest, which somehow makes us feel more exposed.'

Storm from the Sea, Lt-Col. Peter Young

'*Hedgehogs, stakes or tetrahedra will not prevent your beaching provided you go flat out.* Your craft will crunch over them, bend them and squash them into the sand and the damage to your outer bottom can be accepted. So drive on.

'Element C, however, is an obstacle to Mark V L.C.T. though Mark IV and III – at emergency full speed – can bend them and pass partially over them.

'Therefore, avoid *Element C* if you can. If you cannot, try and hit it a glancing blow, preferably near the end of a "bay". This will probably turn it, or drive its supports into the sand. A second blow may enable you to squeeze through or past it.

'Do not worry too much about how you are to get out again. The first and primary object is to get in and land without drowning the vehicles.'

Official rules for guidance

'I remember my motor launch was out amongst this immense throng of craft plunging through heavy seas to the beaches. On one of the landing craft it looked as though something had gone wrong with the rudder because one of the seamen was hanging over the stern in the water steering it with his feet.'

Lt-Comm. Stanbury

'We really had been briefed pretty well to know where we should be from the photographs of the coast. But unfortunately when we were out there looking at all those churches and spires they all looked the same. As we closed in we got into a terrible argument. Some said it was this church, some said it was that. To add to the confusion, the heavy seas meant that people who should have been in front were behind and we ourselves were twenty minutes late.'

A sapper going to Juno beach

'I don't think any of us realized the danger we were in. Nobody ever went to Normandy to die; they went to fight and win a war. I don't think any man that died thought that it was him that was going to be killed. In my opinion, the reason we stormed Normandy like we did was because the soldiers would rather have fought the whole German Army than go back on the ships and be as seasick as they were going over. My God! Those soldiers couldn't wait to get on dry land. Nothing would have got in their way . . . they would have torn tanks to pieces with their bare hands.'

R. McKinley, R.N. Commando

Utah
0630

NAVSITREP 1
TO NAVAL COMMANDER WESTERN TASK FORCE

FORCE U ARRIVED TRANSPORT AREA WITHOUT INCIDENT   COMPLETE SURPRISE ACHIEVED   NO ENEMY ATTACK   FIRST WAVE DESPATCHED TO BEACH AS SCHEDULED

Hitting the beach. The first wave on Utah. In a dramatic aerial photograph, taken minutes after the assault, L.C.T.s are churning the water as troops and the smaller craft push through the surf. At the top of the beach, men are lying prone in the sand, sheltering from German fire coming from the dunes

'Then we all spied it. A red glow lighted the western horizon. Silhouetted by this light was the unmistakable outline of low-lying land. It flashed through my mind that this indelible picture was identical with the silhouettes pasted on the walls of the "Bigot" room, where we studied the intelligence reports describing Utah beach.
'The U.S.S. *Bayfield*, flying our Admiral's two-star flag, had anchored and swung to the gentle breeze. Already her L.C.A.s were lowered away . . . The *Bayfield* marked the transport area. That would be thirteen miles from the beach, and in mineswept waters leading to the boat lanes. At the head of the boat lanes and about four miles seaward from the beach would be the control vessels which would start the assault waves on the scheduled race for glory and victory – or defeat and indescribable slaughter.'
Commodore James Arnold, N.O.I.Y. Utah

This stark message signalled the very first of the D-Day assaults. The easterly movement of the tide in the Channel dictated the priority of the Allied landings. Utah, as the most westerly of the beaches, had H-Hour at 0630 hours. The time was finely calculated to allow the advance demolition teams to deal with the beach obstacles before they were covered by the rising tide.

That Admiral Moon's Force U had arrived 'without incident' was a masterpiece of official understatement. The real drama was more clearly revealed in his own report: 'Force U was the last force to be formed. The craft assigned to it were the last to arrive in England. Arrivals from the Mediterranean, United States and other parts of the United Nations continued up to within a day or two of loading day. In many cases these craft had practically no training.'

That the whole force arrived intact at the lowering points off the Cotentin peninsula on time, was close to a miracle. Constant seasickness during the days at sea had become an unpleasant fact of life for most of the men. Dawn, and sight of land, brought the first prospect of relief – even though it was a hostile shore.

No one saw the sun rise that morning just two minutes before 0600 hours. Heavy cloud and drifting smoke-screens blocked out any cheer it might have given as the long lines of landing craft struggled into formation for the assault waves. A spanking 18-knot breeze blew off the shore, whipping the heavy current into an ugly four-foot sea. It was a miserable, grey experience for the weary troops, only lifted by the mounting crescendo of gunfire through the ninety minutes of the run into the beach.

Commodore James C. Arnold, U.S.N.R. was on an L.S.I. 'For the next half-hour the low-lying coast of France seemed to leap into the air in a sheet of jagged flame and thunder, nor did it settle back until the last bomb bays were emptied by those welcome harbingers of courage to sailor men.

'Meanwhile we headed for the starting line to check the positions of the control ships. Just before we jockeyed into position, a terrific explosion a few hundred yards to starboard rocked our L.C.I. It was the L.C.T. 707. She had hit a mine full and bye, turning her completely over. Then all seemed to cut loose. German shore batteries recovering from the shock of surprise were returning the slugging salvos of the naval fire-support ships, raising great gouts of water as they plumbed for the correct range.'

Admiral Moon, from the bridge of his headquarters, U.S.S. *Bayfield*, followed through binoculars the slow progress of the assault craft on to the beaches. He knew that the journey would be a long one, made far worse by the heavy running sea. The American naval commander, Admiral Kirk, had rejected Admiral Ramsay's advice that the transports should be brought at least eight miles inshore before the launching of the assault. Caution for his ships in the face of German battery fire, and the American need to emphasize their independent command, had decided that American forces would be launched nearly eleven and a half miles out at sea. Deprived of any sheltered water, the soldiers would once again suffer. The rough seas prolonged their agony. Anti-seasick pills gave little relief to the miserable troops. They found their supplies of brown vomit bags more appropriate. Naval doctors later reported that the results of the anti-nausea pills were 'unconvincing'.

Some landing craft started their final trip so far out to sea that their coxswains could not even see the shoreline until they had gone half-way.

Drenching bombardment

To the north a German battery gave some anxious moments in the early stages of the landings, and a grim reminder of what the Atlantic Wall might have been. Fortunately, most of the fortifications were nothing like as impressive. An official report stated: 'A detailed study of the strongpoint in the back of the original Green beach section of the Utah area indicates that this strongpoint is probably typical of those which the Germans have installed along the coast of France.'

In spite of the massive air attack very few of these fortified positions suffered serious damage. Hitler's designs withstood the Allied bombs remarkably well. As an official report noted: 'the large air effort

la Madeleine
Grande Dune

Far left: Wading ashore. G.I.s of the 4th U.S. Division leaving a landing craft on the beach near Les Dunes de Madeleine

Left: Fire support. The battleship U.S.S. *Nevada* firing her big guns during the landings at Utah

Below: Good fortune at Utah. An accidental error in the landing site brought the troops in at a weak spot in the German defences. The low featureless coastline is clearly shown in this photograph. A corresponding detail of the Utah landing map (inset) shows how the defences and obstacles thin out at La Madeleine (for key, see p. 69)

For some Americans it might have been any one of a dozen beaches in the state of Maine back home. At low water, the sandy beach sloped gently up for 400 yards to sand dunes and beach grass. A low concrete wall had been constructed by the Germans facing the sea. The shallows had been planted with long lines of obstacles, stakes and mines. Behind the dunes the meadowland had been flooded for several miles, almost to the nearest village at Varraville.

The teeth of the Atlantic Wall on Utah sector consisted of twenty-eight powerful batteries strung out for miles along the dunes, interspersed with a variety of concrete pillboxes and infantry emplacements. In all some hundred guns could be concentrated on the sector, ranging from 75-mm. guns to the 170-mm. guns of the naval battery at St Vaast-la-Hougue.

The First Wave

of the night before the assault failed to destroy or seriously damage the coast batteries as a group.'

It was left to the bombarding vessels to bring their more accurate fire to bear. 'All available information indicates that the pre-H-Hour aerial and naval bombardment of the assault beaches, while causing no serious damage either to the concrete structures or the guns in the strongpoints behind and adjacent to these beaches, effectively neutralized the positions by terrifying the enemy personnel in them and by preventing them from manning their weapons and firing on the troops during the landings. Before the personnel in these strongpoints could recover sufficiently, our troops were able to use flame-throwers and machine-gunfire against them and to capture the positions with little opposition. It is believed that the reportedly low calibre and morale of the enemy defenders also contributed to the quick capture of these strongpoints.'

It was several hours before the assault waves could neutralize the positions, and some of the batteries proved surprisingly effective in the lulls between the drenching bombardment from sea and air. The destroyer U.S.S. *Corry*, dodging their shellfire, hit a mine and sank. One of the Patrol Craft which had the vital role of guiding the assault waves into the right landing sector, came under heavy and accurate fire:

'At about 0555, while about 7,000–8,000 yards from the beach (about 10–15 minutes behind schedule), P.C. 1261 was hit. She was observed about 30 degrees off-course to starboard, mainmast down and dead in the water. Men could be seen going over the side. Witnesses state she had swung violently to starboard when hit, and that no extensive amount of gunfire was observed. A few shells were falling in the water before and after the hit and it appeared to have been either a chance shell hit or a mine. Later disclosure of a minefield in that area and the way in which 1261 acted after the hit indicated a contact mine on her port bow.

'Shortly thereafter, an L.C.T. directly astern of P.C. 1176 was hit. It also appeared to have been mined, since the entire force of the explosive seemed to go up with little side-effect. The L.C.T. sank almost immediately.'

Breaking through the coast. Far left: Troops of the 8th Infantry Regiment, after a 'breather' in the shelter of the sea-wall, go over the top to push through the sand dunes as (left) waves of follow-up assaults stream ashore
Below: The lucky ones don't even get their feet wet

The loss of the vessel guiding the assault craft in, together with the heavy current sweeping across the landing area, meant that as the leading landing craft approached the shoreline they were, by now, some thousand yards further south of the scheduled landing spots. Had they landed further north in the appointed place they would have faced much stronger German defences.

What could have been more serious was the loss of the L.C.T. carrying four of the D.D. tanks whose job was to clear the beach for the first assault. At the last moment, the surviving L.C.T.s were ordered to close the shore. The calmer water helped the clumsy D.D. tanks. Minutes after the demolition parties waded ashore, all twenty-eight of the surviving Shermans pushed up the beach to bring their fire-power to bear on startled German positions.

Goliath meets David

In minutes, the weight of the assault had all but overwhelmed parts of the defences. In a last desperate attempt to stem the headlong rush, Section Commanders gave the order to release one of Hitler's secret weapons. Americans were half-amused to see squat miniature tanks crawling out off the dunes towards them. Controlled by wires and packed with high explosive, they were intended to tackle full-sized tanks and beached landing craft. These mobile mines were nicknamed 'Goliaths' by cynical German soldiery. On D-Day they were to prove as ineffective as they had on the Russian front.

As the second and third waves began their journey to the shore, Admiral Moon could see that the landings were going ahead with an almost textbook precision.

The official report of the 8th Infantry Regiment underlines the success of the Utah assault in its crispest military detail: 'Approximately half an hour before H-Hour, the first assault waves of the 1st and 2nd Bns rendezvoused and started toward the beach to predetermined points of landing, which were then in the process of being cleared of underwater obstacles by specially trained Navy personnel . . . It was smooth, perfectly co-ordinated

Aftermath of assault. Medics give first aid in the lee of Les Dunes de Madeleine and (right) other landing parties dig into the soft sand of the beach. Below: By late morning, the U.S. 4th Division was moving off the beach and advancing inland

and magnificent . . . Heavy naval fire continued to destroy enemy fortifications and pin down enemy on the beach until just before the landing by the assault troops . . . Although the Navy had previously laid down a heavy barrage which reduced many emplacements on and commanding the beach, many still remained in operation by virtue of deep solid construction.

Not according to the book

Commodore James Arnold, who was to be the naval officer in charge of the beachhead, wrote, 'As the ramp lowered, I was shoved forward up to my knapsack in cold, oily water.

'German 88s were pounding the beachhead. Two U.S. tanks were drawn up at the high-water line pumping them back into the Jerries. I tried to run to get into the lee of these tanks. I realize now why the infantry likes to have tanks along in a skirmish. They offer a world of security to a man in open terrain who may have a terribly empty sensation in his guts. But my attempt to run was only momentary. Three feet of water is a real deterrent to rapid locomotion of the legs. As I stumbled into a runnel, Kare picked me up. A little soldier following grabbed my other arm. Just for a moment he hung on. Then he dropped, blood spurting from a jagged hole torn by a sniper's bullet.'

Brigadier General Theodore Roosevelt Jnr was the hero of Utah beach. A battle-hardened veteran of fifty-seven, he was really far too old to be anywhere near a beach assault, but as former President 'Teddy' Roosevelt's son, he was determined not to miss the action. He had talked his Divisional Commander into letting him go ashore 'to steady the boys' – and it was just as well he did. Not only did he direct and inspire the assault, pacing up and down the beach with his walking-stick – oblivious of the German fire coming from the right flank – but he decided what action should be taken when it was realized that they were a mile away from their correct landing sites.

Sizing up the situation, 'Teddy' Roosevelt was in no doubt that they should go ahead, where they were, rather than attempt to push up on the right flank into the enfilading fire. It would be two hours before the General was proved right. A rapid move inland exploited the easy landings and deepened the beachhead for the assault waves piling up in the shallows. The only problem facing the General was how to re-direct traffic away from the Red-beach sector now under fire. He soon solved that, with the assistance of the N.O.I.C. – Commodore James Arnold – who was sheltering in a beach foxhole:

'An army officer wearing the single star of a Brigadier jumped into my "headquarters" to duck the blast of an 88.

' "Sonsabuzzards," he muttered, as we untangled sufficiently to look at each other. "I'm Teddy Roosevelt. You're Arnold of the Navy. I remember you at the briefing at Plymouth. If you have any authority here, I wish you would stop bringing in my troops down on Red beach. They're being slaughtered. Navy ought to know better than send them into that sector where the darn' Krauts have them bracketed."

'I had in mind to explain to him that N.O.I.C. Utah was not supposed to function until the assault phase was over. Looking at his grim eyes, however, I decided against this procedure.

' "Seems to me, General, there was something in the Plan about your soldiers neutralizing this Kraut artillery. But wait a moment " – I could almost feel the blast he was about to erupt – "I'll shift the unloading from the Red sector over to the Green beach area." "How?" he demanded.

' "By the simple expedient of alerting the Navy beach battalion on Red beach to send the incoming craft over to the Green beach area. I'll station a ship off a couple of hundred yards and divert them. Somebody's going to raise hell because it isn't according to the book, but I have to agree there's no use landing dead men down in that suicide area. Meantime, General, suppose you alert your outfit to change the staging area, or post guides to direct the incoming troops to wherever you want them stage after they land."

'Before he could argue, we were on our way to execute the idea. It was remarkably successful, too, until German spotters finally notified their bat-

teries to shift their fire over to Green beach. That was some three hours later.'

By that time, late in the morning, the troops were fanning out, securing a broad stretch of beach and pushing inland along the weakly defended southern causeway. The road was opening up to relieve the hard-pressed airborne troops of the 101st at Ste Mère-Église.

NAVSITREP 5 summed up the success of that morning's operations at Utah. Incredibly, only forty-three Americans had been killed, and sixty-three wounded.

ALTHOUGH PRIMARY AND SECONDARY CONTROL VESSELS SUNK NORTHERN LIMIT OF ASSAULT BEACH IS ONLY 1000 YARDS SOUTH OF NORTHERN LIMIT AS PLANNED X AND HAS ADDED ADVANTAGE OF FEWER OBSTACLES X HEAVY SHELLING OF BOTH BEACHES HAS COST INCREASING CASUALTIES IN PERSONNEL AND EQUIPMENT X ALTHOUGH THREE ROADS ARE OPEN ACROSS INUNDATED AREA AND VEHICLES ARE MOVING INLAND PROGRESS IS SLOW X CONTINUED BOMBARDMENT WITH ADEQUATE AIRSPOT OF ENEMY IS ESSENTIAL IF BEACHES ARE TO BE PROTECTED AND EARLY ADVANTAGES MAINTAINED

But the Germans were now wide awake.

Omaha
0630

Brink of Disaster

'At approximately 0345 hours the 2nd Battalion and the 3rd Battalion debarked from the U.S.S. *Henrico* and H.M.S. *Empire Anvil* respectively to assault beach Omaha, north of Colleville-sur-Mer, Normandy, France, at 0630 hours. Heavy seas, numerous underwater obstacles and intense enemy fire destroyed many craft and caused high casualties before the assault battalions reached shore. Most supporting weapons, including D.D. tanks, were swamped. The 2nd Battalion, landed 100 yards to 1,000 yards from its scheduled points, was pinned down on the beach by extremely heavy fire from concrete fortifications, machine-gun emplacements and sniper nests which remained intact through severe naval and air bombardment. Casualties were extremely high.'

This was the story of Omaha – written with cold military efficiency in one small part of the U.S. 16th Infantry Regiment's Report. If the Utah landing was a text-book success, then the Americans paid a savage penalty on their other D-Day beachheads. It was almost a disaster. Rough seas, combined with exceptionally strong German opposition, almost gave Rommel the success he had promised the Führer. At Omaha the Germans came very near to 'throwing the Allies into the sea'.

The first phase of the assault, the preparation for the run into the beaches and the embarkation of the troops, went tolerably well in the adverse weather conditions. The Omaha transportation area was more exposed than Utah, and the water rougher. H-Hour had been set for 0630 hours – one hour after low water.

The operational orders detailed with minute precision how the leading wave of landing craft carrying eight battalions would touch down at 0630. Precisely two minutes later, fourteen frogman underwater demolition teams would set to work blowing a path through the extensive obstacles for the following landing craft to reach the shore. This they were expected to complete in half an hour; then the second wave was scheduled to arrive. Then waves of new assaults would come in at intervals of ten minutes until 0930 hours. The whole landing was to be carried out on a four-mile front seaward of the little villages of Vierville in the west

Previous pages: The narrow strip of sand was littered with obstacles and mines, and covered by fire from pillboxes and strongpoints on the high bluffs. Lacking the support of specialized armour, the troops soon found themselves pinned down under devastating fire

Opposite: 'The thin wet line of khaki that dragged itself ashore.' The grim determination of the troops of the Big Red One is summed up by Robert Capa's classic picture, taken during the first hours of the Omaha assault. Trapped between the rising tide and murderous German fire, a group of G.I.s cling for shelter and survival to hedgehog obstacles

Below: The ramps go down and the struggle to reach the shore begins

All boats came under criss-cross machine-gun fire . . . As the first men jumped, they crumpled and flopped into the water. Then order was lost. Some were hit in the water and wounded. Some drowned then and there . . . But some moved safely through the bullet fire to the sand and then, finding they could not hold there, went back into the water and used it as cover, only their heads sticking out. Those who survived kept moving forward with the tide, sheltering at times behind under-water obstacles and, in this way, they finally made their landing. 'Within ten minutes of the ramps being lowered, A Company had become . . . almost incapable of action. Every officer and sergeant had been killed or wounded . . . Within twenty minutes . . . A Company had ceased to be an assault company and had become a forlorn little rescue party bent upon survival and the saving of lives.

General Omar Bradley

'We tried desperately to find the enemy batteries causing all this. A destroyer reported receiving word that the Germans were using a church tower at Vierville as an observation post. The Admiral ordered the ship to open fire. And the first salvo scored a direct hit, knocking off the upper part of the steeple. Another salvo, and that observation post was eliminated.

'Nick Carbone, from Brooklyn, watched a great German shell skip in the water just between the *Texas* and a British cruiser. Imitating a famous American voice, Nick said, "I hate war, Eleanor hates war."

'Now, in rapid succession, our targets were: a mobile battery near Maisy, which we blew into limbo; German troop concentrations in the town of Formigny, which we scattered killing many; truck convoys centering on Trévières, which we smashed completely; and tanks converging on woods near Surrain. In all of these, our R.A.F. spotter, the daring and excitable Englishman, commended our shooting in rapturous tones.

'Finally, he said, "Now I'll try to get you in a new target. I'm diving down to see if these tanks are friendly."

'A few moments later, "They definitely were not friendly. I'm baling out, good-bye!"

'So we sent for a new spotter and kept firing on targets of opportunity from St Laurent-sur-Mer to Pointe-du-Hoc.'

Saturday Evening Post report from U.S.S. *Texas*

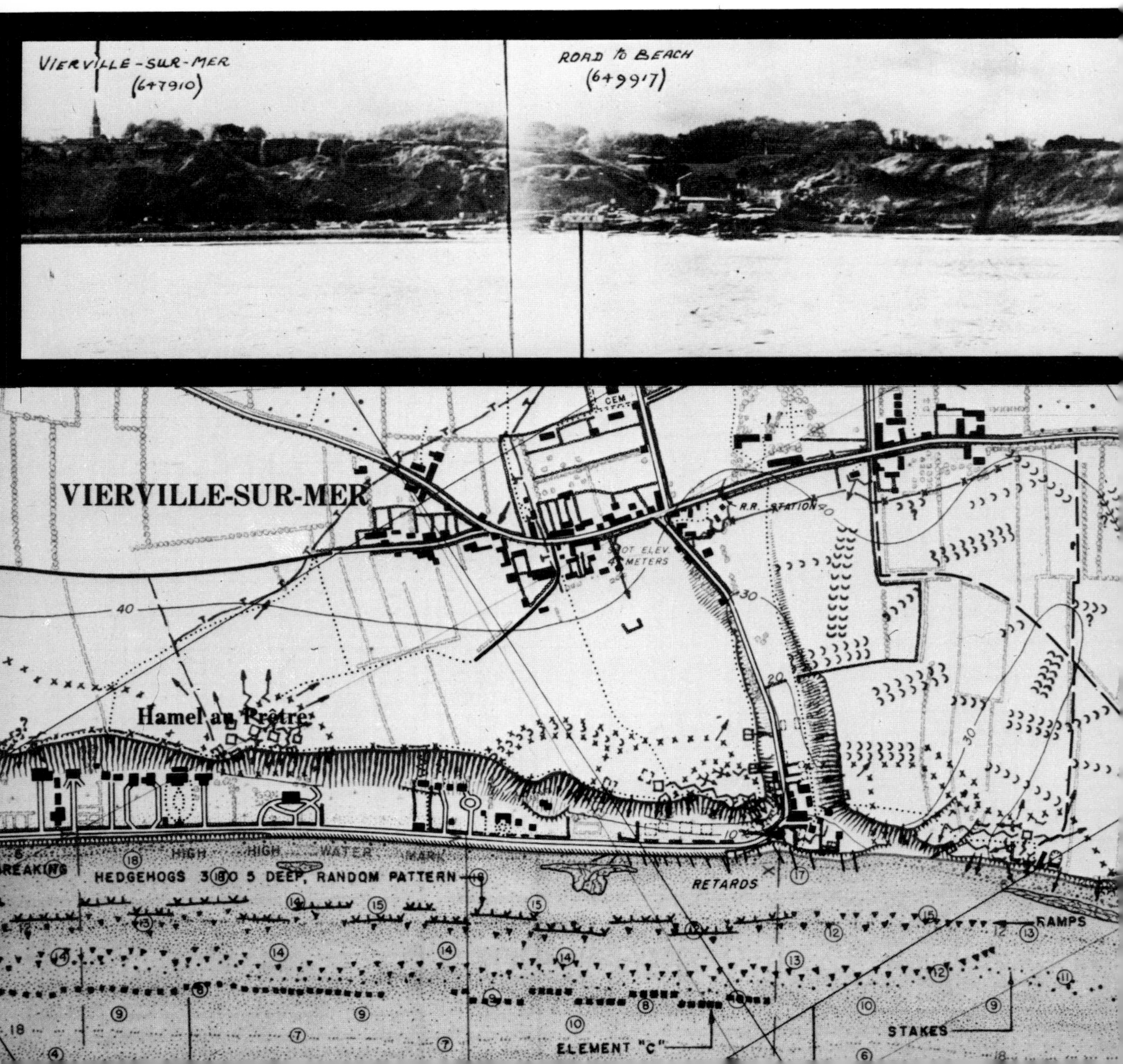

Left: The Pointe-du-Hoc battery, west of Omaha beach, under air attack from Douglas A20 bombers of the U.S. Ninth Air Force

Below: Dog sector of Omaha at Vierville. Left: Pre-invasion reconnaissance photographs show clearly the strongly defended terrain with (right) the battery at Pointe-du-Hoc. Bottom: The corresponding section of the intelligence map indicates how well Rommel had built up the defences. But Allied intelligence did not reveal in time the movement of the crack 352nd Division of German infantry into the sector

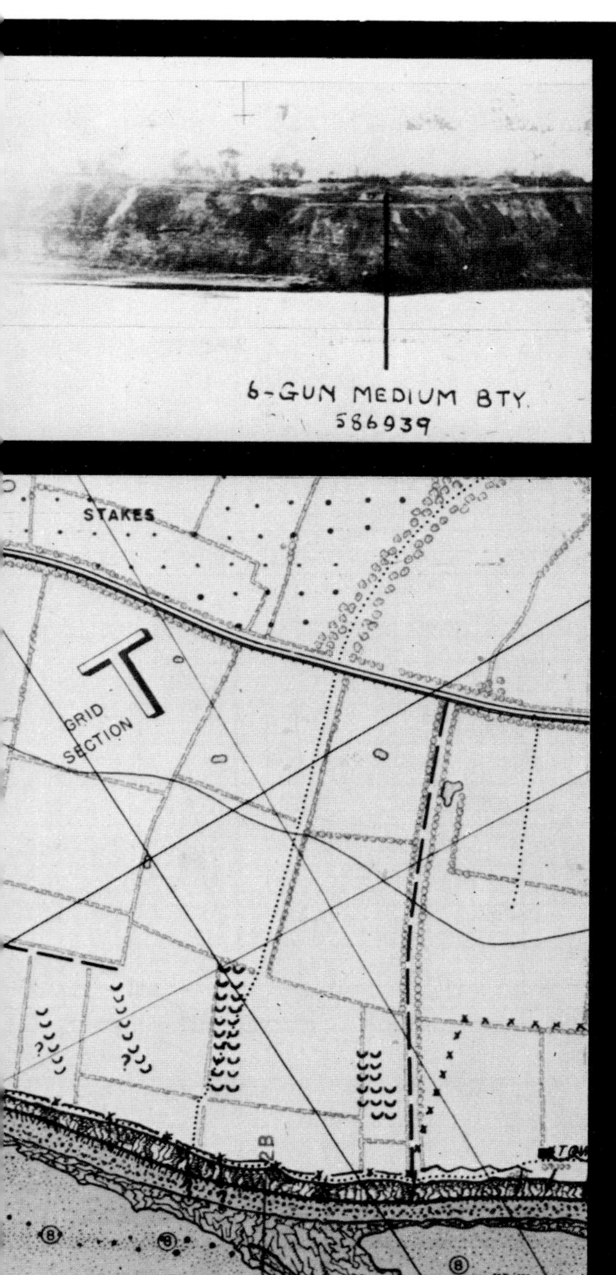

to Colleville in the east. The beaches were split up into six sectors, whose military code names would become engraved in American history: Dog Green, Dog White, Dog Red, Easy Green, Easy Red and Fox Green. The 116th Infantry Regiment was assigned to the western four. The G.I.s of the 16th Infantry Regiment, who stormed the eastern two, joked about the Easy beaches – that was before they reached Normandy on the morning of 6 June.

All units in the Omaha assault were combat-hardened troops. They had seen action in Sicily and that training had been thorough; every man knew his part in the assault plan to the nearest detail. The landing craft commanders knew to the nearest ten yards where they should put their troops ashore. Unlike Utah, the Omaha terrain of cliffs and steeply sloping bluffs was readily recognizable and all landmarks could be clearly identified from briefing photographs.

In spite of the heavy swell and inevitable seasickness, landing craft circled round the transports and U.S.S. *Ancon*, H.Q. of Force O commander, Admiral Hall. Shelling from German shore batteries was almost non-existent. It was ominously quiet.

'The enemy did not want to give away their gun positions during the pre-H-Hour bombardment,' observed one of the American official reports, 'as evidenced by our observation of only one splash from shore batteries during this phase. It was peculiar, because the fire seemed to be coming from behind the hill. Apparently, the enemy had observers either on the crest of the hill or along the slit trenches. They wasted little or no ammunition on ships out of range'.

Overhead, as the assault began its eleven-mile journey to shore, the men heard wave upon wave of heavy bombers. Many men, even among the seasick, were keyed up by the occasion. One officer remembered his troops chatting about 'what a shambles the beach would be from the bombs and ships' guns', although his own impression was 'It looked like another big tactical scheme off Slapton Sands, and I couldn't get the feeling out of my head that it was going to be another miserable two-day job with a hot shower at the end.' A mighty fleet of Eighth Air Force 329 Fortresses thundered

The rocket bombardment fell short and landing craft (below) were raked with murderous fire

towards the shore, obscured by cloud, with orders to smash the German defences. But the heavy cloud meant that the bombing was 'blind'. They did not want to blast the first waves of the morning assault. The drop was postponed by several vital seconds – and 13,000 bombs fell harmlessly into the Normandy meadows. An official assessment dryly records, 'Low ceiling on D-Day prevented beach drenching from the air.' It was not the first failure that morning.

At H minus 40 minutes the battleships U.S.S. *Texas* and *Arkansas*, with supporting cruisers and destroyers, laid down a devastating barrage of fire on beach strongpoints and enemy positions. Ineffective spotting because of low cloud and dust thrown up from the bombing meant that few of the naval broadsides landed accurately on target.

Troops bucketing through choppy green water were cheered by the sound of falling bombs, and the huge dust cloud that rose above the shore. But the impressive pyrotechnics of the rocket launching craft gave them even more cause for satisfaction.

'As we were still 10–15 minutes off-shore, the rocket ships opened up with their thousands of rockets. It certainly was an impressive and cheering sight,' recalled one member of E Company in the first wave. But the rocket craft, like the bombers, were over-cautious about hazarding their own troops, and their projectile batteries were fired too soon. 'Unfortunately, as was later seen, morale effect only was achieved by our rocket ships, for we saw no material effects of their landing – apparently most had fallen into the water.' Other waves of G.I.s would joke about the thousands of dead fish floating on the surface. This turned sour when they soon realized that their rockets had killed fish and not the Germans.

The Americans well knew that the four mile sand crescent of Omaha beach was a good defensive position. Aerial reconnaissance and Resistance reports showed how well the Germans had exploited the high cliffs at either end and the bluffs in the central section for gun emplacements which could sweep the shoreline with murderous fire. Eight big guns were located in concrete bunkers, thirty-five anti-tank guns in smaller pillboxes and eighty-five well-fortified machine-gun nests were concealed in the approaches and on the bluffs. The sandy beach was topped by a belt of shingle too steep for tanks to climb – and to this the Germans had added a concrete wall for most of the length of the beach. Even if an assault forced a landing, there were only three exits inland up narrow valleys to the coast a mile away. Not only the beach, but the exits could be carefully covered by German gunners.

All this had been discovered through intelligence received from aerial reconnaissance, beach parties, the Resistance and simple deduction. If there had been any other choice of beach, SHAEF would have avoided the sandy crescent between Vierville and Colleville. But there was not. High cliffs or rocky shallows prevented a landing being made anywhere else – so Omaha had to be taken.

It was the Americans who chose to crack this

General Bradley (left) watched from U.S.S. *Augusta* with concern the developments on Omaha. He later wrote:
'As the morning lengthened, my worries deepened ove the alarming and fragmentary reports we picked up on the Navy net. From these messages we could piece together only an incoherent account of sinkings, swampings, heavy enemy fire, and chaos on the beaches. V Corps had not yet confirmed news of the landing. We fought off our fears, attributing the delay to a jam-up in communications. It was almost 1000 before the first report came in from Gerow. Like the fragments we had already picked up, his message was laconic, neither conclusive nor reassuring. It did nothing more than confirm our worst fears on the D.D. tanks. "Obstacles, mines, progress slow . . . D.D. tanks for Fox Green swamped." '

tough nut, and General Omar Bradley had given the task to the toughest regiment of his 1st U.S. Army Division, 'The Big Red One'. Battle-hardened in the north African and Sicily campaigns, the divisional commanders reckoned they could take the beach by a massive head-on assault. Rejecting the British and Canadian experiences at Dieppe, the Americans also rejected the British armour that had been specially developed for just such an assault. Refusing the offer of large numbers of Hobart's flails, bobbins and flame-throwing vehicles, the only armour they grudgingly agreed to take was a few dozen D.D. tanks. The 'Big Red One' preferred to trust in the dash and courage of the American infantrymen in direct assault but Dieppe had shown that this was not enough.

As the landing craft came within range of the beach, the men prepared for a tough assault. They had been briefed about the defences in the minutest detail. To within fifty yards, each platoon knew what its task would be and what each man had to do once he hit the beach. They knew it would take plenty of guts to storm the bluffs that loomed through the dust and debris. But what most of the men did not know was that behind the fortifications they would be facing a front-line German infantry. Somehow Allied intelligence had missed the Wehrmachts of the 352nd Division who had been moved up from St Lô to exercise in the Omaha sector in the week just before D-Day. But until just after sailing, Allied intelligence did not realize that they were so close to the beaches. Only General Bradley and a handful of commanders were informed – the news had arrived at Plymouth just as the convoy sailed for France. It had been too late to re-brief the men and might have dented their morale on what was already a difficult assault.

Disaster at H-Hour

Precisely at H-Hour, Omaha had erupted into a frenzied inferno of flying metal and explosive – ripping into landing craft and men. The careful organization of the first wave collapsed with the scores of wounded and dying men falling in the surf. Withering German fire sliced into the demolition teams struggling to clear essential gaps in the tangled steel and concrete of the beach obstacles.

The rising tide and the short time allowed to blow gaps meant that the second wave arrived at 0700 hours to face an almost impenetrable barrier.

In the face of such strong German opposition the American infantry lacked heavy artillery fire. Enough D.D. tanks on the beach might have tipped the balance of the situation. The Force Commander had left it to the individual army commanders on the spot to determine how close the swimming tanks should be launched. It was a costly error. On one battalion front they were not launched for many hours because the water was considered too rough. Worse still on the other flank, where the German fire-power was heaviest on Easy Red, they were landed with the impossible task of swimming four miles through rough, shell-torn water. Of the twenty-nine launched, twenty-one were swamped

' "We were late in getting to the beaches. Our rope ladders got wet on the way over. We were dumped out and had to wade several hundred feet in to the beach, and all the time the Germans were firing at us from the top of the big bluff we had to storm. Some of us were shot crossing the sand to the foot of the cliff. When we climbed, the Germans shot down at us. Finally, we threw grenades at the cliff, making furrows up the side and giving us some protection.

' "Then we all went up and chased those Germans, killing a lot of them. They had left a little dog up there in a shack. He would respond to English, but he would stand up when you talked to him in German." Meccia smiled at that recollection, then his face darkened and he continued, "But that dog turned out to be a fifth columnist. He licked the wounded and annoyed them until we had to slit his throat.

' "I saw a German officer shoot one of his men in the back when he started to walk over to us with his hands up," Meccia said. "One of our guys saw a flag of surrender, and stood up to wave to the Germans to come on over, and was shot between the eyes." '

Ranger Alban Meccia's account, in the *Saturday Evening Post*

Right: The assault on the Pointe-du-Hoc

by the heavy seas, at least one was sunk by a landing craft, two were blown out of the shallows by German gunfire, yet, incredibly, five struggled ashore. One G.I. reported seeing 'five D.D.s on the beach which helped out quite a bit. One was knocked out'.

The dangerous chaos on the Omaha sectors grew much worse, as evidenced in the Force Commander's official report:

'This fire from artillery, mortars, machine-guns, and small arms was heavy and accurate, and casualties were numerous. Many of the tanks which had reached the shore line were knocked out, and losses to the infantry advancing shoreward through the obstacles, and to the demolition parties trying to clear lanes through them, were severe. A considerable portion of the equipment of the demolition parties was lost in the landing due to the surf.'

Chaos on Easy Red

Individual company and battalion accounts give the military details of the nightmare of that morning on 'Bloody Omaha'. The report of the 16th Infantry is particularly telling:

'As the landing craft reached the beach [at Colleville-sur-Mer], they were subjected to heavy artillery, mortar, machine-gun, and rifle fire, directed at them from the pill-boxes and from the cliffs above the beach. Men were hit as they came down the ramps of the landing craft, and as they struggled landward through the obstacles, and many more were killed or injured by the mines attached to the beach obstacles. Landing craft kept coming in with their human cargoes despite the heavy fire and continued to disgorge them on to the narrow shale shelf from which no exits had been opened. Several landing craft were either sunk or severely damaged by direct artillery hits or by contact with enemy mines.

'The enemy now began to pour artillery and mortar fire on to the congested beach with deadly precision and effect. Visibility from the enemy strongpoints was such that the assault groups, armed with rocket launchers, flame-throwers, Browning Automatic rifles, and pole charges of T.N.T. could not approach them directly. A few squads and platoons of infantry gradually and slowly crawled forward from the shelf across the minefields between the enemy strongpoints, and made the slope.' The beach, however, rapidly became congested with the succeeding waves of personnel so that the seven-yard shelf affording the only protection from the enemy's accurate and intense fire became an almost solid mass of bodies, living and dead. Individual units, their assault groups landed at wildly divergent points, found themselves unable to organize because of the density of packed prone men held to the ground by the enemy fire.

It looked so bad at one point that Bradley considered abandoning Omaha. He sent an urgent signal to Headquarters: '0913 Opposition Omaha beach considerable. If required can U.S. Forces be accepted through JIG and KING. Most immediate N.C.E.T.F. pass to G.O.C. 21st A.G.'

The signal did not reach SHAEF Headquarters until late that afternoon. Fortunately, Montgomery never had to authorize a transfer to the British beaches of the Omaha assault. The confusion that would have arisen could have spelt disaster on the scale of Gallipoli.

Pointe-du-Hoc

Unhappily for the American soldiers and General Bradley, their commander, the Omaha crisis was not the only one brewing up on that miserably wet and grey morning. Five miles to the west, on a commanding promontory called La Pointe-du-Hoc, a powerful German battery was under assault by a force of U.S. Rangers led by Colonel Rudder. Approaching the sheer cliffs from the sea, they had the almost impossible task of scaling the strong defensive position and capturing the guns. The official report of the commanding officer of a naval fire support group provides an eyewitness account of the operation:

'The fortifications at Pointe-du-Hoc had been under heavy fire by *Texas* from H minus 40 minutes to H minus 05 minutes. However, this fire had been lifted according to schedule and when the Rangers landed forty-five minutes later, the Germans had filtered back into the fortifications and

were waiting for them with machine-guns, rifles and hand-grenades. At this point the cliff rises abruptly from the water to a height of approximately 100 feet. As the Rangers landed they found themselves pinned under the cliffs and were being rapidly cut to pieces by enemy fire. I immediately ordered *Satterlee* [a destroyer] to close the point and take the cliff tops under main battery and machine-gun fire. This was done. Her fire control was excellent and the Rangers were enabled to establish a foothold on the cliff top.'

In spite of the Rangers' heroism, the Pointe-du-Hoc turned out to be a bitter prize. When Colonel Rudder led his surviving men through the battered concrete casemates, he found the guns gone. The Germans had re-sited them two and a half miles further inland.

The Pointe-du-Hoc was a lesson in co-operation between the assault forces and the naval guns of the Allied fleet. This combination turned the scales at Omaha as the morning wore on. The naval gunners, together with the R.A.F. spotter pilots over the target areas, now began to punch out the German strongpoints one by one with precision gunfire.

'Get the hell out of here!'

Ernest Hemingway, in what survives as the most graphic record of experience of the Omaha landings, recorded what the naval bombardment meant to men going into the blood-stained waters of Omaha.

'Those of our troops who were not wax-grey with seasickness, fighting it off, trying to hold on to themselves before they had to grab for the steel side of the boat, were watching the *Texas* with looks of surprise and happiness. Under the steel helmets they looked like pikemen of the Middle Ages to whose aid in battle had come some strange and unbelievable monster.

'There would be a flash like a blast furnace from the 14-inch guns of the *Texas* that would lick far out from the ship. Then the yellow brown smoke would cloud out and, with the smoke rolling, the

Encouraging News

Omaha extracted a heavy toll during the five terrible hours of chaos and carnage. This is revealed on the faces of survivors of the American infantry (right) as, near exhaustion, they shelter under the chalk cliffs of Colleville. It is brought home by the power of Hemingway's account of the trip to Fox Green, opposite Colleville, to pick up the wounded:

'It was difficult to make our way through the stakes that had been sunk as obstructions, because there were contact mines fastened to them that looked like large double pie-plates fastened face to face. They looked as though they had been spiked to the pilings and then assembled. They were the ugly, neutral grey-yellow colour that almost everything is in war.

'We did not know what other stakes with mines were under us, but the ones that we could see we fended off by hand and worked our way to the sinking boat.

'It was not easy to bring on board the man who had been shot through the lower abdomen, because there was no room to let the ramp down the way we were jammed in the stakes with the cross sea.

'I do not know why the Germans did not fire on us unless the destroyer had knocked the machine-gun pillbox out. Or maybe they were waiting for us to blow up with the mines. Certainly the mines had been a great amount of trouble to lay and the Germans might well have wanted to see them work. We were in the range of the anti-tank gun that had fired on us before, and all the time we were manoeuvring and working in the stakes I was waiting for it to fire.

'As we lowered the ramp the first time, while we were crowded in against the other L.C.V.(P.) but before she sank, I saw three tanks coming along the beach, barely moving, they were advancing so slowly. The Germans let them cross the open space where the valley opened on to the beach, and it was absolutely flat with a perfect field of fire. Then I saw a little fountain of water jut up, just over and beyond the lead tank. Then smoke broke out of the leading tank on the side away from us, and I saw two men dive out of the turret and land on their hands and knees on the stones of the beach. They were close enough so that I could see their faces, but no more men came out as the tank started to blaze up and burn fiercely.

'By then, we had the wounded man and the survivors on board, the ramp back up, and we were feeling our way out through the stakes. As we cleared the last of the stakes, and Currier opened up the engine wide as we pulled out to sea, another tank was beginning to burn.

'We took the wounded boy out to the destroyer. They hoisted him aboard it in one of those metal baskets and took on the survivors. Meantime, the destroyers had run in almost to the beach and were blowing every pillbox out of the ground with their 5-inch guns. I saw a piece of German about three feet long with an arm on it sail high up into the air in the fountaining of one shellburst. It reminded me of a scene in Petrushka.'

concussion and the report would hit us, jarring the men's helmets. It struck your ear like a punch with a heavy, dry glove.

'Then up on the green rise of a hill that now showed clearly as we moved in would spout two tall black fountains of earth and smoke.

' "Look what they're doing to those Germans," I leaned forward to hear a G.I. say above the roar of the motor. "I guess there won't be a man alive there," he said happily.

'That is the only thing I remember hearing a G.I. say all that morning.'

Admiral Hall's report sums up what happened on Omaha: 'Few, if any, of the troops actually crossed the beach during the early hours of the forenoon. The supporting destroyers and gunfire-support craft stood in as close to the beach as the depth of the water would allow and engaged all the defensive installations which they could locate. Despite this, however, little progress had been made prior to 1100 when there was still considerable machine-gun fire, sniping, artillery, and mortar fire on the beaches between the exits, and opposite the exits the condition was critical. A number of enemy strongpoints in the beach were still holding out and our troops were not able to move inland. The first encouraging news came at 1100 from a message to Commander Transport Division.

In the early hours of the afternoon General Bradley knew from the signals coming in that the Americans were indeed making ground; the Big Red One was coming through.

'Had a less experienced division than the 1st Infantry stumbled into this crack resistance, it might easily have been thrown back into the Channel. Unjust though it was, my choice of the 1st to spearhead the invasion probably saved us Omaha beach and a catastrophe on the landing.

'Although the deadlock had been broken several hours sooner, it was almost 1.30 p.m. when V Corps relieved our fears aboard the *Augusta* with the terse message: "Troops formerly pinned down on

beaches Easy Red, Easy Green, Fox Red advancing up heights behind beaches." '

On the beach itself the situation was improving slowly, as an official account of the anti-tank company of the 16th Infantry Regiment relates: 'The Regimental Commander led his staff along the beach over the densely packed men in an effort to find Battalion and Company Commanders and so effect a rapid reorganization of the Regiment. The members of the Medical Detachment brought up the rear, pulling wounded out of the water and rendering first aid as they went. The enemy artillery, machine-gun, and rifle fire depleted the group as it progressed along the beach. When the far end of the beach was reached, three radios were set up and the members of the regimental staff were sent up and down the beach with instructions for Battalion and Company Commanders. Many of the companies were found at this time to be commanded by platoon leaders and their platoons led by the sergeants. Within half an hour reorganization was completed, and the attack was launched. Group after group opened gaps in the wire and crept across the minefield. The Colonel then led his C.P. group back toward the western end of the beach. Three of the D.D. tanks were firing directly at the enemy's reinforced concrete emplacements in an effort to button them up while the infantry advanced to destroy them. Opposite an amphitheatre-like hollow in the cliff-like slope a halt was called and a gap blown in the wire apron by Bangalore torpedoes. The Colonel led the way across the minefield; wounded men marked the path yelling warnings as to where unremoved mines were still emplaced.'

Colonel Taylor's order, given at a critical moment when he sensed the tide of battle was running in the Americans' favour, gave a new dimension to the struggle for Omaha beach:

'Two kinds of people are staying on this beach, the dead and those who are going to die – now let's get the hell out of here!'

Gold

0725

Ashore at Gold. Above: An L.C.A. disembarks commandos; behind, L.C.T.s have landed tanks and vehicles, and a bulldozer is about to emerge from L.C.T. 858. Below: Men of the 56th Infantry Brigade coming in near Asnelles from an L.S.I. For some, like the man who has slipped with his bicycle at the bottom of the ramp on the left, the landing was very wet

H-Hour for Force G, first of the British assaults, was set for 0725 hours. The most westerly of the British beaches, Gold, covered the stretch of sandy shore between the coastal hamlets of Asnelles and La Rivière. The terrain was typical of the sector. A flat beach, heavily sown with obstacles and mines, ended in sand dunes or a sea wall in the built-up villages. Here the Germans had concentrated their crust defences, pillboxes and gun emplacements which allowed them to sweep the beaches with cross-fire. Houses were turned into snipers' nests and strongpoints. More minefields and a pattern of anti-tank ditches criss-crossed the low-lying land on either side of the coastal road, and continued up towards the gentle slope that rose to the inland plateau. Gold beach was dominated by heavy field guns on the heights above Arromanches at the western end, and in the east by large calibre guns in heavy casements on the high ground between Crépon and Ver-sur-Mer.

The assaulting troops at Gold were the British 50th Division, followed by the 7th Armoured Division, the famous 'Desert Rats'. Avenging Dunkirk and Dieppe kept the troops' morale high in spite of seasickness. As the landing craft rode into the first assault, strange sounds echoed over the noise of the bombardment. The tannoys on a rocket barge were defiantly blaring out the strains of 'Roll out the Barrel'.

'Just as it was getting light, a bombing attack was delivered inland of King sector and fires which appeared to come from Ver-sur-Mer and La Rivière could be clearly seen. Apart from some flak, there was no enemy opposition of any sort, although it was broad daylight and the ships must have been clearly visible from the beaches. It was not until the first flight of assaulting troops were away and the cruiser H.M.S. *Belfast* opened fire, that the enemy appeared to realize that something out of the ordinary was afoot. For some time after this the anchorage was ineffectually shelled by the enemy coastal battery situated about three-quarters of a mile inland in the centre of King sector. Shooting was very desultory, and inaccurate, and the guns of only 6- to 8-inch calibre.'

This was how the official observer reported the pre-assault bombardment, which he described in his official record as 'tremendous'. But although the weight of high explosive was intended to fall on German heads, it was unavoidable that many innocent French civilians would suffer its effects too.

Guns at the bottom of the garden

In the straggling farms and villages the French civilians prepared to shelter as best they could in cellars and improvised trenches. Already they had suffered massive air raids and they knew only too well that their houses and gardens would become a battlefield. The diary kept by Mademoiselle Genget, who was living in the village of St Côme-de-Fresne gives some idea of what it was like to be on the receiving end:

'Awakened this morning at 1 a.m. by a distant bombardment, we got dressed thinking we were in for an intense bombing. We heard the big bombers coming in and constantly passing over our heads. We found a corner in one of our rooms where the walls are very thick where we waited. Suddenly the cannon commenced and everything in the house – doors, windows and everything in the loft seem to be dancing. The bombing was intensified and seemed to be coming nearer. We had the impression that all sorts of things were falling in the courtyard. We were not feeling very brave!

'Suddenly a big gun is fired from the sea and the smaller cannon of the Boches were answering. There can be no doubt that a big battle is about to commence. We dare not move and we put cotton-wool in our ears. The noise was terrific and we wondered how it would all end.'

These experiences were shared that morning by hundreds of people in the coastal villages of Normandy. Many civilians – men, women and children – were tragically killed as the tide of battle rolled over them. One person who lived to tell of her incredible experience was Madame d'Anselm. Her house was at Asnelles, not far from Le Hamel on the shore that saw some of the fiercest German resistance. A German gun was stationed at the bottom of the garden and the sector was manned by a unit of the 352nd Field Regiment – the same crack regiment pinning down the Americans at Omaha.

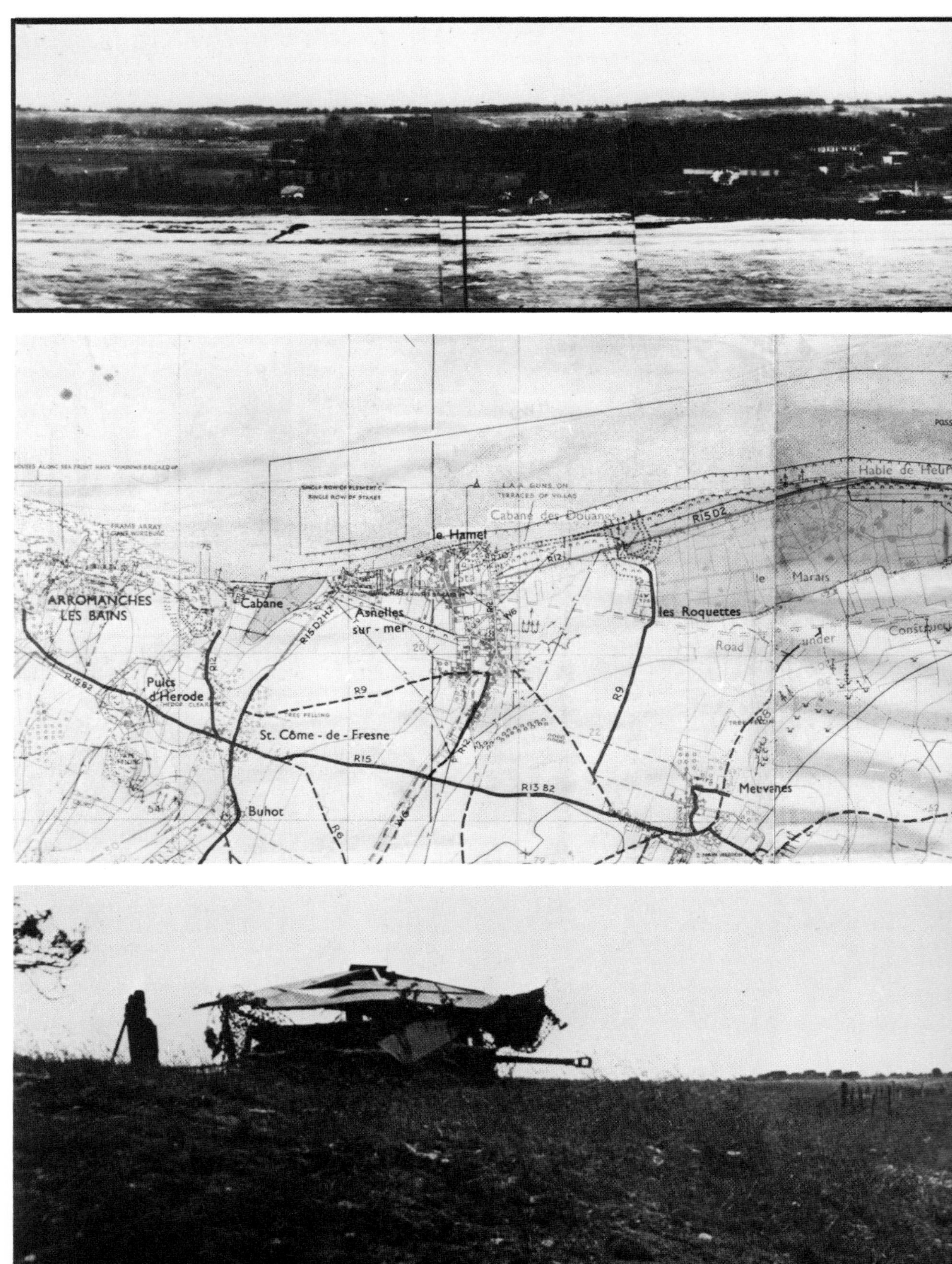
SINGLE ROW OF ELEMENT C
SINGLE ROW OF STAKES
L.A.A. GUNS ON
TERRACES OF VILLAS
Cabane des Douanes
Hable de Heurt
le Hamel
R15 D2
R12
ARROMANCHES
LES BAINS
Cabane
R18
Asnelles
sur - mer
R15 D2 H2
W6
les Roquettes
le
Marais
Road
under
Construction
R15 B2
Puits
d'Herode
R12
R9
TREE FELLING
St. Côme - de - Fresne
R15
R13 B2
R9
Meuvaines
Buhot
R6
W6

Left: Terrain at Gold. A section of the reconnaissance panorama showing building on the outskirts of Le Hamel, which was heavily fortified, as indicated on the intelligence map (below). Many camouflaged anti-tank guns survived the intense naval bombardment, like this one (bottom) on the high ground inland at Mont Fleury strongpoint (see map above)

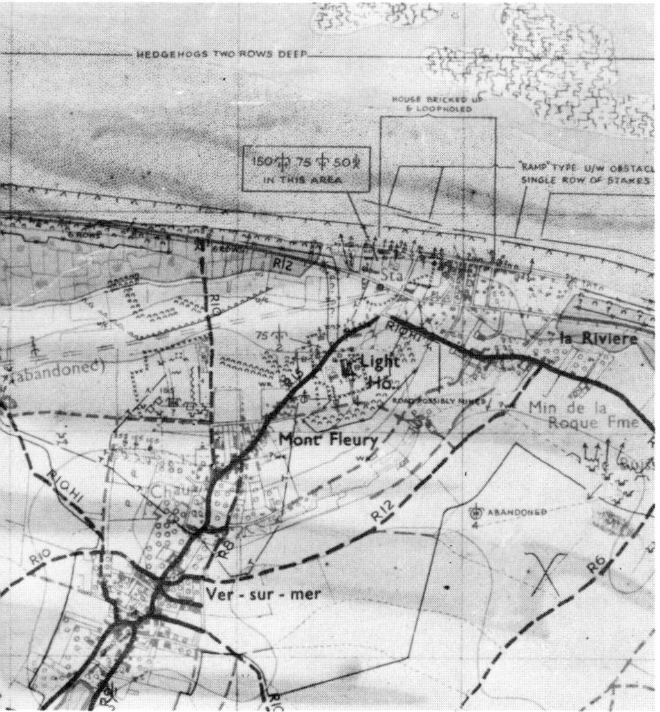

Madame d'Anselm had been urged four days before to take her seven young children to a place of comparative safety by a friend who had had a 'presentiment' that invasion was imminent. Mme d'Anselm refused to leave the family home; her husband and eldest son fighting with the Maquis in the south would not expect her to desert. Sadly, it was her friend and children who were killed as they fled inland on the night of 5 June. Madame d'Anselm had, however, taken the necessary precautions: 'We had dug a little trench in the garden, just big enough to shelter the eight of us and a couple of others. It was not very well protected – or covered. When the bombing attacks started we were in the house, but it was so bad that we had to go into the garden and take refuge in the trench which was fortunate, because the windows and parts of the house were soon smashed. Then, somewhere between three and four o'clock, two of the children took advantage of a pause to go back to the house to fetch something. One of them seized the opportunity to climb on to the garden wall to see what was happening. There was a German gun just on the other side of the garden wall. Suddenly he shouted excitedly, "Mummy, Mummy! Look – the sea – it's black with boats!" '

Clearing a path

The tides, whipped up by strong winds, were rising faster than expected to cover the obstacles. Army sappers and naval frogman demolition teams struggled under heavy fire to clear enough gaps to get through the increasing numbers of landing craft. The obstacles proved thicker than expected and 'heavier than the experimental types made in England'.

When the decision was taken that it was too rough to launch the D.D. tanks, but to land them dryshod later, it looked as though Gold had all the makings of a disaster similar to Omaha. If the infantry were deprived of artillery in close support, the strong defences at La Rivière and Le Hamel would mow down the landing troops with devastating machine-gun and 88-mm. fire. But the British, after the lessons of Dieppe, took no chances. The Funnies, flail tanks, bobbins and the mortar

Survivors of Gold. Right: The battery at Longues-sur-Mer after the effects of bombs and shelling (this is the same battery that survives – see colour section). Centre: The British cruiser, H.M.S. *Belfast*, bombarding a similar German battery at Ver-sur-Mer between Juno and Gold beaches (H.M.S. *Belfast* also survives, as a floating museum on the Thames). Far right: A battered seafront 88mm.-gun emplacement at the eastern end of Gold beach, one of many which today serve as memorials to D-Day

Below: Defence behind the beaches. British troops engaged in fierce house-to-house fighting in streets blocked by anti-tank obstacles, and homes blasted by the bombardment

Pl. 10. A third casemate at Longues showing fragment marks from 1000lb. bomb which exploded alongside the east wall. A second 1000lb. bomb crater can be seen in front of the embrasure.

tanks landed with the first wave. In fact on Jig Green sector, L.C.T.s arrived first and the Funnies were waiting for the infantry. General Hobarts' Funnies had a chance to prove their worth: 'The A.V.R.E.s effectively supported the infantry; the beach-clearance work was hindered by the abnormal tide caused by the onshore wind. It was therefore not possible to clear the beaches properly before the first high water. The Royal Navy accepted the risk involved and beached L.C.T.s which were urgently required, despite these obstacles. Damage and losses were comparatively light (about twenty L.C.T.s were damaged).'

The shore-gun emplacements and the heavily defended sanatorium buildings in Le Hamel fiercely opposed the frontal assault of the 1st Hampshire Regiment which had to capture the seaside village. A unit of the 352nd Division conducted their defence well, with their 88s picking off the British tanks as they tried to leave the congested beach-head. A flail tank had to 'post a letter' through the embrasure of the 88-mm. gun emplacement that was doing all the damage, before the infantry, supported by tanks, could force a flanking movement. They by-passed the centre of Le Hamel and took Asnelles. But the 352nd held out for many more hours of bitter resistance until the Hampshires stormed the village in mid-afternoon from the rear.

On the left, the Dorset Regiment had overrun their weaker opposition in forty minutes. Now they were clearing a route inland towards the battery at Arromanches. The flail tanks rapidly cleared a path through the minefields. The East Yorkshire Regiment and the Green Howards had a similarly easy landing and by mid-morning were firmly established on a ridge a mile inland. One section of La Rivière on the eastern end of Gold had escaped the bombardment and held out against the Yorkshiremen for some time before surrendering. By mid-morning, the landings of the follow-up assault brought the Desert Rats of the 7th Armoured Division into the assault. They rapidly cleared up the last pockets of resistance on the beaches before joining the push inland towards Arromanches and then on towards Bayeux, D-Day's planned objective for the Gold force.

Pl. 11. Casemate type D near La Rivière

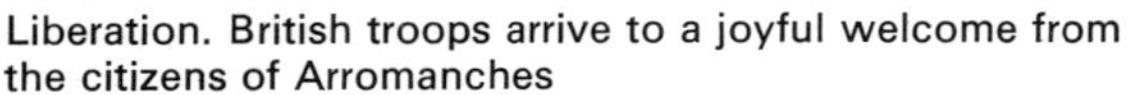
Liberation. British troops arrive to a joyful welcome from the citizens of Arromanches

At the same time, the 47th Royal Marine Commandos had landed near St Côme-de-Fresne on the far right of Gold beach beyond Le Hamel. The beach obstacles had played havoc with their craft, and fifteen out of sixteen had to be abandoned on landing. The first wave came in under such heavy machine-gun fire that one marine was supposed to have called out across to the other boats 'Perhaps we're intruding. This seems to be a private beach.' But, incredibly, the casualties were so light that some of them found it tame, 'like another exercise back home.' The doctors and medical orderlies were surprised to find so little to do and they turned their skills to unloading ammunition!

The commandos' task was to move inland as fast as possible and, by-passing Arromanches, slip behind the coastal belt to capture the small fishing port of Port-en-Bessin, midway between Gold and Omaha beaches. This would lead to a link-up with the Americans. They moved so fast that by 0800 hours in the hamlet behind the beaches of St Côme-de-Fresne, the citizens were able to celebrate their liberation. M. Barron hurried to the church nestling half-way up the hill on the road to Arromanches and set the bells ringing. Across the din of gunfire the pealing of the bells of St Côme signalled the liberation of the eastern beachhead.

'We are at last liberated'

Madame Genget's diary records the joy and happiness that she found in that day of liberation. Before nightfall, 6 June 1944 would mean the same for many thousands:

'What seemed impossible has really happened! The English have landed on the French coast and our little village has become famous in a few hours! Not one civilian killed or wounded. How can we express our surprise after such long hours of waiting in wonderment and fear?

'We got ready in spite of being still very upset and afraid, and got to the Villa St Côme. From there what a sight met our eyes! As far as we could see there were ships of all kinds and sizes and above floated big balloons silvery in the sun. Big bombers were passing and repassing in the sky.

'Nothing has changed at Arromanches but at St Côme up to as far as Courseulles one could see nothing but ships. It is marvellous and an unforgettable sight – a very consoling sight for the sufferings of the last few hours. Whilst we were waiting at the villa we could see tanks and armoured cars passing on the road to Asnelles and coming towards us across the fields we saw a file of soldiers. Going towards the village were the famous D.U.K.W.s, a sort of boat which can sail on the seas and travel on land.

'Finally we go back home, leaving the civilians to show the way to the English soldiers through the garden of the villa to Belle Vue on the cliff, as they must see if there are still German soldiers hiding there . . . the English had thought that all civilians had been evacuated from the coast and were very surprised to find the inhabitants had stayed in their homes in spite of the fierce fighting of the landings. Our little church had received a direct hit on the roof and fire broke out, but with the help of the villagers it was soon overcome. Guns were firing on the big blockhouse between Belle Vue and Arromanches and the underground trenches leading to the munition stacks belonging to the Germans. Soon all was wiped out. What a noise everywhere and smell of burning!

'We return to our rooms and from our windows see a file of tanks passing through the fields opposite on their way to Bayeux. Are we dreaming? Is it all really true? We are at last liberated . . . It is just 7 p.m. The weather is lovely – we only hope other villages will soon be liberated, and finally the whole of France. We are wondering how Radio Paris will announce this arrival of our Allies. What lies are they going to tell?

'. . . the enormous strength that all this war material represents is fantastic and the way it has been handled with such precision is marvellous, and our Allies say it is not yet the real landing. This will come in about ten days' time! The noise continues overhead and in the surrounding fields where the soldiers are busy exploding the mines. A group of Tommies pass and ask us for water. We fill their bottles, say a few words, and, having given chocolate and sweets to the children, they continue on their way. It is very hot . . .'

Juno
0735

The diary of events on the middle of the Juno sector landing beach of the 3rd Canadian Division during the assault gives an immediate and vivid record of the landings in spite of its official terseness. It was compiled by Lt-Cdr Thornton, commanding L.C.H. 168:

'0530 Not the scene I expected. Grey skies, wind and sea; a black coastline ahead. First shots from the cruiser. One can see the tracers going slowly high up into the air.

0532 L.S.I.s anchoring.

0550 Idling along at 5 knots. Cruisers and destroyers inshore but not firing much. Visibility moderate. I doubt if they can see their fall of shot. Church spires can be identified – nearly.

0600 Sporadic bombardment; moving across to Channel 7. Streaky pale sky to the east. Rain clouds ahead. Smoke flowing ahead of *Hilary*. Why? It makes a good screen across the front.

0605 Some aircraft passing towards shore. Wind 280 force 5. No fire from shore yet – hush!

0613 Thick cloud of smoke from where the cruiser's shells falling.

0625 An air strike approaching. We are lounging along and nothing much doing. Too rough for the D.D.s.

0638 Signal that S.P. and L.C.T. (R) are ten minutes late. Bombardment hotting up. Can see water-tower of Courseulles and groynes on the beach by eye. Very dark over land.

0645 It is very difficult to spot targets. No shooting from shore though. What a funny situation!

0701 Force G's L.C.T. (H) firing, or is it bombing? Fog of war or mist over the beaches – dark and grey.

0708 Can see church, the rest is fog of war. Good bombing – black and white smoke.

0715 Good bombing on beach. Can see the obstacles. Cross-wind smoke and dust.

0730 Signal "Deliver D.D.s if you wish" (half D.D.s disembarked and half beached). Fishermen's nets alongside. Hope they are not attached to mines. D.D. going out well.

0750 Yellow dinghy full of men. Presume a D.D.'s crew. 88 mm.? are bursting off beach. Plane down on port beam. One of ours alleged to be hit by a rocket.

0755 Explosion off the mouth of the river. Looks like a controlled minefield; about 50 yards of sea took off just east of the town. Green smoke and flash.

0756 Assaulting infantry on the Mike green.

0805 Machine-gun fire on Mike green. How clear is the air. Well done R.A.F. About sixteen shells a minute falling on Mike green. Some D.D.s firing.

0815 Empty L.C.A. returning. Wind 280 Force 3. (L.C.A. Hedgerow firing on Nan green. Well placed up on the beach defences.) L.C.G.s on Nan right inshore and knocking hard.

0835 Black clouds over the beaches. Wind Force 4. Many flocks of black duck? Moving out to sea.

0840 A small craft inshore passing out situation messages. Most useful.

0855 The black conical buoy off Mike green is there. I am surprised.

0856 No exits. Beach under shellfire.

0900 Beach under mortar fire. Men bunched inside dunes with D.D. and A.V.R.E.s – no movement one can see.

0905 Mike red. Slight opposition only. Beach signal station excellent.

0910 Think things looking a bit better. Report of L.C.A.s having been held on beach obstacle mines. L.C.T. passing with a hedgehog stuck on his bow.'

LCIL 299

Canadian troops pouring ashore near Bernières. During a later wave of the assault, they carried bicycles. It is now high tide and the 'Funnies' have done their job; the difficult sea wall has been climbed by tanks using special bridges (centre) and the troops are already pressing inland

The Juno assaults were essentially an all-Canadian show carried out by the troops of General Crerar's 3rd Canadian Division. The fighting spirit of these tough and highly trained infantry was at a high pitch; after two years' waiting they at last had the chance to avenge the 3,000 Canadian losses at Dieppe.

The Juno beaches, lying on either side of the small fishing port of Courseulles, were partly protected by natural hazards. Off-shore lay rocky shoals; and for this reason H-Hour was set 10 minutes later than for Gold so that the incoming tide gave a few more inches of water over the rocks for safety. Aerial reconnaissance at the left of the sector had shown rocks were apparently far nearer the surface than expected. The landings on this flank were postponed a further 10 minutes until 0745. Later it was discovered that long strands of seaweed had falsified the picture. The delay however meant that the demolition teams would have very little time to clear a way through the obstacles; they would still be exposed to the German guns less than a hundred yards from the shoreline.

Rommel's troops had made a particularly good job of the fortifications along the Courseulles seafront. On either side of the river heavy concrete emplacements housed 88-mm. guns and machine-gun nests. A high concrete wall would have to be bridged or blasted before infantry or tanks could leave the beach which was enfiladed with heavy fire. On the eastern flank of the four-mile Juno beach, which ran from La Rivière to St Aubin, the Germans had sown some 14,000 mines.

The naval bombardment and bombing had seemed impressive and heartening to the men in the landing craft during their four-mile run ashore. But the debris and dust thrown up by the seaside houses had made spotting difficult, and many of the gun emplacements on the shore remained intact. The delayed H-Hour and the fast rising tide meant that when the demolition parties reached the first line of obstacles, they were already under rough water.

One apprehensive Sergeant, in a team of British sappers, was fortunate. 'Our landing craft did get in – just! But on our way up to the beach we met

BERNIERES - SUR - MER

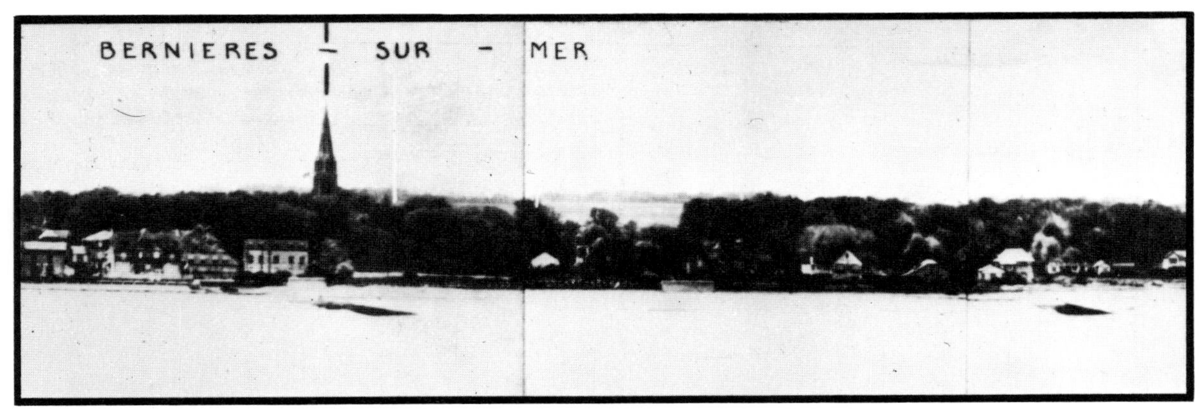

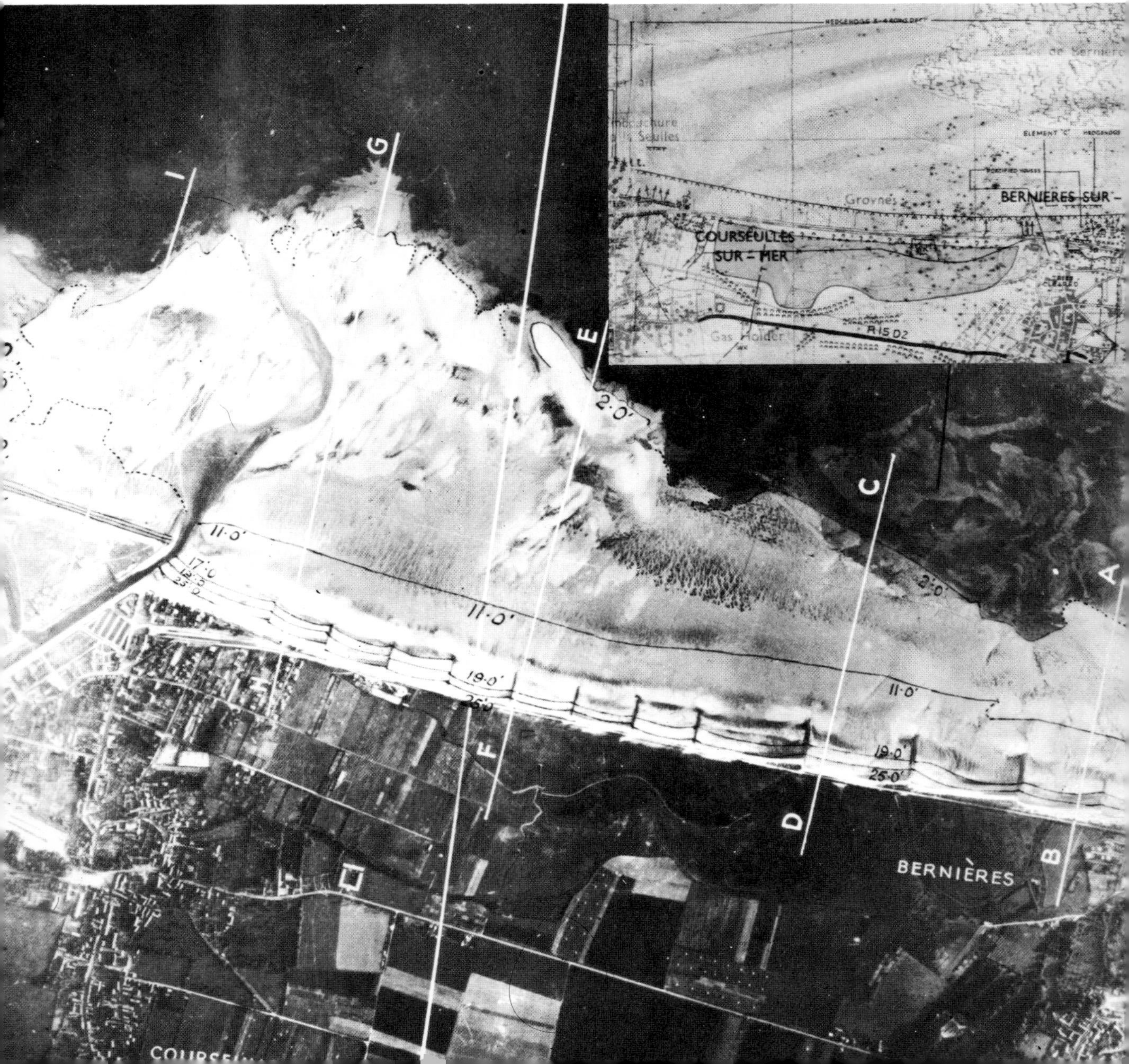
G
I
E
2·0'
11·0'
17·0
23·0
11·0'
19·0'
25·0
F
C
2·0'
A
11·0'
19·0'
25·0'
D
B
BERNIÈRES
ELEMENT "C"
HEDGEHOGS
FORTIFIED HOUSES
Groynes
BERNIERES SUR -
COURSEULLES
SUR - MER
R15 D2
Gas Holder

Left: Reconnaissance panorama of Bernières sector of Juno beach, code-named Nan, showing the flat terrain assaulted by the 8th Canadian Brigade. Below: An aerial intelligence picture of the whole sector, with the fishing village of Courseulles and corresponding invasion map (inset) detailing the obstacles and the underwater rocks at the top right which caused the planners to postpone H-Hour on Juno

an obstacle we had not been told about. They had driven tree-trunks into the shallows with shells fixed to the top. As our ramp was about due to go down, it changed its mind after hitting one – and went up instead. Water poured in the bows and from there we sank. That's where the Marines made a name for themselves. We had a crew of four manning the landing craft – and we looked behind after we heard four splashes – and we had no crew. But one of our lads swam ashore with a rope which he tied to one of the hedgehogs and we used it to get the men ashore including two of our wounded. Bullets were flying everywhere. It was a sandy beach, with dunes and seagrass. But from the water it looked most inhospitable – we could see the barbed wire and pillboxes at the top!'

Canadians hit the beach

Rough seas swept the unwieldy landing craft on to the obstacles. It was a scene repeated many times that morning along the fifty miles from Omaha to Sword. Many craft hit mines, blew up on the shells, or, like the sappers' boat, just sank. Some struggled ashore saving the troops the agony of half-wading, half-swimming ashore weighed down by a sodden kit. Many had cause to bless the rubber sheaths that kept the rifle barrels dry and which had been a standing joke for long training exercises. Soon the tangle of obstacles and wreckage made it difficult for successive craft to find a place to land. The result could have repeated the confused tragedy of the early hours at Omaha and, as the Commanders at Southwick House knew, it could have halted the invasion. But the Canadians were determined to get ashore. Seasickness and blind hatred of the Hun for Dieppe drove them on, often up to their necks in water like the wild Irish Sergeant McQuaid, whose name is venerated in Canadian national folklore: 'Oh, the evil of it,' he was heard to yell struggling ashore with foul oaths, 'they're trying to drown me before I even get up on the beach.'

At Bernières another eyewitness account of the landings tells how the sea resembled a log-covered field, so thick were the mine supports and obstacles. The small craft were the worst hit in the first mad rush for the shore. Pieces of wood from exploding landing craft were hurtled hundreds of feet into the air, showering the troops sheltering against a breakwater with wooden splinters. The experience of the landing craft was typical:

'*L.C.A. 1092.* This craft was holed on some stakes about 20 yards from the beach, which held her. The crew were unable to free her, and so the order to disembark was given. The first soldier through the door was shot dead, and then the craft was lifted clear of the stakes by the surf, and thrown on to the beach. All the Military were disembarked safely and without further casualties. This craft managed to clear the beach, but was holed three times in the process. These holes were successfully plugged and the craft was rehoisted.'

The postponement of the landings had given the Germans time to recover their balance. After the heavy bombardment, they turned the 100 yards of sand into a nightmare of cross-fire. On the right flank, the Funnies were half an hour late in landing. The troops here had to get through the minefields at the extreme risk of being blown sky-high. One gallant dash ended up with fifteen mangled bodies lying in the sand. These dashes across the beach were to cost the Canadians heavily; but were preferable to certain decimation by machine-gun fire at the water's edge. The gallantry of the first assault is evident from one assault-craft commander:

'Owing to the fact that we were twenty minutes late and the south-westerly wind which had been blowing for four days had piled up the sea, we very quickly discovered that far from beaching to seaward of the obstacles, we were ploughing right through them. All craft managed to steer between the obstacles, and the Canadians quickly disembarked, although as I had observed to the unfortunate Coy Comd. there was no support on the beaches for them, and the Germans were anywhere but with their hands down. They had made a rapid recovery from the very heavy bombardment, and were firing very actively, although the firing to start with was hesitant and spasmodic, but mortars were already ranging and machine-guns were firing concentrated bursts.

'The D.D.s for our sector had not been launched owing to the heavy seas, and the L.C.T. carrying them had actually beached not more than one minute before we touched down and in fact three of my Division of Craft beached between two of the L.C.T.s. The first D.D. was on the beach at almost the same time as my Canadians ran out.'

On the eastern sector the Canadians were landing without any fire support at all. Most L.C.T. commanders had decided it was too rough to risk launching the D.D. tanks. Coming in opposite Bernières one company of the Queen's Own Rifles paid the price for the lack of tank support. In minutes it had lost half its men and they only stormed the machine-gun nest when an anti-aircraft ship came close inshore to pour heavy fire into it.

The Nan Red sector, where the L.C.T.s carrying the much-needed armour were struggling ashore, was the scene of all the heavy fighting that day but: 'The L.C.A.s carrying the Assault Companies of the North Shore Regiment on the left touched down without trouble at the right place. By this time, however, considerable machine-gun and mortar fire was being experienced on Nan Red. Several L.C.T. (5)s were hit and the Assault Companies suffered some casualties. The L.C.A.s had to beach amongst the hedgehogs. Although no difficulty was experienced in steering the craft in through them, going astern out of them proved more difficult. A high percentage of L.C.A.s of all the three flights set off mines in this way, causing them to founder.

'The assault companies of the Queen's Own Rifles of Canada touched down about 200 yards east of their correct position (i.e. almost opposite to the strongpoint at Bernières). This meant that initial use could not be made of the excellent

Far left: The landing at St Aubin-sur-Mer with the 48th R.M. Commandos coming ashore to secure the right flank of the Canadian beachhead beyond Bernières. Disembarkation from the assault craft presented special problems for men carrying bicycles (left)

Below: First into Courseulles. Sergeant Leo Gariepy's D.D. tank photographed by a Frenchman as it rolled through the narrow streets of the town in the early morning of 6 June. The dedication reads: 'In recognition of your courage, devotion and your sacrifice'

A.V.R.E. bridge. This in turn caused a delay in the troops getting off the beach and therefore more advance of the Brigade inland.'

In one of the D.D. tanks that survived the rough seas, Sergeant Gariepy approached the sea wall just to the left of Courseulles harbour mouth: 'More by accident than by design, I found myself the leading tank. On my way in I was surprised to see a friend – a midget submarine who had been waiting for us for forty-eight hours. He waved me right on to my target and then made a half turn to go back. I remember him very very distinctly standing up through his conning hatch joining his hands together in a sign of good luck. I answered the old, familiar Army sign – To you too, bud!

'I was the first tank coming ashore and the Germans started opening up with machine-gun bullets. But when we came to a halt on the beach, it was only then that they realized we were a tank when we pulled down our canvas skirt, the flotation gear. Then they saw that we were Shermans.

'It was quite amazing. I still remember very vividly some of the machine-gunners standing up in their posts looking at us with their mouths wide open.

'To see tanks coming out of the water shook them rigid.

'My target was on the sea front. A 75-mm. which was in a position of enfilade fire along the beach like all the guns. The houses along the beach were all full of machine-gunners and so were the sand dunes. But the angle of the blockhouse stopped them firing on me. So I took the tank up to the emplacement, very very close and destroyed the gun by firing at almost point-blank range.'

The Royal Winnipeg Rifles and the Regina Rifles who had landed at the port either side of the river Seulles found the support of the D.D. tanks invaluable. Covered by their fire, they were soon storming through gardens into the little town's narrow streets. Here Sergeant Gariepy nearly got stuck:

'We ended up in a narrow street and there was one of those funny looking trucks with a charcoal burner on the running board. I couldn't get my tank by, and I saw two Frenchmen and a French woman standing in a doorway looking at us. So I took my earphones off and told them in good Quebec French, "Now will you please move that truck out of the way so I can get by?"

'They must have been frightened because they wouldn't budge. So I then called them everything I could think of in the military vocabulary. They were amazed to hear a Tommy – they thought we were Tommies – speak French with the old Norman dialect!' But it had the desired effect, and by mid-morning Gariepy and the Winnipegs and Reginas had pushed two miles inland towards the Caen–Bayeux road.

Dieppe avenged

The dash and bravado of the Canadians that carried them through the beaches swept by the machine-gun fire that morning on Juno made a great impression on the British soldiers who were with them. An engineer Sergeant, from the English sapper squad dealing with the beach minefields owed his life to a quick Canadian reaction. 'We were up in the dunes at the top of the beach, just on the other side of the Seulles river. My task was to deal with the firing pin in this minefield and as we got to the top of a rise I saw my first German. He was alive, but not for very long. These two Canadians who were with me were running up the beach behind me with their rifles. Just as they went up behind me through this opening in the sea wall, the Jerry came up out of the emplacement with a Schmiesser. I thought – Christ! They haven't seen. I hadn't got a sten gun, it had gone in the drink. But they just didn't stop running, they just cracked their rifle butt down on the German and that was that.'

Sword
0725

Tanks of the British 27th Armoured Brigade disembarking from an L.C.T. on a section of Sword beach near Hermanville in front of seaside villas

Lieutenant K. P. Baxter landed on Sword beach on the morning of 6 June 1944 with the 2nd Battalion of the Middlesex Regiment. His task was to coordinate the opening of the exits through the beach defences. His account of the morning's events gives a personal record of 'one man's invasion':

'We could see nothing beyond a horizon of water. Many of us found ourselves mentally checking that the sky was lightening on the port side, showing that we were indeed running south and not back on to an English beach on yet another exercise. The run in was long, and gradually, in the dispersing gloom, we found ourselves joined by more and more craft, whilst from the shore started a crescendo of explosions as the air bombardment carpeted the defences.

'It was now getting quite light and we suddenly came upon the midget submarine X.23, a complete surprise to us as it should have been, and we knew nothing of the long vigil that it had kept awaiting our arrival.

'The shoreline became more distinct, but detailed recognition was still impossible due to the heavy pall of smoke and dust still obscuring the buildings. Stabbing orange flames showed the strike of both artillery and the naval bombardment that had now joined in and then suddenly the air was torn with an ear-splitting roar as the rocket-ships loosed their projectiles.

'Then we saw the first setback: a returning L.C.T. with her ramp seemingly jammed in the half-lowered position. These craft, four to each beach, carried the specially equipped A.V.R.E. tanks that were to work in groups of three, the centre tank being armed with a "snake", a 60-foot long heavy tube of explosive to be pushed through the beach defences and detonated.

'Not only would this breach the wire but the explosion was calculated to set off any mines in the near vicinity. It would then be the job of the Exit Teams to clear and widen the corridors by hand and then to signal in following craft as the exits became operative. That one of these A.V.R.E. carrying craft had been unable to land its tanks meant that at least one of the Beach Teams would have to make its exit the hard way.

'Steadily the flotilla of L.C.A.s pressed onwards towards the beach. Four hundred yards from the shoreline and the Royal Marine frogmen slipped over the side to start the job of clearing underwater obstacles. This would be sufficiently hazardous at the best of times, but add to it the risk from all those churning propellers – with many more following – and their task became most unenviable.

'Closing to the shore rapidly, eyes scanned the clearing haze for familiar landmarks. There were none. A burst of machine-gun fire uncomfortably close overhead brought curses upon those in following craft for their enthusiastic "covering fire". Suddenly a burst ricocheted off the front of the craft, telling us that this was no covering fire. The opposition was very much alive and well.

'We had still been unable to identify our position but we were by now right on top of the beach. The protective steel doors in the bows were opened and everyone waited, tensed for the soft lurching bump. "Ramp down!" – and out into knee-deep water.

Assault on Strongpoint COD

'Ahead, a line of prone figures just above the water's edge and, some 200 yards beyond, a tank was nosed up against the small strip of dunes at the head of the beach.

'The first impression was that the tank had got in ahead of the first wave and they, following the same instructions as given to the Beach Exit Teams, were holding back until the explosive charges had been detonated.

'I had not gone far when I was tripped by some underwater wire, and, with no hope of retaining balance with the heavy Assault Jacket pack that had been issued to us, went flat on my face. Attempting to rise, I was struck a heavy blow on the back which flattened me again. Then suddenly the machine-gun opened up on us once again.

'The fire came from dead ahead and we could now make out the shape of a heavy embrasure in the low silhouette of some concrete fortifications at the top of the beach. We then realized that, by the narrowest of margins, we had landed immediately in front of Strongpoint 0880, code word COD.

'Both mortar and light artillery defensive fire

Right: An oblique aerial view of Queen sector in the middle of Sword beachhead showing the flat coast and the seafront houses, which the Germans had turned into strongpoints. Below: An aerial view of the whole beachhead from Ouistreham and the mouth of the Orne to Lion-sur-Mer. At extreme top centre on the high ground of the Périers ridge, stood the German battery which shelled the beachhead throughout D-Day
Inset: Section of the invasion map for Sword beach

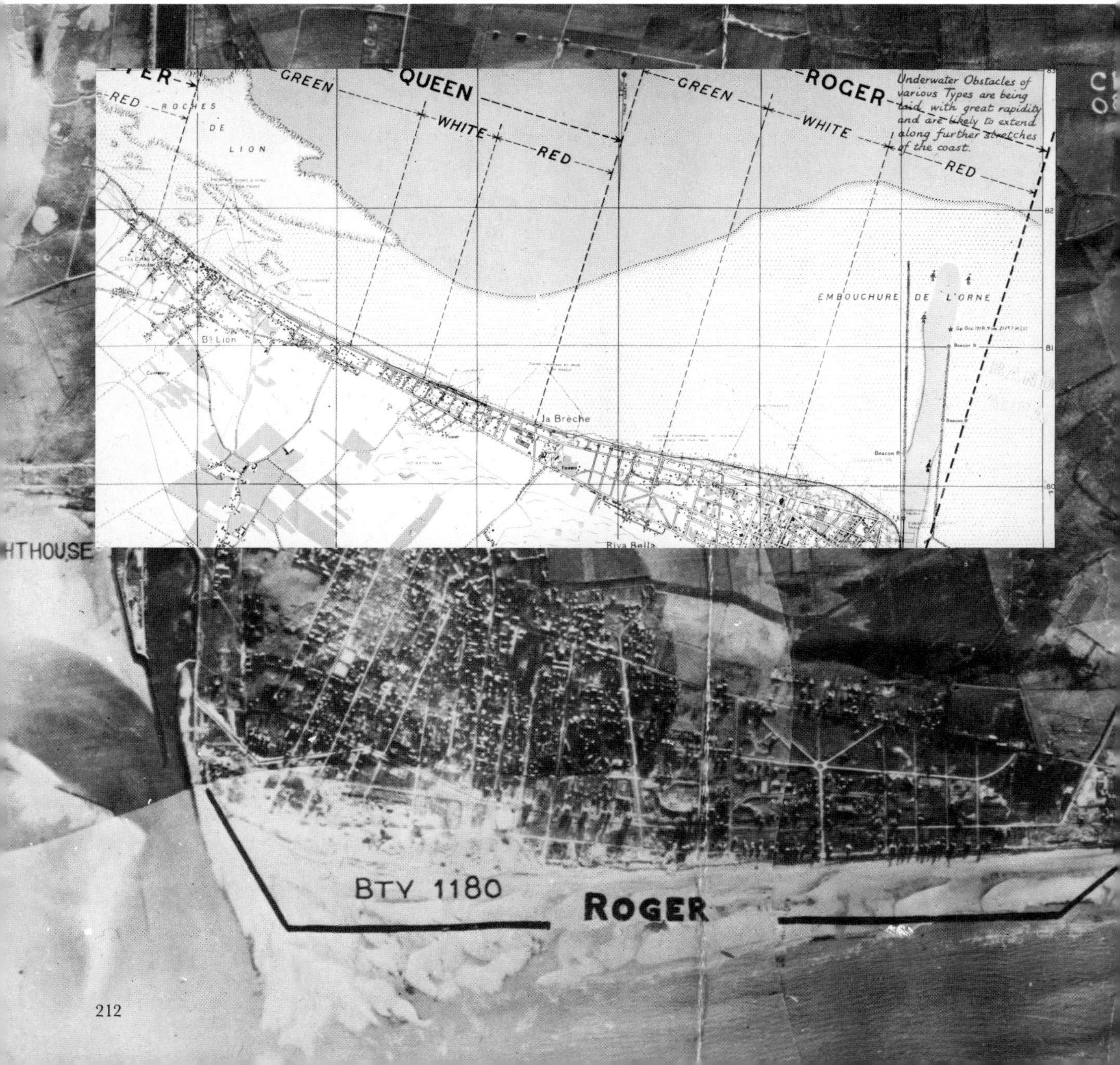

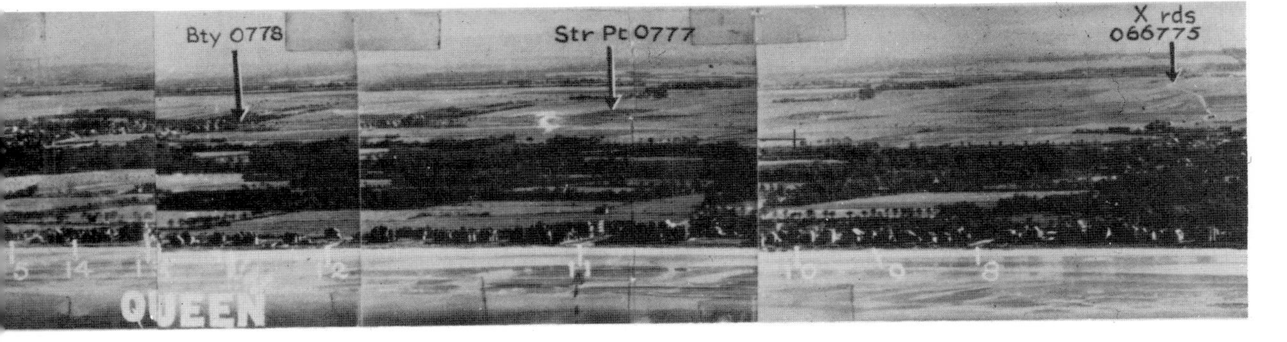
Bty 0778
Str Pt 0777
X rds
066775
14
12
11
10
8
QUEEN

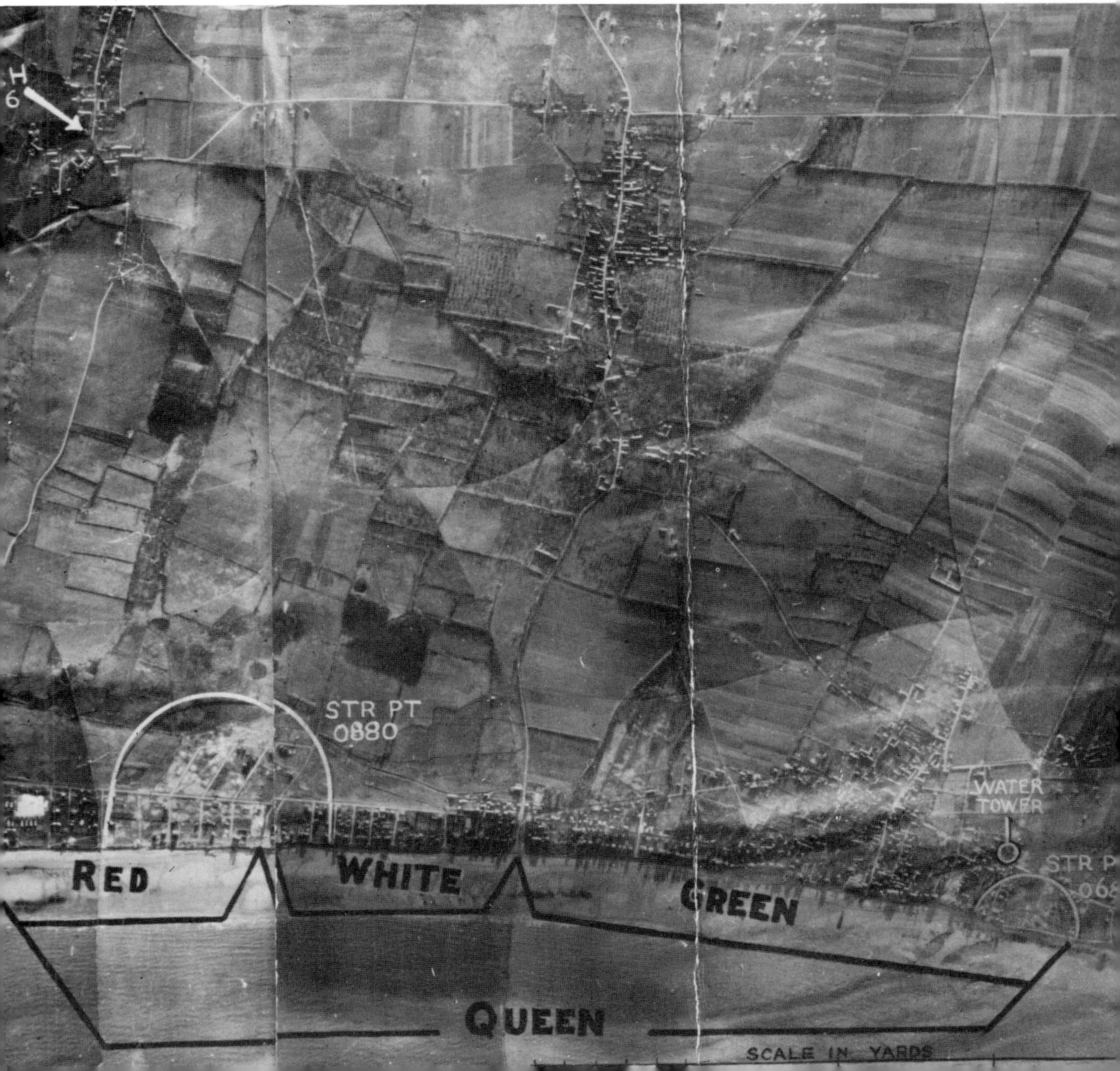

H
6
STR PT
0880
WATER
TOWER
STR P
068
RED
WHITE
GREEN
QUEEN
SCALE IN YARDS

being brought down by the enemy in front of the strongpoint now intensified, and the still unspotted machine-gun made an instant target of anything that moved. The prone figures that had first been seen just above the water's edge, we found to be casualties from the leading craft. Our wireless communication had been lost when the corporal operator, Corporal Roulier, had been hit on leaving our craft, but on White beach to our right, troops could be seen crossing the beach and reaching the top.

'There was a brief lull in the firing and we immediately took this opportunity to make a dash for the top of the beach. Briefly seeking cover behind the motionless tank to count heads, it was found that only the signalman of our group had managed to come through unscathed.

'We had hardly jettisoned our heavy equipment when the strongpoint above our heads sprang to life once more. German stick-grenades somersaulted through the air, their effects being greatly reduced in the soft sand, whilst we in turn desperately sought grenades from amongst the remnants of other detachments now grouping with us.

'However, further action was promptly eclipsed by the arrival of Lieutenant Tony Milne with his machine-gun platoon of the 2nd Bn Middlesex Regt. The platoon was equipped with Bren-gun carriers, having the heavy Vickers mounted above the engine casing, and were the first infantry fighting vehicles to land.

'Without a moment's hesitation, waterproofing shields were ripped away, gun clamps freed and the leading carrier drove straight at the trench line above our heads with a long swinging traverse from the Vickers, depressing into the trench as they closed. A brief pause – silence – then at the end of the trench system some fifteen survivors appeared in hasty surrender. Strongpoint COD had been taken.

'A first-aid post was quickly established in the concrete emplacement of the strongpoint, and then every hand was turned to helping vehicles through the soft sand above the high-water mark. The self-propelled guns of the 76th and 23rd Field Regiments, together with the Royal Marine Artillery, would be coming in at about 0900 hours – and were indeed to establish their first gun line on the water's edge. Already it seemed that we had been there all day.

Bitter fighting on the promenades

H-Hour on Sword had been fixed for 0725 hours. Nearly fifty miles east from Utah, Sword marked the eastern limit of the Allied assault. The five-mile stretch from Juno beachhead at Bernières to Lion-sur-Mer was too shallow and rocky to permit an assault. It had been planned to close the gap here with an assault from each end by the 4th Commando Brigade. Unfortunately, both the commando assaults had been made without tank support and German resistance was stiff at Lagrune and Lion-sur-Mer. Every little villa beside the sea had been turned into a strongpoint of some kind and the streets were blocked with massive concrete walls. The marines' planned pincer movement ground to a halt; German resistance inland was too severe for a flanking movement.

The Germans held on to their four-mile wedge between the two eastern beaches. Inland at Douvres the strongpoint provided an ideal position to interfere with the landings. But they badly needed armoured support. Fortunately for the British, during the critical hours of the landings the sinister black shapes of the 21st Panzer's Mark IVs failed to appear at a time when they could have wrecked the Sword beachhead.

The chief worry of Force S Commander, Rear-Admiral Talbot in H.M.S. *Largs*, was the massive Le Havre battery which could fire directly on to the Sword landing areas. Heavy smokescreens were laid all morning to prevent the Germans ranging. Instead the battery seemed to be content with shelling the warships. Led by H.M.S. *Warspite*, the warships fired heavy salvos back and kept the Germans occupied.

The pre-assault bombardment by the twenty-two ships of Bombarding Force D suffered from the inevitable lack of visibility once the bombing started. According to one official report, not all the bombs landed on target.

'I thought that the air bombardment was placed

rather too far to the westward, but it was difficult to judge through the smoke and dust. Approaching craft reported that they could not recognize the beaches from a distance once the bombardment started. The early waves, however, saw all they needed and all spoke highly of the value of the models and photographs which they were shown in the Commercial Buildings, Portsmouth, prior to sailing. I was surprised to see several houses on the front in Queen sector undamaged and with windows still intact in spite of the bombardment.'

The assault started off in fine style. Brigadier the Lord Lovat led his commandos in with a piper playing Highland reels on the fo'c'sle of his landing craft. One company commander read Shakespeare's fighting speeches from *Henry V*. The men needed to keep their morale high; many had been on the point of physical and nervous exhaustion after the rough crossing. As one naval officer wryly commented, 'the military were mostly seasick'.

According to at least one report this was not a universal experience: 'On 6 June 1944 at 0635 I was lowered in L.C.A. 796 from L.S.I. S.S. *Empire Broadsword* with thirty men and a Captain of the Suffolk Regiment. We formed up and left the lowering position at approximately 0645, commencing the run in to White beach, Sword area, to touch down at H plus 60. The sea was fairly rough but the soldiers, with one or two exceptions, enjoyed the run in.

'At just over 1,000 yards, I signalled all craft to increase to maximum revolutions, and, regardless of our own barrage, some of which fell in our midst, the flotilla hit the beach at full speed, L.C.T. 947 touching down at 0726. Just after the first tank had got ashore from L.C.T. 947, we were hit forward by mortar fire, which exploded the Bangalore torpedoes. The second tank (flail) was put out of action, also the tank astern of it. Three Army personnel were killed, including the Colonel, and seven others wounded.'

In spite of some heavy losses of armour, enough flails, D.D. and mortar tanks crawled up from the

Above left: Marines coming ashore. Above right: The flail tanks and Crocodiles go in. Below: Sheltering from German shellfire on Queen beach

sea to overwhelm the seafront strongpoints and machine-gun positions. The men of the 8th Infantry Brigade slowly fought their way on to the promenades and began a series of vicious hand-to-hand battles for the control of the coastal road. This was fought in and around the seaside villas.

The eastern end of Sword sector saw the landings of the 1st Commando Brigade under the leadership of Brigadier the Lord Lovat.

A commando force was landed at Ouistreham. Denis Glover commanded one of their landing craft and later reproduced a very personal and vivid account of the assault: 'Now eyes for everything, eyes for nothing. The beach looms close, maybe a mile. There are people running up and down it. There are fires, and the bursting of shells. Yes, and wrecked landing craft everywhere, a flurry of propellers in the savage surf among the wicked obstructions. Beach clearance parties I expect, bloody heroes, every one. The special craft stooging quietly in, some of them on fire though. Diesel fuel burns black. That vicious destroyer is irritating me, but the Colonel doesn't seem to mind. He's cool, but I'll bet he's worried. Curious how all these soldiers dislike assault by water. I'd hate to dash out of foxholes at machine-guns. Damn him, I can pretend I'm cool too. It's the noisiest gun – Starboard ten! – it's the noisiest gun in the Navy that 4·7 – Midships Cox'n.

'What a cool disinterested reply he makes. Colonel, you make me grin. I like your nerve.

'We are on those bristling stakes. They stretch before us in rows. The mines on them look as big as planets. And those grey nose shells pointing towards us on some of them look like beer bottles. Oh God, I would be blown up on a mine like a beer bottle.

'Whang – here it comes – those whizzing ones will be mortars – and the stuff is falling all round us. Can't avoid them, but the mines and collisions I can avoid.

'Speed, more speed. Put them off by speed, weave in and out of those bloody spikes, avoid the mines, avoid our friends, avoid wrecked craft and vehicles in the rising water and GET THOSE TROOPS ASHORE . . .

'Everything is working as we've exercised it for so long. Oh hell, this new tin hat is far too big for me – I'll shake it off my head with fright, if I'm not careful.

' "Slow ahead together." Slow down to steady the ship, point her as you want her, then half ahead

'However we were to have one more surprise just before the next echelons were due. The sudden appearance over the top of the low dunes of a gleaming brass fireman's helmet, surmounting the figure of the Mayor of Colleville. He was accompanied by a young French girl, who quickly made her way to render help in the first-aid post. These were the first French people to greet us and all were deeply impressed at the courage of these two who had obviously taken such astonishing risks in exposing themselves to make their way to the beach at such a time.'

Lieutenant J. P. Baxter

Left: French liberators. A Free French commando being welcomed at Riva Bella after Commandant Kieffer's battalion had taken the Casino strongpoint

Below: A bridge-laying tank leads an assault on Sword beachhead; a heavy smokescreen has been laid to seaward to protect the landings but the beach came under heavy shellfire all morning from the German artillery inland at Périers

together and on to the beach with gathering rush. Put her ashore and be damned! She's touched down. One more good shove ahead to wedge her firm. Smooth work! "Now off you go! Good luck, Commandos, go like hell! Next meeting – Brighton!" How efficiently, how quickly they run down the accustomed ramps, not a man hit that I can see, and there they go, slashing through a hundred yards of water, up over more of the flat beach than that and out of sight among the deadly dunes. The Colonel turns to wave and is gone with them. They ignore the beach fire. They have their objective and they are going for it.' This was part of the landing of No. 6 Commando; their objective Ouistreham.

No. 4 Commando had landed earlier than the rest of the brigade, its vital mission being to push inland rapidly and link up with the hard-pressed men of the 6th Airborne Division holding the bridges over the River Orne. The rest of the brigade had the difficult task of prizing the Germans out of their heavily fortified positions at Riva Bella and Ouistreham. The port marked the entrance to the River Orne and the locks to the Caen ship canal.

In a twist of history the local inhabitants had set up a monument to their successful repulse of a British landing attempted on 12 July 1792. Now they were waiting to welcome the British as liberators and, to the great joy of the French inhabitants of Ouistreham and Riva Bella, the new liberators included a Free-French Commando Battalion. Villa by villa they shot it out with the Germans until they were halted by the casino. This had been turned into a strongpoint with guns on its concrete roof. Free French commander, Commandant Kieffer, collected the support of some D.D. tanks and, by 0930, he had stormed the casino.

The shelling of Sword beach made a dramatic improvement suddenly in the middle of the morning. The beach commanders realized that the German artillery was ranging on the barrage balloons flying over the area to provide cover against low-flying aircraft. When they had been cut adrift, the intensity and accuracy declined.

The commandos continued their drive into the town and by midday German resistance spluttered out. Ouistreham was liberated – and Frenchmen had played an important role. The population was overwhelmed. Commandant Kieffer recalled hearing a young French boy say how delighted he was that the English had been so thoughtful as to bring along soldiers who spoke French.

The Philadelphia Inquirer

PUBLIC LEDGER

An Independent Newspaper for All the People

WAR EXTRA

CIRCULATION: May Average: Daily 496,780; Sunday 1,097,774 | TUESDAY MORNING, JUNE 6, 1944 | Copyright, 1944, by Triangle Publications, Inc. Vol. 230, No. 158 | W ★ | THREE CENTS

INVASION

Allies Land in France, Smash Ahead; Fleet, Planes, Chutists Battling Nazis

SUPREME HEADQUARTERS, ALLIED EXPEDITIONARY FORCE, June 6 (Tuesday) (A. P.).—Allied forces landed in northern France early today in history's greatest overseas operation, designed to destroy the power of Adolf Hitler's Germany and wrest enslaved Europe from the Nazis. The German radio said the landings were made from Le Havre to Cherbourg, along the north coast of Normandy and the south side of the bay of the Seine.

Allied Headquarters did not specify the locations, but left no doubt whatever that the landings were on a gigantic scale.

'FULL VICTORY' ASKED

Ringing in their ears, the American, British and Canadian forces who made the landings had these words from their supreme commander, General Dwight D. Eisenhower:

"You are about to embark on a great crusade. The eyes of the world are upon you and the hopes and prayers of all liberty-loving peoples go with you . . .

"We will accept nothing less than full victory."

The German radio filled the air with invasion flashes for three hours before the formal Allied announcement came at 7.32 A. M., Greenwich Mean Time (3.32 A. M., Philadelphia time).

It acknowledged deep penetrations of the Cherbourg peninsula by Allied parachute and glider troops in great strength.

AIDED BY PLANES, WARSHIPS

The assault was supported by gigantic bombardments from Allied warships and planes, which the Germans admitted set the coastal areas ablaze.

A senior officer at Supreme Headquarters said rough water caused "awful anxiety" for the sea-borne troops but that the landings were made successfully, although some soldiers undoubtedly were seasick.

The sun broke through heavy clouds periodically this morning after a daybreak shower. The wind had blown fairly hard during the night, but moderated somewhat with the dawn. The weather outlook remained somewhat unsettled.

Supreme Headquarters' first communique was this single sentence:

"Under the command of General Eisenhower, Allied naval forces supported by strong air forces began landing allied armies this morning on the northern coast of France."

It was announced moments later that Britain's General Sir Bernard L. Montgomery, hero of the Eighth Army victories in North Africa, Sicily and Italy, was in charge of the assault.

TAKE ADVANTAGE OF TIDES

A senior officer at Headquarters said the times of the landings varied to take advantage of the various tide stages at different beaches. Except for the air-borne troops, the first landing times varied from 6 A. M. to 8.25 A. M., British

Continued on Page 2, Column 1

FLASHES

FOUR PARACHUTE DIVISIONS LAND

LONDON, June 6 (A. P.).—The German radio reported today that four British parachute divisions had landed between Le Havre and Cherbourg in France. This was four times the size of the Nazi parachute force dropped on Crete in the Mediterranean.

NAVY, COAST GUARD, MARINES IN BATTLE

Supreme Headquarters, Allied Expeditionary Force, June 6 (A. P.).—United States battleships are supporting the Allied landings in France and U. S. Coast Guard units also are participating in the operations, it was announced today. American Marines likewise are in the fighting, manning secondary guns aboard the big ships.

DIEPPE HIT BY AIR, NAZIS SAYS

NEW YORK, June 6 (A. P.).—The Berlin radio, in a broadcast recorded by N. B. C., said this morning that strong Allied air attacks had been launched on the Dieppe area.

ALLIES GAIN 5 MILES IN ITALY

NAPLES, June 6 (A. P.).—The battle to destroy the German enemy in Italy "continues without pause" and troops of the Fifth Army have advanced some five miles beyond the Tiber, Allied Headquarters announced today.

BERLIN CLAIMS TWO SINKINGS

The Berlin radio broadcast a D. N. B. dispatch today saying that one Allied cruiser and a large landing vessel carrying troops had been sunk in the area of St. Vaast la Hougue, 15 miles southeast of Cherbourg.

LEAVE HOMES, DUTCH TOLD

LONDON, June 6 (U. P.).—Shortly before 7 A. M. (1 A. M., E. W. T.) the B. B. C. broadcast Allied High Command urgent instructions to Holland advising all people living within 35 kilometers (about 18 miles) of the coast to leave their homes immediately and also keep off roads, railways and bridges.

26 WARSHIPS REPORTED OFF COAST

LONDON, June 6 (U. P.).—The German D. N. B. agency said today in a broadcast unconfirmed by Allied sources that six heavy warships and 20 enemy destroyers were lying before the Seine Estuary off the coast of France.

GENERAL DE GAULLE IN ENGLAND

NEW YORK, June 6 (A. P.).—General Charles de Gaulle has arrived in England, it was announced today in a broadcast from Supreme Headquarters, Allied Expeditionary Force. N. B. C. monitored the broadcast.

WHERE ALLIES HAVE LAUNCHED INVASION AGAINST FORTRESS EUROPE

Allied troops are landing on the coast of France, General Dwight D. Eisenhower reported this morning. The heaviest fighting, according to Berlin, is in the area from Le Havre, at the mouth of the Seine, to the Vire River, on the Normandy peninsula, with the center of the battle near Caen. In addition, paratroops are reported landing on the Normandy peninsula near Cherbourg while Abbeville, on the Somme River, is under attack. Naval forces are pounding Le Havre and Allied air fleets are said to be raiding Calais and Dunkirk.

Landings Unopposed,. Eyewitness Asserts

By RICHARD C. HOTTELET

Representing Combined U. S. Press

SUPREME HEADQUARTERS, ALLIED EXPEDITIONARY FORCES, June 6 (Tuesday) (U. P.).—Allied forces landed in France early this morning and from what I could see from a bomber overhead in these first few minutes there was nothing stopping the assault parties from getting ashore.

I watched the first landing barges hit the beach exactly on the minute of H-Hour. I was in a Ninth Air Force Marauder medium bomber flying at 4500 feet altitude along 20 miles of the invasion coast.

I spent about half an hour over enemy territory. We flew over and bombed some of the coastal fortifica-

Continued on Page 2, Column 8

Norwegian King Warns on Revolt

NEW YORK, June 6 (Tuesday) (A. P.).—King Haakon of Norway in an invasion broadcast today to his homeland warned his people against premature uprisings, said a broadcast from Supreme Headquarters, Allied Expeditionary Force, heard by N. B. C.

Big Allied Move Began May 28

By JOHN M. McCULLOUGH

Inquirer Washington Bureau

WASHINGTON, June 6 (Tuesday).—The actual movement for the greatest military operation in history—the invasion of the continent of Europe—began 10 days ago, the War Department disclosed this morning.

It was on May 28 that Allied soldiers stripped for action, backed by the greatest mass of war materiel ever assembled, and began their move to the assault craft which carrid them across the channel to the shores of France.

AIR FORCE STRIKES AHEAD

They were the most heavily armed soldiers in the history of amphibious

Continued on Page 2, Column 4

Eisenhower Summons French People to Posts

NEW YORK, June 6 (Tuesday) (A. P.).—The OWI reported today this statement by General Dwight D. Eisenhower was broadcast by Allied radios in London: "People of western Europe: A landing was made this morning on the coast of France by troops of the Allied Expeditionary Force. This landing is part of the concerted United Nations plan for the liberation of Europe, made in conjunction with your great Russian Allies.

"Although the initial assault may not have been made in your own country, the hour of your liberation is approaching.

ALL HAVE PART TO PLAY

"All patriots, men and women, young and old, have a part to play in the achievement of final victory.

Continued on Page 2, Column 5

Roosevelt Asleep When News Broke

WASHINGTON, June 6 (U. P.).—President Roosevelt was asleep when the word came that the invasion had started, even though he was one of the few persons here who knew about the move in advance.

The White House was dark except for the press room, where a group of reporters sat through the early morning hours, but members of the official staff kept in touch with the Executive Office by telephone.

Allies Order Coast Evacuated

LONDON, June 6 (A. P.).—A spokesman for General Dwight D. Eisenhower, in a London broadcast, told the people living on Europe's invasion coast today that "a new phase of the Allied air offensive has started" and warned them to move inland to a depth of 35 kilometers (about 22 miles.)

In a special broadcast over the B.B.C., directed to France and other coastal countries, the spokesman said:

"A new phase of the air offensive has started. It will affect the entire coastal zone situated not less than

Continued on Page 2, Column 4

1st Communique

The text of Communique No. 1 from Supreme Headquarters, Allied Expeditionary Force:

Under the command of General Eisenhower Allied naval forces, supported by strong air forces, began landing Allied armies this morning on the northern coast of France.

TIME'S REVENGE

14 Day of Destiny

Communiqué no. 1
'Under the command of General Eisenhower, Allied Naval Forces supported by strong Air Forces began landing Allied Armies this morning on the northern coast of France.'

Just before nine in the morning, General Eisenhower ordered the release of the electrifying news that 6 June 1944 was the long-awaited day of destiny – the opening of the second front in Europe. German radio had already broadcast news of an invasion at 0700 hours; but a cautious Eisenhower wanted to see how things settled down before confirming the news of the assault.

Ciphered messages had begun to flow into the Operations Room soon after the first touchdown at Utah and Omaha. Admiral Kirk, U.S. Naval Commander of the Western Task Force, had signalled at 0652 that everything was going 'according to plan'; but the news of the British landings arrived just before 0800. 'It was some time before the signals began to give a sensible picture of what was happening,' recalled Captain Courage who was in charge of signals to the Operations Room. 'I remember the first ones coming through the deciphering machine like ticker-tape. I went into the Operations Room immediately and announced that the first one was coming through and asked whether I should bring in the tape and read it out. I took the tape straight off the machine, it hadn't even been typed and it was difficult to make sense of it as I read it out. But it actually said something like "all going according to plan".' 'We almost felt like cheering,' remembers one of the Wrens in the Operations Room, Mrs Fanny Hughill, 'But we had been too well trained. I do remember that we went out to breakfast feeling nine feet tall, and that we had done it. Although naturally there was concern for what was going to happen in the next few hours which were critical.'

Eisenhower's aide, Captain Butcher, wrote that 'Ike looked in the pink . . . We stood in front of the caravan enjoying the beautiful, oh, what a beautiful day. A G.I. came grinding along with the morning papers from Portsmouth, with headlines of the fall of Rome and the Fifth Army's crashing victory, with a personal statement by Wayne Clark. Ike said, "Good morning, good morning," to the G.I. most cheerfully indeed.

'About then along came Lieutenant-General Morgan, who did much of the hard work on the Great Plan, which Ike reminded him of and to which Morgan said, modestly, "Well, you finished it".'

As the morning wore on and the concern about the American problems at Omaha became apparent, aggravated by a lack of signals on the beach, Eisenhower's mood became noticeably less buoyant. According to a report in *Time Magazine*, 'The Supreme Commander had little to do but wait in galling idleness before the vast fleets of landing craft and gliders could put their troops ashore, and some vestige of order begin to appear out of the vast amphibious chaos. At such times the carefully controlled Eisenhower temper bends under the strain; he hates uncertainty. All he could do now was pace round headquarters, scribble memos to himself. One of his self-memos could stand as a masterpiece of military understatement: "Now I'd like a few reports." '

Praying in the streets
Three thousand miles away across the Atlantic millions of Americans woke up on 6 June to learn that the invasion was under way. The announcement made the early hours of the morning's *New York Times*, and some editions of the morning papers splashed INVASION across their headlines. In New York, people prayed in the streets for success on the beaches.

In Britain, millions in factories and homes paused to catch the morning's radio bulletins. The first communiqué, read by B.B.C. announcer John Snagge, had electrified the nation.

In London, just before midday, the House of Commons assembled in anxious anticipation to hear more news from the Prime Minister. A beaming Churchill appeared, and mischievously made no mention of the invasion in the first part of his speech. Instead he dwelt at some length on the significance of the fall of Rome. Then, pausing for effect, he delivered the words that everyone waited to hear, as cheering rang out around him:

Waiting for the Führer's orders. Rommel's best formations were held in reserve for a rapid counter-offensive before the beachhead could be consolidated. They could not be moved without Hitler's express approval. The Panzer reserves included young and fanatical S.S. infantrymen (right) as well as the 45-ton Mark V Panther tank (far right) armed with a 75-mm. KwK42 gun. They could also deploy the smaller 25-ton Mark IV, with 75-mm. KwK40 gun and the heavy 56-ton Tiger, with its feared 88-mm. high-velocity weapon, capable of out-shooting almost all Allied armour

'In this case the liberating assault fell upon the coast of France. An immense armada of upwards of 4,000 ships, together with several thousand smaller craft, crossed the Channel. Massed airborne landings have been successfully effected behind the enemy, and landings on the beaches are proceeding at various points at the present time. The fire of the shore batteries has been largely quelled. The obstacles that were constructed in the sea have not proved so difficult as was apprehended.'

In Washington, President Roosevelt struck a surprisingly cautious note at his morning press conference. The whole country was 'thrilled by the news of the invasion', he told the correspondents; but he stressed that this should not lead to overconfidence because 'the war is by no means over yet'. Eisenhower was 'up to schedule' – but, 'You don't just walk to Berlin; the sooner this country realizes that the better.'

The absent Field-Marshal

Rommel's plan for dealing with the invasion depended on fully alerted defences containing any assault on the beaches long enough for a swift and crushing counter-attack from the armoured reserves.

Incredibly, and to the intense relief of the British and American commanders, the Germans were taken completely by surprise. Even when they did realize in the early hours of 6 June that something big was under way, with paratroops and fifty convoys approaching the Normandy coast, their reactions were ponderous and confused.

After months of constant alert and exercises, amazingly, the Germans were not expecting an attack on the very day it came. Their whole military machine was overtaken by events and thrown into disarray.

An important factor was their miscalculation about the time of the Allied attack. Rommel expected that the assault would be made at high tide so that the attackers would not have to run the gauntlet of concentrated crossfire over long sandy beaches. In fact, Montgomery had picked a point halfway between low and high water.

One General at least was ready. General Salmuth, commander of the Fifteenth Army guarding the Calais sector, alerted his troops after intercepting the B.B.C.'s signals to the Resistance on the evening of 5 June. Throughout the night of 5/6 June, the Wehrmacht forces north of the Seine waited by their tanks and guns for an invasion that did not materialize; 120 miles to the south the troops were fast asleep. 'The Commander-in-Chief, Western Forces, to whom the codeword was relayed, decided that he would not alert the whole front,' said General Hans Speidel, Rommel's Chief of Staff.

The one man who could have immediately galvanized the whole of the German Seventh Army, Field-Marshal Rommel, had already left France for his home near Ulm on the Danube. Before going on leave he had written to Admiral Rüge, his naval adviser, 'It eases my mind to know that while I'm away the tides will not be suitable for landings. Besides, air reconnaissance gives no reason for thinking they are imminent.'

In the vital hours after the invasion, von Rundstedt and his subordinate commanders in France had to find the answer to one fundamental question: were the landings in Normandy the main Allied effort? The Allied deception schemes were proving so effective that the Generals in France could not give a definite '*schwerpunkt*' – centre for the attack – to Supreme Command headquarters, at that time at Hitler's Berchtesgaden residence. Without this information, considered vital by the Führer, it was impossible to get the Panzer reserves committed to Normandy at an early stage in the Allied landings.

From intelligence and more orthodox assessments, the O.K.W. staff were convinced that the Normandy landings were just a feint.

But by 0600 hours von Rundstedt was satisfied that the invasion was real. Blumentritt, von Rundstedt's Chief of Staff, asked for the Panzer reserves to be released to C.-in-C. West. Warlimont continues, 'This was the first and most important decision which Supreme Headquarters had to take and I therefore immediately got on to Jodl by telephone. It was soon clear that Jodl was fully up to date with the information, but in the light of the latest reports was not yet fully convinced that here and now the real invasion had begun. He did not therefore consider that the moment had arrived to let go our last reserves, and felt that the Commander-in-Chief West must first try to clear up the situation with the forces of Army Group B. This would give time, he considered, to get a clearer picture whether the operation in Normandy was not a diversionary attack prior to the main operation across the Straits of Dover.'

Rommel, with his direct access to Hitler, might have got the right decision taken in time. But he was far from the front, his staff and his maps, relaxing at home. Rommel was first told that the long-expected invasion had come when he was telephoned by General Speidel, his Chief of Staff, shortly after 0600 hours. The Field-Marshal immediately left by car for the long drive back to his battle headquarters at the Château Roche Guyon near Paris.

The best chance for the Germans to subject the British and Americans to another Dunkirk lay in the speedy deployment of the Panzer reserves. These were the élite units of the German army. But the main forces in France, consisting of the 1st S.S., the 12th S.S. Panzer Lehr and the 17th S.S. Panzer Grenadiers, could not be moved without permission of the Supreme Command which meant, in effect, the Führer himself. The Panzer divisions were virtually small armies. Each one was led by an experienced General, capable of acting independently, trained at exploiting battlefield opportunities. Bayerlein, who had been Rommel's Chief of Staff in the desert, commanded Panzer Lehr; the ardent Nazi General Kurt Meyer led the 12th S.S., which was made up of eighteen- and nineteen-year-old fanatics of the Hitler Youth.

Within striking distance of the Normandy coast, these four powerful divisions waited for the Führer's order to move. Both Allied and German Generals knew that they could be the deciding factor in the invasion.

The Führer sleeps

The delay in releasing the Panzer reserves was the first disastrous German error. 'I have been criticized because it was said that I delayed too long in committing my Panzer divisions against the bridgehead,' von Rundstedt said when being cross-questioned after the war. 'Although Panzer Lehr and the 12th S.S. Panzer Divisions were under my command I could not move them until I had received permission from Berlin . . . They hesitated all that night and the next morning were unable to make up their minds. Finally, at four o'clock in the afternoon of 6 June, twelve hours after I had made

'About midday the usual assemblage collected for the briefing conference, but on this particular day there was a Hungarian state visit in honour of which the conference took place in Klessheim castle, at least an hour by road from the offices of those involved. As usual when visitors were involved, it was a showpiece, but in view of events in the west a preliminary conference took place in a room next to the entrance hall. I and many of the others were keyed up as a result of the portentous events which were taking place and, as we stood about in front of the maps and charts, we awaited with some excitement Hitler's arrival and the decisions he would take. Any great expectations were destined to be bitterly disappointed. As so often happened, Hitler decided to put on an act. As he came up to the maps he chuckled in a carefree manner and behaved as if this was the opportunity he had been waiting for for so long to settle accounts with his enemy. In an unusually broad Austrian, he merely said, "so, we're off" '.

General Warlimont

my request, I was told that I could use these Panzer divisions. This meant that a counter-attack could not be organized until the morning of 7 June. By then the bridgehead was over thirty hours old and it was too late.'

Even when the Panzers were moved, they were made unnecessarily vulnerable to air attack. On the afternoon of 6 June when they finally began to roll towards the coast, Allied aircraft took a heavy toll before the Panzers could engage a single enemy tank. General Bayerlein, Panzer Lehr's commander, wrote, 'We moved as ordered, and immediately came under air attack. I lost twenty or thirty vehicles by nightfall. It is hard to remember exactly the figures for each day, but I do remember very well being strafed personally near Alençon.

'We kept on during the night with but three hours' delay for rest and fuelling. At daylight, General Dollmann gave me a direct order to proceed and there was nothing else to do. The first air attack came about 0530 that morning, near Falaise. By noon it was terrible: my men were calling the main road from Vire to Beny-Bocage a fighter-bomber race-course – *Jabo Rennstrecke*.'

In the confused situation there was little that the ground commanders could do except fight as best they could, hoping that the armoured reinforcements would be released as soon as Hitler made up his mind. 'Rommel,' said Speidel, 'had known that every hour would matter in the struggle to destroy the first enemy lodgements and prevent him reinforcing and increasing his foothold. Rommel had telephoned his headquarters urging that the 21st Panzers attack and that High Command must be pressed to release all reserves which should be concentrated under one divisional commander.' But the best that Speidel could do was to get the one Panzer division under Army Group B's control to attack under the command of General Marcks whose LXXXIV Corps was responsible for the Calvados sector.

Vital hours passed and thousands of Allied troops poured ashore. The paratroopers dug in to consolidate their gains on either flank of the bridgehead. The German Generals waited on Hitler to make a decision which would determine the course of the invasion but their Supreme Command structure was totally paralysed. The one man who could initiate action was fast asleep, unaware that his fortress had been breached. Albert Speer was at the Berghof at ten o'clock on 6 June:

' "Has the Führer been awakened?" I asked.

'He shook his head, "No, he receives the news after he has eaten breakfast."

'In recent days,' Speer noted, 'Hitler had kept on saying that the enemy would probably begin with a feigned attack in order to draw our troops away from the ultimate invasion site. So no one wanted to awaken Hitler and be ranted at for having judged the situation wrongly.'

Lost initiative

Within High Command, scattered in various buildings in the little town of Berchtesgaden, urgent messages flowed in from the Normandy front. The morning took on the unreality of a bad dream. At noon, Hitler appeared. But, for those who were eagerly awaiting orders to counter-attack, there was disappointment. In Normandy the German formations wilted under the unprecedented bombardment and tried to hold their ground, awaiting Panzer reinforcements, but Hitler indulged himself in receiving a state visit.

Speer's account of that situation conference reveals how successful Allied intelligence had been in misleading the Führer: 'Hitler seemed more set than ever on his preconceived idea that the enemy was only trying to mislead him. "Do you recall? Among the many reports we've received, there was one that exactly predicted the landing site and the day and hour. That only confirms my opinion that this is not the real invasion yet."

'The enemy intelligence service had deliberately played this information into his hands, Hitler maintained, in order to divert him from the true invasion site.'

But something had to be done about the Normandy landings. Finally Hitler agreed that the O.K.W. reserves should be released to attack the Allied bridgehead. But would this be enough? As Warlimont summed it up, 'The most important step

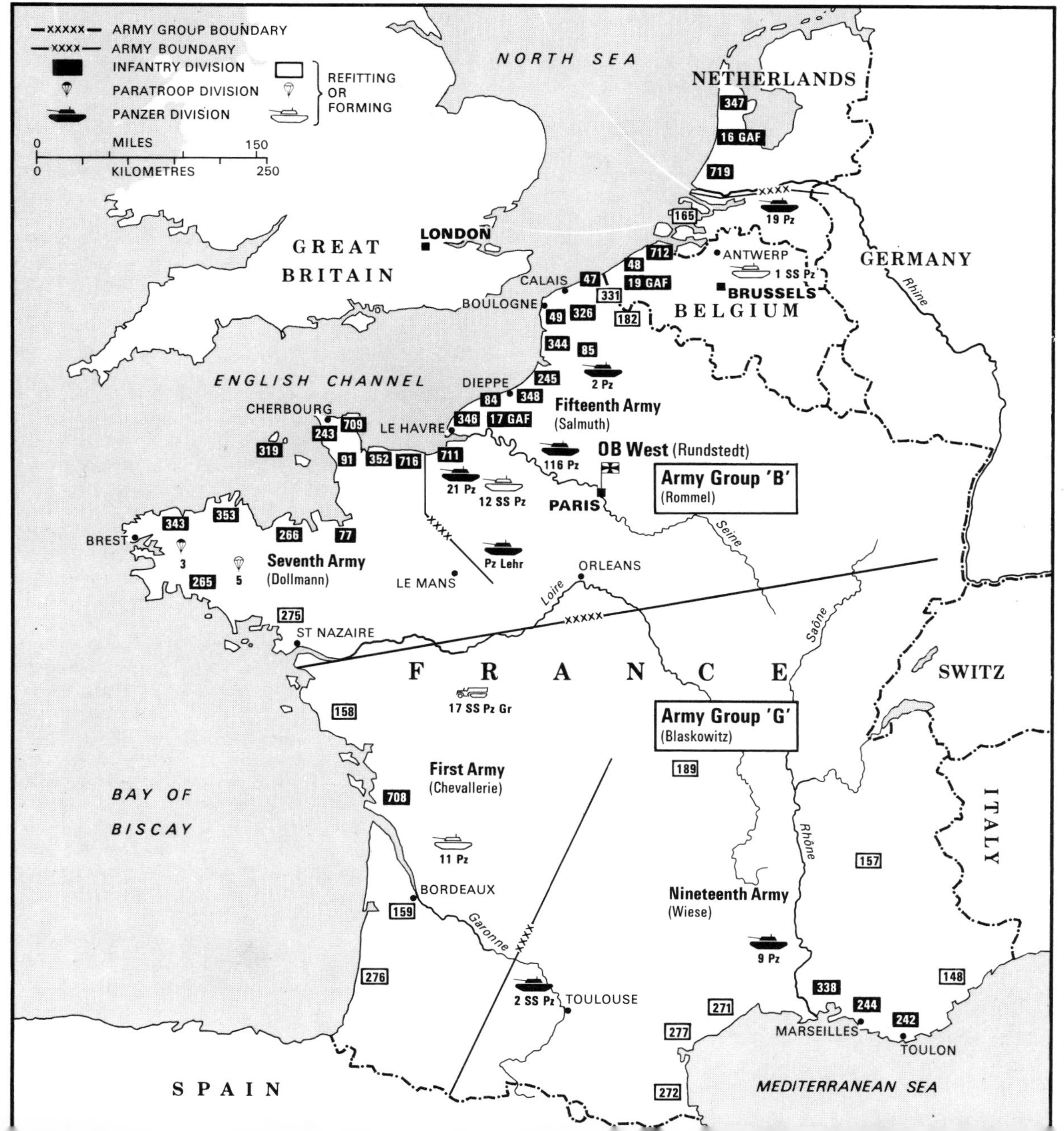

German dispositions to meet a cross-Channel invasion on the eve of D-Day

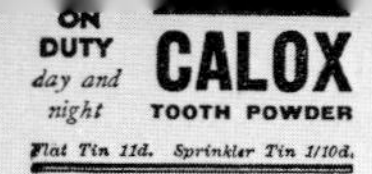

BLACKOUT 10.57 p.m. to 5.0 a.m.
Moon rises 9.48 p.m.
Moon sets 6.31 a.m.

Montgomery Leads British, U.S., Canadian Force

WE WIN BEACHHEADS

4,000 Ships, 11,000 Planes in Assault on France: 'All Going to Plan'—Premier

WE LAND IN JERSEY—Nazis

THE KING ON RADIO AT 9 P.M.

It was officially announced this morning that the King will broadcast at 9 o'clock to-night.

"ALLIES ARE PENETRATING DEEPER INLAND"

Paris radio broadcast these "latest flashes from the invasion area":

"The Germans are putting up very stiff resistance in the Caen area. The town area itself has been sorely tried. The enemy appears to be penetrating deeper inland.

"It has now become clear that the main Allied blow is not against Havre, but that General Eisenhawer is concentrating his efforts to capture Cherbourg.

"Allied paratroopers are now striving to capture the airfields in Normandy."

The London press proclaim a D-Day victory

was to move from the Straits to Normandy the bulk of the Fifteenth Army, then to collect all forces which could be made available rapidly from other parts of France, and so be in a position to launch a decisive counter-attack.' But Hitler refused to countenance the movement of the Fifteenth Army. The bridgehead would have to be annihilated with the forces already in Normandy. The Führer had other grounds for expecting an attack across the Straits of Dover. Fifty-five positions had been prepared, from which several hundred 'flying bombs' were to be launched towards London every day.

When Rommel finally reached his headquarters on the afternoon of D-Day it was already too late for the Germans to regain the initiative. Nevertheless, von Rundstedt passed on Supreme Command's directive to General Dollman's Seventh Army struggling to defend Normandy: 'The beachhead there must be cleaned up by not later than tonight.' It must rank as one of the most incredible commands in military history.

How they told the world

The Allies realized that a skilful use of radio and the press would be an important asset to them in the invasion operations. Eisenhower, in particular, knew the value of good public relations and had always taken the trouble to keep his press corps well briefed, as had Montgomery. They both knew the immense propaganda impact of a successful breakthrough of Hitler's vaunted Atlantic Wall. In Britain and America many people had been caught up in the preparations for D-Day; many had sons, brothers or fathers in the assault troops, and ever since Dunkirk, Britain had been a nation waiting for a cross-Channel attack. It would be an enormous morale booster for the war-weary British to know that 'we had done it at last'. In the oppressed nations of Europe, news that the Allies were poised for a final attack on the Reich would bring relief and stir up resistance to their German masters. Even within the Reich itself, for years indoctrinated by Goebbels' propaganda that the Fortress Europe was unassailable, the news of an Allied landing would be a serious psychological blow.

The B.B.C. used all its immense propaganda power to beam the message of the breach of Hitler's Fortress to all the occupied nations. Its transmitters sent out Eisenhower's message:

'Although the initial assault may not have been made in your own country, the hour of your liberation is approaching. All patriots, men and women, young and old, have a part to play in the achievement of final victory. To members of resistance movements, whether led by nationals or by outside leaders, I say follow the instructions you have received. To patriots who are not members of organized resistance groups, I say continue your passive resistance but do not needlessly endanger your lives. Wait until I give you the signal to rise and strike the enemy.'

Then, perhaps mindful of the feelings of vengeance inside France which could lead to bitter strife as the Germans moved out, Eisenhower said, 'The effective civil administration of France must be provided by Frenchmen. All persons must continue in their present duties unless otherwise instructed. Those who have made common cause with the enemy and so betrayed their country will be removed. When France is liberated from her oppressors you yourselves will choose your representatives and the government under which you wish to live.'

General de Gaulle, too, eventually agreed to make his broadcast to France. Now he meant to convey to the French the message that an independent Free France existed, which would automatically assume power.

'The enemy is to be destroyed; the enemy who bruises and soils our country, the hated and dishonoured enemy. He will do all he can to escape his fate, he will fight desperately to retain his hold on our soil as long as possible . . . France will wage this battle with fury and in good order. We have won our victories in this way for 1,500 years and thus shall we win again – in good order.'

De Gaulle informed the French that there would be no question as to who would assume power. It would not be a patched-up Allied administration. 'For the nation which fights, bound and gagged, against the oppressor armed to the teeth, good order in battle is dependent upon the fulfil-

NS-Kurier

Gauorgan der NSDAP

Stuttgarter Neues Tagblatt

...aufspreis 15 Pfennig | Stadt der Auslandsdeutschen | Mittwoch, den 7. Juni 1944 | Nummer 153 - 14. Jahrgang

Der Invasionstermin wurde von Moskau bestimmt

Landetruppen abgeriegelt oder vernichtet

...r schwere Verluste der feindlichen Verbände / Kämpfe von außerordentlicher Härte / Schwerpunkt der großen Schlacht am Kanal noch nicht zu erkennen / Neue Aktionen werden erwartet

The Nazi *N.S. Kurier* tells a different story – 'landing troops cut off and destroyed'

ment of several conditions; the first is that the instructions given by the French government and by the French leaders whom the government has authorized to give orders locally, must be strictly obeyed. The second is that the struggle carried on by you behind the enemy lines must be co-ordinated as closely as possible with the battles fought by the Allied and French armies.'

Then de Gaulle instinctively understood that this was the moment to re-assert the greatness of France: 'The battle of France has begun. In the nation, in the empire and in the armed forces there is now but one purpose, one desire.

'Look upward. There, where the burden of our blood and tears lie like a lowering cloud upon us – there the light of our greatness is shining through.'

Vichy speaks

General von Stulpnagel, the German military governor of Paris, reacted speedily to the broadcasts by General Eisenhower and de Gaulle and issued a proclamation that was immediately broadcast by French Radio:

'German troops have been given orders to shoot any person who is seen to be co-operating with the Allied invasion forces, or who gives shelter to Allied soldiers, sailors or airmen. Such Frenchmen will be treated as bandits.'

The Vichy authorities throughout France slavishly took up the German line. Prime Minister Laval broadcast a national appeal to his countrymen to ignore de Gaulle's call to resistance.

'With sadness I read today of the orders given to Frenchmen by an American General. These orders imply that Frenchmen should act in contravention of the Hague Convention. The French government stands by the armistice of 1940 and appeals to Frenchmen to honour their country's signature. If you took part in the present fighting, France would be plunged into civil war.'

Vichy knew it was fighting for its life. The aged Marshal Pétain was obliged by conscience and the insistence of the German authorities to broadcast from Paris a 'patriotic' call to Frenchmen to stand behind the Germans: 'The Anglo-Saxons have set foot on our soil. France is becoming a battlefield. Frenchmen, do not attempt to commit any action which might bring terrible reprisals. Obey the orders of the government.'

On 6 June, Dr Goebbels' Ministry of Information and Enlightenment was faced with a seemingly impossible task: that of explaining to the German nation and the world how the impossible had happened – the 'unassailable' Atlantic Wall had been breached, and Allied troops were landing in France in large numbers. Ever resourceful, Dr Goebbels came up with some masterpieces of construction, whose plausibility must have strained the credulity of even the most ardent Nazi. Apparently, the Allies had done precisely what the Germans wanted them to do. They had walked straight into a trap; the invaders were already well on the way to being hurled back into the sea with huge losses.

Berlin Radio claimed that the Allies had only been able to make a minor landing because General Eisenhower had taken advantage of 'an element of surprise'. Although the broadcast stressed that 'of course, complete surprise was impossible because the High Command expected an attempt at the precise place it had been made', they admitted that the High Command had no idea of 'the precise date of the assault'. In fact, the commentator continued, O.K.W.'s 'anxiety has not been that the invasion might come, but that it might evade Germany's Western Army'. The next claim was that the result of the battle was a foregone conclusion, because 'all the German troops are crack veterans hardened in Russia'. They were more than a match for what was claimed as the 'first-class picked men of the Allies'.

On the evening of 6 June, a suitably high-ranking Wehrmacht commander, Lieutenant-General Dettinger, was brought before the microphones to reassure listeners that the Atlantic Wall had after all not been breached: 'Till now, the enemy has at no point been able to cut through the depth of the fortifications. His action up to now has been according to plan – our plan.'

The idea was being propagated, incredibly, that the Führer had actually planned the invasion to trap the Allies into a decisive German victory that would be the turning point of the war.

15 Race Against Time

Widening the beachhead. A few hours after landing, an amphibious Sherman fights its way inland backed by infantry

The first waves of the Allied assault had punched gaping holes in the Atlantic Wall. In a matter of hours, the coastal crust of the German defences had been broken everywhere except at Omaha. Rommel's plan to halt the invasion in the surf had failed. The colossal weight and surprise of the attack overwhelmed the resistance of the static coastal defence regiments. Omaha demonstrated what might have happened if battle-hardened units like the 352nd Division had reinforced the whole of the coastal sector. At Gold beach the units maintained a spirited defence at Le Hamel long after the Slavs, Caucasians and other troops had given up.

Once the crust of the Atlantic Wall had been breached, the Allies rapidly pushed inland towards their D-Day objectives. The British and Canadians in the east struck out towards Caen and Bayeux.

The problem in the mind of the Allied commanders was whether they could achieve their build-up before the Panzers met them in a full counter-attack. Every hour was vital, every tank, gun, man and shell that landed helped to keep up the military balance. When the 'hammer blow' fell, Montgomery and Eisenhower knew that only superiority in the air and the fire-power of naval guns would keep the Germans at bay until they had sufficient land strength to meet it. Meanwhile, the airborne units on the flanks were dangerously exposed. They were encircled by German troops, cut off from the relief that was coming from the coast. At Caen, tanks of the 21st Panzer Division were already moving up to the attack. The British landings were the target. The Germans held a dangerous four-mile strip running down to the sea between Juno and Sword. The marines had failed to break through at St Aubin and Lion-sur-Mer. Inland, German artillery units of the 21st Panzer Division, strategically sited on the ridge above the village of Périers, consolidated their hold on this crucial salient. Adjoining beaches were constantly under fire from guns ranged on the barrage balloons, windsocks and beach markers. For the whole of D-Day this salient was to remain a constant threat to the British beachheads. It offered a chance for a major German counter-attack.

Fortunately, the chronic indecision gripping the High Command that fateful morning effectively paralysed the one Panzer force which could have changed the whole tide of the battle for the beaches. A full hour and a half before the 3rd Division landed at Sword, General Edgar Feuchtinger, 21st Panzer Division Commander, was already moving his forces to the coast when Army Group B confirmed his initiative and ordered him to attack the airborne landings: 'Realizing that my armoured division was closest to the scene of operations, I finally decided at 6.30 in the morning that I had to take some action. I ordered my tanks to attack the English 6th Airborne Division which had entrenched itself in a bridgehead over the Orne. To me this constituted the most immediate threat to the German position.

'Hardly had I made this decision when at seven o'clock I received my first intimation that a higher command did still exist. I was told by Army Group B that I was now under the command of the Seventh Army. But I received no further orders as to my role. At nine o'clock I was informed that I would receive any future orders from LXXXIV Infantry Corps, and finally at ten o'clock I was given my first operational instructions. I was ordered to stop the move of my tanks against the Allied airborne troops, and to turn west and aid the forces protecting Caen.' The result was that the vital hours when the Panzers might have been decisive were wasted back-tracking and re-crossing, tank by tank, the one surviving bridge over the Orne at Caen.

Firmly ashore

Those hours were crucial; on the British beaches the Allies were facing a massive traffic problem, which at times threatened the whole momentum of the invasion. As the tide receded, follow-up landings found it increasingly difficult to struggle ashore through the debris of the first assaults. But one man was extremely glad to find the tide going out; M. G. Gale and his tank crew of the 44th Royal Tank Regiment had begun their invasion, inadvertently, underwater: 'The ship slowed to a halt, the bows opened and down went the flat, and there, just before us in the morning light, was the beach. Fighting was going on just off the beach, we could hear the gunfire, and other tanks were landing to our right, we could see them moving up the beach.

'Sitting in the driver's seat I began to move our Sherman fitted with its new 17-pounder gun (the first we had ever had, up till then we had the 75-mm.) down the ramp. I moved very slowly down the ramp and began to ease her off the end, waiting for the drop into what we had expected to be about 6 ft of water. We were all battened down and waterproofed, which as it turned out was just as well because instead of 6 ft there was 10 or 12 ft of water we fell into. We sat there waiting for the tide to go out for almost two hours. We were able to follow what was going on, on the radio, but seeing nothing except water through our periscope until at last as the water went down we could see and finally, with the better part of our Regiment off the beaches, we were able to rejoin them.'

'Wannsee on a summer's afternoon'

Keeping the vast quantities of men and equipment moving ashore taxed teamwork to its limit. It was not made any easier by rough water and the continuing German attempts at intervention – either by shelling or token appearances by the Luftwaffe.

'We were on the first of the Rhino's . . . my own 3-tonner with petrol and R.E.M.E. supplies and spares and towing a generator, my mate in the vehicle was the Captain's batman,' recalled W. A. Rogers, then a motor transport sergeant with the Royal Artillery. 'Well, as we were coming ashore being shelled from the shore, and we were both standing on the seaward side of the vehicles, one of our warships opened fire. I went to speak to the batman (he was only a small fellow) and I couldn't see him – I thought he had gone overboard, and then I heard his voice say "Has that bloody train gone by yet?" When those shells went overhead you could feel the heat from them – he was under the gun tower and when I thought about it later we were leaning against 5 TONS of 3·7-inch ammo.'

The various nationalities who manned the coastal defences were low-grade units; many surrendered as resistance to the first assault collapsed. Some even gave their captors the impression 'that they had their suitcases packed and white flags ready'. Some were pressed into immediate service to fetch and carry in the clearing-up operations. But the front-line Wehrmacht of the 352nd Division was still proving hostile and held out stubbornly in isolated buildings. Pillbox by pillbox they were flushed out by parties of soldiers and sailors who had lost their units in the rush of the first assault. Roger McKinley, a Royal Navy Commando, who had landed miles away from his beach, joined one of these groups:

'Unfortunately, between us and the battle area were some of the enemy, so we decided to push our way through and do what we could to mop up the Germans on the way. We soon got bogged down by these 88s and machine-gun nests. The Major called me up as the senior N.C.O. and said, "Let's put some grenades in there and get rid of them".

Artillery pours ashore. American self-propelled guns were some of the 81,000 vehicles landed by 16 June. They reinforced the beachhead and played a vital part in checking German counter-attacks. German paratroops (right) from the élite II Parachute Corps were moved into Normandy to contain the American beachhead. They proved unyielding fighters in the ditches and hedgerows of the bocage, and frustrated Bradley's efforts to launch a break-out

'He said, "Use your grenades." But although I had my bomb pouches strapped on, I was not carrying any grenades. "I've only got shoe-cleaning gear and boot polish in one pouch, and my soap and flannel in the other – I'm a sailor and my grenades were in the boxes in the boat." So I had to take the army grenades. I took the pins out with my teeth and held one in each hand and the other in my pouch. I rushed up to the pillbox although they were firing at me and lobbed these grenades in – and we captured a German pillbox.'

In the early hours of the landings, the vulnerable Allied flanks presented the Germans with their best chance to counter-attack and throw the main landings into confusion. Both these flanks were held by scattered and relatively weak paratroop formations.

On the American flank, a failure to appreciate the tactical situation led to the confusion and disorder of the German forces in the Cotentin peninsula on the morning of D-Day, and demonstrated the importance of this element of surprise.

Build-up on Omaha. Hours after the first bloody assault, G.I.s of the 1st U.S. Infantry Division wade ashore to widen the Omaha beachhead

General Dollman, commander of the Seventh Army, had reacted rapidly to the airborne landings by organizing a three-pronged attack from the north, south and west to crush the American forces. These orders were issued in the small hours of the morning, but the division commanders were still hurrying back from their Rennes exercise. Now, in the early morning, faced with a real invasion, they found themselves cut off from their commands and headquarters; the Resistance had cut their communication lines. Confusion reigned.

Major Friedrich-August Freiherr von der Heydte of the 6th German Parachute Regiment finally got his orders to attack the Americans between Carentan and Ste-Mère-Église. He collected his forces. To find out what was happening, he climbed the church tower at St Côme, a little village near Ste-Mère-Église where the 82nd U.S. Airborne Division had dug in. He could see the Utah beach six miles away; the sight was 'overwhelming'. It was the middle of the morning by now, and he could see scores of small craft scurrying to and from the beaches unloading. He was hardly aware that a battle was going on at all; in the warm sun the whole picture was, in his own words, like 'Berlin Wannsee on a summer's afternoon'. He could see no enemy forces inland, nor any sign of the 82nd or 101st Divisions.

By midnight, the first battalion had marched straight through the scattered units of the 101st Division without any difficulty. By then, a sudden landing of gliders and paratroops of the U.S. Airborne Division effectively cut von der Heydte's force in two. In reality the advance inland of the U.S. 8th Infantry Division from Utah had already sealed the regiment's fate, but neither the German troops nor their commander were to realize this until the following morning.

On the coastal strip, a few miles from where von der Heydte's battalions spent the whole day manoeuvring against the American paratroops, the vast bulk of the U.S. VII Corps poured ashore all morning and afternoon. Their only opposition was sporadic shelling from the batteries to the north. Traffic snarl-ups caused by the need to get everything inland through a few beach exits were a far greater problem. The leading battalion of the 8th U.S. Infantry pushed inland to relieve Ste-Mère-Église. Just before nightfall they were halted a few miles south of their objective by stiff German resistance. But for the narrow causeways across the flooded pasture land, seaborne infantry would have achieved their scheduled D-Day penetration to link up with men of the 82nd and 101st Airborne Divisions.

Breakout from Omaha

At Omaha it had been a very different picture. Here, American dead lay scattered over the beach. In the first few hours of the assault, nearly 2,000 casualties had been suffered – one for every six feet of the four-mile beachhead. Except for two platoons east of Dog Green beach which had somehow gained the lower slopes, most of the assault lay pinned down on the shingle or circling helplessly in landing craft unable to get inshore.

Whilst the Generals on the U.S.S. *Augusta* were seriously considering whether or not to abandon the assault and to re-direct the landings to the British beaches, the situation suddenly changed. 'The first encouraging news came at 1100 hours from a message to Commander Transport Division Three, intercepted by the Force Commander to the effect that the German defenders were leaving their posts and surrendering to U.S. troops. Shortly after that another message from a member of V Corps staff embarked in a D.U.K.W. near the shore-line stated that the troops were advancing up the western slopes of the exit from the sector Easy.' The Force Commander's report does not record the dramatic way in which the balance was turned at a crucial moment in the battle. In fact two large landing craft, L.C.T. 30 and L.C.I. (L) 544, had steamed at full speed through the obstacles off the Colleville beaches firing all weapons and drawing the enemy fire even after they were aground. At the same time, two destroyers raced to within 1,000 yards of the shore and shelled the German positions at Les Moulins to the east. Under cover of this burst of firing the assault troops rallied as bulldozers of the engineers' battalions drove two gaps through the St Laurent dunes, filled the anti-tank ditch and

cleared the minefields. With destroyer fire drenching the pillboxes, the 18th Infantry was able to overwhelm the German positions. In less than an hour, this bold drive by sea and land succeeded in bringing the only real breakthrough since H-Hour.

In spite of this, General Dietrich Kraiss, who commanded the sector and the crack 352nd Division, the backbone of the German defences on D-Day, believed that his men had halted the American landings. Reports from the 716th Division in the British assault area were not encouraging. By mid-morning the British 50th Division had penetrated deeply inland and was heading for Bayeux. In the process units of Kraiss's 352nd had been isolated at Le Hamel. They continued a stubborn resistance, but could not stop the advance inland.

The British did not know it, but the collapse of the strongpoint at La Rivière on the eastern flank of Gold beach opened wide the road to Bayeux. Even so, the British 50th Division could not have exploited the situation as their follow-up reserves took two hours to land through the clogged-up beachhead. But for the Germans the situation was serious; the gap had to be plugged before the British could advance and threaten their position at Omaha. Now Kraiss ran into another problem that bedevilled German Commanders on D-Day – lack of adequate reserves. The only forces he had at his disposal were the LXXXIV Corps reserve, the 915th Regiment, which had been stationed at Bayeux. They had often practised this counter-thrust towards the coast. But at 0400 hours that morning they had been sent west to Carentan to deal with reported airborne landings at the base of the Cotentin.

General Kraiss reacted rapidly as the gaping holes opened up in the east of his front, and sent out an order for the 915th to return. But over an hour was lost trying to contact the regiment, now twenty-five miles away from its new objective. Once the orders had got through, there was a pantomime counter-march as the troops, on foot, bicycles and a motley collection of old French lorries, struggled to return to the real battle. It was more than three hours before even a section of the unit was near enough to counter-attack Omaha. Those three hours made the crucial difference between success and failure to the Americans.

The confusion and lack of mobility of the German reserves stopped any reinforcement of the Omaha defences. The long afternoon of D-Day was taken up in the slow process of prizing out the German defences one by one to secure the beachhead. The gunfire from the bombardment force was a decisive factor. A German report stated: 'The fire curtain provided by the guns of the Navy so far proved to be one of the trump cards of the Anglo-U.S. invasion armies.'

Panzer counter-strike

Communication delays and difficulties clouded the information that was reaching Eisenhower and his Commanders back at the SHAEF Advance H.Q. at Southwick House. Montgomery was anxious to sail with his staff for the beachhead to assume his command of the ground forces, and an urgent signal went out to General Bradley for a report:

(1) No news from you since your Sitrep 0730 received here 1454.
(2) Am arriving over myself early tomorrow morning.
(3) Essential I have short report here COMGA. Most Immediate.

Two hours later the long awaited news came back: 'IMMEDIATE
Colleville taken. St Laurent partially occupied. Crust seems to be broken. Considerable mortar and artillery fire falling on beaches. First elements of approximately 4 regiments ashore. At last report no repeat no artillery or anti-aircraft ashore. Many stranded landing craft due to surf and obstacles which were not cleared initially. Destroyers giving close gunfire support. Above for Omaha. On Utah latest reports indicate good progress. No radio reports either airborne division. No hostile air attack yet.'

It was a fair summary of what had happened at Omaha. And it told Montgomery what he wanted to know, that the Americans were firmly ashore and would not easily be dislodged.

Right: New management. American Rangers swarm over the German strongpoint on the Pointe-du-Hoc dominating Omaha beach. The blockhouse had been blasted by 600 shells from the U.S. battleships, *Texas* and *Arkansas*. German prisoners are marched to the beach and captivity

Below: The Wehrmacht begins to crumble. Prisoners are assembled behind a disabled Sherman 'flail' tank. For them the war is over. Some were shipped as far as Canada where they could hardly believe their good fortune

Far right: The 'butcher's bill'. Allied commanders were relieved that there were few casualties on D-Day. Within 90 minutes of the first assault, surgeons were working in field dressing-stations in four of the beachheads. Of the men landed on D-Day, the British and Canadians suffered 3,000 casualties, and the Americans 6,000

On the British front, the critical period of the late morning and early afternoon passed without serious German counter-attack. The 50th Division was only a few miles short of its objective at Bayeux – and would have advanced further if its follow-up forces had not been held on Gold. All day the sappers and naval beach parties worked feverishly to clear the jams and organize the chaos of stranded ships, obstacles, wrecked tanks and assault craft.

Flying high above them with the R.A.F. reconnaissance flights was Richard Dimbleby of the B.B.C.:

'Of enemy troop movements there was, until noon today, little or no sign from the air, even close to the immediate battle area. Long stretches of empty roads shining with rain, deserted dripping woods and damp fields – static, quiet – perhaps uncannily quiet – and possibly not to remain quiet. But here and there a movement catches the eye, as our aircraft on reconnaissance roar over a large suspicious wood – three German soldiers running like mad across the main road to fling themselves into cover. And, near the battle area, much nearer the battle area than they, a solitary peasant harrowing his field, up and down behind the horses, looking nowhere but before him and the soil.'

The occasional stalwart Norman persisted with the day's routine, oblivious to the desperate race around him. The objectives of the Juno and Sword landings had been to take Caen by late afternoon whilst the Germans were still off-balance. Caen was the vital key to the defence of Normandy, dominating the inland plateau; its airfields were strategically positioned and behind the city were miles of open tank country rolling on to the gates of Paris itself. The German Command knew that Normandy was the vital pivot of the battle for France herself.

That afternoon, as the armoured vehicles of the 21st Panzer Division struggled through refugee traffic on the northern outskirts of the city, two powerful prongs of the Allied attack drove towards Caen – from the north-west the Canadian 3rd Division from Juno, and due north the British 3rd Division from Sword. In between, the four-mile salient still remained in German hands in spite of the

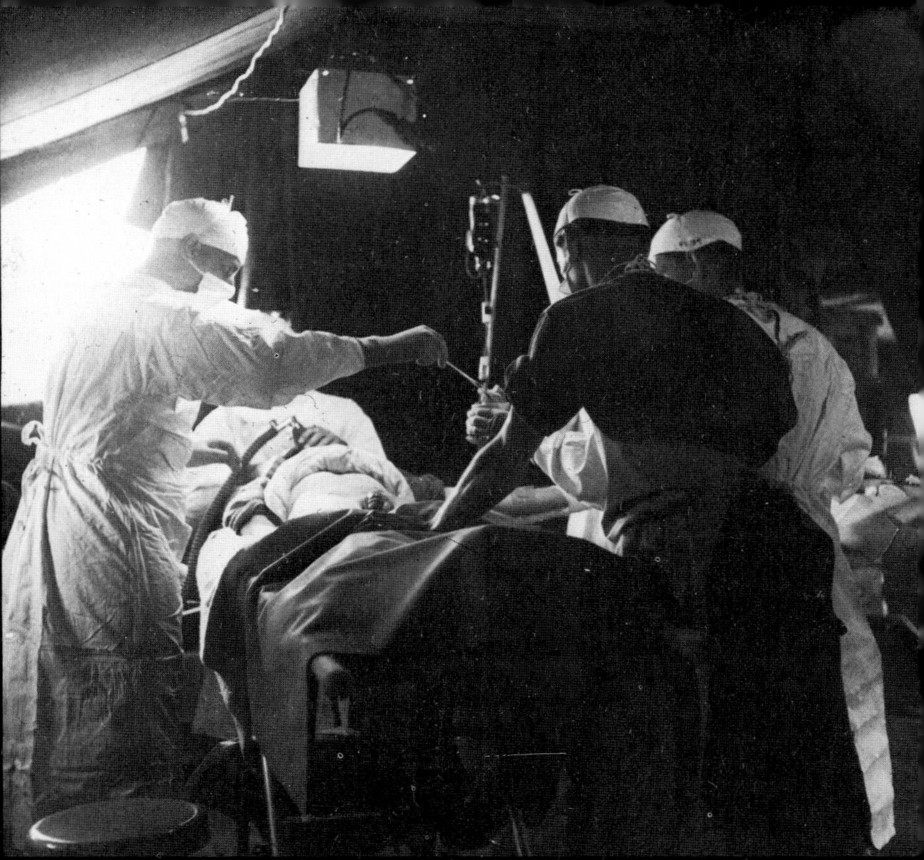

'They haven't come any too soon. There'll be a very unpleasant surprise for the enemy . . . You can hear the aircraft roaring over me I expect as I still speak. I can still see the signs of a typical Panzer battle being raged on the slightly high ground just about three or four miles ahead of me and these paratroops are coming down just between where I'm speaking which is just about above the sand dunes. Down they come. They're being attacked pretty harshly as you'll hear, but they're landing in great force between the sand dunes between the beach area and the battle and they may have a very decisive effect on that battle.'

Alan Melville, B.B.C. correspondent, at Ouistreham

'Another Allied parachute landing on both sides of the Orne, together with a sharp attack by English tanks, forced me to give up my hold on the coast. I retired to take up a line just north of Caen. By the end of the first day my division had lost almost 25 per cent of its tanks.'

General Feuchtinger

Right: On the American beaches by the end of D-Day, organization had been greatly improved, and the Germans pushed back to such an extent that the follow-up forces could walk ashore

fierce fighting by the Royal Marine Commandos.

By late afternoon, when the British and Canadians were within sight of the city, the Panzers struck back. General Feuchtinger threw his tanks into the attack.

'Once over the Orne river, I drove north towards the coast. By this time the enemy, consisting of three British and three Canadian Infantry Divisions, had made astonishing progress and had already occupied a strip of high ground about ten kilometres from the sea. From here, the excellent anti-tank gunfire of the Allies knocked out eleven of my tanks before I had barely started. However, one battlegroup did manage to bypass these guns and actually reached the coast at Lion-sur-Mer, at about seven in the evening.'

Although six tanks and a handful of infantry could hardly smash the beachhead alone, they were a base from which the whole Panzer division might rally to mount a major thrust against the weak flanks of Juno and Sword beaches. It was a threatening situation for the British and one which the Panzer divisions had been trained to exploit.

Another 21st Panzer push heading for Sword beach ran into the British. It was frustrating for the British; they were just five miles from Caen and it was early afternoon. It would take them until early evening to capture the German position. All now depended on the King's Shropshire Light Infantry who, with the tanks of the Staffordshire Yeomanry, set off as soon as the other brigades had run into the opposition. Their orders were to dash to Caen along the western edge of the River Orne. Although it was known from aerial reconnaissance that the German tanks were massing north of Caen for an attack, they set off in high hopes and without full tank cover. Their way inland took them through to the 6th Airborne Division who were holding the Orne bridges under heavy German pressure.

By 1600 hours the British thrust had reached Blainville. Then, on the outskirts of the village, in Liesby wood, just two and a half miles from Caen, they ran up against forty German tanks. In the encounter that followed as the Panzers tried to find a way through the British lines, the Germans lost thirteen tanks. The remaining tanks of the 21st were the only armour that stood between the British and Caen. Their Battalion Commander, Colonel von Oppeln-Bronowski, knew that to press on would decimate his force. Before the attack, General Marcks, the commander of the LXXXIV Corps, had personally told him, 'Oppeln, the future of Germany may very well rest on your shoulders. If you don't push the British back we've lost the war.' As last words, they now had an irony appreciated by von Oppeln as his attack, too, ground to a halt. He might have lost the war, but his tanks had saved Caen. While Caen held, Normandy would hold and whilst Normandy held, France was secure. Caen was in every sense the pivot on which the major battle for France would be fought. But the 21st Panzers were not finished yet. The battle-group which had found the route to the sea could be reinforced. The order went out to the rest of the division to prepare to exploit the position.

Yet, like all the German commanders on D-Day, Feuchtinger had been forced to divide and weaken his counter-attack. At 2000 hours the Panzers were ready for a concerted attack down the salient dividing the British and Canadian divisions. Then suddenly the sky was full with 250 gliders swooping down from the east in over the sea. This massive reinforcement unnerved the leading German tanks. They feared that the airborne landings had been sent to cut them off from Caen. The speed of the Allies' attack amazed them. Low-flying Spitfires dived on the Panzers at almost zero height. The Germans hesitated.

The leading tanks which had reached the sea rapidly withdrew in the face of what they saw as another overwhelming attack.

The following morning they would recover their nerve and try once again to force a gap between the British and Canadians, but by then it was too late. The gap had been closed.

The day's achievement

For thousands of Allied soldiers sunset brought home the full measure of their achievement that day. 'On the beach in that evening it was a marvellous and satisfying sight. It was no exaggeration

to say you couldn't see any sea – it was so full of craft.'

Although records are obviously uncertain, over 130,000 men were landed from the sea (75,000 on the British beaches and 57,500 at Utah and Omaha). In addition, 7,000 British and 15,500 American airborne troops were in action. In view of the strength of the Atlantic Wall and the high risks of the invasion, the casualty rate was far lighter than many experienced soldiers expected. Fears of another Gallipoli were mercifully proved false. Some 3,000 British and Canadians were killed or wounded, as well as 600 men of the 6th Airborne. On the American side over 6,000 men were wounded or lost their lives, including airborne casualties.

Much of the success could be attributed to the Allied Air Forces which from the night of 5 June to the end of D-Day flew 14,000 sorties for the loss of 127 aircraft of all types.

As the forward units in Normandy reported back to 21st Army Group H.Q., the sense of victory was tempered by the knowledge that, in spite of the success of the landings, few of the initial D-Day objectives had been attained.

The British 6th Airborne had done all that was asked of it and had secured the left flank of the beachhead, but the 3rd Division, diving forward from Sword beach, had been halted three miles from Caen, the major D-Day objective. The Canadians had failed to take the important airfield of Carpiquet, three miles west of Caen, even though the forward elements had actually reached the runways. Bayeux was also still in German hands, although the British Army was just one and a half miles away. The Americans, too, had little more than a toehold. At Omaha they had been badly shaken and the Germans were well dug in, barely a mile away. Even at Utah where the landings had gone exceptionally well, the U.S. 4th Division was now fighting hard to link up with the battered 101st and 82nd U.S. Airborne Divisions. They were a long way from cutting off Cherbourg.

The Germans were now moving in their hardened Panzer reserves, the 12th S.S., 2nd S.S., Panzer-Lehr and 17th Panzer Grenadier. These were all en route for the front. The 9th and 10th S.S. Panzers would be brought back from Russia and the 2nd Panzer moved west from Amiens. Other infantry divisions were on the move from Brittany and the Biscay coast. All now turned on the battle of the bridgehead.

16 Break-out to Victory

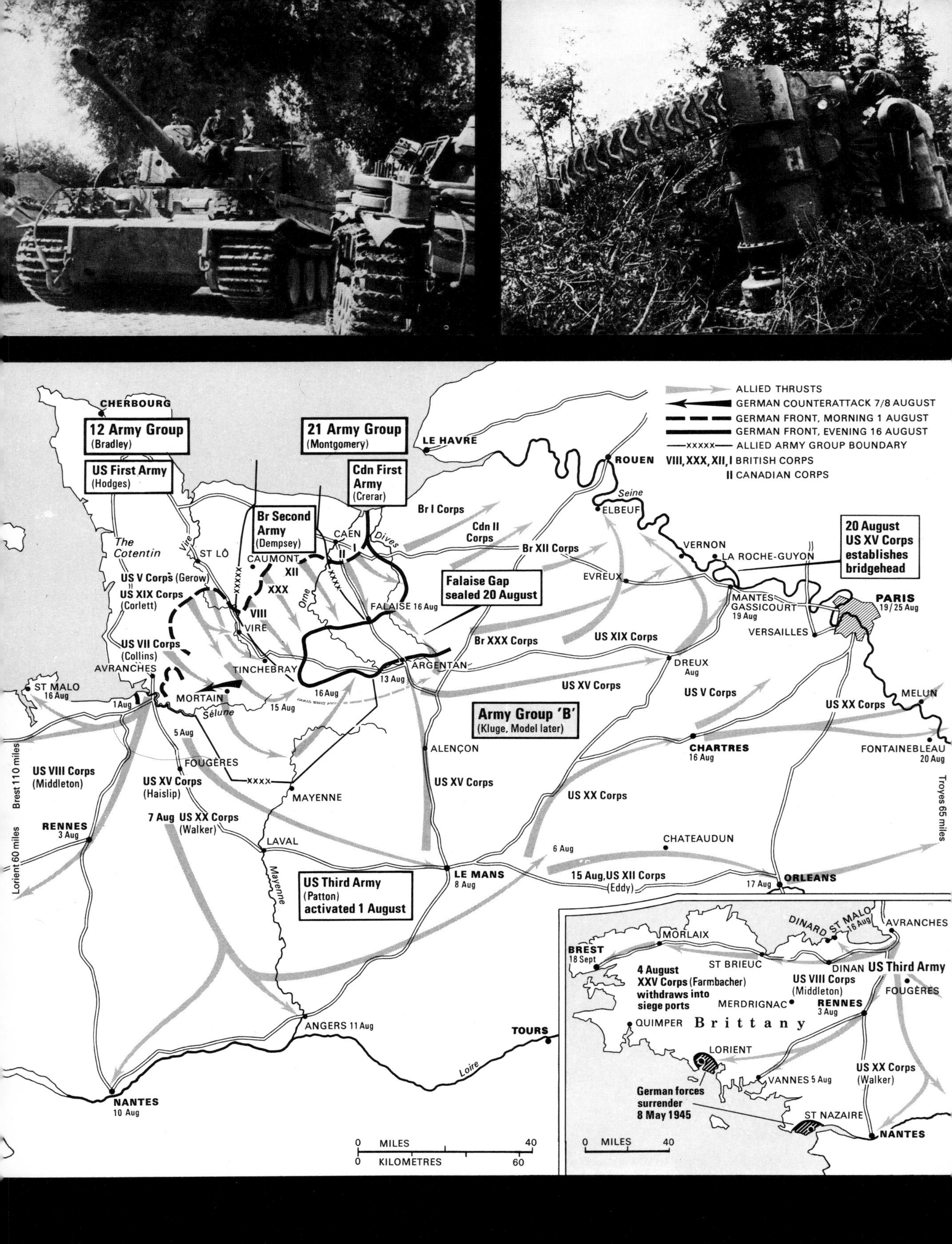

ALLIED THRUSTS
GERMAN COUNTERATTACK 7/8 AUGUST
GERMAN FRONT, MORNING 1 AUGUST
GERMAN FRONT, EVENING 16 AUGUST
ALLIED ARMY GROUP BOUNDARY
VIII, XXX, XII, I BRITISH CORPS
II CANADIAN CORPS
CHERBOURG
12 Army Group (Bradley)
21 Army Group (Montgomery)
US First Army (Hodges)
Cdn First Army (Crerar)
Br Second Army (Dempsey)
LE HAVRE
ROUEN
Seine
ELBEUF
Br I Corps
Cdn II Corps
Br XII Corps
CAEN
Dives
The Cotentin
Vire
ST LÔ
CAUMONT
XII
XXX
VIII
Orne
US V Corps (Gerow)
US XIX Corps (Corlett)
US VII Corps (Collins)
VIRE
FALAISE 16 Aug
Falaise Gap sealed 20 August
VERNON
LA ROCHE-GUYON
20 August US XV Corps establishes bridgehead
EVREUX
MANTES GASSICOURT 19 Aug
PARIS 19/25 Aug
VERSAILLES
Br XXX Corps
US XIX Corps
AVRANCHES
TINCHEBRAY
ARGENTAN
13 Aug
DREUX Aug
ST MALO 16 Aug
1 Aug
MORTAIN
16 Aug
15 Aug
Sélune
US XV Corps
US V Corps
MELUN
US XX Corps
Army Group 'B' (Kluge, Model later)
5 Aug
FOUGÈRES
ALENÇON
CHARTRES 16 Aug
FONTAINEBLEAU 20 Aug
Brest 110 miles
US VIII Corps (Middleton)
US XV Corps (Haislip)
MAYENNE
US XV Corps
US XX Corps
Troyes 65 miles
RENNES 3 Aug
7 Aug US XX Corps (Walker)
LAVAL
CHATEAUDUN
6 Aug
Lorient 60 miles
Mayenne
LE MANS 8 Aug
15 Aug, US XII Corps (Eddy)
17 Aug
ORLEANS
US Third Army (Patton) activated 1 August
ANGERS 11 Aug
TOURS
Loire
NANTES 10 Aug
0 MILES 40
0 KILOMETRES 60
DINARD
ST MALO 16 Aug
AVRANCHES
MORLAIX
BREST 18 Sept
ST BRIEUC
DINAN
US Third Army
4 August XXV Corps (Farmbacher) withdraws into siege ports
US VIII Corps (Middleton)
FOUGÈRES
MERDRIGNAC
RENNES 3 Aug
QUIMPER
Brittany
LORIENT
US XX Corps (Walker)
VANNES 5 Aug
German forces surrender 8 May 1945
ST NAZAIRE
NANTES
0 MILES 40

Previous pages: Bradley's troops widen the bridgehead. Armed with bazookas, infantry cautiously advance towards a knocked-out German tank. The U.S. First Army fought a bitter campaign for six weeks after D-Day, trying to create a major breakthrough to break the German ring in the bocage, which naturally favoured the defenders. Bradley badly needed space in order to build up his forces for a major offensive

Checking the Panzers. Soon after D-Day, Hitler released the Panzer reserves, including battalions of heavy Tigers (left above). They were backed up by S.S. Panzer Grenadiers who were skilled at using camouflage and terrain (right). The Germans were mercilessly harried from the air as they tried to concentrate for a counter-offensive. The Allied Expeditionary Air Force flew thousands of sorties to provide the badly needed time for the D-Day armies to build up to strength

Opposite below: The break-out

The terrifying effect of the bombing attacks on even the most battle-hardened men is described by a staff officer of the 17th S.S. Panzer Grenadier Division based south of the Loire:

'Our motorized columns were coiling along the road towards the invasion beaches. Then something happened that left us in a daze. Spurts of fire flicked along the column and splashes of dust staccatoed the road. Everyone was piling out of the vehicles and scuttling for the neighbouring fields. Several vehicles were already in flames. This attack ceased as suddenly as it had crashed upon us fifteen minutes before. The men started to drift back to the column again, pale and shaky, wondering how they had survived this fiery rain of bullets. This had been our first experience with the Jabos [fighter-bombers]. The march column was now completely disrupted and every man was on his own to pull out of this blazing column as best he could'

The most crucial phase of the western campaign immediately followed the landing. The Allied armies had to be built up through the Normandy bridgehead. Mobile Panzer divisions were now ordered to move north and west from all over France. The eighteen divisions of the Fifteenth Army, north of the Seine, the best German units in France, were to be transferred to the bridgehead once Hitler realized there was no attack coming across the Pas de Calais.

After 13 June Hitler was more certain than ever that the Allies would make a second assault. On that day he ordered the launching of the first of the new terror weapons at London.

Under pressure from von Rundstedt and Rommel, the Germans began to reach deep into France to concentrate reserves against the invasion. The 3rd Parachute Division was marching from the west to attack the base of the Cotentin and to form the nucleus of the parachute army. Further afield, other divisions set out for Normandy. On urgent appeals from Rommel, Hitler ordered the 9th and 10th S.S. Panzers to move west from Russia on 11 June to make up a II S.S. Panzer Corps.

As the Panzer divisions edged north they were attacked incessantly by the Allied Air Forces in what the Panzers called a 'fighter-bomber race track'.

The closer the Panzers approached the Allied beachhead the more difficult their progress became. General Bayerlein, commanding the Panzer Lehr Division coming up from Lisieux on 7 June, found that incessant air attack virtually halted his advance: 'Every vehicle was covered with tree branches and moved along hedges and the edges of woods. Road junctions were bombed, and a bridge knocked out at Condé. This did not stop my tanks, but it hampered other vehicles. By the end of the day, I had lost forty tank trucks carrying fuel, and ninety others. Five of my tanks were knocked out, and eighty-four half-tracks, prime-movers and self-propelled guns . . .

'These were serious losses for a division not yet in action. I was just east of Tilly on 6 June and ready to attack. My attack took Ellon, and I could have gone straight to the sea down the corridor between the American and British forces, splitting them apart. I was ordered to hold at Ellon because units on my right flank had been delayed. I was a day behind schedule myself, because of air-harassment.'

Ten miles from the coast the tanks would come under heavy bombardment from the sea. Naval gunfire had been completely underrated by the Germans.

It affected Rommel's plans. He reported to O.K.W. on 11 June: 'The guns of most enemy warships have so powerful an effect on areas within their range that any advance into this zone dominated by fire from the sea is impossible.'

In spite of the powerful interdiction of Allied air- and sea-power, the German forces began to march for a determined counter-attack to drive the invaders into the sea. After the triumph of D-Day itself, the Allied soldiers knew they would have to face the battle-hardened troops and tanks of Hitler's élite divisions. As the Allies settled down for the night, clinging to a narrow strip of coast, they knew the Germans were rushing up with weapons which were often far superior to those of the British and Americans.

The fall of Bayeux

The British soon achieved one of the first objectives of their assault – the capture of Bayeux. General Kraiss, whose 915th Division was fully committed, had no reserves to defend it, and evacuated. Early on D plus 1, the ancient city of Bayeux, with its historical connections with William the Conqueror, fell to British troops.

Lt-Colonel Stanley Christopherson of Wye, Kent, was a tank squadron commander. 'We were the first troops into the town. We were given a most enthusiastic and spontaneous reception by the inhabitants who appeared genuinely delighted to welcome us and demonstrated their joy by throwing flowers at the tanks and distributing cider and food among the men.

'One enemy machine-gun post concealed in a house held out in the south of the town, which caused the building to catch fire as a result of our gunfire. After a very short space the clanging of a bell heralded the arrival of the Bayeux Fire Bri-

'My most vivid memory is of coming in through the swirling smoke and a roughish sea on to a beach littered with wrecked craft, debris of all kinds, bodies and the beach obstacles, most of which had mines or explosives attached to them, about which we had been warned. I was twenty-two and completely on my own so far as the job was concerned.'

Lieut. David Nicolson, R.N.

'The first evidence of their emotions came from a woman living in a village. Her husband had been severely wounded in the last war. Her son, a prisoner in this war and still held in a German prison camp. "God has sent the British and Americans," she said in a trembling voice. "The Germans are afraid. I tell you they are afraid. They told me as they came over here. The Allies have so many men, so much material, the sea is filled with ships."'
The Times, June 1944

Below left: Return in triumph. De Gaulle enters Bayeux on 14 June. He was determined to make his presence felt as the new leader of liberated France
Right: The port they took with them. The British Mulberry at Arromanches. It could provide sheltered water for landing craft and quays for merchant ships and transports. The blockships and concrete caissons (Phoenix) can be seen forming the sea wall on the right, whilst the piers and roadways (Whales) stretch towards the shore. A second American Mulberry was in use off Omaha beach. Mulberries helped to supply the army long after D-Day
Below right: Royal visit. The King visits his armies in the beachhead, welcomed by General Montgomery and Admiral Ramsay

gade, manned by a full team all wearing shiny helmets. Regardless of the machine-gun fire, they held up the battle, entered the house, extinguished the fire and brought out the German machine-gun section.'

The Times correspondent described the liberation of the first French city: 'Crowds of young and old people stood today in the cobbled streets of this town from which Allied troops had just driven the Germans. Some of the French people had tears streaming down their faces; all were shouting "*Vive l'Angleterre*", "*Vive l'Amérique*", "*Vive La France*!" and raising their fingers in the Victory-V sign.

'An old woman whose face was lined by years and sorrow told me that the national flags had been hidden away for years, "Now we can bring them out without fear of Boche reprisals."

'Frenchmen, Frenchwomen and children embraced British soldiers and showered them with flowers or pressed bottles of wine into their hands.'

The Channel life-line

By the evening of 7 June, the Allied Armies had begun to create a continuous beachhead, the British and Americans linking up south of Port-en-Bessin. On the left flank, east of the Orne, a strong force of the 21st Panzer Division and three infantry divisions threw everything they had against the airborne bridgehead, now being reinforced by I British Corps. The German thrusts were countered only with great difficulty. The accurate artillery fire of I Corps, supplemented by the bombardment of warships, kept the Germans in check. On the west, the 'Big Red One' and the U.S. 29th Division began to move forward from Omaha and were soon pressing down the road to St Lô, but the VII U.S. Corps in the Cotentin, after its trouble-free landing was now meeting determined German resistance, and making little progress towards the vital port of Cherbourg. A major problem for the Americans was the natural defensive character of the Normandy landscape. The experienced Wehrmacht infantry, now being pushed into the Cotentin from Brittany, took great advantage of the excellent natural defences. They lay in wait, expertly camouflaged, until the American soldiers were within a few yards before opening up with their Schmiessers and Spandaus.

Allied Headquarters became deeply anxious over the rate of Allied build-up within the restricted beachhead. The Americans at Omaha had managed to land only a fraction of their planned tonnage of vehicles and stores, and immediately after the landings Montgomery was two divisions short of his planned requirements.

Montgomery's problem was that everything needed by his armies had to be ferried from England. Although divisions landed with full petrol tanks and a week's rations, a growing army could consume an immense amount of stores even if it sat on the beach and did nothing. Once it engaged the Germans, petrol, ammunition and supplies were used up at a prodigious rate. This battle to build up supplies was one of the underestimated parts of the Normandy campaign.

With a front line just a few miles from the sea, SHAEF was far more anxious about the possibility of the Allied armies keeping a foothold in France than Montgomery. Eisenhower distrusted the Channel weather which could interrupt the over-the-beach supplies and stop the Allied Air Forces providing continuous support to the attacking armies. The weather, however, was only one constant threat.

The Luftwaffe rarely put in an appearance by day, but the Kriegsmarine was still a force to be reckoned with in its attempts to interfere with the Allied sea shuttle.

Every night Krancke sent his E-boats into the attack against the densely packed sea lanes off the Isle of Wight. Although of only 90 tons displacement, the E-boats were like hornets round the invasion fleet. Carrying two torpedo tubes and a 3·7-inch gun, they were hard to catch because of their high speed of 40 knots.

The objective was to strike hard and fast at the 'Spout' as the edge of the rendezvous point off the Isle of Wight was called. There were many night skirmishes between Krancke's E-boats and the navy's destroyers and M.T.B.s. Occasionally they broke through and hit several landing craft, but it was the E-boats that suffered heavy casualties; some seventeen were sunk and thirteen damaged in the first weeks of the invasion.

The hopes of the German Navy rested once again on the U-boat. Doenitz, the Supreme Commander German Navy, deployed a special invasion fleet, known as the Landwirt, based at Brest. Sixteen U-boats were ordered into the Channel. They were hunted as they made for the Spout and only one ever arrived. Most of the others turned back or were sunk.

A threat was posed by the German mines, especially the new types, called 'Oysters'. The passage of a vessel over the mine caused a change in pressure to detonate it. The Allies were fortunate when one was dropped on Sword beach and recovered intact. It was immediately shipped back to Britain for analysis and counter-measures worked out. Ships were given instructions to proceed as slowly as 2·3 knots in shallow water but mines were never completely avoided and they accounted for the loss of twenty-one ships between D-Day and 16 June, four of which were destroyers. The Luftwaffe continued to lay large numbers of oyster mines in the bay of the Seine and across the invasion routes at night. These meant further restrictions on Allied ship movement.

'Planting' a port

The Mulberry harbours and the associated Gooseberries were vital in ensuring a rapid Allied build-up. Their assembling began on D plus 1. Ramsay reported: 'The first convoy of forty-five blockships arrived in the assault area at 1230 on 7 June and the sinking of these ships was commenced at once according to plan.'

According to Rear-Admiral Tennant's report to the Admiralty: 'The military required to disembark 3,000 tons per day of stores by D plus 4, 7,000 tons per day of stores, 2,500 vehicles per day by D plus

A close-run thing. British armour had a hard struggle against the German Panzer reserves massed against them in the eastern sector of the beachhead. After the first few days of the Normandy campaign, British commanders became seriously worried about the ability of the Allied Shermans, Churchills and Cromwells to stand up to the stronger Tigers and Panthers, although the 17-pounder Sherman did something to redress the balance. The experienced British divisions like the 7th Armoured (Desert Rats) had to fall back on skills learnt in the desert war, but the Second Army was to suffer heavy tank losses south of Caen

8 and finally 12,000 tons per day of stores and 2,500 unwaterproofed vehicles per day within the shelter of these harbours.'

Each day convoys of eight Phoenix, eight bombardons, four Whale pierheads, ten Whale roadways and two miscellaneous units were towed across the Channel by the fleet of tugs. The planned speed of $3\frac{1}{2}$ knots was increased to $4\frac{1}{2}$ which reduced the turn-around time. Losses of twenty to twenty-five per cent were expected on the crossing, but very few units sank, apart from half the floating Whale roadway.

The skill demanded in assembling the harbours on the far shore is brought out in Commodore Hughes-Hallett's report. A key ship had first to be sunk very accurately in position. The initial attempt to do this at Mulberry stage failed; the tugs at the stern of the first ship, the *Alynbank*, let go early and, as she was settling down rather more slowly than was anticipated, the tide turned and swung her almost at right angles to the required position. As it turned out, this was a fortunate mishap because she formed a most useful shelter from the west and her behaviour during sinking was salutary.

'At Mulberry A, the planting went ahead at considerable speed and, at the end of the first week, the powers that be were enquiring why Mulberry B was not keeping pace. The officers responsible replied that they were satisfied with the progress and the results so far, but, on further pressure from above, endeavoured to plant an extra Phoenix the following day with the result that, in failing light and falling tide, a large unit was poorly planted near the main entrance. The truism, "more haste and less speed" was proved to be right after all.'

Montgomery still lacked his planned reinforcements, but the battle was beginning to swing his way. As the Panzer divisions arrived in Normandy, Rommel was forced to commit them piecemeal to hold the British drive on Caen. This flouted all the rules of armoured warfare, since this static task of containment was best performed by infantry. The German infantry divisions, without adequate motor transport, had great difficulty getting to the battlefield and Hitler refused to move the Fifteenth Army.

Break-out

On 10 June Montgomery made his first concerted attack to deepen the bridgehead. Since Caen could not be taken by frontal assault, he decided to attack around each side of the city. The 51st Division and 4th Armoured Brigade would attack from the airborne lodgement east of the Orne. By now, Bailey bridges allowed its continuous reinforcement. This left hook would move on Cagny. Meanwhile, a right swing was to be led by the famous 7th Armoured Division, the Desert Rats. It was to advance on the key village of Villers Bocage behind Bayerlein's crack Panzer Lehr, holding high ground. If the two spearheads broke through and joined up, the 1st British Airborne Division would be flown from England and dropped between them to close the ring. Rommel and von Rundstedt also planned a counter-attack in exactly the opposite direction to the British and Canadians. Panzer Lehr would move forward against the 7th Armoured, and the 21st Panzer Division was ordered forward once again to clear the airborne bridgehead. This was to be a major thrust to push the British back into the sea. The attack failed.

On the left flank the assault by the 21st Panzers had the effect of spoiling the organized drive of the

'The morale of the men was very low indeed. So many of their long-time comrades had stayed behind on the battlefield, the battle itself had been so savage, so furious, that every man felt that the 12th S.S. Panzer had a personal grudge against our tanks. Silently, grimly, we were looking at each other, knowing exactly what was in the other man's mind. They simply lay there, not sleeping, eyes opened, just staring into space. A poet or a writer would have found the proper words to describe this vacant look and what was going through their minds, but other than a few comforting words from the Padre, Major Creelman, not much was said. Mostly, everyone was rather vindictive, and silently swearing revenge.'
Sergeant Leo Gariepy, Winnipeg Rifles

Highlanders. Werner Kortenhaus, of the 22nd Panzer Regiment, described an attack on 9 June by the Battlegroup Luck of the 21st Panzers in their Mark IVs: 'We rolled through the gap one after the other, the Panzer Grenadiers storming on behind us, weapons at the ready, trying to shelter behind their tanks as they deployed into broad front formation on the other side of the attack which was to steamroller us into Ranville. The firing began when we were only 30 yards from the hedge, and the first grenadiers dropped groaning to the ground. Tank 432 was hit, and lost track. Thirty seconds later tank 400 was hit and our company commander, Lieutenant Hoffmann, was staring in horror at the bloody mess which had been his leg, while tank 401 exploded, blowing open the hatches and literally flinging the crew out.'

Eventually the Panzers were forced back. Other attacks were mounted by the Canadians towards Bretteville, only to be checked savagely.

The attack of the 7th Armoured almost led to humiliation for Montgomery. The Division was a splendid sight advancing down the road to Villers Bocage. They had now been re-equipped with lighter Cromwell tanks instead of their desert Shermans. Suddenly, as the vehicles were moving along an open road, they came upon a company of heavy S.S. tanks; Oberstürführer Michael Wittman opened fire from his Tiger with his 88-mm. high-velocity gun. The unprotected half-tracks carrying the British infantry burst into flames, smoke and debris were everywhere. Wittman swung his heavy 50-ton tank out of cover as the Cromwells deployed to attack.

The British guns were as effective as pea-shooters against the Tiger armoured vehicles. The 7th Armoured lost twenty-five tanks, fourteen half-tracks and fourteen Bren gun-carriers in the battle. The British withdrew and heavy fighting went on inside Villers Bocage, where they hit back at the Tigers with their Piat anti-tank rockets, and 6-lb. anti-tank guns.

The 7th Armoured Division was now in a perilous position since, to the surprise of Montgomery and Dempsey, a new German Panzer division had arrived from Amiens. Luttwitt's 2nd Panzer was identified on the 7th Armoured's front. The British were almost surrounded by Panzer Lehr and 2nd Panzer and the heavy S.S. tanks. But with the build-up two days late and the 50th Division bogged down, the British reverted to their desert training and formed an 'island' which was attacked from three sides.

The 7th Armoured Division pulled back seven miles after intense air bombardment. Whilst the 2nd Panzer struck towards Caumont and the sea, Montgomery was fighting four Panzers on his sector.

In the western sector Bradley was making progress. Although the drive on St Lô was bitterly contested, by 18 June the Cotentin had at last been sealed off. Now Major-General Collins prepared to wheel his VII Corps north against Cherbourg.

Calamity on the beaches

Montgomery, not surprisingly, began to feel confident enough to mount a limited offensive using the newly arrived British VIII Corps, which included the 43rd (Wessex) Division. On the night of 19 June, however, what SHAEF feared, perhaps most of all, finally happened – a Channel storm.

Right: Withdrawal forbidden. Hitler was taking the key decisions in the Wehrmacht's Normandy battle. In spite of desperate pleas from Rommel and von Rundstedt for the army to be pulled back to a new defence line, to be reinforced from the idle Fifteenth Army in the Pas de Calais, Hitler nevertheless insisted on ordering a counter-offensive. Von Rundstedt was soon to be dismissed for urging the High Command to make peace, whilst Rommel was put out of action by an Allied fighter bomber
Far right: Sack Monty! The British C.-in-C. was severely criticized at SHAEF headquarters for his slow progress in breaking out of the beachhead. Eisenhower and Tedder believed Montgomery was far too cautious and that he should have captured Caen shortly after D-Day. Montgomery, however, claimed that he was soaking up the German reserves to help Bradley make progress in the west

Ironically, this struck the Mulberry operation just as 'all possible tugs were mobilized and set out with a record number of units including 22 tons of roadway, each 480 feet long, making a total of nearly two miles. But not one yard of roadway reached the far shore because at 0300 hours on the Monday morning (D plus 13), it commenced to blow and it blew a full gale for three days, such as had not been known in the Channel in summer for eighty years.'

By early afternoon the wind was blowing at 30 knots, raising breakers eight feet high. For the next three days the storm caused havoc on the invasion beaches. Five hundred landing craft rode through the storm inside the British Arromanches Mulberry B harbour, where the blockships had been strengthened by a row of heavy concrete caissons. The port was damaged, six caissons were lost on the western side, and piers and roadheads were badly mauled.

The Americans were harder hit than their British allies. The Utah Gooseberry lost several blockships which were torn open by the gale, and the Mulberry harbour off St Laurent on Omaha beach was devastated. The breakwaters were overwhelmed by vast masses of water. Two of the blockships broke their backs and of thirty-five huge Phoenix caissons, only ten remained in position. The piers and bombardons were wrecked and the harbour was a write-off. As the storm blew itself out, Bradley went down to the beach to see the damage for himself: 'I was appalled by the desolation for it vastly exceeded that on D-Day.'

The calamity seriously affected the Allied build-up. The arrival of men and supplies fell to only a fraction of the daily average which had been built up in the second week of the landing. From 15–18 June, 15,774 British and 18,938 Americans had been landed every day; this fell to 3,982 and 5,865 respectively in the next three days. The number of vehicles was halved, and stores coming in at 25,000 tons on average every day were reduced to 7,000 tons.

Bradley now had only three days' supply of ammunition left and Montgomery, already two brigades behind the planned build-up, was now three divisions short.

Confrontation at Soissons

The disruption of the Mulberry harbours caused by the storm and the resulting dangerous rundown in supplies underlined the urgent Allied need to capture the port of Cherbourg. On 18 June, the eve of the storm, Major-General Lawton Collins' 82nd Airborne and 9th Division struck across the Cotentin. The 9th Division reached the west coast of the Cotentin at Baronville. The Germans defending Cherbourg were now cut off. At great speed, Collins turned his forces north. Supported by massive air strikes in which medium and heavy bombers unloaded hundreds of tons of bombs on the twenty square miles of German defences, the American units were soon fighting in the suburbs of the French port. On 21 June the garrison was finally summoned to surrender by loud-speaker broadcast.

'It was scheduled to begin at seven o'clock in the morning but hardly had the tanks assembled when they were attacked by fighter-bombers. This disrupted the troops so much that the attack did not start again until 2.30 in the afternoon. But even then it could not get going. The murderous fire from naval guns in the Channel and the terrible British artillery destroyed the bulk of our attacking force in its assembly area. The few tanks that did manage to go forward were easily stopped by the English anti-tank guns.'

Obergruppenführer Paul Hausser, reporting on the Panzer counter-offensive

The final battle did not last long. By the 25th the Americans had taken the centre of the town. In spite of the Führer's orders: 'It is your duty to defend the last bunker and leave the enemy not a harbour, but a field of ruins', General Schlieben realized the position was growing increasingly hopeless, and by the evening of the 26th almost all opposition had ceased.

But, in one respect, the defenders had carried out Hitler's orders to the letter: they had reduced the port to a complete shambles.

On the British front in the east, Montgomery had been delayed launching his first major offensive, code-named Epsom. Its aim was to advance towards Caen, drawing the German Panzers on to the British whilst the Americans made progress in the west. The Panzers had to be kept continuously engaged on the front line to prevent Rommel regrouping for a counter-offensive. The Führer himself, at a crucial meeting with Rommel and von Rundstedt on 17 June at Soissons, had decided to maintain the front-line battle. Urgent requests by the two commanders had brought the Führer hurrying to France to answer their demands that German forces should be pulled back to a new defence line well beyond the range of naval guns.

Talking to his Generals in the headquarters which, ironically, he had prepared to direct the invasion of Britain, the Führer forbade withdrawal. He insisted that the Panzers should be pulled back for a strong counter-thrust at the sensitive point where the American and British forces were linked. But with Montgomery keeping up the pressure, it proved impossible to pull back the tanks in the absence of the reserves. Nor would the Führer allow reserves to be drawn from the Fifteenth Army which was still guarding his vaunted V-weapon landing sites. One misguided V-weapon landed in the vicinity of the headquarters and a shaken Hitler left France for the safety of the Reich.

The Scottish corridor

At the end of June, Montgomery launched Epsom to capture Caen by driving south to the River Odon, and then outflanking the city. The Operation was led by General O'Connor who had just brought his VIII British Corps across the Channel. O'Connor was one of the most successful British tank leaders, having brilliantly defeated the Italians in the desert during 1942.

O'Connor attacked the next day, receiving little air support because of the bad weather. The 15th Scottish Division was in the van, supported by the 11th Armoured and 43rd Wessex Division. Bitter fighting took place between the Scots and the Hitlerjugend infantry of the 12th S.S. Panzer. But the Germans failed to hold O'Connor's thrust forward. Soon they reached the Odon and the 11th Armoured Division's tanks pressed forward towards the menacing Hill 112, lynchpin of the German line. By now, the Germans had thrown almost the whole of their armour against the British thrust. But the British offensive had struck at a critical moment for the Germans, just as they were moving the 2nd, 9th and 10th S.S. Panzer of General Hausser's II S.S. Panzer Corps for a thrust to the sea, in fulfilment of the Soissons decision.

Dempsey, Commander of the British Second Army, now became anxious about the exposed position of the 'Scottish Corridor' forced by the 11th Armoured and 15th Scottish Divisions to Hill 112. Hausser had enough armour to cut them off and inflict a disastrous reverse. Accordingly, O'Connor pulled back to a defensive position on the line of the Odon. Eisenhower and SHAEF were furious. Montgomery had let slip another chance of a break-out.

But when the Panzer counter-offensive came, it was a failure.

Montgomery received little thanks for his spoiling action. Eisenhower wanted action all along the front. He believed that Montgomery was too slow in going in to exploit army gains, and the Supreme Commander received the support of many powerful voices at SHAEF headquarters, British as well as American.

But the Allies were winning the battle of the build-up. By the end of June, 875,000 men had been landed in Normandy as well as thousands of vehicles and tons of stores. The American and British Armies each had sixteen divisions, yet the Germans had only twenty in the whole battle area.

'I met Jeanne rushing down a village street, hair awry, her coat torn on barbed wire. She was clutching at the arm of a German prisoner who was being marched to the coast.

'She was not alone. Seven other women were doing the same to seven other German prisoners. Presumably for the same reasons as Jeanne.

'The war? There was no war in Normandy when we marched in . . .'

Rex North, *Sunday Pictorial,* 18 June

Below: Liberated Caen. The central pivot of the Normandy battle since D-Day, Caen was finally captured on 9 July, after fierce fighting in which the British and Canadians suffered almost 5,000 casualties. Although the city had suffered heavy bombing and shelling, the inhabitants turned out in force to welcome the liberators. After the fall of Caen, the battle for Normandy was decided in the open country to the south and east of the city

Right: Patton unleashed. After Bradley's successful offensive on 25 July, General George C. Patton's Third U.S. Army streaks out of the beachhead. It swung west and south in a huge arc to cut behind the Wehrmacht's Normandy front. By 20 August, the Americans had joined up with the First Canadian Army to trap the Germans at Falaise

At the end of June, Rommel and von Rundstedt demanded to see Hitler, who appeared blissfully ignorant of the true state of affairs on the front, hundreds of miles from his Berchtesgaden retreat. The two Field-Marshals drove 600 miles to urge some sanity on the High Command. They pressed for a tactical withdrawal to a new line on the Seine; Rommel wanted to strengthen the weakened Seventh Army and Panzer Group West with reserves from the Fifteenth Army and the unused divisions in southern France. Yet Hitler would not hear of any withdrawal, not even of tactical adjustments of the line for better defence. Goering and Doenitz were told to intensify their efforts, although Sperrle, Commander-in-Chief of the Luftwaffe in the west, said that he would need an additional 1,200 to 1,400 fighters to provide defended air corridors for the reinforcement of the Wehrmacht.

Rommel and von Rundstedt returned to France, 'angry and disgruntled'. Von Rundstedt held the most pessimistic views of Germany's military fortunes.

The Prussian Field-Marshal had a deep contempt for the supine staff officers serving Hitler, particularly the Chief of Staff, Field-Marshal Keitel. Once, when Keitel complained about von Rundstedt's progress in Normandy, the old Prussian merely said, 'If you think you can do better you had better come down here and lead this filth yourself.' This outspokenness hardly endeared the C.-in-C. to Hitler, and on 1 July von Rundstedt went too far when he told Keitel, in answer to his urgent queries on how to shore up the crumbling German front, 'Make peace, you fools'. Twenty-four hours later, von Rundstedt was sacked, and Field-Marshal von Kluge, a stocky commander from the Russian front, took over.

The world's press had centred its attention on Caen as the expected breakthrough point and began to wonder why the British were taking so long to capture the lynchpin of Normandy's coastal communications. Montgomery, however, was choosing his own time.

In the west, the American attack was equally slow. Bradley was fighting over very difficult terrain. Apart from the hazards of the bocage, there

were large areas of marshland on the lower Vire with only one road-crossing.

In early July, Bradley tried to seize the two points of La Haye du Puits and St Lô, which controlled the exits from the Cotentin. The fighting was bitter; by 6 July, German LXXXIV Corps was reporting to Seventh Army headquarters: 'The enemy controls the air to such an extent that movement on the roads is impossible.'

By 10 July, the American operation ground to a halt; the Germans still held the Allies' objective of St Lô. In the east, Montgomery made another attempt on Caen.

Preceded by an immense air bombardment on 7 July in which 2,573 tons of bombs were dropped by R.A.F. Lancasters and Halifaxes, and followed by an all-night artillery barrage from the massed guns of the British I and VIII Corps as well as H.M.S. *Rodney*, and *Roberts* and cruisers, the 3rd and 59th Canadian Divisions moved forward, backed by the 33rd Armoured Brigade. The Germans fought savagely, 12th S.S. Panzer losing sixty-five out of 150 tanks; the 16th Luftwaffe Division was destroyed. By 9 July, after thirty-three days, one half of Caen and the airfield at Carpiquet were at last in British and Canadian hands.

The inhabitants crept out of the ruins of their devastated city to welcome the liberators.

French bullets

Not all the French were alleged to have greeted the Allies with such ecstasy. The British War Cabinet, anxious about the effect of the air and naval bombardment of Normandy, had been disturbed by press reports concerning French hostility to British troops. On 20 June, the War Cabinet had considered an article in the *Sunday Pictorial* of 18 June by Rex North. Headlined 'These people terrify me', and datelined Normandy, North had written: 'I thought I should be sitting here on the beaches of France reporting the war. But I am forced to the conclusion that there is another and possibly even more important story to write today.

'It is a grave and disturbing story; of a people who are divided among themselves – and divided to a large degree against us.

'Soberly and factually, I must set it down. Six out of ten of the people over here distrust and detest us, and I have carefully checked the figure . . .

'Like so many others, I expected everyone to fete our victorious forces as they come in. Instead, I have spent a week wondering where the next French bullet was coming from . . .

' "Don't go down that side street," I was warned. "Keep to the main road . . . These French snipers have killed a dozen of our blokes in the last two days."

'It is not nice to be shot at from back and front by the people you have come to liberate.'

This was so disturbing that an enquiry was ordered by British intelligence. The War Cabinet was given a more realistic assessment on 21 June.

'Taking into account the naturally cold and reserved disposition of the Normans, the troops have received an enthusiastic welcome. The first British troops entering Bayeux were cheered and embraced, flowers were showered on them and a demonstration celebrating the liberation was held three days after D-Day, at which a British civil affairs officer was tempestuously cheered. Everywhere the reception was friendly . . .'

The intelligence corps also found, 'Not a single shred of evidence . . . at SHAEF nor at 21st Army Group confirming any of the stories about the sniping of our troops by French women, although full reports have been called for. It has been suggested by one reliable British officer that these stories may have been deliberately manufactured by the Germans.

'It was thought that German stragglers "may have been sniping and that some of them at any rate have been dressed in women's clothes".'

The intelligence corps also threw an interesting sidelight on the reaction to General de Gaulle. One bilingual British officer was sent to Bayeux where he reported, 'there is no really furious hatred of the Germans or fervid enthusiasm for General de Gaulle, but the vast majority are in favour of General de Gaulle's provisional government, for want of a better substitute.'

The slogging match in Normandy went on into July, becoming increasingly hard for the people at

De Gaulle enters Paris in triumph, 24 August 1944

home in America and Britain to understand. They had been accustomed to expect fast mobile warfare, with lightning armoured strikes achieving quick and comparatively bloodless results.

Montgomery's underlying strategy was working well. The great bulk of German armour had been drawn on to the British who were trying to knock out the German defences around Caen. On 30 June and the following weeks, the British Second Army faced no less than 725 German tanks, whilst the Americans confronted a smaller number – 190 – on their front.

The Americans badly needed St Lô, as a starting line for their break-out. Roads radiated in all directions, particularly to Coutances and Brittany, from the small battered town. The fortified Hill 192 also had to be taken. On 18 July, after a hard-fought battle, Bradley's army finally succeeded in taking the key communications centre.

The plan for two operations at each end of the Allied bridgehead was put into effect. In the east, under Operation Goodwood, Dempsey's armoured spearhead of three British divisions, the 11th Armoured, the 7th and the Guards Armoured, would advance across the Orne east of Caen from the airborne bridgehead. They would drive through the dense German defences and aim 'to engage German armour and to write it down to such an extent' that it could not be used to resist Bradley's break-out.

The American offensive, which was to strike for open country, was code-named Operation Cobra. It was timed to follow Goodwood on 20 July but bad weather forced Cobra's delay to 25 July. Montgomery had marshalled 750 guns, 750 tanks and 4,000 aircraft to deliver 2,500 tons of bombs. But the bombing was not completely effective against Eberbach's strong defences, strengthened by the 88-mm. flak guns of the Luftwaffe used in an anti-tank role.

Although the British attack started well, gaining six miles in under two hours, they soon ran into stubborn resistance. The Canadians slowly occupied the remainder of Caen, but the British divisions made little headway. The British VIII Corps lost 131 tanks in one day to the Tigers and 88s.

By 21 July Goodwood had reached a stalemate, with the loss of 500 British tanks and 4,000 men. The Germans also suffered. Rommel wrote to von Kluge, 'The situation on the Normandy front is growing worse every day and is now approaching a grave crisis. The troops are fighting heroically but the unequal struggle is approaching its end. It is urgently necessary for the proper conclusion to be drawn from this situation.'

Von Kluge passed this on to Hitler with his own comments, but by that time the Germans had lost Rommel. He was shot up by Allied fighters while driving and was withdrawn to hospital on 17 July.

Once again, Montgomery had failed to make a breakthrough. At SHAEF, the demand for his replacement rose.

The trap closes

On 25 July, the Americans launched their break-out attack on a narrow 6,000-yard front. Fortresses and Liberators bombed the German defences in an area 4 miles long and 1½ miles deep. Although some of the leading American elements were bombed by their own air force, the effect on the Germans was overwhelming.

Then the American armoured spearheads went in and, after the first indecisive day, broke the Wehrmacht's defensive crust. The German LXXXIV Corps disintegrated and von Kluge was left without reserves. Frantic attempts to switch the 2nd and 17th S.S. Panzer from the Orne to the Vire were halted by the Allied Air Forces; nothing could stop the Americans thrusting out into France. Now Patton raced for the key town of Avranches with the Third U.S. Army fanned out into Brittany.

Nothing could stop the Americans now. Patton's tanks tore through open country, by passing pockets of German resistance. Rennes fell on 4 August and Patton's columns reached the Atlantic. In another thrust towards Le Mans, he swung behind the German front.

At the same time, the British attacked and drew off the armoured reinforcements despatched to stem the American break-out.

Now Hitler tried one last gamble to save Normandy. On 4 August, von Kluge was ordered to

scrape all his Panzer divisions together for a big counter-offensive towards the pivotal town of Mortain, to cut off the American corridor. The German Generals were aghast and said it would be putting the Wehrmacht's head into a noose; Hitler merely complained, 'my Generals think of nothing but retreat'.

The Wehrmacht launched its counter-attack with 250 tanks and fought with desperate courage, but the attempt was a disaster. Von Kluge knew this, but the fanatical General Paul Hausser issued the following order to the Seventh Army: 'On the successful execution of the operation [breakthrough to the sea] the Führer has ordered, depends the decision of the war in the west, and with it perhaps the decision of the war itself.'

In spite of these fanatical exhortations, the German armies had now delivered themselves up to destruction; as they drove north to counter-attack, the jaws of the immense trap closed round them – the British and Canadians from the north, the Americans from the south and west. The First U.S. Army closed the ring, moving through Alencon and then north of Falaise. At the same time, the Canadians drove hard on Falaise to meet the Americans. Too late, the Germans began to withdraw. The Falaise pocket became a terrible slaughter ground. Von Kluge became an immediate scapegoat for the failure of Hitler's Mortain counter-offensive. '15 August was the worst day of my life,' Hitler said later. A new C.-in-C. replaced the unfortunate Kluge who was summoned to Berlin. He killed himself before he got there, disgraced, and under suspicion for involvement in the Generals' abortive plot to assassinate Hitler. General Model was ordered to leave the Russian front to take command in the west, but he could do little better.

The desperate remnants of once-proud Wehrmacht divisions fought desperately to break out, but they were trapped in the wreckage of their own transport and destroyed tanks. The scenes were frightening, even to the hardened German infantry. On one bridge over a ravine, men and vehicles were pushed over the side to avoid blocking the road. They made a grisly pile of carnage below. It was now every man for himself as the noose tightened and determined groups, sometimes led by a full General, tried to infiltrate the Allied lines.

By 22 August it was all over. Some Germans managed to escape the fearful Allied fire-power, but over 50,000 surrendered. Others were not so fortunate: between 10,000 and 12,000 Germans were killed. The battle area was littered with the fighting equipment of Hitler's legions. To the British, it was a fitting revenge for Dunkirk.

Within days, Allied forces, spearheaded by Leclerc's Free French Armoured Division, were welcomed by the ecstatic citizens of liberated Paris. The invasion had achieved its first great victory. France was soon to be free, and, in less than a year, the Thousand-year Reich would be brought to an end.

Author's Note concerning the little known part played by the writer of the Foreword in ensuring the success of D-Day and Overlord.

Admiral of the Fleet The Earl Mountbatten of Burma,
K.G., P.C., G.C.B., O.M., G.C.S.I., G.C.I.E.,
G.C.V.O., D.S.O., F.R.S.

On 12 June 1944, after a visit to the D-Day beaches of Normandy, the Allied war leaders sent a combined signal to Admiral Mountbatten, then Supreme Allied Commander, South-East Asia:

'To-day we visited the British and American Forces on the soil of France. We sailed through vast fleets of vessels with landing craft of many types pouring more and more men, vehicles and stores ashore. We saw artificial harbours in the process of rapid development. We have shared our secrets in common and helped each other all we could. We wish to tell you at this moment in your arduous campaign that we realize that much of the remarkable technique and therefore the success of the venture has its origin in the developments effected by you and your Staff of Combined Operations.'

It was signed, in alphabetical order by:

General Arnold Chief of the U.S. (Army) Air Staff
Field-Marshal Brooke Chief of the Imperial General Staff and Chairman of the British Chiefs of Staff Committee
Winston Churchill Prime Minister
Admiral King Chief of U.S. Navy Operations
General Marshall Chief of the U.S. Army Staff
Field-Marshal Smuts Prime Minister South Africa

They all knew at first hand the importance of Mountbatten's contribution to the great success of D-Day.

In his Foreword, Lord Mountbatten describes how he was sent for by Winston Churchill to take over Combined Operations in October 1941 and the dramatic and imaginative instructions he received to plan and prepare for a re-entry into the Continent of Europe.

This operation, which originally had the code name 'Round Up', was given a new name, 'Overlord', in May 1943. Churchill had not liked the original name and had asked, 'Who will be Rounded Up, the Germans or ourselves?'

Overlord was to become by far the biggest 'Combined Operation' for an amphibious invasion in all recorded history. As the moving spirit, Churchill had chosen a forty-one-year-old naval Captain who had never done a staff course. But even Mountbatten's infectious enthusiasm could not overcome conventional delays and opposition, so in March 1942 Churchill gave him the acting rank of Vice-Admiral, the honorary ranks of Lieutenant-General and Air Marshal, and made him Chief of Combined Operations and the fourth member of the Chiefs of Staff Committee. This put him almost a 'generation up' and gave him immense power to get things done which, as the above signal testifies, he proceeded to do.

It is not surprising that when the U.S. Chiefs of Staff sent over Major-General Eisenhower to discuss Allied invasion plans, he proposed that Mountbatten should be given the overall command, little realizing that by the time the American contribution exceeded that of the British and Canadian, he himself would be appointed Supreme Allied Commander.

In April 1942 Mountbatten persuaded the U.S. Chiefs of Staff to select officers from their three services to join his British staff, thus creating the first Inter-Allied Inter-Service H.Q. which became the prototype of all the Allied Headquarters in every theatre of war.

In his Foreword, Lord Mountbatten briefly recounts the immense struggle he had to stop plans being made for our landings in the Pas de Calais area and to insist that the landings take place on the Normandy beaches. Who can now doubt that, but for him, no one could have planned the great thirtieth-anniversary celebration to commemorate our successful landing at Arromanches and the neighbouring beaches. No wonder this little town has an 'Avenue Amiral Mountbatten'. And yet the fact that he was fighting his campaign against the Japanese in Burma when D-Day finally took place meant that most people have overlooked the part he and his valiant, expert 'Combined Operations Command' played in making the invasion possible, let alone such a success.

Let us look at one great concept, without which no successful invasion could have taken place. Weather statistics showed that not more than four consecutive days could be expected in the Channel on which it would be possible to continue landing vital reinforcements, munitions and supplies. If they were stopped the enemy could build up enough force, however good any deception plan might be, to throw the invaders back into the sea. So some form of port had to be available for the invaders.

The Dieppe raid showed that a port could not be captured by frontal assault without such heavy bombardment from the sea and air as to destroy the port facilities. As far back as December 1941 the staff in C.O.H.Q. were investigating the possible use of a 'Bubble Breakwater' to produce a sheltered area of water by surrounding it with pipes laid on the bottom, pierced with holes, through which compressed air could be pumped. The idea was to produce a curtain of aerated water, which, being compressible, would prevent the transmission of wave motion through it. However, it required large powerful air pumps in vessels to be moored off the beaches, which, if knocked out by the enemy, would cause the 'Bubble Breakwater' to collapse. Mountbatten rejected it on this account.

Various forms of floating or sunken breakwaters and floating piers were investigated before the Dieppe operation in 1942 confirmed that a mobile port would be indispensable.

General Eisenhower, in his book *Crusade in Europe*, wrote: 'Since the nature of the defenses to be encountered ruled out the possibility of gaining adequate ports promptly, it was necessary also to provide a means of sheltering beach supply from the effect of storms . . . To solve this apparently unsolvable problem we undertook a project so unique as to be classified by many scoffers as completely fantastic. It was to plan to construct artificial harbors on the coast of Normandy.

'The first time I heard this idea tentatively advanced was by Admiral Mountbatten, in the Spring of 1942. At a conference attended by a number of Service Chiefs he remarked, "If ports are not available, we may have to construct them in pieces and tow them in". Hoots and jeers greeted his suggestion but two years later it was to become reality.'

During the conference (Rattle) called by the Chief of Combined Operations at the end of June 1943 at Largs, the subject was seriously discussed by the responsible authorities under Admiral Mountbatten's chairmanship.

Brigadier Sir Bernard Fergusson (now Lord Ballantrae), in his book, *The Watery Maze*, described briefly the discussion: 'The magic phrase "artificial ports" provided the ray of hope referred to, and in the course of RATTLE both Hughes-Hallett and Hussey (two naval captains in "Combined Operations") were called on to speak about them. Various experiments had been going on for over a year.' Fergusson describes them and goes on:

'Mountbatten had drawn up a list of ideal requirements: his dream pier would be a mile long, able to withstand winds of gale force, and capable of berthing large coasters. The Prime Minister thought this was splendid, only let's have three or four miles instead of one. "Pray do not lightly turn this aside," he minuted on 26th September, 1942, and "Press on; when will the four miles be ready?" on 1st December.'

Two mobile ports were in fact towed over in pieces, immediately the beachheads had been secured. One was moored unsuccessfully off the American beaches, where it was destroyed by a gale. The other Mulberry was successfully installed off the British and Canadian beachheads at Arromanches, where it gave vital and indispensable service making it possible for reinforcements and supplies to be poured in during the many days of rough weather.

Admiral Mountbatten's decision to get all the senior officers of all the Allied Services up to the Rattle Conference at one of his establishments at Largs in Scotland was in fact crucial in convincing the senior officers of all the Allied Services that an invasion of Normandy was not only possible but could be highly successful if all the techniques developed by Combined Operations were used in the Normandy and not the Pas de Calais area.

Acknowledgements

In assembling an account of an historical event of such epic proportions as Operation Overlord, which involved millions of people in many countries, the authors are aware of the impossibility of doing justice to every detail of this vast subject. However, we have tried to give a broad perspective in narrative and pictures drawn from eye-witness accounts, despatches and official reports, radio and press coverage, as well as drawing on the rich reserves of published memoirs and histories.

In attempting to convey the atmosphere of this memorable day in world history, we are particularly indebted to all those who gave us their personal accounts, either by letter or interview; regrettably, it has only been possible to include a small proportion of this vivid material. But it is our intention that all these accounts will become part of the D-Day Museum planned for Portsmouth.

There is a famous D-Day museum at Arromanches in Normandy, and the authors have received great encouragement and research assistance from its director, Mlle Antoinette de Bearenger, and the Comité du Débarquement. The recently opened British Archives covering the period have formed an important part of the book, and considerable help and advice was generously given by the staff of the Public Records Office, the Imperial War Museum and the D-Day Fellowship. The authors would like to thank Lord Mountbatten's archivist and the distinguished military historian, Major J. G. D. Haswell, for their constructive comments on the manuscript.

We are particularly grateful for the important assistance given by the staff of the Royal United Service Institute Library, the Ministry of Defence Library and the Royal Naval Historical Branch. It would have been impossible to have collected the great wealth of material without the expert assistance of our research team: Judy Harkison in the United States; Jonathan Moore, Andrew Mollo, David Rowley and Graham Sargent in Europe.

The presentation of this complex story has been skilfully and patiently organized by the designer, Paul Watkins, and editor, Jan Widdows. Finally, no book would have been possible without the dedicated effort of those who typed the manuscript: in this case, Jeanette Childs, Frances Leach and Mrs Iris Hughes.

We are grateful to the following for permission to reproduce extracts from the books listed below:
William Collins Ltd and Charles Scribner's Sons for Ernest Hemingway's *By-line*, ed. William White, 1968; Dept. of the Army, Washington, for *The United States Official History*, 1954; Gerhard Stalling Verlag for *Invasion – They're Coming* by Paul Carell, 1962; Kurt Vowinckel Verlag for *Die Invasion* by Friedrich Hayn, 1954; Commodore James Arnold and the *Washington Naval Review* for the article published in 1962; Hutchinsons for *The Story of Landing Craft* by Lt-Comm. T. Blore, 1946; Dept. of the Army, Washington, for *U.S. Navy in World War II* by Samuel Elliot Morrison, 1954; Cassell & Co. and Houghton & Mifflin for *The Second World War* by Winston Churchill, 1950; A. D. Peters for *Overture to Overlord* by General Sir Frederick Morgan, 1950; Heinemann and Doubleday for *Crusade in Europe* by General D. Eisenhower, 1948; Cassells and Little, Brown for *With Prejudice* by Lord Tedder, 1966; Oxford University Press for *B.B.C. War Report*, 1946; Weidenfeld and Nicolson and Macmillan Inc for *Inside the Third Reich* by Albert Speer, 1970; Weidenfeld and Nicolson and Praeger for *Inside Hitler's Headquarters* by Walter Warlimont, 1968; Heinemann and General H. C. Butcher for *Three Years With Eisenhower* by Gen. Butcher, 1946; Harper & Row for *Soldier* by General M. B. Ridgway, 1956; Collins and Holt, Rhinehart & Winston for *The Watery Maze* by General Sir Bernard Fergusson, 1961; Ballantine and Coronet for *Defeat in the West* by Milton Schulman, 1973.

Selected Bibliography

BBC War Report, BBC War Reporters, BBC, 1946
Caen, Anvil of Victory, A. McKee, Souvenir Press, 1964
The Challenge of War, Guy Hartcup, David & Charles, 1970
Commando, Peter Young, Ballantine, 1969
Crusade in Europe, Dwight D. Eisenhower, Heinemann, 1948
Decisive Battles of World War II, The German View, Ed. Jacobsen and Rohwer, André Deutsch, 1965
Full Cycle, The Biography of Admiral Sir Bertram Ramsay, W. S. Chalmers, Hodder and Stoughton, 1959
Grand Strategy, Vol V, Edward Ehrman, HMSO, 1956
History of US Naval Operations in World War II, Samuel Elliot Morrison, OUP, 1957
Inside Hitler's Headquarters, W. Warlimont, Weidenfeld, 1968
Inside the Third Reich, Albert Speer, Weidenfeld, 1970
Invasion – They're Coming, P. Carell, Gerhard Stalling, 1962
The Longest Day, C. Ryan, Gollancz, 1970
The Mediterranean Strategy in the Second World War, Michael Howard, Weidenfeld and Nicolson, 1968
Memoirs, Viscount Montgomery, Collins, 1968
Overlord Revisited, Richard N. Leighton, *The American Historical Review*, July 1963
Overture to Overlord, General Sir Frederick Morgan, Hodder and Stoughton, 1950
The Papers of David Dwight Eisenhower, John Hopkins Press, 1970
The People's War, Angus Calder, Jonathan Cape, 1969
The Red Beret, H. St George Saunders, Michael Joseph, 1950
Report by Supreme Commander Allied Expeditionary Force General Eisenhower, HMSO, 1946
The Rommel Papers, ed. G. H. Liddell Hart, Collins, 1953
S.O.E. in France, M. R. D. Foot, HMSO, 1956
The Second World War, Winston Churchill, Cassell, 1950
The Secret War, Gerald Pawle, Harrap, 1956
The Secrets of D-Day, G. Perrault, Presses de la Cité
Soldier, General Matthew B. Ridgway, Harper and Row, 1956
A Soldier's Story, General Omar Bradley, Eyre and Spottiswoode, London, 1951
The Strategic Air Offensive Against Germany 1939–1945, Vols I and II, Sir Charles Webster, Noble Frankland, HMSO
The Struggle for Europe, Chester Wilmot, Collins, 1952
The Supreme Commander, Stephen E. Ambrose, American Heritage Publishing Co. Inc., 1969
Three Years with Eisenhower, General Harry C. Butcher, Heinemann, 1946
Triumph in the West, Arthur Bryant, Collins, 1959
U.S. Army in World War II, Department of the Army, Washington, 1954
The Supreme Command, Vol I, Forrest C. Pogue, 1954
Cross Channel Attack, Vol II, Gordon A. Harrison, 1954
The Victory Campaign (Official History of the Canadian Army in World War II), Colonel C. P. Stacey, Queen's Printer, Ottawa, 1966
Victory in the West, Vol I, Major L. F. Ellis, HMSO, 1956
War Memoirs, General de Gaulle, Librairie Plon
The War at Sea, Vol II, Pt 2, Captain Roskill, HMSO, 1961
The Watery Maze, Gen. Sir Bernard Fergusson, Collins, 1961
We Defended Normandy, H. Speidel, Jenkins
With Prejudice, Lord Tedder, Cassell, 1966

List of Regiments

AMERICAN D-DAY ASSAULT DIVISIONS

OMAHA BEACH

1st U.S. Division

116 Infantry
16 Infantry
18 Infantry
26 Infantry
115 Infantry
2nd Rangers
5th Rangers
741 Tank Bn.
111 Field Artillery Bn.
7 Field Artillery Bn.
81 Chemical Bn.

UTAH BEACH

4th U.S. Division

8 Infantry
22 Infantry
12 Infantry
359 Infantry (attached from 90th Div.)
70 Tank Bn.

BRITISH D-DAY ASSAULT DIVISIONS

SWORD BEACH

3rd British Division

8th Bde.
1st Bn. The Suffolk Regt.
2nd Bn. The East Yorkshire Regt.
1st Bn. The South Lancashire Regt.

9th Bde.
2nd Bn. The Lincolnshire Regt.
1st Bn. The King's Own Scottish Borderers
2nd Bn. The Royal Ulster Rifles

185th Bde.
2nd Bn. The Royal Warwickshire Regt.
1st Bn. The Royal Norfolk Regt.
2nd Bn. The King's Shropshire Light Infantry

Divisional Troops
3rd Reconnaissance Regt. R.A.C.
3rd Divisional Engineers
3rd Div. Signals
7th, 33rd and 76th Field, 20th Anti-Tank and 92nd Light Anti-Aircraft Regts. R.A.
2nd Bn. The Middlesex Regt. (Machine Gun)

JUNO BEACH

3rd Canadian Division

7th Bde.
The Royal Winnipeg Rifles
The Regina Rifle Regt.
1st Bn. The Canadian Scottish Regt.

8th Bde.
The Queen's Own Rifles of Canada
Le Régiment de la Chaudière
The North Shore (New Brunswick) Regt.

9th Bde.
The Highland Light Infantry of Canada
The Stormont, Dundas and Glengarry Highlanders
The North Nova Scotia Highlanders

Divisional Troops
7th Reconnaissance Regt. (17th Duke of York's Royal Canadian Hussars)
3rd Canadian Div. Engineers
3rd Canadian Div. Signals
12th, 13th and 14th Field, 3rd Anti-Tank and 4th Light Anti-Aircraft Regts. R.C.A.
The Cameron Highlanders of Ottawa (Machine Gun)

GOLD BEACH

50th British (Northumbrian) Division

69th Bde.
5th Bn. The East Yorkshire Regt.
6th and 7th Bn. The Green Howards

151st Bde.
6th, 8th and 9th Bns. The Durham Light Infantry

231st Bde.
2nd Bn. The Devonshire Regt.
1st Bn. The Hampshire Regt.
1st Bn. The Dorsetshire Regt.

Divisional Troops
61st Reconnaissance Regt. R.A.C.
50th Div. Engineers
50th Div. Signals
74th, 90th and 124th Field, 102nd Anti-Tank and 25th Light Anti-Aircraft Regts. R.A.
2nd Bn. The Cheshire Regt. (Machine Gun)

OTHER FORMATIONS

79th Armoured Division

30th Armoured Bde.
22nd Dragoons
1st Lothians and Border Horse
2nd County of London Yeomanry (Westminster Dragoons)
141st Regt. R.A.C.

1st Tank Bde.
11th, 42nd and 49th Bns. R.T.R.

1st Assault Bde. R.E.
5th, 6th and 42nd Assault Regts. R.E.
79th Armoured Div. Signals
1st Canadian Armoured Personnel Carrier Regt.

1st Special Service Bde.
Nos. 3, 4 and 6 Commandos
No. 45 (Royal Marine) Commando

4th Special Service Brigade
Nos. 41, 46, 47 and 48 (Royal Marine) Commandos

Royal Marine
Armoured Support Group: 1st and 2nd Royal Marine Armoured Support Regts.
Units of the Royal Artillery and Royal Engineers

AIRBORNE FORCES

6th Airborne Division

3rd Parachute Bde.
8th and 9th Bns. The Parachute Regt.
1st Canadian Parachute Bn.

5th Parachute Bde.
7th, 12th and 13th Bns. The Parachute Regt.

6th Airlanding Brigade
12th Bn. The Devonshire Regt.
2nd Bn. The Oxfordshire and Buckinghamshire Light Infantry
1st Bn. The Royal Ulster Rifles

Divisional Troops
6th Airborne Armoured Reconnaissance Regt. R.A.C.
6th Airborne Div. Engineers
53rd Airlanding Light Regt. R.A.
6th Airborne Div. Signals

U.S. 101st and 82nd Airborne Divisions

Allied Naval Forces – Operation Neptune

BRITISH

Battleships

RAMILLIES
RODNEY
WARSPITE

Cruisers

AJAX
ARETHUSA
ARGONAUT
BELFAST
BELLONA
BLACK PRINCE
DANAE
DIADEM
EMERALD
ENTERPRISE
FROBISHER
GLASGOW
HAWKINS
MAURITIUS
ORION
SCYLLA
SIRIUS

Monitors

EREBUS
ROBERTS

HQ Ships

BULOLO
HILARY
LARGS

Destroyers

ALGONQUIN
ASHANTI
BEAGLE
BLANKNEY
BLEASDALE
BRISSENDEN
CAMPBELL
CATTISTOCK
COTSWOLD
COTTESMORE
DUFF
EGLINTON
FAULKNER
FURY
GRENVILLE
HAIDA
HAMBLEDON
HOTHAM
HURON
IMPULSIVE
ISIS
JERVIS
KELVIN
KEMPENFELT
MELBREAK
MIDDLETON
OBEDIENT
OFFA
ONSLAUGHT
ONSLOW
OPPORTUNE
ORIBI
ORWELL
PYTCHLEY
SAUMAREZ
SAVAGE
SCORPION
SCOURGE
SERAPIS
SIOUX
STEVENSTONE
SWIFT
TALYBONT
TANATSIDE
TARTAR
ULSTER
ULYSSES
UNDAUNTED
UNDINE
URANIA
URCHIN
URSA
VENUS
VERSATILE
VERULAM
VESPER
VIDETTE
VIGILANT
VIMY
VIRAGO
VIVACIOUS
VOLUNTEER
WENSLEYDALE
WESTCOTT
WRESTLER

Frigates

CHELMER
HALSTED
HOLMES
RETALICK
RIOU
ROWLEY
STAYNER
THORNBOROUGH
TORRINGTON
TROLLOPE
NITH

Corvettes

ALBERNI
ARMERIA
AZALEA
CAMPANULA
CLARKIA
CLEMATIS
CLOVER
GODETIA
KITCHENER
LAVENDER
MIGNONETTE
MIMICO
NARCISSUS
OXLIP
PENNYWORT
PETUNIA
PINK

Sloops

HIND
MAGPIE
REDPOLE
STORK

Asdic Trawlers

BOMBARDIER
BRESSAY
COLL
DAMSAY
FIARAY
FLINT
FOULNESS
FUSILLIER
GAIRSAY
GATESHEAD
GRENADIER
HUGH WALPOLE
LANCER
LINDISFARNE
LORD AUSTIN
NORTHERN FOAM
NORTHERN GEM
NORTHERN GIFT
NORTHERN PRIDE
NORTHERNREWARD
NORTHERN SKY
NORTHERN SPRAY
NORTHERN SUN
NORTHERN WAVE
OLVINA
SAPPER
SKYE
TEXADA
VELETA
VICTRIX

Fleet Minesweepers

ARDROSSAN
BANGOR
BEAUMARIS
BLACKPOOL
BLAIRMORE
BOOTLE
BOSTON
BRIDLINGTON
BRIDPORT
BRITOMART
CARAQUET
CATHERINE
CATO
COCKATRICE
COWICHAN
DORNOCK
DUNBAR
EASTBOURNE
ELGIN
FANCY
FORT WILLIAM
FORT YORK
FRASERBURGH
FRIENDSHIP
GAZELLE
GEORGIAN
GLEANER
GORGON
GOZO
GRECIAN
GUYSBOROUGH
HALCYON
HARRIER
HOUND
HUSSAR
HYDRA
ILFRACOMBE
JASON
KELLET
KENORA
LARNE
LENNOX
LIGHTFOOT
LLANDUDNO
LOYALTY
LYDD
LYME REGIS
MALPEQUE
MELITA
MILLTOWN
MINAS
ONYX
ORESTES
PANGBOURNE
PARRSBORO
PELORUS
PERSIAN
PICKLE
PINCHER
PIQUE
PLUCKY
POOLE
POSTILLION
QUALICUM
RATTLESNAKE
READY
RECRUIT
RIFLEMAN
ROMNEY
ROSS
RYE
SALAMANDER
SALTASH
SEAGULL
SEAHAM
SELKIRK
SHIPPIGAN
SIDMOUTH
SPEEDWELL
STEADFAST
SUTTON
TADOUSSAC
TENBY
VESTAL
WASAGA
WEDGEPORT
WHITEHAVEN
WORTHING

U.S.A.

Battleships

ARKANSAS
NEVADA
TEXAS

Cruisers

AUGUSTA
QUINCY
TUSCALOOSA

Destroyers

BALDWIN
BARTON
BUTLER
CARNICK
CHERARDI
CORRY
DOYLE
ELLYSON
ENDICOTT
FITCH
FORREST
FRANKFORD
GLENNON
HAMBLETON
HARDING
HERNDON
HOBSON
JEFFERS
LAFFEY
MCCOOK
MEREDITH
MURPHY
NELSON
O'BRIEN
PLUNKETT
RODMAN
SATTERLEE
SHUBRICK
THOMPSON
WALKER

HQ Ship

ANCON
BAYFIELD

Frigates

BORUM
MALOY

Patrol Craft

484	617	1233
552	618	1252
564	619	1261
565	1176	1262
567	1225	1263
568	1232	

Minesweepers

AUK
BROADBILL
CHICKADEE
NUTHATCH
PHEASANT
STAFF
SWIFT
THREAT
TIDE

FRENCH

Cruisers

GEORGES LEYGUES
MONTCALM

Destroyer

LA COMBATTANTE

Corvettes

ACONIT
RENONCULE

Frigates

LA DECOUVERTE
L'AVENTURE
LA SURPRISE
L'ESCARAMOUCHE

POLISH

Cruiser

DRAGON

Destroyers

KRAKOWIAK
SLAZAK

NORWEGIAN

Destroyers

GLAISDALE
STORD
SVENNER

GREEK

Corvettes

KRIEZIS
TOMPAZIS

NETHERLANDS

Sloops

FLORES
SOEMBA

Other vessels

4,126 Landing Ships and Craft; 736 Ancillary Ships and Craft; 864 Merchant Ships.

ALLIED EXPEDITIONARY AIR FORCE

Royal Air Force, Second Tactical Air Force
Royal Air Force, Air Defence of Great Britain
Royal Air Force, Airborne and Transport Forces
United States Ninth Air Force

ALLIED STRATEGIC AIR FORCE

Royal Air Force. Bomber Command
United States Eighth Air Force

ROYAL AIR FORCE COASTAL COMMAND

List of Contributors

Abbott, A. E.
Abbott, Mrs
Adams, Mrs
Allan, W.
Anselm, Mme d'

Bace, F.
Badgery, Mrs
Baines, W.
Bakker, G. R.
Baldwin, N. W.
Balfour, Rear-Admiral G. I. M.
Barber, C.
Barclay, H. L.
Barnett, Mr
Baxter, K. P.
Belchem, Maj.-Gen.
Bearenger, A. de
Betts, B.
Bishop, Mrs
Blanc, R. le
Blomfield, Rev.
Bourbel, Miss de
Bourgoing, Senator P. de
Bowers, H. W., M.M.
Bowring, G.
Bowring, Mrs
Box, M.
Brewer, V.
Brien, W. J.
Brierly, D. S. C.
Briggs, H. J.
Broadhead, Mr
Brock, Mr
Brookes, Mr
Brough, A.
Brown, R.
Buffett, Rev.
Burrell, D.

Cairns, A.
Carman, Mrs
Carpentier, F.
Chodzko, M. A.
Christopherson, S
Claus, Mr
Cole, Mrs G.
Cole, R.
Corrie, Mrs
Coste, J. H.
Courage, Capt. R. H., R.N.
Coyne, Mrs D.
Crabb, Mrs B. L.
Cullingford, L. H.
Curtis, R.
Cutty, W.

Davies, G. R.
Divine, D.
Dodd, Mrs
Douglas, G. N.
Douglas, J.
Druce, Mr

Edwards, Mrs E.
Evans, Mr J.

Fairlie, G.
Faulconbridge, R. C.
Flint, G.
Foulser, Mrs
Fowkes, Mrs
Fox, Mrs J.
French, J. J.
Fuller, J.

Gale, M. G.
Gardiner, Mr
Gariepy, L.
Georget, Mlle
Gibson, R.
Gilbert, A. D.
Gilbert, Cdr D., R.N.
Gillard, Mrs
Gillbard, R. G.
Ginger, D. W.
Glover, Wing Cdr
Goodeve, Sir C.
Gordon, Mrs
Gosling, G.
Gould, Miss
Grant, G. S.
Gray, E. A. W.
Grocott, Mrs Nora
Gueritz, Rear-Admiral E. F.

Hackett, I.
Haig-Brown, R.
Hansdoerfer, P. A.
Hardie, Lt-Col. I. G. G. S.
Harrison, Mrs
Hawkins, Lt-Cdr
Heard, Mrs
Hickling, R. H.
Hiett, T. R.
Hodgkin, Dr K.
Hodgson, Mrs
Holley, Mr
Honour, Lt-Cdr
Hughill, Mrs
Hugill, J. A. C.
Humphries, P. H.
Hunter, J.
Hyde, M.

Irwin, H. M.

Jacob, Maj.
Jefferson, A.
Jenkins, Cdr D.
Jennings, M. H.
Johnson, A. E.
Johnson, B.
Johnstone, F. D.
Jones, J. C.
Juniper, Cdr

King, B. L.
King, J. E.
King, K. M.
Knapfield, Mrs

Lam, Capt. A. C.
Langdon-Davies, Mrs
Langridge, A.
Lanng, Mrs O.
Latimer, J. C.
Lawford, Cdr
Lay, Mrs
Leaney, Mrs
Legg, Mr
Leyman, R.
Little, R. A.
Lloyd, R. G.

Mackenzie, Mrs
McKinley, R. H. G.
Mallett, S. B.
Martin, J. P.
Masey, J.
Maude, R. M. S.
Maxwell, Mrs
Michel, Cdr D.
Mills, G.
Murch, F. J.
Murrin, R. J.
Myers, L.

Naunton, Dr W. J.
Nease, Lt G. E.
Nelson, J.
Newton, Mrs
Nicolson, C. N.
Nissan, Audrey
Noone, J.
Norwich, Bishop of
Nowlan, Mrs

Oldaker, Mrs Jean
Owens, P.

Palmer, Mr
Palmer, W. J.
Parham, Rear-Admiral F.
Parker, Audrey
Paton, Dr
Pawle, G.
Pearce, G. R.
Phillips, Mr R.
Pickett, D.
Potter, D. C.
Potter, Mr
Potts, Cdr
Prendergast-Arnold, Mrs
Prosser, O. H.
Purchase. E.

Reading, Mr
Rees, K. C. L.
Rees, Mr
Ridley, Mr
Ridley, R.
Rogers, W. A.
Rooke, D.

Salter, K. W.
Sander, C.
Sanders, G. J. St J.
Saxby, T. G.
Scheider, O.
Scriven, Maj.
Seymour, J.
Shackell, Mrs E.
Shanton, A. E.
Shepheard, M.
Short, Mrs
Sissons, Mr A.
Smith, C.
Smith, Mrs
Sproull, Mrs
Stagg, J. M.
Stanbury, Cdr
Stanier, Brig. Sir A.
Stannard, Mrs
Stansfield, Grp-Capt. P. W.
Stone, Maj. B.
Strangeways, Rev.
Strong, Mrs M.
Stubbs, R. F.
Sumption, D.
Sutton, Lt-Col. S. P. M.
Swain, Mr

Tennent, Mrs R. M.
Tewsons, Peter
Thompson, E. J.
Thornton, M.
Thornton, Mrs
Tiltman, Mrs
Tones, R. E.
Triboulet, R.
Tucker, Mr

Upward, E. H.
Uttley, D.

Vaisey, T. H. F.

Wakefield, Mrs L.
Walters, P. E.
Watts, Captain O. M.
Weston, R. V.
White, J. N.
Whitehouse, C.
Williams, Mrs
Winckworth, J.
Witrand, Vice-Admiral J.
Woodward, C. J.

Young, A. F. C.

Index

Africa, north 21, 22, 24, 25, 28–9
Alençon 222, 249
Alexander, Gen. 16, 57
Algeria 24
Allied Air Forces 92–93, 94, 96, 105, 107, 239, 248
Allied Naval Forces 100–5
Anderson, Gen. Sir Kenneth 28
Antwerp 53, 68
Anvil, Operation 39, 91–92
Arnold, Commodore James C. 177, 182
Arromanches 197, 200, 202, 244
Asnelles 64, 197
Atlantic, Battle of the 19, 36
Atlantic Charter 18
Atlantic Wall 26, 44, 45, 46, 48–50, 52, 53, 66, 67, 75, 205, 225
Avranches 156, 248

Balkans 31
Barbarossa: see Russia, German invasion
Baronville 244
Bassett, Col. Sam 62, 63, 65
Bayeux 200, 227, 232, 235, 239–40
Bayerlein, Gen. 221, 222, 239, 242
Beaches, fortifications: see Atlantic Wall
Beaches, reconnaissance 36, 37, 62, 63, 64, 65, 67
Bedell Smith, Gen. 58, 145
Belle Vue 202
Bernal, Prof. J. D. 64
Bernières 207, 208
Beny-Bocage 222
Bigot 84–5
Blainville 234
Blaskowitz, Gen. 53
Blumentritt 221
Bobbin tanks 65
Bodell, Stanley C. 152
Bolero: see U.S. forces in Britain
Bombardons 241
Boulogne 49
Bowden, Maj. Scott 64
Bracken, Brendan 59
Bradley, Gen. Omar 58, 79, 83, 98, 191, 192, 194, 243, 244, 246–247, 248
Brest 52
Bretteville 243
Britain, Battle of 14
Britain, German invasion plans 15
British Army:
21st Army Group 64, 235, 247
Second Army 58, 248
Corps: I 99; VIII 243, 245, 247, 248; XXX 99
Armoured Divisions: 7th 197, 200, 242, 243, 248; 11th 245, 248; 79th 65; Guards 248
Airborne Divisions: 1st 242; 6th 99, 158, 161, 217, 227, 234, 235
Infantry Divisions: 3rd 232, 235; 5th 58; 50th 99, 197, 232; 51st 242; 15th Scottish 245; 43rd Wessex 243, 245
Armoured Brigades: 4th 99, 242; 8th 99
Infantry Brigades: 1st Commando 216; 4th Commando 214; 12th Parachute 159
Armoured and Infantry Regiments: 44th Royal Tank 227–8; Dorset Regiment 200; East Yorkshire Regiment 200; Green Howards 200; Hampshire Regiment 200; 51st Highland Regiment 99; King's Shropshire Light Infantry 234; Middlesex Regiment 211, 214; Staffordshire Yeomanry 234; Commandos: 9, 99, 215, 228; No. 4 217; No. 6 217 (see also Royal Marines)
Royal Artillery 228: 23rd Field Regt. 214; 76th Field Regt. 214
British Broadcasting Corporation (B.B.C.) 63, 146, 148, 155, 160, 166, 219, 220, 224, 232
British Expeditionary Force (B.E.F.) 9–10, 17
Brittany 248
Brooke, Field-Marshal Sir Alan, Chief of Imperial General Staff (C.I.G.S.) 16, 23, 39, 40, 92
Brown, Admiral Sir Andrew 28
Bucknall, Gen. 99
Butcher, Capt. Harry 155, 219

Caen 38, 62, 156, 158, 217, 227, 232, 234, 235, 242, 245, 246, 247, 248
Cairo Conference 57
Calais 220
Canadian Army:
First Canadian Army 59
Infantry Divisions: 3rd Canadian 99, 205, 232, 247; 59th Canadian 247
Regiments: 6th Canadian Armoured 99; 10th Canadian Armoured 99; North Shore Regiment 99, 206; Queen's Own of Canada Regiment 99; Queen's Own Rifles 208; Regina Rifles 99, 209; Royal Winnipeg Rifles 99, 209
Canaris, Admiral 86
Cap Gris Nez 49
Carentan 38, 67, 166
Carpiquet 247
Casablanca Conference 31, 35
Casualties 235
Caumont 243
Cherbourg 36, 38, 39, 52, 62, 243, 244
Churchill, Rt Hon. Winston 13, 14, 15, 16, 18, 19, 21, 23, 24, 25, 38, 57, 91, 152
Chief of Staff to the Supreme Allied Commander (COSSAC) 35, 36, 37, 38, 62, 91
Cobra, Operation 248
Colleville-sur-Mer 98, 186, 189
Collins, Maj-Gen. Lawton 243, 244
Combined Operations Conference 72
Combined Operations Pilotage Parties (COPP) 64
Coningham, Air Marshal 79
Copeland, Miles 87
Cotentin 38, 91, 157, 158, 177, 229, 239, 240, 243, 244, 247
Courage, Capt. Richard 112, 155, 219
Courseulles 202, 205
Coutances 248
Creasey, Admiral 97
Crépon 197
Crerar, Gen. 205
Crete 15
Crocker, Gen. 98, 99
Crocodile tanks 75

de Gaulle, Gen. Charles 13, 68, 87–8, 106–7, 224–5, 247
Dempsey, Gen. M. C. 98, 243, 245, 248
Dettinger, Lt-Gen. 225
Deyo, Admiral 97
Dieppe raid 26, 44
Dill, Field-Marshal 24
Directorate of Combined Operations 4–5, 25
Doenitz, Admiral 241, 246
Dollman, Gen. 156, 222, 224
Douglas, Air Chief Marshal Sholto 23
Douvres 214
Dragoon (Anvil) 92
DUKW (amphibious vehicle) 75, 202
Dunkirk: see British Expeditionary Force
Duplex drive (D.D.) tanks 75

Eberbach 248
E-boats 241
Eisenhower, Gen. Dwight 28, 33, 57, 58, 74, 79, 94, 97, 112, 145, 146, 148, 155, 170, 219, 224, 227, 241, 245
Epsom, Operation 245
European Theatre of Operations United States Army 23

Fabius 83
Falaise 222, 249
Feuchtinger, Lt-Gen. 165, 227, 234
Flail tank (Crab) 75
Fortitude, Operation 89
France: surrender 9; Vichy government 24, 28–9, 225; Resistance 13, 62, 65–6, 68, 148, 158, 220; reaction to landings 105–7, 160, 197, 199, 202, 209, 217, 247
Free French 65:
Armoured Division 249; Navy, F.F.S. *Montcalm* 103; F.F.S. *Georges Leygues* 103; Commando Battalion 217

George VI 97
German Army:
Afrika Korps 15, 53
Army Group B 67, 166, 221, 222, 227
Army Group G 53, 54
Panzer Group West 246
Seventh Army 166, 224, 227, 246, 249
Fifteenth Army 89, 148, 220, 224, 239, 242, 245, 246
Corps: LXXXIV Corps 165, 166, 222, 227, 234, 247, 248; II S.S. Panzer Corps: 239, 248
Armoured Divisions: Panzer Divisions 53, 54, 89, 221, 239; 9th S.S. Panzer 235, 239, 245; 10th S.S. Panzer 235, 239, 245; 12th S.S. Panzer 166, 221, 235, 245; 17th S.S. Panzer 248; 21st Panzer 89, 165, 214, 222, 232, 234, 240, 242, 243; 352nd Panzer 191, 197, 200, 227; Panzer Lehr 166, 242, 243; 1st S.S. Panzer Lehr 235, 243, 245; 2nd S.S. Panzer Lehr 235, 243, 245, 248; 12th S.S. Panzer Lehr 247
Infantry Divisions: 91st 89; 716th 156; 915th 239
Airborne Divisions: 3rd Parachute Division 239; 91st Airborne Division 67, 158
Regiments: 6th Parachute 50; 919 Infantry 166; 22nd Panzer 243; 17th S.S. Panzer Grenadiers 221, 235, 243
Germany, peace offer to Britain 13
Gliders 158–9, 234
Glover, Wing Commander L. C. 168–9
Goebbels 224, 225
Goering 14, 246
Gold Beach 98, 99, 197–202, 227
Goodwood, Operation 248
Gooseberries 73, 241, 244
Governments in exile 13
Guderian, Gen. 54

Halder, Gen. 54
Hall, Admiral 189, 194
Harris, Sir Arthur 93
Hauser, Gen. Paul 249
Haw-Haw, Lord 73
'Hill 112' 245
'Hill 192' 248
Hitler, Adolf 9, 10, 12, 13, 14, 48, 53, 54, 67, 222, 239, 245, 246, 248, 249
Hobart, Maj-Gen. Percy 75
Hoffman, Admiral 165
Home Guard 13
Hopkins, Harry 22, 24
Hughes-Hallett, Commodore John 37, 72, 242
Husky, Operation 31, 33
Hussey, Capt. 72

Intelligence: Allied 45, 86–7; German 86, 88–9
Inter-Services Topographical Unit 62, 63, 64
Inter-Services Training and Development Centre (I.S.T.D.C.) 19
Invasion of Britain (Plans) 10, 13–14, 15
Invasion (D-Day): briefing 97–8; dummy 35, 89, 155, 156; forces 22, 35, 36, 38, 58, 68, 72, 74–5, 79, 91, 98, 235, 241–2, 244, 245; rehearsals 82–3; postponement 112, 145
Ireland 87
Italy 33, 39, 40, 91, 219

Japan, war against 19, 21, 24
Jodl, General Alfred 221
Juno Beach 98, 99, 203–9, 227, 232, 234

Keitel, Field-Marshal 165, 246
Kesselring, Field-Marshal 40
Keyes, Admiral Sir Roger 4, 25
Kieffer, Commandant 217
King, Admiral Ernest J. 21, 24, 36
Kirk, Admiral 100, 112, 177, 219, 245
Koenig, Gen. 68, 88, 96
Kraiss, Gen. 239
Krancke, Admiral 156, 241
Kriegsmarine 241

Lagrune 214
La Haye du Puits 247
Landing craft 17, 74, 152
La Pointe-du-Hoc 167, 192, 193
Largs, Combined Operations Training School conference 37, 72
La Rivière 64, 197, 199, 200, 205
La Roche Guyon 54
Laval, Pierre 225
Lease-Lend 18
Le Hamel 199, 200, 202, 227
Le Havre 36, 168, 214
Leigh Mallory, Air Marshal 16, 57, 94, 96, 97, 107, 145, 157
Le Mans 248
Liesby wood 234
Lion-sur-Mer 214, 227, 234
Lovat, Brig. The Lord 215, 216
Luftwaffe 54, 57, 68, 228, 241, 247, 248

Maginot Line 9, 49
Marcks, Gen. 156, 158, 160, 165, 234
Marshall, Gen. 22, 23, 31, 36, 57, 91
Mediterranean 24, 35
Merville 159
Meyer, Kurt 221
Middle East 15, 21
Model, Gen. 249
Molotov 23
Montgomery, Gen. Sir Bernard 16, 33, 58, 79, 97, 145, 146, 220, 224, 227, 240, 243, 244, 245, 246, 247, 248
Moon, Admiral 177
Morgan, Lt-Col. Frederick 17, 35, 37, 74, 83
Mountbatten of Burma, Earl 4–5, 37, 62, 250
Mulberry harbours 37, 38, 72, 73–4, 89, 241, 242, 244

Naval bombardment 161, 164, 167, 205, 240
Neptune, Operation 100, 146
Newfoundland meeting 18
Normandy 37, 38, 224, 232, 234, 248

O'Connor, Gen. 245
Odon 245
Ogden-Smith, Sgt B. 64
Oberkommando des Heeres (O.K.H.) 86
Oberkommand Wehrmacht (O.K.W.) 10, 54, 67, 68, 89, 146, 160, 221, 222, 225, 239
Omaha Beach 98, 167, 186–95, 219, 227, 235, 240, 244
Orne 68, 158, 165, 217, 227, 240, 242, 248
Otway, Lt-Col. 159
Ouistreham 168, 217
Overlord, Operation 33, 35, 38
Oyster mines 214

Pacific, war in 15, 21, 24
Paget, Gen. Sir Bernard 5, 23
Pas de Calais 36, 52
Patton, Gen. 79, 248
Pearl Harbour 19
Pétain, Marshal 225
Phoenixes 72, 73, 241, 244
Pluto pipeline 37, 74, 89
Pointblank 94
Pondrardier, Dominic 65, 66
Portal, Sir Charles 93
Port-en-Bessin 202, 240

Quebec Conference 38, 39, 72
Quinéville 166

Ramsay, Admiral 16, 33, 57, 63, 65, 79, 97, 100, 145, 146, 170, 177, 241
Rankin, Operation 35
Ranville 159, 161, 243
Rattle Conference (Largs) 37
Rennes 248
Richter, Colonel 156
Ridgway, Gen. Matthew B. 98, 153, 158
Riva Bella 217

Rommel, Field-Marshal 21, 51–2, 53, 54, 66, 67, 110, 220, 221, 222, 224, 239, 242, 245, 246, 248
Roosevelt, President 18, 22, 57, 96, 220
Roosevelt, Brig.-Gen. Theodore Jr 182
Rouen 156
Round-up 23, 31, 33, 35
Royal Air Force 105: Bomber Command 93, 94; Bombing policy 36, 37, 94, 96; Second Tactical Air Force 57, 93
Royal Marines: Royal Marine Artillery 214; 41st Royal Marine Commando 99; 47th Royal Marine Commando 202, 234; 48th Royal Marine Commando 99
Royal Navy: landing plans 100–5; Convoy S, 7; Ships: *Ajax* 103; *Arethusa* 103; *Argonaut* 103; *Belfast* 103, 152, 167, 197; *Black Prince* 103, 167; *Clan Lamont* 145, 170; *Danae* 103; *Diadem* 103; *Emerald* 103; *Erebus* 103; *Enterprise* 103; *Frobisher* 103, 168; *Glasgow* 103; *Hawkins* 103; *Largs* 214; *Mauritius* 103; *Nelson* 102; *Orion* 103, 167; *Pelorus* 152; *Ramilies* 102; *Roberts* 103, 247; *Rodney* 102, 247; *Scylla* 103; *Warspite* 102, 168, 169, 214
Rudder, Col. 192
Rüge, Admiral 220
Russia 15, 16, 17, 22, 23, 24, 25, 88

St Aubin 205, 227
St Côme-de-Fresne 197, 202
St Lô 156, 166, 240, 243, 247, 248
St Malo 66
Ste Mère-Église 157, 183
St Pierre-sur-Dives 165
Salmut, Gen. 220
Schlieben, Gen. 245
Sea-Lion, Operation 13, 14
Seine 52, 220, 246
Seulles 209
Sicily 31, 33
Slapton Sands 83
Sledgehammer, Operation 23, 24
Soissons 245
Somme 52
Spaatz, Gen. Carl 93, 96
Speer, Albert 48, 222
Speidel, General Hans 220, 221, 222
Sperrle, Field-Marshal Hugo 246
Spud pier 73
Stalin 16, 25
Starkey (mock invasion) 35
Stimson, Henry 33, 39
Strongpoint 0880 (COD) 211, 214
Supreme Headquarters Allied Expeditionary Force (SHAEF) 58, 62, 68, 93, 241, 245, 247, 248
Sword Beach 98, 99, 159, 168, 211–17, 227, 232, 234, 241

Talbot, Rear Admiral 214
Taylor, Col. 195
Tedder, Air Chief Marshal 28, 33, 57, 79, 93, 94, 96, 97, 145
Tehran Conference 40
Tennant, Rear Admiral 241
Thompson, Commander 152
Todt Organization 45, 68
Torch, Operation 25, 28–9
Tracy-sur-Mer 156
Transportation Plan 94, 96
Tunis 54

U-boat attacks 13, 15, 22, 241
United Nations 57
U.S.A.:
  Declaration of war 21
  forces in Britain 21, 23, 25, 33, 58, 59, 98
  Air Force: 105; U.S. Eighth Air Force 93, 189
  Army: First Army 249; Ninth Army 57, 93; Corps: V U.S. Corps 98, 194; VII U.S. Corps 98, 240, 243
  Airborne Divisions: 6th 79; 82nd 98, 153–5, 235, 244; 101st 98, 148, 157, 183, 235; 82nd Paratroop Division 156–7
  Divisions: 1st U.S. Army Division 191; 1st Infantry Division 98; 2nd Infantry Division 98; 4th Infantry Division 98, 235; 9th Infantry Division 98, 244; 29th Infantry Division 98, 240; 79th Infantry Division 98; 90th Infantry Division 98
  Infantry Regiments: 8th Infantry Regiment 181; 16th Infantry Regiment 186, 189, 192, 195; 116th Infantry Regiment 189
  16th Regimental Combat Team 98
U.S. Marine Corps: U.S. Rangers 98, 192–3
U.S. Navy: ships: U.S.S. *Ancon* 189; *Augusta* 103, 194; *Arkansas* 102, 190; *Bayfield* 177; *Corry* 180; *Empire Anvil* 186; *Henrico* 186; *Nevada* 102; *Quincy* 103, 167; *Satterlee* 193; *Texas* 102, 167, 190, 192, 193; *Tuscaloosa* 103, 167
Utah Beach 98, 157, 167, 177–83, 219, 235, 244

V-weapons 44, 53, 245
Ver-sur-Mer 197
Verteidigungsbereich 48
Vian, Admiral 100
Vierville-sur-Mer 98, 186
Villers Bocage 242, 243
Villerville 168
Vire 39, 68, 222, 246, 248
Von Kluge 246, 248, 249
Von Oppeln-Bronowski 234
Von Rundstedt, Field-Marshal 35–6, 44, 50–2, 54, 67, 68, 146, 148, 160, 166, 220, 221–2, 224, 239, 242, 245, 246
Von Schweppenburg, Geyr 53–4, 68
Von Stulpnagel 225

Warlimont, Gen. 67, 221, 222–3
Washington Conference 1941 21
Washington Conference 1943 31
Wedemeyer, Gen. Albert C. 22
Wells, Frederick 62
Wehrner, Maj.-Gen. Sir Harold 73
Whales (pierheads) 72, 73, 241
Widewing, Operation 58
Wiederstandsnest 48
Willmott, Lt-Commander 64

Zuckerman, Prof. 94

Photo acknowledgements

Title pages: Süddeutscher; pages 6–7 Popperfoto, London; 8 Imperial War Museum (IWM), London; 9 Daily Mail; 10–12 IWM; 12 (top) Süddeutscher Verlag, Munich; 13 Etablissement Cinématographique & Photographic, France; 14–15 (top) Süddeutscher; 15 (bottom) Ullstein GmbH, Berlin; 16–17 IWM; 18 Fox Photos, London; 19 Popperfoto; 20 (left) US Library of Congress, Washington; 20 (right) Keystone Press Agency, London; 22 Novosti Press Agency, London; 24 (top) IWM; 24 (bottom) Daily Mail; 25 (top) Popperfoto; 25 (bottom) Punch; 26–29 IWM; 30 (top) Novosti; 30–31 (top) IWM; 31 (bottom) Fox; 32 Camera Press/IWM; 33 IWM; 34 (top) US Army, Washington; 34 (bottom) IWM; 36–37 IWM; 39 Keystone; 40–41 (top) IWM; 40–41 (bottom) US Army; 41 IWM; 42–43 IWM; 45 Historical Research Unit (HRU), London; 46 (top) HRU; 46–47 (top) Süddeutscher; 46 (bottom) Public Records Office, London; 46–47 (bottom) Süddeutscher/HRU; 47 (top)–49 Süddeutscher; 48 (bottom) PRO; 49 IWM; 50 Süddeutscher; 50–51 HRU; 51 (top) Süddeutscher; 51 (bottom) HRU; 52(top) HRU; 52 (bottom) Süddeutscher; 52–53 HRU; 54 Psywar Society, St Albans; 55 Ullstein; 56 IWM, US Nat Archives; 58–59 Fox; 59 Punch; 60 IWM; 61 IWM/USAF; 62–63 PRO; 63 PRO; 64 Musée du Debarquement Arromanches; 65 Illustrated London News (ILN); 66 Ullstein; 67 Süddeutscher; 69 US Air Force, Washington; 70–71 ILN; 72 IWM; 72–73 IWM; 73 PRO; 75–77 IWM; 78 (inset) IWM; 78–79 US Navy, PRO; 80 (top left) IWM; 80 (top right) IWM; 80–81 US Army; 81–82 (top) IWM; 82 (bottom) PRO; 83 Punch; 85 Punch; 86–90 IWM; 88 (top) Punch; 92 IWM; 93 Keystone; 94 (top left & centre) IWM; 94 (top right) IWM; 95 USAF; 96 HRU; 98–99 IWM & US Army; 100–103 IWM; 104 IWM; 107 Camera Press/IWM; 108–111 US Army; 112 (top) Camera Press/IWM; 112 (bottom) IWM; 113 HMS Dryad, Royal Navy; 114 HRU; 115 HRU; 116 (top) IWM; 116 (below left) IWM; 116–117 IWM; 117 (top) Conway Picture Library, London; 118 HRU; 118–119 (top) HRU; 118–119 (bottom) HRU; 119 HRU; 120 IWM; 120–121 Popperfoto; 121 IWM; 122 IWM; 122–123 (top & bottom) IWM; 124–125 USAF; 125 USAF; 126–127 IWM; 128–129 Popperfoto; 130–131 HRU; 132–133 (top) HRU; 132–133 (bottom) HRU; 133 HRU; 134 IWM; 134–135 Popperfoto; 135 HRU; 136–137 Conway; 137 HRU; 138 US Army; 139 US Army; 140 (top) IWM; 140 (bottom) IWM; 141–142 US Army; 143 Nautic; 144 IWM; 145 Nautic; 147–148 IWM; 148–149 USAF; 150–151 HRU; 152–153 IWM; 154 (top) PRO; 154 (bottom) US Army; 156 USAF; 157 IWM; 158 Süddeutscher; 159 IWM; 160–161 PRO; 161 IWM; 162–163 HRU; 164 HRU; 164–165 IWM; 165 US Navy; 165–168 Süddeutscher; 169 IWM; 169 (bottom) IWM; 170–171 IWM; 171 PRO; 172–173 US Coast Guard, Washington; 174 (left) US Coast Guard; 174 (right) IWM; 175 US Coast Guard; 176 USAF; 178–179 US Navy; 180 US Army; 180–181 US Navy; 181 Camera Press/IWM; 181 US Army; 183 (top) IWM; 184–185 IWM; 186–187 US Army; 188–189 PRO; 189 USAF; 190 IWM; 190–191 US Army; 191 Keystone; 193–195 US Army; 196 (top & bottom) IWM; 198–199 PRO; 200 PRO; 200–201 Popperfoto; 201 (top left) IWM; 201 (top right) PRO; 202 Musée du Debarquement; 204–205 IWM; 206–207 PRO; 208 IWM; 209 IWM; 210 PRO; 212–213 (top & bottom) PRO; 212–213 (middle) IWM; 214–217 IWM; 218 US LofC/IWM; 219 Punch; 220–221 Süddeutscher; 224 John Frost Newspaper Library/Evening News, London; 225 HRU; 226 Camera Press/IWM; 228–229 IWM; 229 (top) HRU; 230–231 US Army; 232–233 (top) US Army; 232–233 (bottom) IWM; 233–236 IWM; 238 (top) Süddeutscher; 238 (bottom) IWM; 240 IWM; 241 (top) PRO; 241 (bottom) IWM; 242–243 IWM; 244 Süddeutscher; 245–246 IWM; 247–249 IWM.